THE PERSISTENCE OF PARTY

Political parties are taken for granted today, but how was the idea of party viewed in the eighteenth century, when core components of modern, representative politics were trialled? From Bolingbroke to Burke, political thinkers regarded party as a fundamental concept of politics, especially in the parliamentary system of Great Britain. The paradox of party was best formulated by David Hume: while parties often threatened the total dissolution of the government, they were also the source of life and vigour in modern politics. In the eighteenth century, party was usually understood as a set of flexible and evolving principles, associated with names and traditions, which categorised and managed political actors, voters, and commentators. Max Skjönsberg thus demonstrates that the idea of party as ideological unity is not purely a nineteenth- or twentieth-century phenomenon but can be traced to the eighteenth century.

MAX SKJÖNSBERG is a postdoctoral research associate in the Department of History at the University of Liverpool. An intellectual and political historian of the eighteenth century, he has published articles in *The Historical Journal, Journal of British Studies, History of Political Thought, Modern Intellectual History,* and *History of European Ideas.* He has previously lectured in history and political theory at the University of St Andrews and the University of York. In addition to being awarded the 2013 Skinner Prize from the University of London, he was David Hume Fellow at the Institute for Advanced Studies in the Humanities at The University of Edinburgh in 2018, and received the Parliamentary History Essay Prize in 2020.

IDEAS IN CONTEXT

Edited by David Armitage, Richard Bourke and Jennifer Pitts

The books in this series will discuss the emergence of intellectual traditions and of related new disciplines. The procedures, aims and vocabularies that were generated will be set in the context of the alternatives available within the contemporary frameworks of ideas and institutions. Through detailed studies of the evolution of such traditions, and their modification by different audiences, it is hoped that a new picture will form of the development of ideas in their concrete contexts. By this means, artificial distinctions between the history of philosophy, of the various sciences, of society and politics, and of literature may be seen to dissolve.

The series is published with the support of the Exxon Foundation.

A full list of titles in the series can be found at:
www.cambridge.org/IdeasContext

THE PERSISTENCE OF PARTY

Ideas of Harmonious Discord in Eighteenth-Century Britain

MAX SKJÖNSBERG

University of Liverpool

CAMBRIDGE
UNIVERSITY PRESS

CAMBRIDGE
UNIVERSITY PRESS

University Printing House, Cambridge CB2 8BS, United Kingdom

One Liberty Plaza, 20th Floor, New York, NY 10006, USA

477 Williamstown Road, Port Melbourne, VIC 3207, Australia

314–321, 3rd Floor, Plot 3, Splendor Forum, Jasola District Centre, New Delhi – 110025, India

79 Anson Road, #06–04/06, Singapore 079906

Cambridge University Press is part of the University of Cambridge.

It furthers the University's mission by disseminating knowledge in the pursuit of education, learning, and research at the highest international levels of excellence.

www.cambridge.org
Information on this title: www.cambridge.org/9781108841634
DOI: 10.1017/9781108894500

© Max Skjönsberg 2021

First published 2021

A catalogue record for this publication is available from the British Library.

Library of Congress Cataloging-in-Publication Data
NAMES: Skjönsberg, Max, 1987– author.
TITLE: The persistence of party : ideas of harmonious discord in eighteenth-century Britain / Max Skjönsberg.
DESCRIPTION: Cambridge, United Kingdom ; New York, NY : Cambridge University Press, 2021. | SERIES: Ideas in context | Includes bibliographical references and index.
IDENTIFIERS: LCCN 2020037941 (print) | LCCN 2020037942 (ebook) | ISBN 9781108841634 (hardback) | ISBN 9781108794992 (paperback) | ISBN 9781108894500 (epub)
SUBJECTS: LCSH: Political parties–Great Britain–History–18th century. | Party affiliation–Great Britain–History–18th century. | Political culture–Great Britain–History–18th century. | Great Britain–Politics and government–18th century.
CLASSIFICATION: LCC JN1119 .S55 2021 (print) | LCC JN1119 (ebook) | DDC 324.241009/033–dc23
LC record available at https://lccn.loc.gov/2020037941
LC ebook record available at https://lccn.loc.gov/2020037942

ISBN 978-1-108-84163-4 Hardback

To Janet

Contents

Contents

Figures

All of the above are part of William Hogarth's series
of election paintings.

Acknowledgements

This book is an expanded and revised version of my PhD thesis which I wrote at the London School of Economics and Political Science (LSE) between 2014 and 2018. First, I would like to thank my supervisor, Tim Hochstrasser, who was not only the ideal supervisor but also became a dear friend along the way. I would also like to give special thanks to Richard Whatmore and Brian Young, who examined the thesis and gave me invaluable advice.

In addition, I would like to single out three academics. My greatest academic debt I owe to Richard Bourke, who has been exceptionally supportive of my career in many ways and remains my greatest inspiration among historians. Writing my MA dissertation on 'David Hume on Party' under Richard's supervision at Queen Mary University of London (QMUL) in 2012–13 worked as a springboard for the present project. I have also benefited tremendously from Richard's work on Edmund Burke and eighteenth-century politics and political thought. Second, Robin Douglass – with whom I have been organising a reading group in London since 2014 on various themes – has been a wonderful interlocutor and supporter in several ways. Third, I was very lucky to belong to the same batch of PhD candidates at the LSE as Ian Stewart, with whom I have continuous discussions and conversations about historiography and other things, and who has directed my attention to many important sources. I am especially indebted to Ian for advising me at the final stages of producing this book.

I also wish to thank my former teachers, especially Iain McDaniel, Maurizio Isabella, Quentin Skinner, Gareth Stedman Jones and Georgios Varouxakis, in particular Quentin, who has been a great source of inspiration and support, and Georgios, who stimulated my interest in the history of political thought at QMUL as an undergraduate in 2009.

I am grateful to the International History department at the LSE for funding my PhD research, and to all my colleagues and friends at the LSE, especially Bastiaan Bouwman, Alex Dab, Cees Heere, Anne Irfan, Alex Mayhew, Tommaso Milani, Michael Rupp, Isaac Scarborough and Eline Vo. Among these, Isaac provided vital help with reading parts of the book before submission. Among the members of staff in the department, Paul Keenan and Paul Stock gave great advice and encouragement. In London I had the privilege of belonging to an illustrious network of early-career historians of political thought. These have included Signy Gutnick Allen, Caroline Ashcroft, Conor Bollins, Alexandra Chadwick, Stephanie Conway, Adela Halo, Shane Horwell, Catherine Hulse, Vanessa Lim, Shiru Lim, Giorgio Lizzul, Julia Nichols, Evangelos Sakkas, Emily Steinhauer and Sarah Wilford.

I would like to thank Cambridge University Press, in particular Liz Friend-Smith and Atifa Jiwa, and the two anonymous reviewers of the manuscript. Further thanks are due to Thomas Ahnert, David Allan, David Armitage, Alex Barber, Adrian Blau, Harald Braun, Monica Brito-Viera, Simon Burrows, Elaine Chalus, Danielle Charette, Alvin Chen, J.C.D. Clark, John Clark, Greg Conti, Hugo Drochon, Robin Eagles, Knud Haakonssen, James Harris, Heikki Haara, Rachel Hammersley, Marc Hanvelt, Randal Hendrickson, Mark Hill, Joseph Hone, Tom Hopkins, Colin Kidd, Minchul Kim, Robert Ingram, Melissa Lane, Mads Langballe Jensen, Sophie Jones, Avi Lifschitz, Felicity Loughlin, Robin Mills, Alex Murdoch, Steve Murdoch, Laura Nicolì, Johan Olsthoorn, Niall O'Flaherty, Giulia Oskian, Joanne Paul, Jason Peacey, Malcolm Petrie, Jacqueline Rose, Lucia Rubinelli, Andrew Sabl, Paul Sagar, Matthew Sangster, Will Selinger, Mira Siegelberg, Mark Spencer, Tim Stanton, Tim Stuart-Buttle, Angie Sutton-Vane, Stephen Taylor, Mikko Tolonen, Sylvana Tomaselli, Mark Towsey, Pedro Vianna Faria, Felix Waldmann, Lina Weber, Blair Worden and Bill Zachs for camaraderie, inspiration and advice. Johan read key passages of the book before submission and gave important advice.

This work would not have been possible without my parents, Åsa and Hans, who taught me to love books, and the unflinching support of my wife Janet Chan, to whom this book is dedicated.

Note on the Text

Eighteenth-century spelling has been kept in citations, in English and in French, and I have not made any attempts to 'correct' the grammar in eighteenth-century citations. I have, however, avoided reproducing graphical signs such as 'y^e' and 'y^t'. '[Sic]' has sometimes been inserted for clarity. When deemed necessary, 'cf.' has been used in the footnotes to indicate contrasting views. Old-style dates have usually been converted to new style in the sense that I have taken each year to start on 1 January rather than 25 March (which was generally the case in Britain until 1752). In order to remain faithful to the historical sources I have treated, and not to mischaracterise the period, it has not always been possible to avoid gendered language and use gender neutral pronouns. I have also occasionally used eighteenth-century expressions such as 'man of letters'. For most citations in French, I have used reliable and reasonably literal translations, but I have kept some shorter quotations from correspondence and lesser known works in French. For the sake of economy, I have used short titles and surnames in the footnotes, apart from when the full title has been deemed to be of extra significance.

Abbreviations

Add	Additional
Anecdotes	William King, *Political and Literary Anecdotes of His Own Times* (London, 1818)
BJECS	*British Journal of Eighteenth-Century Studies*
BL	British Library, London
Bodleian	Bodleian Library, Oxford
Commons, 1690–1715	*History of Parliament: The House of Commons, 1690–1715*, ed. Eveline Cruickshanks, Stuart Handley, and David Hayton (5 vols., Cambridge, 2002)
Commons, 1715–54	*History of Parliament: The House of Commons, 1715–54*, ed. Romney Sedgwick (2 vols., London, 1970)
Commons, 1754–90	*History of Parliament: The House of Commons, 1754–90*, ed. Lewis Namier and John Brooke (3 vols., London, 1964)
Contributions	Bolingbroke, *Contributions to the Craftsman,* ed. Simon Varey (Oxford, 1982)
Correspondence	*The Correspondence of Edmund Burke*, ed. Thomas W. Copeland et al. (10 vols., Chicago, 1958–78)
Dissertation	Rapin, *An Historical Dissertation upon Whig and Tory*, translated by Mr Ozell (London, 1717). (Rapin, *Dissertation sur les Whigs et les Torys* (The Hague, 1717))
ECS	*Eighteenth-Century Studies*
Egmont Papers	Aubrey N. Newman (ed.), 'Leicester House Politics, 1750–60, from the Papers of John, 2nd Earl of Egmont', *Camden Fourth Series,* 7 (1969), 85–228

EHR	*English Historical Review*
ESRO	East Sussex Record Office, The Keep
Essays	David Hume, *Essays, Moral, Political and Literary*, ed. Eugene F. Miller (Indianapolis, 1987)
Estimate	John Brown, *An Estimate of the Manners and Principles of the Times* (2 vols., London, 1757–8)
Fox Memorials	*Memorials and Correspondence of Charles James Fox*, ed. Lord John Russell (4 vols., London, 1853–7)
Further Letters	*Further Letters of David Hume*, ed. Felix Waldmann (Edinburgh, 2014)
Hearne's Recollections	*Remarks and Collections of Thomas Hearne*, ed. C.E. Doble et al (11 vols., Oxford, 1885–1921)
HEI	*History of European Ideas*
Hervey's Memoirs	Lord Hervey, *Some Materials towards Memoirs of the Reign of King George II*, ed. Romney Sedgwick (3 vols., London, 1931)
Histoire	Rapin, *Histoire d'Angleterre* (10 vols., The Hague, 1724–7)
History	David Hume, *The History of England from the Invasion of Julius Caesar to the Revolution in 1688* (6 vols., Indianapolis, 1983 [1754–61])
HJ	*Historical Journal*
HMC	Royal Commission on Historical Manuscripts
HPT	*History of Political Thought*
JBS	*Journal of British Studies*
Letters	*The Letters of David Hume*, ed. J.Y.T. Greig (1932), (2 vols., Oxford, 2011)
Marchmont Papers	*A Selection from the Papers of the Earls of Marchmont, in the Possession of the Right Honourable Sir George Henry Rose: Illustrative of Events from 1685 to 1750* (3 vols., London, 1831)
Memoirs of George III	Horace Walpole, *Memoirs of the Reign of King George III* (4 vols., London, 1845)
MS	Manuscript(s)
New Letters	*New Letters of David Hume*, ed. Raymond Klibansky and Ernest C. Mossner (1954), (Oxford, 2011)
NLS	National Library of Scotland, Edinburgh
ODNB	*Oxford Dictionary of National Biography*

Parl. Hist.	*The Parliamentary History of England from the Earliest Period to the Year 1803*, ed. William Cobbett (36 vols., London, 1802–20)
PH	*Parliamentary History*
Political Writings	Bolingbroke, *Political Writings,* ed. David Armitage (Cambridge, 1997)
RA	Royal Archives, Windsor Castle
TCD	Trinity College Dublin
Tory and Whig	*Tory and Whig: The Parliamentary Papers of Edward Harley, 3rd Earl of Oxford, and William Hay, MP for Seaford, 1716–53,* ed. Stephen Taylor and Clyve Jones (Woodbridge, 1998)
Treatise	Hume, *A Treatise of Human Nature,* ed. L.A. Selby-Bigge and P.H. Nidditch (Oxford, 1978 [1739–40])
Unpublished Letters	*The Unpublished Letters of Henry St John, First Viscount Bolingbroke,* ed. Adrian Lashmore-Davies (5 vols., London, 2013)
W&S	*The Writings and Speeches of Edmund Burke,* ed. Paul Langford et al. (9 vols., Oxford, 1970–2015)
Waldegrave Memoirs	*The Memoirs and Speeches of James, 2nd Earl Waldegrave, 1742–63,* ed. J.C.D. Clark (Cambridge, 1988)
Works	*The Works of the Late Right Honourable Henry St. John, Lord Viscount Bolingbroke,* ed. David Mallet (5 vols., London, 1754)
WWM	Wentworth Woodhouse Muniments, Sheffield City Archives

Introduction
Party in History and Politics

The influence of races in our early ages, of the church in our middle, and of parties in our modern history, are three great moving and modifying powers, that must be pursued and analysed with an untiring, profound, and unimpassioned spirit, before a guiding ray can be secured.

Benjamin Disraeli, *Sybil; or the Two Nations* (1845)

What is called union in a body politic is a very equivocal thing. The true kind is a union of harmony, whereby all parts [*les parties*], however opposed they may appear, cooperate for the general good of society – as dissonances in music cooperate in producing overall concord.

Montesquieu, *Considérations sur les causes de la grandeur des Romains et de leur décadence* (1734)

While there are no timeless arguments in the history of political thought, there may indeed be perennial questions. If anything is recurrent throughout Western thought, it is likely to be the abhorrence of conflict and the quest for stability and peace. Political societies require a degree of internal peace to function. Since they imply division, political parties thus pose a problem for political theory. Extreme partisan divisions threaten to undermine trust among citizens, tear societies apart and constitutions asunder, and degenerate into violent strife and even civil war. Yet parties can also help to pacify and domesticate conflict. Party is an instrument for organising competition and adjudicating between interests and opinions. Any politics worthy of the name entails competition between 'ins' and 'outs', involving a mixture of interest and principle. Politics is not *just* about competition, but this is a crucial aspect of any politics that would be recognisable to us in the twenty-first-century Western world, as in many other parts of the world. In modern large-scale societies, effective political action requires numbers and organisation. Moreover, parties and partisanship are natural concomitants of modern understandings of liberty: in liberal regimes we have the right to form opinions and associate with others of similar views. Securing political stability has been a concern for political thinkers since at least Thucydides, but the role played by parties in channelling or augmenting division is a more recent concern – one on which this book is focused.

First and foremost, this book is intended as a contribution to the still limited literature on the notion of party in the history of political thought, with a focus on the eighteenth century, when parliamentary parties emerged as stable features of politics.[1] In the eighteenth century, the question of whether party was beneficial or pernicious to political life dominated political discourse. Second, this book engages with political history, a field in which studies of party once dominated, but where they have since fallen out of fashion together with parliamentary history more broadly. We will additionally need cultural and social histories of party,[2] but this book concentrates on politics and political thought. Few attempts are now likely to be made to write about politics in the eighteenth century without reference to party, as Lewis Namier prescribed but did not practice.[3] However, a question as complex as that of party in this period needs to be revisited because there is no consensus about its importance or even what it meant.

While we take party for granted – for us politics simply is *party* politics – party was not taken for granted by the men and women of the eighteenth

---

[1] Ihalainen, *The Discourse on Political Pluralism in Early Eighteenth-Century England* (Helsinki, 1999); Ball, 'Party', in *Political Innovation and Conceptual Change* (Cambridge, 1989), 155–76; Klaus von Beyme, 'Partei, Faktion', in *Geschichtliche Grundbegriffe* (7 vols., Stuttgart, 1972–92), IV (1978), 689–90; Gunn, 'Introduction', in *Factions No More* (London, 1971); Gunn, 'Party before Burke', *Government and Opposition*, 3 (1968), 223–42; Harvey Mansfield, *Statesmanship and Party Government* (Chicago, 1965); Robbins, 'Discordant Parties', *Political Science Quarterly*, 73 (1958), 505–29; Thomson, *The Conception of Party in England, in the Period 1740 to 1783* (D. Phil. thesis, Cambridge, 1938). There are more recent works in political theory; see Rosenblum, *On the Side of the Angels* (Princeton, 2008); Muirhead, *The Promise of Party in a Polarized Age* (Cambridge, MA, 2014); White and Ypi, *The Meaning of Partisanship* (Oxford, 2016).

[2] For such contributions, see esp. Wilson, *The Sense of the People* (Cambridge, 1995); Rogers, *Whigs and Cities* (Oxford, 1989); De Krey, *A Fractured Society* (Oxford, 1985); Brewer, *Party Ideology and Popular Politics at the Accession of George III* (Cambridge, 1976).

[3] Namier, *The Structure of Politics and the Accession of George III* (2 vols., London, 1929), I, vii. See also Namier, 'Monarchy and the Party System', *Personalities and Powers* (London, 1955), 13–38. The vocabulary of Tory and Whig is not absent from his writings, however; importantly, see Namier, *England in the Age of the American Revolution* (London, 1930), 206–33, which *inter alia* includes the statement: 'The division between Whigs and Tories existed in 1761, as before, and as it still exists in the body politic of England; it was latent in temperament and outlook, in social types, in old connexions and traditions' (207). This statement is quickly qualified by the observation that personal factionalism had increasingly replaced party as the relevant division in politics. This is discussed at length in Chapters 8–11.

century. This meant that political writers devoted many pages to trying to comprehend this 'modern' aspect of politics. This book focuses on the case study of eighteenth-century Britain, a composite monarchy and imperial state which came into being after the Anglo-Scottish Union of 1707. It will thus contribute to the field of British history, roughly as defined by J.G.A. Pocock.[4] This approach acknowledges that there is a political system (and community of sorts) known as Britain to be studied – existing institutionally and in the imagination – not in isolation from European and world history, but as a unit suitable for independent historical study nevertheless. It also recognises the disproportionate weight of the English component in this composite monarchy and imperial state. The eighteenth century is generally held to be a crucial period for the birth of modern politics. This is largely – if to an exaggerated degree – regarded as the product of the transatlantic revolutions at the end of the century rather than Britain's parliamentary system. For histories of party, however, the British case study has always and rightly been central. For good or ill, Britain was the parliamentary system par excellence for most of the eighteenth century, and was known as such by foreign commentators such as Voltaire, Montesquieu, Jean-Louis de Lolme, and Anders Nordencrantz. Only excessive fear of British exceptionalism and Whig history could lead to the absurdity of denying or depreciating this obvious fact.[5]

My own home country, Sweden, had a different and more short-lived experience of parliamentary sovereignty and party politics in the eighteenth century during its 'Age of Liberty' (1718–72). This experiment is likely to have been inspired by the Anglo-British example to an extent that Swedish historiography has yet to appreciate. As the example of Sweden illustrates, the history of party in Britain is not only of concern to the British but to everyone interested in modern, parliamentary politics. Variants of the Westminster model and other representative assembly-based systems, and along with them party politics, have spread around the world, because of empire – British, French, and American, formal as well as informal – and imitation.

From a historical perspective, the main reason to study eighteenth-century attitudes towards party is because the topic was considered by political writers and actors at the time to be profoundly important. Political life in the period simply cannot be understood without reference

---

[4] Pocock, *Discovery of Islands* (Cambridge, 2005).
[5] For the importance of the British political system in French liberal political thought, see Selinger, *Parliamentarism* (Cambridge, 2019).

to party, at least not in a way that eighteenth-century men and women would have recognised. An additional reason for undertaking a study of this kind is that the question of party is still relevant. Party conflict and partisanship remain the stuff of political theory today. Parties are a funda-mental part of representative governments, and they feature in any state that calls itself democratic.[6] Despite this, political philosophers – past and present – have generally been reluctant to embrace parties, both as nor-matively desirable in politics and as a subject worthy of study.[7] The eighteenth century is thus a crucial period because of the ubiquity of focus on the topic, as well as Edmund Burke's famous embrace of parties.

This book does *not* argue that there were stable Whig and Tory parties throughout the eighteenth century. Although these terms were almost continuously in use, their meanings were contested, and the Whig–Tory polarity in parliament was sometimes dwarfed by so-called Court and Country alignments, as well as factionalism within the Whig family. During the age of Whig Supremacy (*c.*1714–60), there were both Tory and Whig groupings in opposition, which occasionally cooperated. By around 1760, moreover, both parties had lost most traces of parliamentary unity, although the party names survived, as did party organisations in localities. Such significant changes will be considered along with important continuities. They belie any notion of a two-party *system*, which is why I prefer to speak of a party *framework*. But the basic insight is that the idea of party dominated political discourse in eighteenth-century Britain. This will lead us to reject claims that party-based politics was 'unanticipated' when it 'emerged' in the nineteenth century.[8] Indeed, any stark contrast between the eighteenth century as a period without meaningful party politics and the nineteenth century as a time with a stable two-party system is misleading, since historians have long recognised that parties, especially in the beginning of the nineteenth century, were still 'loosely cast confederations' and a far cry from twentieth-century organisations.[9] Indeed, it has been argued that the 'modern party system', whereby parties

---

[6] Undemocratic and quasi-democratic states often involve one party in permanent government and a handful of affiliated sister parties – which is a rather different phenomenon than party competition – but is nevertheless testimony to how important the vocabulary of party has become in the modern world, and not exclusively in the West.

[7] Rosenblum, *On the Side of the Angels*, introduction.

[8] Cf. Scarrow, 'The Nineteenth-Century Origins of Modern Political Parties', in *Handbook of Party Politics* (London, 2006), 22.

[9] Bentley, *Politics without Democracy* (Oxford, 1984), 26. On the problem of interpreting the middle decades of the nineteenth century as a two-party system, see Hilton, *A Mad, Bad, and Dangerous People* (Oxford, 2006), 517–24.

are supported by central bureaucracies and mass membership, aspire to ideological homogeneity and have MPs who are expected to speak and vote as a bloc in parliament has only become dominant since the 1880s.[10] Accordingly, when linking this study of the past with the present we must remember that eighteenth-century parties were different from the parties of today. In terms of leadership and organisation, they were much looser than present-day political parties, without parliamentary whips, mass membership, or official manifestos. However, even though parties have changed and developed more sophisticated organisations, the question of internal division has independent merit on a theoretical plane, as Nancy Rosenblum has argued.[11] For this reason we should not be too quick to dismiss the 'aristocratic' parties of the eighteenth century as irrelevant for modern politics, as Moisey Ostrogorsky and Max Weber did in an earlier era.[12]

For political historians, the first age of party in England and Britain – the 'Rage of Party' – has attracted a great deal of interest.[13] This is the period from the Glorious Revolution of 1688–9 to the death of Queen Anne in 1714. During this period, British political culture was divided into a fairly neat two-party framework, with the Whigs and Tories alternating in holding the key positions in government.[14] By contrast, for political theorists, the writings of Edmund Burke (1729/30–97) from the second half of the century have usually been the starting point. Partly as a counterweight to the current literature, this book places plenty of emphasis on the intermediate period from the Hanoverian succession in 1714 until the accession of George III before finishing with four chapters on Burke.

I was initially drawn to the subject of party via the writings of David Hume, when I observed that Hume's essays on party from 1741 had been left comparatively neglected by scholars. To argue that Burke was the first to have had anything interesting to say about party would be to overlook the apparent fact that such a notable political analyst as Hume had earlier spent so much time and effort on the topic. My main focus is on specific thinkers, principally Paul de Rapin-Thoyras, Bolingbroke, Hume, John

---

[10] Hawkins, *British Party Politic, 1852–86* (Basingstoke, 1998). This was a gradual process, as party organisations, both local and central, had become more sophisticated earlier in the nineteenth century; see Gash, 'The Organisation of the Conservative Party, 1832–46', *PH*, 2 (1983), 131–52.

[11] Rosenblum, *On the Side of the Angels*, 13.

[12] Ostrogorsky, *La Démocratie et l'organisation des partis politiques* (2 vols., Paris, 1903), I, viii–x; Weber, *Political Writings* (Cambridge, 1994), 336–8.

[13] Following Holmes's pathbreaking *British Politics in the Age of Anne* (London, 1967). For its impact, see Jones (ed.). *Special Issue: British Politics in the Age of Holmes, PH*, 28 (2009), vii, 1–208.

[14] For qualification see Chapter 2.

Brown, and Burke. To identify authorial intentions, I have considered the contributions of these writers in their intellectual and political contexts. As the question of party concerns how people were analysing a phenomenon they saw at work, context has been understood in expansive terms. This book is not exclusively meant as a study of how political thinkers responded to others' arguments – although it is that too – it is also about how they understood their practical politics and how they thought it had come into being. For this reason, in this book we will encounter under-studied political writers such as Thomas Carte, John Perceval, and Catharine Macaulay, along with key political actors, including not only Walpole, the Foxes, and the Pitts, but also Harley, Pulteney, and Portland.

My starting point is the deliberately Whiggish question of how party, initially seen as pernicious and wholly negative, could become something tolerable and even advantageous, as viewed in the writings of Burke. Since history is about tracing both continuities and discontinuities between past and present, I agree with John Dunn that the history of political thought is best when it is Whig regarding subject matter and Tory regarding truth.[15] While my question may be Whiggish, this history is not a straightforward narrative of intellectual progress. The question of party was never really settled in the eighteenth century. Arguments in favour of party competition were put forward at the start of the period and arguments against were still heard towards the end of the century. The American Founders, who inherited the British debate about party, were deeply ambivalent, as were Francophone liberals such as Germaine de Staël.[16] In their own specific circumstances, James Madison and de Staël both shared many of Hume's anxieties about factionalism, as well as some of the solutions he proposed, which revolved around how political systems could accommodate rather than eradicate party division.

If we were to read only Burke, the question of party might appear settled. It would be unduly anti-Whiggish, however, to suggest that attitudes did not change during the course of the eighteenth century. On 10 February 1780, more than 600 men and women from all walks of life gathered for a meeting of a debating society, the School of Eloquence, in Soho Square, London, to discuss 'whether parties were beneficial in a free state'. After a 'curious' two-hour debate, the majority

---

[15] Dunn, 'The Identity of the History of Ideas', *Philosophy*, 43 (1968), 98.
[16] Spencer, 'Hume and Madison on Faction', *The William and Mary Quarterly*, 59 (2002), 869–96; Fontana, *Germaine de Staël* (Princeton, 2016), 75.

decided that parties were indeed beneficial.[17] Such an outcome would have been unlikely a hundred years earlier, when the party names of Whig and Tory emerged in England during the Exclusion Crisis (1679–81), initially as terms of abuse, and borrowed from earlier usages in Scotland and Ireland.[18] From then on, discussions of party would be partisan in a strong sense. The press that developed in the wake of the lapsing of the Licensing Act in 1695 was a party press, and it is difficult to find non-partisan political writings before Hume. During the 'Rage of Party' in the reign of Anne (1702–14), most printed statements about party were routinely denunciations of the other side and frequently of party as such.

With the exception of an opening contextual chapter, this book is structured chronologically, covering a short eighteenth century from roughly 1714 to 1797. This chronological approach has been chosen to keep in mind changing political circumstances and to avoid giving statements the appearance of timelessness. As all chapters will reflect, the post-revolutionary period and the reign of Anne was indeed the moment when the terms of British political debate were shaped, but discussions of party only matured subsequently. Most of the thinkers in this study put forward different visions of what I call harmonious discord. This phrase is inspired by a passage from Montesquieu, which is the epigraph at the head of this introduction and is discussed in Chapter 1. As will be shown in Chapter 2, the French Huguenot Rapin broke new ground as he tried to understand British party mechanics in a more detached and analytical fashion than domestic writers had achieved during the 'Rage of Party'. Rapin argued that the two parties in Britain, the Whigs and Tories, represented the two pillars of the mixed constitution – parliament on the one hand and monarchy on the other – and that both parties were necessary for equilibrium between these two parts of the constitution. Both parties were likewise necessary for balance in the religious sphere, which was as important as the secular in public life at the time. One party favoured the

---

[17] *The Letters of Sir William Jones* (2 vols., Oxford, 1970), I, 346. With the American War going badly for Britain, and the North ministry facing fierce opposition in parliament, several debates on similar topics were held in London in 1779–80, e.g., 4 February 1779, Coachmaker's Hall: 'Has a British King more to fear from the flattery of his courtiers, or the opposition of parties?'; 20 January 1780, Coachmakers Hall: 'Is it not a criminal indifference to be of no party in the present alarming and divided state of the nation?'; 22 February 1780, Old Theatre, Portugal Street, Lincolns Inn Fields: 'Which has been the more prejudicial to Great Britain, the influence of the crown or the spirit of party?'; 23 March 1780, Coachmakers Hall Society: 'Which is the most to be dreaded in this country, the influence of the Crown, or the spirit of party?' For these debates, see Andrew (ed.), *London Debating Societies, 1776–1799* (London, 1994).

[18] Willman, 'The Origins of "Whig" and "Tory" in English Political Language', *HJ*, 17 (1974), 247–64.

Church of England and the other toleration for Protestant Dissenters, and
the only way to achieve a sustainable medium between two extreme
positions, according to Rapin, was competition and mutual checking
and balancing between Tory and Whig.

Bolingbroke (Chapter 3) and Hume (Chapters 4 and 6–8) followed
Rapin's example, the former no doubt for partisan purposes but in a new
analytical manner and depth compared with the partisan literature of
Jonathan Swift, Daniel Defoe, and others during the reign of Anne.
Against the grain of the literature on the subject, I argue that
Bolingbroke made the case for organised partisan opposition to Walpole
under the banner of a 'Country party'. In the context of Whig supremacy,
Bolingbroke had to think hard about how to justify opposition in a
political landscape where party names had become entrenched, but where
systematic opposition was viewed as morally and legally dubious. In
Chapter 5, I consider the pamphlet war and political changes prompted
by the fall of Walpole, especially John Perceval's notorious *Faction Detected*
(1743), which sought to define legitimate opposition along more restricted
Whiggish lines. Perceval was answered by Tories and Country party
writers, armed with a host of Bolingbrokean arguments. Bolingbroke,
moreover, provoked Hume's early writings on party. Hume disliked party
in many ways but treated it as an inevitable component of parliamentary
politics. He believed that parties – or factions, terms he used interchangeably – based on 'principles' were especially pernicious and unaccountable.
The danger was that religious principles had the potential of making
people fanatical and ready both to proselytise and persecute dissidents.
The parties which Hume viewed as more excusable were those based on
'interests', meaning different economic interests. In Chapter 8, Hume's
last and highly significant essay on party is considered together with
Burke's first, unpublished essay on the subject, which was written at about
the same time. In this early essay, written before Burke began his political
career, he distinguished faction from party and made a non-partisan case
for the benefit of party conflict in a mixed system of government.

In Chapter 9, John Brown's influential anti-party writings are considered in the context of the Seven Years' War and the accession of George
III. Few writers abhorred political division as much as Brown, and in his
last political text – *Thoughts on Civil Liberty, on Licentiousness, and Faction*
(1765) – he sought to demonstrate that a political society could be both
free and united by pointing to the ancient republic of Sparta. This text was
written against the Rockingham Whig administration, with the chief
publicist of which, Edmund Burke, Chapters 10–13 are concerned. As

will be seen, Burke's main intention when writing his *Thoughts on the Cause of the Present Discontents* (1770) and other famous texts was not so much to innovate as to revive the principles of party and Whiggism in a new political climate after the accession of George III. Burke later split with his party over the French Revolution, believing that this event rendered old party distinctions by and large irrelevant. However, Chapter 12 shows that he never really lost faith in party as such. In Chapter 13 – which considers Burke in the context of thinkers associated with the umbrella term the 'Scottish Enlightenment', especially Hume and Adam Smith – I demonstrate that Burke returned to his earlier, more sceptical appraisal of the benefits of party towards the end of his life, when he was himself liberated from partisanship. He now argued that the balance of Britain's mixed constitution had not been maintained by one party alone but by competition between Whig and Tory.

By unearthing the sustained theoretical engagement with the concept of party during most of the eighteenth century, this book demonstrates that attitudes to party, although they could be damning, were more multifaceted and complicated than scholars have often thought. These findings will pose problems for those seeking to understand eighteenth-century politics solely on the basis of power politics, patronage, and family networks. Although 'Namierism' is today perhaps more often denigrated than emulated,[19] many of its elements still recur in the most unexpected places.[20] This is all for the better, because my point is not that these aspects of politics were trivial, or that Namier's contribution to eighteenth-century historiography was insignificant. If anything, this study reflects the complexity of British politics before the age of mass suffrage. The eighteenth century was the time when the institutions of parliamentary democracy were trialled, but it was not a democratic age.

When political historians used to look for the origin of the 'modern' political party, they tended to focus on organisation rather than principles. In this respect, I disagree with the classic Namierite formulation that '[t]he durability of Parties depends less on the ideas they represent than on the

---

[19] For the relative eclipse of Namier, see Hayton, *Conservative Revolutionary* (Manchester, 2019), 391–8.

[20] Chalus, *Elite Women in English Political Life* (Oxford, 2005), 4, 6–7, 10–11. To be sure, even though Namier understood his ambitions as 'sociological', Chalus's work is more concerned with political culture and society beyond parliament, and so should not be called neo-Namierite in a strong sense (12).

strength and coherence of party organizations'.[21] As illustrated by the split between the Portland and Foxite Whigs in the 1790s, discussed in Chapter 12, even the most organised parties can become divided as a result of disagreement about ideas and policy. In recent British history, splits have occurred within the Labour and Conservative parties over questions such as 'Brexit', or the ideological direction under specific leaders. Most notably, disagreement caused by Labour's move to the left in the early 1980s led to several senior Labour politicians leaving the party and setting up the Social Democratic Party, which joined the Liberal Party in 1988 to form the Liberal Democrats. Economic and trade policy divided the Labour and Liberal parties during the Great Depression in the 1930s, when two National Governments were formed between 1931 and 1935. In the nineteenth century, Robert Peel's repeal of the Corn Laws caused divisions within the Tory-Conservatives, and William Gladstone's Irish Home Rule proposal split the Liberal Party. In all these cases, strategy and selfish calculations played their part, but the basic point that ideological and principled ruptures have changed the course of political history still stands.

Perhaps the most important conclusion of my study is that party in the eighteenth century was not only, and perhaps not even mainly, understood in terms of organisation. Rather, it was usually thought of as a set of flexible and evolving principles, associated with names and traditions, which categorised and managed political actors, voters, and commentators. In other words, the idea of party as ideological unity is not purely a nineteenth- or twentieth-century phenomenon but a way of thinking that can be traced to the eighteenth century. If we are to understand eighteenth-century politics, we need to understand the political arguments of the period. This is not to say that principles determine political behaviour *on their own*, but rather that they play a crucial role in circumscribing, prompting, and delaying action. For this reason, ideas matter even if power politics is the ultimate motivating factor – one of Quentin Skinner's most valuable insights.[22] Historians can thus learn much from

---

[21] *Commons, 1754–90*, I, 186. Having said that, eighteenth-century parties were often more organised than frequently assumed. For the beginning of the century, see Jones, 'The Parliamentary Organisation of the Whig Junto in the Reign of Queen Anne', *PH*, 10 (1991), 164–82; Jones, 'The Extra-Parliamentary Organisation of the Whig Junto in the Reign of William III', *PH*, 32 (2013), 522–30. For the later eighteenth century, see Ginter (ed.), *Whig Organisation in the General Election of 1790* (Berkeley, 1967).

[22] Skinner, *Visions of Politics* (3 vols., Cambridge, 2002), I, 145–57. Namier's scepticism about the agency and importance of ideas and principles in politics and history is succinctly formulated in 'Human Nature in Politics', *Personalities and Powers*, 1–7.

Namier, including his still unmatched archival research, while taking political thought and principles seriously. Ideas may not cause historical change and events single-handedly, but they certainly influence when they happen and how they unfold. In the eighteenth century, historians and political commentators believed that party conflict and partisanship, principled as well as self-interested, had shaped their political environment, and this exerted a powerful grip on their imagination as to what they thought they could expect in the present and in the future(s).

CHAPTER I

Background, Contexts, and Discourses

A King or Queen of England must govern by the Bulk of their people, & must never be tied to one or t'other party, which made King W[illia]m & all the Kings his Predecessors change from one to the other party, as they had the majority in the Nation & Parliament.

The Earl of Strafford to Sophia of Hanover (1714), BL Stowe
MS 242, f. 106

It gives me serious concern to see such a spirit of dissention in the country; not only as it destroys virtue and common sense, and renders us in a manner barbarians towards one another, but as it perpetuates our animosities, widens our breaches, and transmits our present passions and prejudices to our posterity ... I am sometimes afraid that I discover the seeds of civil war in these our divisions.

Joseph Addison, *The Spectator* (1711)

The Parties and Divisions which reign among us may several Ways bring Destruction upon our Countrey, at the same Time that our united Force would be sufficient to secure us against all the Attempts of a foreign Enemy. Whatever expedients therefore can be found to allay those Heats and Animosities, which break us into different Factions and Interests, cannot be but useful to the Publick, and highly tend to its Safety, Strength, and Reputation.

Joseph Addison, *The Freeholder* (1716)

Party What?

Party is a crucial theme in William Hogarth's four election paintings from the second half of the 1750s (see Figures 1.1–1.4). The paintings were in part inspired by the controversial Oxfordshire election of 1754, one of the last major strongholds of Tory-Jacobitism in eighteenth-century England. The four paintings depict how Tories dressed in blue and Whigs in orange entertain and canvass voters, the polling where Tories and Whigs alike engage in dubious practices to gain votes, and finally the 'chairing' of the

Figure 1.1 *An Election Entertainment* (1755), by William Hogarth. A chaotic political banquet modelled on Leonardo's *Last Supper*. A Tory crowd is demonstrating outside.

Figure 1.2 *Canvassing for Votes* (1758), by William Hogarth. A farmer is being bribed by two innkeepers from the Crown (Whig) and the Royal Oak (Tory), respectively.

Figure 1.3 *The Polling* (1758), by William Hogarth. The blue and orange flags represent Tory and Whig, respectively.

Figure 1.4 *Chairing the Member* (1758), by William Hogarth. The winning member depicts George Bubb Dodington. The procession turns into a riot.

winning candidate. The Oxfordshire election is often said to have been violently partisan to an unusual degree for mid-century politics, but it was mirrored by comparable developments elsewhere at the same time, notably in Bristol and Nottingham.[1] In any event, Hogarth clearly captured something peculiar about eighteenth-century Britain: its party-dominated politics.

Parties or partisanship in a broad sense may be as old as the earliest societies where there was competition for office. But what did 'party' mean in eighteenth-century Britain? Some historians have applied lists of criteria to identify specific parties at particular moments, but such an approach may say more about how we understand the concept than about the period of enquiry. Having said that, it would not be difficult for the Whig and Tory parties for much of the period to qualify for the characteristics of the 'First Whigs', as proposed by J.R. Jones: recognised leader(s), organisation, political platform, propaganda organs, and political philosophy.[2] Yet we must stress that people in the eighteenth century tended to think of party in more flexible terms. A recent historian, borrowing Benedict Anderson's vocabulary, has defined eighteenth-century party as an 'imagined community of shared but not rigid national priorities'.[3]

When people in the eighteenth century themselves sought to define 'party' they were often slightly more specific, even though they were never as rigid as Jones. Out of the eight definitions of party in Samuel Johnson's *Dictionary*, only one, the first, relates directly to political party: '[a] number of persons confederated by similarity of designs or opinions in opposition to others; a faction'.[4] This ostensibly simple definition hints that political party in the eighteenth century carried more than one meaning in British discourse, although many of them overlapped. (1) Party could simply mean internal division in general terms. (2) It could more specifically refer to the Whig and Tory parties. (3) It frequently related to religious divisions, such as Anglicans and Dissenters – a crucial division since the 'Clarendon Code' in the 1660s – or high churchmen and latitudinarians,

---

[1] Poole and Rogers, *Bristol from Below* (Woodbridge, 2017), 94, 133–6; Harris, *Politics and the Nation* (Oxford, 2002), 46. We should also note that the paintings were only partly inspired by the 1754 Oxfordshire election. The fourth instalment in the series, on the front cover of this book, is likely to depict George Bubb Dodington, who was defeated in Bridgwater but secured a victory at Weymouth in 1754. See Paulson, *Hogarth* (Cambridge, 1993), 152–84.

[2] Jones, *The First Whigs* (Oxford, 1970 [1961]), esp. introduction.

[3] Graham, *Corruption, Party, and Government in Britain, 1702–13* (Oxford, 2015), 26.

[4] Johnson, *Dictionary of the English Language* (2 vols., London, 1755). Other definitions included persons engaged against each other, for instance, in legal cases or war, and a detachment of soldiers.

with countless theological subcategories.[5] (4) It could refer to the Court and Country 'parties', in other words those of government and opposition. (5) It could refer to the Jacobite threat. (6) It could mean political or parliamentary connection, that is, a smaller political group led by an identifiable leader, for example the Rockingham party connection. (7) It more rarely denoted different parts of the constitution, as in Commons and Lords. (8) Lastly, it could be synonymous with faction.

Historians have often stressed the importance of separating party in the 'real sense' from connections and factions,[6] but this is a distinction many in the period would not have recognised, although some would have, including Bolingbroke and Burke. 'Faction' in turn did not strictly correspond to our modern usage, when it denotes a splinter group or a party within a party. In the eighteenth century it could broadly mean four things. First, it could denote the Whig and Tory *factions*, in other words be interchangeable with party. Second, it could mean something akin to 'interest group', notably an economic interest. Third, it could refer to a party connection purely motivated by ambition and self-interest, with little or no interest in principles or opinions. This was sometimes described as a degenerated *party*, underlining the loose terminology. Finally, it could imply the even more negative connotation of a conspiracy within the state to destroy the constitution. Frederick Barlow's *Dictionary* (1772) defined faction as 'a tumult, discord, confusion or dissension'.[7]

Following Namier, the eighteenth century is often described as a period of personal factionalism followed by a clear two-party system in the nineteenth century. The truth is that the entire eighteenth century can be viewed as a period of fluctuation between personal factionalism and two-party division.[8] Although 'party spirit' waxed and waned, and the British press was often quick to celebrate when it diminished,[9] 'party' was a persistent key word in political debate.[10] Moreover, the British parties continuously confounded foreign visitors and commentators in the

---

[5] Gascoigne, *Cambridge in the Age of the Enlightenment* (Cambridge, 1989); Bradley, *Religion, Revolution and English Radicalism* (Cambridge, 1990); Young, *Religion and Enlightenment in Eighteenth-Century England* (Oxford, 1998); Clark, 'Church, Parties, and Politics', in *The Oxford History of Anglicanism* (5 vols., Oxford, 2017), II, 289–313.

[6] Graham, *Corruption, Party, and Government*, 30; Cannon (ed.), *The Whig Ascendancy* (London, 1981), ch. 8.

[7] Frederick Barlow, *The Complete English Dictionary* (2 vols., London, 1772).

[8] A similar point has been made about the period from 1760 to 1830 in Sack, *The Grenvillites 1801–29* (Urbana, 1979), xii.

[9] Harris, *London Newspapers in the Age of Walpole* (Toronto, 1987), 124.

[10] Cf. Langford, *Public Life and the Propertied Englishman* (Oxford, 1991), 118–38.

Hanoverian period. Voltaire observed that the prevalence of party spirit in the country meant that '[o]ne half of the nation [was] always the enemy of the other'.[11] In a similar vein, the Swiss travel writer César de Saussure remarked in 1729 that the 'two parties [we]re so opposed to each other that nothing but a real miracle could cause them to become united'.[12]

One of the implications of this book is that the period after 1714 should not be described as a time of political tranquillity, which used to be a dominant framework.[13] In the wake of the fall of Sir Robert Walpole in 1742, Johnson commented that '[i]t has been for many Years lamented, by those who are the most eminent among us for their Understanding and Politeness, that the Struggles of opposite Parties have engrossed the Attention of the Public, and that all Subjects of Conversation, and all kinds of Learning have given way to Politicks'.[14] As late as 1758, James Ralph spoke of party as the defining concept in the world of letters: 'we have a many-headed Intruder amongst us, call'd P[art]y In [teres]t, which, by the irresistible Power of two magical Monosyllables [Whig and Tory], has subdued all Things to himself'.[15] While a leading revisionist historian has pointed out that most people in the eighteenth century defined themselves by church rather than party membership,[16] and that court politics was an important alternative to parliamentary politics,[17] it is clear that the political nation viewed politics from a Whig–Tory perspective, with a remarkable degree of continuity, even beyond the disintegration of the Tory party as a coherent unit around 1760. What is more, the same historian has elsewhere pointed out that party played a key role, more important than the electorate, in the formulation of policy and in setting the terms for debate in the eighteenth century.[18]

---

[11] Voltaire, *Philosophical Letters* (Indianapolis, 2007), 92.
[12] Saussure, *A Foreign View of England in the Reigns of George I and George II* (London, 1902), 348.
[13] Following Plumb, *The Growth of Political Stability in England, 1675–1725* (London, 1967). Cf. Harris, *Politics and the Nation*.
[14] Preface to *Gentleman's Magazine*, XIII (1743).
[15] [Ralph], *The Case of Authors by Profession or Trade, Stated* (London, 1758), 65.
[16] Clark, *English Society, 1660–1832* (Cambridge, 2000 [1985]), 482.
[17] Clark, 'Introduction', in *Waldegrave Memoirs*, 1–21.
[18] Clark, 'A General Theory of Party, Opposition and Government, 1688–1832', *HJ*, 23 (1980), 295–325. We must add that the parties did not operate independently of the electorate, the importance of which should not be underestimated. Although only about 20–25 per cent of adult males had the vote, the early eighteenth-century electorate in England and Wales was larger and more diverse than at any time before 1868 (1832 brought it back to the level at the beginning of the eighteenth century). Floating voters numbered between 10 and 20 per cent of voters in an average county, as has been shown in Holmes, *Making a Great Power* (London, 1993), 329–33.

While the British parties were aristocratic and elitist in terms of their leadership, they had supporters from across society. Voters and writers identified themselves and their opponents along these lines.[19] For this reason, it has been argued that the parties were imperative in the creation of a 'public sphere' (*Öffentlichkeit*) in Britain, as they drew 'a broader public into debates over national issues, politicizing and at the same time educating it'.[20] Moreover, party was not an exclusive domain for men. Indeed, it was a significant component of what Elaine Chalus has dubbed 'social politics', a sphere in which women played prominent roles.[21] As Chalus rightly argues, the familial structure of eighteenth-century politics gave women (as wives, sisters, mothers, and daughters) at the top of society a clear position close to politics. At the same time, she may have under-estimated the place of party. For example, Sarah Churchill, Duchess of Marlborough, continued to meet and correspond with members of parliament long after her husband, the great general and statesman, passed away. She was seen as a Whig heroine, and the hack John Oldmixon dedicated to her his posthumous political testament, in which he described her as the most glorious asserter of the 'Whig cause'.[22] On the opposite side of the political spectrum, the Duchess of Buckingham, the illegitimate daughter of James II/VII, was *la grande dame* of the opposition to Walpole in the 1720s and 1730s.

The main context in which writers analysed party was historical discussions and studies centred on the seventeenth century and the reigns of William III/II and Anne. However, rival historical parallels, as well the party terminology itself, could be found in the ancient world, to which we will now briefly turn.

Greece and Rome

'Party' could be said to be between the first and second categories of political concepts discussed by Reinhart Koselleck: it is neither unchanged, nor radically changed (at least not in every aspect), nor entirely new.[23]

---

[19] For party politics among the 'middling sort' and the 'crowd' in various contexts in the period, see Wilson, *The Sense of the People* (Cambridge, 1995); Rogers, *Whigs and Cities* (Oxford, 1989).
[20] Melton, *The Rise of the Public in Enlightenment Europe* (Cambridge, 2001), 21.
[21] Chalus, 'Elite Women, Social Politics, and the Political World of Late Eighteenth-Century England', *HJ*, 43 (2000), 669–97.
[22] Oldmixon, *Memories of the Press, Historical and Political, for Thirty Years Past, from 1710 to 1740* (London, 1742).
[23] Koselleck, *Futures Past* (New York, 2005), 88.

While organised parliamentary parties can hardly be said to have existed before the late seventeenth century, the question of internal division has a longstanding tradition in the history of political thought. Internal conflict was theorised as *stasis* in Ancient Greece, notably in book three of Thucydides' history of the Peloponnesian War, written in the fifth century BC.[24] The Greek context was sometimes used in the eighteenth century to point to the danger of party strife.[25] The Roman context was arguably more important, however, and the terms 'party' and 'faction' are derived from Latin. The best known ancient account of factional strife in the early Roman Republic is book two of Livy's *History of Rome*. Livy spoke of a division of fathers (*patres*),[26] or senators, and plebs in 494 BC, springing from disagreement about the burden of debt held by the plebeians, leading to their secession and, eventually, the creation of the tribunes of the plebs.[27] Livy condemned 'factionalism' along with private interestedness as things always hurtful to the public.[28] The Roman historian also spoke of 'intestine discord' (*discordiae intestinae*), which would come to be a key phrase in later debates about party strife.[29] According to Livy, such discord in the city equalled disagreement among various body parts, which would lead to starvation.[30] By contrast, in his well-known commentary on the first ten books of Livy, Machiavelli praised such discord for leading to the creation of the tribunes of the plebs which made Rome a perfect commonwealth.[31]

In the second century BC, long-term political groupings in Rome developed, which were being described as *factio* and *pars* or *partes* (from *partire*, meaning to divide). As with the eighteenth century, *factio* did not correspond directly to the way we use 'faction'. *Partes* was the term Cicero

---

[24] *Stasis*, literally 'standing', has often been translated as 'civil war' and sometimes as 'faction'. The authoritative edition by Jeremy Mynott (Cambridge, 2013, 212 note 1) translates it as 'civil strife' and questions 'civil war' as an appropriate term because of scale. See also David Armitage, *Civil Wars* (Padstow, 2017), ch. 1, and note that *stasis* can also mean the opposite, that is, peace; see Schmitt, *Politische Theologie II*, 116–18.

[25] Brown, *Estimate*, I, 124; Burke, *Thoughts on French Affairs* (1791), in *W&S*, VIII, 343.

[26] Usually translated as 'patricians'.

[27] Livy, *History of Rome: Volume I* (Cambridge, MA, 1989), bk 2, chs. 23–33.

[28] 'sed factione respectuque rerum privatarum, quae semper offecere officientque publicis consiliis'. Ibid., ch. 30.2.

[29] Ibid., ch. 31.10.

[30] Ibid., ch. 32.9–12. Shakespeare would later employ this bodily metaphor in the first scene of *Coriolanus*.

[31] Machiavelli, *Discourses on Livy* (Chicago, 1998), 16–23. Although Machiavelli was primarily known as a defender of civil discord, he differentiated between beneficial and harmful divisions in *Istorie fiorentine* (1525), as Jean-Louis de Lolme picked up in the eighteenth century; see Whatmore, *Against War and Empire* (New Haven, 2012), 117.

commonly utilised when describing the 'personal parties' of Marius, Sulla, Sertorius, and Caesar. Sallust, on the other hand, preferred to write of *partes* in the sense of the dichotomy of senate and people, corresponding roughly to Cicero's *optimates* and *populares*. Originally, *factio* appears to have had a neutral meaning, but it gradually acquired a negative connotation, which it kept in the early-modern period.[32] Another key Roman substitute for 'party' was *amicitia* (friendship), an ideal depicted in Cicero's *De amicitia*.[33] The vocabulary of friendship was also frequently used as a euphemism for political grouping in the eighteenth century.[34] This did not necessarily have a positive connotation, however; note Burke's use of the phrase the 'king's friends' for the king's faction (see Chapter 11). According to Sallust, unanimity of purpose was *amicitia* among good people and *factio* among the bad. Sallust, a partisan of Caesar, frequently used *factio* to refer to self-proclaimed good men with oligarchical tendencies, so-called *optimates*. This usage was also common among 'optimate' partisans, for example when Cicero defined *factio* as representing a monopoly of power on the part of a clique of *optimates* in *De re publica*.[35]

At least as often read in the eighteenth century as Machiavelli's *Discorsi* was Montesquieu's short history of Rome, which repeated the Florentine's praise of internal discord. Montesquieu described how a secret war had been going on within the walls of Rome when it conquered the universe.[36] Paraphrasing Machiavelli, the Frenchman said that '[w]e hear in the authors only of the dissensions that ruined Rome, without seeing that these dissensions were necessary to it, that they had always been there and always had to be'.[37] Montesquieu stressed that these divisions had been necessary to the martial spirit of Rome. Moreover, he contended that 'whenever we see everyone tranquil in a state that calls itself a republic, we can be sure that liberty does not exist there'.[38] It is important to note, however, that while these 'Machiavellian' passages may sound straightforward, they are found in a chapter entitled 'Deux causes de la perte de Rome'. For a while, this dissension could produce harmony, 'as dissonances in music cooperate in producing overall concord'.[39] In the longer run, however, the expansion of Rome changed the nature of the republic;

[32] Ross Taylor, *Party Politics in the Age of Caesar* (Los Angeles, 1968 [1949]), 8–9.   [33] Ibid., 7.
[34] Bourke, *Empire and Revolution*, 270.   [35] Ross Taylor, *Party Politics in the Age of Caesar*, ch. 1.
[36] Montesquieu, *Considerations on the Causes of the Greatness of the Romans and their Decline* (Indianapolis, 1999 [1734]), 83.
[37] Ibid., 93.   [38] Ibid.
[39] Ibid., 94. The musical imagery suggests a commentary on Cicero's *De re publica* (2.69a), preserved and transmitted to us (and Montesquieu) via Augustine's *De civitate Dei contra paganos* (2.21).

'good laws, which have made a small republic grow large, become a burden to it when it is enlarged. For they were such that their natural effect was to create a great people, not to govern it.'[40] In other words, Rome was made for expansion, not for maintaining peace and stability: '[Rome] lost its liberty because it completed the work it wrought too soon.'[41] Importantly, for Montesquieu, Rome was an anachronistic model of government, whereas for Machiavelli it presented a blueprint for success.

Although Montesquieu's alleged agreement with Machiavelli is often highlighted, the Frenchman's account shares some of the complexity with the writings of his compatriot Jacques-Bénigne Bossuet, the seventeenth-century champion of royal absolutism. Bossuet had argued that Rome 'portait en son sein la cause de sa ruine, dans la jalousie perpétuelle du peuple contre le sénat, ou plutôt des plébéiens contre les patriciens'.[42] The extreme positions espoused by each side, and the embracing of particular interests, led directly to the rise of Caesar and the fall of the Republic, according to Bossuet.[43] A similar portrayal of internal discord in Rome was repeated in Adam Ferguson's history of the Roman Republic, a historian who viewed his work as an elaboration of Montesquieu's enterprise.[44] In short, eighteenth-century supporters of civilised monarchy such as Montesquieu and Ferguson were rarely straightforward Machiavellians, even if their language sometimes gave that impression.

Many eighteenth-century writers approached internal conflict between political parties from the prism of factional strife in the Roman Republic, and the commentators contributing to this tradition include Jonathan Swift and Thomas Gordon. Most discussions of party strife had at least some references to the tumults of Rome, although this may in hindsight be viewed as a partially misleading comparison, since the Roman divisions were so different from the parliamentary parties in eighteenth-century Britain. Roman tumults, at least of the kind Machiavelli condoned, were first and foremost social forces representing different orders in the state and parts of the constitution. By contrast, the British parties were parliamentary and had supporters among the aristocracy, gentry, middling sort, and even the crowd – as can be seen in Hogarth's election paintings (see Figures 1.1–1.4). Some, though not all, were acutely aware of this difference. As Hume put it, the contest in Rome 'was founded more on form [of government] than party'.[45] As we shall see, the British parties were not

---

[40] Ibid.   [41] Ibid., 95.   [42] Bossuet, *Discours sur l'histoire universelle* (Paris, 1966 [1681]), 413.
[43] Ibid., 415.
[44] Ferguson, *The History of the Roman Republic* (5 vols., Edinburgh, 1825 [1783]), I, xxv.
[45] Hume, 'Of Some Remarkable Customs' (1752), *Essays*, 373.

unrelated to the form of government, but they represented something other than parts of the constitution. For this reason, ancient political groupings were often translated simply as 'factions'.

Faction and Party

As mentioned above, many eighteenth-century writers used the terms party and faction interchangeably, although 'faction' generally had a more negative connotation than 'party'. The practice of treating them as synonyms had a longer history in the English language, however. In the 1640s, the Levellers would in passing refer to 'parties' and 'factions' as synonyms for parliamentary groups pursuing interests distinct from those of the people they were supposed to represent.[46] Much of the Levellers' programme, including annual elections and a ban on serving in parliament for two consecutive terms, was indeed intended to counteract the formation of such groups.[47] Around the same time, Thomas Hobbes criticised 'faction', and what he meant by this was related to the later concept of political party, as he referred to formations in assemblies based on policy difference. Interestingly, he also seems to have conceived of a more modern idea of faction, since he argued that such groups were always controlled by a minority, referred to as 'a faction within the faction'. Faction was anathema for Hobbes, who defined it as a commonwealth within a commonwealth, because it required citizens to form a new union and an alliance separate from the state.[48] This was entirely at odds with Hobbes's absolutist political theory. 'Princes who permit faction are as good as admitting an enemy within the walls', he warned.[49] It was also the major disadvantage of democracy, according to Hobbes. Deliberation in a large assembly was a source of factions, which in turn caused sedition and civil war. In a somewhat similar vein, Sir William Temple (1628–99), Swift's one-time patron, condemned 'faction' in the same breath as 'popular discontents'.[50] 'Divisions of Opinion, though upon Points of common Interest or Safety, yet if pursued to the Height, and with Heat of Obstinacy on both Sides, must end in Blows and Civil Arms', he concluded.[51]

---

[46] *The English Levellers* (Cambridge, 1998), 29, 99, 176.   [47] Ibid., 170–1.
[48] Hobbes, *On the Citizen* (Cambridge, 1997 [1642]), 149, 140.
[49] Ibid., 149. See also Hobbes, *Leviathan* (Cambridge, 1999 [1651]), 164, 228.
[50] 'Of Popular Discontents', *The Works of Sir William Temple* (2 vols., London, 1720), I, 255–71. Temple used 'party' to denote a political group, and occasionally synonymously with faction (261, 263, 266, 270).
[51] Ibid., 270.

One of the first to write about 'party' rather than 'faction' was George Savile, 1st Marquess of Halifax (1644–95), known as the 'Great Trimmer' for his bipartisanship. Halifax's language was in many ways similar to Hobbes's, as he believed that '[t]he best Party is but a kind of Conspiracy against the rest of the Nation'.[52] Be that as it may, he held that citizens sometimes had to side with the party they disliked the least.[53] The extreme aversion to the term 'faction' survived into the eighteenth century, even among Whig thinkers wedded to the mixed constitution.[54] According to E.W. Montagu, writing at the beginning of the Seven Years' War, factions originated in the 'lust of dominion', since 'the man, who is actuated by that destructive passion, must, of necessity, strive to attach to himself a set of men of similar principles, for the subordinate instruments'. For Montagu, faction was synonymous with iniquitous combination and he described the typical factious leader as someone who 'will court the friendship of every man, who is capable of promoting, and endeavour to crush every man, who is capable of defeating his ambitious views'.[55]

In contradiction with what he had said a few sentences earlier about 'similar principles', Montagu contended that 'private interest is the only tye which can ever connect a faction', particularly 'the lust of wealth'.[56] He further argued that even in a state immersed in luxury and corruption, such as Britain, 'the man who aims at being the head of a faction for the end of dominion, will at first cloak his real designs under an affected zeal for the service of the Government'.[57] Once in power, such a factious leader would not be esteemed by his faction for the good he would do to his country, but rather for the extent of which he could gratify his friends.[58] Montagu's views were not particularly purist but fairly mainstream. On the other side of the Whig spectrum, a Walpole-sponsored journal had earlier defined faction as 'the Struggle of a *private Interest* against a *Publick Good*'.[59] The major disagreement was not about the nature of faction, but rather *who* was factious: for Montagu it was Walpole-like leaders and for the Walpole press it was the opposition. This is discussed at greater length later in the book, especially in Chapter 3.

---

[52] Halifax, *Complete Works* (London, 1969), 209. [53] Ibid., 210.
[54] The holistic ideal within the idiom of the mixed constitution was classically expressed by Viscount Falkland and Sir John Culpepper in *His Majesties Answer to the XIX Propositions of Both Houses of Parliament* (1642), cited in Nelson, *The Royalist Revolution* (Cambridge, MA, 2014), 11.
[55] Montagu, *Reflections on the Rise and Fall of the Ancient Republicks: Adapted to the Present State of Great Britain* (Indianapolis, 2015 [1759]), 177.
[56] Ibid. [57] Ibid., 178. [58] Ibid., 178–9. [59] [Arnall], *Free Briton*, No. 125, 20 April 1732.

The same attitude is present in the Tory-Jacobite Roger North's apologia for Charles II. According to North, 'the ordinary Policy of Faction is to bring ruin to a Nation'.[60] The common usage of faction was to refer to a party that was 'unquiet, malecontent, ravenous, incroaching, querulous' in opposition and 'cruel' in power.[61] North was clear, however, that some 'Party-Men' were 'excusable', since it could also refer to such people who are 'desirous of Justice, Peace and good order'.[62] In his account of the Exclusion Crisis, he described the Whigs as a 'factious *Trojan*-Horse' and the Tories as engaged in 'a just Cause, and in good Company, [comprising] the Majority of the best Persons in the Nation'.[63] In other words, there was nothing wrong with taking sides if it meant 'the Side of the established Religion and Government, and for the Continuance of it in Peace'.[64]

While this anti-factional and holistic idiom survived into the eighteenth century, as is demonstrated by the example of such disparate writers as North and Montagu, there was a different strand of thought, fairly common among so-called Commonwealth thinkers, which associated internal conflict with liberty. Such ideas originated with Machiavelli's *Discorsi*, although Montesquieu became a key reference after his *Considérations*. As has been made familiar by J.G.A. Pocock, Machiavelli's arguments were taken up in English discourse in the seventeenth century.[65] The exponents of this tradition appear to have disagreed about the role of internecine conflict, however, with James Harrington preferring internal tranquillity and Algernon Sidney believing that it could be harmless and even beneficial.[66] The best example of a 'Machiavellian' argument in favour of civil discord is Walter Moyle's *Essay upon the Constitution of the Roman Government.*[67]

A parliament with real power is widely believed to be a precondition for the emergence of political parties and what above all made Britain different from other European powers in the eighteenth century.[68] Although absolutist France represented the 'other' for most Britons, the exceptionalism of

---

[60] North, *Examen: Or, An Enquiry into the Credit and Veracity of a Pretended Complete History; shewing the Perverse and Wicked Design of it ... All tending to Vindicate the Honour of the late King Charles II, and his Happy Reign ...* (London, 1740 [1713]), 51.

[61] Ibid., iii.   [62] Ibid., iii–iv.   [63] Ibid., 323–5.   [64] Ibid., 323, iv.

[65] Pocock, *The Machiavellian Moment* (Princeton, 1975), part three.

[66] Harrington, *The Commonwealth of Oceana* (Cambridge, 2001 [1656]), 29, 155, 158; Sidney, *Discourses concerning Government* (Indianapolis, 1996 [c.1698]), 159–61.

[67] Sullivan, 'Walter Moyle's Machiavellianism', *HEI*, 37 (2011) 120–7.

[68] Colley, *Britons* (Avon, 1992), 50; Habermas, *The Structural Transformation of the Public Sphere* (Cambridge, 1989 [1962]), ch. 3.

Britain in this regard can be oversold. While France and Spain famously dispensed with national assemblies, the Dutch Republic, the Holy Roman Empire, Switzerland, Poland-Lithuania, Hungary, Sweden, Sicily, and Ireland retained representative assemblies in the eighteenth century.[69] Some of these assemblies were more active and powerful than others, but political parties did have as much weight as in Britain in at least one other country. In the next section, we will briefly look at eighteenth-century Sweden.

Comparative Perspective: Sweden

Sweden's politics was dominated by the Hat and Cap parties (*Hatt och Mösspartierna*) during a great proportion of the so-called Age of Liberty (*Frihetstiden*) between 1718 and 1772.[70] The reasons why Sweden temporarily diverted from absolute monarchy were contingent. In 1718, the unexpected death of the heirless Charles XII, the warrior king immortalised by Voltaire in his *Histoire de Charles XII*, instigated, in the words of a prominent historian of Sweden, 'an experiment in parliamentary sovereignty destined to last for just over half a century'.[71] The death of Charles XII caused a succession crisis, with both his sister, Ulrika Elenora, married to Frederick, Landgrave of Hesse-Kassel in the Holy Roman Empire, and his nephew, Charles Frederick, Duke of Holstein-Gottorp, also in the empire, claiming a right to the throne. Ulrika Elenora struck a deal with the Swedish *Riksdag* of the Estates to succeed her brother, the outcome of which was a written constitution (1719 *års regeringsform*, revised in 1720) setting out a power-sharing agreement between the monarch and the assembly. In contrast with the British experience, the power of the Swedish monarch was severely limited, both in theory and practice.[72] This experiment involved a gradual development of party politics. Sweden's *Riksdag* was a legislative assembly of four estates: nobility, clergy,

---

[69] France kept a degree of representative institutions at the local level; see Hayton, Kelly, and Bergin (eds), *The Eighteenth-Century Composite State* (New York, 2010).

[70] Metcalf, 'The First "Modern" Party System?', *Scandinavian Journal of History*, 2 (1977), 265–87. For a recent study which downplays the 'modernity' of the Swedish eighteenth-century parties, see Winton, *Frihetstidens politiska praktik* (Uppsala, 2006).

[71] Metcalf, 'The First "Modern" Party System?', 265.

[72] For comparisons between the British and Swedish systems of government in the eighteenth century, see Ihalainen, *Agents of the People* (Leiden, 2010); Roberts, *Swedish and English Parliamentarism in the Eighteenth Century* (Belfast, 1973); Brolin, 'Svenskt och engelskt sjuttonhundratal: en jämförelse', *Historielärarnas föreningsårsskrift* (1971), 77–97.

burghers, and peasants. It was generally dominated by the nobility – and criticised on these grounds by Jean-Louis de Lolme[73] – and so were the parties. Besides mechanisms in favour of the nobility, they were numerically superior to the other estates put together by virtue of the fact that all noble families of Sweden could sit in the *Riksdag*.

Unsurprisingly, the first political parties that emerged after 1719 were dynastic parties: a Court party (*Hovparti*) attached to Ulrika Elenora and her husband who became Frederick I of Sweden in 1720, and the Holstein party, which championed Charles Frederick as heir to the throne. Meanwhile, the 1720–38 period was dominated by Arvid Horn, often compared to Walpole, and his personal following, known as 'Horn's friends'. Historians have questioned whether these early dynastic groupings and personal followings could be thought of as political parties in any meaningful way.[74] The twilight years of Horn's political career, however, saw the rise of the more concrete Hat and Cap parties.[75] The Hat party consisted of a coalition of former members of the Holstein party, which had been dissolved in 1727, and other opposition groups, united in their hostility to Horn's peace politics, particularly vis-à-vis Russia. They called their opponents 'nightcaps' (*nattmössor*), insinuating that they were asleep when the enemy advanced, and in contrast styled themselves as 'hats', referring to military headgear.[76] The 'Hats' supplanted the 'Caps' in 1738–9 in power and managed to monopolise rule until the mid-1760s, when the Cap party capitalised on Sweden's costly involvement in the Seven Years' War, known in Sweden as *Pommerska kriget* against Prussia, a war which had brought about ruptures within the Hat party.[77] The 'Caps' won the 1771 election, but only a year later the Age of Liberty, and the first age of party, came to an end in Sweden after Gustavus III's *coup d'état*.[78]

Unlike in Britain, Swedish print operated under strict censorship until 1766, but there was plenty of privately circulated and 'unprinted' literature.[79] The debate about party in Sweden appears to have shared some

---

[73] De Lolme, *A Parallel between the English Constitution and the Former Government of Sweden* (London, 1772).

[74] Hammarlund, *Politik utan partier* (Stockholm, 1985).

[75] Carlsson, *Parti – partiväsen – partipolitiker, 1731–43* (Stockholm, 1981).

[76] This straightforward division is a simplification, as has been emphasised by Nilzén, *Studier i 1730-talets partiväsen* (Stockholm, 1971).

[77] It has been argued that it was in the 1760s when the Swedish parties became organised for the first time, Brolin, *Hattar och mössor i borgarståndet, 1760–66* (Uppsala, 1953).

[78] A Swedish historian has made a speculative but not entirely implausible claim that Gustav III studied Bolingbroke's *Patriot King*; see Kjellin, 'Gustaf III, den patriotiske konungen', in *Gottfried Carlsson* (Lund, 1952), 323–38.

[79] Carlsson, *Frihetstidens handskrivna politiska litteratur: En bibliografi* (Göteborg, 1967).

common ground with the equivalent debate in Britain, although it has recently been argued that attitudes in Sweden were far more positive.[80] While a larger-scale and more systematic comparative study would be needed to corroborate this argument, it is certainly true that there was much anti-party rhetoric in eighteenth-century Britain, which is discussed in the next section.

Why Were Parties Detested?

Denouncing party division was a commonplace in eighteenth-century political discourse, and suspicion of party would remain strong at the end of the century, among 'moderates' such as the Federalists, as well as more 'radical' thinkers such as Thomas Paine and Condorcet.[81] Partisans from the Whig John Tutchin to the Tory-Jacobite Nathaniel Mist paid lip service to the ideal of consensus.[82] The most fundamental reason why parties were so widely disliked was that division was seen as posing an existential threat to the political community. Machiavelli may have been a popular author, but he was controversial and could not rival the influence of classical historians and philosophers such as Livy and Cicero, or the Bible. It was common to quote or paraphrase Mark 3:24 and Matthew 12:25: 'If a Kingdom is divided against itself, it cannot stand.'[83] Like Hobbes and Temple in the seventeenth century, many in the eighteenth century associated party conflict with civil war, and, as we shall see, Rapin and Hume traced the beginning of the British parties to the Cavalier–Roundhead division in the Wars of the Three Kingdoms. Britain's mixed and limited monarchy was celebrated, but the civil war and religious conflicts of the seventeenth century – spawned by the Reformation – left repercussions. In the wake of increased 'party spirit' in the context of the peace negotiations concluding the Seven Years' War, a Butite pamphlet complained that 'Everything was attempted, to throw us back into the barbarity of the last century.'[84]

---

[80] Metcalf, 'Hattar och Mössor 1766–72', in *Riksdag, Kaffehus och Predikstol* (Stockholm, 2003), 39–54.

[81] Urbinati, *Representative Democracy* (Chicago, 2006), 139–40, 159–60. It should be noted, however, that after the French Revolution and the advent of a representative system of government, Sieyès recognised that parties had become a necessity; see *Political Writings*, ed. Sonenscher (Indianapolis, 2003), introduction, xxxiiii.

[82] Black, *The English Press in the Eighteenth Century* (London, 1987), 305.

[83] Hobbes, *Leviathan* (Cambridge, 2011 [1651]), 127; Gordon, *Political Discourses on Tacitus and Sallust* (Indianapolis, 2013 [1728–44]), 243; Paine, *Common Sense* (Boston, 1856 [1776]), 23; Ferguson, *The Roman Republic*, II, 221.

[84] *A Full and Free Enquiry into the Merits of the Peace; With Some Strictures on the Spirit of Party* (London, 1765), 54.

From a mainstream Anglican perspective, viewing the state as a single, religious body, personified by the monarch, the connotation and association of party division with sectarianism and religious schism was anathema and a threat to the unified church-state.[85] What is more, 'party spirit' was deemed to be at odds with the Christian message of benevolence and brotherly love. Some divines dedicated entire sermons to the subject and preached the expulsion of parties.[86] One such sermon preached that party spirit 'lessens our Concern for Things of Great Moment, and increases it for Matters of no Consequence . . . inclines to Bigotry and Superstition . . . tends to confound the very Distinctions of Good and Evil . . . undermines Justice and Mercy . . . roots up our kind Affections, and good Dispositions; and instead of them fills our Hearts with Rage and Rancour'.[87] It further argued that party spirit corrupted the mind and vitiated judgement.[88] On a societal level, 'nothing can have a greater Tendency to embroil a State, and throw it into the utmost Disorder'.[89] Even the best constitution in the world could be destroyed by parties, the sermon warned. The only strife that should be permitted was among those 'who shall be most zealous and active in the Service of the Public', a type of strife that was believed could take place without parties.[90] The need to distinguish public spirit from party was a commonplace argument in the period.[91] In general, party strife was seen as especially illegitimate in times of national crisis, as was stressed by writers from Joseph Addison to William Eden (later Baron of Auckland).[92]

Parties were also disliked for what we may call lesser reasons. One of the most common criticisms of party was that it impeded independence as it encouraged a form of herd mentality. Halifax had likened parties to 'an Inquisition, where Men are under such a Discipline in carrying on the common Cause, as leaves no Liberty of private Opinion'.[93] Swift argued similarly in his first political pamphlet, in which the future Tory sought to defend the Whig Junto from impeachment. To follow a party blindly was

---

[85] Clark, *The Language of Liberty* (Cambridge, 1994), ch. 2.

[86] *The Duty of Benevolence and Brotherly Love, and the ill Effects of a Party Spirit. Considered in a Sermon Preached at the Assizes held at Newcastle upon Tyne, on Tuesday the 8th of August, 1727* (N.p., 1727), 104–5. See also Secker, *A Sermon preach'd before the University of Oxford, at St Mary's, on Act Sunday in the afternoon, July 8, 1733* (1733), 20, warning about the 'rage of party zeal' with particular reference to the Jacobites in Oxford.

[87] *The Duty of Benevolence*, 106.   [88] Ibid., 105.   [89] Ibid., 106.   [90] Ibid., 110.

[91] See, e.g., *The Present Necessity of Distinguishing Publick Spirit from Party* (London, 1736).

[92] See the first letter in Eden's *Four Letters to the Earl of Carlisle* (London, 1779), entitled 'On certain perversions of political reasoning; and on the nature, progress, and effect of party spirit and of parties.'

[93] Halifax, *Complete Works*, 211.

'below the Dignity both of Human Nature, and Human Reason', according to Swift.[94] John Trenchard contended along similar lines in *Cato's Letters*.[95] Later in the century, Johnson, via James Boswell, would voice a comparable complaint when discussing the Rockinghamite Whig Burke, a member of Johnson's club: 'Dr Johnson now said a certain eminent political friend of ours [Burke] was wrong in his maxim of sticking to a certain set of men on all occasions.'[96]

To some observers, attachment to party seemed inexplicable and random. 'There is a sort of Witchcraft in Party, and in Party Cries, strangely wild and irresistible', wrote Thomas Gordon. 'One Name charms and composes; another Name, not better nor worse, fires and alarms.'[97] Gordon's 'First Discourse: On Party and Faction', prefixed to his translation of Sallust, presented one of the most vehement criticisms of party in the century, but it was by no means atypical. To him, parties were pernicious for two broad reasons. In the first instance, they led to zealous disputes among enthusiastic followers. Party thus meant the triumph of passion over reason. These passions could be used by ambitious leaders to further their own interest at the expense of the public. According to Gordon, Caesar was a 'great Party-Man ... who, by the Force and Improvement of Party, put an End to Liberty'.[98] Parties thus presented a double menace: they could either represent extreme convictions and overconfidence in one's beliefs, or no beliefs at all, but simply a veil for naked self-interest and ambition. Both types were believed to endanger *salus populi*. As this book demonstrates in later chapters, Hume was particularly concerned with the former and Bolingbroke with the latter.

Both Swift and Gordon were suspicious and critical of party leaders. This remained a prominent theme in anti-party rhetoric throughout the century.[99] Indeed, William Cleghorn defined the spirit of party as 'Attachment to certain particular Men or Leaders', as opposed to principles.[100] The absence of independence that came with party membership was a common objection. The orientalist William Jones said that he would not 'enlist under the banners of a party ... because no party

---

[94] Swift, *A Discourse of the Contests and Dissensions ... in Athens and Rome* (London, 1701), 56.
[95] *Cato's Letters* (2 vols., Indianapolis, 1995 [1720–3]), I, 117–22. (No. 16, 11 February 1721.)
[96] *To the Hebrides: Samuel Johnson's Journey to the Western Iceland of Scotland and James Boswell's Journal of a Tour of the Hebrides* (Edinburgh, 2007 [1775 and 1785]), 30.
[97] Gordon, *Political Discourses*, 237.   [98] Ibid., 318.
[99] *The True Whig Displayed. Comprehending Cursory REMARKS on the Address to the Cocoa-Tree. By a TORY* (London, 1762), 8.
[100] Cleghorn, *The Spirit and Principles of the Whigs and Jacobites Compared* (London, 1746), 16–17.

would receive a man determined, as I am, to think for himself'.[101] At the same time, Jones relished hearing his friend Burke give speeches in parliament, and even if he was critical of the Irishman's defence of party, he 'envied [Burke's] access to political power', according to Jones's biographer.[102]

We should not exaggerate the dislike of party, since it could also be a powerful principle for rallying support, long before the time of Burke and the Rockingham Whigs. Walpole's speech to followers and potential followers, at the height of the Excise Crisis of 1733, ahead of a crucial vote in the Commons, is a case in point. Walpole professed that he was 'not pleading [his] own cause, but the cause of the Whig party', adding that 'it is in Whig principles I have lived, and in Whig principles I will die'.[103] Lord Hervey commented that the speech reignited 'party spirit' and helped secure a favourable outcome. Burke was thus not being anachronistic when he said that Walpole had governed by 'party attachments'.[104] This example shows that it would be too simplistic to conclude that 'party' was simply an 'accusatory term' at the time.[105] At certain times and in certain settings, it formed part of the glue which helped maintain what Joanna Innes has called the 'more or less informal co-operation between leading statesmen' on which the distribution of political power was dependent in the eighteenth century.[106] But even though party was an important organisational principle, the term carried negative connotations, which is why euphemisms were often used. The Tories and Whigs in Oxford, for instance, were called the Old and New Interest, respectively.[107] Whigs often referred to Tories as the high or haughty party, and Tories themselves preferred to style themselves as the 'True Blues' or simply the country gentlemen.[108] In the next section, I consider one further and highly significant reason why party was often seen as pernicious by looking at Jacobitism.

Jacobitism

A crucial phenomenon which encumbered positive appreciations of party in the first half of the eighteenth century was the menace of Jacobitism, the

---

[101] *Letters of William Jones*, I, 344.   [102] Franklin, '*Orientalist Jones*' (Oxford, 2011), 164.
[103] *Hervey's Memoirs*, I, 182–3.
[104] Burke, *An Appeal from the New to the Old Whigs* (1791), *W&S*, IV, 416.
[105] Cf. Rosenblum, *On the Side of the Angels*, 21.   [106] Innes, *Inferior Politics* (Oxford, 2009), 50.
[107] Smollett, *Continuation of the Complete History of England. Volume the First* (London, 1760), 236–7.
[108] In Norwich, however, blue and white were the colours of the local Whigs; see *The Diary of Windham* (London, 1866), 100.

movement that sought to restore the Stuart royal family after the Glorious Revolution.[109] The enduring strength of Jacobitism meant that it took a long time before the Protestant settlement was on a sure footing, and Britain suffered two major Jacobite risings and several plots and near-invasions in the eighteenth century. In many ways, the precise end of the Jacobite cause as a real threat to the Hanoverian regime, at least in England, was neither the defeat at Culloden in 1746 nor the accession of George III in 1760, but the abandoned Elibank Plot in the early 1750s, thus called after Hume's longstanding friend Lord Elibank, even if his brother Alexander Murray was more deeply involved in the plotting.[110] In its aftermath, the Highlander Dr Archibald Cameron became the last Jacobite rebel to be executed for his role in the 'Forty-five'.[111] After this event, Jacobitism survived for a long time as a bogeyman and as a sentimental attachment, especially in Scotland. Shelburne wrote in an autobiographical sketch: 'All Scotland was enthusiastically devoted to the exiled family, with a very few exceptions. In 1756 going through the country as a traveller, I heard many of them, sober as well as drunk, avow it in the most unreserved manner.'[112] When the Select Society, the famous debating club which included Hume, Smith, and the Jacobite Elibank, was founded in Edinburgh in 1754, it was decided that all topics could be debated 'except such as regard Revealed Religion, or which may give occasion to vent principles of Jacobitism'.[113] Even though the Elibank Plot was the last serious Jacobite plot on English soil, a French invasion with Jacobite involvement was planned during the Seven Years' War in 1759, but it was aborted.[114]

Jacobitism was the defining political question in Britain in the first half of the eighteenth century. It is a key context for party strife in the period, especially since many Tories were periodically involved in Jacobite plotting, and as a party routinely associated with the movement by their

---

[109] For the importance of dynastic politics at the start of the eighteenth century, see Hone, *Literature and Party Politics at the Accession of Queen Anne* (Oxford, 2017).

[110] Mossner, 'New Hume Letters to Lord Elibank, 1748–76', *Texas Studies in Literature and Language*, 4 (1962), 431–60. Little is known about the plot itself, but see Charles Petrie, 'The Elibank Plot, 1752–3', *Transactions of the Royal Historical Society*, 14 (1931), 175–96. Earlier generations of political historians used to date the end of Jacobitism as a 'serious menace' even earlier, often to the defeat of the Atterbury Plot in 1720–2; see Foord, *His Majesty's Opposition* (Oxford, 1964), 75, 467.

[111] Harris, *Politics and the Nation*, 36.

[112] Fitzmaurice, *Life of Shelburne* (3 vols., London, 1875), I, 50.

[113] Robertson, *The Scottish Enlightenment and the Militia Issue*, 85.

[114] Nordmann, 'Choiseul and the Last Jacobite Attempt of 1759', in *Ideology and Conspiracy* (Edinburgh, 1982), 201–17.

opponents. However, identifying *consistent* Jacobites among parliamentary Tories has been notoriously difficult, although there certainly were such ones, including William Shippen and Charles Somerset, Duke of Beaufort.[115] Significantly, there were also men of letters committed to Jacobitism with evident links to the Tory party, notably Thomas Carte, which shows that the association between Jacobitism and Toryism was not only Whig propaganda. When William King, principal of St Mary Hall at Oxford, gave a controversial speech in Latin at the opening of the Radcliffe Camera Library in 1749 – in which he repeated the word *redeat* ('that he may return') six times – it was attended by Tory MPs and peers such as Beaufort, the Earl of Oxford, Sir Watkin Williams Wynn, and Sir Walter Bagot.[116] Oxford was a stronghold of Jacobitism for much of the eighteenth century. It was intermingled with High Church Toryism and sometimes caused public disturbances. William Bromley, MP for Oxford University, wrote in May 1715 to Arthur Charlett, Master of University College, Oxford: 'I have such Reports of Riots & Disorders committed at Oxon [Oxford], & the Scholars having been concerned in them, that I shall be glad to be favoured with a particular Account of them from you.'[117] The Oxford non-juror Thomas Hearne described these riots enthusiastically: 'The People run up and down crying King James the 3d, the true King, no Usurper, the Duke of Ormond, &c. & Healths were every where drank suitable to the Occasion, & every one at the same time Drank to a new Restauration, which I heartily wish may speedily happen.'[118]

The behaviour of Tory MPs could be contradictory. Sir John Hynde Cotton, for example, was actively involved in Jacobite plotting when he briefly served in Henry Pelham's broad-bottom administration in 1744–5.[119] We should thus note that the connection between Tories and Jacobitism was often opportunistic rather than principled, and may have stemmed partly from the fact that the death or replacement of a

[115] The optimistic headcount of Jacobite Tories by Eveline Cruickshanks in *Commons, 1715–54* and *Political Untouchables* (London, 1979) and the conclusion that the Tories were consistently committed to Jacobitism as a party have been criticised; see, e.g., *Tory and Whig*, xxxix–xlii and Hanman, '"So Few Facts"', *PH*, 19 (2000), 237–57 (cf. Cruickshanks, 'Jacobites, Tories and "James III"', *PH*, 21 (2002), 247–54). In an important study of the 1710–14 Tory ministry, Daniel Szechi identified the existence of Hanoverian and middle-of-the-road Tories along with Jacobites, and argued that the latter did not view themselves as separate from the Tories; see *Jacobitism and Tory Politics, 1710–14* (Edinburgh, 1984), 76, 146–7.
[116] Robson, *The Oxfordshire Election of 1754* (Oxford, 1949), 5.
[117] MS Ballard 38, Bodleian, f. 94.   [118] *Hearne's Recollections*, V, 62.
[119] Glickman, 'The Career of Sir John Hynde Cotton (1686–1752)', *HJ*, 46 (2003), 817–41.

monarch was the most straightforward way to effect a change in ministry and policy at this time, especially after 1714. This explains why many Tories went to court upon the death of George I in 1727, in vain as it turned out, and why opposition leaders and parties so often in the eighteenth century associated with the Hanoverian successor to the throne (the 'reversionary interest').[120] Few parliamentary Tories took an active part in rebellious acts; on the contrary, many appear to have wavered when it really mattered. For example, John Perceval wrote of Thomas Rowney, MP for the borough of Oxford in 1722–59, that 'It is remarkable of this man … allways reputed a rank Jacobite, who has drunk the Pretenders health 500 times, that when the Pretenders son came into England [during the "Forty-five"], he was frightened out of his wits – and ordered his chaplain to pray for King George which he had never suffered him to do in his life before.'[121] Also of note is Johnson's exaggerated yet illustrative remark to Boswell in 1777 that the people 'would not give twenty shillings a piece to bring about [a Jacobite restoration]. But, if a mere vote could do it, there would be twenty to one [in favour].'[122] Much Jacobitism was indeed passive, and often simply an excuse for sociability and drinking. Even at times when Jacobitism was more a spectre than reality, it was a potent one. Crucially, it informed George I's and George II's suspicion of Tories and effectively resulted in the proscription of the party until the accession of George III in 1760. Jacobitism remains centre stage in the next section, which considers the dynamics within the different national components of the British Isles.

Scotland, Wales, Ireland, and the British State

As set out in the Introduction, this study is a contribution to British history. Much of the book will focus on London and Westminster politics. This may be criticised as Anglo-centric, but the ambition is not to capture an 'English' party debate. As Joanna Innes has stressed, English-language print culture was British rather than merely English, and England itself was governed by a British state after 1707.[123] Moreover, the names of Whig

---

[120] *Egmont Papers*; *Tory and Whig*, lii–lv; Eagles, 'Loyal Opposition? Prince Frederick and Parliament', *PH*, 33 (2014), 223–42; Eagles, 'Frederick, Prince of Wales, the "Court" of Leicester House and the "Patriot" Opposition to Walpole', *The Court Historian*, 21 (2016), 140–56.

[121] *Egmont Papers*, 149–50. [122] Boswell, *The Life of Johnson* (2 vols., London, 1791), II, 145.

[123] Innes, *Inferior Politics*, 9. The Scottish contribution to eighteenth-century British print culture was disproportionately large; see Allan, *The Making of British Culture* (London, 2008) and Sher, *The Enlightenment and the Book* (Chicago, 2006).

and Tory originated in Scotland and Ireland, respectively, even if these names were applied to political parties in the English context of the Exclusion Crisis and became entrenched after the Glorious Revolution. 'British' in this study refers mainly to Anglo-British. As Colin Kidd has shown, the British identity which was slowly being fostered in the wake of the Anglo-Scottish Union of 1707 was largely based on the English constitution, and the North British writers of the Scottish Enlightenment 'adopted an Anglo-British institutional identity'.[124] Scottish and Irish thinkers made a disproportionately large contribution to British political debate, however, and this is reflected in the present study, which pays a great deal of attention to the Scot Hume and the Irishman Burke in particular. In this section, I argue why Scotland merits close attention, before adumbrating the party-political contexts of Wales and Ireland.

The debate about party in the eighteenth century had at least the potential to be more impartial in Scotland than in England. When setting out to write about politics in the late 1730s, Hume's main focus was English rather than Scottish politics.[125] Had Scotland retained its parliament after 1707, his focus may have been different, although he also wanted to target the London book market. As Hume himself emphasised, political opinion south of the border was always party-political. According to his friend Adam Smith, Scotland had benefited enormously from the decline of party spirit since the abolition of the Scottish parliament in 1707.[126] The standard identification of the 'Scottish Enlightenment' with Whiggism, although a more 'sceptical' or 'scientific' kind, which was less tribal, has become a historical commonplace but needs to be more qualified. As we shall see in Chapters 6–8, if Whiggism is understood in the sense of ancient constitutionalism and glorification of the English past,[127] then Hume was certainly not a Whig. If it is taken in the more partisan sense of defending the 1688–9 Revolution Settlement, then Hume can be perceived as a 'sceptical Whig' – a phrase Hume used once to label the conclusion of one of his essays.[128] As becomes clear from his letters, however, this is the only time he used the term to describe himself, and he became disenchanted with the word after he had written his *History of England*, and expected to receive greater acclaim from Tories such as

---

[124] Kidd, *Subverting Scotland's Past* (Cambridge, 1993), 1, 99.
[125] This is particularly true in the essays he published in 1748, which are discussed in Chapter 6.
[126] See Chapter 13.   [127] Kidd, *Subverting Scotland's Past*, 5–6.   [128] *Letters*, I, 111.

Johnson than Whigs.[129] When applied to Hume, the Whig label is so thin and provokes too many unhelpful connotations to be helpful, unless it is used within the precise and local context which Hume himself intended. This is discussed in greater detail in the Hume chapters, especially Chapter 6.

After the Union of 1707, Scotland sent sixteen peers to the Lords and forty-five members to the Commons, a disproportionately small number chosen by a puny electorate of less than 1 per cent of the population. But even though the Union with England transformed the nature of Scottish party politics, it did not abolish it.[130] The most important party division in Scotland was that between Whigs and Jacobites. Jacobitism in Scotland was not confined to the Highland clans but permeated throughout Scottish society.[131] Scotland was centre stage of the two major risings of 1715 and 1745, and Scots were involved in the assassination attempt of William of Orange in 1695, the minor risings in 1708 and 1719, the Jacobite plots of 1703, 1706, 1717, 1723, and 1751–2, as well as the two abortive French invasions of 1744 and 1759. As a recent survey summarised the dynamics within the three kingdoms, 'whereas the English drank for Jacobitism and Irish dreamt of Jacobitism, the Scots died for Jacobitism'.[132]

Scotland also had personal factionalism in abundance. Walpole devolved Scottish patronage to Archibald Campbell, 1st Earl of Ilay and 3rd Duke of Argyll (after 1743), one of the sixteen Scottish peers. Argyll was the most powerful Scottish politician until his death in 1761.[133] Under George III, his favourite Lord Bute emerged as a key political figure for some years in the 1760s, and in the final decades of the century Henry Dundas, the Younger Pitt's ally, became known as the uncrowned king of Scotland.[134] In this environment, the politics of patronage, within the Church of Scotland especially but also within the universities, law, and the arts, was the source of personal partisanship in Scotland.[135] Moreover, from the 1730s the Kirk was divided into Moderate and Popular (or evangelical) parties.[136]

---

[129] *Boswell's Edinburgh Journals 1767–1786* (Edinburgh, 2013), 258.
[130] Allan, *Scotland in the Eighteenth Century* (Abingdon, 2002); Shaw, *The Political History of Eighteenth-Century Scotland* (New York, 1999).
[131] Macinnes, 'Jacobitism in Scotland', *Scottish Historical Review*, 86 (2007), 225–52.
[132] Ibid., 230.
[133] Murdoch, *'The People Above'* (Edinburgh, 1990); Emerson, *An Enlightened Duke* (Kilkerran, 2013).
[134] Fry, *The Dundas Despotism* (Edinburgh, 1992).
[135] Emerson, *Academic Patronage in the Scottish Enlightenment* (Edinburgh, 2008).
[136] Sher, *Church and University in the Scottish Enlightenment* (Edinburgh, 2000 [1985]).

Eighteenth-century Wales was dominated by influential gentry families, many of whom were members of the Commons rather than the Lords.[137] While the Welsh gentry had been distinguished in the seventeenth century, no MP for a Welsh constituency sat in the Cabinet from Robert Harley's elevation to the Lords in 1711 until 1822.[138] For much of the eighteenth century, the most prominent Welsh politicians were in opposition. Like Scotland and Ireland, Wales was a hotbed for Jacobitism with many Welsh Jacobite MPs, including Wynn, who publicly burned a picture of George I in 1722 and corresponded with the Jacobite court in the 1740s.[139] In the Wars of the Three Kingdoms, Wales had been strongly royalist, and most of its MPs were Tories in the reign of Anne (for instance, twenty-three out of twenty-seven MPs after the election of 1710).[140] By 1727, a little more than a decade into the Age of Whig Supremacy, the Whigs won a majority of Welsh seats, but they were never as strong as the Tories had been under Anne.[141] Moreover, Toryism and Jacobitism remained vibrant at the local level and in parliament, notably in the shape of Sir John Philipps. Monarchism and the Church of England were popular in the principality, and religious toleration did not become a significant question until the later decades of the century. What is more, nominal Tories and Whigs often cooperated locally when it suited them. It has been argued that Welsh politics became increasingly anglicised during the course of the eighteenth century, as the Welsh gentry spent more time in London during parliamentary sessions and married English wives. In the twilight years of George II, ancient Tory families had evolved into supporters of Whig ministries, reflecting the decline of the importance of the Whig–Tory dichotomy in national politics in the immediate years prior to the accession of George III.[142] This event in a sense 'restore[d] Tory interests' in the principality, and indeed turned many traditional Whig families away from the Duke of Newcastle, the Whig magnate, to the young monarch.[143]

Unlike Scotland, Ireland retained its own parliament during the eighteenth century, even though it was subordinated to Westminster, especially before a series of constitutional changes in 1782, initiated by the second Rockingham ministry's repeal of the Declaratory Act. Irish political debate was closely bound up with England's, and some Irish political

---

[137] The key study is Thomas, *Politics in Eighteenth-Century Wales* (Cardiff, 1998).   [138] Ibid., 10.
[139] Although, like many Tory-Jacobite MPs, he did not take an active part in the 'Forty-five'; see Chapter 5.
[140] Thomas, *Politics in Eighteenth-Century Wales*, 74.   [141] Ibid., 93.   [142] Ibid., 131.
[143] Ibid., 204.

figures such as Robert Molesworth were MPs in Dublin as well as Westminster. As Catholics were excluded, the Irish parliament embodied the Protestant Ascendency. The importance of the Irish parliament should not be underestimated, however. Having met infrequently in the seventeenth century, and not at all from 1666 to 1689, the Irish parliament became a regular part of Anglo-Irish politics in the eighteenth century.[144] As its leading historian has demonstrated, the contrast between the Rage of Party during the Reign of Anne and the Whig Supremacy after 1715 was even starker in Ireland than in England.[145] Irish Protestantism was not the same as Irish Whiggism, as an Irish Tory 'High Church' party was formed within the Protestant ranks after 1692 in response to the question of Dissent.[146] Although individual Tories remained, this Anglican Tory party declined in the context of the crisis over the Hanoverian Succession between 1713 and 1715. The opposition in parliament then usually called itself Country or Patriot. Towards the end of the century, a Whig party was forming in Ireland, modelled on Burke's *Thoughts on the Cause of the Present Discontents* and with close links to Burke's English Whig connection.[147]

Ireland was another potential stronghold for Jacobitism thanks to the Catholicism of the Stuarts, although its prominence is disputed.[148] The bloodiest battles after the so-called Glorious Revolution took place in Ireland between 1689 and 1691, ending with the Treaty of Limerick and followed by what has been described as a decade-long English occupation of Ireland.[149] The outcome was that the Catholic interest was annihilated as a political force.[150] Since the Irish Whigs and Tories in a sense represented the Protestant community in opposition to the Catholic majority, Irish Tories tended to support the Protestant Succession from the start. The Irish diaspora, on the other hand, at the exiled Stuart court and in the French army, was more involved in Jacobite activities.[151]

What brought William victory was the creation of a continental-style war apparatus paid for by English taxes of unprecedented size, in other words, the creation of what has become known as a fiscal-military state.[152] The Williamite revolution was consummated by the creation of the Bank

---

[144] See Hayton (ed.), *The Irish Parliament in the Eighteenth Century* (Edinburgh, 2001), esp. introduction.
[145] Hayton, *Ruling Ireland, 1685–1742* (Woodbridge, 2004).   [146] Ibid., 94.
[147] O'Gorman, *The Whig Party and the French Revolution* (New York, 1967), 218–32.
[148] See, however, Ciardha, *Ireland and the Jacobite Cause, 1685–1766* (Dublin, 2000).
[149] Szechi, *The Jacobites* (Manchester, 1994), 50.   [150] Hayton, *Ruling Ireland*, 31.
[151] Szechi, *1715* (New Haven, 2006), 44–6.   [152] Brewer, *The Sinews of Power* (London, 1989).

of England and the national debt in the 1690s – the so-called financial revolution[153] – and it became the target of Country, Tory, and Jacobite denunciations for half a century, and of 'radical' ones subsequently. John Brewer's fiscal-military state framework has been influential in eighteenth-century historiography in recent decades. The viability of this thesis has, however, recently come under criticism by the leading economic historian Julian Hoppit, who argues that the eighteenth-century British state was a fragmented entity and not a mighty leviathan.[154] By focusing on economic legislation, Hoppit aptly demonstrates that the British fiscal regime in the eighteenth century was more irregular and patchy than what is conjured up by the image of Brewer's fiscal-military state. However, this important revisionism, inspired by Paul Langford's work on the 'local' nature of eighteenth-century politics,[155] does not undermine the fact that the British state was widely perceived as growing exponentially after the Glorious Revolution.[156] An anti-executive language was formed – building on the seventeenth-century Country tradition – which was perfected by Bolingbroke, the vestiges of which survived in the writings of Burke.

The final theme we look at briefly in this chapter is the question of human sociability – one of the most prominent subjects of recent historiography of political thought.[157]

Sociability and Partisanship

One underlying dimension of the debate about parties in the eighteenth century was the belief that partisanship was a key component of man's social nature. Adam Ferguson is often credited with what has been described as 'antagonistic sociability',[158] but he was drawing on a long-standing tradition in English and Scottish enlightenment debates. Notably, the 3rd Earl of Shaftesbury had argued that everyone was imbued with a *'combining* Principle' since neither the interests of the world in general nor those of the nation were easily apprehended by the

---

[153] The classic study remains Dickson, *The Financial Revolution in England* (London, 1967).
[154] Hoppit, *Britain's Political Economies* (Cambridge, 2017), 22–3.
[155] Langford, *Public Life and the Propertied Englishman.*
[156] For an attempt to reconcile these interpretations, see Innes, 'Polite and Commercial's Twin', in *Revisiting the Polite and Commercial People* (Oxford, 2019), 241–58.
[157] Hont, *Jealousy of Trade* (Cambridge, MA, 2005); Hundert, *The Enlightenment Fable* (Cambridge, 1994); Sagar, *The Opinion of Mankind* (Princeton, 2018).
[158] Kalyvas and Katznelson, *Liberal Beginnings* (Cambridge, 2008), 71–6.

individual.[159] This combining principle gave rise to 'the most generous Spirits', but also '*Love of Party,* and Subdivision by *Cabal*', or '*Wheels within Wheels*', according to Shaftesbury.[160] In other words, party was a sign of sociability rather than selfishness, and the 'true *Men of Moderation*' and 'the least forward in *taking Party*' were also the most selfish.[161] In the Scottish context, Francis Hutcheson took issue with Shaftesbury on this score. While Hutcheson conceded that association was often 'amiable and good', including 'Cabals for Defence of Liberty against a Tyrant', he believed that party spirit in general represented a corruption of the moral sense.[162] Being biased to one party or sect would pervert 'our natural Notions of Good and Evil', Hutcheson claimed.[163] Although Smith dis-agreed with Hutcheson about much, he concurred with his old teacher in viewing 'party spirit' as destructive of morality.[164] Other thinkers such as Ferguson sought to strike a balance between Shaftesbury and Hutcheson on this question. Hume, who said that the 'social sympathy in human nature' gave rise to 'party zeal, [and] a devoted obedience to factious leaders',[165] was clear that human beings were inclined to gregarious as well as conflictual dispositions. This line of thinking prompted statements such as Thomas Jefferson's that 'the terms whig and tory belong to natural as well as to civil history'.[166]

While the debate about human sociability no doubt informed such philosophically minded political thinkers as Hume and Burke, the more common way to discuss and write about political parties in the century was in political, historical, and constitutional terms, and this book will focus more closely on these expressions, starting with Rapin in Chapter 2. It will be argued that the French historian of England did more than anyone to shape the debate about party in the first half of the eighteenth century.

---

[159] Shaftesbury, '*Sensus Communis*' (1709), in *Characteristicks of Men, Manners, Opinions, Times* (3 vols., Indianapolis, 2001 [1711]), I, 70.

[160] Ibid., 71–2.   [161] Ibid., 72.

[162] Hutcheson, *An Inquiry into the Original of our Ideas of Beauty and Virtue* (Indianapolis, 2004 [1725]), 141–2.

[163] Ibid., 142.   [164] See Chapter 13.

[165] Hume, *Enquiry Concerning the Principles of Morals* (Oxford, 1975 [1751]), 224.

[166] Cited in Rosenblum, *On the Side of the Angels*, 18.

CHAPTER 2

Rapin on the Origins and Nature of Party Division in Britain

Rapin seems to be the most candid of all those who have wrote on the affairs of England.

Adam Smith, *Lectures on Rhetoric and Belles Lettres* (1762–3)

Introduction

Paul de Rapin-Thoyras (1661–1725) – often mentioned, but rarely studied in detail – is known for having written the pre-Macaulay Whig interpretation of the history of England.[1] A French Huguenot, Rapin had been driven out of his native country after the revocation of the Edict of Nantes in 1685. He first went to England, but moved quickly on to the Dutch Republic, where the majority of the Huguenot diaspora resided along with many exiled Whigs.[2] He returned to England as part of William of Orange's invasion in 1688, and then served William as a soldier in Ireland, taking part in the battles of the Boyne and Limerick. From 1693 to 1704, he worked as a tutor to the son of the king's favourite, William Bentinck, 1st Earl of Portland.[3] His *Histoire d'Angleterre* (10 vols., 1724–7) was a truly European enterprise: written in the French language, in Germany, and published in the Dutch Republic.[4] The thrust of his thesis was that England was the only European country to have preserved the free constitution which had been the common inheritance of the

---

[1] Trevor-Roper, *History and the Enlightenment* (New Haven, 2010), 194–5; Trevor-Roper, 'Our First Whig Historian: Rapin', in *From Counter-Reformation to Glorious Revolution* (London, 1992), 252; Franchina, 'Entering the Republic of Letters: The Backstage of Paul Rapin Thoyras' *Histoire d'Angleterre*', *Erudition and the Republic of Letters*, 3 (2018), 315–47.

[2] Koselleck, *Kritik und Krise* (Sinzheim, 2013 [1957]), 51. For context, see Marshall, *John Locke, Toleration and Early Enlightenment Culture* (Cambridge, 2006), esp. part one.

[3] This son served as a Whig MP from 1705 to 1709, when he inherited his father's earldom and took his seat in the Lords. At the end of his life he was governor of Jamaica.

[4] For the success of the *Histoire*, see Sullivan, 'Rapin, Hume and the Identity of the Historian in Eighteenth-Century England', *HEI*, 26 (2002), 145–62.

conquerors of Rome. He thus agreed with his fellow Huguenot François Hotman (*Franco-Gallia*, 1573) that France had had an ancient constitution which involved power sharing, but unlike England's constitution it had been lost. Rapin had English predecessors, notably James Tyrrell and Laurence Echard,[5] but his became the standard Whig history for a generation. His thesis can helpfully be seen in contrast to that of the royalist historian Robert Brady, who had effectively refuted the idea that parliament was of immemorial antiquity in the 1680s.[6] Even if Rapin claimed to have written 'impartial' history, and was celebrated for this by Voltaire and others,[7] the Whig stamp is hard to avoid.[8] Yet Rapin was not just any Whig historian. Adam Smith regarded him as far superior to the 'party writers' Lord Clarendon and Gilbert Burnet, and the most candid historian of England before he was surpassed by Smith's friend Hume.[9] Joseph Priestley called Rapin's history the most 'impartial', also in contrast with Clarendon and Burnet.[10]

Quickly translated into English and 'continued' by Nicolas Tindal, the brother of the famous Deist, the work was particularly influential for two of the central writers in this book: Bolingbroke and Hume.[11] Before Rapin's *Histoire*, the Frenchman had made his name from a pamphlet entitled *Dissertation sur les Whigs et les Torys*, written in February 1716 and published the following year.[12] This text was often published together with his *Histoire*; in the original French edition in the tenth and final volume, and in Tindal's translation in the penultimate fourteenth volume (1731), dealing with the last twelve years of Charles II's reign. The main aim of this chapter is to reconstruct the historical and political arguments in the *Dissertation*, which will serve as a backdrop for the later discussions of party in the works of Bolingbroke and Hume. It is necessary to treat this text at length, because it was foundational for party thought in the eighteenth

---

[5] Hicks, *Neoclassical History and English Culture* (Basingstoke, 1996), 146–50.

[6] Pocock, *The Ancient Constitution and the Feudal Law* (Cambridge, 1987 [1957]), ch. 8.

[7] Voltaire, *Philosophical Letters* (Indianapolis, 2007), 92; Wallace, *The Doctrine of Passive Obedience and Non-resistance Considered* (Edinburgh, 1754), 23n.

[8] Trevor-Roper, 'Our First Whig Historian', 262–5; Kenyon, *The History Men* (London, 1993 [1983]), 41; Okie, *Augustan Historical Writing* (Lanham, 1991), ch. 3. Cf. Sullivan, 'Rapin, Hume and the Identity of the Historian', 153–5.

[9] Smith, *Lectures on Rhetoric and Belles Lettres* (Indianapolis, 1985), 116.

[10] Priestley, *Lectures on History* (Birmingham, 1788), 209.

[11] Bolingbroke was one of the subscribers to the first edition of the *Histoire*; see Cazenove, *Rapin-Thoyras, sa famille, sa vie et ses œuvres* (Paris, 1866), 365. He referred to Rapin several times in his *Dissertation upon Parties* (1733–4). Hume had read Rapin early, at least by 1730; see Hume to Michael Ramsay, [1730], *Letters*, II, 337. On the continent, it made a strong impression on Montesquieu; see Girard d'Albissin, *Un précurseur de Montesquieu* (Paris, 1969); Erich Haase, *Einführung in die Literatur des Refuge* (Berlin, 1959), 401, 524.

[12] The *Dissertation* was translated into English by John Ozell the same year as it was published. It was also translated into Dutch, Danish, Spanish, and German, and became a bestseller across Europe.

century. It would provide an intellectual context for later writers, and a historical backdrop against which the origins and nature of party were understood. While the *Dissertation* could not possibly have been entirely accurate, the strength of the pamphlet was that it explained with clarity what seemed to many unintelligible, and it came closer than anyone before Hume to capturing both the essence and nuances of British party politics. This chapter will also consider Rapin's discussion of party in the *Histoire* in the context of its immediate predecessors, but that work deserves a more detailed and holistic analysis than can be offered here.

Contexts of the *Dissertation*

Anyone expecting to find a wholehearted endorsement of the Whig party in Rapin's *Dissertation* will be disappointed. Instead, writing as the relatively detached foreigner he was,[13] at least by this stage in his life, he argued that total domination of either party should be avoided. He wanted to see the defeat of what he regarded as the extreme wing of the Tories, which had become strongly associated with Jacobitism, but he was equally critical of the small and declining republican clique within the Whigs.[14] The *Dissertation* was written when single-party government, or at least near-single-party government, was beginning to be practised in Britain. Although all ministries between 1689 and 1710–11 had been mixed, that is, containing both Whigs and Tories, one party was usually more dominant, like the Tories after 1690, and the Whig Junto between 1693–4 and 1700.[15] After the resignation of Robert Harley (later Earl of Oxford) and Henry St John (later Viscount Bolingbroke) in 1708, the government was dominated by the Whigs, even if the nominal Tory Sidney, 1st Earl of Godolphin, remained a leading figure. Both Godolphin and Harley can be seen as royal servants and managers rather than as party leaders. They sought to achieve a balanced ministry comprising moderates from both parties. This proved difficult, however, at a time when Parliament was divided into Whig and Tory.[16]

---

[13] He said that 'neither his Inclination nor his Interest has attached him to either of the two Parties'; see *Dissertation*, vii. I have cited from the reasonably literal English translation of the *Dissertation* from 1717, by Ozell, with references to the French edition in brackets.

[14] For this minority within the Whigs after the Revolution, see Goldie, 'The Roots of True Whiggism, 1688–1694', *HPT*, 1 (1980), 195–236.

[15] Claydon, *William III* (London, 2002), ch. 4.

[16] The best study remains Holmes's *British Politics in the Age of Anne* (London, 1987 [1967]).

In the wake of the High Church Tory reaction to the Whig impeachment of Henry Sacheverell – who had preached non-resistance and attacked Dissenters on Gunpowder Plot Day[17] – the Godolphin–Marlborough administration crumbled, and Harley was back in office in August 1710. In October of the same year the Tory party won by a landslide at the general election, and soon formed something akin to a single-party administration. It was, however, led for the most part by the moderate Harley, who was reluctant to remove all Whigs to the irritation of the High Church elements of the Tories.[18] Bolingbroke, who served as secretary of state in 1710–14, was the strongest advocate of single-party government and vied with Harley for the leadership of the Tories in 1714. He described the Tory 'revolution' of 1710 in the following way:

> I am afraid that we came to court in the same dispositions as all parties have done; that the principal spring of our actions was to have the government of the state in our hands; that our principal views were the conservation of this power, great employment to our selves, and great opportunities for rewarding those who had helped to raise us, and of hurting those who stood in opposition to us.[19]

The Tory triumph proved short-lived, however, and the Hanoverian accession after Queen Anne's death in August 1714 eventually marked the beginning of the Whig Supremacy and the proscription of the Tory party from office, which, with some exceptions, was to last until 1760. This was far from a predetermined outcome when George I ascended the throne, however. Prior to his accession, Georg Ludwig had initially sought to keep both parties at an equal distance, but he came to regard the Peace of Utrecht of 1713 as the Tories betraying their continental allies. The Whigs grasped this opportunity and pitched themselves as the true friends of Hanover. Notably, John Churchill, 1st Duke of Marlborough, showered Jean Robethon, George's private secretary, with letters warning of 'the designs of the English Ministry to bring in the Pretender'.[20] As a result, Bolingbroke and nearly all Tory ministers had either resigned or been dismissed even before George I had arrived in England.

For Rapin, writing in February 1716 without the benefit of hindsight, more ministerial 'revolutions' and further alternations between Whig and

---

[17] Sacheverell, *The Perils of False Brethren, both in Church, and State: Set forth in a Sermon preached . . . at the Cathedral-Church of St. Paul, on the Fifth of November, 1709* (London, 1710).
[18] Bennett, *The Tory Crisis in Church and State* (Oxford, 1975), chs. 7–9; Szechi, *Jacobitism and Tory Politics, 1710–14* (Edinburgh, 1984),123, 153, 161–3.
[19] Bolingbroke, *Letter to Sir William Windham* (1717), *Works*, I, 8–9.
[20] BL Stowe MS 242, f. 47.

Tory administrations seemed highly likely.[21] Indeed, one reason the Whigs gave for introducing septennial parliaments in April–May 1716 was that frequent parliaments impaired Britain's reputation abroad: 'Foreigners, who see that we have scarce *Two Parliaments together of the Same Mind*; and that everything is manag'd according to the *Humour of the prevailing Party*, are apt to *think* that not only our *Parliaments*, but our *Government is Triennial.*'[22] The Septennial Act was designed to end ministerial alterations, which had been perfectly natural in the 1689–1714 period. As Strafford explained to Sophia of Hanover in May 1714: 'A King or Queen of England must govern by the Bulk of their people, & must never be tied to one or t'other party, which made King W[illia]m & all the Kings his Predecessors change from one to the other party, as they had the majority in the Nation & Parliament.'[23]

The second and decisive justification for the Septennial Act was the Jacobite threat, as the country had recently suffered a rebellion, the so-called 'Fifteen', defeated at the beginning of February 1716, and to which Rapin referred in the *Dissertation*. Even if the 'Fifteen' failed, a restoration of the House of Stuart did not look inconceivable when Rapin started writing his text. The Tories were around this time split into (1) outright Jacobites, (2) Hanoverians, and (3) undecided or 'whimsical' Tories, who did not desire to be under a king who was German, Lutheran, and, in their eyes, unlawful, but who saw the Pretender's conversion to Anglicanism as a *sine qua non*.[24] As we shall see, Rapin believed that the Jacobite cause was doomed *if* the Whigs made the right choices and did not alienate moderate Tories and Church members. Rapin may have addressed the Whigs partly because they were in government, but it is evident from his tone and emphasis (as well as his background) that he sympathised with that party, although not as much as one might expect.[25] It should be noted,

---

[21] Rapin himself spoke of 'la force du parti des Torys' in May 1717; see Rapin to Jean Robethon, secretary to George I, BL Stowe MS 230, f. 118. The Tories themselves expected to gain office on several occasions after the Hanoverian succession, especially after the Whig split of 1716–17, even if they became less optimistic as time wore on; see HMC, *Stuart Papers* (7 vols., London, 1907–23), III, 379, IV, 221–2, VI, 405; Colley, *In Defiance of Oligarchy* (Cambridge, 1982), 25–50.

[22] *A Letter to a Country Gentleman, shewing the inconvenience, which attend the last part of the Act for Triennial Parliaments* (London, 1716), 35.

[23] BL Stowe MS 242, f. 106.

[24] D'Iberville to de Torcy, 6 March 1714, BL Add MS 34495, ff. 12–14.

[25] This is even more evident in his private correspondence; see Rapin to Robethon, BL Stowe MS 230, ff. 114–21.

moreover, that other Huguenot refugees with a stake in England were more eager to glory in Whiggism.[26]

Rapin's pamphlet was successful in Britain because the country was still learning how to live with party conflict and the phenomenon was poorly theorised. The main reason for Rapin composing the *Dissertation*, however, was the Treaty of Utrecht of 1713. This treaty concluded Britain's participation in the War of the Spanish Succession, a war which involved virtually all the great European powers against France, and had made the British parties relevant on the European stage. The reason was that a Tory administration had negotiated a peace which was detested by the oppositional Whig party. The two parties had disagreed for years about how the war should be waged, with most Tories favouring a naval, 'blue-water' strategy, while the Whigs supported a land war.[27] They then clashed over how urgently and upon which terms Britain should seek peace, with the Whigs famously wanting 'no peace without Spain'. Long before the Treaty of Utrecht was concluded, the Tories were known as the 'peace party', and when Harley became the Queen's first minister in 1710, it was widely expected that peace-making would be his first priority.[28] The peace was vital for the Tories, since they believed that the country gentlemen, in their view the backbone of the country, were being ruined by heavy wartime taxation.[29]

Around this time, Rapin was present at the house of the Prussian governor of Wesel, where he was residing, when the nature of the British parties had been debated.[30] The Frenchman went away with the impression that the discussants knew little about the Whigs and Tories, and wrote a paper to clarify his own ideas. The Whig courtier Sir Andrew Fountaine was shown the paper when visiting Wesel, and convinced Rapin to publish it.[31] In the 'Avertissement' to the *Dissertation sur les Whigs et les Torys*, Rapin duly remarked that the 'English' party division had been of little interest to foreigners before Utrecht.[32] After this event, even foreigners started to be partial in British domestic politics and 'take party' (*prendre parti*), since one party was for peace and another for war.[33]

---

[26] Dubourdieu, *Apologie de nos Confesseurs qui etoient aux galères, au mois de Janvier 1714* (London, 1717), esp. part three: 'On confond la Neutralité recommandé aux Réfugiez, par le Sir R[iva]l'.
[27] For a recent discussion, see Black, 'Foreign Policy and the Tory World in the Eighteenth Century', in *The Tory World* (Farnham, 2015), 33–68.
[28] Holmes, *British Politics in the Age of Anne*, 64–81.
[29] Szechi, *Jacobitism and Tory Politics, 1710–14*, 34.   [30] Cazenove, *Rapin-Thoyras*, 228.
[31] Ibid., 237–8.   [32] Rapin, *Dissertation*, [iii] (n.p.).
[33] *The Whigs Appeal to the Tories in a Letter to Sir T[homas] H[anmer]* (London, 1711), 2–3.

Partisans of France embraced the Tories, and their enemies the Whigs. Even if Rapin pointed out that both parties were equally in favour of Protestantism, foreign Catholics supported the Tories because of that party's penchant for Jacobitism, which meant the backing of a Catholic monarch (James 'III', the Old Pretender).[34] In Britain, or England as he almost invariably referred to it, Rapin remarked in a 'Spectatorial' manner that many were Tories and Whigs 'without having a clear Notion of the Party they have embrac'd'.[35] However, he stressed that he was not writing for an English audience.[36] Since Utrecht had demonstrated that the party that was victorious domestically could influence and indeed decide the most important affairs of Europe, Rapin's intention of publishing was to instruct the European public about the exact nature of these two 'factions' or parties.[37] He believed himself to be singularly suited to offer an 'impartial' analysis of the parties as a foreigner, since everything published in Britain was written by partisans of either party.[38] He also assured his readers that he had spent a long time in England and studied its history with care.[39]

Rapin was not alone in attempting this. In the same year, *Histoire du Whiggisme et du Torisme* was published in Leipzig by Emmanuel de Cize, another Huguenot refugee who had served in the British army.[40] It was dedicated to Jakob Heinrich von Flemming, a Saxon military officer in the Great Northern War, and republished in The Hague in 1718. De Cize's

[34] Rapin, *Dissertation*, iv (n.p.) The association between Toryism and Jacobitism was cemented in the wake of a Jacobite plot to assassinate William III/II in 1696, when the Whig Junto rose to power, and asked members of parliament to subscribe to 'the Association' to defend their 'rightful and lawful monarchy' against Catholics. About a hundred Tories in both chambers, principally the lower, refused to sign. See Holmes, *Religion and Party in Late Stuart England* (London, 1975), 24.

[35] Rapin, *Dissertation*, v (n.p.)

[36] Ibid., vii. This is more strongly expressed in the French original, whereas the English translation said that the work was not *only* for an English readership.

[37] At first glance, it appears as if Rapin was utilising 'party' and 'faction' interchangeably, but as Girard d'Albissin has remarked, we should note that he only used 'faction' three times in the *Dissertation*, twice in the preface and once in the text and then to avoid repetition of party; see *Un précurseur de Montesquieu*, 99 and note 335.

[38] Rapin, *Dissertation*, vi (n.p.) For examples of such partisan descriptions of party in this period, see [Davenant], *The Old and Modern Whig Truly Represented. Being a Second Part of His Picture. And a Real Vindication of his Excellency the Earl of Rochester* [i.e. the Tory leader] ... *and of Several Other True Patriots of our Establish'd Church, English Liberty, and Ancient Monarchy* [i.e. Tories] (London, 1702); [Swift], *The Public Spirit of the Whigs* (London, 1714), written when Swift was employed by the Tory government.

[39] He had begun working on his *Histoire* perhaps around 1707, and announced it in 1714. BL Stowe MS 230, f. 121.

[40] For de Cize, see Yardeni, 'The Birth of Political Consciousness among the Huguenot Refugees and their Descendants in England', in *From Strangers to Citizens* (Portland, 2001), 404–11.

detailed work follows the history-writing conventions of the time, which meant the inclusion of long speeches and original documents; conventions which Rapin would follow in his *Histoire* but dispense with in his fast-paced though slightly repetitive *Dissertation*. More than twice as long as Rapin's pamphlet, it does not appear to have had the same impact, at least not in Britain. Ephraim Chambers cited de Cize in his *Cyclopaedia* (1738), but not at the same length as Rapin's *Dissertation*.[41] De Cize presented a more straightforward condemnation of parties, of which there was no lack in Britain, and many of his insights were virtually the same as Rapin's.[42] He could of course have come up with them independently, but internal evidence suggests that it may have been written and published after Rapin, although this cannot be said for certain since de Cize's narrative finishes in 1714 and he does not comment on events after the accession of George I.[43] Also, *Histoire du Whiggisme et du Torisme* contains much content absent in Rapin, notably more information about the political allegiance of the twenty-four English bishops, the majority of whom he classified as Tory, singling out Francis Atterbury, bishop of Rochester, as the most 'furious'.[44] One source for de Cize is likely to have been the contemporary hack-historian Abel Boyer, another French Huguenot who had settled in England in 1689.[45]

The Rise of Party in England

The *Dissertation* began with 'l'origine du gouvernement d'Angleterre'. Its two first sentences summarised the thesis which would make Rapin famous as a Whig historian *par excellence*: 'The Government of *England* is of a particular kind, and the only one of the Sort in the World. 'Tis nevertheless the same that was formerly settled in all the kingdoms formed in *Europe*, out of the *Roman* Empire. The Difference [is that] ... the *English* have preserved the Form of their Government.'[46] This type of

---

[41] See the entries for 'Whig' and 'Tory' in Chambers, *Cyclopaedia* (2 vols., London, 1738).

[42] For example, that 'il est possible que ceux qui sont *Toris* ou *Whigs* en matiere Politique, suivent des maximes matiere de Religion, mais cela est rare'. De Cize, *Histoire du Whiggisme et du Torisme* (Leipzig, 1717), 2.

[43] On the first page, he lists Rapin's party categories: *Rigides*, *Outrez*, *Mitigez*, and *Moderez* (which are discussed at greater length below), as if referring the reader to Rapin's work. Ibid., 1.

[44] Ibid., 25.

[45] His works include *The History of King William the Third* (3 vols., 1702–3); *The History of the Reign of Queen Anne Digested into Annals* (1703–13); *The Political State of Great Britain, being an Impartial Account of the most material occurrences, Ecclesiastical, Civil, and Military, in a monthly letter to a friend in Holland* (38 vols., 1711–29).

[46] Rapin, *Dissertation*, 1 (1–2).

government was partly monarchical and partly republican, in other words 'un Gouvernement Mixte'. Rapin then offered a brief summary of the history of England, from the Saxon period to his own time. The crucial century for party formation in this narrative was the seventeenth century. This was the time when James I/VI, under the pernicious influence of his favourite Buckingham, began to seek to diminish the power of parliament.[47]

Rapin then described how James's son and successor, Charles I, pursued a project of becoming 'Absolute and Independent of the Laws'.[48] In 1640, he was forced to call his first parliament since 1629 to pay for a war against Scotland, on which he sought to impose Anglicanism. Rather than aiding the king, the new parliament was eager to assure 'the Liberties of the Nation' by circumscribing royal power.[49] The real tussle between the privileges of the people and the prerogative of the crown began at this point, according to Rapin. That was when 'deux Partis' were formed in England, one for the king and the other for parliament, or rather the lower house of parliament. There was no doubt in Rapin's mind that these parties were the ancestors of the later parties: 'The King's Friends were at first called *Cavaliers*, which name was afterwards changed into that of *Tories*. Those of the Parliament, who were then called *Roundheads*, afterwards received the Name of *Whigs*.'[50] Rapin also traced the *names* of Tory and Whig to this early stage, remarking that the appellations were as old as these 'troubles'. Admitting that he was unable to say exactly when it happened, Rapin believed that Cavalier and Roundhead lasted until Charles II's reign and were then 'peu-à-peu' replaced by Tory and Whig.[51] In the *Histoire*, he was able to trace the beginning of Tory and Whig more accurately, as we see in the next section. Already in the *Dissertation* he was convinced, however, that the division that had begun before the Commonwealth era was fundamentally the same that still divided England in 1716.

Rapin supported the connection he made between these two sets of party names by pointing to shared political and religious principles. The king's party during the civil war (the Cavaliers) consisted of two sorts of people: those attached to the interest of the crown and those attached to the interest of the Anglican Church. This mixture of two different points

---

[47] Ibid., 14 (22).   [48] Ibid. (23).   [49] Ibid., 18 (28).   [50] Ibid., 21 (34).
[51] From the start of Charles II's reign, he called them Tories rather than Cavaliers. It long remained common to call the parliament elected in May 1661 a 'Tory' parliament, as Carte complained in *A Full Answer to the Letter from a Bystander* (London, 1742), 79. De Cize was more precise in dating the birth of the Tory and Whig appellations to 1678 in *Histoire du Whiggisme et du Torisme*, 50–1.

of view, one monarchical and one religious, was still a cause of confusion among Tories in the eighteenth century, he argued.[52] Rapin thus made a distinction between *Cavaliers Politiques*, or *d'Etat*, and *Cavaliers Ecclésiastiques*, or *d'Eglise*, each of which was subdivided into two further categories. Among the political Cavaliers were the likes of Buckingham, Bishop Laud, and the Earl of Strafford, who strove for absolute monarchy and the destruction of parliament. Such extremists were in the minority, however, and he called them *Cavaliers Outrez*.[53] Most of the political Cavaliers were moderates (*modérez*), who wanted to reinforce the power of the monarch, but as part of the ancient constitution, which included an important role for parliament.[54] The ecclesiastical Cavaliers were also divided into two groups: one 'rigid' and one 'mitigated'.[55] As we shall see, Rapin believed that he could trace the same division between moderate and extreme elements within the Tories in the different ministries of Queen Anne: first Godolphin and the moderate Tories who joined the Whig Junto to form the queen's first ministries in 1702–10, and then the so-called high-flying Tories who ruled in a (near) single-party government in 1710–14, when Dissenters were attacked and a Jacobite restoration became an alternative.

The Roundheads, on their part, were divided into two groups along similar lines: one political, which championed the rights of the people (*les droits du peuple*), and one ecclesiastical, which sought to advance Presbyterianism. Among the political Roundheads were both republicans, wanting to destroy royal power, and moderates, merely seeking to prevent the king from abusing it.[56] Finally, there were both rigid and moderate Presbyterians, the former seeking to abolish bishops and the latter wanting toleration. These different labels and their principles are discussed at greater length below.

---

[52] Rapin, *Dissertation*, 22 (36).

[53] From the verb *outrer* ('to go to excess'). Translated as *arbitrary* Tories in the English translation by Ozell (ibid., 23), and as *furious* Tories by Tindal, see *Dissertation*, in *History of England* (15 vols., London, 1727–31), XIV, 440. Around this time, 'furious' was commonly used in contradistinction with 'moderate' and in a similar sense to the way we would use 'extreme'; see, e.g., the sub-title of Mary Astell's *A Fair Way with Dissenters and their Patrons: Not writ by Mr. L[esle]y, or any other Furious Jacobite, whether Clergyman or Layman; but by a very Moderate Person and Dutiful Subject to the Queen* (1704).

[54] Others, like Brady and Filmer, disagreed about the antiquity of Parliament and the Commons in particular; see Brady, *Introduction to the Old English History* (London, 1684), esp. *The First, An Answer to Mr. Petyt's Rights of the Commons Asserted*; Filmer, *Patriarcha* (Cambridge, 1991), 54.

[55] Rapin, *Dissertation*, 23 (37–8). 'Les Rigides' was the standard term used by l'Hermitage, a Dutch agent in London, for the Tories. See Holmes, *British Politics in the Age of Anne*, 460 note 28.

[56] Rapin, *Dissertation*, 23 (38–9).

Rapin skated over the civil war and the 'unfree' Commonwealth era fairly quickly.[57] In the reign of Charles II, Rapin singled out the Duke of York (the future James II/VII) as the leader of the Tories.[58] The main project of the duke, according to Rapin, was to establish Catholicism in England, a religion James had embraced during his exile, as he made public in 1676. The Whigs regarded him as a threat to the state as well as the Protestant religion and prepared a bill to exclude him from succession to the throne. They were not successful, however, and as James II/VII he proclaimed liberty of conscience to all his subjects, and permitted people of all faiths to worship publicly. The aim of this policy was twofold, according to Rapin: to favour the papists and placate the Presbyterians. The Tories, who had hitherto supported James, began to repent their past actions, as they saw how each step of the king tended to the dissolution of the established government and the ruin of Protestantism.

Not willing to sacrifice their religion and liberty to ensure the destruction of the Whigs, the Tories united with their nemesis and invited William of Orange, the Dutch Stadtholder and James's son-in-law and nephew. The king's party was weak at this stage, consisting only of Catholics, the *Torys Outrez*, and a few courtiers.[59] Rapin contended that the Glorious Revolution demonstrated that the English, although still divided into two parties, prioritised saving their (Protestant) religion and liberty over defeating their counterparts.[60] Under William and Mary (1689–94), and later under William alone (1694–1702), moreover, moderate men from both parties were employed, especially before the rise of the Whig Junto in 1694. Since it was impossible to make both parties content at the same time, as there were not enough offices to dispose, William 'affected to change his Ministry often, and to make use of the two Parties by turns'.[61]

Division did not come to an end, however, and it was mainly religion that helped to sustain the parties. The ecclesiastical Tories of the rigid kind were furious to see Presbyterians enjoying complete liberty of conscience, worshipping publicly, and holding office, despite the Act of Uniformity 1662.[62] The extremists among the political Tories, who advocated

---

[57] The first historian to defend the 'Rump Parliament' was Catharine Macaulay, many years later; see Pocock, 'England's Cato', *HJ*, 37 (1994), 935.

[58] Rapin, *Dissertation*, 28 (45).   [59] Ibid., 34 (57).

[60] As we see in Chapter 4, Hume would mirror this analysis closely in 'Of the Parties of Great Britain' (1741).

[61] Rapin, *Dissertation*, 36 (61).

[62] They were granted exemption from the penalties of the Test Act under the Toleration Act, which was not as far-reaching as James II's Declaration of Indulgence of 1687. Occasional conformity became common practice from 1689 onwards.

absolutism and had seen James II/VII as their leader and defender, became Jacobite. The slogan among these discounted Tories was '*the Church* [is] *in Danger*'.[63] It would be wrong, however, to view the continuous division as an exclusively religious disagreement, Rapin stressed, as was evidenced by the existence of the *Torys Outrez* and the *Whigs Républiquains*, even if the latter faction was minuscule.

William's successor Anne – the daughter of James II/VII – was raised in the religious principles of the *Torys Rigides* and political principles similar to the *Torys Outrez*, Rapin claimed.[64] Surprisingly, in the first part of her reign she chose not to rely on such Tories, among whom her uncle the Earl of Rochester was regarded as the leader.[65] The reason was that she was pressurised by a coalition between the moderates of both parties.[66] Accordingly, Anne turned to Godolphin, Marlborough,[67] and other moderate Tory leaders,[68] in conjunction with Whigs. From this time forth, moderate Tories and Whigs looked almost like the same party, Rapin remarked, doubtlessly thinking of Godolphin and Marlborough, whose party identities are hard to classify even for modern scholars.[69]

Marlborough, Godolphin, and Harley formed what contemporaries called a triumvirate until 1708. If this administration had stayed in power until the death of Anne, the *Torys Outrez* and *Rigides* would have seen their

---

[63] Ibid., 37 (63).

[64] Ibid., 39 (65–6). It was a common opinion among Whigs that the queen was a Tory, and this was expressed by Lord (William) Cowper and Lord (Thomas) Coningsby, both of whom were Whigs who presented 'histories of parties' to George I early in his reign. Cowper, 'An Impartial History of Parties' (1714), manuscript printed in Campbell, *The Lives of the Lord Chancellors and Keepers of the Great Seal of England* (10 vols., London, 1846), VI, 421–9; Coningsby, 'History of Parties; presented to George the First' (1716), manuscript printed in *Archaeologia, or Miscellaneous Tracts relating to* Antiquity (110 vols., London, 1770–1992), XXXVIII, 3–18 (also in BL Lansdowne MS 885, ff. 65–74).

[65] Laurence Hyde, 1st Earl of Rochester (1642–1711), son of Edward Hyde, 1st Earl of Clarendon, had held high office under Charles II and James II/VII, served as Lord Lieutenant of Ireland in 1700–3, and returned to the cabinet as Lord President of the Council in 1710 until he died the following year. William had been compelled to rely on Rochester from the end of 1700, but Rochester resigned from the government in 1703.

[66] Rapin did not think highly of the queen but some modern historians have given Anne more credit; see esp. Gregg, *Queen Anne* (New Haven, 2001 [1970]).

[67] However, Marlborough's wife, Sarah, Duchess of Marlborough, was a staunch Whig, and Marlborough himself became a Whig hero after his victories against the French in the War of the Spanish Succession; see Cruickshanks, 'Religion and Royal Succession', in *Britain in the First Age of Party, 1680–1750* (London, 1987), 33.

[68] Rapin, *Dissertation*, 40–1 (67–8). The administration also included Harley and Henry St John (Bolingbroke) between 1704 and 1708. The concept of 'moderation' was ridiculed by High Church men; see Shippen, *Moderation Displayed* (London, 1704); Downie, *Robert Harley and the Press* (Cambridge, 1979), 81.

[69] In the words of Holmes, their Toryism had ceased by the time of Anne's accession and was merely nominal; see *British Politics in the Age of Anne*, 189–90.

numbers depleted, Rapin speculated. He suggested that more extreme
Tories came back into power by convincing the queen that she was a slave
to an administration that went against her inclinations. She thus replaced
them with the 'furious' and rigid Tories in 1710. It was also during the
1710–14 administration that the Tories took the decisive step towards
Jacobitism, fearing that their day in the sun would come to an end under
the Elector of Hanover, set to ascend the throne on Anne's death, in
accordance with the Act of Settlement 1701.[70] Rapin conceded, however,
that it was uncertain whether the 'cunning Gentleman [*Ministre*] in the
Tower was of the same mind', referring to Harley/Oxford, imprisoned in
the Tower of London at the time of the composition of the text.[71]

Having taken his historical narrative up to the time of writing, Rapin
proceeded to consider the principles of the two parties in greater detail. He
began with the *Torys Outrez*, or the high-flying (*volant haut*) Tories, thus
unflatteringly called after a bird lost in the clouds and flying outside the
common sphere of other birds.[72] Rapin was sure that these Tories wanted to
establish absolutism of the French kind in England. This party was not
numerous but remained considerable. Rapin gave three reasons to account
for this. First, their leaders usually held high office at court and church, and
from there could direct those below them. That is why the Tory party as a
whole was often but unfairly accused of advocating despotic government,
when this was only the objective of a minority.[73] Second, this Tory branch
had often been aided by the ecclesiastical Tories, whose numbers were much
greater, in preaching the dogma of passive obedience to the monarch, especially
under Charles II, James II/VII, and at the end of Anne's reign.[74] Finally, the
high-flying Tories tended to become powerful when they were backed by the
monarch, as they had been under Charles I and James II/VII (as well as Richard
II, Edward II, and Henry III, 'For the Party of *arbitrary Tories* is more ancient
than is generally imagin'd').[75] More recently, they had pushed Anne into
creating twelve new peers in 1711 to break the Whig control of the Lords.[76]

---

[70] The Hanoverian dynasty represented Anne's nearest Protestant relatives.

[71] Ibid., 44 (74). Harley corresponded with the Pretender in 1710–14, but his intentions remain
uncertain; see Bennett, 'English Jacobitism, 1710–15', *Transactions of the Royal Historical Society*, 32
(1982), 137–51. It has been suggested in Cruickshanks, 'Religion and Royal Succession', 37 that he
embraced Jacobitism more wholeheartedly after his imprisonment.

[72] Rapin, *Dissertation*, 46 (78).   [73] Ibid., 47–8, 68 (80–1, 112–13).   [74] Ibid., 48 (81).

[75] Ibid. (82). One of Rapin's signature techniques was to apply the vocabulary of post-revolutionary
politics to much older events to make them more comprehensible; see Sullivan, 'Rapin, Hume and
the Identity of the Historian', 150.

[76] Many considered this to be unconstitutional at the time, e.g., [Steele], *Letter to Sir Miles Wharton,
Concerning Occasional Peers* (Fleet Street, 5 March 1713).

The second category of political Tories, the *Modérez*, were also monarchical and protective of the royal prerogative, but not at the expense of the monarch's subjects. Perhaps surprisingly, Rapin had nothing but admiration for these Tories, who had often saved the state from *Torys Outrez* and republican Whigs alike, both of whom wanted to *change* the government.[77] It would be a grave injustice to confound these Tories with their high-flying namesakes, Rapin highlighted. The moderate Tories wanted to conserve the just prerogatives of the crown and were prepared to join with moderate Whigs to maintain the mixed and balanced constitution.[78]

As Rapin had already stated, the republican Whigs were a small minority in their party, even if the Tories sought to persuade the public that all Whigs were republicans.[79] The moderate Whigs were roughly of the same principles as the moderate Tories and '*véritables Anglois*' for the same reasons: they wanted to maintain the government on its ancient foundations. This was a common way to distinguish between moderate and extreme positions at the time: a moderate wanted to preserve the constitution and an extremist change it. As the Whig James Tyrrell put it, 'I am not what the world calls a *Republican* or *Commonwealthsman*, nor do I design or desire alterations in the government either of Church or State'.[80] The ancient constitution could be interpreted in different ways, and the views of Tyrrell and Rapin differed from those of Thomas Salmon and Thomas Carte.[81] The latter claimed to be as opposed to alterations as Tyrell and Rapin, however, writing in 1722 that 'all experiments of Alterations in any Essential Part [of the constitution] have been always thought of a very dangerous nature & wise men ever tremble at them'.[82]

So far Rapin had mainly analysed the parties' political principles, but party formation was as much about church as state affairs. As he put it, 'what contributes most to make them be looked upon as two different Parties, is Religion'.[83] Turning to religion, Rapin began by disputing the idea that all Episcopalians were Tory and all Presbyterians Whig. Indeed, some could be Tory regarding the church but Whig vis-à-vis the

---

[77] Rapin, *Dissertation*, 49 (82).   [78] Ibid., 51 (86).

[79] See, e.g., [Leslie], *A View of the Times, their Principles and Practices, in the Rehearsals* (3 vols., London, 1750), II, 218 (5 June 1706).

[80] Tyrrell, *Bibliotheca Politica* (London, 1718 [1694]), vi.

[81] Salmon, *The History of Great Britain and Ireland … The Second Edition, with a Preface wherein the Partiality of Mons. Rapin and other Republican Historians, is demonstrated* (London, 1725); [Carte?], *A Defence of English History, against the Misrepresentations of M. de Rapin Thoyras, in his History of England* (London, 1734), 11, 65–6.

[82] Carte MS 230, Bodleian, f. 362.   [83] Rapin, *Dissertation*, 77–8 (128).

government, and vice versa.[84] The main reason why rigid Episcopalians tended to be Tory and Presbyterians Whig, however, was the question of hierarchy (bishops), which generally conformed to their political beliefs, even if they sometimes clashed as in the Convocation Controversy of 1697–1701.[85]

The division between Whig and Tory could be traced not only to the conflict between king and parliament in the seventeenth century, but also the religious rift between two different visions of what road the church should take in the wake of the Reformation in the sixteenth century. Unlike in Scotland, the reformed English church retained its bishops. Separatists were called Presbyterians because they refused to submit to the authority of bishops, arguing that Presbyteries, or a body of ministers and lay-elders, held the same rank. Two parties were thus formed: Episcopalians and Puritans, the latter being denominated as such because of their conviction that bishops went against the *purity* of Christianity.[86] The Wars of the Three Kingdoms began initially when Charles I sought to reform the Scottish church along Episcopalian lines, as was stressed by Rapin. When the English parliamentarians needed the aid of Scotland, they promised to bring Presbyterianism to England. The division between Episcopalians and Presbyterians, neither of whom tolerated one another, had lasted until Rapin's day and still worked to underpin the split between Whig and Tory.[87]

The ecclesiastical Tories included *almost* the entire country, since they could be considered to be made up of all the members of the Anglican Church, according to Rapin.[88] They were thus far superior to the Presbyterian Whigs: the Dissenting vote is estimated to have been between 15 and 20 per cent of the total electorate in the reign of Anne.[89] In short, it was religion that made the Tory party powerful.[90] Rapin believed that if

---

[84] Ibid., 51–2 (87–8).
[85] For the Convocation Controversy, see Smith, *The Gothic Bequest* (Cambridge, 1987), 28–38.
[86] Rapin, *Dissertation*, 53–4 (91).   [87] Ibid., 57 (96).
[88] Ibid., 69 (114–15). It has often been said that the Tories enjoyed a natural majority in early eighteenth-century England and perhaps beyond. The Tories themselves at least were confident that they constituted 'the vast majority' of the population; see Thomas Blackwell to unidentified, 14 April 1717, in HMC, *Stuart Papers*, IV, 214. Bolingbroke reportedly said that the Tories outdid Whigs by eight to one in the country, and were roughly equal in London; see d'Iberville to de Torcy, 6 March 1714, BL Add MS 34495, ff. 12–23. Tories were also confident that they enjoyed a strong majority in Scotland: 'The proportion between Whig and Torie in Scotland ... may be, at most, one to three, even whilst the government of the State, Church [i.e. the Presbyterian Church] and army, is in their hands, and if it were otherways, scarce one to five.' 'History of Whigs and Tories in Scotland' (*c.*1702), BL Add MS 61136, f. 201.
[89] Holmes, *Politics, Religion, and Society in England, 1679–1742* (London, 1986), 201.
[90] Rapin, *Dissertation*, 72 (118).

the *Tory Outrez* were far less numerous than the moderates among political Tories, the opposite could be said for church Tories, among whom *Torys Rigides* outnumbered the *Torys Mitigez*.[91] High Church (*Haute Eglise*) Tories made up almost all of the lower clergy (*le bas Clergé*), many of the bishops, and Oxford University.[92] Rapin defined High Church as a church without any mixture of Presbyterianism; indeed, he believed that many of them would rather see England Catholic than Presbyterian. They were less driven by religious zeal than by party spirit, however, because their hatred of Presbyterianism stemmed not only from different opinions about bishops but more importantly from the fact that most Presbyterians were Whigs. Catholics formed another branch of the Tory party. They were often united with the *Torys Outrez*, since they could only hope to make Catholicism dominant in a Protestant country with the aid of an absolute king, according to Rapin.[93] Even if the Catholics had little political sway in England, being disenfranchised they played a role in attaching the Tory party to Catholic powers abroad, especially France. This was useful occasionally but came at a dear price, since it made them an easy target for Whig criticism.[94]

The ecclesiastical Whigs were divided into two categories: rigid and mitigated Presbyterians. The former rejected all forms of ecclesiastical hierarchy and all Anglican ceremonies. These were fairly numerous in England, but what made them more considerable was their real power base in Scotland, united with England in a union of crowns since 1603 and a parliamentary (but not ecclesiastical) union since 1707.[95] In the other group, the mitigated Presbyterians, Rapin also included all nonconformists, such as Quakers and Anabaptists. They were less fiery than their rigid brethren and could easily blend in with the Anglican Church when they needed to, Rapin wrote with a clear reference to occasional conformists. Such ecclesiastical Whigs wanted to see Presbyterianism become dominant but rejected violent means to achieve this end. They were the biggest threat to the *Torys Outrez* and *Rigides*, because they made it harder to complain that the Whigs sought to ruin Anglicanism.[96]

---

[91] Ibid., 72–3 (118–19).
[92] Ibid.; 75 to 80 per cent of the parish clergy voted Tory in Anne's reign; see Holmes, *The Making of a Great Power*, 343.
[93] Rapin, *Dissertation*, 73–4 (120–1).
[94] Anti-Catholicism was widespread in the eighteenth century and one of the few things which many Tories and Whigs agreed about; see Clark, *English Society, 1660–1832* (Cambridge, 2000 [1985]); Harris, *Politics under the Later Stuarts* (London, 1993), 70.
[95] Rapin, *Dissertation*, 79 (130).   [96] Ibid., 80 (133).

It was against these Whigs that the Tories attempted to strike when they passed an act against Occasional Conformity in 1711.[97] Occasional conformity had been a way for nonconformists to circumvent Charles II's Test Acts and attain state employment. The Act of 1711 was an attempt by the Tories to deal a decisive blow to the Whigs by excluding all nonconformists from holding office and requiring actual membership of the Church of England rather than a single act of conformity. The Act was still in place at the time of Rapin's writing but was repealed a year after the *Dissertation* was published. Somewhat surprisingly, Rapin recommended the Whigs to keep the Act so as to pre-empt the Tory complaint that they threatened the established church.[98] As long as king and parliament worked in unison and refrained from interfering with the church, the Pretender's cause was doomed, Rapin was convinced.[99] He repeated similar views in correspondence with George I's private secretary in 1717.[100]

Rapin also considered the motives and interests of the two parties. Naturally, they both professed to be more just and equitable than their adversary and that they fought for the glory of God, honour of the king, and the public good. Rapin was sceptical about such motivations, and argued instead that, since the parties were made up of people, they were mainly moved by self-interest (*l'intérêt propre*).[101] The influence of Pierre Bayle, Rapin's fellow Huguenot, is detectable here.[102] While Rapin did not mean to exclude other motivations entirely, including the well-being of the state and religious beliefs, he maintained that these were of secondary importance.[103]

Rapin believed that if the Tory party only aimed at the maintenance of the royal prerogatives and protection of the Church they would be invincible, because these were the true interests of the kingdom. As it happened, however, the Tories had sometimes used these policies as a fig leaf for absolutism and even Jacobitism.[104] When the monarch favoured the Tories in general, it was difficult for the moderates to detach themselves from the high-flying Tories because of their self-interest and desire for

---

[97] Holmes, *The Trial of Doctor Sacheverell* (London, 1973), 268–75.

[98] Rapin, *Dissertation*, 80 (133–4). Despite this, a Tory critic would present Rapin as straightforwardly pro-Dissent and anti-Church of England. [Carte?], *Defence of English History*, 149, 152.

[99] Rapin, *Dissertation*, 81 (136).

[100] 'L'Angleterre est Episcopale, c'est le gros de l'arbre, où, selon mon petit avis, le Roi le doit toujours tenir attaché'. BL Stowe MS 230, f. 119.

[101] Rapin, *Dissertation*, 60 (100–1).

[102] Bayle, *Miscellaneous Reflections, Occasion'd by the Comet, which appear'd in December 1680* (London, 1708), esp. sect. CLXI.

[103] Rapin, *Dissertation*, 62–3 (105).   [104] Ibid., 74 (121–2).

office.[105] Rapin here undoubtedly referred to the Tory administration of 1710–14, when the moderate Harley had been caught up with *Torys Outrez*, and Bolingbroke attached himself to the latter faction in opposition to Harley.[106] Self-interest also explained why they would consider restoring a Catholic king, in opposition to their religious inclinations: if they helped to restore the Stuarts, they could expect to be rewarded. At this juncture, after the accession of George I, the *Torys Outrez* found themselves completely out of favour, and they could not be expected to remain tranquil when being excluded from office and honours, the attainment of which were their main motivation.[107] That is why many Tories had played such a rash part in the late *Troubles*, meaning the 'Fifteen'.

Moving on to consider personalities and character traits in the two parties, Rapin described Tories as proud, haughty, and passionate.[108] Since they were the Church of England party, and had a natural majority in the nation, they saw themselves as dominant and could not stand being equal, let alone inferior, to their adversaries.[109] Another characteristic of the Tories was that they changed their principles depending on whether they were in or out of government.[110] When they had the monarch's favour, they pushed for passive obedience, a doctrine they were quick to forget when in opposition. Having been established during the *Troubles* of Charles I's reign, for instance in the preaching of Laud, Rapin pointed out that passive obedience came back into fashion in the last years of Anne, and the English translation points more precisely to the case of Sacheverell.[111] In short, Rapin's Tories were distinguished by ideological flexibility. In contrast with the Tories, the Whigs had not been led by their extreme wing since the Long Parliament. The Whig leaders were thus more moderate than their Tory counterparts, and they were characteristically slow in contrast to the passionate speed by which the Tories acted.[112]

In terms of foreign connections, Rapin said that everyone knew the Estates General of the United Provinces to be friends and partisans of the Whigs. This was natural since the Whigs routinely supported their interests in England.[113] The reason was straightforward: '*France*, the everlasting Foe to Holland, has constantly supported the *Tories*'.[114] Despite his Catholic religion, the Holy Roman Emperor had to be an ally of the

---

[105] Ibid., 68–9 (113).   [106] Dickinson, *Bolingbroke* (London, 1970), 111–33.
[107] Rapin, *Dissertation*, 75 (124).   [108] Ibid., 83–4 (140).   [109] Ibid.   [110] Ibid., 85 (145).
[111] Ibid., 87. It is uncertain whether this was the example Rapin had in mind, since Sacheverell gave his notorious sermon in 1709, when the Tories were in opposition, and it fits uneasily with Rapin's contention that this was an argument Tories used in government rather than in opposition.
[112] Rapin, *Dissertation*, 86–7 (149).   [113] Ibid., 97 (165).   [114] Ibid., 98 (166).

Whigs by virtue of being sovereign of the Austrian Low Countries. In his bid to establish a universal monarchy in Europe, the recently deceased Louis XIV had forged a coalition with Charles II and his (*avant la lettre*) Tory ministers against Holland in 1672, but since 1689 his policy had simply been to cause as much unrest as possible in England to achieve this aim, which, according to Rapin, explained his attachment to Jacobitism.[115]

At the time of the composition of the *Dissertation*, France was at a crossroads since Louis XIV had died in September 1715.[116] Rapin argued that if his successor, Louis XV, five years old on his accession, gave up the aim of achieving universal monarchy in Europe, France would no longer have an interest in inflaming disturbances in England. Unfortunately, the Regent of France, Philippe II, Duke of Orléans, continued to support, at least indirectly, the Pretender's cause. Rapin believed that the Regent may have been badly informed about the state of the parties in Britain and that he could have been deceived by the Pretender himself. A footnote was added to this passage, stressing that the *Dissertation* was written in February 1716 and that Britain, France, and Holland formed an alliance in January 1717.[117] This alliance meant that France had taken the path Rapin wanted. The relationship between the French and the Stuarts had soured in the wake of the Treaty of Utrecht, and the Jacobite court, which between 1689 and 1713 had resided at France's second palace at Saint-Germain-en-Laye, moved to the Duchy of Lorraine, then Avignon, then Urbino in the Papal States, before settling permanently in Rome in 1719. Be that as it may, as the leading Catholic power in Europe and Britain's greatest rival, in many respects France continued to be a nerve centre for Jacobitism in the coming decades.[118]

Rapin's *Dissertation* was strongly entrenched in its immediate political context. In the *Histoire*, to which we will turn next, he would return to the seventeenth century and, within the framework he had already set out, refine his views on the rise of party in certain aspects.

Party in Rapin's *Histoire*

As a historian of party, Rapin was not entirely without predecessors. His main contemporary French rival historian of England was the Protestant

---

[115] Ibid., 100–3 (170–7).
[116] His death was described by Bolingbroke in *Letter to Windham*, *Works*, I, 48 as a big blow to the Jacobite cause.
[117] *Dissertation*, 104n (177n).   [118] Szechi, *The Jacobites* (Manchester, 1994), 90–104.

Isaac de Larrey, who published his *Histoire d'Angleterre* at Rotterdam in four volumes between 1697 and 1713. De Larrey's rendition of the rise of party was taken verbatim from Roger Coke, whom he cited.[119] What is more, we find in de Larrey an eagerness to praise the Whigs, which does not occur to the same degree in Rapin.[120] The most relevant among British historians for Rapin was Laurence Echard, who published a three-volume *History of England* between 1707 and 1718, the two last volumes of which dealt with the seventeenth century. Echard also translated the Jesuit Pierre-Joseph d'Orléans's Jacobite *Histoire des révolutions d'Angleterre* into English, which contributed to the debate about whether Echard wrote Tory or Whig history.[121] This did not lessen Rapin's admiration, who himself pondered translating Echard into French. Echard was no admirer of parties, writing that '[t]he Extremities of Parties are the Scandals and Excrescencies of Human Nature ... it is more eligible and less slavish to write for Bread, than for a Party'.[122]

Rapin (d. 1725) lived just long enough to have been able to read the first volume of Gilbert Burnet's posthumous *History of His Own Time* (1724), which was cited in the ninth and tenth volumes of his *Histoire*.[123] Like Rapin, Burnet was in exile in The Hague along with other Whigs in the late 1680s, and also like Rapin, he landed in Torbay with William on 5 November 1688. The first volume of Burnet's *History* dealt with the 1660–89 period. It was questioned at the time whether Rapin had actually read Burnet or whether the quotations were inserted afterwards, since the ninth and tenth volumes were published after Rapin's death.[124] Whether he read him or not, there was nothing in Burnet's *History* that brought to bear on Rapin's discussion of party. The Scot Burnet explained the origin of the word 'Whig' in the context of Scotland in 1648, in the preamble to the real beginning of the *History* in 1660. Rapin also referred to the Scottish origin of the term Whig, but his source was probably Echard rather than Burnet, since the Frenchman, with Echard, traced it to 'sour milk' rather than to 'Whiggamore' (a term for horse driver that became associated with a Scottish faction that took part in the Whiggamore's Raid

[119] Coke, *A Detection of the Court and State of England* (2 vols., London, 1694).
[120] De Larrey, *Histoire d'Angleterre, d'Ecosse et d'Irlande* (4 vols., Rotterdam, 1697–1713), IV, 543.
[121] Stephan, 'Laurence Echard', *HJ*, 32 (1989), 843–66.
[122] Echard, *Appendix to Echard's History of England* (London, 1720), 36.
[123] Rapin, *Histoire*, IX, 567–78; X, 83–96. In the earlier volumes, he had cited Burnet's *The History of the Reformation of the Church of England* (3 vols., 1679–1714).
[124] [Carte?], *Defence of English History*, 134.

of 1648).[125] Burnet remarked that 'from *Scotland* the word was brought into *England*, where it is now one of our unhappy terms of distinction'.[126] Party played a prominent role in Burnet's second volume, which dealt with the reigns of William and Mary, and Anne, but it was first published in 1734, nine years after Rapin's death.

In the words of Laird Okie, Rapin represented a 'substantial advance over his predecessors', partly because he 'developed themes and made an effort to interpret the facts rather than simply list them'.[127] In the *Histoire*, Rapin once again traced party division far back in the seventeenth century, as far as the reign of James I/VI, in which he observed a curious mixture of puritanism in politics and religion in parliament. This confusion of ideas had continued (*s'est conservée*) until Rapin's day.[128] There was no doubt in his mind that the parties that arose under James I/VI represented something in addition to religious sentiments, even if he by no means wanted to downplay the importance of religion. Two parties were properly formed in the third parliament of James I/VI, who Rapin regarded as intent on securing absolute power, in 1621, 'l'un pour la Cour, l'autre pour le Peuple'.[129]

In contrast to the *Dissertation*, Rapin was less explicit in emphasising continuity between Cavalier–Roundhead[130] and Tory–Whig, although, as we shall see, he pointed out that this was a connection the latter parties made themselves, when they arose. He now described the divisions within the parliament called in 1640 without any references to later party divisions.[131] Moreover, rather than calling the parties Tory and Whig from the start of Charles II's reign as in the *Dissertation*, he referred to high churchmen and Presbyterians. Since he had already pointed to continuity between the parties that arose under James I/VI and the Tories and Whigs in the eighteenth century, he probably felt that it was unnecessary to make the same argument when discussing the civil war.

Another reason may have been that he had now acquired the knowledge, perhaps thanks to Echard, to be more precise regarding *English*

---

[125] *Bishop Burnet's History of His Own Time* (2 vols., Dublin, 1724–34), I, 26. This long passage was included in Johnson's *Dictionary* (1755) under the entry for 'Whig'.
[126] Ibid.   [127] Okie, *Augustan Historical Writings*, 47.   [128] Rapin, *Histoire*, VII, 131.
[129] Ibid., 152.
[130] He used these terms, but more sparingly than in his *Dissertation*, preferring to talk of royalists and parliamentarians, and, even more frequently, of Episcopalians and Presbyterians (rigid and moderate).
[131] Rapin, *Histoire*, VIII, 4–7.

parties[132] when tracing the beginning of the Tory and Whig appellations to the Exclusion Crisis.[133] Closely following Echard's narrative, he described how in late 1679 and early 1680, Country sympathisers petitioned for a parliament to be called by Charles II, who responded that such interventions represented an invasion of the royal prerogative. Court sympathisers agreed and made addresses in which they expressed abhorrence that some people made these demands on the king.[134] These 'Adresseurs' and 'Abhorans' (*petitioners* and *abhorrers* in the English translation) gave each other names of reproach, namely Whig and Tory. The Whigs viewed their opponents as 'entirely devoted to the Court and the *Popish* Faction [*Parti Catholique*], [and] gave them the Name of *Tories*, a Title given to the *Irish* Robbers'. These Tories viewed their opponents 'as Men entirely in the Principles of the Parliament of 1640, and *Presbyterians* in their Hearts, [and] gave them the Name of *Whig*, or *Sour-Milk*, formerly appropriated to the *Scotch Presbyterians* and *rigid Covenanters*'.[135]

From this time, the Tories sought to unite the two interests of monarchy and religion, until the revolution, 'when there was no longer a Possibility of keeping them united, without overturning at once the established Government and Religion'.[136] In a similar vein to the *Dissertation*, Rapin contended that the strength of the Tories consisted entirely of this union, since they represented the established Church, to which a majority of people belonged. By contrast, the Whigs, perceiving that this union was entirely to the benefit of the Tories, 'seem to have lessened their Pretentions with regard to Religion, contenting themselves with procuring the *Presbyterians* a bare Liberty of Conscience'.[137] Since the greatest part of the Whigs comprised either Presbyterians or people inclined that way, and the Tories were victorious in the Exclusion Crisis, a violent persecution of all nonconformists ensued.[138] The *Torys Outrez* were not satisfied, however, and aimed to make the king absolute, as if it was the only way to save the Church from the Presbyterians.[139]

---

[132] Whig was an older Scottish term, as was highlighted by Burnet, and also in *The Character of an Honest Man; whether stiled Whig or Tory, and his Opposite, the Knave* (1683), in *A Collection of Tracts on all Subjects* (London, 1748), IV, 278; 'History of Whigs and Tories in Scotland', BL Add MS 61136, ff. 199–203.

[133] Rapin, *Histoire*, IX, 484.

[134] Neither side ought to be viewed as a reliable measurement of the true sentiment of *the* people, as was demonstrated by their mutual existence, according to Rapin. Ibid., 485.

[135] Rapin, *The History of England*, XIV, 244; Rapin, *Histoire*, IX, 485–6.

[136] Rapin, *The History of England*, XIV, 300; Rapin, *Histoire*, IX, 522.   [137] Ibid.

[138] Rapin, *Histoire*, IX, 529.   [139] Ibid., 529–30.

The Tories had been deluded when thinking that the Court had the same interest as them. It became clear that they did not align when the Catholic James II/VII ascended the throne.[140] The principle of passive obedience could be seen as the 'chief Source of the Nation's Misfortunes', and the turning point came when churchmen realised that they had to dispense with it to save their Protestant religion from a Catholic king.[141] The first step was thus an anti-Catholic union between the Church of England and nonconformists, followed by political reconciliation between Tories and Whigs. This reconciliation was a decisive blow to the king, 'since his great Strength lay in their Division'.[142] While it was debatable whether a union, or league, against the king, was permissible in other monarchies, Rapin remarked in what can be read as either a Whiggish or a relativist manner that it was fully justifiable in the circumstances and under such a constitution as England's, since James II/VII had violated the constitution of church and state.[143] It has been argued that 'relativism' had a long prehistory in Huguenot political thought; Moïse Amyraut (1596–1664) supported royal absolutism in France but saw it as a given that the English monarchy should be limited and monitored by parliament.[144]

Rapin's argument rested on a contrast between Elizabeth I and the Stuarts, a contrast Bolingbroke would endorse and Hume would reject. However, both Bolingbroke and Hume would follow Rapin in arguing that the Glorious Revolution was the product of a union between the two great parties. Previous histories of England said little about this alleged union between Whigs and Tories, and many Whigs argued long after that the Revolution was 'entirely owing' to the Tories.[145] After Rapin, this

---

[140] Ibid., X, 2–3.   [141] Rapin, *The History of England*, XV, 150; Rapin, *Histoire*, X, 102–3.

[142] Rapin, *The History of England*, XV, 151; Rapin, *Histoire*, X, 104.

[143] Rapin, *Histoire*, X, 104. He also noted that several had persisted to this day in the opinion that it was unjust, and together with Catholics they formed 'le Parti des *Jacobites*'.

[144] Yardeni, 'The Birth of Political Consciousness', 405. Rapin wrote the following in the preface to the *Dissertation*: 'Some may, perhaps, think it strange that the Author, who was born the Subject of a Government purely Monarchical, shou'd upon some Occasions write in such a Manner, as may induce People to believe he does not approve that sort of Constitution. To prevent this Suspicion, he desires the Reader to remember, that he cou'd not speak pertinently upon this Subject, without putting on the Spirit of an *Englishman*, and confirming himself to the Principles that are common in *England*' (viii). In general, Huguenot political thought was absolutist prior to the revocation of the Edict of Nantes; see Tim Hochstrasser, 'The Claims of Conscience', in *New Essays on the Political Thought of the Huguenots of the Refuge* (Leiden, 1995), 17–20.

[145] *The Whigs Appeal to the Tories*, 7; Coningsby, 'History of Party' (1716), 8. As Goldie has shown, this was also a commonplace argument among Augustan Tories, and modern historiography has tended to corroborate this view; see *Tory Political Thought, 1689–1714* (PhD thesis, Cambridge, 1977), 65.

union became a staple historical argument.[146] In a throwaway comment, though the sincerity of which we should not doubt, Rapin said that it was unfortunate that the union between Whigs and Tories did not last beyond the Revolution.[147] Rapin also damned the effect of 'party' on history writing itself.[148] A major, final assessment of parties of the kind in Burnet's conclusion to the *History of His Own Time* is lacking in the *Histoire*.[149] This can be explained by the fact that Rapin only oversaw the publication of the first eight volumes of the work before his death, in other words up to and including the reign of Charles I. The final two volumes of the French edition were published posthumously from his manuscripts.[150] For this reason, we have to view the *Dissertation* as his key statement on party.

Rapin and the Party Structure

Rapin viewed the categorisation of the two parties into distinct groupings – *Tories Outrez*, rigid church Tories, moderate Tories in church and state on the one hand, and republican Whigs, rigid Presbyterian Whigs, moderate Whigs in church and state on the other – as the key contribution of his 'petite Dissertation'.[151] Perhaps with a tinge of false modesty, he said that '[t]out le reste n'est qu'un accessoire où il peut y avoir plus ou moins que ce que j'en ay dit'.[152] This is not to say that he invented these terms, however; the Whig Lord Coningsby spoke of 'moderate Whigs', and the Huguenot René de Saunière de l'Hermitage referred to the Tories as 'les Rigides', just to give two examples. There is little doubt, however, that Rapin's specific way of using the nomenclature had resonance, as can be seen in the de Cize's *Histoire du Whigisme et du Torysme*, most likely published shortly after Rapin's work.[153]

The division and subdivision of different groupings and factions within the Tories and Whigs should not confuse us into believing that there was something akin to a multi-party system in early eighteenth-century England or Britain, or that Rapin held such an opinion. There was no

---

[146] Bolingbroke, *Dissertation upon Parties*, 72; Hume, *History*, VI, 502–3. It became the dominant view in the nineteenth century. See Okie, *Augustan Historical Writing*, 215–16.
[147] Rapin, *Histoire*, X, 104.   [148] Ibid., IX, 184–5.
[149] *Burnet's History of His Own Time*, II, 393–4, 396–7.
[150] Okie believes that the treatment of James II/VII and the Revolution was 'very probably compiled after his death and tacked on to the main body of his narrative'; see *Augustan Historical Writing*, 59.
[151] Rapin to Robethon, BL Stowe MS 230, f. 114.   [152] Ibid.
[153] De Cize, *Histoire du Whiggisme et du Torisme*, 1.

doubt in his mind that virtually all members of the political class were either Tory or Whig. His point was that the parties were not monolithic, although more disciplined and organised than we might imagine.[154] Subcategories and labels were used as an explanatory device to make sense of varieties within the parties, and especially to explain why opinions he considered extreme, particularly absolutism and Jacobitism, could have sway in a Protestant country with a mixed constitution. As we have seen, the reason he gave was that a small clique could control a larger body of people simply by virtue of being in leadership positions.

Rapin did not refer to Court or Country parties in his *Dissertation*, as he had done briefly in his *Histoire*, giving the impression that he thought that Tory and Whig had supplanted them. When he spoke about the Court, he often simply referred to the centre of government, or the ministry, comprising the monarch and his or her ministers, including junior ones. Court party usually denoted little more, since there was no alternative centre of government to the Court, and 'Court' was often used synonymously with 'ministry'. It could also refer to those members who invariably voted with the king's or queen's government, which, although a small minority, constituted a source of stability in the first age of party.[155] There were Court Whigs and Court Tories, but on major ideological issues such as the Sacheverell trial, Whig and Tory mattered more.

'Country party' could have a variety of meanings, but was commonly used as a euphemism for oppositions combining Whigs and Tories.[156] Country principles entailed suspicion of central government and particularly government spending, and related issues such as the standing army, placemen in parliament, the moneyed interest, and the national debt.[157] As Rapin demonstrated in his *Histoire*, the Whig party had begun its life as a Country party,[158] but from the reign of William III/II it became

---

[154] See, e.g., the work of Jones, including 'The Extra-Parliamentary Organisation of the Whig Junto in the Reign of William III', *PH*, 32 (2013), 522–30.

[155] Holmes, *British Politics in the Age of Anne*, 345–403.

[156] This was a platform rather than an organised party; see Hayton, 'The "Country" Interest and the Party System', in *Party and Management in Parliament* (Bath, 1984), 37–85; Hayton, 'Moral Reform and Country Politics in the Late Seventeenth-Century House of Commons', *Past and Present*, 128 (1990), 48–91.

[157] Tories had been against the standing army from the start, as they associated it with Cromwell and Commonwealth England; see Harris, *Politics under the Later Stuarts*, 100.

[158] A leading historian of the period has referred to *A Letter from a Person of Quality to his Friend in the Country* (1675), by Locke or someone else in the Shaftesbury circle, as the manifesto of the Whig party (*avant la lettre*); see Goldie, 'Priestcraft and the Birth of Whiggism', in *Political Discourses in Early Modern Britain* (Cambridge, 1993), 226.

increasingly associated with the Tories and even Jacobitism.[159] Indeed, country gentlemen became a synonym for Tories.[160] The most prominent example of such an opposition in the period was Harley's 'New Country party'.[161] Rapin may have referred to this type of alliance indirectly,[162] but it was not a major part of his narrative. Country members remained Whig or Tory primarily,[163] and in the context of 1716 it made little sense to talk of Court and Country when the most prominent question of the day was the Protestant Succession.

Rapin was clear that people were attached to the same party for different reasons, and the division between the political and ecclesiastical branches within the parties is therefore relevant. Rapin concluded his *Dissertation* by saying that while he was convinced that the entire people (*tout le Peuple*) enlisted themselves in one or the other 'faction', from interest or inclination, it did not follow that everyone acted from the views that he had attributed to the parties. In fact, '[i]t is certain that most of them suffer themselves to be led they know not wither, without examining into the Tendency of the Steps they are made to take'.[164] For example, a person attached to the Anglican Church was often a committed Tory, and by association obliged to support the *Torys Outrez* and *Rigides*, even if it was against their inclinations.[165] In theory, a person could thus be a Church Tory and a political Whig, or vice versa, but in practice Whig and Tory were separated, for historical reasons, and as party strife tended to produce a dichotomy.

Rapin was in many ways as critical of party intrigue as most British writers, especially, as we saw in the previous section, in the *Histoire*. Even in the *Dissertation*, he suggested that twelve neutral Lords, that is, the size of the cabinet, would suffice to break the power of the two parties, implying that this was a desirable outcome.[166] It was very difficult to achieve neutrality, however, since there were so few people without ambition and avarice.[167] The days when a 'trimmer' (Halifax) held high

---

[159] Monod, 'Jacobitism and Country Principles in the Reign of William III', *HJ*, 30 (1987), 289–310.
[160] Holmes, *British Politics in the Age of Anne*, 120.
[161] Hill, *Robert Harley* (New Haven, 1988), 34–61.   [162] Rapin, *Dissertation*, 93 (158).
[163] As the Country Whig E.W. Montagu conceded: 'The Country Whigs and Country Tories were not very different in their notions, and nothing has hindered them from joyning but the fear that each have of the others bringing in their whole party.' See 'On the State of Affairs when the King Entered' (1715?), manuscript source printed in *The Letters and Works of Lady Mary Montagu* (2 vols., London, revised edn., 1898), I, 21.
[164] Rapin, *Dissertation*, 105 (178).   [165] Ibid., 105 (179).   [166] Ibid., 61–2 (103).
[167] Modern research has confirmed that there was only a handful of people with no party ties in the political nation in the early part of the eighteenth century; Holmes, *British Politics in the Age of Anne*, 13–50.

office were over. Since the dominant party employed and promoted their
friends and backers, *les Neutres* found themselves out of office. Moreover, the
parties often accused each other of extreme positions which only few people in
either party actually espoused. But since both sides accused their adversaries of
seeking to destroy church and state, it was hard for people not to take sides
when such great dangers appeared to be at stake.[168] Accordingly, Rapin was
reluctant to blame the rank and file for these party divisions, described here as
unnatural (*dénaturées*). Instead, the blame should be reserved for the leaders,
who fomented division to advance their own interests.

The *Dissertation*, with all its flaws, is a crucial text because it was the
most extensive historical treatment of the parties to date. In addition, the
Frenchman stood out by offering a defence of the British party structure as
he understood it. This was unusual at a time when most political literature
was written to justify one party in opposition to the other, or alternatively
to lambast party as such.[169] Even if Rapin believed that the moderate
branches of the two parties were roughly of the same sentiments *politically*,[170] the fact that they argued for the rights of monarchy and parliament respectively maintained a balance between the two branches of the
constitution. When the safety of the state demanded it, these two parties
joined forces, as at the Glorious Revolution. In general, however, the
raison d'être of the political Tories was to defend the authority of the
monarch from Whig attacks, and this was what gave them their reputation
and credit at court and among the people.[171] On their part, the moderate
Whigs defended parliament against royal encroachments. If neither side
prevailed completely, the ancient constitution and the Anglican Church
would be protected. The Whigs had indeed been favoured by the court to
a considerable degree, especially since 1693 in England and since 1688–9
in Scotland, but it remained common to argue that the Whigs wanted to
'use that very power and authority . . . to cutt the sinews of the Royalty'.[172]

Consequently, Rapin argued, '[i]t may be positively affirmed, it is not
the Interest of the kingdom that one of the Parties shou'd become so
superior as to meet with no Contradiction'.[173] Crucially, this did not only

---

[168] Rapin, *Dissertation*, 106 (180).
[169] See, e.g., *The Spectator*, nos. 125 and 126 (24 and 25 July 1711). Addison was himself a Whig MP
and a member of both the Kit Cat and the Hanover Club. He held office before 1710 and again
after 1714, notably as secretary of state for the Southern Department in 1717–18. His *Spectator*
colleague Steele was also a Whig MP.
[170] Rapin, *Dissertation*, 51 (86).   [171] Ibid., 69 (114).
[172] 'History of Whigs and Tories in Scotland', BL Add MS 61136, f. 201. The author of this
manuscript viewed the Whigs as the ancestors of the Roundheads.
[173] Rapin, *Dissertation*, 106 (181).

apply to the extreme wings of the two parties: if moderate Tories became too superior, their penchant for the royal prerogative risked making the king powerful enough to abolish parliament. On the other hand, if the moderate Whigs had complete power, they would attack royal power, turning the sovereign into the condition of the Doge of Venice.[174] The same logic applied in the religious arena: exclusive reign of either Episcopalians or Presbyterians would mean the ruin of their adversaries. Rather than one party becoming superior, 'it will always be safer [plus avantageux] for the State, that the Division shou'd continue as it is at present'. According to Rapin, 'the Equality their Discord keeps them in' was preferable to the dominance of a single party.[175]

On the other hand, Rapin was clear that 'a Spirit of Party, the Cabals of their Leaders, the Intrigues of the Court, the Interests of private Men, have but two [*sic*] much influence over the Deliberations of that Assembly, which represents the *English* Nation'.[176] This was largely inevitable, however, since parliament was made up of people who could not be expected to be dispassionate. All that could be done was to reform abuse. The primary abuse as he saw it was court influence over the election of the Commons, as it upset the balance of the constitution. The ruling party could spend money and exert influence in constituencies to ensure the election of the members of parliament it wanted.[177] They could therefore control deliberations in parliament. Thus it happened that ordinarily the parliament was Whig when the ministry was Whig, and Tory when the ministry was Tory.[178] This seems obvious from a modern point of view, but this was a time when ministries were formed *before* elections,[179] and Rapin and many others assumed that the mixed constitution, while balanced, implied a degree of 'Lockean' separation between its legislative and executive powers. The creation of twelve Lords under Anne was an

---

[174] Ibid., 107 (182).   [175] Ibid., 108 (183–4).   [176] Ibid., 92 (155).

[177] As Cowper put it, the governing party would have 'a clear majority, as it will always happen whenever the Court have a mind to have it so' ('An Impartial History of Parties', 426). Both Rapin and Cowper may have exaggerated the influence of the Court on elections, however. The leading modern historian of the period has described most elections before 1722, when a party won a majority for the first time since 1681 that was clearly disproportionate to its strength in the country, as popular triumphs. See Holmes, *The Making of a Great Power*, 329–32.

[178] Rapin, *Dissertation*, 92–3 (157–8).

[179] A Jacobite wrote the following in December 1716, when the fall of Townshend from the Whig ministry looked like a dandy opportunity for the Tories: '[I]f a Tory Ministry can be had, a new Parliament must be of course, for they can never make any thing of this flaming Whig one.' J. Menzies to Michel Fribourgh (L. Inese), 20 December 1716, in HMC, *Stuart Papers*, III, 378.

example of an attempt by the executive to disturb the balance of the constitution by controlling the legislature, according to Rapin.[180]

The *Dissertation* finished on an ambivalent note. The only thing that could put an end to Britain's 'intestine' war (*Guerre intestine*) – a phrase often used with reference to factional strife in the Roman republic – was a just, equitable, and moderate king, who loved Protestantism and sought to ensure the well-being of his subjects, he argued.[181] Rapin thus ended with an homage and an exhortation to the newly crowned George I, to whom he would later dedicate his *Histoire*.[182] Perhaps this was simply a conventional way to round off a fairly controversial pamphlet, like Machiavelli in *Il Principe*, or Lord Chancellor Cowper, who in the conclusion of a memorandum for George I talked of 'means to extinguish the being and the very name of party amongst us', just after he had advised the king to employ nominal Whigs.[183] However, it is also fully conceivable that Rapin believed that this was possible to achieve, if the new government addressed the abuses in the political system he had listed in the pamphlet, and if the beliefs of the extreme wings of the two parties were revealed for what they were: a way to gather support to further private ambitions. Most statements in his *Histoire* corroborate the view that Rapin disliked party division and that his defence of the British party structure was strictly a 'lesser evil' argument. Even so, it was momentous.

Rapin on Ideology

As has been shown, Rapin was prepared to vindicate the moderate aims of the two parties: the preservation of the 'ancient', mixed constitution as he understood it, and the protection of the Anglican Church combined with toleration for Dissenters.[184] If the equilibrium of the constitution and the balance between Church and Dissent could only be secured through a compromise between the two parties, they were both necessary to control and check each other, and make sure that neither side became superior. Although he believed that whereas the moderates of both parties were cut from the same cloth, the political Whigs were somewhat superior to the political Tories, even if this was mainly due to the fact that extreme Tories

---

[180] Rapin, *Dissertation*, 93–4 (158). Other abuses Rapin pointed out included the inequality in size between different constituencies, bribery at elections, and the inability of constituents to instruct or hold their representatives accountable.

[181] Ibid., 108 (184).   [182] Ibid.   [183] Cowper, 'An Impartial History of Parties', 429.

[184] The term 'ideology' in the section heading is an anachronism, being coined in the 1790s, but the concept is arguably older; see Kelley, *The Beginning of Ideology* (Cambridge, 1981), 4.

were in the leadership of their party whereas the republican Whigs, although equally pernicious, were barely noticeable within the Whigs. Moreover, the religious Tories were in many ways preferable to the religious Whigs, since they encompassed almost the entire established Church.[185] Introducing Presbyterianism in an Anglican country would be as extreme and impracticable as introducing Catholicism, according to Rapin.

Rapin's starting point, however, was that the most obvious difference between the parties in Anne's reign had been foreign policy, essentially different ideas about how the Protestant interest in Europe was best protected.[186] The Tory party was fundamentally against entanglements on the continent. In other words, it was a party for peace, alternatively for naval as opposed to land warfare, which is not the same as a xenophobic or anti-trade party, even if some modern scholars, unlike Rapin, seem to think that.[187] The Whigs, on the other hand, were interventionist and for war against France. This was the division that mattered to Europeans on the continent. Rapin sought to explain these contrasting views on foreign policy through a historical analysis of the parties' traditions and ideas.

While Rapin paid attention to ideas and principles, he did not seem to think that they were prime movers in high politics. Rather, he believed that they were a way to gather support to satisfy personal ambitions. By contrast, the Whig Lord Cowper informed George I that 'it has been often said, that the only difference is about places; but this is either a superficial judgment, or a desire to hinder the true causes from being discerned'.[188] Before we blame Rapin for either accusation, we should remember that he did not dismiss the influence of ideas entirely. While leaders may have used them to gain support, they were not without influence on policy and

---

[185] Rapin to Robethon, BL Stowe MS 230, ff. 114–21.

[186] See Thompson, *Britain, Hanover and the Protestant Interest, 1688–1756* (Woodbridge, 2006).

[187] Jupp, *The Governing of Britain, 1688–1848* (New York, 2006), 69; Hill, 'Parliament, Parties, and Elections 1688–1760', in *A Companion to Eighteenth-Century Britain* (Oxford, 2002), 61. The Tory-Jacobite William King (1685–1763) of Oxford retold an anecdote about the Jacobite hero Archbishop Fénelon in which the Frenchman was quoted as having said that 'You should endeavour to divest yourself of all national prejudices, and never condemn the customs and manners of a foreign people, because they are altogether different from your own. I am a true *French*-man, and love my country; but I love mankind better than my country.' King, *Anecdotes*, 21.

[188] Cowper continued: 'For if that was true, then the struggle would only be between individuals, and not between two set of parties of men, which can only be kept up by some diversity of opinion upon fundamentals' ('An Impartial History of Parties', 427). By contrast, his fellow Whig Lord Coningsby put more emphasis on personality and court intrigue in his 'History of Parties', which he also presented to George I.

political developments. Even if he was sceptical about the sincerity of principles held by top politicians, he was convinced that opinions and beliefs (political and religious) divided and united the rank and file and more widely the people.[189]

Rapin's investigation into beliefs and principles was limited, however. While he referred repeatedly to the doctrine of passive obedience, he did not seek to probe further into divine right theories of kingship that underpinned this principle.[190] Interestingly also, while referring to the right to resistance recognised by the Whigs, Rapin made in the *Dissertation* no reference to contract theory. In the *Histoire*, the debate about the 'original contract' at the Convention Parliament of 1689 was mentioned, but Rapin did not link this notion specifically to the Whigs. His relative silence on these questions, at least in the *Dissertation*, may have several explanations. It seems questionable that he would not have been sufficiently informed about them considering his extensive knowledge of British politics. It is also clear that he was aware of different versions of absolutist arguments in the seventeenth century, as he compared England to France.[191]

Regarding contract theory, Rapin is likely to have been aware of John Locke's *Two Treatises of Government* (written *c.*1680–3), either its English edition, or perhaps the 1791 French translation of the *Second Treatise* by David Mazel, a Huguenot pastor in London.[192] Rapin was also acquainted with Jean Le Clerc, who edited and disseminated Locke's works for a Protestant audience on the continent.[193] Rapin's fellow Huguenot and party historian de Cize mentioned Locke's death in 1704 as a significant event and singled out the *Treatises* 'où il refute les opinions du Chevalier

---

[189] As discussed in the Introduction, Skinner has forcefully argued that ideas are important even for actors who are purely motivated by self-interest, since the range of actions open to them is determined and circumscribed by the principles they appeal to in order to justify their actions, whether or not the principles are sincerely believed.

[190] De Cize referred to 'droit divin' numerous times in his *Histoire du Whigisme et Torisme*, a phrase that never occurs in the *Dissertation*.

[191] Rapin, *Dissertation*, 86–7 (146).

[192] Laursen, 'Introduction', in *New Essays on the Political Thought of the Huguenots*, 10. We know that Rapin was aware of Locke's writings on philosophy and religion; see Rapin to Jacques Lenfant, 1723, in 'Receuil de lettres et fragments poétiques', in Cazenove, *Rapin-Thoyras*, xxix. For Rapin as a political disciple of Locke, see Girard d'Albissin, *Un précurseur de Montesquieu*, 12, 110–13.

[193] However, when Le Clerc's summary of the *Two Treatises* appeared in *Bibliothèque universelle* in December 1690, Rapin was in Kinsale, Ireland. Le Clerc later became a key source for Rapin's historical enterprise and crucially obtained for him Thomas Rymer's *Foedera* (Okie, *Augustan Historical Writing*, 53). For Le Clerc and the reception of Locke in the Francophone world, see Soulard, 'The Reception of Locke's Politics', in *Politics, Religion and Ideas in Seventeenth- and Eighteenth-Century Britain* (Woodbridge, 2019), 201–18.

Filmer ... [and] etablit l'origine des gouvernements, comme je l'ay expli-
quee dans les maxims des Whigs [i.e. contract theory], & justifia la
revolution'.[194] Moreover, Locke was not the only contract theorist at the
time and it is likely that Rapin would have known about Benjamin
Hoadly.[195]

Why did Rapin not spend more time on the parties' speculative systems
of government, if we assume that he was aware of them? Was he frightened
of contract theory and did not want to draw attention to it? That seems
implausible considering his approval of the Glorious Revolution. We can
therefore consider the possibility that Rapin may have diagnosed that the
'original contract' and 'divine right' theories were relatively unimportant in
the context in which he was writing, since he believed that extreme
partisans were mainly motivated by self-interest or religious sectarianism,
and moderate ones by ancient constitutionalism. In this area, Hume, who
in many respects built on Rapin, would go beyond the Frenchman and
offer a more sustained discussion of the speculative systems of the two
parties.[196] Rapin and Hume agreed that principles mattered more for the
rank and file and that party leaders were mainly motivated by self-interest.
It should not surprise us that the Frenchman put more emphasis on the
latter and Scotsman on the former. As Smith put it, Rapin's drawback as a
historian vis-à-vis Hume was that Rapin 'has entered too much into the
private affairs of the monarchs and the parties amongst the severall great
men concern'd, so that his history as many others is rather an account of
the Lives of the princes than of the affairs of the body of the people'.[197]

Conclusion

One of the most important moves that Rapin made was to connect the
eighteenth-century Tory–Whig polarisation to the 'Court' and 'Country'
parties that he saw emerging in the early 1620s, as a result of James I/VI's
ambition to become an absolute monarch and expand Anglicanism, on the
one hand, and popular Puritanism, on the other. The party divide thus had
its roots in the split between Episcopalians and Presbyterians after the
Reformation in England and Scotland in the sixteenth century. The visible
division that emerged under James I/VI fed into the civil war parties, or

---

[194] He added that Locke 'gagna plus de prosélites au Party *Whig* qu'aucun homme qui ait jamais écrit.'
De Cize, *Histoire du Whiggisme et du Torisme*, 263–4, 3–5.
[195] E.g., Hoadly, *The Original and Institution of Civil Government* (London, 1710).
[196] See Chapter 6. [197] Smith, *Lectures on Rhetoric and Belles Lettres*, 116.

combatants, of Cavalier and Roundhead. As Rapin stressed in the *Histoire*, the civil war connection was one that the parties of the 1680s made themselves, especially the Tories. The relationship between the Roundheads and Cavaliers and the Whigs and Tories was taken for granted by many in the eighteenth century.[198] That the pre-Revolutionary Whigs and Tories were essentially the same as those of his own time, Rapin regarded as a given. As we have seen, the dividing lines he identified between the parties, for the seventeenth century and his own time, were religious and political. Modern scholarship has, with good reason, tended to stress the primacy of religion over politics in the early history of party formation,[199] as a reaction to an older historiographical tradition, which saw the seventeenth-century struggles as mainly constitutional. For Rapin, the parties had always contained a mixture of political and religious principles, but as his terminology shows, he saw these principles as distinct and believed that one set of principles could be more dominant than the other.

In the nineteenth and early twentieth centuries, many British historians believed that their own party framework was more or less prefigured in the seventeenth century, even if some looked to the civil war and others to the Restoration period for the watershed moment.[200] Some even argued that '[t]he germs of party, in the councils and Parliament of England, – generated by the Reformation, – were first discernible in the reign of Elizabeth', for Rapinesque reasons.[201] As a reaction to this presentism, famously criticised by both Herbert Butterfield and Lewis Namier in the interwar period, later historians have tended to stress discontinuity

---

[198] Later, Chambers, who quoted from Rapin's *Dissertation* at length in his entries for both Whig and Tory, wrote in his *Cyclopaedia* (1738) that 'England has, for upwards of a century, been divided into two *parties*'. The connection was naturally not Rapin's invention; Clarendon's *History of the Rebellion* (published in 1702–4) became a key text for Tories, and the legacy of the civil war was debated between the Whig White Kennett and the Tory Mary Astell in 1704.

[199] Goldie, 'Danby, the Bishops and the Whigs', in *The Politics of Religion in Restoration England* (Oxford, 1990), 75–105.

[200] Cooke, *The History of Party* (3 vols., London, 1836–7), I, preface; Macaulay, *The History of England from the Accession of James II* (5 vols., Chicago, 1890 [1848]), I, 100; Abbott, 'The Origin of English Political Parties', *American Historical Review*, 24 (1919), 578–602; Trevelyan, *The Two-Party System in English Political History* (Oxford, 1926). Many who were more cautious about drawing parallels with their own time still argued for continuity between the seventeenth and the beginning of the eighteenth century; see Hallam, *The Constitutional History of England* (2 vols., Cambridge, 2011 [1827]), II, 549–657; Feiling, *A History of the Tory Party, 1640–1714* (Oxford, 1924).

[201] Erskine May, *The Constitutional History of England* (2 vols., New York, 1874 [1861]), II, 19.

between the seventeenth and eighteenth centuries.[202] The most extreme version of this tendency in relation to party has been the attempt to deny that political parties existed in any organisational sense in the late Stuart period.[203] But writers in the eighteenth century were not so interested in organisation. When Rapin and others tentatively before him searched for the origin of party, they looked for ideological polarisation, although Rapin largely saw this as a fig leaf for the pursuit of power. For Rapin and others of his generation, party meant primarily ideological allegiance under a banner, or a party name. What Rapin tried to do in his *Dissertation* was to show the relevance of pre-revolutionary issues for post-revolutionary ones.[204] He is thus a key historical thinker for helping us not to lose sight of how people in the eighteenth century themselves believed that seventeenth-century issues, and by extension those of the Reformation, had been carried into their own time. Whether he was right or merely helped to sustain a myth, continuity in this limited sense is worth highlighting, which is not the same as pointing to an unbroken chain of development towards the current Westminster model of politics.

The emphasis in Rapin's historical narrative was thus on continuity. While he did not disregard context and contingency, one can certainly argue that he underplayed the role of the Glorious Revolution as a turning point for the parties, as regular sessions of parliament after 1688–9 enabled the development of a clearer two-party structure. Others may have been guilty of the converse, however. As I argue in Chapter 3, Bolingbroke, no doubt for partisan purposes, attempted to accentuate the effects of the Revolution in his own *Dissertation upon Parties*.

Rapin's *Dissertation* was read immediately in Britain, as can be seen in an unpublished Tory-Jacobite commentary on the British constitution,

---

[202] The generation of political historians succeeding Namier stressed the limitations of his method, but were still writing against Whig historians, and wanted to show how the eighteenth century was different to the previous century; see Plumb, *The Growth of Political Stability* (London, 1967); Holmes, *British Politics in the Age of Anne*. However, some historians have been willing to recognise continuity between the seventeenth and eighteenth centuries, but they have generally been disinclined to go further back than the Restoration; see Harris, *Politics under the Later Stuarts*; Clark, *English Society*.

[203] This case has been made by Scott, *Algernon Sidney and the Restoration Crisis* (Cambridge, 1991), 9–17, 21–5. Scott has been criticised and responded to this criticism in a series of articles in a special issue of *Albion*, including Harris, 'Party Turns? Or, Whigs and Tories Get Off Scott Free', *Albion*, 25 (1993), 581–91. If we use a looser eighteenth-century understanding of party, it is clear why people at the time regarded them as parties. Scott's thesis only holds up if we apply a stricter, modern-day definition of party, borrowed from political science.

[204] This was something Whigs sought to refute, as they were eager to dissociate themselves from the regicide and republican principles, e.g., in Cowper, 'An Impartial History of Parties', 421, 428.

written in the same year as the publication of the *Dissertation*.[205] Although this Jacobite writer was critical, especially of Rapin's 'keep[ing] company mostly with the Whigs',[206] the long-term impact of Rapin was colossal. For example, Rapin's influence, at least indirectly, is evident in the case of the Court Whig scribbler-historian Samuel Squire, Bishop of St David's in 1761–6, who argued that 'the two parties of *Whig* and *Tory*, were first virtually formed' in the sixteenth century in the shape of 'the *Puritans* and *Church-of-England-men*'.[207] These parties were initially 'entirely religious' but were divided into religious and civil branches, *'Church-whigs'* and *'State-whigs'*, in the reign of James I/VI.[208] Moreover, as late as 1819, Abraham Rees borrowed the lion's share of his material on the British parties in the *Cyclopaedia* from Rapin's *Dissertation*, supplemented with references to de Cize, Hume, and Gregory Sharpe's translation of Ludvig Holberg's *Introduction to Universal History*, which was itself reliant on Rapin.[209]

In the sphere of political theory, Rapin's *Dissertation* can be regarded as a milestone as it was the first recommendation of balance between parties, as distinct from Machiavelli's social orders, as a way to achieve proper balance in a mixed constitution. As we have seen, however, Rapin ended the pamphlet on an ambivalent note by appealing to unity, which ultimately appears to have been his highest ideal. In the *Histoire*, he deplored that the union between Whigs and Tories, which he saw as a catalyst for the Revolution, had not been maintained after the event. However, it is questionable whether he saw unity as a realistic objective. He knew from his own experience that it was not an attainable religious ideal. At the same time he sought to prop up unity by suggesting a compromise between the moderate wings of the two parties. In the religious sphere he advocated support for the national church combined with toleration for Dissenters. If the ruling Whigs desisted from repealing the Occasional Conformity Act 1711, they might be able to defeat the *Torys Outrez* in general and

---

[205] *A View of the English Constitution with some Facts not generally known* [c.1717], in NLS MS 296, ff. 22–35. Although the advertisement is dated 1749–50, the main text is dated 1717. The copy in the NLS is followed by a postscript dated 1747, in which the author refers to the *Histoire* ('since that time Monsr. Rapin has produced a much greater Work' (f. 46)).

[206] Ibid., f. 28.

[207] [Squire], *Historical Essay upon the Ballance of Civil Power in England ... in which is introduced a new Dissertation upon Parties* (London, 1748), 60–1. The *Dissertation* alluded to in the title was that written by Squire's nemesis Bolingbroke.

[208] Ibid., 61–3.

[209] Rees, *The Cyclopaedia* (39 vols., London, 1819), XXXVI; Holberg, *Introduction to Universal History ... with Notes Historical, Chronological, and Critical by Gregory Sharpe* (London, 1755), 210–14.

Jacobitism in particular, by not giving the Church of England a reason to associate with the extreme Tory forces. Church and Dissent could then coexist, and moderate Whigs and Tories could cooperate in politics, as they had on several occasions, notably in 1704–8.

We can be sure, however, that Rapin did not think that the disputes between High Church and Dissent, or those about the proper balance between monarchical and parliamentary power, were going to disappear in the foreseeable future. In the unlikely event that they did, he believed that office-seeking would help to maintain the parties, since they competed about employment and shared the spoils of victory with their supporters. Parties were here to stay, and his *Dissertation* tried to understand them and explain how they had originated, not how they could be exterminated. We must remember that his intention behind publishing the *Dissertation* was to instruct Europeans in British party strife as they had proved to be important in European affairs and were likely to continue to be so.

Finally, Rapin's correspondence with George I's secretary Robethon suggests that the message of the pamphlet may have been communicated or even shown to the first Hanoverian king, who was as perplexed as other continental Europeans by the British parties.[210] Shortly after his accession and some years thereafter, the king was exposed to several memoranda about the history and state of the British parties.[211] By proscribing the Tories, he followed the advice of Cowper and Coningsby rather than Rapin.[212] Moreover, the Stanhope–Sunderland ministries from 1717 went against Rapin's advice of leaving the Church of England alone, as they repealed the Occasional Conformity and Schism Acts.[213] This reform

[210] Rapin's letter to Robethon in May 1717 is a response to a letter in which George I's private secretary must have asked Rapin about his *Dissertation* and appears to have wanted policy advice. Like Rapin, Robethon was a French Huguenot in exile, who had been private secretary to William III/II before entering the service of Hanover; see Thompson, *Britain, Hanover and the Protestant Interest*, 50–1, 69. His ties with Rapin appear to go a long way back: they both accompanied the Earl of Portland on his mission to Paris in 1698. On his grand tour in 1701–3, Rapin's pupil Lord Woodstock (later 2nd Earl of Portland) visited Celle (where Robethon was working for George I's uncle, Georg Wilhelm of Celle), but at that stage Rapin had already left his pupil for Holland. BL Egerton MS 1706, ff. 127–30, 164.

[211] Cowper's 'Impartial History of Parties' (1714) and Coningsby's 'History of Party' (1716) have been cited earlier in this chapter.

[212] Many believed that the initial intention of George I was to employ both Whigs and Tories; see Montagu, 'On the State of Affairs when the King Entered', 15. For the important local dimension of Tory proscription, see Landau, *The Justices of the Peace* (Berkeley, 1984).

[213] Champion, *Republican Learning* (Manchester, 2003), ch. 6; Townend, 'Religious Radicalism and Conservatism in the Whig Party under George I', *PH*, 7 (1988), 24–44; Bennett, *The Tory Crisis in Church and State*, 205–22; Holmes, *The Trial of Doctor Sacheverell*, epilogue. The Whig government also introduced the Act for Quieting and Establishing Corporations as a 'bonus' to the Dissenters. Plans to regulate Oxford and Cambridge were dropped, however.

agenda – effectively a reversal of the 1710–14 Tory ministry's crackdown on nonconformity – slowed down under Walpole, but the proscription of Tories remained a dogma, and a significant portion of the Tory party was so estranged that many of them continued to be periodically tangled up with Jacobitism until the abandoned Elibank Plot in the early 1750s.

CHAPTER 3

Bolingbroke's Country Party Opposition Platform

The natural Result of which is a Spirit of Opposition; however pernicious this may seem to be in general, yet in some particular Cases, as, where the *Honour* and *Welfare* of our *Kings* and *Country* is at Stake, through the *Blunders* and *Mismanagement* of an *ignorant, overbearing Minister*; in such Cases, I say, a Spirit of Opposition may be judg'd commendable; for if *Falshood* be not oppos'd, *Truth* cannot appear . . . there must be Parties, or Difference of Principles, unless it can be suppos'd, that Good and Bad do not contradict each other, which is absurd. As, therefore, Men's Actions be distinguish'd by *Good* and *Bad*, so are these Parties by the known Titles *Tory* and *Whigg*.

Fog's Weekly Journal, 6 March 1731

The *Coalition of Parties* seems indeed a Thing very *capable* of being effected. Interest or Conviction may cause Men to lay aside their *peculiar* Differences, and may make them unite in some *common* Maxims and Designs. But Principles are invariable: and as Truth and Falshood, Liberty and Slavery, true *Whiggism* and staunch *Toryism* are necessarily and immutably different, and quite irreconciliable with each other; it is impossible they can ever *coalesce*, or be brought into a real Union and Friendship.

The Old Whig, 11 September 1735

The Life and Times of Bolingbroke

Henry St John, 1st Viscount Bolingbroke (1678–1751), has commonly been portrayed as the paradigmatic anti-party writer of the eighteenth century.[1] It has also often been suggested that he tried but failed to

---

[1] Hofstadter, *The Idea of a Party System* (Berkeley, 1970), 10, 18; Ball, 'Party', in *Political Innovation and Conceptual Change* (Cambridge, 1989), 170. One exception to the prevalent view of Bolingbroke as an anti-party thinker is Kluxen, *Das Problem der Politischen Opposition* (Munich, 1956), 103–19.

illustrate the ideal of a non-party state.[2] In his own lifetime, however, Bolingbroke was more often seen as a party man and a party writer. This chapter demonstrates that Bolingbroke was in fact the promoter of a very specific party: a systematic parliamentary opposition party under the banner of the Country party in resistance to what he perceived as the Court Whig faction in power. When this political party has been acknowledged in the existing literature, it has usually been construed as 'a party to end all parties'.[3] Moreover, Bolingbroke has been associated with the anti-party catchphrase 'not men, but measures'.[4] This chapter shows not only that these slogans were never used by Bolingbroke but also that they are arguably incompatible with his political writings.[5]

First, however, we need to say something more about Bolingbroke's formation and political career, which was already touched upon in Chapter 2. His upbringing was unorthodox, to say the least. With a Whig father and possibly education at a Dissenting academy, his background 'promis'd that he would one Day be a Pillar of the common Cause' of Whiggism, in the words of the Whig hack John Oldmixon.[6] In the event, however, as a parliamentarian in 1701–8 and 1710–15, Bolingbroke cut a figure as a loyal Tory, although it was mainly in the latter period that he became associated with the *Torys Outrez*. For a large part of the early period he was closely allied with the moderate Country Tory Robert Harley, with whom he served in the mixed ministry as Secretary at War in 1704–8. His friendship with Harley deteriorated and turned into rivalry during the administration of 1710–14, however.[7] Bolingbroke aimed for leadership of the High Church Tories, which was ironic considering his own lack of religious sympathies. Pocock commented that '[w]hat so outspoken a deist as Bolingbroke had been doing at the head of an Anglican party in Anne's reign is a question that seems to transcend any

---

[2] Robbins, 'Discordant Parties', *Political Science Quarterly*, 37 (1958), 507; Fieldhouse, 'Bolingbroke and the Idea of Non-party Government', *History*, 23 (1938), 41–56.

[3] Rosenblum, *On the Side of the Angels* (Princeton, 2008), 35–6; Muirhead, *The Promise of Party in a Polarized Age* (Cambridge, MA, 2014), 39.

[4] Mansfield, *Statesmanship and Party Government* (Chicago, 1965), 179.

[5] On the only occasion I have found Bolingbroke using 'men' and 'measures' in the same sentence, he spoke of their interrelation: 'do not drop your protest against the *men & the measures* that ruine it [the country]', see Bolingbroke to Wyndham, 18 November 1739, *Unpublished Letters*, V, 249.

[6] Oldmixon, *Memories of the Press, Historical and Political* (London, 1742), 17. Dickinson has shown that one of St John's fellow travellers on the grand tour in 1698–1700 was shocked by him joining the Tory ranks when entering parliament in 1701; see 'Henry St. John: A Re-appraisal of the Young Bolingbroke', *JBS*, 7 (1968), 52.

[7] For Bolingbroke's criticism of Harley, see Bolingbroke, *Of the State of Parties at the Accession of King George the First* (1739), in *Works*, III, 134–5. (Hence: *State of Parties*.)

answer (however justified) in terms of political duplicity'.[8] We should remember, however, that Bolingbroke's religious freethinking was publicised posthumously in the 1750s, and Tocqueville was thus exaggerating when he said that '[i]t was Bolingbroke who completed Voltaire's education', with reference to his heterodox views on religion.[9] In terms of his outspoken policy during his lifetime, Bolingbroke was not an odd one out in the Church of England party (as Tocqueville acknowledged). In October 1710, he wrote to one of his earliest political friends, Sir William Trumbull, that 'I have resolv'd to neglect nothing in my power wch may contribute towards making the Church interest the prevailing one in our Country'.[10]

Having been a prominent member of the Tory administration of 1710–14 and the chief negotiator of the Treaty of Utrecht, Bolingbroke fled to France about six months after George I ascended the British throne in August 1714, an event which instigated what he would later describe as 'the millenarian year of Whiggism'.[11] His decision to take up a position at the court of James 'III', the Stuart Pretender, whom he served for less than a year, prevented him from returning to Britain until the mid-1720s. Shortly after his dismissal following the failed Jacobite rebellion of 1715, Bolingbroke defended his conduct by arguing that he was acting in the belief that he was helping the Tory party in England.[12] This may have been at least partly genuine; in October 1714 he had dramatically written to his political ally Bishop Atterbury that 'the grief of my soul is this, I see plainly that the Tory party is gone ... where are the Men of Business, that will live and draw together[?]'[13] Bolingbroke had communicated with the Stuart court and Jacobite agents prior to the Hanoverian Succession, but his flirtations with Jacobitism appear to have been opportunistic rather

---

[8] Pocock, *Virtue, Commerce, and History* (Cambridge, 1985), 240.

[9] Tocqueville, *The Ancien Régime and the French Revolution* (Cambridge, 2011 [1856]), 140.

[10] *The Correspondence of Henry St. John and Sir William Trumbull, 1698–1710*, ed. Lashmore-Davies, *Eighteenth-Century Life*, 32 (2008), 172.

[11] 'Letter addressed to an unnamed Lord', [c.1750], printed in *Unpublished Letters*, 304–10. In contrast with Lashmore-Davies, I believe that this letter should be regarded as a draft of a political essay, though probably not intended for wider publication, rather than a piece of correspondence. In terms of tone, style, spelling, and grammar, it is much closer to Bolingbroke's political writings than his private correspondence. I will henceforth refer to it as ['Reflections on Walpole'].

[12] Bolingbroke, *Letter to Windham*, in *Works*, I, 37, 39, 83, 87. Bolingbroke said that there was neither a conspiracy to overthrow the Hanoverians nor an organised Jacobite party before the violence of the Whigs 'forced them [the Tories] into the arms of the pretender' (31). See also, Bolingbroke, *State of Parties*, in *Works*, III, 130–3.

[13] Stowe MS, BL, f. 177. This letter is not included in either *Unpublished Letters* or *Letters and Correspondence, Public and Private, of Bolingbroke* (4 vols., London, 1798).

than principled.[14] Indeed, the diehard Jacobite Carte was convinced that '[t]he Design of L[ord] B[olingbroke] at the time [of Anne's death] was to bring about the Hanover Succession'.[15]

Bolingbroke put on a brave face – 'Wise men are certainly superior to all the evils of exile'[16] – but there was no secret that he actively sought to return to Britain. When he was eventually allowed to return, he remained barred from taking up his seat in the Lords. Deprived of a political voice in parliament, he launched the *Craftsman* journal with the opposition Whig William Pulteney in 1726. Bolingbroke and the *Craftsman* were part of a wider intellectual opposition against Walpole and the Whig political order. It was to become the bestselling publication in the country for many years, and won the respect even of its fiercest enemies, with Lord Hervey remarking that it was 'a much better written paper than any of that sort that were published on the side of the Court'.[17] The literary part of this opposition comprised such luminaries as Jonathan Swift, Alexander Pope, John Gay, Dr Arbuthnot, and, at a later stage, James Thomson, Samuel Johnson, and Henry Fielding.[18] Bolingbroke had known many of these wits since his time in government, as he was a supporter and member of what would later be known as the Scriblerus Club. Many of these figures did seek patronage from the Hanoverian regime and Walpole himself, and turned to opposition when their aspirations were disappointed. 'Bob, the Poet's Foe', a phrase from Swift's poetry, thus became a common complaint in opposition literature and propaganda during the Walpole era.

What did Bolingbroke mean by the 'millenarian year of Whiggism', and what was this new political order to which he was so vehemently opposed? The main development in party-political discourse in the early eighteenth century, in the words of an expert scholar, was that 'the Whigs, once the party of populist resistance to oligarchy, gradually became oligarchs themselves, while the Tories picked up the populist mantle'.[19] This process was

---

[14] Szechi, *Jacobitism and Tory Politics, 1710–14* (Edinburgh, 1984), 190–1. He later became dismissive of Jacobitism publicly, but appeared to have been more flexible behind the scenes; see Cruickshanks, 'Lord Cornbury, Bolingbroke and a Plan to Restore the Stuarts 1731–1735', *Stuart Papers*, 27 (1986), 1–12. Moreover, he did not cut his ties with his Jacobite friends, including Carte and Corbett Kynaston; see BL Add MS. 21500, f. 15 (6 September 1729).

[15] Carte MS 231, Bodleian, f. 92 (30 May 1726).

[16] Bolingbroke, 'Reflections upon Exile' (1716), *Works*, I, 113.   [17] *Hervey's Memoirs*, I, 263.

[18] Gerrard, *The Patriot Opposition to Walpole* (Oxford, 1994); Pocock, *The Machiavellian Moment* (Princeton, 2003 [1975]), 477–86; Kramnick, *Bolingbroke and his Circle* (Ithaca, 1992 [1968]), 205–35; Goldgar, *Walpole and the Wits* (Lincoln, 1976).

[19] Hayton, 'Introduction', *Commons, 1690–1715*, I, 463. See also Goldie, *Tory Political Thought, 1689–1714* (PhD thesis, Cambridge, 1977), ch. 6 and epilogue; Rogers, 'The City Elections Act (1725) Reconsidered', *EHR*, 100 (1985), 604–17.

intensified and accelerated after the Hanoverian Succession. Rapin had written his *Dissertation* in February 1716 and it is only with the benefit of hindsight that we know that the age of Whig supremacy had already begun by this point. The cementation of this new epoch took place a few months later when the Septennial Act was introduced, prolonging the life of parliament until 1722. The ministry had already cracked down on extra-parliamentary discontent with the introduction of the Riot Act, which erased the distinction between public and private disorder, and made it a capital felony for a group of more than twelve people to fail to disband within one hour if so instructed by the authorities.[20]

In exile, Bolingbroke mellowed from his one-time tribal Toryism. He may to a small degree have been influenced by Rapin's *Dissertation*, but the main reason behind the shift was unquestionably his personal circumstances. In any event, some of the sentiments in Rapin's *Dissertation* were repeated by Bolingbroke in a letter to John Dalrymple, 2nd Earl of Stair, on 18 August 1718.[21] Stair was at this point the British ambassador to France and his main mission was to combat Jacobitism. For this purpose, Stair cultivated Bolingbroke and the Earl of Mar, who had succeeded Bolingbroke as the Pretender's secretary. Bolingbroke did not need Rapin to enlighten him about the state of British politics, but the similarities are still striking, and it would not be rash to assume that Bolingbroke had read the *Dissertation* at this point since it had been a bestseller across Europe the previous year, and Bolingbroke was one of the original subscribers to Rapin's *Histoire* only a few years later.[22] The former Tory secretary of state was now intent on 'breaking the Confederacy of Party'. This was not an unselfish goal since partisanship obstructed his return to England; most Whigs naturally viewed him as *persona non grata* and many Jacobites blamed him for the failure of the rising in 1715.[23] Conspicuously, Bolingbroke argued in the letter that 'the object of the Tories is Jacobitism, and that of the Whiggs some fantastical alterations in the Constitution of our Laws & Government'. Similarly to Rapin, Bolingbroke held that 'many go on with the two Partys, who do not mean either of those two things, but the seamen will be Hurried out of their Depths by the Torrents of Party unless they go ashoar in time'. The king was in the shackles of his ministry because he could not submit to the

---

[20] Rogers, *Whigs and Cities*, 29.
[21] DAN/394, ESRO. This letter is missing from the various collections of Bolingbroke's correspondence, including the recent *Unpublished Letters* and earlier collections which included letters between Bolingbroke and Stair.
[22] See Chapter 2, note 11.   [23] *Unpublished Letters*, V, 30, 47.

Tories without losing his crown, or to the discontented Whigs without becoming contemptible. Bolingbroke's solution was nevertheless to 'emancipate' the king by choosing Tories *and* Whigs 'ready to Support the Government in opposing extream of all Sides'. Nothing other than this coalition comprising the moderates of both parties could save the country from 'running into Immediate Confusion', he concluded.[24]

Some years later, owing to the delays to his return by party politics in England, Bolingbroke became even more forthcoming in his condemnation of party, writing to Swift in August 1723 that 'I forget I was ever of any Party myself; nay ... I am ready to imagine that there never was any such Monster as Party.'[25] At the end of his life, he wrote in his own epitaph that he had been 'the enemy of no national party; the friend of no faction' during the Hanoverian era.[26] This distinction between national party and faction had been at the heart of his political writings. As we shall see, although Bolingbroke's starting point as a political writer was a critique of Whig and Tory, he condoned and indeed advocated a systematic opposition *party*. In order to give 'party' a positive connotation, he had to distinguish it carefully from 'faction'. We now turn to these endeavours.

Historian of Faction and Party

History for Bolingbroke was 'philosophy teaching by examples', and party and faction were always integral to his historical enquiries.[27] Already in March 1729 in the *Craftsman*, he used the technique of pointing out '*Parallels*' in the past as a way to 'forewarn all *Ages* against *evil Counsels* and *corrupt Ministers*'.[28] The reason why such an indirect approach had to be adopted was that even though the press had been unlicensed since 1695, publications critical of government were often prosecuted as seditious libel, a practice which began at the turn of the eighteenth century under Lord Chief Justice John Holt.[29] This paved the way for a golden age of political satire and irony, and the age of Defoe and Swift was also the age of Bolingbroke and the *Craftsman*. The tactic was not entirely risk-free,

---

[24] DAN/394, ESRO, n.f.   [25] *The Correspondence of Pope* (5 vols., Oxford, 1956), II, 187.
[26] Cited in Dickinson, *Bolingbroke* (London, 1970), 295.
[27] Bolingbroke, *Letters on the Study and Use of History* (1735), in *Works*, II, 9.
[28] Bolingbroke, *Contributions*, 82–3. The idea of 'counsel' had been crucial in the prefaces to the most significant historical works published during Bolingbroke's formative years: Clarendon's *History of the Rebellion* (3 vols., 1702–4), with prefaces written by his son, the Earl of Rochester, a Tory leader.
[29] Hamburger, 'The Development of the Law of Seditious Libel and the Control of the Press', *Stanford Law Review*, 37 (1985), 661–765.

however, and the ministerial press busied itself with reading Jacobite hints into oppositional statements, as Bolingbroke complained in the *Craftsman* in October 1730.[30] Nathaniel Mist had been prosecuted and obliged to go into exile in Paris after having printed the Duke of Wharton's ('Amos Dudge') 'Persian Letter' in August 1728, as it was interpreted as an indirect commentary on the royal family and Walpole.[31]

From June 1730 to May 1731, Bolingbroke's first major political work, the *Remarks on the History of England*, was serialised in the *Craftsman*.[32] The *Remarks* abounds with references to contemporary political disputes, as when he referred to ministerial writers who defended the maintenance of a standing army in peacetime as 'doctors of slavery'.[33] Being actively engaged in opposition at a time when such activities were regarded as morally and legally dubious, and indeed often prosecuted,[34] Bolingbroke's most important intention in the *Remarks* was to show that oppositional activity had historically not been factious but had on the contrary been necessary for liberty, which for him meant the survival of the free and mixed constitution.[35] Bolingbroke conceived of England's history as a perennial battle between the spirit of liberty and the spirit of faction. As Duncan Forbes has pointed out, this was essentially 'diluted Rapin', the *Craftsman*'s favourite historian.[36] In the *Craftsman*, Bolingbroke often transcribed entire passages from Rapin,[37] although he mixed Rapinesque Whiggism with a tinge of Harringtonian economic analysis, with the latter

---

[30] Bolingbroke, *Contributions*, 119.

[31] 'Wolf [Mist] the Printer to S[i]r R[obert] W[alpole]', [*c*.1728], MS Eng. Hist. C. 374, Bodleian, ff. 21–2. The manuscript is in Carte's handwriting and was probably dictated to him by Mist as Carte himself was in exile in Paris until November 1728.

[32] Bolingbroke enjoyed a sustained reputation as a historian on the basis of the *Remarks*. Pitt the Elder recommended them to his nephew 'before any other reading of history', despite being 'warped' as they contained 'the truest constitutional doctrines' and were 'to be studied and almost got by heart, for the inimitable beauty of the style, as well as the matter'; see *Correspondence of William Pitt* (4 vols., London, 1840), I, 107–9.

[33] Bolingbroke, *Remarks on the History of England* (1730–1), in *Works*, I, 490. (Hence: *Remarks*.) For the ministerial press, see Browning, *Political and Constitutional Ideas of the Court Whigs* (Baton Rouge, 1982); Targett, 'Government and Ideology during the Age of Whig Supremacy', *HJ*, 37 (1994), 289–317.

[34] The *Craftsman*'s printer Richard Francklin was tried and freed in 1729, but two years later the Walpole ministry managed to secure a verdict against him. Henry Haines, who took over the printing after Francklin, was sentenced in 1737.

[35] For Bolingbroke's linkage between liberty and the preservation of the integrity of the constitution, see Bolingbroke, *A Dissertation upon Parties* (1733–4), in *Political Writings*, 169. (Hence: *Dissertation*.) For Bolingbroke as a theorist of opposition, see also Skinner, 'The Principles and Practice of Opposition', in *Historical Perspectives* (London, 1974), 93–128.

[36] Forbes, *Hume's Philosophical Politics* (Cambridge, 1975), 241.

[37] Bolingbroke, *Contributions*, 116–17.

being entirely absent in Rapin.[38] In any event, Carte was unhappy with the *Craftsman*'s idolising of the French Huguenot and complained about it in a letter to the Tory MP Corbett Kynaston on 4 July 1738.[39]

Although 'party' and 'faction' were often used interchangeably in the period, Bolingbroke distinguished between the two terms. Such a distinction had been expressed as early as 1717 by William Paterson, a founder of the Bank of England, who argued that parties were usually harmless and 'capable of Good, as well as Hurt, of Love as well as Hatred', unlike factions, which 'hate, but love not, are hurtful in their Nature, and chiefly produces Enmity'.[40] Bolingbroke's own journal, albeit when he was in exile, defined party as 'a national Division of Opinions, concerning the *Form* and *Methods of Government*, for the benefit of the *whole Community*', and faction as 'a Set of Men arm'd with *Power*, and acting upon no one Principle of *Party*, or any Notion of *Publick Good*, but to preserve and share the Spoils amongst *Themselves*, as their only Cement'.[41]

Bolingbroke's distinction between party and faction runs along similar lines. In his ironic dedication to Walpole prefixed to the publication of the *Dissertation upon Parties* in book form in 1735,[42] Bolingbroke said that '[t]here may be such a conduct, as no national party will bear, or at least will justify. But faction hath no regard to national interests. Factions therefore will bear any thing, justify any thing.'[43] Factions struggled for power, not principle, Bolingbroke argued.[44] He believed that numbers were a good benchmark for whether a cause was national or factional: '[p]rivate motives can never influence numbers. When a nation revolts, the injury is national.'[45] Bolingbroke's favourite historical example of a national party that had degenerated into faction was the Whigs under Anne, who, in Bolingbroke's rendition, had initially adhered to the Protestant Settlement out of honourable zeal for the nation's liberty and religion, but this 'national interest became soon a secondary and subservient motive' and they started to care more about the establishment of their own power.[46] This spirit of faction is what had ended his own political

---

[38] The same mixture would reappear in the Court Whig writer Samuel Squire, one of Bolingbroke's foes.

[39] BL Add MS 21500, f. 117.

[40] Paterson, *Enquiry into the State of the Union of Great Britain* (London, 1717), 45.

[41] *The Country Journal, or the Craftsman*, No. 674, 9 June 1739.

[42] Bolingbroke referred to the work as his 'Epistle to Sir Rob'; see *Unpublished Letters*, V, 123.

[43] Bolingbroke, *Dedication to Sir Robert Walpole* (1735), in *Works*, II, 14–5. (Hence: *Dedication*.) See also Bolingbroke, ['Reflections on Walpole'], *Unpublished Letters*, V, 307.

[44] Bolingbroke, *Dissertation*, 76. See also ['Reflections on Walpole'], *Unpublished Letters*, V, 308.

[45] Bolingbroke, *Dissertation*, 86.   [46] Bolingbroke, *State of Parties*, in *Works*, III, 137–8.

career, Bolingbroke was convinced (and, as we have seen, he was not entirely unjustified in thinking that).

The key message Bolingbroke wanted to convey in the 1730s was that Walpole was not the leader of a national party but a court faction, which was something completely different. According to Bolingbroke, a national party 'will always retain some national principles, some regard to the constitution', which meant that 'a national party will never be the instruments of completing national ruin', unlike a faction.[47] Accordingly, 'the minister who persists in so villainous a project ... will be found really at the head of a faction, not of a party'.[48] For Bolingbroke, 'the difference between one and the other is so visible, and the boundaries where party ceases and faction commences, are so strongly marked, that it is sufficient to point at them',[49] even though a faction will always seek to hide 'under the name and appearance of a national party'.[50]

Bolingbroke viewed the spirit of faction as the prioritising of private interest at the expense of the public good, and the spirit of liberty as a willingness to do whatever it takes to put the common good first. The two spirits 'are not only different, but repugnant and incompatible: so that the life of either is the death of the other'.[51] Throughout history, the spirit of liberty had often found its outlets in opposition to powerful monarchs, he argued. Bolingbroke sought to reinvigorate this jealous spirit of liberty in his contemporaries but directed at the chief minister rather than the monarch. In his historical writings, he often drew attention to unpopular ministers and Court favourites in the past, particularly Buckingham,[52] Rapin's favourite target. Unlike many court favourites in previous centuries, Walpole did not hold a formal court position, but the historical parallel could not have been missed.[53]

Being in opposition to the Court Whigs, Bolingbroke had to explode the belief that faction was only found in opposition to the Court and demonstrate that it could equally be found *at* Court. One of his tactics was to associate the ministerial position against 'factious opposition' with absolutist theories, of which he saw James I/VI as an exponent.[54] '[H]e,

---

[47] Bolingbroke, *Dissertation*, 99–100.   [48] Ibid., 100.   [49] Ibid..
[50] Bolingbroke, *Dedication*, in *Works*, II, 15.   [51] Bolingbroke, *Remarks*, in *Works*, I, 292.
[52] Ibid., 515.
[53] While it became less common for politicians of the top rank to hold place at court in the early Hanoverian period, the favour of and closeness to the monarch remained key for political influence. Smith, *Georgian Monarchy* (Cambridge, 2006), ch. 5.
[54] Bolingbroke, *Dissertation*, 120; Bolingbroke, *The Idea of a Patriot King* (1738), in *Political Writings*, 243. (Hence: *Patriot King*.)

who confines his notions of faction to oppositions made to the crown, reasons, in an absolute monarchy, in favour of the constitution', he wrote in the *Remarks*.[55] Bolingbroke's intention was to show that the reigns of James I/VI and Charles I demonstrated how the spirit of faction *at* Court could lead the country wayward. In presenting the first Stuart kings as 'innovators', Bolingbroke followed Rapin. It was not solely the royalist faction that was responsible for pushing the country into civil war at mid-century, but Bolingbroke believed that '[t]he faction of the court tainted the nation, and gave life and strength, if it did not give being, to the factions in the state'.[56] Opposition could thus be a counter-factional measure: 'If there had not been an early and honest opposition, in defence of national liberty, against King James, his reign would have sufficed to establish him in the seat of arbitrary power.'[57]

The key move made by Bolingbroke was to associate opposition to the court with the spirit of liberty. He began the *Remarks* by setting out that 'liberty cannot be long secure, in any country, unless a perpetual jealousy watches over it'.[58] This jealousy has to be 'permanent and equal'.[59] The reason is straightforward: Bolingbroke viewed the love of power as natural and insatiable. Consequently, liberty was always 'in some degree of danger under every government'.[60] The fear of losing liberty is common to all and 'may become a general principle of union'.[61] This perpetual jealousy, if well grounded, 'may have the good effect of destroying a wicked minister, of checking a bad, or of reclaiming a misguided prince'.[62] James I/VI was an epitome of the latter and Walpole of the former. In the ministerial press, the jealous spirit of liberty was equated with 'opposition' and 'contention' and was described as a *'dreadful State'*.[63]

There is little doubt that Bolingbroke's main aim was the destruction of Walpole and his Whig ministry.[64] Bolingbroke has misleadingly been associated with the 'not men, but measures' opposition slogan, for example by Harvey Mansfield.[65] This slogan entailed that oppositions should criticise and seek to change specific measures rather than focusing on censuring (and attempting to replace) the ministry, either in part or in whole. While Bolingbroke never used this catchphrase in his public writings, it is true that he paid lip service to similar lines of thought, for

---

[55] Bolingbroke, *Remarks*, in *Works*, I, 439.   [56] Ibid., 460–1.   [57] Ibid., 492.   [58] Ibid., 278.
[59] Ibid.   [60] Ibid., 284.   [61] Ibid., 282.   [62] Ibid., 288.
[63] The *London Journal*, No. 570, 4 July 1730.
[64] Bolingbroke to Wyndham, 25 January 1740, in Coxe, *Memoirs of Walpole* (3 vols., London, 1798), III, 554.
[65] Mansfield, *Statesmanship and Party Government*, 179.

instance when he discussed the Wars of the Roses in the *Remarks*. He described the war as a conflict about who should govern rather than how they should be governed, and he argued that the latter was worth contending for, as in the civil war preceding the Magna Carta, whereas the former 'ought always to be looked upon with great indifference'.[66] However, certainly with Walpole in mind, Bolingbroke added a crucial qualification: 'except in cases where [the personnel] has so immediate and necessary a relation to the [measures of government], that securing the first depends, in a great measure, on settling the last'.[67] This position was later adopted by the Patriot opposition, which Bolingbroke did so much to inspire. As Stair would put it five years later, 'there is a preliminary absolutely necessary to the saving of the nation, and that is, the removing of Sir Robert'.[68] As Chapter 9 demonstrates, the slogan 'not men, but measures' is more appropriate for discussing the political writings of John Brown, who did indeed use this catchphrase.

It is not without significance that Bolingbroke in the *Remarks* cited Machiavelli, who had notoriously argued that tumult in the Roman Republic between different orders in the state had been a blessing rather than a curse.[69] Bolingbroke did not draw attention to this controversial teaching, but instead referred to another lesson from Machiavelli's *Discorsi sopra la prima deca di Tito Livio*, namely that the best governments are such 'which by the natural effect of their original constitutions are frequently renewed or drawn back ... to their first principles'.[70] The fact that the state has subsisted is sufficient evidence that its first principles are sound. In other words, the purpose of Bolingbroke's politics was not to innovate but to reform the state by drawing it back to its foundation, by which he meant the Revolution Settlement of 1688–9. Unlike some ministerial writers, Bolingbroke regarded this settlement as a reassertion of ancient liberties rather than a new beginning.[71] His oppositional theory, which will be discussed at greater length below, is thus related to his adherence to the ideology of the ancient constitution.[72] Bolingbroke's

---

[66] Bolingbroke, *Remarks*, in *Works*, I, 336.   [67] Ibid.   [68] *Marchmont Papers*, II, 171.

[69] Machiavelli, *Discourses on Livy* (Chicago, 1998), 16–17.

[70] Bolingbroke, *Remarks*, in *Works*, I, 289. See also Machiavelli, *Discourses*, 209. As so often, Bolingbroke's references have echoes in the 1701–14-period; his friend Swift had cited exactly the same lesson from Machiavelli in his *Project for the Advancement of Religion and the Reformation of Manners* (London, 1709), 61–2.

[71] For the ministerial counter-argument, see [Hervey], *Ancient and Modern Liberty* (London, 1734), 4–5.

[72] For Bolingbroke's ancient constitutionalism, see *Dissertation*, 81–2, 114–5. His views on the ancient constitution were of a peculiar kind: on the one hand, there was no need to look further

main inspiration in this respect was Rapin, but also domestic historians such as Nathaniel Bacon, known for *An Historical Discourse of the Uniformity of the Government of England* (1647–51).

Bolingbroke was guarded about associating himself with Machiavelli, and he felt obliged to qualify his reference by saying that he 'would not advise you to admit the works of MACHIAVEL into your cannon of political writings; yet ... in them, as in other apocryphal books, many excellent things are interspersed'.[73] One of those excellent things was Machiavelli's argument about first principles, and it was also considered a safe reference in an age where innovation was widely seen as evil and zeal for the Revolution Settlement was mainstream. At this point, opposition had to take the form of 'zeal for the constitution' rather than 'zeal for this or that party'.[74] This elucidates why so much of Bolingbroke's later *Dissertation upon Parties* was taken up by his explanation of the British constitution, which was far from unambiguous. The notion that the 'mixed constitution' – combining monarchy, aristocracy, and democracy – was the optimal way to prevent decline seriously crystallised in English discourse with *His Majesty's Answer to the Nineteen Propositions* (1642), drawing on book six of Polybius' *Histories*.[75] In the eighteenth century, the British constitution was universally described as mixed or balanced – since monarch, Lords, and Commons shared legislative power – but it was uncodified and there was no unanimity as to how the mixture ought to work in practice.[76]

In the third letter of the *Remarks*, Bolingbroke hit out at the ministerial writer James Pitt ('Francis Osborne').[77] In July 1730, Pitt had claimed in the *London Journal* that 'a Man of Sense ... had much rather have liv'd under the Pacific Reign of *Augustus*, tho' cloath'd with all Power, than under *a Mob Government*, always quarrelling at *Home*, or fighting *Abroad*', referring to the 'perpetual Struggles between the *Senate* and the *People*', which had been defended by Machiavelli.[78] In return, Bolingbroke recommended Thomas Gordon's 'excellent' discourses, prefixed to his

---

back than 1688–9, on the other, the Glorious Revolution had been a reassertion of ancient liberties, see Pocock, *The Ancient Constitution* (Cambridge, 1987 [1957]), 231–2.

[73] Bolingbroke, *Remarks*, in *Works*, I, 164–5.

[74] Bolingbroke, *Dissertation*, 122. See also, Bolingbroke, *Dedication*, in *Works*, II, 24–5.

[75] Sabbadini, 'Popular Sovereignty and Representation in the English Civil War', in *Popular Sovereignty in Historical Perspective* (Cambridge, 2016), 166.

[76] See Vile, *Constitutionalism and the Separation of Powers* (Indianapolis, 1998 [1967]), esp. ch. 3.

[77] Targett, 'Government and Ideology', 290.   [78] The *London Journal*, No. 570, 4 July 1730.

translation of Tacitus, in which he portrayed Augustus as a tyrant.[79] For all of Gordon's sneers at parties and factions, he nevertheless held that 'a free State the worst constituted, as was that of Florence, is, with all its disorders, factions, and tumults, preferable to any absolute Monarchy, however calm'.[80]

Bolingbroke's explicit intention in his next central opposition tract, *A Dissertation upon Parties*, serialised in the *Craftsman* between October 1733 and December 1734, was to make 'an enquiry into the rise and progress of our late parties; or a short history of Toryism and Whiggism from their cradle to their grave, with an introductory account of their genealogy and descent'.[81] The kernel of the argument is that Tory and Whig had become redundant as national parties since there was no disagreement about the fundamentals of the British constitution among honest people. When the parties had come into being during the Exclusion Crisis, there had been real differences at stake, with the Tories espousing divine right monarchy, lineal succession, and passive obedience, and the Whigs seeking to exclude the Catholic Duke of York from the succession to the throne.[82] Bolingbroke described the Glorious Revolution, which he, following Rapin, believed was carried out by a coalition of parties, as 'a fire, which purged off the dross of both parties; and the dross being purged off, they appeared to be the same metal, and answered the same standard'.[83] The Whigs and Tories had no need to fear each other after the Revolution, as they both had rid themselves of their extreme doctrines: republicanism and divine right theory, respectively. While the real essence of the parties had been destroyed, the names had survived for factious purposes and continued to haunt and divide the political nation like ghosts, according to Bolingbroke.[84] More specifically, he accused the Court Whigs in power for having turned into a faction that sought to keep alive artificial party distinctions for their own benefit.[85]

The claim that Whig and Tory had become redundant was not new and little more than a repetition of that in *Cato's Letters* more than a decade earlier.[86] It was a powerful tool for Bolingbroke's polemical purposes,

---

[79] Bolingbroke, *Remarks*, in *Works*, I, 310. In the following issue of the *London Journal* on 18 July, Pitt defended and repeated his claim but toned it down by removing the phrase 'mob government' as a description of the Roman Republic.

[80] Gordon, *The Works of Tacitus* (2 vols., London, 1728–31), I, 60.

[81] Bolingbroke, *Dissertation*, 12.   [82] Ibid., 5.   [83] Ibid., 65.   [84] Ibid., 70, 61.

[85] Bolingbroke, *Dedication*, in *Works*, II, 12.

[86] Trenchard and Gordon, *Cato's Letters* (2 vols., Indianapolis, 1995 [1720–3]), II, 583–7 (No. 80, 9 June 1722).

however, as it allowed him to portray Walpole as a divider.[87] As mentioned in the introduction, Bolingbroke has often been portrayed as an anti-party writer. This is true if we take it to mean a denial of the relevance of the Whig and Tory labels in the context of the 1730s. Importantly, however, Bolingbroke's criticism of Whig and Tory should not necessarily be construed as an attack on party in every sense of the term. For all his scorn of party passion, he differentiated between a national party seeking to address general grievances and a faction only interested in maximising its power. Unsurprisingly, Bolingbroke's attack on Whig and Tory was reported by ministerial pamphleteers as a partisan rather than anti-party position.[88]

As the old parties had long been irrelevant, a national union had become a possibility, Bolingbroke argued. The political nation was still divided, however, and instead of Whig and Tory, Bolingbroke believed that 'new combinations force themselves upon us', namely the Country and Court parties.[89] It is to these parties that this chapter now turns.

Advocate of the Country Party

The *Dissertation upon Parties* abounds with anti-party comments, as when Bolingbroke speaks of the 'spirit of party' as a spirit that '[i]nspires animosity and breeds rancour, which hath so often destroyed our inward peace, weakened our national strength, and sullied our glory abroad'.[90] He also made a distinction between moral and party justice, with the former being based on reason, while the latter 'takes its colour from the passions of men, and is but another name for injustice'.[91] The historical example of the Whigs in the wake of the accession of George I in 1714 was the one that mattered for Bolingbroke, who wrote that he wanted 'to change the narrow spirit of party into a diffusive spirit of public benevolence'.[92] For this purpose, he invoked the memory of Halifax, the great Trimmer, as someone who tried to 'allay this extravagant [party] ferment'.[93]

Yet Bolingbroke did not simply say that Britain was divided into Court and Country parties – he also promoted the latter.[94] He separated the political landscape into three camps: (1) enemies of the government but friends of the constitution, referring to his own Country party; (2) enemies

---

[87] Bolingbroke, *Dissertation*, 3. See also Bolingbroke, *Dedication*, in *Works*, II, 13.
[88] [Arnall], *Opposition No Proof of Patriotism: With Some Observations and Advice Concerning Party-writings* (London, 1735), 18.
[89] Bolingbroke, *Dissertation*, 5.   [90] Ibid., 6.   [91] Ibid., 17.   [92] Ibid., 6.   [93] Ibid., 48.
[94] Ibid., 61, 187.

of both, meaning the Jacobites; and (3) friends of the government but enemies of the constitution, that is, the Court Whigs.[95] He claimed that he was only interested in the first and the third division since the Jacobites were so few and insignificant.

Importantly, Bolingbroke's utterances on Jacobitism in the 1730s should not be viewed as statements of facts; dynastic politics still remained an important aspect of politics, even though it would be an exaggeration to claim that the Tory party was consistently and without exceptions committed to principled Jacobitism. However, the relevance of the dynastic dimension – not least in the general political imagination – along with his own past made it all the more important for Bolingbroke to downplay the significance of Jacobitism. We should also note that the Jacobites saw themselves as invested in the same parliamentary strife against Walpole. As the 5th Earl of Orrery wrote to Carte in January 1733: 'A bad minister who has been long the Woolsay [*sic*] of my Father's affairs, has left me to say with Hamlet: The Times are out of Joynt; Oh! cursed Spight! | That ever I was born to set 'em right. However the greater Labour, the greater glory, nor do I at all doubt but at last we shall bring him to Justice.'[96] Carte himself referred to Walpole as 'that detestable corrupter of the virtues of his Country' upon his resignation.[97] The Oxford Jacobite Thomas Hearne described Walpole as 'a wicked man, & imployed to do all the dirty tricks that can be thought of to inrich miserably covetous Princes, and to drain the Subject'.[98]

Bolingbroke was far from neutral when he argued that the first division – in other words, those who were enemies of the government but friends of the constitution – 'might hope to unite even the bulk of the nation to them, in a weak and oppressive regime', in opposition to the third, around which 'our greatest and almost our whole danger centres'.[99] In sharp contrast to the Court party, '[a] Country party must be authorized by the voice of the country'.[100] Such a party had the potential to unite Whigs and Tories, as '[i]t must be formed on principles of common interest. It cannot be united and maintained on the particular prejudices, any more than it can, or ought to be, directed to the particular interests of any set of men whatsoever.'[101] The Country party was an opposition party whose core principle was to defeat what was perceived as Walpole's system of corruption. By corruption, Bolingbroke meant executive influence over

---

[95] Ibid., 85, 177.   [96] Carte MS 227, Bodleian, f. 66.   [97] Carte MS 230, f. 200.
[98] *Hearne's Recollections*, XI, 174.   [99] Bolingbroke, *Dissertation*, 85, 86.   [100] Ibid., 37.
[101] Ibid.

the legislature as well as the Machiavellian sense of degeneration of civic *virtù*.

The Country party had a distinct ideology that emphasised the importance of independence of parliament from crown influence, support of the landed and traded interests in opposition to the moneyed interest, and a preference for a citizen militia and a strong navy as opposed to the standing army.[102] Both the Whig and Tory parties had had Country elements since the Glorious Revolution, but they had usually only collaborated on specific issues, for example the standing army question in 1697–8. From the reign of Queen Anne onwards, Country sentiments were more dominant among Tories than Whigs, with the former becoming known as the 'country gentlemen'.[103] Bolingbroke wanted to turn the occasional Country coalition into a permanent political force and this was the aspiration of his joint enterprise with Pulteney.[104] The enterprise of bringing Tories and Whigs together in opposition was for a limited time successful. Stair wrote to the 2nd Earl of Marchmont – both Scottish opposition Whigs – in 1736: '[i]t is true, that in the opposition we have made to the ministers' measures, we have had the assistance of many persons, who have been called by [the] name of Tories; but I am very far from being ashamed to take the assistance of Tories to preserve our constitution'.[105]

The Court Whigs under Walpole had moved closer to the Church of England. Since they thought that they could count blindly on the support of the Protestant Dissenters, Walpole paused further legislative measures in their favour. Some Whigs appear to have pondered removing the bishops from the upper house at George I's accession, but Walpole had then protested that 'turning them out of the H. of Lords would give a general distaste; & that tho' many of the B[isho]ps were at present ag[ain]st them, yet their number would lessen every day, & a new set might be put in that would be entirely subservient to the Court measures'.[106] Between

---

[102] Dickinson, *Liberty and Property* (London, 1977), 163–92.

[103] Hayton, 'The "Country" Interest and the Party System', in *Party and Management in Parliament* (Bath, 1984), 40–4.

[104] David Mallet, who edited Bolingbroke's collected works, believed that the idea of a coalition of parties originated with Harley/Oxford, a leading figure in the Country opposition to the standing army in the 1690s, see Mallet, *Memoirs of the Life and Ministerial Conduct* (London, 1752), 337. As Dickinson has pointed out, Bolingbroke seemed to have been genuinely won over by Harley's moderation when entering the mixed ministry as Secretary at War in 1704; see 'Henry St. John', 52.

[105] *Marchmont Papers*, II, 81. Both Stair and Marchmont were staunch Whigs and acquainted with Sarah Marlborough.

[106] [Notes on conversation with Sir John Hynde Cotton MP], 5 August 1737, Carte MS 266, ff. 29–32.

1723 and 1736, Walpole formed a formidable alliance with his 'pope' Edmund Gibson, Bishop of London.[107]

Bolingbroke sought to convince Protestant Dissenters, the natural enemies of High Church Tories and key allies of the Whigs, that they had nothing to fear from this new Country platform, even if it contained a prominent Tory element: 'The principal articles of your [the Dissenters'] civil faith, published some time ago, or, to speak more properly, the civil faith of the Old Whigs, are assented and consented to by the Country party.'[108] Bolingbroke here referred to the age-old union between Whiggism and Dissent, going back to the first formation of the Whigs under Shaftesbury in the 1670s. Bolingbroke attempted to persuade the Dissenters that there could be no doubt about which side they should now espouse, as the principles they believed in were 'manifestly pursued' by the Country party whereas the Court party pursued 'those which they have opposed, or others equivalent to them in their effect'.[109] This was an important argument since, as the ministerial press constantly pointed out, he had once been the head of the Church party. As William Arnall ('Walsingham') wrote in 1731: 'What would be the Case of the *Protestant Dissenters*, should the Patron of the *Schism Bill* [1714] come again into the Management of Parliamentary Councils.'[110]

Bolingbroke qualified his defence of the Country party by arguing that '[a] party, thus constituted, is improperly called party. It is the nation, speaking and acting in the discourse and conduct of particular men.'[111] Be that as it may, he then continued to call it a 'party'.[112] Bolingbroke concluded the *Dissertation* by arguing that both sides should agree 'to fix upon this principal and real distinction and difference; the present division of parties; *since parties we must have*; and since those which subsisted formerly are quite extinguished, notwithstanding all the wicked endeavours by some men [i.e. the Court Whigs and their hired pens] ... to revive them'.[113] Just as nothing could be more 'ridiculous' than to preserve the nominal division of Whig and Tory when the difference of principles no longer existed, 'so nothing can be more reasonable than to admit the nominal division of constitutionists and anti-constitutionists, or of a Court and a Country party, at this time, when an avowed difference of

---

[107] Taylor, '"Dr Codex" and the Whig "Pope"', in *Lords of Parliament, 1714–1914* (Stanford, 1995), 9–28.
[108] Bolingbroke, *Dissertation*, 8–9.   [109] Ibid., 8, 187.
[110] [Arnall], *Remarks on the Craftsman's Vindication of his Two Hon[oura]ble Patrons* (London, 1731), 58.
[111] Bolingbroke, *Dissertation*, 37.   [112] Ibid.   [113] Ibid., 185–6. (My emphasis.)

principles make this distinction possible'.[114] This Country–Court polarity would be applicable as long as there were people 'who argue for, and who promote even a corrupt dependency of the members of the two houses of Parliament on the crown'.[115] The Court party had to be opposed by the Country party, for if the independency of parliament was lost, the constitution would be a 'dead letter'.[116] The rationale for and the nature of this opposition party is further explored in the next section.

Theorist of Opposition

Bolingbroke was the most prominent theorist of formal opposition of his generation. This was urgently needed from the point of view of those discontented with Walpolean Britain. In the words of Carte, one of the major reasons why 'the corrupt & distructive measures of ministers' prevailed was 'the want, as well of a proper method of Union among the principal members of the opposition & concert of their measures'.[117] The problem was not only that opposition members were lured with places and pensions, significant as that was, but also the fact that 'fox-hunting, gardening, planting, or indifference having always kept our people in the country, till the very day before the meeting of the Parliament', as Chesterfield complained in 1741.[118] Already in the *Remarks*, Bolingbroke had spelled out what he regarded as the proper characteristics of the business of opposition: opposition had to commence early and be vigorous if the free constitution was being attacked.[119] In one of his earliest political writings in the *Craftsman*, Bolingbroke criticised neutrality per se when he referred to ancient Athens where the citizen who took no side 'was branded for his infamous neutrality'.[120] Bolingbroke believed that '[o]ur duty must oblige us in all public disputes to take the best side, and to espouse it with warmth'.[121]

The main enterprise of the *Dissertation*, besides demonstrating the redundancy of the names of Tory and Whig and the relevance of the Court–Country division, was to specify why it was necessary to oppose Walpole, or the 'prime, or sole minister' as Bolingbroke mockingly

---

[114] Ibid., 186.   [115] Ibid., 186–7.   [116] Ibid., 187.
[117] 'Scheme for the Counties' [*c.*1730?], in Carte MS 237, f. 27. Carte himself proposed a triennial council of eleven gentlemen representing and instructed by the counties and the opposition, or the 'Country interest'.
[118] Chesterfield, *Letters* (Oxford, 1998), 24.   [119] Bolingbroke, *Remarks*, in *Works*, I, 492.
[120] Bolingbroke, *The Occasional Writer in the Craftsman*, No. 3, 13 February 1727, *Works*, I, 180.
[121] Ibid.

referred to him at a time when the office of prime minister had no official place in the British constitution.[122] As we saw in the previous section, Bolingbroke made use of the Country ideology to legitimise opposition. The ministerial press responded by labelling the opposition Jacobite and republican, and portrayed Walpole and the Court Whigs as the only ones who could be trusted as custodians of the Glorious Revolution, the Act of Settlement 1701, and the Hanoverian succession of 1714.[123] Bolingbroke had to find responses to all three points.

First, Bolingbroke argued that Walpole and the Court Whigs had not lived up to the principles of the Revolution. More specifically, he saw the chief end of the Revolution as securing the nation against corruption, by which he meant a dependency of parliament on the court. The Revolution was thus incomplete since the means for this technical sense of corruption (or influence) had increased immensely in the decades after 1688–9, because of the larger revenue of the crown and the proliferation of government offices and employments, which had produced higher taxes and debt.[124] In other words, Bolingbroke remained a 'Queen Anne Tory' in the sense of being an enemy of the so-called financial revolution, which had seen the erection of the Bank of England and national debt in the 1690s, and the creation of a 'moneyed interest' in opposition to the landed and traded interests.[125] In short, he believed that landowners and traders had to bear the cost of an ever-expanding state – what John Brewer dubbed the fiscal-military state.[126] One of the reasons why his Country opposition was such a fierce opponent of Walpole's proposed extension of excise in 1733 was that the scheme would increase the number and powers of revenue officers and effectively the government's size and reach.[127] Moreover, the Revolution had provided for frequent parliamentary sessions and elections, but this had partly been overturned by the Septennial

---

[122] Bolingbroke, *Dedication*, in *Works*, II, 8.

[123] Bolingbroke, *Dissertation*, 49. For the ministerial case, see, e.g., [Hervey], *The Conduct of the Opposition and the Tendency of Modern Patriotism* (London, 1734), 37, 40.

[124] Bolingbroke, *Dissertation*, 84, 174, 177, 180. In Letter XII of the *Dissertation*, Bolingbroke replied to an article in the *London Journal* on 28 September 1734 (No. 796) which defended this type of influence (121).

[125] Bolingbroke, *Contributions*, 34, 57–8; Bolingbroke, *Some Reflections on the Present State of the Nation* (1749), in *Works*, III, 174. See also Dickson, *The Financial Revolution in England* (London, 1967), 18–28.

[126] Brewer, *The Sinews of Power* (London, 1989).

[127] Bolingbroke, *Contributions*, 145–6; Bolingbroke, *Dissertation*, 175; Pulteney, *A Review of the Excise Scheme* (London, 1733), 53–4. Excise was a question which could unite Whigs and Tories, since tradesmen and shopkeepers of both persuasions were strong opponents; see Langford, *The Excise Crisis* (Oxford, 1975).

Act 1716.[128] In a word, Bolingbroke wanted to show that the opposition could be better trusted to cherish the legacy of the Glorious Revolution, as 'the settlement then made is looked upon by the whole Country party as a new Magna Carta'.[129]

Second, Bolingbroke repeatedly argued that the Jacobite party had become an inconsiderable faction in the state, and that Jacobitism had nothing whatsoever to do with either him or his Country platform, as when he ridiculed the writings of the Jacobite Charles Leslie, writer of the notorious *Rehearsal* at the beginning of the century.[130] This was an essential move by Bolingbroke, as he had served the Pretender in 1715–16, and Walpole and the ministerial press never tired of portraying him as a Jacobite and a traitor.[131] We have also seen that many of his Jacobite acquaintances saw themselves as being involved in the same struggle against Walpole, and Bolingbroke needed thus to distance himself from them.[132] Already in his 1717 apologia, he had said that he was as anti-Catholic as any sensible Englishman and that he had tried to convince James 'III' to convert to Protestantism.[133] In private, however, the Court Whigs knew that Bolingbroke was no principled Jacobite and that his periodic involvement in the cause was largely opportunistic. Hervey likened Bolingbroke's mobility and flexibility to Handel: 'His fortune in music is not unlike my Lord Bolingbroke's in politics. The one has tried both theatres, as the other has tried both Courts. They have shone in both, and been ruined in both; while everyone owns their genius and sees their faults, though nobody either pities their fortune or takes their part.'[134]

Third, although the revenue of the crown had increased, Bolingbroke contended that the present royal family had not flourished under Walpole.

---

[128] Bolingbroke, *Dissertation*, 101–10. Frequent elections meant that 'there is not sufficient time given, to form a majority of the representatives into a ministerial cabal' (104). Bolingbroke recommended annual or at least triennial parliaments.

[129] Ibid., 9.

[130] Ibid., 5, 9, 198; Bolingbroke, *Remarks*, in *Works*, I, 277, 299. These views were by and large consistent with those Bolingbroke expressed in private; see, e.g., Bolingbroke to Wyndham, 25 January 1740, in Coxe, *Memoirs of Walpole*, III, 555. Leslie had been part of the Jacobite court when Bolingbroke served it, and they appear to have disagreed about whether the Old Pretender should have been pressurised into converting to Anglicanism. See *Letter to Windham*, in *Works*, I, 92.

[131] Walpole's speech on the Excise Crisis in *Hervey's Memoirs*, I, 183–4; [Arnall], *Remarks on the Craftsman's Vindication*, 6, 28; [Hervey], *The Conduct of the Opposition*, 57–8; [Arnall], *Opposition No Proof of Patriotism*, 17–8.

[132] However, see note 14 in this chapter.

[133] Bolingbroke, *Letter to Windham*, in *Works*, I, 90–1, 104–5.

[134] Hervey to Digby, 25 November 1735, in *Lord Hervey and His Friends, 1726–38* (London, 1950), 239.

In his dedicatory letter to the *Dissertation*, he argued that the security of the House of Hanover depended on the full completion of the Revolution.[135] Just as the violence of the Whigs had turned many Tories into Jacobites, the proscription of Tories had created unnecessary enemies for the royal family.[136] The message was that George II could effectively kill off all remnants of Jacobitism within the Tories by ending proscription.

In *A Letter on the Spirit of Patriotism* (1736), Bolingbroke would elaborate on his oppositional theory. Bolingbroke had written about the 'Godlike Spirit of *Patriotism*' since his early writings in the *Craftsman*, as in his eulogy to Nicholas Lechmere on 15 July 1727.[137] His 1736 text was originally not written for general distribution but for a smaller readership and this gave him more freedom. The *Letter* is in one sense pessimistic in tone, which is not strange considering that Bolingbroke had a year earlier gone into a second exile in France, mainly because of the revelation of his closeness to the French government,[138] but perhaps also partly because the opposition had failed to bring down Walpole at the general election of 1734. He did not hold back when describing the gravity of the state of Britain, which he thought had 'lost the spirit of [its] constitution' and become an oligarchy in the hands of '[o]ne party [the Court Whigs, which have] given their whole attention, during several years, to the project of enriching themselves, and impoverishing the rest of the nation'.[139] Bolingbroke expressed disappointment with the Country Tory–Whig coalition he had forged with Pulteney in 1726, which had missed a golden opportunity to defeat Walpole. 'I expect little from the principal actors that tread the stage at present', he said, 'these men have been clogged, or misled, or overborne by others; and, seduced by natural temper to inactivity.'[140]

Bolingbroke's second exile in France in conjunction with the bad health of Pulteney was a major blow for the opposition. As Hervey put it,

> Lord Bolingbroke's going out of England on account of the bad situation both of his public and private affairs slackened, too, extremely the spirit of the public papers; and Mr. Pulteney, partly from a very ill state of health,

---

[135] Bolingbroke, *Dedication*, in *Works*, II, 11.   [136] Ibid., 14.

[137] Bolingbroke, *Contributions*, 22. Bolingbroke hailed Lechmere for opposing the Septennial Act 1716, and for being of '*no Party*, nor attached to any Interest, but that of his Country'.

[138] *The Grand Accuser the Greatest of All Criminals* (London, 1734).

[139] Bolingbroke, *Letter on the Spirit of Patriotism* (1736), in *Political Writings*, 206, 198. (Hence: *Spirit of Patriotism.*)

[140] Ibid., 207–8.

and partly, as some people thought, from being weary of the opposing part
he had so long unsuccessfully acted, withdrew himself the greatest part of
the session from all attendance in the House of Commons ... Sir William
Wyndham [a Tory leader], deprived of his private prompter, Lord
Bolingbroke, and his coadjutor in public action Mr. Pulteney, made a very
inconsiderable figure, and was as little useful to the party he espoused as
formidable to that he opposed.[141]

Stair, who had previously been optimistic about the opposition coalition
with the Tories, was pessimistic at the start of 1738. While he spoke of the
necessity of unity in the opposition, he admitted 'that it may prove a very
difficult matter to unite all the different pieces, of which the opposing
party is made up, into one body, nay, it may be impossible'.[142]

   While Bolingbroke appears to have given up his coalition with Pulteney
at the beginning of 1736 – he said that he was 'quits with [his] friends,
party friends I mean'[143] – the *Letter* is not defeatist. 'I turn my eyes from
the generation that is going off, to the generation that is coming on the
stage', he wrote, referring primarily to the twenty-six-year-old Lord
Cornbury, the addressee of the *Letter*, who, as Clarendon's grandson and
MP for Oxford University, was one of the most promising young Tories in
parliament.[144] Cornbury had been involved in Jacobite intrigues, but
seems to have stopped corresponding with the Stuart court from
1735.[145] Bolingbroke may also have alluded to a group of young opposition politicians led by Lord Cobham, the so-called 'Boy Patriots', which
included William Pitt and George Lyttelton, who would later create an
opposition group centred around Frederick, the Prince of Wales. These
young men, especially Cornbury, were destined to be 'the guardian angels
of the country they inhabit'.[146] It was the duty of such people 'to oppose
evil, and promote good government'.[147] Bolingbroke emphasised repeatedly that this opposition had to be strong and persistent, as he was
convinced that not even the worst thinkable minister could do harm unless
others supported him in his mischief, and unless those who oppose him
were 'faint and unsteady' in their conduct.[148] For Bolingbroke, there was
'little difference ... between opposing faintly and unsteadily and not
opposing at all'.[149]

[141] *Hervey's Memoirs*, 529.   [142] Stair to Marchmont, 1 January 1738, *Marchmont Papers*, II, 91.
[143] Bolingbroke to 3rd Earl of Essex, 30 May 1736, *Unpublished Letters*, V, 168.
[144] Bolingbroke, *Spirit of Patriotism*, 208.   [145] Cruickshanks, 'Lord Cornbury, Bolingbroke', 9.
[146] Bolingbroke, *Spirit of Patriotism*, 193, 195.   [147] Ibid., 197.   [148] Ibid., 198.
[149] Ibid., 200. See also *Unpublished Letters*, 210.

Bolingbroke equated opposition with duty to one's country. He feared, however, that many undertook opposition 'not as a duty, but as an adventure'.[150] These people 'look[ed] on themselves like volunteers, not like men listed in the service'.[151] Bolingbroke sought to encourage young noblemen such as Cornbury to view opposition as an even higher duty than office. It was a tangible worry in the period that able opposition politicians could be bought off by bribes, government positions and sinecures, since the executive had a great deal of patronage at its disposal. He asked rhetorically: 'To what higher station, to what greater glory can any mortal aspire, than to be, during the whole course of his life, the support of good, the control of bad government, and the guardian of public liberty?'[152] It was the duty of every politician 'to promote good, and to oppose bad government; and, if not vested with the power of a minister of state, yet vested with the *superior* power of controlling those who are appointed such by the crown'.[153]

One obvious objection to the centrality of Bolingbroke's theory of opposition in the intellectual history of party is that he may have meant opposition by individual members of parliament and that he was as opposed as anyone to concerted opposition. Towards the end of the *Letter*, however, Bolingbroke went beyond everything he had written about opposition thus far. He dismissed the widespread idea 'that opposition to an administration requires fewer preparatives, and less constant application than the conduct of it'. This way of thinking was a 'gross error' and a 'false notion of opposition', he stressed, warning that '*Want of concert* ... [and] want of preliminary measures' would lead to failure.[154] Opposition was not to be undertaken in a haphazard way: '[e]very administration is a system of conduct: opposition, therefore, should be a system of conduct likewise'.[155] As Burke was to do more than three decades later, Bolingbroke compared the struggle between opposition and administration to military combat.[156] The moral of this metaphor is straightforward: oppositions and governments are like armies with generals; in other words, they are like parties and not made up of mavericks.

Bolingbroke stressed that opposition needed to be as systematic as government, and suggested that an organised party was acceptable to achieve concerted action: '[t]hey who engage in opposition are under as great obligations, to prepare themselves to control, as they who serve the

---

[150] Bolingbroke, *Spirit of Patriotism*, 201.　[151] Ibid.　[152] Ibid., 202.
[153] Ibid., 215–16. (My emphasis.)　[154] Ibid., 215. (My emphasis.)　[155] Ibid.
[156] Ibid. For Burke, see Chapter 11.

crown are under, to prepare themselves to carry on the administration, *and that a party formed for this purpose*, do not act like good citizens nor honest men, unless they propose true, as well as oppose false measures of government'.[157] At the end of the *Letter*, Bolingbroke said that he had demonstrated 'the duty of an opposing *party*', and that such 'a party who opposed, systematically, a wise to a silly, an honest to an iniquitous scheme of government, would acquire greater reputation and strength, and arrive more surely at their end, than a party who opposed occasionally ... *without any general concert, with little uniformity*'.[158]

Further evidence that Bolingbroke thought of opposition in terms of concerted activity can be found in his private correspondence. For example, he wrote the following to his close friend Sir William Wyndham, one of the leaders of the Tories in the Commons, in May 1737, after the opposition had supported the Prince of Wales in his request of an increased allowance: 'when your Party appeared lately in the Prince's cause, I took it for granted, as I do still, that this step was part of a *scheme*, and the *scheme* that might follow it, & be built upon it, easily occurred to my mind'.[159] The episode had frightened Walpole, who had felt compelled to produce a compromise over Prince Frederick's allowance.[160] Bolingbroke believed that the bad health of George II, fifty-five years old at the time, had rocked Walpole's confidence. In a later letter to Wyndham, Bolingbroke continued to press for an organised opposition centred around Frederick: 'this affair would have alarmed, and have done more than alarm them, in what ever state the Kings health had been, if it had been the first measure of a scheme of conduct wisely formed, and *concerted among all those that stand in opposition to the present administration*'.[161] A formal opposition with Prince Frederick as figurehead was formed the same year.[162]

Another obvious objection to the importance of Bolingbroke's conception of an oppositional Country party is that the Bolingbrokean party was

---

[157] Bolingbroke, *Spirit of Patriotism*, 216. (My emphasis.)   [158] Ibid. (My emphasis.)

[159] Bolingbroke to Wyndham, 11 May 1737, *Unpublished Letters*, V, 204. (My emphasis.)

[160] Langford, *A Polite and Commercial People* (Oxford, 1989), 236–7.

[161] Bolingbroke to Wyndham, 9 June [1737], *Unpublished Letters*, V, 211. (My emphasis.) Lack of concert was a persistent worry in opposition correspondence in the late 1730s; see, e.g., James Erskine to Marchmont, 8 September 1739, Stair to Marchmont, 9 December 1739, in *Marchmont Papers*, II, 161–2, 169. Stair echoed Bolingbroke when he said that to remove Walpole, 'there must be a perfect union amongst the leaders of the country party ... all the operations must be directed by one common council'. *Marchmont Papers*, II, 171–2.

[162] Glickman, 'Parliament, the Tories and Frederick, Prince of Wales', *PH*, 30 (2011), 120–41.

meant to be a party to end all parties.[163] It is important to note, however, that Bolingbroke never used a phrase corresponding to this evocative and oft-repeated slogan. Although he was sanguine about what the Country party could achieve, he never expressed any belief in an end to political conflict. On the contrary, he said that although the constitution was near-perfect, people could never allow themselves to rest on their laurels.[164] Bolingbroke appears to have accepted continued political conflict in a limited monarchy such as Britain, where the 'struggle between the spirit of liberty and the spirit of dominion ... always hath subsisted, and ... must always subsist'.[165] Such conflicts could in the future even encompass the dethronement of a monarch as in the Glorious Revolution, as long as all parties recognised the overall constitutional framework: 'Better ministers, better Kings, may be hereafter often wanted, and sometimes found, but a better constituted government never can.'[166]

Finally, it is worth drawing attention to one of Machiavelli's teachings that Bolingbroke firmly believed in: the natural mortality of states, which is closely linked to the argument about 'first principles' discussed above.[167] 'The best instituted governments, like the best constituted animal bodies, carry in them the seeds of their destruction', Bolingbroke wrote. 'All that can be done, therefore, to prolong the duration of a good government, is to draw it back, on every favourable occasion, to the first principles on which it was founded.'[168] Consequently, Bolingbroke must have accepted that even if his opposition party had successfully rolled back Walpole's allegedly corrupt regime and managed to bring the state back to its first principles, decay and decadence would likely return at some stage, as all states contain the seeds of their own destruction. There could therefore never be a party to end all parties and the rationale for opposition could not be forever eradicated.

On balance, the evidence presented here suggests that it is an overstatement to view the Bolingbrokean opposition party as a party to end all parties. This interpretation stands in sharp contrast to that of Shelley Burtt, who reads Bolingbroke as a thinker who rejected 'the inevitability of conflict'.[169] Burtt's analysis hinges on *The Idea of a Patriot King*, as she sees the patriot king as someone who 'can and will govern in such a way as to transcend the usual adversarial nature of government.'[170] The *Patriot*

---

[163] Rosenblum, *On the Side of the Angels*, 36; Hofstadter, *The Idea of a Party System*, 18.
[164] Bolingbroke, *Dissertation*, 84.   [165] Ibid., 91.   [166] Ibid., 86.
[167] Machiavelli, *Discourses*, 10–14. See also Pocock, *The Machiavellian Moment*, 217–18.
[168] Bolingbroke, *Patriot King*, 252.   [169] Burtt, *Virtue Transformed* (Cambridge, 1992), 96.
[170] Ibid., 95.

King is the text commonly used to demonstrate Bolingbroke's alleged belief in absolute unity and harmony without party-political conflict. This chapter now turns to this famous but enigmatic text.

The *Patriot King*

Many interpretations of Bolingbroke as an anti-party writer are based on *The Idea of a Patriot King* (1738). It is indeed in this text that we find some of his most negative comments about parties, for instance that they are political evils, and such statements cannot be ignored. It remains clear, however, that Bolingbroke had not ceased to differentiate party and faction, even if the distinction became more minimal: 'faction is to party what the superlative is to the positive: party is a political evil, and faction is the worst of all parties'.[171] He now maintained that '[p]arties, even before they degenerate into absolute factions, are still numbers of men associated together for certain purposes, and certain interests, which are not, or which are not allowed to be, those of the community of others'.[172] Bolingbroke believed himself to be particularly suited to understanding the inner workings of political parties, since he had seen 'the inside of parties'.[173] As we shall see, however, this state of mind led him neither to reject the inevitability of conflict nor prescribe a non-party state.

The *Patriot King* is a mirror-for-princes, modelled on Machiavelli's *Il principe* (*c.*1513) and influenced by Fénelon's *Les aventures de Télémaque* (1699).[174] It has commonly been read as an abstract political text.[175] By contrast, I argue that it should be read as a highly topical oppositional tract written for a small circle consisting of Prince Frederick and his advisers, at a time when the prince was seen as a figurehead of the opposition. Some of Bolingbroke's friends would have read a Jacobite message into the text, but there is no evidence that Bolingbroke had any Jacobite intentions at this time. His main objective remained the replacement of Walpole, to whom

---

[171] Bolingbroke, *Patriot King*, 257.   [172] Ibid., 258.   [173] Ibid., 268.

[174] Butterfield, *The Statecraft of Machiavelli* (London, 1960 [1940]), 149–65; Hart, *Viscount Bolingbroke* (Toronto, 1965), 83–143. Bolingbroke's choice of genre was not idiosyncratic in the context of the 1730s. Fénelon's mirror for princes *Les aventures de Télémaque* (1699) had been published in several translations and editions in early Hanoverian Britain, notably Charles Forman's *Protesilaus: Or, the Character of an Evil Minister. Being a Paraphrase of the Tenth Book of Telemachus* (1730). Like the book form of Bolingbroke's *Dissertation*, Forman's adaptation of Fénelon was dedicated to Walpole and part of the literary opposition to the Court Whigs, see Ahn, 'From Idomeneus to Protesilaus', in *Fénelon in the Enlightenment* (Amsterdam, 2014), 99–128.

[175] See, e.g., Gerrard, *The Patriot Opposition to Walpole*, 186.

he gave the full responsibility for the corrupt state of the nation, 'since he has been so long in possession of the whole power' and 'corrupt[ed] the morals of men'.[176] Bolingbroke's wish was that '[a] wise and honester administration may draw us back to our former credit and influence abroad'.[177] If we are to believe the author himself, he never wanted to publish the *Patriot King*, but only did so to correct an unauthorised version printed and distributed by his friend Pope.[178] The *Patriot King* is rightly considered as Bolingbroke's most utopian writing; for example, he calls the patriot king 'the most uncommon of all phenomenon in the physical or moral world' and even a 'standing miracle', but there is not sufficient textual evidence to support the claim that Bolingbroke rejected the inevitability of political conflict.[179]

Like Elizabeth I, the paradigmatic patriot princess, the patriot king would be a unifier and a healer.[180] The patriot king has a duty 'to govern like the common father of his people ... he who does otherwise forfeits his title'.[181] He – as was customary at the time, Bolingbroke uses the masculine pronoun, although he thought that Elizabeth had been the greatest patriot monarch – would not 'be exposed to the temptation, of governing by a party; which must always end in the government of a faction'.[182] We should note that Bolingbroke had a specific precedent in mind. In *Of the State of Parties at the Accession of George I* (1739), written a year after the *Patriot King* and published together with it in 1749 with the explicit intention to complement the sections on party in the *Patriot King*, he attacked the policy of George I, a policy of which he himself had been a victim.[183] Upon George I's accession, Bolingbroke was shocked to find that the king would 'immediately let loose the whole fury of party, suffer the queen's servants, who had surely been guilty of no crime against him, nor the state, to be so bitterly persecuted, and proscribe in effect every man

---

[176] Bolingbroke, *Patriot King*, 219.   [177] Ibid.
[178] Bolingbroke to Lyttelton, 15 April 1748, in *Memoirs and Correspondence of George, Lord Lyttelton, from 1734 to 1773* (2 vols., London, 1845), II, 429–30. For the complicated printing history of the *Patriot King*, see Barber, 'Bolingbroke, Pope, and the Patriot King', *The Library*, 19 (1964), 67–89.
[179] Bolingbroke, *Patriot King*, 221, 251.
[180] Ibid., 271–3. For the Elizabethan cult in the 1730s, see Gerrard, *The Patriot Opposition to Walpole*, 150–84.
[181] Ibid., 257.
[182] Ibid. John Toland wrote a pamphlet entitled *The Art of Governing by Partys* (London, 1701), in which he used language which Bolingbroke may have tried to imitate, e.g., 'a King can never lessen himself more than by heading of a Party; for thereby he becomes only the King of a Faction, and ceases to be the common Father of his People' (41).
[183] Bolingbroke, *State of Parties*, in *Works*, III, 129.

in the country who did not bear the name of whig'.[184] Bolingbroke contrasted this conduct with that of Charles II upon the Restoration in 1660, and that of Henry IV of France, who 'not only exercised clemency, but shew[ed] favour to those who had stood in arms against them' after coming to the throne.[185] He believed that the accession of George I and the subsequent violent behaviour of the Whigs drove the Tories into rebellion, a direct effect 'of maintaining divisions in a nation, and of governing by faction'.[186]

Bolingbroke concluded the *State of Parties* by saying that 'division has caused all the mischief we lament, [and] that union can alone retrieve it'.[187] By 'union', however, he meant the ascendency of 'the coalition of parties, so happily begun, so successfully carried on, and of late so unaccountably neglected', meaning the Country platform, combining Tories and opposition Whigs. Bolingbroke was explicit that this union would not incorporate the Court Whigs, and probably not even George II, who he thought had turned into a party king resembling his father: 'such a union can never be expected till patriotism fills the throne, and faction be banished from the administration'.[188]

To return to the *Patriot King*, while such a king, according to Bolingbroke's advice, was not at liberty to espouse or proscribe any party, '[h]e may favour one party and discourage another, upon occasions wherein the state of his kingdom makes such a temporary measure necessary'.[189] This implies that there would be political parties under the patriot king. Moreover, personnel and measures remained intertwined in Bolingbroke's thinking. The first action of the patriot king would be 'to purge his court, and to call into the administration such men as he can assure himself will serve on the same principles on which he intends to govern'.[190] By this he meant that Walpole and his supporters, or 'the prostitutes who set themselves to sale' as he referred to them, would be banished.[191] Entire parties were not to be proscribed, however, and the patriot king must distinguish 'between those who have affected to dip

---

[184] Ibid., 139. Bolingbroke's friend Jonathan Swift, who had worked as a government hack for the Tory administration in 1710–14, ridiculed George I's approach to parties in *Gulliver's Travels* (1726). On the island of Lilliput, although the Tramecksans, or the High Heels, were widely seen as being 'most agreeable to our ancient Constitution', the king only employed Slamecksans, or Low Heels. The king himself wore lower heels than anyone at his court. *Gulliver's Travels* (London, 2003), 47.

[185] Bolingbroke, *State of Parties*, in *Works*, III, 139.   [186] Ibid., 140.   [187] Ibid., 141.
[188] Ibid.   [189] Bolingbroke, *Patriot King*, 263.   [190] Ibid., 253.   [191] Ibid.

themselves deeply in precedent iniquitous, and those who have had the virtue to keep aloof of them'.[192]

There has been a tendency among readers of the *Patriot King* to focus on the sweeping statements about the patriot king's ability to unify and purify the nation.[193] The all-important qualifications have sometimes been neglected. For Bolingbroke, it was axiomatic that '[a] people may be united in submission to the prince, and to the establishment, and *yet be divided about general principles, or particular measures of government*'.[194] Accordingly, under such a reign, people 'will support or oppose particular acts of administrations, and defend and attack the persons employed in them; *and both these ways a conflict of parties may arise*'.[195] The patriot king must 'pursue the union of his subjects, and the prosperity of his kingdoms independently of all parties', but Bolingbroke recognised that in practice this meant that he would choose the best side rather than no side when two parties are clashing: 'When parties are divided ... He may and he ought to show his dislike or his favour, as he judges the constitution may be hurt or improved, by one side or the other.'[196]

Bolingbroke believed that under a patriot king 'the opportunities of forming an opposition ... will be rare, and the pretences generally weak'. But importantly he stressed that '[s]uch opportunities ... may happen; and there may be reason, as well as pretences, sometimes for opposition even in such a reign ... Grievances then are complained of, mistakes and abuses in government are pointed out, and ministers are prosecuted by their enemies.'[197] The patriot king 'knows that neither he nor his ministers are infallible, nor impeccable. There may be abuses in his government, mistakes in his administration, and guilt in his ministers, which he had not observed.'[198] On the rare occasion when an opposition would be justified in such an illustrious reign, the patriot king will not 'treat those who carry on such prosecutions in a legal manner, as incendiaries, and as enemies of his government', as Bolingbroke and Pulteney had been treated in the ministerial press.[199]

To conclude this section, although the *Patriot King* is Bolingbroke's most anti-party writing, he does not in it appear to conceive of a state

---

[192] Ibid., 254. Bolingbroke remained a friend and admirer of Hardwicke, Lord Chancellor under Walpole from 1737. He was careful to differentiate Hardwicke from 'the narrowness, & lowness ... of the people with whom he acts', see *Unpublished Letters*, V, 201. For their correspondence, see Harris, *The Life of Lord Chancellor Hardwicke* (3 vols., London, 1847).

[193] Armitage, 'A Patriot for Whom?', *JBS*, 36 (1997), 405.

[194] Bolingbroke, *Patriot King*, 259. (My emphasis.)   [195] Ibid. (My emphasis.)

[196] Ibid., 259–60.   [197] Ibid., 260.   [198] Ibid., 261.   [199] Ibid.

without either parties or opposition. As we have seen, many of his anti-party comments have contextual explanations and can be seen as part of his general discontent with George I and George II, both of whom he regarded as (Court) Whig kings.[200] In case Prince Frederick would ascend the throne, Bolingbroke was eager to ensure that he would not be captured by Walpole, as had happened to George II upon his accession in 1727, when many expected at least some changes in the administration.[201] Moreover, the naming of his paradigmatic ruler as a *patriot* king was not a neutral move, since 'patriotism' had been the watchword of Bolingbroke's earlier coalition, and the new generation of politicians in Prince Frederick's circle were known as the 'boy patriots'. This group included Lyttelton, Frederick's secretary at the time of the *Patriot King*'s composition and originally intended as the dedicatee of the work. When the work was finally about to be published in an authorised version a decade later, Lyttelton wrote to Bolingbroke to turn down this 'honour', since he was no longer in Frederick's service and instead connected with many of the late Walpole's close friends, meaning that he had joined Henry Pelham's ministry.[202] This episode demonstrates that the *Patriot King* was far from an abstract political text about how to avoid conflict and achieve harmony in a polity. It was an oppositional tract and a contribution to the party-political struggle of the day.

The Impact of Bolingbroke

Although Bolingbroke was an influential voice in the opposition, not all Tories adopted his argument that Court and Country had entirely superseded Whig and Tory.[203] But eventually many did. Sir Roger Newdigate, MP for the Tory stronghold of Oxford University between 1751 and 1780, has often been described as a diehard Tory, but in fact he complained that those who resisted the Whig 'system of corruption' were

> ridiculously called Tories, unjustly called Jacobites, but who deserve civic crowns as the genuine friends of their country . . . Thence they have their true distinction, the *Country party* as opposed to administration, to watch the encroachments which power, the great corruptor of the human mind is always at work to make. No other names nor distinction as a party will they

---

[200] He also lamented that Britain's interests abroad had been subordinated to those of Hanover since 1714; see Bolingbroke to Lyttelton, 4 November 1741, *Correspondence of Lyttelton*, I, 196.
[201] Langford, *A Polite and Commercial People*, 11–15.
[202] Lyttelton to Bolingbroke, 14 April 1748, in *Correspondence Lyttelton*, II, 428.
[203] See, e.g., *Fog's Weekly Journal*, 6 March 1731, and Shippen's speeches in parliament.

acknowledge. They equally disdain the names of Tory and Jacobite. They abhor the principles of both. They are the disinterested friends of their country, unmoved by all the discouragement of power or opprobrium of the vulgar who follow or admire it. Declared enemies to bad men and bad measures and trusting that under the shadow of the Revolution they may venture to judge of worth in the highest and to love and respect even Kings themselves as they shall deserve.[204]

Bolingbroke's impact was enormous in several other ways. The importance of the idea of 'opposition' can be seen in the case of his friends Pope and Wyndham. Writing to Lyttelton in November 1738 about a meeting with Wyndham, Pope said that the Tory leader was worried about 'the present State & Conduct of the Opposition', and more particularly that it 'would be drawn off from the Original Principle on which it was founded, by two Persons [Carteret and Pulteney]'. Under the direction of these opportunistic Whigs, 'the Opposition ... would become nothing more than a Bubble-Scheme, wherein multitudes who intended the publick Service, would be employ'd to no other purpose than to service private Ambition'.[205] The letter proved prophetic since Pulteney and Carteret left their Tory allies in the opposition after the fall of Walpole in 1742, as we shall see in Chapter 5. The letter testifies, moreover, that both Wyndham and Pope were comfortable to view the Patriot Prince (Frederick) as 'the Head of the Party'; indeed, Pope thought 'it a Nobler Situation, to be at the head of the best Men of a Kingdom than at the Head of any Kingdom upon earth'.[206]

Bolingbroke's impact on the next generation of opposition wits was colossal. George Lyttelton rehashed Bolingbroke's analysis of party in his Montesquieu-inspired *Letters from a Persian in England* (1735), along with many of Bolingbroke's other ideas, as was pointed out in the pamphlet *The Persian Strip'd of his Disguise* (1735). Although the idiom of opposition Toryism had been replete with populist and 'libertarian' rhetoric prior to Bolingbroke, there is no doubt that he perfected the language of liberty. 'Old Whig' Jacobites such as Wharton had already espoused a union of opposition Whigs and Tories,[207] but after Bolingbroke this idea became the favoured policy, or at least rhetorical technique, even among Tory-

---

[204] Cited in Thomas, 'Sir Roger Newdigate's Essays on Party, c.1760', *EHR*, 102 (1987), 398. (My emphasis.) Unlike Bolingbroke, Newdigate seems to have been genuinely uninterested in office.
[205] *Pope Correspondence*, IV, 142–3. [206] Ibid., IV, 144.
[207] *His Grace the Duke of Whartons [sic] Reasons for leaving his native Country & espousing the Cause of his Royal master K. J.3. in a Letter to his friends in G. Britain & Ireland* [c. 1727], English History MS C 374, Bodleian, f. 26.

Jacobites. As William King, principal of St Mary Hall at Oxford, wrote to James Edgar, clerk to the Pretender, in November 1736:

> I could heartily wish some proper steps were taken to unite Garth [the Jacobites] and Mercer [the Whigs] in the same interest, which I conceive would not be at all difficult to be affected at this juncture. I mean the same Mercer [the opposition Whigs], who is such a professed enemy to all the measures of 500 [George II] and 503 [Walpole]. I cannot help intimating this, because I am fully persuaded 473 [the Stuart restoration] in a great measure depends on that union.[208]

The following year, the Pretender sponsored the opposition journal *Common Sense, or the Englishman's Journal*, under the editorship of Charles Molloy, the erstwhile editor of the *Fog's Weekly Journal*, successor to the more openly Jacobite *Mist's Weekly Journal*.[209] King contributed at least one piece to *Common Sense*, while the opposition Whigs Chesterfield and Lyttelton wrote more regularly.[210] The journal in some ways continued the legacy of Bolingbroke and the *Craftsman*, which ran out of steam after Bolingbroke's second exile in France. King's one known essay in *Common Sense*, appearing in May 1737, has many similarities with Bolingbroke's *Patriot King* but with a stronger anti-Hanoverian undertone.[211]

Bolingbroke's influence extended well beyond his circle and he quickly became an authority on the subject of party. In *Lettres d'un François* (1745), the Abbé Le Blanc hailed Bolingbroke's works 'pour l'élégance du style & la solidité du Raisonnement, est au-dessus de tout ce que les Anglois ont produit en ce genre'.[212] For decades, everyone dealing with party had to respond to Bolingbroke. In 1750, Thomas Pownall wrote a noteworthy treatise which was largely a response to Bolingbroke. His major objection to Bolingbroke, and all writers wedded to the mixed government, was his acceptance of the inevitability of conflict. In the preface he attacked what he perceived as an anti-Harringtonian message in the *Patriot King*, which had the previous year been published in an

---

[208] Cited in Greenwood, *William King* (London, 1969), 75. The letter is deciphered with the help of a key from the Stuart papers, provided by Greenwood.

[209] Hilton Jones, 'The Jacobites, Charles Molloy, and *Common Sense*', *The Review of English Studies*, 4 (1953), 144–7; Lockwood, 'The Life and Death of *Common Sense*', *Prose Studies*, 16 (1993), 78–93.

[210] Greenwood, *William King*, 77–8. Although the Pretender had been involved in setting up *Common Sense*, the Jacobite Carte referred to it as an 'Old Whig' journal. BL Add MS 21500, f. 114.

[211] On the article, see Greenwood, *William King*, 78–80.

[212] Blanc, *Lettres d'un François* (3 vols., The Hague, 1745), II, 28 (note).

edition authorised by Bolingbroke for the first time.[213] By encouraging the patriot king to make appointments based on talent rather than property, Pownall argued that 'the Measures recommended to the Patriot Prince, instead of healing, uniting and restoring, do seem more likely to run ALL into *Party*'.[214] Pownall's main target, however, was the *Dissertation upon Parties*, which had been printed for the seventh time in 1749, and more specifically he criticised Bolingbroke's firm belief in the mixed constitution.[215] In short, Pownall found it unsound to perceive of king and people as separate estates. '[I]t is of the very Essence of these Governments to subsist, and be carried on, by Parties and Opposition, as the noble Author of the Dissertation on Parties hath fully shown', he wrote.[216] For Pownall, Bolingbroke's principles were essentially conflictual, 'calculated for an opposition' and 'incompatible with establish'd Power'.[217]

This chapter has argued that Pownall's critical reading was in many ways closer to Bolingbroke's own intentions than has been realised by later commentators. Pownall was right to view the Bolingbrokean party as an opposition party, which is not necessarily the same as a party to end all parties. Bolingbroke's raison d'être as a political writer was opposition to Walpole and the Court Whigs. All his major political writings extol the virtues of opposition. We have also seen that Bolingbroke conceived of opposition as organised and concerted, to be undertaken by a party of political actors (who could be drawn from several parties in the sense of Whig and Tory) disciplined by leadership. He often referred to this opposition as a Country party, which, in contrast to the Court faction, was a national party seeking to address national grievances. The Country party was also equipped with principles, which, unlike the Whig and Tory creeds, were fit for the political climate of the 1730s.

Bolingbroke had little to say about what would happen if this oppositional Country party was successful. Would it become a party of government, a new Court party? Some historians have speculated that it is likely that Bolingbroke would have followed a similar path as Walpole if he had been in power.[218] It did not fit his polemical purposes to spell out how the Country party would behave after the fall of Walpole and the Court Whigs. The closest we come to a description of a future political order

---

[213] [Pownall], *A Treatise on Government* (London, 1750), 12–13.
[214] Ibid., 14. Harrington had influentially stated that '[d]ominion is property' in *The Commonwealth of Oceana* (Cambridge, 2001 [1656]), 11.
[215] One can thus argue that Pownall fits better than Bolingbroke in Rosenblum's anti-party tradition of 'holism'; see *On the Side of the Angles*, ch. 1.
[216] [Pownall], *Treatise on Government*, 22–3.   [217] Ibid., 32.   [218] Dickinson, *Bolingbroke*, 192.

in Bolingbroke's writings is the *Patriot King*. This text has often been read as a pie-in-the-sky attempt to abolish parties and political conflict as all political actors would unite in awe of the virtuous patriot king. This chapter has shown, however, that the *Patriot King* should be read as an opposition tract. Crucially, it has been demonstrated that Bolingbroke, even in this somewhat utopian text, emphasised that causes for opposition may arise even in the reign of the patriot king. He was explicit that parties divided over political issues would survive in such a reign, and while the patriot king would not govern by party – like Bolingbroke thought the Georges had done – he would be at liberty to take sides in political disputes.

It remains true that Bolingbroke sometimes appeared to have damned party while condoning opposition, and evidence in favour of that view has not been concealed within the analysis in this chapter. The ambition has been, however, to explode the persistent myth of Bolingbroke as the paradigmatic anti-party thinker, because his views on these subjects were more complex. His writings were calculated to legitimise opposition and a specific kind of political party: the Country party. Finally, his writings on the Court and Country party division in British politics, and his constitutional thought more generally, would provoke and influence writers for decades.[219] Notably, Hume, to whom we now turn, used them as his starting point – and targets of criticism – when writing his first batch of political essays in the early 1740s.

---

[219] For Bolingbroke's influence on Montesquieu, see Shackleton, *Montesquieu* (Oxford, 1961), 297–8; Hammersley, *The English Republican Tradition and Eighteenth-Century France* (Manchester, 2016 [2010]), 73–8.

CHAPTER 4

David Hume's Early Essays on Party Politics

To determine the nature of [the British] parties is, perhaps, one of the most difficult problems, that can be met with, and is a proof that history may contain questions, as uncertain as any to be found in the most abstract sciences.

Hume, 'Of the Parties of Great Britain' (1741)

Introduction

Few, if any, political thinkers of the eighteenth century dealt as thoroughly and extensively with party as David Hume (1711–76). Not only did he write three essays exclusively devoted to the subject, but the genesis of party also played a significant part in his *History of England*, especially the two Stuart volumes published as *The History of Great Britain* in 1754 and 1756. This book deals with Hume's diverse contribution in a series of chapters, starting here with his first batch of political essays published in the beginning of the 1740s. Chapter 6 considers a series of essays written by Hume in the wake of the Jacobite rebellion of 1745–6, and Chapter 7 Hume's history of the seventeenth century, which put party at the centre. Finally, in Chapter 8, Hume's essay 'Of the Coalition of Parties' (1758) is studied alongside Edmund Burke's first (and unpublished) essay on the subject of party. It will become evident that Hume equated modern, parliamentary politics with party politics.

Hume was in London between August 1737 and February 1739, and, on his return to Ninewells, Scotland, he began drafting essays in the summer of 1739 at the latest.[1] Many at the time, especially those in opposition to Walpole's Whigs, denied the relevance of the party distinctions of Whig and Tory. This used to mislead historians into believing that Court and Country represented the only 'real' division in the mid-

---

[1] Hume to Kames, 4 June and 1 July, 1739, *New Letters*, 5–7.

Hanoverian era, rather than an additional dimension of party conflict.[2] As we saw in Chapter 3, this was a tactic associated with Bolingbroke, while the government position was that Whig and Tory were still relevant, and that the Tories were predominantly Jacobite. However, Hume arrived in London hot on the heels of the debate over the Mortmain and Quakers' Tithe Bills in 1736, which had made it hard for even the opposition to deny the survival of Whig and Tory as it had divided Parliament along such lines.[3] The former was a technical piece of legislation intended to regulate the transfer of lands, goods, and money for charitable purposes. The Tories viewed this as part of an anti-clerical onslaught. For Edward Harley, 'the true Design' of the bill was evident from the '[s]peeches against the two Universities [Oxford and Cambridge], the Charity Schools, Queen Annes Bounty to the poor Clergy, and to the Clergy in General', adding that '[n]one [were] more forward in those Invectives than Mr Sandys and the Patriots', with the latter referring to opposition Whigs.[4] The Quakers' Tithe Bill, introduced a week later, would remove the jurisdiction of the payment of tithes (a religious tax) from the ecclesiastical courts to the justices of peace. The Tories viewed this bill as a further attack on the clergy, members of which signed several petitions against it. Once again it split the opposition, and Harley lamented in his diary that 'all the discontented Whigs joined with the Court'.[5] These episodes caused Bolingbroke to berate his brother-in-law Robert Knight, an opposition Whig and MP for Great Grimsby: 'if you have broke the coalition by stating high whig points, while Torys have been kept so long from their old follys that they are weaned almost from 'em, the damage is great, & such as I apprehend it will be hard to repair'.[6]

As we shall see, for Hume Whig–Tory as well as Court–Country alignments were integral to British politics, with the former dividing the political nation along religious and at least to an extent dynastic lines, and the latter reflecting parliamentary conflict and the workings of the mixed constitution. Hume's analysis can thus be read as a compromise between Bolingbroke and Walpole. Yet it was something more than that and

---

[2] Speck, *Stability and Strife* (London, 1977), 7; Dickinson, *Liberty and Property* (London, 1977), part two.

[3] Taylor, 'Sir Robert Walpole, the Church of England, and the Quakers Tithe Bill of 1736', *HJ*, 28 (1985), 51–77; Kendrick, 'Sir Robert Walpole, the Old Whigs and the Bishops, 1733–1736', *HJ*, 11 (1968), 421–45.

[4] *Tory and Whig*, 19.   [5] Ibid., 22.   [6] *Unpublished Letters*, V, 171.

arguably the most ambitious attempt to make sense of party in British politics since Rapin.[7]

Hume's first collection of political essays tells us much about the impact of Bolingbroke. By the time Hume arrived in London in 1737, Bolingbroke had gone into a second exile in France. When Hume wrote and published his first essays between 1739 and 1741, however, it was still within the framework established by Bolingbroke in the heyday of his journalism in the 1730s, even if it was a framework Hume sought to supersede.[8] Unlike the government hacks, of whom he did not think highly, Hume did not seek to smear Bolingbroke as a Jacobite, but instead engaged with his arguments. He wanted to go beyond Bolingbroke's partisanship and aimed to establish a science of politics expressed in Addisonian polite prose rather than a party-political programme. Be that as it may, we should not minimise the fact that it was Bolingbroke who had set the terms for political debate.

While Bolingbroke was Hume's main interlocutor, his principal factual source for his first pronouncements on the British parties is likely to have been Rapin. We know that Hume had read Rapin's *Histoire* at an early stage,[9] and we can take for granted that he had also seen the *Dissertation sur les Whigs et les Torys* (1717), which was included within the *Histoire*. This *Dissertation* would have given Hume the insight that the study of politics in Britain was the study of party. It also meant that Hume, as Nicholas Phillipson has noted, looked back on the reign of Anne as the time when the agenda of modern political discourse had been set.[10] After having written the Stuart volumes of the *History of England*, Hume added a footnote at the end of 'The Parties of Great Britain', saying that he had come to revise some of the conclusions reached in the essay, apologising in effect for vulgar Whiggism.[11] Despite Hume's fairly Whiggish, or at least Rapinesque, account of seventeenth-century events at this stage of his

---

[7] Gunn is thus wide of the mark when arguing that Hume's views on party are 'quite unremarkable'; see *Factions No More* (London, 1972), 258.

[8] The most important study of Hume's engagement with Bolingbroke remains Forbes, *Hume's Philosophical Politics* (Cambridge, 1975), 193–223. After the publication of Bolingbroke's posthumous *Works*, with which Hume was not impressed, in 1754, Hume and Bolingbroke were often bundled together owing to their controversial views on religion; see *Admonitions from the Dead, in Epistles to the Living . . . to Promote the Cause of Religion and Moral Virtue* (London, 1754); *The Beauties of Hume and Bolingbroke* (London, 1782).

[9] Hume to Michael Ramsay, [1730], *Letters*, II, 337.

[10] Phillipson, 'Propriety, Property and Prudence', in *Political Discourse in Early Modern Britain* (Cambridge, 1993), 304.

[11] Hume, 'Parties of Great Britain', *Essays*, 72n. 'Vulgar Whiggism' is Forbes's term; see *Hume's Philosophical Politics*, 150–1.

career, it would be a mistake to think that he was not making a genuine attempt to give a disinterested account, starkly different both in tone and content from both the ministerial and the oppositional press.[12]

Parties in General

As has often been pointed out, Hume adopted the essay format from Addison's and Steele's polite essays in the *Tatler* (1709) and *Spectator* (1711–12).[13] The idea was to write about politics in a polite manner, but with a more philosophical and non-partisan bent than in Bolingbroke's political writings.[14] Hume publicised these intentions in the advertisement to the first edition of the first volume of *Essays, Moral and Political* (1741). '[T]he READER may condemn my Abilities, but must approve of my Moderation and Impartiality in my Method of handling POLITICAL SUBJECTS', he wrote.[15] What Addison and Bolingbroke had in common, however, was that they in their respective contexts called for all honest men to unite into what Addison called a 'neutral body' and Bolingbroke a 'Country party'.[16] Hume took a more realistic, or sceptical, view. For him, party was both an intrinsic part of the British constitution, and a reflection of the fact that people were naturally inclined to conflict as well as gregarious sentiments.[17] The goal of the philosophically minded writer was simply to promote moderation – a controversial message if considered in context.

Hume's first extensive discussion of parties, or factions, came in 'Of Parties in General' (1741).[18] Hume opened the essay with a curious tribute to lawgivers, who otherwise play no role in his political thought. He then proceeded to castigate parties in a well-known passage:

> As much as legislators and founders of states ought to be honoured and respected among men, as much ought the founders of sects and factions to be detested and hated ... Factions subvert government, render laws impotent, and beget the fiercest animosities among men of the same nation, who ought to give mutual assistance and protection to each other ... And what

---

[12] See, e.g., the *London Journal*'s articles in response to Bolingbroke's *Dissertation upon Parties*, where the Tories are called 'tyrants' in power and 'deceivers' out of it (No. 779, 1 June, 1734).

[13] For the impact of Addison and Steele on Hume, see Phillipson, *David Hume* (London, 2011 [1989]), 24–7.

[14] Hume, 'Advertisement' (1741), iii.   [15] Ibid., iv.   [16] *The Spectator*, No. 126, 25 July 1711.

[17] Hume, *Enquiry Concerning the Principles of Morals* (Oxford, 1975 [1751]), 224, 275.

[18] In contrast with Bolingbroke, Hume used the two terms interchangeably. As Forbes pointed out, he frequently changed 'factions' into 'parties' and vice versa when editing his essays; see *Hume's Philosophical Politics*, 202.

should render the founders of parties more odious is, the difficulty of extirpating these weeds, when once they have taken root in any state.[19]

His first more balanced observation was that parties 'rise more easily, and propagate themselves faster in free governments [i.e. mixed governments[20]], where they always infect the legislature itself, which alone could be able, by the steady application of rewards and punishments, to eradicate them'.[21] What some readers may have expected after such a grand opening was a more precise explanation by Hume for how the legislature could go about 'eradicating' parties. Nothing of that kind followed, however.

Instead Hume stayed true to the title of the essay and proceeded to analyse the phenomenon of party supported by examples from history. He divided parties into *personal* and *real*, adding that most parties were a mixture of both.[22] Personal factions were most common in small republics, where every domestic quarrel became an affair of state. Hume believed that people had 'such a propensity to divide into personal factions, that the smallest appearance of real difference will produce them', and like Jonathan Swift he referred to the Prasini and Veneti factions, which had begun as different teams wearing different colours, green and blue, in chariot racing, but culminated in what we call the Nika riots.[23] Hume duly listed personal factions of the Italian city states, most of which emerged in the *Trecento*: the Neri and Bianchi of Florence, the Fregosi and Adorni of Genoa, and the Colonesi and Orsini of Rome (in the second edition of the essay, he also referred to the Castellani and Nicollotti of Venice later in the essay). The Colonesi (Colonna) and Orsini were the leading families of the notorious Guelph and Ghibelline factions, which began as two sides supporting the Pope and the Holy Roman Emperor respectively in the twelfth century and created a division that spread beyond Rome and lasted until the sixteenth century.[24] Hume commented that '[n]othing is more usual than to see parties, which have begun upon a real difference, continue even after that difference is lost', the reason being that after a division has occurred, people 'contract an affection to the persons with

---

[19] Hume, 'Parties in General', *Essays*, 55.

[20] For Hume's understanding of free governments as mixed governments, see 'Of the Origin of Government' (1777), *Essays*, 40–1. For Hume's approval of such a government, see 'Politics a Science', *Essays*, 18. It should be noted, however, that Hume differed from many thinkers in the period by arguing that civilised monarchies such as France were also legitimate; see 'Of Civil Liberty' (1741), *Essays*, 94.

[21] Hume, 'Parties in General', *Essays*, 55–6.   [22] Ibid., 56.   [23] Ibid., 56–7.

[24] Modern scholarship tends to view these factions as more ideological; see Ferente, 'Guelphs! Factions, Liberty and Sovereignty', *HPT*, 28 (2007), 571–98.

whom they are united, and an animosity against their antagonists', sentiments which are often transmitted to posterity.[25] That is why such parties are categorised as *personal*, although they differed in opinion from the outset.

Hume's main interest, however, was parties he classified as *real*, meaning those representing a more tangible difference. In this category, he made a tripartite classification into parties from *interest, principle*, and *affection*. Those from interest he called 'the most reasonable, and the most excusable' of all factions.[26] This was a bold step by Hume, since at this time, as Pocock has reminded us, '[p]arty was for most men tolerable only when it embodied principle and so was capable of virtue', whereas parties representing interests were seen as perpetuating 'the reign of corruption'.[27] The virtue–corruption dichotomy had been at the heart of Bolingbroke's enterprise. However, Hume did not think that Bolingbroke's platform passed the test of objectivity and moderation; the erstwhile Tory was simply making a partisan case against the government, according to Hume.

Why, then, were parties from interest the most excusable? First, they were inevitable. With the history of the Roman republic before his eyes, Hume argued that when parties represented different orders in the state, such as nobles and people (or *nobili* and *plebe* in Machiavelli's idiom), and when these orders had a part in government, 'they naturally follow a distinct interest'.[28] Considering the 'selfishness implanted in human nature', it would be vain to expect anything else.[29] Indeed, he further commented that it would require great skill on the part of the legislator to prevent such parties, and that many philosophers believed it impossible to achieve in practice. Signalling his agreement with this notion, Hume argued that such parties of interest existed even in despotic governments, similarly to Montesquieu in *Considérations sur les causes de la grandeur des Romains et de leur décadence* (1734).

Hume followed Bolingbroke in criticising the 'attempt' to divide England into landed and trading interests.[30] Both would probably have been familiar with Charles Davenant's influential demonstration of the correlation between increases in land prices and expansion of trade.[31]

---

[25] Hume, 'Parties in General', *Essays*, 58.   [26] Ibid.
[27] Pocock, *The Machiavellian Moment* (Princeton, 2003 [1975]), 483–4.
[28] Hume, 'Parties in General', *Essays*, 59.   [29] Ibid.
[30] Ibid., 60; Bolingbroke, *Contributions*, 142, 145.
[31] Langford, *Public Life and the Properties Englishman, 1689–1798* (Oxford, 1991), 42. For Davenant's influential economic and political writings, see Hont, *Jealousy of Trade* (Cambridge, MA, 2005), ch. 2.

Hume's main point in the present context was that the British parties were not parties based on interest in this economic sense of land versus trade. The British Whig and Tory parties, as we will see, were a mixture of the two other forms of real parties, namely those of principle and affection. At the same time, the Court and Country polarity, the government–opposition dimension, was to a great extent based on interest in the sense that they competed for office. This is most likely what Hume referred to when he said that such factions were 'the most reasonable, and the most excusable'; interest was more rational and accountable than principles. As Tocqueville would later write, interest was 'not very lofty, but clear and sure'.[32]

In contrast with parties from interest, parties from principle, 'especially speculative principle, are known only to modern times, and are, perhaps, the most extraordinary and unaccountable *phœnomenon,* that has yet appeared in human affairs'.[33] Divisions from principle gave rise to madness and fury, according to Hume, who explicitly linked ideological differences to 'religious controversies'. The reason was that such partisans, like religious fanatics, were intent on making everyone a convert to their beliefs. Most people were eager to debate and dispute, even those with the most speculative opinions, because the human mind was 'wonderfully fortified by an unanimity of sentiments' and 'shocked by any contrariety'.[34] That is why two people of opposite principles of religion could not pass each other when travelling in different directions on a highway without arguing, although Hume believed that the road was 'sufficiently broad' for them to pass without disruption.[35]

While it may appear frivolous, this tendency in human nature 'seems to have been the origin of all religious wars and divisions', Hume believed.[36] He had earlier in the same essay broached the questions of both civil and religious wars, two concepts inescapably and fatally linked to party division in the most extreme form as he understood it. Europeans were wrong to laugh at the racial civil wars of Morocco of 1727 when their own religious wars had been even more ridiculous. Whereas skin colour is a real difference everybody can observe, 'the controversy about an article of faith, which is utterly absurd and unintelligible, is not a difference in sentiment, but in a few phrases and expressions, which one party accepts of, without understanding them; and the other refutes in the same manner'.[37] The

---

[32] Tocqueville, *Democracy in America* (Chicago, 2000 [1835–40]), 502.
[33] Hume, 'Parties in General', *Essays*, 60.   [34] Ibid., 60–1.   [35] Ibid., 60.   [36] Ibid., 61.
[37] Ibid., 59.

racial war in Morocco was also more 'reasonable' because neither the 'whites' nor the 'blacks' sought to convert their opponents.[38]

The rise of Christianity explained why parties from principle were known only in modern times, whereas the ancients had parties from interest such as nobles versus people, and personal factions such as those of Caesar and Pompey, although the latter were not discussed by Hume in this particular essay. In antiquity, '[t]he magistrate embraced the religion of the people, and entering cordially into the care of sacred matters, naturally acquired an authority in them, and united ecclesiastical with the civil power'.[39] Christianity arose, however, in opposition to the established religion and government, and priests could thus monopolise power within this new sect. The fact that priestly government continued after it had become the established religion led to a spirit of persecution at the heart of this religion, according to Hume.[40] This spirit of persecution had 'ever since been the poison of human society, and the source of the most inveterate factions in every government'.[41] Hume thus believed that 'parties of religion' were 'more furious and enraged than the most cruel factions that ever arose from interest and ambition'.[42] The Reformation worsened religious division. Hume believed that such religious factions could be classified as factions of principle on the part of the followers but factions of interest on the part of the priest-leaders. As we shall see, he would make the same argument about the British parties.

Hume concluded the essay with a paragraph on the third kind of real party: parties from affection, by which Hume meant dynastic parties.[43] It may be difficult to distinguish this category of *real* party from the *personal* factions that Hume referred to earlier in the essay, but from the example he gives it is clear that he had different kinds of parties in mind. The key example of a real party from affection at the time was the Jacobite faction with its attachment to the Stuarts. The question of Jacobitism was always prominent in Hume's thinking, even if this essay was written four years before the Jacobite rebellion in 1745, and Hume was eager to downplay the significance of Jacobitism in his native Scotland. Hume had little sympathy with this type of party as it was often 'very violent'. The attachment could be good-natured or ill-natured. Activated by the splendour of majesty and power, it could be based on an imaginary interest which makes people attached to a single person and gives them the impression that they have an intimate relationship with him or her. But

---

[38] Ibid., 610 (variant readings).   [39] Ibid., 61.   [40] Ibid., 62.   [41] Ibid.   [42] Ibid., 63.
[43] Ibid.

it could also arise 'from spite and opposition to persons whose sentiments are different from [their] own'. In general, this inclination was often found in people with 'no great generosity of spirit' who are not 'easily transported by friendship beyond their own interest'.[44] The allusion to Jacobitism is an appropriate segue into Hume's second major essay on party, to which we now turn.

The Parties of Great Britain

'Of the Parties of Great Britain' (1741) is one of the most heavily edited of Hume's essays, which is not strange considering how much the state of parties changed between the first edition of the *Essays* (1741) and the final version of his *Essays and Treatises on Several Subjects* (2 vols., 1777). Crucially, he never withdrew the essay, but instead sought to amend it. Hume began the essay by arguing that party division was inevitable in mixed governments such as the British, delicately balanced between its monarchical and republican elements. In addition to this uncertain balance, people's passions and prejudices would necessarily generate different opinions concerning the government, even among people of the best understanding. While all reasonable people would agree to maintain the mixed government, they would disagree about specifics. Those with a mild temperament, who love peace and order and detest sedition and civil war, would incline towards monarchy and entrust greater powers to the crown than those bolder and more passionate lovers of liberty.[45] In short, 'there are parties of PRINCIPLE involved in the very nature of our constitution, which may properly enough be denominated those of COURT and COUNTRY'.[46] The Court and Country parties would always subsist as long as Britain remained a limited monarchy, that is to say, as long as it retained its parliament, Hume believed, in this regard echoing Bolingbroke and the opposition press.[47] This analysis was starkly different from that of the ministerial press, which called Bolingbroke's Court–Country distinction 'wicked', since it suggested that the interests of the king and court were opposite to those of the country.[48]

---

[44] Ibid.
[45] Smith would follow Hume closely in these descriptions in his *Lectures on Jurisprudence* (Indianapolis, 1978), 219–21.
[46] Hume, 'Parties of Great Britain', *Essays*, 65.
[47] Berkeley would also say that 'There is and ever will be a natural Strife between Court and Country' in *Maxims Concerning Patriotism* (Dublin, 1750), 6.
[48] *London Journal*, No. 767, 9 March 1734.

Arguing for a Court–Country division was just to say that there would always be parties of government and opposition. Since there was no alternative centre of government than the monarch there would always be a Court party, and since the Country party platform represented the standard set of opposition arguments, there would constantly be a Country party. In all editions of the essay up until and including the one published in 1768, Hume emphasised that he did not attach any value judgement to the appellations but simply used them because they were prevalent. He was clear that the Court party may occasionally look after the interest of the *country* and the Country party oppose it.[49] He believed that Cicero, whose oratory if not philosophy Hume admired,[50] had spoken as a 'true party man' when he defined the *Optimates* as 'the best and worthiest of the ROMANS'.[51] In opposition to Bolingbroke's *Dissertation upon Parties*, which Hume was to cite later in the same essay, he added that the term 'Country party' may have a positive connotation in the same manner as the term *Optimates,* '[b]ut that it would be folly to draw any argument' on account of names given by partisans.[52]

Similarly to Rapin's analysis of Whig and Tory, Hume continued by highlighting that the Court and Country parties were mixed parties, that they were not just motivated by principle, but also by interest, 'without which they would scarcely ever be dangerous or violent'.[53] The statement appears to be at odds with Hume's argument in the previous essay when he expressed a preference for parties of interest over parties of principle. However, we must remember that he never said that interested parties were less 'dangerous or violent', simply that they were 'the most reasonable, and the most excusable'. We should also note that not all principles are equally dangerous. The Court and Country parties represented a struggle between the monarchical and republican elements of the constitution (exactly what Rapin thought that Tory and Whig had done in his day), but their disagreement was not extra-constitutional. This division did not involve principles regarding religion or dynastic conflict to the same extent as Whig and Tory.

Like Rapin, Hume believed that leaders of factions were mainly motivated by interest, because they were closer to power, whereas inferior members were more attached to principles. The crown would naturally give government positions to those most favourable to monarchical power,

---

[49] Hume, 'Parties of Great Britain', *Essays*, 610 (variant readings).
[50] Hume, 'Of the Standard of Taste', *Essays*, 243.
[51] Hume, 'Parties of Great Britain', *Essays*, 610 (variant readings).   [52] Ibid.   [53] Ibid., 65.

who at this time paradoxically were the Whigs because of Jacobitism and proscription of the Tories. Hume hinted that the Whigs in government had shifted ground somewhat, as he highlighted that 'this temptation will naturally engage them to go greater lengths [*sic*] than their principles would otherwise carry them'.[54] Likewise, '[t]heir antagonists, who are disappointed in their ambitious aims, throw themselves into the power whose sentiments incline them to be most jealous of royal power, and naturally carry those sentiments to a greater height than sound politics will justify'.[55] In the original edition of the essay, Hume, echoing Rapin as well as the *Spectator*, added that 'the greatest part are commonly men who associate themselves they know not why; from example, from passion, from idleness'.[56]

Hume then turned to the religious dimension of party politics, highlighting that 'in all ages of the world, priests have been enemies to liberty', since freedom of thought always posed a threat to priestly power.[57] For this reason, 'the established clergy, while things are in their natural situation, will always be of the *Court*-party; as, on the contrary, dissenters of all kinds will be of the *Country-party*; since they can never hope for that toleration, which they stand in need of, but by means of our free government'.[58] The Swedish sixteenth-century king Gustavus Vasa may have been the only king who managed to supress both the established church and liberty at the same time, according to Hume.[59] The natural order would be the opposite, as in the situation in the Dutch Republic. As we shall see, however, religion and dynastic conflict had interrupted the natural development of politics in Britain. Although Hume agreed with Bolingbroke that the Dissenters should normally side with the 'Country party', he differed starkly from the Englishman by acknowledging and analysing the religious and dynastic aspects of politics.

Having outlined what he referred to as a 'general theory', Hume went on to explain 'the first rise of parties in ENGLAND'. Much like Rapin's *Dissertation*, Hume related the rise of party to the division between Roundhead and Cavalier during the great rebellion.[60] '[T]he species of government gave birth to them, by a regular and infallible operation', Hume contended.[61] Hume was never more Whiggish as when he described Charles I as '[a]n ambitious, or rather a misguided prince ... who ... openly acted in violation of liberty'.[62] However, his larger point

[54] Ibid.   [55] Ibid.   [56] Ibid., 610 (variant readings).   [57] Ibid., 65–6.   [58] Ibid., 66.
[59] Ibid.   [60] Ibid., 67.   [61] Ibid.
[62] Ibid., 68. For Hume's revision on this score, see Chapter 7.

was that it was not strange that the civil war divided the people into 'parties', since even the impartial in his own day could still not make up their minds about the event. Both king and parliament threatened to break the balance of the constitution by their respective absolutist and republican aims. Since the contest was so equal, interest played no role, but 'men naturally fell to the side which was most conformable to their usual principles'.[63] Hume did not describe Roundhead and Cavalier as extremists but instead argued that neither 'disowned either monarchy or liberty' but simply reflected inclinations.[64] That is how they fitted into his 'general theory' of party: 'they may be considered as court and country-party, enflamed into civil war, by an unhappy concurrence of circumstances, and by the turbulent spirit of the age'.[65] They also fitted the religious aspect of his theory, as the established clergy joined the king's party, and the nonconformists were on parliament's side.

The civil war was fatal to the Cavaliers first, as the king was executed in 1649, and the Roundhead cause second, as the royal family was restored in 1660. According to Hume, however, 'Charles II was not made wiser by the example of his father; but prosecuted the same measures, though at first, with more secrecy and caution'.[66] This seems to have been why new parties arose 'under the appellations of *Whig* and *Tory*, which have continued ever since to confound and distract our government'. It was at this stage that Hume's general theory of party became problematic, as he acknowledged that '[t]o determine the nature of these parties is, perhaps one of the most difficult problems, that can be met with, and is a proof that history may contain questions, as uncertain as any to be found in the most abstract sciences'.[67] At this point in the essay, Hume stayed close to the *Spectator*'s polite prose, when writing that 'we are at a loss to tell the nature, pretensions, and principles of the different factions', even if partisans of both parties were ubiquitous.[68] It remains clear, however, that he took them more seriously than previous essayists, because he proceeded to try and explain these pretensions and principles.

Since Whig and Tory had been preceded by Roundhead and Cavalier, Hume began by comparing them. His first, somewhat surprising and exaggerated, claim was that 'the principles of *passive obedience*, and *indefeasible right*, which were but little heard among the CAVALIERS ... became the universal doctrine ... of a TORY'.[69] Pushed to its extremity, this would imply an absolute as opposed to a limited monarchy, and 'a formal renunciation of all our liberties', since a *limited* monarchy which

---

[63] Ibid.   [64] Ibid., 69.   [65] Ibid.   [66] Ibid.   [67] Ibid.   [68] Ibid., 70.   [69] Ibid.

cannot be resisted would be an absurdity.[70] Quoting Bolingbroke directly for the first time in the essay, Hume added that passive obedience was bizarre enough to disturb the common sense of comparatively uncivilised peoples such as the Samoyedes or the Hottentots.[71] Fortunately, the Tories never carried this doctrine into practice, for '[t]he TORIES, as men, were enemies to oppression; and also as ENGLISHMEN, they were enemies to arbitrary power'.[72] They may not have been as zealous for liberty as their antagonists, but were sufficiently flexible to forget about passive obedience and indefeasible right 'when they saw themselves openly threatened with a subversion of the ancient government'.[73] Hume here referred to the alleged attempts by James II/VII to impose a form of absolutism, which prompted the invitation of William of Orange by the 'immortal seven' and the Glorious Revolution.

From the Revolution, 'the firmest foundation of BRITISH liberty' as Hume described it in this early essay, a great deal could be learned about the Tories. The Revolution showed that the Tories were 'a genuine *court-party*, such as might be expected in a BRITISH government'. In other words, while attached to monarchy they were also attached to liberty.[74] Hume is here highly critical of the Tories, as he believed that they 'carried their monarchical principles further, even in practice, but more so in theory, than was, in any degree, consistent with a limited government'.[75] However, while they may have been doubted before the Revolution, their active part in it seems to have vindicated them in Hume's eyes.[76]

Hume acknowledged, however, that neither the Revolution nor the Hanoverian Settlement were entirely satisfactory to the Tories, because they were at odds with their principles of passive obedience and indefeasible hereditary right, as well as their affections for the Stuart family. They compromised because 'any other settlement . . . must have been dangerous, if not fatal to liberty'. On this basis, Hume arrived at a general definition of a Tory since the Glorious Revolution as 'a lover of monarchy, though without abandoning liberty; and a partizan of the family of STUART'. From this he also derived his definition of a Whig as 'a lover of liberty

---

[70] Ibid.   [71] Ibid., 70, 611; Bolingbroke, *Dissertation upon Parties*, in *Political Writings*, 15.

[72] Hume, 'Parties of Great Britain', *Essays*, 70. Hume was closely following Rapin at this point; see Rapin, *Dissertation*, 49.

[73] Hume, 'Parties of Great Britain', *Essays*, 70. Hume would put more emphasis on religion in his account of the same episode in his *History*.

[74] Ibid., 71.   [75] Ibid.

[76] At least two of the 'immortal seven' (Danby and Compton) have generally been considered as Tories.

though without renouncing monarchy; and a friend to the settlement in the PROTESTANT line'.[77] The parties were different in degree rather than kind.

At this stage Hume signalled his main disagreement with Bolingbroke, who had argued that the real difference between Whig and Tory had disappeared after the Revolution. If Bolingbroke were right, it 'would turn our whole history into an ænigma', Hume said, and, in the 1741 and 1742 editions of the essay, he added that it was also 'so contrary to the strongest Evidence, that a Man must have a great Opinion of his own Eloquence to attempt proving it'.[78] A crucial piece of evidence for the continuing existence of the Tory party was their Jacobitism: '[h]ave not the TORIES always borne an avowed affection to the family of Stuart, and have not their adversaries always opposed with vigour the succession of that family?'[79] How could Hume be so confident that the Tories were, at heart, Jacobite? As Walpole, convinced of the reality of the Jacobite threat,[80] put it, '[n]o man of common prudence will profess himself openly a Jacobite', as doing so was not only treason and carried the death penalty, but could also hurt the cause.[81] In the earlier paper war, Bolingbroke had denied the prominence of Jacobitism as much as the ministerial press had warned about it.[82] In parliament, Walpole identified it as the top threat while William Wyndham of the Hanoverian Tories – although he himself had a Jacobite past – said it was merely a ghost haunting the Court Whigs.[83] Without hard evidence, Hume had to make a judgement call. Jacobitism was simply the only thing that could explain why the Tories, whose principles were more favourable to monarchy, had been hostile to all monarchs since the Revolution with the exception of Anne, who was both a Stuart and a devout Anglican, and selected a Tory

---

[77] Ibid.

[78] Hume, 'Parties of Great Britain', *Essays*, 611–12 (variant readings). Hume expressed his admiration for Bolingbroke's 'genius for oratory' twice in the original version of 'Of Eloquence' (1742). In the edition of the essay published in *Essays and Treatises on Several Subjects* (4 vols., 1753–4), he added that Bolingbroke's works contained 'defects in argument, method and precision'; see *Essays*, 621, 622 (variant readings).

[79] Hume, 'Parties of Great Britain', *Essays*, 612 (variant readings).

[80] Fritz, 'The Anti-Jacobite Intelligence System of the English Ministers, 1715–45', *HJ*, 16 (1973), 265–89.

[81] *Commons, 1715–54*, I, 68–9.

[82] The ministerial press continued to warn about Jacobitism after Bolingbroke's second exile; see *Daily Gazetteer*, No. 883, 4 May 1738.

[83] *Parl. Hist.*, X, 445.

administration in 1710–14.[84] In other words, during the reign of Anne, affection, principle, and interest coalesced for the Tories. During his stay in London, Hume may also have been convinced of the prominence of Jacobitism among Tories by members of the Marchmont family, the powerful Scottish Whig political dynasty, with whom Hume was on familiar terms and indeed distantly related.[85] The Marchmonts were in opposition to Walpole and remained in opposition until coming to terms with Pelham in 1747.

Hume recognised that 'the TORY party seem, of late, to have decayed much in their numbers; still more in their zeal; and I may venture to stay, still more in their credit and authority'.[86] Most educated people and at least most philosophers since the time of John Locke[87] would be ashamed to be associated with the Tory party, he argued. By contrast, 'in almost all companies the name of OLD WHIG is mentioned as an uncontestable [*sic*] appellation of honour and dignity'.[88] That is why some members of the opposition referred to the courtiers as true Tories and themselves true Whigs.[89] Hume was fully aware, however, that the Tories had a power base which was more consistent and reliable than Jacobitism: High Church Anglicanism. The popularity of journals such as *Mist's Weekly Journal* (1716–28) and *Fog's Weekly Journal* (1728–37), which differed widely from Bolingbroke's *Craftsman* in their attitude to Protestant Dissenters, demonstrates the ubiquity of this tradition, which was linked to royalism in general and Jacobitism in particular, even if the latter association was veiled.[90] Hume was by no means saying that Toryism

[84] Hume, 'Parties of Great Britain', *Essays*, 612 (variant readings). Unlike Bolingbroke, Hume did refer directly to proscription.

[85] Hume, 'My Own Life', *Essays*, xxxii; Hume to George Carre of Nisbet, 12 November 1739, *Letters*, I, 36.

[86] Hume, 'Parties of Great Britain', *Essays*, 614 (variant readings).

[87] Locke was clearly seen as a Whig hero at this stage; see, e.g., *Craftsman*, No. 540, 6 November 1736.

[88] Hume, 'Parties of Great Britain', *Essays*, 614 (variant readings).

[89] A writer in the *Craftsman* described himself as 'a Whig after the old fashion'. *Craftsman*, No. 512, 24 April 1736.

[90] These journals had Jacobite links, but their clericalism could be expressed more openly. For the relationship between High Church and Jacobitism, see Sharp, '"Our Church"', *Royal Stuart Papers*, 57 (2000), 1–21; Black, 'An Underrated Journalist: Nathaniel Mist and the Opposition Press during the Whig Ascendency', *ECS*, 10 (1987), 27–41. Few contemporaries would have doubted the Jacobite sympathies of *Fog's*. In August 1729 it devoted the weekly issue to a eulogy of the Stuart family, opening with a complaint against Whig 'Rancour ... against the *Royal Family* of the STUARTS ... abusing and insulting the *Memories* of the best-natured PRINCES that have set upon any throne in *Europe*'. With a clear reference to the Hanoverians, the journal applauded Charles II, who truly merited the title of '*Father of his People*' for making '*no Demands upon his People for Deficiencies in his* CIVIL LIST'. *Fog's Journal*, 16 August 1729.

had become irrelevant; if that was what he thought then he would not have treated it so seriously.[91] Hume was clear that '[t]here are . . . very considerable remains of that party in ENGLAND, with all their old prejudices'.[92]

While Hume believed that the Whig–Tory dichotomy was real in the 1740s, he was fully aware that the fact that the Whigs had become a Court party, and many Tories resorted to Country party politics, caused problems for his general theory. ''Tis monstrous to see an established episcopal clergy in declared opposition to the court, and a non-conformist presbyterian clergy in conjunction with it', he wrote.[93] The only thing that could have produced 'such an unnatural conduct in both', was that 'the former espoused monarchical principles too high for the present settlement, which is founded on the principles of liberty: And the latter, being afraid of the prevalence of those high principles, adhered to that party from whom they had reason to expect liberty and toleration'.[94] As we have seen, Bolingbroke knew that he had to win over the sizeable voting bloc of Dissenters to create a viable Country party that could unite opposition Whigs and Tories. As noted, however, in 1736 the opposition split along Whig and Tory, or Low and High Church, and Gibson and Walpole fell out,[95] dealing a blow to Bolingbroke's hopes for such a union, at least for the time being.

The most important evidence for Hume showing that the British party division had not turned into Court and Country was that almost all Dissenters sided with the Court, that is to say, the Whigs, and all the lower clergy of the Church of England (and the non-jurors)[96] with the opposition and the Tories. 'This may convince us, that some biass [sic] still hangs upon our constitution, some extrinsic weight, which turns it from its natural course, and causes a confusion in our parties', Hume concluded.[97] The extrinsic weight was religion, which Hume would analyse in greater detail in 'Superstition and Enthusiasm' (1741) as well as his *History*.

In a passage indicative of Rapin's influence, Hume argued briefly that foreign policy differentiated the two parties, as he saw France as the natural ally of the Tories and Holland the natural ally of the Whigs.[98] Indeed,

---

[91] Modern research has indeed shown that the Tory party remained buoyant in parliament long after the Hanoverian Succession; see Colley, *In Defiance of Oligarchy* (Cambridge, 1982); *Tory and Whig*, xxvii–lix.

[92] Hume, 'Parties of Great Britain', *Essays*, 72.

[93] Hume, 'Parties of Great Britain', *Essays*, 612 (variant readings).   [94] Ibid.

[95] See note 3 in this chapter.

[96] Although non-jurors did not attend public churches, they regarded themselves as the 'true Church of England'. *Hearne's Recollections*, XI, 131, 212.

[97] Hume, 'Parties of Great Britain', *Essays*, 72.   [98] Ibid., 612 (variant readings).

Whig pamphlets from the War of the Spanish Succession to War of the Austrian Succession had argued that opposition to France was the *only* real criterion of Whiggism.[99] France was indeed the country where James II/ VII had first gone into exile, and where the Jacobite court had been located until it moved in 1713. France remained a hotspot for Jacobites, however, and the French government continued to support Jacobitism periodically.[100] Such well-known Jacobite writers as the Chevalier Ramsay and Nathaniel Hooke were given titles and jobs by the French court. France was also the country to where many Jacobite conspirators fled, including Francis Atterbury and Nathaniel Mist. Holland was the native land of William III/II, and also a commercial republic, with which many Whigs would naturally sympathise. Once again, the ascendency of Walpole had produced a change in this respect. While foreign policy was not Walpole's main area of interest, at least not before the dismissal of Townsend in 1730, the initial focus of his foreign policy had been friendship with France.[101] This friendship was increasingly strained after 1731, however, and by the time Hume's essay was published the two countries were on opposite sides in the Anglo-Spanish conflict, the 'War of Jenkins' Ear' (1739–48), as France was allied with Spain. Yet the passage on foreign policy looked rather out of place in the essay, and seems like it could have been taken from, and was more suitable to the period of, Rapin's *Dissertation*, where the Frenchman had gone into more detail to make the same point.

In the last pages of the essay, Hume returned to the dynastic question, re-emphasising that this was the main dividing line between the parties. Importantly, however, the Whigs were attached to the Hanoverian succession only as a means to support liberty. He acknowledged that the Whig government may have taken steps inimical to liberty,[102] but only in the belief that this would support the present royal family and thus liberty, since the Stuarts posed a threat to the Revolution Settlement. He then continued, with a nod to his preceding essay 'Of Parties in General', to argue that the Tories' attachment to the Stuarts was based on affection.[103]

---

[99] *The Whigs Appeal to the Tories in a Letter to Sir T[homas] H[anmer]* (London, 1711), 2–3. In Chapter 5 we consider Perceval, *Faction Detected* (London, 1743), covering the later period.

[100] Szechi, *The Jacobites* (Manchester, 1994), 90–104.

[101] The death of Louis XIV in 1715 and the Anglo–French alliance in 1716–31 kept the Jacobite court south of the Alps.

[102] He probably referred to such common oppositional complaints as the Septennial Act 1716, the question of influence (see below), and borrowing (see 'Of Public Credit' from 1752).

[103] Hume, 'Parties of Great Britain', *Essays*, 614 (variant readings).

The conclusion that Hume kept in the last edition of the essay simply stated that the Tories had 'so long [been] obliged to talk in the republican stile, that they seem to have been made converts of themselves by their hypocrisy'.[104] What did it mean to talk in the republican style? In its simplest form, it meant that the Tories had sided with the people versus the Court, as they had been in opposition. Yet Hume may have had a more specific political programme in mind.

As Montesquieu had done when visiting England, Hume may have attended parliament and perhaps the debate about the King's Speech at the opening of the new session of parliament on 24 January 1738, since he was in London at the time and, we can safely assume, deeply immersed in the study of British politics.[105] In that debate, the leading Tory-Jacobite Watkin Williams Wynn attacked Walpole's ministry for curtailing freedom of speech,[106] allowing public debt to rise, and corrupting parliament and the people, while stressing the importance of the 'the preservation of our excellent constitution'.[107] When the reduction of the standing army was debated on 3 February 1738, William Shippen, another leading Tory-Jacobite, said that the maintenance of the standing army 'produces but one single good, which is security of the [Whig] administration'.[108] By 'the republican stile', Hume may have meant that Wynn, Shippen, and other Tories had adopted the Country party rhetoric. This tactic, which had been Whig at the time of the Exclusion Crisis and then viewed by Tories as quasi-republican, was recommended by Bolingbroke, and had been staple Tory rhetoric since the beginning of the eighteenth century.

In the conclusion of the various editions of the essay prior to 1770, Hume turned to his native Scotland, arguing that there were never any

---

[104] Ibid., 72.

[105] Hume's essay 'Of Eloquence' suggests that he had attended parliamentary debates. Even if he did not attend these particular debates in person, these and other debates would have been discussed in London circles at the time. During his 1737–9 stay in London, Hume was acquainted with certain Scottish members of parliament, notably the Marchmont family (see note 85 in this chapter). From the early 1740s, some of his friends sat in the Commons, e.g., William Mure and James Oswald. Moreover, although direct parliamentary reporting was not allowed until 1771, Johnson satirised parliamentary debates ('the senate of Lilliput'), or reported during recess, in the *Gentlemen's Magazine* from the mid-1730s, to circumvent the laws. We also know that Hume later frequented the Commons. Hume to William Robertson, *Letters*, I, 300.

[106] Wynn referred to the censorship of stage plays and parliamentary reporting, issues which may well have occasioned Hume's essay 'Of the Liberty of the Press' (1741). The Licensing Act 1737 placed control of censorship under the Lord Chamberlain. The first play to be banned under the new legislation was *Gustavus Vasa* by Henry Brooke. What is more, a Commons resolution on 13 April 1738 ruled parliamentary reporting to be illicit. *Parl. Hist.*, X, 800.

[107] Ibid., 371–2.   [108] Ibid., 380.

Tories in that country but only Whigs and Jacobites.[109] An outright Jacobite differed from a Tory by having 'no regard to the constitution, but is either a zealous partizan of absolute monarchy, or at least willing to sacrifice our liberties to the obtaining the succession in that family to which he is attached'.[110] We have seen that the Tories were not prepared to push things to that extreme. The reason behind the difference was that the political and religious divisions corresponded to each other in Scotland unlike in England. All Presbyterians were Whigs and all Episcopalians were Jacobites in Scotland. Since the governance of the Presbyterian Church had been decided at the Williamite Revolution, Scottish Anglicans had no motivation to swear oaths to William III/II.[111] The Jacobites had thus been more violent in Scotland than their Tory 'brethren' in England, wrote Hume, with a reference to the rebellion of 1715, which had been centred on Scotland.

Writing in 1741, Hume believed that the Jacobite party was almost entirely extinguished in Scotland, and that 'the Distinction of *Court* and *Country*, which is but creeping in at LONDON, is the only one that is ever mention'd in this *kingdom*'.[112] At least this was the message Hume wanted to convey to his London readers, because Jacobitism remained important in eighteenth-century Scotland, even in the lowlands. A humorous unpublished pamphlet from 1744 divided Edinburgh's 'ladies' fairly evenly into Jacobites and Whigs (despite its title).[113] In Edinburgh in the first half of the eighteenth-century, the quasi-Jacobite *Caledonian Mercury*, printed by Thomas Ruddiman, competed with the

[109] The same argument was made by Cleghorn (chosen for the moral philosophy chair at Edinburgh ahead of Hume in 1745) in *The Spirit and Principles of the Whigs and Jacobites Compared* (London, 1746), and Reid, invoking Cleghorn, in his *Lectures on Politics* (1765–6); see *Reid on Society and Politics* (Edinburgh, 2015), 50.
[110] Hume, 'Parties of Great Britain', *Essays*, 615 (variant readings). In other words, they were either infatuated with principle or affection.
[111] In 1712, under Queen Anne, these non-jurors formed the Scottish Episcopal Church, but the split had taken place after the Revolution when the episcopal, or Anglican, segment of the Kirk were unwilling to swear allegiance to William and Mary, and became exterior to the state-church, which from then on became wholly Presbyterian. According to modern scholarship, it was the Jacobitism of the Scottish bishops that motivated William of Orange to break their control and hand it over to the Presbyterians instead; see Lenman, 'The Scottish Episcopal Clergy and the Ideology of Jacobitism', in *Ideology and Conspiracy* (Edinburgh, 1982), 39. As Lenman put it, 'A Scots episcopalian was, in some cases until Prince Charles died in 1788, more often than not a Jacobite at heart' (46).
[112] Hume, 'Parties of Great Britain', *Essays*, 616 (variant readings).
[113] *An Impartial and Genuine List of the Ladys on the Whig ... or ... Jacobite Partie. Taken in hand merely to show that the Common Accusation and Slander, Rashly Thrown on the ... Female ... Sex. As to their being all Jacobites is False and Groundless. As upon a Calculation the Whigs are Far Superior in numbers and not inferior either in Rank, Beauty or Sollidity.* NLS MS 293, ff. 1–5.

Whig *Evening Courant*. The former reported enthusiastically about the Jacobite advances during the 'Forty-five'. After the Jacobite takeover of Edinburgh in September 1745, it was reported that 'All the publick Offices continue their Business, nor is any Person molested or injured in Person or Property'.[114] It also assisted the Jacobite propaganda campaign by printing Charles Stuart's proclamations and reviving the controversy of the Glencoe Massacre of 1692.[115] The 'unhappy troubles'[116] of the 'Forty-five' would prove Hume badly wrong, and his reflections about the decline of Jacobitism in Scotland naturally did not survive in the third edition of the *Essays*, published in 1748. We return to the question of Jacobitism in Scotland in Chapter 6.

The main point Hume promoted in the conclusion of the original essay was the distinction between Court, representing monarchy, and Country, representing liberty, with which he had begun the essay. This conclusion brings Hume closer to the person who is usually seen as his *bête-noire*, namely Bolingbroke. It is important to stress, however, that Hume was, and viewed himself as, making a very different argument from Bolingbroke, whom he believed was disingenuously arguing that Tory and Whig had disappeared when everyone could see that they had not. Convinced of the danger of religious principles, it should not surprise us that Hume was willing to promote a Court–Country polarity. As we have seen, however, religion prevented the disappearance of Whig and Tory.

Superstition and Enthusiasm

Hume's two essays on party are immediately followed by 'Of Superstition and Enthusiasm', which, as Pocock has pointed out, 'offers to explain the reasons why an unnatural bias or extrinsic weight still hangs upon the British constitution'.[117] Together they form a trilogy as all essays deal with the genesis of the British party division. More broadly, Hume attempted in this essay to explain the impact of the 'two species of false religion', superstition and enthusiasm, defined as excessive fear and hope respectively, on government and society.[118] The two sentiments were opposite in

---

[114] *The Caledonian Mercury*, Edinburgh 18 September 1745, No. 3891. Aberdeen University Library, MacBean Collection.

[115] See, e.g., 7 October 1745, No. 3898; 9 October 1745, No. 3899; 14 October 1745, No. 3901; 16 October 1745, No. 3902.

[116] Hume to Sir James Johnstone, 19 September 1745, *Letters*, I, 63.

[117] Pocock, *Barbarism and Religion* (6 vols., Cambridge, 1999–2015), II, 193.

[118] Hume, 'Superstition and Enthusiasm', *Essays*, 73, 75.

the sense that superstition had a bias towards priestly power whereas enthusiasm was a friend of civil liberty. The most extreme kind of superstition was 'popery', but Hume was clear that it also applied to the Church of England with its 'Propensity to Priestly Power and Dominion'.[119] The most extreme forms of enthusiasm were the various Protestant sects that had rebelled against the king in the Wars of the Three Kingdoms, including the Presbyterians in Scotland. In that conflict, superstition had prevailed within the royalist and Church party, or the Cavaliers, and enthusiasm within their antagonists, the parliamentary party, or the Roundheads.

Since the origin of Whig and Tory, the leaders of the Whigs had either been deists or moderate Anglicans, who were 'friends to toleration, and indifferent to any particular sects of *christians*'.[120] For that reason, the various Protestant sects 'who have all a strong tincture of enthusiasm, concurred with that party [the Whigs], in defence of civil liberty'.[121] Hume believed that the 'tolerating spirit' of the Whigs had led to a rapprochement between that party and the Catholics, who had previously been united with 'high-church *tories* ... in support of prerogative and kingly power'.[122] This was especially the case at the inception of the party appellations, during the Exclusion Crisis of 1679–81, when those called Whigs sought to exclude the Duke of York from the succession to the throne due to his Catholicism, while those called Tories defended the royal succession.[123]

The main conflict when Hume wrote this essay, however, was not between prerogative and privilege, but between High Church, on the one hand, and Low Church and Dissenters, on the other (and Episcopalians and Presbyterians in Scotland). Rather than trying to make a point about Protestantism versus Catholicism, it is possible that Hume's main intention was to point to the importance of this tripartite division within Protestantism, which was more relevant in the British context. The gulf between High Church and Dissenters helped explain why the Tory and Whig parties had survived. Religious beliefs would trump political considerations for those disposed to either superstition or enthusiasm. The High Church Tories opposed the Whigs because they believed that the Church was undermined by the Dissenting interest. The key slogan of the Tory party in the first age of party had been 'the Church is in danger', as we saw in Chapter 2. Once the Tories formed the government

---

[119] Ibid., 617 (variant readings).   [120] Ibid., 79.   [121] Ibid.   [122] Ibid.
[123] This episode will be dealt with in greater detail in Chapter 7.

in 1710–14, their main reforms were against Dissenters, including the Occasional Conformity and Schism Acts, both of which were repealed by the Sunderland–Stanhope Whig government in 1718 and 1719. While the Whigs managed to build up a strong power base among bishops after 1714, and in particular under Walpole, most of the lower clergy remained Tory.

These ecclesiastical divisions help to explain the political situation in Britain in the early Hanoverian period, when the Court party was made up of Whigs and the Country party predominantly of Tories, and were a strong reason why the latter could not support the Court. This may have been 'unnatural' as the Whigs were the party of civil liberty and the Tories the party of royal power, but their respective policies vis-à-vis Protestant Dissenters explain why this division endured. They also shed light on what Hume meant when he said that even if the Tories had long talked in the republican style, a considerable chunk of 'that party in ENGLAND, with all their old prejudices' remained. As the rift over the Mortmain and Quakers' Tithe Bills in 1736 demonstrated, religion continued to separate opposition Whigs and Tories.

Party Politics at the End of the Walpole Era

Hume's claim that Whig and Tory still mattered may have placed him in the Whig camp,[124] but it did not necessarily make him a government supporter.[125] The local nature of Hume's self-labelling as a sceptical Whig is discussed in Chapter 6. Many have attempted to portray him as a supporter of the Court Whig government, or at least an exponent of establishment Whiggism.[126] His early essays, however, especially 'A Character of Sir Robert Walpole' (1742), gave an ambivalent impression.[127] As M.M. Goldsmith has pointed out, Hume was received by some as an opposition writer.[128] Moreover, Hume heaped praise over the

---

[124] *Common Sense, or the Englishman's Journal*, 17 July 1737, in vol. I (London, 1737), 172.

[125] As Forbes has remarked, as soon as one has found enough evidence that points in one ideological direction, evidence pointing in the opposite direction, from the same chronological phase, will be found; see *Hume's Philosophical Politics*, 135.

[126] Pocock, *Virtue, Commerce, and History* (Cambridge, 1985), 138, 250; Dickinson, *Liberty and Property*, 132–3.

[127] This essay first appeared in the second volume of *Essays, Moral and Political*, which was published early in 1742 just before the fall of Walpole. Hume then turned it into a footnote to 'That Politics may be reduced to a Science' (1741), before dropping it completely in 1770. Hume's correspondence suggests that he was even more damning of Walpole in private. Hume to Colonel Abercromby, 7 August 1747, *Letters*, I, 103.

[128] Goldsmith, 'Faction Detected', *History*, 64 (1979), 15–16.

giants of the literary opposition, on Swift, Pope, and even, albeit with qualifications, Bolingbroke.[129] While some commentators have endeavoured to classify Hume as either a Whig or a Tory,[130] instead of a philosopher above party as Hume believed himself to be, more recent scholars have rightly pointed out that Hume's main intention in his early essays was to teach lessons of moderation to government and opposition alike.[131] This is the line Hume explicitly took in the original introduction to his essay 'Of the Independency of Parliament' (1741), where he compared the Court and Country parties.[132] Hume began by arguing that he had found the Court party 'less assuming and dogmatical in conversation' than the Country party.[133] He added that this only applied 'to Conversation, and to Gentlemen, who have engag'd by Interest or Inclination in that Party'.[134] The Court party's 'hir'd Scribblers' were 'altogether as scurrilous as the Mercenaries of the other Party', and in that sense the government-funded *Daily Gazetteer* had no advantage over *Common Sense, or the Englishman's Journal* of the opposition.[135] Generally speaking, however, Court politicians were more apt to make concessions than their more zealous adversaries. The opposition would say that their party was founded on public spirit and that they could not endure any doctrines pernicious to liberty. The Court would refer to Shaftesbury's description of a clown who could not support his cause by arguments and instead became violent.[136]

Characteristically, Hume contended that we should believe neither opinion.[137] Instead, Hume thought that he could explain the difference in conduct between Court and Country without offending either side. He argued that Country had usually been 'the most popular' party, in both

---

[129] Hume, 'Civil Liberty', *Essays*, 91; Hume, 'Eloquence', *Essays*, 99, 108. Although he was not impressed by his philosophy, he kept using Bolingbroke, along with Pope, as a reference for style. Hume to Andrew Millar, 20 June 1758, *Letters*, I, 282–3.

[130] Conniff, 'Hume on Political Parties: The Case for Hume as a Whig', *ECS*, 12 (1978–9), 150–73; Grene, 'Hume: Sceptic and Tory?', *Journal of the History of Ideas*, 4 (1943), 333–48.

[131] Harris, *David Hume* (Cambridge, 2015); Wulf, 'The Skeptical Life in Hume's Political Thought', *Polity*, 33 (2000), 89–94.

[132] This introduction was removed after 1760, and is overlooked by Goldsmith (see note 128 in this chapter).

[133] Hume, 'Independency of Parliament', *Essays*, 607 (variant readings).   [134] Ibid., 608.

[135] Ibid., 608–9. The *Daily Gazetteer* was a Walpole-funded newspaper where Ralph Courteville, under the pseudonym of Algernon Sidney, was the main writer. For the latter journal, see Hilton Jones, 'The Jacobites, Charles Molloy, and *Common Sense*', *The Review of English Studies*, 4 (1953), 144–7. For a contemporary assessment of party writers, from a ministerial point of view, see *An Historical View of the Principles, Characters, Persons, &c of the Political Writers in Great Britain* (London, 1740).

[136] Shaftesbury, *Characteristicks of Men, Manners, Opinions, Times* (3 vols., Indianapolis, 2011 [1711]), III, 67.

[137] Hume, 'Independency of Parliament', *Essays*, 608 (variant readings).

senses of the word. Since they were used to prevailing in public debates, they became overconfident in their opinions and could not stand being challenged. The Court party, however, was so accustomed to being 'run down by popular talkers' that they were always surprised when met with moderate arguments and concessions, and would then return like for like. Hume expanded this thought into a general observation: 'In all controversies, we find, without regarding the truth or falshood [*sic*] on either side, that those who defend the established and popular opinions, are always the most dogmatical and imperious in their stile.'[138] That is why the religious freethinkers,[139] who 'oppose the exorbitant power of the clergy', were more moderate and good-mannered compared to 'the furious zeal and scurrility of their adversaries'.[140] Similarly, in relation to the ancient–modern debate in France at the beginning of the century, Hume believed that those making the case for modern learning, the less popular side, 'never transgressed the bounds of moderation and good breeding', in stark contrast to those in favour of the ancients. In both controversies, there is little doubt that Hume was on the side of gentlemanly moderation in opposition to what he saw as popular cant.[141] Religious freethinking was a minority, elite movement at this time, unlike High Church Anglicanism, which is why Cruickshanks may not be wide of the mark when remarking that the Tories would have won every election between 1715 and 1745 if the voting system had been more proportional, as they tended to represent counties and larger constituencies.[142]

Hume went on to consider one of the most heated party-political disputes of his time, that of influence (or corruption) of parliament. As we have seen, this had been integral to Bolingbroke's attack on Walpole's government. Hume followed the Court position in arguing that such influence, as long as it was confined to offices and honours as opposed to outright bribes, actually helped to maintain the balance of the mixed constitution. Hume had already established in 'Of the Liberty of the Press' (1741) that liberty, or parliament, as opposed to authority, or monarchy, predominated in the British constitution, which he emphasised again in 'The Independency of Parliament'.[143] Fortunately, the crown's patronage

---

[138] Ibid.

[139] Hume listed the deists Anthony Collins and Matthew Tindal, and such freethinking clergymen as Benjamin Hoadly and James Forster.

[140] Hume, 'Independency of Parliament', *Essays*, 608 (variant readings).

[141] For Hume as a 'modern', see Harris, *Hume*, 186–95, 284–5.

[142] Cruickshanks, *Political Untouchables*, 5. See also Colley, *In Defiance of Oligarchy*, 296.

[143] Hume, 'Liberty of the Press', *Essays*, 11–12.

prevented the body of the Commons from scuppering the entire constitution, by appealing to the self-interest of individual members.[144] Rather
than attacking this type of influence, 'the country-party should have made
some concessions to their adversaries, and have only examined what was
the proper degree of this dependency, beyond which it became dangerous
liberty'.[145] This essay is sometimes read as Hume inventing a new type of
justification, a 'Humean' defence, of crown influence. We have long
known, however, that he simply adopted a familiar Court Whig argument,
which he applied with more panache than his predecessors.[146] The essay,
especially in its original form and context, was meant as a case study of the
excesses of party-political debate to demonstrate that 'moderation is not to
be expected in party-men of any kind'.[147]

The essay on the independence of parliament can helpfully be read in
conjunction with 'Whether the British Government Inclines More to
Absolute Monarchy, or to a Republic', which immediately followed. If
Hume came across as a Court Whig in the former essay, the latter essay,
which was reprinted in the *Craftsman*, gave the opposite impression. In
this essay he established, somewhat contrary to elsewhere in his early
essays, that Britain inclined more to absolute monarchy than a republic.
Hume did so by following the Harringtonian argument that power follows
property, but amending it by saying that less property in a single hand
could counterbalance more property in several hands. In other words, the
king could use the size of the civil list of £1 million per annum, along with
an additional £2 million from taxes and funds to pay for salaries in the
army, navy, and the church, to create dependencies, even if the Commons
had a greater annual income in total.[148] It is not odd that the opposition
found this essay palatable; in the same essay Hume reported arguments
against luxury, corruption, and the standing army.[149] It is evident, however, that Hume attempted to strike a balance between the two sides,
highlighting that while all these things may have been dangerous in a
usurped power, the same cannot be said for a 'legal authority' with
limitations.[150] Moreover, due to 'a sudden and sensible change in the
opinions of men within the last fifty years ... Most people ... ha[d]

---

[144] Hume, 'Independency of Parliament', *Essays*, 45.   [145] Ibid.
[146] Kramnick, *Bolingbroke and his Circle*, 123–4.
[147] Hume, 'Independency of Parliament', *Essays*, 45.
[148] Hume, 'British Government', *Essays*, 47–9.
[149] For Hume on the standing army, see Robertson, *The Scottish Enlightenment and the Militia Issue*
(Edinburgh, 1985), 60–97.
[150] Hume, 'British Government', *Essays*, 50.

divested themselves of all superstitious reverence to names and author-ity'.[151] Accordingly, the clergy's 'talk of a king as GOD's vicegerent on earth ... would but excite laughter in every one'.[152] This may have been out of hope as much as belief, however, and in any event he would come to revise this statement after the 'Forty-five', as we shall see in Chapter 6.

Hume agreed with the Country party that 'the power of the crown, by means of its large revenue, is rather upon the encrease [sic]'.[153] This may seem paradoxical seeing what Hume had just said about people's opinion about monarchy. There was little doubt, however, that the revenue of the crown had inflated in recent years. Upon the accession of George II in 1727, after he had hinted at a change of government, Walpole managed to double the size of the civil list and ensured an extra £100,000 for his close ally Queen Caroline.[154] It is less clear why the remainder of the essay would have pleased the readers of the *Craftsman* journal. Since no states last forever, Hume speculated that absolute monarchy would be the preferable '*Euthanasia*' rather than a republic. An imagined ideal republic would have been preferable still, but that was not something Britain could hope for. The example of Oliver Cromwell's dictatorship of the previous century was a more likely outcome, according to Hume. If the House of Commons ever dissolved itself in such a scenario, each election would lead to a civil war. If it maintained itself, 'we shall suffer all the tyranny of a *faction*, subdivided into new factions'.[155] In the end, an absolute monarchy would have to be set up to re-establish order. Britain could therefore avoid many convulsions and civil wars by establishing an absolute monarchy from the start. The takeaway point, however, should not be that Hume was recommending either form of government. Rather, the intention was, as ever, to 'teach us a lesson of moderation in all our political controver-sies'.[156] Put differently, Hume was seeking to steer a course between Court and Country.

Hume believed that disagreements between the Court and Country parties in the Walpole period were on many issues not as significant as both sides pretended. The upshot was that the debate became 'a very frivolous one, and can never be brought to any decision, as it is managed by both parties'.[157] The solution was not to abolish parties, however. The conclusion of one of his most famous essays, 'That Politics May Be Reduced to a Science' (1741), was also intended as a lesson of moderation

---

[151] Ibid., 51.   [152] Ibid.   [153] Ibid.
[154] Langford, *A Polite and Commercial People* (Oxford, 1989), 15.
[155] Hume, 'British Government', *Essays*, 52. (My emphasis.)   [156] Ibid., 53.   [157] Ibid.

for government as well as opposition. Towards the end of the essay, after Hume had established that constitutional design mattered more than personnel in free/mixed governments, he proceeded to direct his attention to the Court and Country parties. Although the parties were united in extolling the British constitution as the envy of the world, those in opposition to Walpole 'carr[ied] matters to an extreme', Hume complained, and accused the minister not just of 'mal-administration' but also of 'undermining the best constitution in the world'.[158] On the other hand, others defended Walpole just as excessively, and praised him for 'a religious [i.e. strict] care of the best constitution in the world'.[159] Hume contended that the arguments of the accusers *and* the defenders were at variance with their hostility to each other: if the constitution was so excellent, 'it would never have suffered a wicked and weak minister to govern triumphantly for a course of twenty years, when opposed by the greatest genius in the nation' – including Bolingbroke, Pope, and Swift.[160] If Walpole was as wicked as the opposition claimed, the constitution must be faulty if it allowed him to remain in office, since a 'constitution is only so far good, as it provides a remedy against mal-administration'.[161] Likewise, if the constitution was as good as the government held, '[t]hen a change of ministry can be no such dreadful event'.[162]

Hume was careful to underline that he did not wish to argue 'that public affairs deserve no care and attention at all'.[163] But he wanted to 'persuade men not to contend, as if they were fighting *pro aris & focis* [for God and Country, or, literally, for altars and hearths], and change a good constitution into a bad one, by the violence of their factions'.[164] In summary, then, Hume was neither arguing against Court and Country distinctions nor party per se. These constitutional debates that divided people along Court and Country lines were different from the Whig–Tory dichotomy in that, as long as they were kept within certain bounds, they did not pose an existential threat to the constitution. Hume realised that it was immensely difficult to define these bounds, but this is exactly what he tried to do in the essays discussed in this section. He wanted to give examples of when both the Court and the Country parties had good arguments, and that is why some essays may seem irreconcilable. The two sides were frequently not as far apart as they purported to be, as on the question of instructions

---

[158] Hume, 'Politics a Science', 27–8.   [159] Ibid., 28.   [160] Ibid., 29.   [161] Ibid.
[162] Ibid., 30.   [163] Ibid.   [164] Ibid., 30–1.

to representatives.[165] The key point he wanted to hammer home was that these debates should be conducted in a civilised manner and not carried to extremes.

Conclusion

Hume occasionally seemed to be as disapproving of parties as Addison had been in the *Spectator*. As he set out in the advertisement to the first edition of *Essays, Moral and Political*, Hume believed that public spirit meant 'bear[ing] an equal Affection to all our Country-Men; not to hate one Half of them, under the Pretext of loving the Whole'.[166] The greatest danger, as he repeatedly stressed, was that honour as a check on behaviour was largely ignored 'when men act in faction'.[167] To partisans, it only mattered to be of service to their own party and to promote the interests of that body. He realised, however, that party was an intrinsic part of the British constitution, as he argued at the beginning of his essay on the British parties. As Pierre Bayle, writing about religious division at the end of the seventeenth century, had put it, perfect unity 'is a thing more to be wish'd than hop'd for'.[168] Hume's intention was thus not to recommend the abolition of parties but simply to 'repress [party rage] as far as possible' and he hoped that his approach would be 'acceptable to the moderate of both Parties; at the same Time, that, perhaps, it may displease the Bigots of both'.[169] Echoing Mandeville, Hume believed 'every man ought to be supposed a knave' in politics.[170] The point of his science of politics was to make it in the interest of even bad people to act for the public good, hence the emphasis on institutions and constitutions that could bring this about.[171]

---

[165] Hume, 'Of the First Principles of Government', *Essays*, 606 (variant readings; this original conclusion was removed in 1770).

[166] Hume, 'Advertisement' (1741), iv–v.

[167] Hume, 'First Principles of Government', *Essays*, 33; Hume, 'Independency of Parliament', *Essays*, 43.

[168] Bayle, *A Philosophical Commentary* (Indianapolis, 2005 [1686–9]), 208. For Hume and Bayle, see Robertson, *The Case for the Enlightenment* (Cambridge, 2005), ch. 6.

[169] Hume, 'Advertisement' (1741), v.

[170] Hume, 'Independency of Parliament', *Essays*, 42. For Mandeville, see Robertson, *The Case for the Enlightenment*, 266. See also Tolonen, *Mandeville and Hume* (Oxford, 2013).

[171] Hume, 'Politics a Science', *Essays*, 16; Hume, *Treatise*, 537; Hume, *Enquiry Concerning Human Understanding* (Oxford, 1975 [1748]), 90. See also Bourke, 'Theory and Practice', in *Political Judgement* (Cambridge, 2009), 73–109. It should be noted that Hume elsewhere stressed that 'the science of politics affords few rules, which will not admit of some exception, and which may not sometimes be controuled by fortune and accident.' See Hume, 'Of the Original Contract', *Essays*, 477.

The Hume that emerges from this investigation is a careful anatomist of politics who analysed parties in a more detached manner than perhaps anyone had done before him. The only one who had come close was Rapin. Hume's rejection of Bolingbroke's analysis, which he viewed as a partisan appeal, did not make him a Court Whig. He was not finished with his analysis of party, however, and would continue this enterprise not only in his *History of Great Britain*, but also in a series of essays on party ideology written in the wake of the 'Forty-five'. Before turning to these endeavours, Chapter 5 briefly focuses on the party-political developments between the fall of Walpole in 1742 and the Jacobite rising of 1745–6.

CHAPTER 5

Faction Detected? Pulteney, Perceval, and the Tories

Let the honest *Whigs* consider, how often their Firmness and good Sense have saved their Country, and whether any thing but Union among themselves can do it now?

John Perceval, *Faction Detected* (1743)

They desire to be called *Whigs*, that they may be thought Friends to Liberty, as the old *Whigs* were; they would have them that oppose them stiled *Tories*, that they may not be thought Friends to Liberty, as they really are.

Anon, *The Desertion Discussed* (1743)

Pulteney's Desertion

The most significant figure in the opposition to Walpole besides Bolingbroke and its parliamentary focal point was William Pulteney. According to Shelburne, Pulteney was 'by all accounts the greatest House of Commons orator that had ever appeared', but alas 'he never did any good nor attempted any' in his 'long opposition'.[1] Pulteney had once been one of Walpole's allies when they went into opposition together in the Whig schism of 1717.[2] They fell out quickly, however, because Pulteney at this stage was against cooperation with the Tories in opposition.[3] When Walpole rose to prominence, he left Pulteney in the cold. The major rift between the two occurred in 1724, when the Duke of Newcastle rather than Pulteney replaced Carteret as secretary of state for the Southern Department. The following year Pulteney went into open opposition together with his cousin Daniel Pulteney and a splinter group of Whigs.

---

[1] Fitzmaurice, *Life of Shelburne* (3 vols., London, 1875), I, 45.
[2] There is no modern biography of Pulteney. The standard sources for his public life are Coxe, *Memoirs of Walpole* (3 vols., London, 1798), I, 352–66, and Sedgewick's sketch in *Commons, 1715–54*, the latter being largely based on the former, with some modification.
[3] *Commons, 1715–54*, II, 375.

Chesterfield, who joined the opposition to Walpole during the excise crisis, described Pulteney as being driven by 'resentment': 'He had thought himself slighted by Sir Robert Walpole, to whom he publicly avowed not only revenge, but utter destruction.'[4] Perhaps as an act of defiance, Pulteney was alone among the opposition's main speakers to retain his seat on the treasury bench, close to Walpole, throughout his seventeen years in opposition.[5]

The staunch Hanoverian Whig Pulteney united with the erstwhile Jacobite and renegade Tory Bolingbroke in opposition to Walpole.[6] As Walpole had realised in 1717–20, cooperation between Whigs and Tories was necessary for any opposition to be viable due to the numerical strength of the Tories.[7] Upon Bolingbroke's return to England, he was almost immediately rumoured to be 'caballing … with Mr Pulteney',[8] and the *Craftsman* was launched at the end of 1726, as we saw in Chapter 3. It has been argued that the draconian City Elections Act of 1725 had previously paved the way for cooperation between Tories and opposition Whigs.[9] In an unpublished essay, Bolingbroke waxed lyrical about Pulteney: 'The Whigs … owe to him the honour of having kept up & supported the true Spirit & Credit of their Party, whilst so many under that denomination, were prevaild on some how to shew, though to their own dissatisfaction, the utmost passive obedience even to the Ministry.'[10]

Pulteney's involvement with Bolingbroke's Country party platform, whose raison d'être was to unite Tories and Whigs, ended upon the fall of Walpole. Bolingbroke had already begun to feel dissatisfied with

---

[4] *Characters by Chesterfield* (London, 1778), 27. Chesterfield wrote for the oppositional *Common Sense* after 1737, and was often identified as a contributor to the *Craftsman*, although this is unlikely; see Varey, 'Introduction' to Bolingbroke, *Contributions*, xvii. He said he made his portrait of Pulteney 'to the best of my knowledge, from very long acquaintance with, and observation of, the original.' See *Characters by Chesterfield*, 28.

[5] Foord, *His Majesty's Opposition* (Oxford, 1964), 156.

[6] One early mentioning of a meeting between Pulteney and Bolingbroke occurs in an undated letter from Pulteney to George Berkeley: 'Mrs. Pulteney and I propose dining at Cranford to-morrow, and if Lord Bolingbroke is not there, I will wait on him at Dawley.' It is dated as 1730 in *Letters to and from Henrietta, Countess of Suffolk, and George Berkeley* (2 vols., London, 1824), I, 406–7, but this is unlikely considering that Bolingbroke only stayed temporarily at Cranford in 1726–7 when Dawley was being renovated. A much likelier date would be between 14 April and 3 November 1726, due to the context and its place in the manuscript collection. BL Add MS 22628, f. 69.

[7] See, for example, HMC, *Stuart Papers*, IV, 300, 331.

[8] *The Correspondence of Pope* (5 vols., Oxford, 1956), II, 291.

[9] Rogers, *Whigs and Cities* (Oxford, 1989), 41.

[10] Senate House Library MS 533, f. 19. For attribution, see Hone and Skjönsberg, 'On the Character of a "Great Patriot"', *JBS*, 57 (2018), 445–66.

Pulteney towards the end of the 1730s.[11] By then, Pulteney had been dispirited for some time; he wrote to his fellow opposition Whig George Berkeley in November 1735 to admit that 'you may have perceived this resolution arising in me for some years, it is in vain to struggle against universal corruption, and I am quite weary of the opposition'.[12] After Walpole's resignation, Pulteney was seen as abandoning the Tories when he resisted attempts to prosecute Walpole, and accepted a seat in the Lords as the Earl of Bath. Other opposition Whigs, notably Carteret, made the same transition. The ministerial Whig MP William Hay described the transaction as the intention 'to introduce into the Ministry some of the Patriots (as they were now called) whose regard for the Royal Family was as undoubted as their Aversion to the Minister [Walpole]: and to exclude the Tories who were averse to the Hanover Succession at First; and had shewn no regard to the Family since'.[13]

Alexander Pope, who was active in opposition politics at the time, made his discontent clear in a letter of December 1742: 'I am sick of *this* World & the Great ones of it, tho they have been my intimate Acquaintance.'[14] William King wrote in his posthumous anecdotes:

> By his opposition to a mal-administration for near twenty years, he [Pulteney] had contracted an universal esteem, and was considered as the chief bulwark and protector of the British *liberties*. By the fall of WALPOLE, he enjoyed for some days a kind of sovereign power. During this interval, it was expected that he would have formed a patriot ministry, and have put the public affairs in such a train as would necessarily, in a very short time, have repaired all the breaches in our constitution. But how were we deceived! He deserted the cause of his country: he betrayed his friends and adherents: he ruined his character; and from a most glorious eminence sunk down to a degree of contempt.[15]

Bolingbroke was even more distressed. In November 1742 he penned an attack on Bath in the form of an epistle. A version of this text was published in the *Westminster Journal* in 1747 with author, addressee, and Bath's name suppressed.[16] In this epistle Bolingbroke sought to shame Bath for apostasy, reminding him of his previous commitment to the opposition and how he had 'resolutely continued the Battle' after Bolingbroke had retired.[17] He slated him for now adhering to measures that he had formerly opposed, most notably septennial parliaments and the

---

[11] Bolingbroke to Wyndham, 23 July 1739, in Coxe, *Memoirs*, III, 522; Pope to Lyttelton, [*c*.1 November 1738], in *Pope Correspondence*, II, 142.
[12] BL Add MS 22628, f. 73.   [13] *Tory and Whig*, 177.   [14] *Pope Correspondence*, IV, 431.
[15] King, *Anecdotes*, 42–3.   [16] *Unpublished Letters*, V, 276.   [17] Ibid., 274–5.

maintenance of the standing army. The biggest betrayal for Bolingbroke, however, appears to have been Bath's abandonment of the Tories. According to Bolingbroke, one week's conduct had ruined ten years of fame as 'Mr Pulteney was on a sudden against a Coalition of Parties which with me he had so often & often approved Prosecuted & determined to obtain, what could I say but in Imitation of Shakespear Frailty thy name is Man.'[18]

Shelburne later queried Bath on why he had not done more for the public upon the resignation of Walpole, whereupon Bath had answered that 'there was no comprehending or describing the confusion that prevailed' when Walpole resigned, and 'that he had lost his head, and was obliged to go out of town for three or four days to keep his senses'.[19] The only victory Bath could claim was a limited Place Bill, which the Tories described as 'a sham bill'.[20] Bath and Carteret were removed from the government in a reshuffle in 1744. When Walpole as Lord Orford met Bath in the upper chamber he allegedly told his former rival: 'My Lord BATH, you and I are now two as insignificant men as any in England.'[21]

Faction Detected and Leicester House

John Perceval (later the 2nd Earl of Egmont) wrote a notorious pamphlet defending Pulteney/Bath, entitled *Faction Detected by the Evidence of Fact* (1743). Perceval and his father had been in opposition to Walpole since the general elections of 1734, when the son was not elected to the seat of Harwich from which the father retired. Perceval was subsequently elected as an opposition candidate for Westminster in 1741, but *Faction Detected* made him unpopular with the opposition, particularly the Tories, and he lost his seat in 1747. In *Faction Detected*, Perceval distinguished between legitimate and factious opposition, associating the former with Whigs and the latter with Tories and Jacobites.[22]

Perceval began the pamphlet by arguing that opposition was inevitable due to the ambitious and restless nature of human beings, and this was especially the case in trading nations. Opposition could be either 'pernicious' or 'very beneficial', in other words, it could either be opposition or faction.[23] Faction in Britain was of two kinds, either republican or

---

[18] Ibid., 276.   [19] Fitzmaurice, *Life of Shelburne*, I, 46–7.   [20] *Whig and Tory*, 58.
[21] King, *Anecdotes*, 43.
[22] Perceval recognised that not all Tories were Jacobites, but that virtually all Jacobites disguised as Tories, and that the Jacobite leaders often directed duped Tories. *Faction Detected*, 168–9.
[23] Ibid., 7.

Jacobite. Republicanism had brought 'miserable consequences' in England between 1642 and 1660, but it had had been toothless subsequently, since it was 'chiefly confined to Men of an inferior Class'. Moreover, although the republican principle was 'mistaken', it could inspire 'very great and glorious things ... [and] it clashed in its Pursuit, neither with the Honour nor the Independency of their Country'.[24] Jacobitism, however, rested on 'no Principle at all' besides 'the Interest of one Man, and of one Family ... who by their Education and Religion were nourished in a fatal Enmity to their Country'. Because of their association with France and Catholicism, Jacobite opposition 'tended in every Step to destroy the Honour and Independency of their own Country'. Even though 'the two great parties', Whig and Tory, were neither republican nor Jacobite, he argued that the Whigs often joined with the former and the Tories with the latter for reasons that would be evident to anyone acquainted with British history. Accordingly, he contended that '[a] Whig Opposition is ... the only one with which [the people] can *for a Moment* concur safely'.[25]

According to Perceval, both republican and Jacobite oppositions had to mask their true principles since they were generally so detested. For this reason, politicians must be judged 'not upon what Men call themselves, but upon what they do'. Whig and Tory were fundamentally divided over how Britain should relate to the power of France, and how the Protestant interest should be best protected in Europe. For Whigs, the greatest danger came from Catholic France, whereas for Tories Dissenters represented the biggest threat. As he put it: 'the Criterion of a Whig Conduct *is ... to resist and reduce the Power,* and the Criterion of a Jacobite or Tory Faction, *directly or indirectly, to assist, encourage, and support the Interest of* France'.[26] When the opposition to Walpole commenced in the 1720s, there would still be those who would remember how the Tories had obstructed supplies and eventually 'deserted their Allies' as a 'Sacrifice to France', Perceval wrote with reference to the Treaty of Utrecht.[27]

The fault of Walpole was that he had 'neglected Popularity too much, and studied only how to avoid War', with the upshot that 'the two Powers, from whom we have to fear the most, the *French* and the *Spaniards*, play'd him off unmercifully'.[28] A Whig opposition was justified to Walpole, since

[24] Ibid., 8.   [25] Ibid., 9.
[26] Ibid., 10. An unmistakably Tory response to Perceval retorted: 'This exorbitant Power of France has now, more than half a Century, been set up as a Bugbear, wherewith, to frighten this Nation out of its Treasure as well as Senses.' *The Opposition Rescued from the Insolent Attacks of Faction Detected* (London, 1744), 10.
[27] Perceval, *Faction Detected,* 13.   [28] Ibid., 15.

he was neither firm enough against France nor supportive enough of Austria, the natural ally, and in effect carried out a Tory foreign policy.[29] The opposition to Walpole had included Tories, but it had been led by Whigs, Perceval argued, with allusions to Pulteney and Chesterfield.[30] The Tories joined this opposition for opportunistic reasons, and realising the ascendency of Whig principles, they went 'silent upon the Topicks of *Passive Obedience, Non-resistance*, and the *Danger of the Church*'.[31] The removal of Walpole signalled a natural end point of the Whig opposition: 'the plain Origin, and avowed Views of this Opposition, were the Removal of the Minister, and the Change of his Measures'.[32] When this was done, it would have been 'inconsistent with their avowed Professions' to persist in opposition. Those who remained opposed to the government were simply 'a Faction, and that of the most dangerous kind to this Nation'.[33]

The limited nature of Pulteney's Place Bill along with the continued proscription of the Tories – except for Gower – meant that many argued that the measures had not properly changed at all. The author of one of the many attacks on Perceval's pamphlet distinguished between party and faction in a similar way to Bolingbroke:

> A *Party* is, when a great Number of Men join together *in professing a Principle, or Set of Principles*, which they take to be for the *publick Good*, and therefore endeavour to have them established and universally professed among their Countrymen. *Faction* ... is, when a Number of Men unite together *for their own private Advantage*, in order to force themselves into Power, or to continue themselves in Power after they have once got it.

According to this writer, Perceval had been wrong to only focus on opposition: '[f]rom hence one may see, that *a Set of Ministers, or a Prime Minister and his Tools*, may be *a Faction*'; indeed, this was likelier to be the case, since a ministry 'can give *present Rewards*, [an opposition] nothing but *distant Hopes*'.[34] Moreover, this writer agreed with Bolingbroke that the Whigs in government had increased the power of the crown and that '*our Liberties are not a Bit the more secure, because those who formerly called themselves* Whigs *are employed in the Administration*'.[35] Another response to Perceval upheld Bolingbroke's argument that Court and Country had supplanted Whig and Tory, or at least that they should.[36] This pamphlet quoted at length from Bolingbroke's *Final Answer to the Remarks on the Craftsman's Vindication* (1731). A third pamphlet against Perceval had the

---

[29] Ibid., 17.   [30] Ibid., 11.   [31] Ibid., 18.   [32] Ibid., 20.   [33] Ibid., 21.
[34] *The Detector Detected* (London, 1743), 58.   [35] Ibid., 60.
[36] *A Defence of the People* (London, 1744), 13–14.

telling title *Opposition not Faction: Or the Rectitude of the Present Parliamentary Opposition* (1743).

Although Perceval was answered with Bolingbrokean arguments, he had concurred with Bolingbroke that opposition could be legitimate and must be distinguished from faction, even though they may have agreed about little beyond this. Like Walpole, Perceval associated Toryism with Jacobitism and invested Whiggism with a great deal of positive connotation. In the conclusion of *Faction Detected*, he stressed how often the 'Union' and 'firmness' of the 'honest *Whigs*' had saved the country.[37] However, few would have described Perceval's character as firm. Indeed, he made enemies easily and changed sides repeatedly. Upon his death, Horace Walpole described Perceval as 'a man always ambitious, almost always attached to a court, yet, from a singularity in his turn, scarce ever in place'.[38] Like many of such temperament, Perceval became part of the Leicester House opposition to Pelham in the 1740s. Somewhat ironically, in this position he sought the cooperation of Tories, with mixed results. The Tory MP Charles Gray wrote to Perceval (now Egmont) in 1749 of 'the difficulties of carrying on [the present opposition] by reason of the coldness and negligence of some, and the want of confidence and a closer connexion among the rest'. The cloud still hanging over any opposition coalition between Whigs and Tories remained what the latter viewed as Pulteney's betrayal, which, according to Gray, 'troubled the air too so much as that it has quite choked us ever since'. He remained persuaded, however, that Perceval 'in a little time [would] have it in [his] power to do what Lord Bath should have done'. What was needed was a set of agreed guarantees in advance on constitutional questions, and intriguingly the Tory Gray highlighted the need to rationalise the franchise. '[T]he very root of corruption should be struck at, by enabling freeholders of a certain value to vote jointly with the Burghers in every corporation in the country', he argued.[39]

It was not to be. The rather sudden death of Frederick in 1751 put an end to this specific reversionary opposition. This shattered the fortunes of Perceval and others associated with Frederick's court, notably his rival George Bubb Dodington, for the time being. Dodington's diary reveals the importance of the general concept of party to politicians at the time, even if Tory and Whig had started to decrease in importance. After Frederick's death, Dodington was 'persuaded of the necessity of forming

[37] Perceval, *Faction Detected*, 169.   [38] Cited in *Commons, 1754–90*, 266.
[39] *Egmont Papers*, 180–2.

a party, united by constitutional principles', and he made plans with major opposition figures, including the Earls of Shaftesbury and Westmorland.[40] For this group, as with the Bolingbroke–Pulteney opposition, party activity extended beyond parliamentary tactics: '[i]f a party should be formed, then [it was agreed] to fix the subscription for a paper by Mr. [James] Ralph, to be supported by about twenty of us', Dodington wrote.[41] Not much came of this proposed opposition. In 1754, Dodington lost his seat at Bridgwater to his bitter rival Perceval, but he was elected for Weymouth with the support of Newcastle, and is depicted in Hogarth's fourth election painting (Figure 1.4). Eventually both Dodington and Egmont gained government employments. A Leicester House opposition was reignited in 1756 when the future George III reached his maturity, as briefly discussed in Chapter 9.

Transitory Broad-Bottom

As Perceval had pointed out, the opposition Whigs had not quite abandoned all Tories upon the fall of Walpole, but had allegedly 'intend[ed] to have promoted the most moderate of that Party'.[42] Notably, the Tory leader Lord Gower was made Lord Privy Seal in 1742. Linda Colley dates Gower's real defection to 1745 as the Tories wanted someone on the inside in 1742.[43] But there is little doubt that the Whigs sought to break the Tories by poaching Gower and his followers. Chesterfield, now in government, wrote to Newcastle in March 1745: '[p]lease Gower and his detachment, I beseech you; which will at last break the Tory party, so as to make the other part of it absolutely inconsiderable'.[44] According to Johnson, 'Gower forsook the old Jacobite interest'. In his *Dictionary*, Johnson added to the entry for *renegado*, '*Sometimes we say a* GOWER', but the publisher did not print it.[45] Beaufort emerged as Tory leader in the Lords after

---

[40] *The Diary of George Bubb Dodington* (London, third edn., 1785), 107.

[41] Ibid. Ralph had been the chief writer and editor of the Leicester House opposition's paper *The Remembrancer* in 1747–51.

[42] Perceval, *Faction Detected*, 49.

[43] Colley, *In Defiance of Oligarchy* (Cambridge, 1982), 240–1. See also Cruickshanks, 'Tory and Whig "Patriots"', in *Samuel Johnson in Historical Contexts* (London, 2002), 146–68.

[44] Lodge (ed.), *Correspondence of Chesterfield and Newcastle* (London, 1930), 20. The following month he wrote: 'do all that is possible naturally to satisfy the reasonable part of that party [the Tories], and then you may with safety and even with advantage despise the rest.' (Ibid., 44.) At this point, there were an estimated 136 Tories in the Commons; see Owen, *The Rise of the Pelhams* (London, 1957), 66.

[45] Boswell, *The Life of Johnson* (2 vols., London, 1791), I, 164.

Gower's defection; symbolically the former replaced the latter as head of the Tory club the Honourable Brotherhood.[46]

In 1744, when Carteret and Bath were dismissed, a 'broad-bottom' administration entered office, comprising a coalition between Chesterfield, who had remained in opposition up until this point, and Court Whigs such as Pelham, Hardwicke, and Newcastle, the so-called 'Old Corps'. Importantly, a few Tories joined this administration as individuals in lesser positions, including two suspected Jacobites: Sir John Hynde Cotton as treasurer of the Chamber and John Philipps on the Board of Trade.[47] Sir Watkin Williams Wynn, another prominent Tory-Jacobite, declined a peerage but began voting with the government for the first time in his life.[48] As was the case with Pulteney, this was frowned upon among parts of the opposition: if you '[had done] the Nation's Business before you did your own; you [would] have made a true Coalition of Parties, and thereby put an End to Faction', one writer complained.[49]

A pamphleteer, suspected to be Thomas Carte, defended the Tories taking office by contrasting it with Pulteney's 'desertion' in 1742. Rather than abandoning their principles, the Tories only wanted to relieve Britain from a costly land war (the War of the Austrian Succession), and had insisted on the addressal of constitutional grievances, notably the employment of new justices of peace for the counties 'without distinction', in other words, an end to Tory proscription, which was as deeply felt at the local level as nationally.[50] Notably, the same Tory/Country pamphlet encouraged solidarity among the Tories: '[i]f Men break with their Friends, as often as Opinions differ about the Means of attaining the same Ends, no Business will ever be carried into Execution'.[51] The pamphlet sought to turn the many years in the wilderness into a point of strength: '[w]e have for *Thirty* Years persevered in a constant Opposition against all incroachments of Power', adding that '[w]e have the same *English* Hearts we ever had' in echo of Queen Anne's famous words.[52]

In the end, however, with little constitutional redress, Tory inclusion in the 'broad-bottom' did not last long, and Tory proscription in a broader

---

[46] Colley, 'The Loyal Brotherhood and the Cocoa Tree', *HJ*, 20 (1977), 81; *Correspondence of Chesterfield and Newcastle*, 40–1.
[47] Interestingly, Bolingbroke was involved, and is even believed to have 'set on foot', the negotiations which culminated in the formation of the short-lived broad-bottom ministry; see *Tory and Whig*, 71; Dickinson, *Bolingbroke* (London, 1970), 282–7.
[48] Thomas, *Politics in Eighteenth-Century Wales* (Cardiff, 1998), 174.
[49] *An Expostulatory Epistle to the Welsh Knight* [Wynn] (London, 1745), 26.
[50] [Carte?], *The Case Fairly Stated*, 11.   [51] Ibid., 35.   [52] Ibid., 38.

sense did not come to an end.[53] The Tories' return to systematic opposition in 1746 led to Pulteney (now Bath) becoming significant again during an infamous two-day 'ministry', which, according to one ironical pamphlet, lasted 'forty-eight Hours, three Quarters, seven Minutes, and eleven Seconds'.[54] Bath's failure to form an administration paved the way for the consolidation of power for Pelham and his brother Newcastle.

Some Tories had already left the 'broad-bottom' government after only a few months. Philipps resigned before the outbreak of the 'Forty-five'.[55] Cotton returned to opposition in 1745 as well, but kept his employment until June 1746, when he was dismissed. What Tory-Jacobites were doing as part of the administration is a conundrum, since some of them were simultaneously involved in negotiations with the Jacobite court about a French invasion in 1744. While it is evident that many prominent Tory parliamentarians were involved in Jacobite intrigue at this time, there is no consensus about either the significance or the representativeness of this behaviour.[56] To some historians their actions are signs of principled Jacobitism, and to others those of opportunism. The evidence is patchy, and while it is undisputable that many Tories had longstanding Jacobite sympathies and inclinations, it is plausible that most of them kept their options open – similarly to Bolingbroke and Harley/Oxford in 1710–14 – and that negotiations with the Stuarts recommenced after the disappointments in 1742. Cotton and Wynn did not take an active part in the 'Forty-five', since the French involvement they demanded did not materialise. John Murray of Broughton, Jacobite secretary of state, was arrested in Scotland in the wake of the defeat at Culloden. In exchange for a pardon, he revealed the Jacobite involvement of Cotton, Wynn, Lord Barrymore, and others.[57] Lord Lovat was arrested and executed with the aid of

---

[53] New justices of peace were appointed in 1745 which reinstated Tories in a handful of counties, but Lord Chancellor Hardwicke laboured to maintain Whig predominance on the benches; see Landau, *The Justices of the Peace* (Berkeley, 1984), 107–36. For Edward Harley's disappointment, see *Tory and Whig*, 73.

[54] *The Surprising History of a Late Long Administration* (London, 1746), 37.

[55] Though there is evidence of Jacobite sympathies, there is none of him taking an active part in plotting. After the outbreak of the 'Forty-five', he was a member of a Commons committee that ordered the Pretender's proclamation to be burned, but he later obstructed emergency measures and represented the Jacobite agent Alexander Murray at his trial in 1751. Thomas, *Politics in Eighteenth-Century Wales*, 180–1, 185–8.

[56] Colley, *In Defiance of Oligarchy*, 41–2, 58; Thomas, *Politics in Eighteenth-Century Wales*, 140–3. Cruickshanks, *Political Untouchables* (New York, 1979).

[57] *Memorials of John Murray of Broughton, Some-time Secretary to Prince Charles Edward, 1740–1747* (Edinburgh, 1898), 424, 426. Tory Lords implicated in Jacobite plotting at the time were Beaufort, Lichfield, and Orrery. See ibid., 510 and Cruickshanks, *Political Untouchables*.

Murray's evidence, but the Pelham ministry did not take legal action against Cotton, Wynn, and Barrymore, partly because of the lack of decisive evidence, and partly because of strategic reasons. Instead, their names were divulged when they were present in the Commons, stamping them with notoriety.[58] Many of the Tories implicated in Jacobite intrigue became involved in Frederick's Leicester House opposition after 1747, which to a degree supports the case of them being opportunistic.[59]

As Bob Harris has stressed, although a significant minority of Tories had Jacobite connections – perhaps a slender majority even had such sympathies – what the Tories predominantly stood for in national terms at this stage was the 'country interest' or 'old interest', which were indeed the preferred terms of the Tories themselves. This entailed protection of the gentry against corruption, costly wars, high taxes, and the 'moneyed interest'.[60] It should be added that this remained intertwined with the Church of England interest, and especially that of the lower clergy. This is what Hume meant when he said that '[t]here are ... very considerable remains of that party in ENGLAND, with all their old prejudices', as we saw in Chapter 4. The Jacobite association was strong enough for the Tories to remain in the cold as a party. In Chapter 5, we see how many of the ideas some believed to have been extinguished, including divine right monarchy and passive obedience,[61] resurfaced, especially in Scotland as we turn to Hume's essays written in the wake of the 'Forty-five'. As Hume's new essays imply, the 'Forty-five' also reminded the Whigs of the essence of their political creed.

---

[58] Cruickshanks, *Political Untouchables*, 104–5. See also *ODNB* entries for Wynn and Barrymore, written by P.D.G. Thomas and Stephen W. Baskerville, respectively.

[59] Owen, *The Rise of the Pelhams*, 312–14.

[60] Harris, *Politics and the Nation*, 44–5. For discussion, see also *Tory and Whig*, xxxvii–xxxix, xlii–xlvii. *Common Sense or the Englishman's Journal* of 12 February 1743 (issue 313) equated the Tories with 'the *landed interest*' in opposition to an anti-Tory pamphlet entitled *A Compleat View of the Present Politicks of Great Britain* (London, 1743).

[61] *The Detector Detected*, 61.

CHAPTER 6

Hume on the Parties' Speculative Systems of Thought

[T]here can be no Dispute, but that the first Man *Adam,* was the first civil Governor, and that Monarchy is as old as the Creation of *Eve,* and an Addition of his Subjects made at the Birth of every one of his Descendant ... I ... shall therefore conclude that Government was of God's own Institution, and that Monarchy was what he appointed, and *Adam* the first King[.]

Mitre and Crown, March 1749

Introduction

In his magisterial study of British high politics in the 1740s, John Owen said that it was difficult to define 'Tory' and impossible to define 'Whig' in this period.[1] *Pace* Owen, if we want to begin to understand these mid-century party creeds, we could do worse than consider the writings of Hume. For the 1748 edition of the *Essays, Moral and Political,* Hume removed some essays he regarded as 'frivolous and finical', and inserted three new ones.[2] Of the new essays, one was '*against* the original Contract, the System of the Whigs, another *against* passive Obedience, the System of the Tories'.[3] In terms of the content of the essays, however, the separation is not as clean as their titles suggest, and, as we shall see, he dealt with both parties' respective speculative systems in the first, longer essay 'Of the Original Contract', and then the practical consequences of these systems in 'Of Passive Obedience'. He had also completed a third essay on the Protestant Succession, in which he 'treat[ed] that subject as coolly and indifferently, as I would the dispute between Caesar and Pompey'.[4] Hume

---

[1] Owen, *The Rise of the Pelhams* (London, 1957), 69–70.
[2] He kept all political essays. The three new essays, 'Of the Original Contract', 'Of Passive Obedience', and 'Of National Characters', had already appeared as *Three Essays, Moral and Political,* published earlier in 1748.
[3] Hume to Lord Tinwald, 13 February 1748, *Letters,* I, 112. (My emphasis.)
[4] Hume to Kames, 9 February 1748, ibid., 111.

said that '[t]he conclusion shows me a Whig, but a very sceptical one', hence Forbes's influential labelling of Hume.[5] Hume discussed 'Of the Protestant Succession' with his friends, most of whom thought that it would be 'extremely dangerous' to publish, and therefore it did not appear until the publication of his next essay collection: the *Political Discourses* (1752).[6] As this chapter will emphasise, the Glorious Revolution remained integral to British political debate in the mid-century.[7] It will begin by setting out the contexts of Hume's discussion of the speculative systems of the Whigs and Tories respectively, and then treat the three essays in turn. Writing in the wake of the 'Forty-five', Hume now focused on politics in his native Scotland, and in particular the Scottish version of Toryism, which, as he had stated in his earlier essays, was synonymous with Jacobitism, and different from the more populist form of Country Toryism which prevailed south of the border.

'Of Passive Obedience' and 'Of the Original Contract'

The demolition of the 'original contract' is one of the interventions that Hume is most famous for in the history of political thought.[8] The idea that government was founded on and received its legitimacy from a conditional contract between governors and the governed had long been a shibboleth of the Whig party. Half of a sample of 139 pamphlets defending the 1688–9 revolution and three-quarters of Whig pamphlets between 1689 and 1694 based their claim on contractual resistance.[9] The term 'original contract' later played a role in the prosecution of the High Church Tory Henry Sacheverell, impeached by the Whigs in 1709–10 for preaching non-resistance, notably in the speeches of Nicholas

---

[5] Ibid.; Forbes, 'Sceptical Whiggism, Commerce and Liberty', in *Essays on Adam Smith* (Oxford, 1975), 179–201.

[6] Hume to Lord Tinwald, 13 February 1748, *Letters*, I, 112–13.

[7] This has also been emphasised recently by Glickman, 'Political Conflict and the Memory of the Revolution in England, 1689–c.1750', in *The Final Crisis of the Stuart Monarchy* (Woodbridge, 2013), 243–71.

[8] Jeremy Bentham hailed Hume for this achievement in *A Fragment on Government* (Cambridge, 1988 [1776]), 51.

[9] Goldie, 'The Revolution of 1689 and the Structure of Political Argument', *Bulletin of Research in the Humanities*, 83 (1980), 490. Seventy-three per cent of Whig defences affirmed contract theory. We have to bear in mind, however, that the phrase 'original contract' at this time often referred to a coronation oath to preserve the ancient constitution, as opposed to Locke's theoretical contract that explained the origin of government; see Pocock, *The Ancient Constitution* (Cambridge, 1987 [1957]), 251.

Lechmere, one of the managers of the trial.[10] The independent Whig journal *Cato's Letters* (1720–3) asserted the existence of an original contract and defended the right to resist.[11] Few people in Hume's lifetime would have struggled to recognise the original contract, and by extension the right to resist, as a Whig doctrine, and passive obedience as a Tory doctrine, although it was often pointed out that practice rarely corresponded to theory. While Hume targeted the speculative systems of the two parties and not the precise articulations of any particular philosopher, he singled out John Locke as the Whig contract theorist par excellence, and in this regard he was followed by Adam Smith.[12] The significance of Locke in the formation of Whig principles is a scholarly discussion in its own right.[13] Locke's thought appears to have played a marginal role in the immediate aftermath of the Glorious Revolution.[14] In the early eighteenth century, however, the *Two Treatises of Government* (*c.*1680–3) began to receive attention, as can be seen in the hostility they received from the Jacobite Charles Leslie.[15] In Scotland, the *Two Treatises* were recommended by the Advocates Library in Edinburgh already in 1695, and shortly afterwards Gershom Carmichael and later Francis Hutcheson incorporated the text into their teaching at Glasgow University.[16]

While the related doctrines of divine right, indefeasible hereditary right, non-resistance, and passive obedience had been ridiculed by many in the 1730s and 1740s, Hume among others,[17] it is safe to assume that many still believed in such theories. The notion of hereditary right is theoretically distinct from divine right, but in practice divine right was commonly thought to be transmitted by hereditary succession.[18] Bolingbroke did not speak for all Tories when he renounced these ideas.[19] Divine right Toryism and its twin Jacobitism remained buoyant in church circles and at the University of Oxford, with the latter being a training ground for the

---

[10] Walpole, another manager of the trial, did not evoke the contract; see Holmes, *The Trial of Doctor Sacheverell* (London, 1973), 132, 139–40.

[11] Trenchard and Gordon, *Cato's Letters* (2 vols., Indianapolis, 1995 [1720–3]), II, 916.

[12] Hume, 'The Original Contract', *Essays*, 487; 'The Parties of Great Britain', *Essays*, 614 (variant readings); Hume to Francis Hutcheson, 10 January 1743, *Letters*, I, 48; Smith, *Lectures on Jurisprudence* (Indianapolis, 1982), 314–21.

[13] See Goldie (ed.), *The Reception of Locke's Politics* (6 vols., London, 1999), I, introduction.

[14] Kenyon, *Revolution Principles* (Cambridge, 1977), 1–2. See, however, Ashcraft and Goldsmith, 'Locke, Revolution Principles, and the Formation of Whig Ideology', *HJ*, 26 (1983), 773–800.

[15] Goldie (ed.), *The Reception of Locke's Politics*, xxxi.   [16] Ibid., xxxiv.

[17] Hume, 'Whether the British Government inclines more to Absolute Monarchy or to a Republic', *Essays*, 51.

[18] McLynn, 'The Ideology of Jacobitism on the Eve of the Rising of 1745', *HEI*, 6 (1985), 1–18.

[19] Bolingbroke, *A Dissertation upon Parties*, in *Political Writings*, 5, 22.

former. Edward Gibbon, himself from a Tory family and a student at Magdalen College in 1752–3, attested that such theories survived until the accession of George III in 1760, the first Hanoverian king born in England.[20]

Divine right (*divino jure*) is the idea that the monarch was accountable to God alone and could not be opposed by their subjects. Such a theory should not necessarily be conflated with unchecked or arbitrary royal power, however. In its eighteenth-century form, divine right was closer to the arguments about legitimate kingship by the non-juror Leslie (1650–1722) than the in some ways atypical Sir Robert Filmer,[21] who had explicitly defended arbitrary monarchy in the previous century.[22] Indeed, the Jacobite movement conceived of itself as combatting the 'arbitrary power of Foreigners'.[23] It is also doubtful whether post-1689 divine right in the British setting should be associated with the absolutist theories of Jean Bodin and Hobbes.[24] By contrast, in the eighteenth century it was usually combined with mixed constitutionalism. An anonymous Scottish Jacobite, for example, writing in 1746 to justify his conduct in the 'Forty-five', described 'the British Constitution, as it stood in the year 1688' as 'a mixture of monarchy, aristocracy, & Democracy'.[25] A key pledge of the Jacobite court was a 'free & legal Parliament' without placemen.[26] Moreover, the Stuarts could argue that they aspired to more power sharing than afforded by the Whig–Hanover axis since they promised to recall the Convocations of Canterbury and York to settle Church affairs.[27] As the Old Pretender put it, 'If any one Article of the least moment to the Wellfare, and Security of the Church, or State, should be wanting, Let the blame lay at your own doors, to whose Wisdome and

[20] Gibbon, *Memoirs of My Life* (London, 1990), 80, 90–1.

[21] See Monod, *Jacobitism and the English People* (Cambridge, 1989), 17–23.

[22] Filmer, *Observations Concerning the Orginall of Government* (1652), in *Patriarcha and Other Writings* (Cambridge, 1992), 281.

[23] *Hearne's Recollections*, V, 38.

[24] Unlike divine right, royal absolutism did not survive in its seventeenth-century sense in eighteenth-century Britain; see Daly, 'The Idea of Absolute Monarchy in Seventeenth-Century England', *HJ*, 21 (1978), 227–50. A new form of absolutism, which saw the legislative power, consisting of king, lords, and commons, as absolute, came to the fore, however.

[25] NLS MS 296, f. 8. The same writer says repeatedly that it was the constitution that had been 'violated' in 1688–9 (f. 10).

[26] If restored, the Stuarts promised to 'refuse nothing a free Parliament can ask, for the Security of their religion, Laws & Liberty or the People'; see *Declaration of Charles Prince of Wales . . . Unto all his Majesty's Subjects . . .* [1745], in *English Jacobite Ballads, Songs & Satires, etc. From the mss. at Towneley Hall, Lancashire* (printed for private circulation, 1877), 132, 137.

[27] *The Kings* [i.e. James 'III'] *Letter to the Archbishop of Canterbury*, 27 December 1722, in Rawlinson MS 909, Bodleian, n.f.

Consciences we referr it; Make yourselv's happy'.[28] In other words, we need to recognise that constitutionalism and political reform were integral to the clearest expression of divine right politics, namely the Jacobite movement. As with the original contract, the flexibility of divine right theory ensured its survival.

The immediate reason why thinkers opposed to divine right theory of monarchy in the second half of the 1740s felt that they had to treat it seriously as opposed to mocking it was the Jacobite rising in 1745,[29] which was initially successful, especially in Scotland. Scottish Whigs could no longer pretend that Jacobitism was not a serious 'party' north of the border. '[T]he number of the Jacobites in Scotland is so great and their interests so considerable that I will honestly confess it gives me a great deal of uneasiness', wrote Robert Wallace shortly after the outbreak of the rebellion in an unpublished pamphlet.[30] While Wallace countered the theoretical arguments for Jacobitism in the first half of his text, he spent the second half attempting to demonstrate that industry had increased at a faster pace than population growth in Scotland since 1688–9, in opposition to recently published pamphlets such as *Some Considerations on the Present State of Scotland* (Edinburgh, 1744) and *The Present State of Scotland Consider'd: And Its Declining and Sinking Condition charged upon the Conduct of the Landed Gentlemen* (Edinburgh, 1745). According to Wallace, the Jacobites made use of these pamphlets to demonstrate that Scotland was in a state of decline which created discontent and made the country ripe for rebellion, although he stressed that he did not believe that this had been the intention of either author.[31]

The Jacobite defeat at Culloden in April 1746 and the bloody clampdown on Jacobitism that followed did not immediately sound the death knell for Jacobitism, as popular riots in the years that followed attest.[32] In his first essays from 1741, Hume had treated Jacobitism seriously in the

---

[28] Ibid.

[29] I disagree with Harris's suggestion that Hume concentrated more on the Whig than the Tory doctrine because the latter 'look[ed] mostly irrelevant' after the failure of the 'Forty-five'; see Harris, *David Hume* (Cambridge, 2015), 239.

[30] Wallace, *An Address to the Jacobites in Scotland. In which among other reasons offered to perswade them to acquiesce in the Revolution and the Settlement of the Crown in the Protestant line it is proved that Scotland has not declined in wealth since the Revolution but is richer att present than att that period* (c.1745), Edinburgh University Library, La.II.97/5, f. 6.

[31] Ibid., f. 27.

[32] Monod, *Jacobitism and the English People*, 195–232. The 1748 Act for Disarming the Scottish Highlands included attacks on the Scottish Episcopalian Church, the parishioners of which were part of the Jacobite stronghold north of the border; see Ingram, *Religion, Reform and Modernity in the Eighteenth Century* (Woodbridge, 2007), 203.

sense that he linked the Tory party with the movement. In the Scottish context, however, he had underestimated, or at least downplayed, the threat of Jacobitism in his early essays, as we saw in Chapter 4. The 'Forty-five' proved that the theory of divine right continued to have more sway in Britain than he had previously thought, or perhaps hoped. One rebel executed after the 'Forty-five' declared that 'the *Cause* for which I suffer is divine' and died convinced that he would go to heaven for his deeds.[33] The last words of another insurgent were that 'the thinking Few, who have not forsaken their Duty to God and their King, will ... look upon [his execution] as being little inferior to MARTYRDOM itself'.[34]

On a superficial reading it may not be evident that Jacobitism and passive obedience were compatible, since the former was a rebellious movement. How could Hume and most of his contemporaries, including many Jacobites themselves, treat them as part of the same ideological package? The simplest answer is that passive obedience referred to 1688–9: the Hanoverians were seen as German usurpers and taking up arms against them meant fighting for the royal cause as they understood it. As Wallace put it, 'if the Revolution is overturnd and declared rebellion and the pretenders title recogniz'd on account of his Hereditary Indefesible and Divine right the doctrine of none resistance is Establishd for ever'.[35] Passive obedience played an essential role in Jacobite propaganda in 1745, as far as evidence is extant.[36] An anonymous Jacobite writing in October 1745 argued that '[i]f the Doctrines of the Church, & the Laws of the Kingdom do concur to assure us, that Subjects must not take Arms, or rebel against their King ... then it is evident that ... the revolution in 1688 was against all rules of our established Religion & Policy'.[37] Longevity did not give legitimacy, according to this pamphleteer: the

---

[33] *True Copies of the Papers wrote by Balmerino, Syddall, Morgan, Fletcher, Berwick, Deacon, Chadwick, Dawson, and Blyde; and delivered by them to the Sheriffs at the Places of their Execution* (N.p., 1746), 22, 23. A recurrent theme in these 'vindications' is that the rebels believed that they had done what their 'conscience' (for them a religious concept) told them and many stressed their commitment to the Church of England (6, 8, 21, 22, 32, 33, 37).

[34] Ibid., 27.   [35] Wallace, *Address to the Jacobites in Scotland*, f. 21.

[36] Monod, *Jacobitism and the English People*, 15–44.

[37] *A Letter to the Archbishop of York: humbly offering to His Grace's Solution some doubts and scruples suggested by his late Speech to the Grand Meeting of the County of York, called to subscribe an association for supporting the German Government in England* [1745], in *English Jacobite Ballads*, 168. Unlike government propaganda, explicit Jacobite propaganda could not be safely printed, and we must thus rely on manuscripts. Songs and poems, communicated *viva voce*, played an important part in making the case for the Jacobite cause. There were exceptions, however, including the short-lived *The National Journal, or Country Gazette* (1746), which was suppressed, and *Mitre and Crown* and the *True Briton*, edited by George Osborne.

throne was either hereditary or elective, and if the former, 'the Prince who sits in it at present, has no right'.[38]

In the aftermath of the 'Forty-five', a literary controversy erupted between the Scottish minister George Logan and the Jacobite scholar Thomas Ruddiman, who immediately preceded Hume as Keeper of the Advocates Library in Edinburgh.[39] Ruddiman made use of divine right arguments in response to Logan's challenge that the Scottish crown was not strictly hereditary.[40] The Jacobite rebellion compelled Scottish writers in particular to respond to these arguments, which clearly had influenced many people. Hume's friend Henry Home (later Lord Kames) wrote a publication during the Jacobite rebellion which treated 'hereditary and indefeasible right' in an extensive appendix.[41] By concentrating on the legal side of the argument,[42] Kames sought to refute the widespread view that the succession to the British crown prior to the Glorious Revolution had been lineal. Hume expressed his approval of his friend's *Essays*,[43] although he himself would take a different approach and seek not only to refute the religious and philosophical underpinnings of Tory-Jacobitism, but also Whiggism. In addition to Kames and Hume, we have already noted that Wallace wrote an *Address to the Jacobites* in 1745. While this text was not published, Wallace returned to the debate in *The Doctrine of Passive Obedience and Non-resistance Considered* (1754), recycling many of his arguments about the advantages of the 1688–9 Revolution, this time in response to Lord Dun's *Friendly and Familiar Advices* (Edinburgh, 1754). He prepared a second edition in 1762, which, although never published, demonstrates the longevity of debates about these matters in Scotland.[44]

Hume's starting point was that 'no party, in the present age, can well support itself, without a philosophical or speculative system of principles, annexed to its political or practical one'.[45] He had already dealt with the parties' respective political and practical systems in his earlier essays. He now proceeded to deal with their speculative systems, religious and

---

[38] Ibid., 169.   [39] See Duncan, *Thomas Ruddiman* (Edinburgh, 1965).

[40] Ruddiman, *Dissertation concerning the Competition for the Crown of Scotland* Edinburgh, 1748), 88–90.

[41] [Kames], *Essays upon Several Subjects concerning British Antiquities … With an appendix upon Hereditary and Indefeasible Right. Composed anno MDCCXLV* (Edinburgh, third edn., 1747), 193–216. Hume's friend Kames had inherited Jacobite opinions, which he held onto until the early 1730s; see Ross, *Lord Kames and the Scotland of His Day* (New York, 1972), 44–58.

[42] The legal argument, i.e. that the Stuarts had a hereditary right to the throne by the law of succession, was as important as the religious one; see Erskine-Hill, 'Literature and the Jacobite Cause', in *Ideology and Conspiracy* (Edinburgh, 1982), 51.

[43] Hume to Kames, June 1747, *New Letters*, 25.   [44] Edinburgh University Library, La.II.96/6.

[45] Hume, 'Original Contract', *Essays*, 465.

philosophical. Divine right theory and the original contract represented such religious and philosophical systems of principles for the Tories and the Whigs respectively, with passive obedience being a practical consequence of the former theory and resistance of the latter. Hume revised his earlier ridicule of divine right theory, now simply stating that 'one party [the Tories], by tracing up government to the DEITY, endeavour to render it so sacred and inviolate, that it must be little less than sacrilege, however tyrannical it may become, to touch or invade it'.[46] The Whigs, on their part, 'by founding government altogether on the consent of the PEOPLE, suppose that there is a kind of *original contract*, by which the subjects have tacitly reserved the power of resisting their sovereign, whenever they find themselves aggrieved by that authority'.[47]

Hume's main intention was as ever to promote moderation, as he explicitly set out at the start of the essay. In the first instance, he contended that both systems were just, but not in the ways interpreted by the parties. Second, both sets of practical consequences – passive obedience and resistance – were prudent, but not to the extreme to which each party carried them.[48] How could divine right theory be described as just by someone who famously did away with God in his own philosophy? Hume distinguished between divine right *kingship* and divine right *government*. For religious people, it would be appropriate to regard the deity as the author of all governments, and since the human race depended on government for comfort and security, it would be perfectly consistent for believers to view this as intended by a beneficent being. Finally, as government existed in all countries and all ages, this could also be ascribed to the intention of an omniscient being, for those who believed in such a thing, Hume argued.

The problem with this theory was the belief in *providence*, which Hume regarded as at odds with the importance attached to lineal succession, and he consequently exploded the anti-Hanoverian case of the Jacobite Tories. For those who believed in providence and divine intention, 'the greatest and most lawful prince' must be incorporated in the same divine plan as usurpers, robbers, and pirates.[49] Many divines had relied on providence when shifting their allegiance from James to William and Mary after the Revolution. Notably, William Sherlock, Dean of St Paul, took the new oaths after one year's hesitation and defended the new regime on the basis of providential conquest and deliverance.[50] Another problem for the Tory

---

[46] Ibid., 466.   [47] Ibid.   [48] Ibid.   [49] Ibid., 467.

[50] For Sherlock's *Case of the Allegiance Due to Sovereign Powers* (1691), see Straka, 'The Final Phase of Divine Right Theory in England, 1688–1702', *EHR*, 77 (1962), 646–7. For a different variety of

system as Hume saw it was that if authority per se was regarded as divine, this would have to apply to 'every petty jurisdiction ... and every *limited* authority' within a state, and even a constable would thus act 'by a divine commission'.[51]

Hume then moved on to the original contract, with which he had already dealt at length in the third book of his *Treatise of Human Nature* (1739–40). In the *Treatise*, Hume had referred to the original contract, or the idea that government received its legitimacy from the consent of the governed, as 'the foundation of our fashionable system of politics' and 'the creed of a party amongst us, who value themselves, with reason, on the soundness of their philosophy, and their liberty of thought', that is to say, the Whigs.[52] In a similar vein to his earlier treatment, Hume argued that if the contract was interpreted in what we may call the Hobbesian sense, with the people originally giving rise to government by having 'voluntarily, for the sake of peace and order, abandoned their native liberty, and received laws from their equal and companion', then 'all government is, at first, founded on a contract'.[53]

The mistake philosophers, 'who have embraced a party (if that be not a contradiction in terms)',[54] made was to believe that government continued to rest on no other foundation than a contract.[55] More precisely, Hume wanted to expose the absurdity that people 'owe allegiance to no prince or government, unless bound by the obligation and sanction of a *promise*', a promise from which they may free themselves.[56] In the *Treatise*, Hume had argued that civil duties of obedience 'soon detach themselves from our promises, and acquire a separate force and influence'.[57] In short, we disapprove of rebellion because the execution of justice would be impossible without submission to government.[58] 'Tho' there was no such thing as a promise in the world, government wou'd still be necessary in all large and civiliz'd societies', he asserted.[59] Allegiance to government rested

---

the conquest argument, one that took its cue from Hugo Grotius, see Goldie, 'Edmund Bohun and *Jus Gentium* in the Revolution Debate, 1689–93', *HJ*, 20 (1977), 569–86.

[51] Hume, 'Original Contract', *Essays*, 467.   [52] Hume, *Treatise*, 542.

[53] Hume, 'Original Contract', *Essays*, 468. This did not apply to 'all the governments, which exists at present, or of which there remains any record in story,' almost all of which had 'been founded originally, either on usurpation or conquest, or both' (471). Moreover, in his final word on this topic, his posthumous 'Of the Origin of Government', he did away with even this minimal form of contract.

[54] Undoubtedly a reference to Locke, whom he quoted at the end of the essay.

[55] Hume, 'Original Contract', *Essays*, 469.   [56] Ibid.   [57] Hume, *Treatise*, 544.

[58] Ibid., 546. Similarly, we condemn breach of faith in business because human commerce depends on promise-keeping.

[59] Ibid., 546.

entirely on opinion, of right and interest, and it was underpinned by habit, according to Hume.[60] In 1748, he appears to have been even more eager than in the *Treatise* to dispute the idea that the sovereign promised justice and protection, and that if the subject believed they failed to deliver on this promise, the subject 'has thereby freed his subject from all obligations to allegiance'.[61] If interpreted this way, contract theory implied a charter of rights that could be invaded and a *right* of resistance in such cases.

Hume's objection to the original contract interpreted in this Lockean fashion was twofold: it was a historical absurdity that did not exist and had never existed anywhere,[62] and moreover, it posed a threat to the stability of government by encouraging rebellion. As he later put it in his *History*, the idea that the people were the origin of all just power was a noble principle in itself, but belied by all history and experience.[63] Hume was clear that resistance would occur when real oppression was taking place, and no one could condemn it in such cases, but there was no reason to encourage this behaviour, as resistance would always take place when necessary.[64] The contract was also mistaken in placing so much emphasis on consent. Hume remarked that Henry IV and Henry VII were elected kings by parliament, but never acknowledged this because they believed that it would weaken their authority. 'Strange, if the only real foundation of all authority be consent and promise', Hume scorned.[65] This type of Whiggism further bred a form of nationalism based on the idea that the British post-revolutionary regime was unparalleled. Hume agreed that it was to some extent, but not in the sense commonly thought,[66] and he was always eager to put notions of English exceptionalism to the test. Here he reminded his readers that the Glorious Revolution was not founded on universal consent, but the majority of 700 MPs who decided the fate of the entire nation.[67]

In the following essay, 'Of Passive Obedience', Hume repeated the argument that, 'as government binds us to obedience only on account of

---

[60] Hume, 'Of the First Principles of Government', *Essays*, 33; Hume, *Treatise*, 548; Hume, 'Of the Origin of Government', *Essays*, 37, 39. For the centrality of opinion in Hume's account of political obligation, see Buckle and Castiglione, 'Hume's Critique of the Contract Theory', *HPT*, 12 (1991), 457–80.

[61] Hume, 'Original Contract', *Essays*, 469.

[62] Hume believed that this belief would result in imprisonment in most parts of the world if propagated.

[63] Hume, *History*, V, 533.   [64] Hume, *Treatise*, 552–3; Hume, *History*, V, 544.

[65] Hume, 'Original Contract', *Essays*, 473.

[66] '[T]he English Government is certainly happy, though probably not calculated for Duration, by reason of its excessive Liberty'. Hume to William Strahan, 3 March 1772, *Letters*, II, 261.

[67] Hume, 'Original Contract', *Essays*, 472.

its tendency to public utility', obedience ceases when it would lead to public ruin.[68] Hume followed Hobbes and Locke in quoting from Cicero's *De Legibus* that *salus populi suprema lex esto*.[69] He then used the same examples as when covering similar ground in the *Treatise*: no one would condemn those who rebelled against Nero and Philip II, however 'infatuated with party-systems' they may be.[70] 'Even our high monarchical party [the Tories], in spite of their sublime theory [of passive obedience], are forced, in such cases, to judge, and feel, and approve, in conformity to the rest of mankind', Hume argued. Accordingly, in 'extraordinary emergencies', 'when the public is in the highest danger, from violence and tyranny', Hume granted that resistance would be permitted, which his modern readers are often keen to emphasise.[71] This was mainstream Scottish Whiggism, or indeed English establishment Whiggism.[72] Hume's larger point, however, was that 'obedience is our duty in the common course of things' and that 'it ought chiefly to be inculcated'.[73] His main intention was to show that the respective systems of both parties contained a grain of truth, but that both could be equally dangerous if carried to extreme lengths.[74]

Nevertheless, Hume closed the essay on passive obedience with some arguments in favour of the Whigs. The first was that the Tories erroneously sought to exclude the exceptions to the general rule of obedience.[75] It is likely that Hume here meant the Tory fiction that no resistance had taken place in 1688–9 and that James II/VII had abdicated the throne. This enabled Tories to obey William as king de facto, while James remained king de jure, a way of thinking which continued to be a

---

[68] Hume, 'Passive Obedience', *Essays*, 489.

[69] As the examples of Hobbes of Locke show, *salus populi* arguments could be used by 'resistance' and 'non-resistance' advocates alike. In the wake of the Revolution, it was utilised by those arguing that passive obedience had not been breached in 1688–9: while people were not allowed to act against the prince, they did not need to actively support him. Goldie, 'Edmund Bohun and *Jus Gentium*', 583.

[70] Hume, 'Passive Obedience', *Essays*, 490; Hume, *Treatise*, 552.

[71] Hume, 'Passive Obedience', *Essays*, 490; Whelan, 'Hume and Contractarianism', *Polity*, 27 (1994), 201–24. Phillipson, 'Propriety, Property and Prudence' (Cambridge, 1993), 302–20; Hont, 'Commercial Society and Political Theory in the Eighteenth Century', in *Main Trends in Cultural History* (Amsterdam, 1994), 77–8.

[72] Wallace made a similar argument, emphasising that resistance was only lawful on 'extraordinary occasions' of tyranny, in *Address to the Jacobites in Scotland*, ff. 8–14.

[73] Hume, 'Passive Obedience', *Essays*, 490.

[74] Conniff thus misses the point when arguing that Hume gave the Whig doctrine serious consideration while rejecting the Tory doctrine out of hand in 'Hume on Political Parties', *ECS*, 12 (1978–9), 160–1. Conniff also anachronistically conflates the Whig party with the 'progressive movement of [Hume's] day' (173).

[75] Hume, 'Passive Obedience', *Essays*, 491.

prominent part of Tory discourse for a long time after the Revolution.[76] It was a potentially destabilising fiction, however, since James's 'abdication' did not apply to his offspring. Accordingly, after the death of Anne, the last Stuart monarch, Jacobites argued that James 'III/VIII' (the Old Pretender) was the rightful sovereign, despite the Act of Settlement of 1701. Hume concluded that the Whigs should be applauded for insisting on exceptions to the rule of obedience, because they consequently defended both truth (James II/VII had been deposed) and liberty (the power of parliament).

Second and finally, Hume believed that the nature of the British constitution was more favourable to the Whig system since the king was above the law only regarding his own person.[77] The king's government, on the other hand, was subject to the full force of the law, and if the king attempted to usurp more legislative power than the mixed constitution allowed, as Charles I and James II/VII had done in the seventeenth century, it would become 'necessary to oppose them with some vehemence'.[78] Hume thus concluded that resistance to monarchs was necessarily more common in mixed forms of government than in simple ones, where monarchs had little incentive to run into difficulties that would warrant resistance.[79] As has often been pointed out, this appears to contradict Hume's earlier statement that resistance was only justified as a last resort 'when the public is in the highest danger, from violence and tyranny'.[80] This apparent contradiction may have stemmed from Hume's ambition to give both parties their due. While his final pronouncements on these matters are to be found in his *History of Great Britain* (1754–6) and 'Of the Coalition of Parties' (1758), in the next section we investigate Hume's attempt to go beyond this inconsistency, in book III of the *Treatise* and his essay 'Of the Protestant Succession'.

'Of the Protestant Succession'

The two essays discussed in the previous section were meant to be accompanied by a third and related essay on the Protestant Succession,

---

[76] Kenyon, *Revolutionary Principles*, 32–3; *Whig and Tory Principles of Government fairly stated in a Dialogue between an Oxford Scholar and a Whig Parson* (n.p., 1716), 33–5, 40–1. Despite its title, we can easily identify it as a Tory pamphlet, since the 'Oxford scholar' is doing most of the talking and winning all the arguments.

[77] Hume, 'Passive Obedience', *Essays*, 491.   [78] Ibid., 492.   [79] See also Hume, *Treatise*, 564.

[80] Hume, 'Passive Obedience', *Essays*, 490. McLynn has called Hume's thinking on resistance 'muddled', and Forbes has called it 'ambivalent'; see 'Jacobitism and Hume', *Hume Studies*, 9 (1983), 194 and *Hume's Philosophical Politics* (Cambridge, 1975), 101, respectively.

which Hume intended to include in the 1748 edition of the *Essays*, but the publication of which he postponed until 1752. The succession to the throne was a party-political issue and Hume believed that he had to deal with it to achieve his aim of mollifying party animosity. The essay was provocative because Hume by his own admission treated the subject 'coolly and indifferently' – a precarious enterprise in the aftermath of the 1745–6 Jacobite rising. Like the contract, Hume had already dealt with the topic in *Treatise* book III.[81] In his earlier treatment, he had been clear that a disputed succession presented a near-intractable problem. When the principles deciding who should govern (most importantly long possession, present possession, and positive law) pointed in different directions, that is, long possession for the Stuart family, and present possession and positive law (the Act of Settlement) for Hanover, 'an impartial enquirer, who adopts no party in political controversies' would never be satisfied by any answer.[82]

Hume made several concessions to the Jacobite case in his contentious essay, in which he imagined himself a member of parliament between 1689 and 1714, the period between the Revolution and the Hanoverian accession. A restoration of the Stuart family at this time would have had the advantage of 'preserv[ing] the succession clear and undisputed, free from a pretender', Hume acknowledged.[83] Bloodline was the most straightforward indicator of legitimacy in the minds of the multitude and strong feelings for the 'true heir of their royal family' were precisely what rendered monarchical government stable, according to Hume. It was foolish to place kings on the same level as the meanest of mankind, even if 'an anatomist finds no more in the greatest monarch than in the lowest peasant or day-labourer; and a moralist may, perhaps, frequently find less'.[84] Such reflections are largely pointless, Hume argued, since 'all of us, still retain these prejudices in favour of birth and family'.[85] He gave the rather trivial but telling example that everyone prefers to see plays about kings rather than sailors, views later echoed by Smith.[86]

By comparison with the Stuarts, the Hanoverian succession 'violate[d] hereditary right; and place[d] on the throne a prince, to whom birth gave no title to that dignity'.[87] In contrast to his essays of the early 1740s, Hume was now prepared to defend the actions of the Stuart kings in the

---

[81] Hume, *Treatise*, 553–67, esp. 563–7.   [82] Ibid., 562–63.
[83] Hume, 'Protestant Succession', *Essays*, 503.   [84] Ibid., 504.   [85] Ibid.
[86] Smith, *The Theory of Moral Sentiments* (Indianapolis, 1982), 53.
[87] Hume, 'Protestant Succession', *Essays*, 505.

seventeenth century. Anticipating his later historical writings, Hume argued that James I/VI and Charles I viewed England as a simple monarchy, based on the precedent of the Tudors and comparisons with other monarchs in Europe at the time. These ideas were bolstered by the flattery of courtiers, 'and, above all, that of the clergy, who from several passages of *scripture* . . . had erected a regular and avowed system of arbitrary power.'[88] On the other hand, Hume argued that a limited monarchy, which he saw as an important achievement, could never have been established within that royal line. The Stuart family was simply too bound up with the doctrine of divine right. Indeed, the last Stuart monarch, Anne, revived the practice of touching for the king's evil, whereby the monarch touched subjects to cure scrofula, which William had previously discontinued because he viewed it as popish superstition.[89] While Hume unsurprisingly regarded the royal touch as an 'ancient superstition', many educated people still believed in the practice at the time, including Carte.[90] According to Hume, '[t]he only method of destroying, at once, all these high claims and pretensions, was to depart from the true hereditary line, and choose a prince, who [was] plainly a creature of the public'.[91] This 'secured our constitutional limitations' and a peculiar, but in Hume's view salutary, situation whereby '[t]he people cherish monarchy, because protected by it, [and t]he monarch favours liberty [i.e. parliament, representing the people], because created by it'.[92] As in his essays from 1741, and *Treatise* book III, Hume thus came down firmly on the side of the Revolution Settlement.[93]

Be that as it may, Hume went on to consider that the Hanoverian monarchy had further disadvantages, chiefly the question of foreign dominions, which would engage Britain in intrigues and wars on the continent.[94] From George I's accession in 1714 up until the start of Queen Victoria's reign in 1837, Britain shared its monarch with the German state of Hanover. The first Hanoverian monarch to be born in Britain was George III, who ascended the throne in 1760. His two predecessors were German Lutherans, who spent a significant amount of time in Hanover and were, according to their critics, more interested in their native land than their new kingdom. These were constant themes in Jacobite propaganda, especially secret poems full of sarcasm: 'Lest Rights

---

[88] Ibid.   [89] David Green, *Queen Anne* (London, 1970), 105.
[90] Hume, *History*, V, 491; Carte, *A General History of England* (4 vols., London, 1747–55), I, 291–2 (note 4). See also MS Carte, Bodleian, ff. 247–8. For a discussion of rationality within irrational contexts, see Skinner, *Visions of Politics* (3 vols., Cambridge, 2002), I, 27–56.
[91] Hume, 'Protestant Succession', *Essays*, 505–6.   [92] Ibid., 506.   [93] Ibid.   [94] Ibid.

& Liberties be in danger | They must be gifted to a German Stranger'.[95] The *Fog's Weekly Journal* (1728–37), the somewhat milder successor to *Mist's Weekly Journal,* gloried in the memory of the last Stuart monarch, described as 'that entirely English Queen', implicitly in contrast with her German successors.[96] Jacobite rebels executed in 1746 saw the Old Pretender as not only their 'rightful' and 'lawful' sovereign but also 'native' and 'British' in contrast to George II, invariably referred to as the Elector of Hanover.[97]

Foreign influence had been a worry from the start of the reign of William III/II, who had largely relied on Dutch advisers and fought wars on the continent. As a response, the Act of Settlement barred foreigners from becoming privy councillors and MPs. The Act also forbade the monarch from engaging the nation in a war in defence of foreign territories without the consent of parliament. Nevertheless, shortly after the Hanoverian succession in 1714, disagreement over the influence of Hanover on British foreign policy brought about a split within the Whigs.[98] In 1715, Hanover became involved in the Great Northern War (1700–21) against Sweden. The main reason why the small state of Hanover was accepted into the alliance with Russia and other big powers was that George I had the British navy at his disposal. Britain's naval engagement gave ammunition to oppositional attacks on the ministry. In the editions of the essay up until and including the one published in 1768, Hume remarked that 'it would be difficult to show any harm we have ever received from the electoral dominions, except that short disgust in 1718, with [the Swedish king] CHARLES XII'.[99] In the first half of the 1740s, the payment of Hanoverian troops in the War of the Austrian Succession was a major issue of political debate.[100] Elsewhere in the *Political Discourses* (1752), Hume referred to the parliamentary ruling in 1742 to pay for 16,000 Hanoverian troops as a 'factious vote'.[101]

---

[95] BL Add MS. 14854, f. 142.

[96] *Fog's Weekly Journal,* 11 October 1729, in *Select Letters Taken from the Fog's Journal* (2 vols., London, 1732) I, 136. As Hannah Smith has demonstrated, however, not all British discourse was xenophobic and anti-German. Indeed, some German princes were widely hailed as Protestant heroes in eighteenth-century Britain, including Frederick the Great, and, for loyalists, George I and II belonged to the same tradition; see *Georgian Monarchy* (Cambridge, 2006).

[97] *True Copies of the Papers wrote by Lord Balmerino,* 27, 32.

[98] Speck, *Stability and Strife* (London, 1977), 187.

[99] Hume, 'Protestant Succession', *Essays,* 646 (variant readings). Sweden became involved in Jacobite plotting as a direct result of Hanover's part in the Great Northern War; see Szechi, *The Jacobites* (Manchester, 1994), 104–7.

[100] Harris, *A Patriot Press* (Oxford, 1993), 74.   [101] Hume, 'Of the Balance of Power', *Essays,* 339.

The main disadvantage of the House of Stuart, according to Hume, was their Catholicism. The Act of Settlement declared that 'whosoever shall hereafter come to the possession of this crown, shall join in communion with the church of England, as by law established'.[102] The whole point behind the legislation was to secure the *Protestant* Succession, hence the title of Hume's essay. The Hanoverian succession was only on the agenda because Anne's last surviving child died in 1700. The importance of not having another Catholic on the throne after what was perceived as the disastrous experience of James II/VII was realised by both parties and the Act of Settlement had been supported by virtually all Tories.[103] On the two main occasions when Bolingbroke dabbled in Jacobite intrigue, he sought to convince the Stuart Pretender to change either his own religion or that of his sons because he understood that it was the only way to feasibly bring about a restoration.[104] Two of the more optimistic Jacobite scholars have argued that a Stuart restoration would have been fully possible in 1714 had the Old Pretender given up his religion as Bolingbroke urged him.[105] Hume had already contended in 1741 that Catholicism was an enemy of civil liberty and here he argued that Catholicism 'affords no toleration, or peace, or security to any other communion'.[106]

Hume pointed out that almost all Jacobites regarded the Catholicism of the Stuarts as problematic,[107] as much as Hanoverian loyalists admitted that foreign dominions presented a difficulty.[108] He then picked up the gauntlet he himself had thrown down in the *Treatise*, saying that '[i]t belongs, therefore, to a philosopher alone, who is of neither party, to put all the circumstances in the scale, and assign to each of them its proper poise and influence'.[109] Hume began by criticising the reign of the Stuarts as a period when 'the government was kept in a continual fever, by the

---

[102] Williams (ed.), *The Eighteenth-Century Constitution* (Cambridge, 1960), 59.

[103] Harris, *Politics under the Later Stuarts* (London, 1993), 157.

[104] Bolingbroke, *Letter to Windham* (1717), in *Works*, I, 90; Cruickshanks, *Political Untouchables* (New York, 1979), 12–13.

[105] Cruickshanks and Erskine-Hill, *The Atterbury Plot* (Basingstoke, 2004), 7.

[106] Hume, 'Superstition and Enthusiasm', *Essays*, 78; Hume, 'Protestant Succession', *Essays*, 506.

[107] This would of course exclude the Catholics themselves, e.g., Hume's one-time acquaintance the Chevalier Ramsay. The Stuarts could usually rely on the Catholics for support, but they represented a small part of the population. Nevertheless, when Charles Stuart was planning an invasion with the help of France in 1743, the Privy Council ordered the Earl of Cholmondeley, *Custos Rotulorum* of the county of Chester, to enforce punitive laws against Papists and suspected Papists. BL Add MS 33954, ff. 7–8. See also Glickman, *The English Catholic Community, 1688–1745* (Woodbridge, 2009).

[108] Hume, 'Protestant Succession', *Essays*, 506–7.   [109] Ibid., 507.

contention between the privileges of the people and the prerogatives of the crown', a domestic quarrel which allowed France to erect itself as a European superpower 'without any opposition from us, and even sometimes with our assistance'.[110] In contrast, in the sixty-year period after the Glorious Revolution, here referred to as a 'parliamentary establishment', 'an uninterrupted harmony has been preserved between our princes and our parliaments'.[111] In short, Britain in these years had enjoyed a longer period of glory and liberty than any other nation, according to Hume. This outcome stood in sharp contrast with the turbulence of the seventeenth century.

On the other hand, because of the exiled royal family, the same period had seen 'two rebellions [the "Fifteen" and "Forty-five"] ... besides plots and conspiracies without number'.[112] In other words, Hume would hardly have recognised J.H. Plumb's 'political stability'. Britain had so far been fortunate, but Hume feared that 'the claims of the banished family ... are not yet antiquated' and he had no reason to believe that the 'Forty-five' would be the last major Jacobite rebellion or invasion. As he had said in the *Treatise*, 'a century is scarce sufficient to establish any new government, or remove all scruples in the minds of the subjects concerning it'.[113] Hume believed that dynastic conflicts were even more dangerous than disputes between privilege and prerogative, because they could only be settled by war rather than debate and compromise.[114] What is more, a prince with a disputed title would not dare arm his subjects and set up a militia, an institution of which Hume approved.[115] Hume further argued that the 'precarious establishment' of the Hanoverians explained Britain's eagerness to contract debt to support the regime, a hazardous way of raising money in Hume's mind, as he expressed in 'Of Public Credit', also appearing in 1752.[116]

The situation of Hanover was precarious because even if Hume believed that a parliamentary title may be more advantageous to a hereditary one in theory, he was clear that most people would not see it that way.[117] As we have seen, he believed that bloodline was key in the eyes of the multitude. Why, then, had the Stuarts not been restored? The answer was that anti-Catholic sentiments in Britain were simply too strong. The real reason for the exclusion of the Stuart family was entirely their religion, Hume

---

[110] Ibid.   [111] Ibid., 508.   [112] Ibid.   [113] Hume, *Treatise*, 557.
[114] Hume, 'Protestant Succession', *Essays*, 508.
[115] Robertson, *The Scottish Enlightenment and the Militia Issue* (Edinburgh, 1985), 60–97.
[116] Hume, 'Protestant Succession', *Essays*, 509.   [117] Ibid., 646 (variant readings).

concluded, which threatened the country 'with much more dismal consequences' than the Hanoverian connection.[118] This was all for the better,
Hume believed. In addition to being more expensive and less tolerant than
Protestantism, the most important argument against Catholicism was that
it was *Roman* Catholicism, which not only separated the head of church
from the regal office, something Hume regarded as pernicious, but also
bestowed the sacerdotal, or priestly, office on a foreigner (the Pope), who
had a separate and sometimes opposite interest to that of the British
state.[119] Moreover, even if Catholicism had been advantageous to society,
it would be a mistake to have a sovereign of that religion when the great
majority of the people were Protestant, especially since the spirit of
moderation had made such slow advances in Europe.[120] The Stuarts were
aware of this problem. After landing in Scotland in 1745, Charles Edward
Stuart pledged 'not to impose upon any a religion they dislike, but to
secure them all the enjoyment of those which are respectively at present
establish'd among them, either in England, Scotland, or Ireland'.[121] In
desperation, Charles even converted to Anglicanism in the early 1750s, but
this backfired since it was seen as unprincipled.[122]

Although anti-Catholicism was the decisive factor for most people,
Hume gave one final reason why the balance tipped in favour of
Hanover, namely that they had attained longevity.[123] Hume believed that
the Hanoverians were now rightful kings according to the *imagination* of a
slender majority.[124] While it may have been difficult for an 'impartial
patriot' to choose between Hanover and Stuart immediately after the Act
of Settlement, the Hanoverian regime had now been more or less consol-
idated and it would be highly unwise to restore the Stuarts by way of civil
war.[125] Time had given legitimacy to the settlement, even if no one could
have known at the outset that it would turn out to be beneficial. For
Hume, a government had to be judged on its present merit; its foundation
was to a large degree irrelevant. As he had set out in the *Treatise*, few, if
any, governments in history had a better foundation for their authority
than present possession, and a sudden change would result in confusion
and bloodshed.[126] In the final analysis, then, Hume's intention was to
undermine the Jacobite case.

---

[118] Ibid., 510.   [119] Ibid.   [120] Ibid.
[121] He further promised 'to pass any law, that his Parliament shall judge necessary' for the protection
of Protestantism in *Declaration of Charles Prince of Wales* [1745], in *English Jacobite Ballads*, 131–2.
[122] McLynn, *Bonnie Prince Charlie* (London, 2003), 399.   [123] See also Hume, *Treatise*, 566.
[124] For Hume's justification by psychology, see Forbes, *Hume's Philosophical Politics*, 91–101.
[125] Hume, 'Protestant Succession', *Essays*, 510–11.   [126] Hume, *Treatise*, 558, 557.

We have to remember, however, that his intention was to refute the speculative systems of both parties, and his approval of the Hanoverians was a balance sheet assessment which boiled down to the avoidance of a bloody counter-revolution.[127] Indeed, Hume himself said that he 'very liberally abused both Whigs and Tories' in the essay.[128] In comparison with establishment discourse in the aftermath of the 'Forty-five', his treatment of Toryism and Jacobitism was fairly balanced and respectful. It would thus be an exaggeration to speak of Hume's 'utter lack of sympathy with the Jacobite cause', as Hume's latest biographer has done.[129] Hume had many Jacobite friends,[130] and he sent the new essays discussed in this chapter to the known Jacobite Lord Elibank in January 1748, joking that 'I am afraid that your Lordship will differ from me with regard to the Protestant Succession, whose Advantages you will probably rate higher than I have done.'[131]

Hume's approach can helpfully be contrasted with his fellow Scotsman Thomas Gordon's narrative of the rise of the Tory party in the fourth volume of the *Independent Whig*, written after the Jacobite rising of 1745–6 and mainly a commentary on that event. Rather than depicting the Tories as lovers of British liberty, as Hume had done in 1741, Gordon only viewed them as 'fierce Enthusiasts for Popish and Arbitrary Princes' in the reigns of Charles II and James II/VII and later 'Enthusiasts, more fierce, if possible, against a zealous Protestant Prince [William III/II]'.[132] Anti-Catholicism, which was the key Hanoverian argument in the 1740s,[133] was part of Hume's case, but his was a more complex argument which did not simply equate Catholicism with despotism, and he also emphasised the importance of longevity. Finally, he refrained from the temptation to point to what could be presented as a glaring contradiction between the belief in passive obedience and resistance to Hanover.[134] Hume's approach was in some ways close to that of his countryman

---

[127] Wallace warned the Jacobites that 'there are many thousands in Britain who will spill the last drops of their blood to support the Revolution', adding that 'I don't write in this manner from an inclination to Bully but to set before you the difficulties you may expect'. *Address to the Jacobites*, ff. 23–4.

[128] Hume to John Clephane, 4 February 1752, *Letters*, I, 167.   [129] Harris, *Hume*, 234.

[130] Mossner, *The Life of Hume* (Oxford, 1954), 177–86.

[131] Mossner, 'New Hume Letters to Lord Elibank', *Texas Studies in Literature and Language*, 4 (1962), 437.

[132] Trenchard and Gordon, *The Independent Whig* (4 vols., London, 1741–7 [1720–47]), IV, 352.

[133] Cleghorn, *The Spirit and Principles of the Whigs and Jacobites Compared*, 41–4; Monod, *Jacobitism and the English People*, 43.

[134] This was an argument employed by Henry Fielding in his ironically entitled *Jacobite's Journal* (1747–8); see *The Jacobite's Journal* (Oxford, 1974), 158.

Wallace, who also made the effort to seek to understand the Jacobites, asserting his belief that their conviction must have stemmed from 'mistaken views of the Interest of your Country … without any wicked intention'.[135] Like Hume, Wallace also stressed the importance of longevity.[136]

In the aftermath of the Jacobite rebellion Hume was critical of the vindictive behaviour of many Whigs. In October 1747, Hume wrote a lesser-known pamphlet in which he defended his friend Archibald Stewart, former Lord Provost of Edinburgh, who surrendered the city to the Jacobite army. As part of a wider crackdown on Jacobitism after Culloden, Stewart found himself imprisoned and tried.[137] Hume argued that Stewart had done a noble deed by avoiding a bloodbath since Edinburgh was so poorly defended. As Stewart was acquitted before Hume had published the pamphlet at the start of 1748, Hume added a postscript in which he noted that the trial had become a party-political affair, and Stewart's acquittal had been bemoaned by certain Whigs while celebrated by the Tory-Jacobites.

In the postscript, Hume, echoing Rapin's *Dissertation*, made a distinction between political and religious Whigs: 'The Idea I form of a political *Whig*, is that of a Man of Sense and Moderation, a Lover of Laws and Liberty, whose chief Regard to particular Princes and Families, is founded on a Regard to the publick Good'.[138] By contrast, Hume believed that the characteristics of a religious Whig were 'Dissimulation, Hypocrisy, Violence, Calumny, [and] Selfishness'.[139] According to Hume, '[t]his Species of *Whigs* … form but the Fag-end of the Party, and are, at the Bottom, very heartily despised by their own Leaders'.[140] He compared such Whigs to leading 'Roundheads' and 'Covenanters' from the Wars of the Three Kingdoms and Commonwealth era, including Oliver Cromwell, Henry Ireton, and Archibald Johnston of Wariston. These could presumably be regarded as Whigs *avant la lettre* for Hume because of their anti-Episcopalian bias. On this basis, he argued that the 'religious *Whigs* … are

---

[135] Wallace, *Address to the Jacobites*, f. 7. Wallace was bending over backwards to treat the Jacobites respectfully. When discussing the religion of kings in his unpublished pamphlet, he struck out 'a bigotted' before 'Papist', clarifying in a note to the editor that 'to avoid offence I shall not call him a bigoted [Papist]'). He also changed 'his own Bigotry' to 'his attachment to popery' (ff. 10–11).

[136] Ibid., f. 24.

[137] For the immediate context and the punitive action against Jacobitism in Scotland, see Bruce Lenman, *The Jacobite Risings in Britain* (London, 1980), 260–82.

[138] Hume, *A True Account of the Behaviour and Conduct of Archibald Stewart, Esq: Late Lord Provost of Edinburgh* (London, 1748), 33.

[139] Ibid., 33–4.   [140] Ibid., 34.

much worse than the religious *Tories*; as the political *Tories* are inferior to the political Whigs'.[141] In this context, Hume was eager to point out, maybe as a provocation since his friend had already been acquitted, that he regarded divine right Tories as superior to Whig extremists: '[A] Zeal for Bishops, and for the Books of Common-Prayer, tho' equally groundless, has never been able, when mixt up with Party Notions, to form so virulent and exalted a Poison in human Breasts, as the opposite Principles.'[142] Hume concluded that all *political* Whigs, unlike *religious* Whigs, were pleased with the acquittal of Stewart because he was innocent, adding, 'I am charitable enough to suppose, that the Joy of many of the *Tories* flowed from the same Motive.'[143]

The postscript thus offered a classic Humean paradox: the Whigs may have had the soundest politics, but some of their supporters, the fanatic Presbyterians, were more violent and zealous than even the High Church followers of the Tory party. As Hume had set out in 'Superstition and Enthusiasm', Protestant sects may have been conducive to civil liberty, but they were also violent, as he would elaborate in his *History*. In other words, Whigs were not necessarily more tolerant of their ideological opponents just because they were tolerant of various Protestant Dissenters, who were their supporters. Indeed, Hume evidently believed that the contrary was the case. 'Passion and Party-Zeal' when carried too far had little regard for justice, he lamented: 'many of the *Whigs* have betrayed such a furious Zeal on this Occasion, that they are mortified, or rather indeed inraged to the last Degree, that an innocent Man has been found innocent'.[144] At the same time, he was prepared to vindicate moderates in both parties in a Rapinesque manner. This episode and pamphlet can only strengthen our conviction that Hume sought to give a fair hearing to Whigs and Tories alike, even as he was writing *against* both parties' systems. On a personal level, he was as relieved as he was surprised that both Whigs and Tories supported his election as Keeper of the Advocates Library in Edinburgh in 1752.[145] He had expected to be opposed by both sides.

Conclusion

To conclude, Hume never seemed to have believed that Toryism had become indistinguishable from the patriot creed in the 1740s, as has been

---

[141] Ibid., 33.   [142] Ibid.   [143] Ibid., 34.   [144] Ibid., 32–3.
[145] Hume to Clephane, 4 February 1752, *Letters*, I, 167.

argued by Robert (Bob) Harris.[146] Nor did Hume think that the Whigs had become Tories by virtue of having become a Court party and pursuing such seemingly authoritarian policies as the Riot Act, which was a common opposition rant. For Hume, an analysis of the parties' speculative systems of thought in many ways helped to explain their more practical commitments, which he had sketched in his earlier essays. To generalise and simplify, Tories believed in divine right because they were High Church, and the concrete consequences of such a belief were indefeasible hereditary right and passive obedience, which in turn explained their penchant for Jacobitism. Conversely, being Low Church, Whigs regarded government as man-made and based on a conditional contract which gave subjects the right to withdraw their consent and resist authority. In their minds, James II/VII had broken the contract and was justly opposed and replaced. Their allegiance to Hanover was thus unproblematic.

Fully aware that party passion was not going to disappear, Hume's intention was to sound a note of moderation in the midst of division, and pacify party animosity by revealing the strengths and weaknesses of both parties' ideologies and worldviews, both of which could be beneficial if not taken too far. Neither speculative system held water if philosophically and historically probed, which Hume was keen to demonstrate, being convinced that the political legitimacy of states and political systems had to be divorced from their foundations. His way of discussing politics and comparing parties set him apart from virtually all his contemporaries. Hume even discussed the Protestant Succession in a cool and indifferent manner. The main reason he gave against a Jacobite restoration was the overarching need to avoid a civil war, and he arrived at this conclusion after he had offered several concessions to the Jacobite case. He was clear that obedience was the general rule and that armed resistance to the established government was only permitted in cases of egregious tyranny like that of Nero, and the Hanoverian kings did not come close.[147] That may well be

---

[146] Harris, *A Patriot Press*, 48–83. It may well have been the case that 'patriotism' motivated a substantial body of people 'without doors' (82), but many people remained motivated by Tory-Jacobitism. It also played a large part at elections. For example, when Charles Lennox, courtier and friend of the Pelhams, wrote to John Hill in June 1747 to advise him who to vote for in impending elections in Westminster and Middlesex, he had no qualms about the fact that ''tis the honest old Whig cause I recommend to you in opposition to the Jacobite schemes'. BL Stowe MS 155, f. 116. Moreover, it is clear from Perceval's and other diaries that the Tories remained a parliamentary bloc in the late 1740s and early 1750s. *Egmont Papers*, 108–11, 159, 178, 204.

[147] It is doubtful whether James II/VII qualified as a tyrant according to Hume's criteria, but his point was that this mattered little sixty years later. James was a harmless if not a good man in his private character, but he had mistaken the nature of the constitution and lacked due regard for the nation's religion; see Hume, *Essays*, 492; Hume, *History*, VI, 520–1.

why he called his essay 'Passive Obedience' as opposed to 'Divine Right', even if both aspects of the Tory doctrine were part of his discussion. He wanted to encourage Tory-Jacobites to limit their resistance to making disloyal toasts and not taking oaths, which was indeed what most Jacobites did.[148] Although Hume's exact arguments only come alive when considered in their specific contexts, he set a gold standard for all subsequent debaters aspiring to moderation amid tribal strife. While it may not be possible to label even a balance sheet Hanoverian a non-partisan in an age still dominated by dynastic conflict, he may have approximated that ideal as far as was possible in a divided society.[149]

---

[148] Hume's emphasis on obedience can thus be read as a message to the Jacobites; see Forbes, *Hume's Philosophical Politics*, 91–101.

[149] This description is more commonly associated with an earlier period; see Holmes and Speck (eds), *The Divided Society* (London, 1967).

CHAPTER 7

Hume and the History of Party in England

This parliament [of 1621] is remarkable for being the epoch, in which were first regularly formed, though without acquiring these denominations, the parties of court and country; parties, which have ever since continued, and which, while they oft threaten the total dissolution of the government, are the real causes of its permanent life and vigour.

Hume, *The History of England* (1754–61)

Background and Contexts

Hume's *History of England* (6 vols., 1754–61) has commonly been hailed as a cosmopolitan history,[1] which may be true but should not distract us from the fact that domestic politics was a vital part of the work. As Richard Bourke has put it, 'politics, for Hume, had a very specific meaning centred on the dynamics of "party" or factional struggle'[2] – an approach shared by Rapin. Hume explained to Smith that he began his historical investigation with the Stuart period partly because the factions, which he believed still informed British politics in the eighteenth century, arose at that time.[3] His own historical work, however, was a conscious attempt to rise above faction and to see things both ways,[4] which he believed English

---

[1] O'Brien, *Narratives of Enlightenment* (Oxford, 1997), ch. 3; Forbes, 'The European, or Cosmopolitan, Dimension in Hume's Science of Politics', *BJECS*, 1 (1978), 57–60; Forbes, 'Introduction', in Hume, *The History of Great Britain* (Middlesex, 1970); Meinecke, *Historism* (London, 1972 [1936]), 176.

[2] Bourke, 'Pocock and the Presuppositions of the New British History', *HJ*, 53 (2010), 747–70.

[3] Hume to Smith, 24 September 1752, *Letters*, I, 168. He later came to regret that he had not begun with Henry VII, since that was when 'modern History commence[d]'; see Hume to Andrew Millar, 20 May 1757, *Letters*, I, 249. He further believed that he would have escaped many objections by beginning with the Tudors, because it could then be shown that James I/VI's ideas about the royal prerogative differed little from his illustrious predecessor, Elizabeth I. Hume to Clephane, 3 September 1757, *Letters*, I, 264; Hume to Catharine Macaulay, 29 March 1764, *New Letters*, 80–2. See also Hume, *History*, IV, appendix III.

[4] He later admitted that he fell short of his own standard of impartiality when he originally started, as he believed that he was too infected with Whiggism. Hume to Gilbert Elliot, 12 March 1763, *New Letters*, 69–70.

historiography had failed to do before him.[5] Not only did the factions emerge in the Stuart period, 'the misrepresentations of faction [in history writing] began chiefly to take place' at that time.[6]

According to Smith, it had been the fate of all modern histories of England to be written in a 'party spirit', and Rapin had been 'the most candid' before Hume.[7] Even if it would be a mistake to see Rapin as a straightforward party writer in the same mould as Bishop Burnet, the Frenchman had clearly not been entirely free from partiality and Hume sought to improve on the Huguenot in this regard. Hume was well acquainted with Rapin's writings when he began his historical work.[8] Having been a friendly critic and even an admirer, he became increasingly disapproving as time wore on.[9] He downgraded Rapin to a 'compiler',[10] for him in the same category as Carte and Echard.[11] We shall see, however, that Hume remained indebted to Rapin's framework to an extent. Just as he believed that he could rely on Carte for background without subscribing to Jacobitism,[12] so the same could be said of Rapin and Whiggism.

As we have seen, Hume believed that embracing a party was out of the question for a philosophically minded anatomist of politics. As Pierre Bayle had put it, '[t]he very perfection of a good history is to be disagreeable to all sects and to all nations, given that it proves that the author flatters neither one party nor the other, but has given his frank opinion of each'.[13] While Hume's obsession with impartiality was not novel in the eighteenth century,[14] the way he pursued this goal was. Being disinterested for Hume

---

[5] For statements of this intention, see *Letters*, I, 171, 179; 185, 193, 210, 226, 235, 242, 244, 461; New *Letters*, 231. See also Pocock, *Barbarism and Religion* (6 vols., Cambridge, 1999–2015), II, ch. 11.

[6] Hume, 'My Own Life', *Essays*, xxxvi.

[7] Smith, *Lectures on Rhetoric and Belles Lettres* (Indianapolis, 1985), 116.

[8] Hume to Michael Ramsay, [1730], *Letters*, II, 337. As we saw in Chapter 4, his historical account in 'Of the Parties of Great Britain' was heavily indebted to Rapin, and he had also referred to the Frenchman approvingly in 'The Original Contract' and 'The Protestant Succession', discussed in Chapter 6.

[9] *Letters*, I, 170, 179, 258.

[10] For a distinction between 'compilers', whose work contained large chunks of transcriptions from other works and primary documents, and lacked a clear narrative voice, on the one hand, and genuine Enlightenment historians, on the other, see Okie, *Augustan Historical Writing* (Lanham, 1991), 210. For Hume's ambition to go beyond 'compiling-history' and write 'polite' history, see Hicks, *Neoclassical History and English Culture* (Basingstoke, 1996), ch. 7.

[11] Hume to [John Francis Erskine], 26 July [*c*.1755–8?], *Further Letters*, 33.

[12] Hume was greatly indebted to Carte, particularly for the mediaeval segment of the *History*. See Harris, *David Hume* (Cambridge, 2015), 390–1.

[13] Bayle, *Political Writings* (Cambridge, 2012), 331.

[14] Hugh Blair listed 'Impartiality, Fidelity, and Accuracy' as the fundamental qualities of a historian. He also said that a historian 'must not enter into faction, nor give scope to affection' in *Lectures on Rhetoric and Belles Lettres* (Carbondale, 2005 [1783]), 397.

did not mean never taking sides or favouring a particular policy of any party, but rather avoiding following a consistent party line; in other words, being independent.[15] Hume's *History* puzzled many readers by containing a mixture of traditional Whig and Tory positions, sometimes in close proximity. Hume himself said that '[m]y view of *things* are more conformable to Whig principles; my presentations of *persons* to Tory prejudices', referring to the combination of his balance sheet defence of the Glorious Revolution with his sympathy for at least some of the Stuart kings in the seventeenth century.[16] He also came to believe that the first and second Stuart volumes – the *History of Great Britain*, which later became volumes five and six of the *History of England* – should have been published together, because whereas the first volume was more favourable to Tory opinion, the second one was more Whig.[17] If considered together, he believed that the right balance had been struck. Historians disagree about Hume's success in this respect.[18]

Hume's *History of Great Britain* caused an outcry, chiefly among Whigs, among them Robert Wallace, because of his unwillingness to villainise the Stuarts, at least James I/VI and Charles I, leading to suspicion of Jacobitism.[19] Hume complained in a letter to an ex-Jacobite that he was unfairly conflated with Carte, who in a notorious footnote claimed that the Stuart Pretender had cured a man of scrofula by the royal touch.[20] For Hume, it was vulgar to think that 'the Cause of Charles the I and James the 2 were the same, because they were of the same Family'.[21] Hume said that all revisions he made to his *History* were 'invariably to the Tory party', meaning that he became less and less inclined to blame the Stuart

---

[15] Hume to James Oswald, 28 June 1753, *Letters*, I, 179, 189; Hume, 'My Own Life', xxxviii.

[16] Hume to Clephane, 1756, *Letters*, I, 237.

[17] Hume to Millar, 12 April 1755, *Letters*, I, 217–18. Hume predicted that this would be the case after having finished the first volume; see Hume to Clephane, 28 October 1753, *Letters*, I, 180.

[18] For accounts that put emphasis on Hume's 'Tory' leanings, see Giarrizzo, *David Hume politico e storico* (Turin, 1962); Okie, *Augustan Historical Writing*, 195–207. For the opposite view, see Wootton, 'Hume, the Historian', in *The Cambridge Companion to Hume* (Cambridge, 2006).

[19] Wallace, *Characteristics of the Present Political State of Great Britain* (London, 1758), 56–8. For accusations of Jacobitism, see *Letters*, I, 222, 263–4, 314. The cold reception was only initial, however. The complete *History* replaced Rapin's as the standard history of England, and became the most popular such work ever written, until it was eclipsed by Macaulay in the nineteenth century. Okie, *Augustan Historical Writing*, 195.

[20] Hume to Balcarres, 17 December 1754, *Letters*, I, 214; Carte, *A General History of England* (4 vols., London, 1747–55), I, 291–2 (note 4). Carte's *History* received financial backing from people and institutions with Tory-Jacobite backgrounds such as Cotton, Wynn, Beaufort, Oxford University, and the City of London, but also the Whig Speaker Arthur Onslow. Carte MS 175, Bodleian.

[21] Hume to Strahan, 30 November 1756, *Letters*, I, 235.

monarchs for the turbulent seventeenth century.[22] What is more, he allegedly told Boswell that 'he became a greater friend to the Stuart family as he advanced in studying for his *History*; and he hoped he had vindicated the two first of them so effectually that they would never again be attacked'.[23] What underpinned this disinclination to blame the early Stuart monarchs, and even 'shed[ding] a generous tear for the fate of Charles I',[24] was not Jacobitism in any meaningful sense but his disbelief in the myth of the ancient constitution.[25] For Hume, there was no ancient constitution, but a series of constitutions.[26] Burke remarked that this did not mean that Hume let the Stuarts off the hook entirely; they could still be duly criticised for 'not having sagacity enough to see that they had fallen in the times, when, from the opinions and fashions of the age, it behoved them to slacken and remit of the authority exercised by their predecessors'.[27]

It may be hard to understand why Hume was so harshly criticised by Whigs for breaking with the ancient constitution tradition. Brady had been appropriated by Whigs as far back as the Convocation Controversy of 1697–1701, in opposition to the 'ancient liberty' argument by the Tory and future Jacobite Francis Atterbury.[28] Tories had long been eager to argue for ancient liberties such as fair and frequent elections, notably in the debates about the Septennial Act 1716.[29] As we saw in Chapter 3, ministerial Whigs in the 1730s had embraced a 'modern liberty' thesis in opposition to Bolingbroke, notably in Hervey's *Ancient and Modern Liberty* (1734). The Court Whigs still differed from Hume, however, because they were never prepared to vindicate the Stuart kings in any way, even if this would have been a logical extension of their argument.[30] Moreover, that ancient constitutionalism had had a renaissance as Whig

---

[22] Hume, 'My Own Life', xxxviii. See also Mossner, 'Was Hume a Tory Historian?', *Journal of the History of Ideas*, 2 (1941), 225–36, which shows that a great majority if not all of Hume's revisions can be labelled as 'Tory' in accordance with Hume's own understanding of the term. However, Forbes has demonstrated that many changes were simply stylistic and that Hume's main thesis remained the same; see *Hume's Philosophical Politics*, 324–6.

[23] *Boswell's Edinburgh Journals 1767–1786* (Edinburgh, 2013), 258.

[24] Hume, 'My Own Life', xxxvii.

[25] Johnson, a royalist and Jacobite of sorts, knew that he had no ally in Hume; 'Sir, the fellow is a Tory by chance', as he had said to Boswell. *Boswell's Edinburgh Journals*, 258.

[26] Hume, *History*, IV, 355 (note l). Cf. Pocock, *Barbarism and Religion*, II, ch. 14.

[27] Review of the *History* in the *Annual Register*, vol. 4, December 1761, in *Early Responses to Hume* (10 vols., Bristol, 2005), VII, 264.

[28] Smith, *The Gothic Bequest* (Cambridge, 1987) 28–38.

[29] See the speeches of Shippen, Bromley, Nottingham, and others in *Parl. Hist.*, vol. VII.

[30] Forbes, *Hume's Philosophical Politics*, 248–9.

orthodoxy in Hume's day can be seen from George Lyttelton's *History of Henry II* (1767–71), whose Whiggery Hume ironically recommended to Smith.[31]

Hume's *History* acquired a persistent reputation of being Tory and royalist, as can be seen in the way it was interpreted by Gilbert Stuart later in the eighteenth century and George Brodie in the nineteenth century.[32] However, Hume's *History* was Whig in the sense of defending the Revolution Settlement of 1688–9, even if it sought to demonstrate its accidental nature. This was comparable to the Court Whig position personified by Hervey and was called 'true Whig principles' by the Jacobite Sir James Steuart.[33] It stood in sharp contrast with Bolingbroke, who had described the settlement as a confirmation of Magna Carta.[34] Hume may well have had Bolingbroke in mind when he scoffed at '[t]hose who, from a pretended respect to antiquity, appeal at every turn to an original plan of the constitution, only cover their turbulent spirit and their private ambition under the appearance of venerable forms'.[35] As we saw in Chapter 4, the paper war between the Court Whigs and Bolingbroke was in many ways the immediate context for Hume's early essays. It is evident that Bolingbroke was still on Hume's mind when he turned to history, as he referred to the *Dissertation upon Parties* in the second Stuart volume.[36] While he agreed with Bolingbroke that history was philosophy teaching by example,[37] they drew different lessons from their respective studies, even if there was also common ground.

As will become clear, when describing the rise of party in English history Hume was not partial to either the Whigs or the Tories, or to any of their predecessors. His key concern was to investigate how religion, faction, and interest were all connected and mutually supportive principles that produced 'party spirit'. Bolingbroke would have agreed with him in this respect. However, Hume also explained in more detail and with greater

---

[31] *Letters*, II, 150.

[32] Stuart, selections from *A View of Society in Europe in its Progress from Rudeness to Refinement* (1778) and Brodie, selections from *History of the British Empire* (1822), in *Early Responses*, VIII, 50–5, 217–72. See also Richard Hurd's critique of Hume's alleged Toryism in *Early Responses*, VII, 173–80, and Kidd, *Subverting Scotland's Past* (Cambridge, 1993), 240, 244. For the multifaceted reception of Hume's *History* among various reading communities, see Towsey, *Reading History in Britain and America* (Cambridge, 2019), esp. ch. 3.

[33] Steuart to Hume, 10 November 1767, *Letters of Eminent Persons to Hume* (Edinburgh, 1849), 175–6.

[34] Pocock, *The Ancient Constitution* (New York, 1987 [1957]), 231–2.   [35] Hume, *History*, II, 525.

[36] Ibid., VI, 377.

[37] Hume, *History*, V, 545. See also Hume, *Enquiry concerning Human Understanding* (Oxford, 1975 [1748]), 83.

sophistication how the constitution of England, at the time uncertainly balanced between royal prerogative and parliamentary privilege, gave birth to parties of government and opposition. Hume's history of party in the seventeenth century will be reconstructed at length below, because it is arguably the most refined eighteenth-century account of the non-linear emergence of party.

'Court' and 'Country' under James I

The crucial difference between Hume and Rapin (and his 'disciple' Bolingbroke) was that the latter believed that the first Stuart kings had actively tried to stretch the royal prerogative. Hume's denial of this claim put him closer to his contemporary compatriot William Guthrie, who published *A General History of England from the Invasion of Julius Caesar to 1688* in four volumes between 1744 and 1751.[38] While Hume diverged from Rapin's ancient constitutionalism, in his account of the rise of party in the seventeenth century, we shall see that he remained indebted to Rapin's narrative in some important respects.[39] This is not strange; he also shared Smith's low opinion of Burnet,[40] but nevertheless referred to him frequently, particularly in the second Stuart volume. Hume followed Rapin in arguing that 'party' as a parliamentary phenomenon began in the reign of James I, and that the underlying facilitators could be traced to the previous century: the split in the Protestant church between Episcopalians and Puritans, and a gradual revolution in learning and manners.[41] The Elizabethan age was thus the dawn of the mixed constitution, as the 'precious spark of liberty' had been kindled and preserved by the Puritan sect.[42] As a result of differences in religious opinions, England 'contained the seeds of intestine discord', which is why the Stuart volumes should not be considered in isolation from the Tudor volumes.[43]

These novelties in the Tudor period, which truly took hold in the seventeenth century, meant that 'the love of freedom . . . acquired new force' in the shape of 'a passion for a limited constitution'.[44] As Hobbes had been dismayed

---

[38] Forbes, *Hume's Philosophical Politics*, 253–8. Hume likened Tudor England to Turkey and Elizabeth to Peter the Great in *History*, IV, 360, 364.

[39] The fact that he did not refer to Rapin in the footnotes does not mean much. Hume was criticised by Horace Walpole and others for omitting references in general. *Letters*, I, 284–5.

[40] Hume to Millar, 4 December 1756, *Letters*, I, 235–6.

[41] Hume, *History*, III, 81–2, 211–12, 290, 339, 347, IV, 123, 167, 278, 384–5.

[42] Ibid., IV, 145–6. This perspective had been anticipated by the Dissenting minister Daniel Neal in his *History of the Puritans* (1732); see Okie, *Augustan Historical Writing*, 85–91.

[43] Hume, *History*, IV, 147.   [44] Ibid., V, 18.

to see, men of high birth and education were particularly fond of reading Greek and Roman authors, who, according to Hume, encouraged an emulation of 'manly virtues'.[45] Even if James I's accession in 1603 had been smooth, Hume emphasised that the new king was not popular enough to keep 'this rising spirit' within narrow bounds as his prudent predecessor.[46] The king, who 'had established within his own mind a speculative system of absolute government', found himself of an 'opposite disposition' from his parliament.[47] The 'spirit of liberty' that became increasingly dominant, particularly in the Commons, was the beginning of a 'more regular plan of liberty'.[48] It was now evident that leading members 'less aspired at maintaining the ancient constitution, than at establishing a new one, and a freer, and a better'.[49]

Hume was clear that zeal for civil liberty and religious principles had been conflated in the 'great revolution of manners, which happened during the sixteenth and the seventeenth centuries', across Europe but particularly in England.[50] At this point the Commons became increasingly powerful, as the balance of property had shifted in their favour.[51] In his essays, Hume had modified Harrington's thesis that power followed property by arguing that this was only the case when the original constitution allocated a share of power to the order of 'men' concerned, as with the lower house in England.[52] All this produced a much different political and intellectual climate at the beginning of the seventeenth century. As Hume said plainly in private, this was the time when England became a cultivated nation; by contrast, '*When good Queen Elizabeth sat on the Throne*, there was very little good Roast Beef in [England], and no Liberty at all.'[53]

Hume stressed that even though the 'spirit of liberty' had been kindled under Elizabeth by the Puritans,[54] it was now it truly became a force to be reckoned with. The opposing doctrines of divine right and passive obedience could be traced to homilies in Elizabeth's reign.[55] Rather than being invented in the Stuart age, they 'were only found by the court to be more necessary at that period, by reason of the opposite doctrines, which *began* to be promulgated by the puritanical party'.[56] In this clash of contrasting

---

[45] Ibid., 19. For the role of humanist rhetoric in this period, see Peltonen, *Rhetoric, Politics, and Popularity in Pre-Revolutionary England* (Cambridge, 2013).
[46] Hume, *History*, V, 3, 19.   [47] Ibid., 19.   [48] Ibid., 40.   [49] Ibid., 42.   [50] Ibid., 80.
[51] Ibid., 40. See also ibid., III, 77, 80; 'Of Refinements in the Arts' (1752, originally 'Of Luxury'), *Essays*, 278.
[52] Hume, 'First Principles of Government', *Essays*, 33, 35.
[53] Hume to Thomas Percy, 16 January 1773, *New Letters*, 198.   [54] Hume *History*, IV, 146.
[55] Ibid., IV, 357, V, 563 (note q). Hume also stressed that patriarchal theory was not invented by Filmer.
[56] Ibid., V, 127. As Forbes pointed out, 'began' was not italicised in the first edition.

principles, religious and political, the first Stuart monarch could not resist putting his head above the parapet. James I/VI – a scholar in his own right[57] – had an unfortunate fondness for discussing theology. From the Hampton Court Conference at the beginning of his reign, the king 'showed the strongest propensity to the established church'.[58]

All these factors combined to produce an environment conducive to the birth of parties. Like Rapin, Hume identified the parliament of 1621 as 'the epoch, in which were first regularly formed, though without acquiring these denominations, the parties of court and country', or parties of government and opposition.[59] Closely paraphrasing the Frenchman, Hume stressed that these were 'parties, which have since continued'.[60] These formulations were originally part of the main text of the *History*, but were later moved to an endnote, as Hume did not want to interrupt the narrative with too many digressions.[61] They should not be regarded as views he later repudiated, however, and he kept them in the note because they were 'important'.[62] Moreover, a similar statement was retained in the main body of text towards the end of the same chapter.[63] The immediate context for the advent of these 'parties' was public displeasure over the king's policy towards Spain and Roman Catholics in England, as James I/VI sought to bring about a marriage treaty with Philip III. This stirred up anti-Catholic sentiments and brought parliamentary opposition to the king to a new level, according to Hume. Whether Hume and Rapin were correct to identify 1621 as the beginning of the Court–Country party system does not concern us here since our interest is the way 'party' was understood in the eighteenth century.[64]

Hume's argument was not entirely taken from Rapin. In a significant modification, he argued that parliamentary 'parties' emerged under James I/VI because parliament became important for the first time.[65] Under the feudal constitution, parliament only sat for a few days and no one would then have dared oppose the monarch as he would have found himself unprotected upon the dissolution of parliament a few days after. Even under the Tudors, parliament was not a road to either honour or

---

[57] Albeit a 'middling' one, according to Hume; see ibid., 154.   [58] Ibid., 12.

[59] Ibid., 556. By contrast, Guthrie pointed to the parliamentary session of 1614 as the beginning of 'constitutional opposition' to James I; see *A General History of England* (4 vols., 1744–51), IV, 703.

[60] Hume, *History*, V, 556.   [61] Hume to William Robertson, 25 January 1759, *Letters*, I, 294.

[62] Hume, *History*, V, 558.   [63] Ibid., 121.

[64] However, recent work suggests that the political culture of the early Stuart age became increasingly adversarial; see Peltonen, *Rhetoric, Politics, and Popularity*.

[65] For the servility of parliaments in the Tudor era, see Hume, *History*, III, 264, 323, IV, 144–5, 346, 374.

preferment, as it was merely an 'organ of royal will and pleasure'.[66] In such a situation, '[o]pposition would have been regarded as a species of rebellion'.[67] It had been perfectly natural for James 'to take the government as he found it', but alas 'neither his circumstances nor his character could support so extensive an authority' as exemplified by Elizabeth.[68] Due to his small revenue and lack of frugality, he became increasingly dependent on parliament. Thanks to a general spread of knowledge and greater emphasis on civil liberty, the outcome was that 'a party, watchful of a free constitution, was regularly formed in the house of commons'. Crucially, these political considerations intermingled with religious views. Hume believed that royal authority remained so extensive that few would have considered 'resisting it, had they not been stimulated by religious motives, which inspire a courage unsurmountable by any human obstacle'.[69] Importantly, Hume's choice of words is indicative of intellectual distance between him and Bayle, who argued against the importance of religion in human motivation.[70] Accordingly, Episcopalians rallied behind the Court party, and the Puritans behind the Country party. The 'bold, daring, and uncontrouled' spirit of the latter made them inclined towards republican principles.[71] Similarly, the alliance between monarchical power and ecclesiastical authority was a natural one.[72]

Even if Hume believed that a parliamentary party system of sorts was now emerging, it remained irregular. This was a time when parliamentary sessions were short, and most saw England as an unmixed monarchy, and parliament as a mere ornament.[73] This general perception was key, as government was entirely founded on opinion, according to Hume.[74] He did not just think that the Court and Country parties that emerged in the parliament of 1621 still informed British party politics. Even more strikingly, he claimed that 'while they [the parties] oft threaten the total dissolution of the government, [they] are the real causes of its permanent life and vigour'.[75] This statement, a classical Humean paradox, was more positive than anything he had written in his previous essays about parties.[76]

---

[66] Ibid., V, 557 (note j).   [67] Ibid. See also Ibid., IV, 368.   [68] Ibid., V, 558.   [69] Ibid.
[70] Bayle, *Miscellaneous Reflections, Occasion'd by the Comet* (London, 1708), esp. section CLXI.
[71] Hume, *History*, V, 559.   [72] Ibid., 558.   [73] Ibid., 127.
[74] Ibid., 128; Hume, 'First Principles of Government', *Essays*, 32–3.   [75] Hume, *History*, V, 556.
[76] Despite this statement, many scholars, even those citing from the *History*, persist in arguing that Hume simply 'condemned parties'; see, e.g., Halliday, *Dismembering the Body Politic* (Cambridge, 1998), 8.

A similar wording can be found in Montesquieu's *De l'esprit des lois*, which had made a major intellectual impression on Hume between his early political essays and the publication of the *History*. After having described the British constitution (or the English constitution, as he called it) in book eleven of his *chef-d'œuvre*, Montesquieu proceeded in the final chapter of book nineteen to adumbrate how Britain was perpetually divided into two 'parties', one inclining to the executive and the other to the legislative power.[77] With the power of patronage, 'all those who would obtain something from [the executive] would be inclined to move to that side, and it could be attacked by all those who could expect nothing from it'.[78] The competition generated 'hatred, envy, jealousy, and the ardor for enriching and distinguishing oneself ... to the full extent'.[79] However, since Montesquieu saw liberty as the principle of the British constitution, 'if this were otherwise, the state would be like a man who, laid low by disease, has no passions because he has no strength'.[80] Montesquieu's discussion of the executive and legislative partisans is believed to have been derived from Bolingbroke's Court–Country analysis of British politics in the *Craftsman*, with which Hume had already engaged in his essays.[81]

Hume had read *De l'esprit des lois* in the autumn of 1748, the same year the book was published. The following spring he wrote a lengthy letter to Montesquieu, congratulating him for having written a work 'qui sera l'admiration de tous les siècles'.[82] He then proceeded to give Montesquieu detailed feedback on specific passages, before returning to flattery, noting that Bath (Pulteney) had quoted the Frenchman in the Lords.[83] Hume believed that the French aristocrat, with some justification, had made the English proud of their beloved form of government. However, this pride should not lead to complacency: 'Mais ne peut-on pas remarquer que, si les formes simples de gouvernement sont par leur nature sujettes à l'abus, parce qu'il n'ya aucun contrepoids, d'un autre côté les formes compliquées où une partie réprime l'autre, sont, comme les machines compliquées, sujettes à déranger par le contraste et l'opposition des parties.'[84] In other words, Hume believed that Montesquieu had been

---

[77] Montesquieu, *The Spirit of the Laws*, (Cambridge, 2015 [1748]), 325.   [78] Ibid.
[79] Ibid., 325, 156.   [80] Ibid.   [81] See Chapter 3, note 219.   [82] *Letters*, I, 133.
[83] Hume could not help mocking Bolingbroke's erstwhile opposition colleague who had joined the government side upon the fall of Walpole in 1742 but was 'à présent dans le opposition; vous avez que ces distinctions ne sont pas souvent de longue durée parmi nous et sont très casuelles.' Ibid., 138.
[84] Ibid.

too optimistic about the pacific nature of British party strife. While Hume was eager to stress the disruption (*déranger*) of party politics in mixed constitutions in his letter to Montesquieu, it is possible that Montesquieu's choice of words left a lasting impression on Hume. As we have seen, Hume had earlier held that party politics was an inescapable part of Britain's mixed government. In his *History* he took one further step and explicitly argued, with Montesquieu, that it also gave 'life and vigour' to the government.

Hume argued that while 'the wise and moderate in the nation endeavoured to preserve, as much as possible, an equitable neutrality between the opposite parties ... they regarded the very rise of parties as a happy prognostic of the establishment of liberty'.[85] In other words, a mixed government and a parliamentary system required partisans, and parties were a price worth paying for such an 'invaluable blessing'.[86] As Hume saw it, 'Governments, especially those of a mixed kind, are in continual fluctuation: The humours of the people change perpetually from one extreme to another'.[87] As we shall see, however, his *History* would also put emphasis on the destructive role of party. The balance between parliamentary privilege and royal prerogative was at this time so uncertain that not only was it inevitable that the people became divided, but a 'civil war must ensue; a civil war, where no party or both parties would justly bear the blame'.[88] We now turn to Hume's treatment of that unhappy episode.

Charles I and Civil War

Charles I inherited a parliament possessed by a jealous 'spirit of liberty'.[89] This Bolingbrokean phrase, which Bolingbroke had seen as constantly present in the history of England, now began to become truly relevant for the first time, according to Hume. Discontent was not restricted to the lower house, but 'diffused itself over the nation'.[90] This 'republican spirit' was countered by a 'monarchical spirit', for instance in the shape of sermons preaching that parliamentary consent was not a prerequisite for the imposition of taxes, as the sovereign needed to have access to all the nation's property when deemed necessary. These opposite spirits tended to augment each other, 'and the just medium was gradually deserted by all men'.[91] Two ideological polar opposites, some aspects of which could be detected already in the previous reign, became increasingly prominent.

---

[85] Hume, *History*, V, 95.   [86] Ibid.   [87] Ibid., 353.   [88] Ibid., 96.   [89] Ibid., 191, 221.
[90] Ibid., 203.   [91] Ibid., 199.

That the Commons 'seriously formed a plan for reducing their prince to subjection' was evident when they declared it illegal to levy tonnage and poundage, a form of taxation, without the consent of parliament, in the face of the precedent of many reigns.[92] The *Puritans* at this time were made up of three *parties* that became united: political Puritans, attached to civil liberty; Puritans in discipline, who opposed the ceremonies and hierarchy of the Episcopalians or the Anglicans; and the doctrinal Puritans, who defended the speculative system of the first reformers.[93] As had been common since the time of Elizabeth, 'the puritanical party' was dominant in the Commons. This party was opposed by the Court party, the hierarchy (i.e. the established Episcopalian church), and the Arminian sect. Hume believed that the last sect gradually incorporated itself into the established church, as it found 'more encouragement from superstitious spirit of the church than from the fanaticism of the puritans'.[94] The supporters of episcopal government, including Bishop Laud, 'were the strenuous preachers of passive obedience'.[95] Theological and metaphysical controversies were carried out together with the debates on tonnage and poundage.

Charles dissolved parliament in 1629 and did not call another one for eleven years, resorting to ship money for finance. Hume argued that the king now 'entertained a very different idea of the constitution, from that which *began*, in general, to prevail among his subjects', that is, the spirit of liberty.[96] Hume was careful to stress, however, that the situation would have been sustainable had it not been for the fact that discontent broke out in Scotland, as a result of the king seeking to introduce Episcopalian uniformity in the northern kingdom. Lack of funds to support war with Scotland obliged Charles to summon a parliament in 1640. Unfortunately for the king, the majority elected to this parliament were not compliant but 'stubborn patriots' and country gentlemen outside the reach of crown influence.[97] Realising that his enemies in parliament outnumbered his friends, the king violently and abruptly dissolved parliament (but not Convocation), producing further discontent among the people.[98]

The king was shortly obliged to call another parliament, which became known as the 'Long Parliament'. It began by prosecuting some of the king's closest men, Strafford and Laud, for high treason and seeking to introduce arbitrary monarchy.[99] The belief that the king could do no wrong, and only his ministers and servants could be found culpable, had

---

[92] Ibid., 208.   [93] Ibid., 212.   [94] Ibid., 211.   [95] Ibid., 212–13.   [96] Ibid., 236.
[97] Ibid., 271.   [98] Ibid., 276.   [99] Ibid., 290.

thus far retained its prominence.[100] In a bid to weaken the king's already small 'party', projectors and monopolists were expelled from the Commons. The king had to acquiesce to the Triennial Act and give up his independent right to tonnage and poundage. The Star Chamber and the Court of High Commission, seen as instruments of discretionary royal and ecclesiastical power respectively, were abolished. In hyperbolic language, Hume argued that the changes undertaken at the beginning of the Long Parliament changed the country instantly 'from a monarchy almost absolute, to a pure democracy'.[101]

The popular leaders in parliament, seized by passion for Presbyterianism and the wild enthusiasm that accompanied this religion, soon began to plan for abolition of the entire monarchy.[102] They also attacked 'the hierarchy' (the bishops) in the Lords. The king was so emasculated at this point that 'the fears and jealousies, which operated on the people, and pushed them so furiously to arms, were undoubtedly not of a civil but a religious nature'.[103] The 'dread of popery' was the foremost concern among the populace, even if this was often a 'groundless charge', such as when Laud was executed.[104] The 'party-names' of Roundhead and Cavalier emerged in the context of the run-up to the civil war, as Hume had already pointed out in his *Essays*. These were initially terms of reproach, but allowed 'the factions [to] rendezvous and signalize their mutual hatred'.[105] The king sought to strike back by prosecuting five popular leaders in parliament, including Pym, Hollis and Hampden, and a civil war in England began to look imminent, and duly commenced in 1642.

Sometimes when referring to 'the people' as opposed to the king, Hume referred to one segment of the population, as both sides attempted to 'gain the people's favour and good opinion', and both sides had their partisans.[106] As he put it, '[w]hen two names, so sacred in the English constitution as those of KING and PARLIAMENT, were placed in opposition, no wonder the people were divided in their choice, and were agitated with the most violent animosities and factions'.[107] The religion of the people 'corresponded exactly to these divisions': 'The Presbyterian religion was new, republican, and suited to the genius of the populace: The other [Episcopalian] had an air of greater show and ornament, was established on ancient authority, and bore an affinity to the kingly and aristocratical parts of the constitution.'[108] Other sects hid among the

---

[100] Ibid., 291.   [101] Ibid., 293.   [102] Ibid., 348.   [103] Ibid., 380.   [104] Ibid., 457.
[105] Ibid., 363.   [106] Ibid., 380.   [107] Ibid., 386.   [108] Ibid., 387.

Presbyterians, notably the Independents, among whom Oliver Cromwell was a leader.[109] As already mentioned, most nobles sided with the king, whereas the City of London had adopted republican principles and sided with parliament. Hume described the manners of the two 'factions' of Roundhead and Cavalier as being 'as opposite as those of the most distant nations'.[110] The Cavaliers were fond of pleasure; the Roundheads were gloomy enthusiasts, opposed to all forms of recreation.[111] Hume was clear that most advantages laid with the parliamentary party, especially since the veneration for parliaments was generally 'extreme' at this time, and '[m]en considered the house of commons, in no other light than as the representatives of the nation'.[112] Crucially, thanks to their 'popularity', this party acquired the power to affix epithets: the king's adherents were called 'wicked' and 'malignant', and his adversaries 'godly' and 'well-affected'.[113]

For evident reasons, the two parties, or ideological counterparts, at this point started to look less like *political* parties and more like two warring parties. The fact that a clear distinction between the two was difficult to make for the seventeenth century is important when we assess how people in the eighteenth century understood 'party'. Parliamentary parties were, in historical and political writing, related to civil war 'parties', which is why a discussion of Whig and Tory was usually incomplete without reference to Cavalier, Roundhead, and the civil war.[114] For similar reasons, mentions of the factions that brought down the Roman Republic were also common in discussions of British party politics.[115] We now turn to the second half of the seventeenth century, and Hume's second Stuart volume, and see how the survival of religious parties once again produced a Court and Country polarity, which in turn would give way to Tory and Whig.

Restoration

After eleven years of republican rule, many under the essentially military government of Cromwell,[116] monarchy was restored with the aid of General Monck, lavishly praised by Hume.[117] Reconciliation between

---

[109] Ibid., 441–4.   [110] Ibid., VI, 141.   [111] Ibid., 141–2.   [112] Ibid., V, 388.
[113] Ibid., 389.   [114] *Spectator*, No. 125, 24 July 1711.
[115] Gordon's 'First Discourse: On Party and Faction', in *Political Discourses on Tacitus and Sallust* (Indianapolis, 2013 [1728–44]).
[116] Hume, *History*, VI, 5, 54, 74, 85–6, 93.
[117] In an extensive footnote, Hume attacked the 'factious spirit' of Bishop Burnet for treating Monck with 'malignity'. The Whig Burnet's treatment was 'a singular proof of the strange power of faction', according to Hume; see *History*, VI, 247 (note g).

erstwhile rival parties paved the way for the Restoration.[118] Upon his restoration, Charles II 'admitted the most eminent men of the nation, without regard to former distinctions'.[119] Hume was clear that Cavalier and Roundhead expired at the Restoration, as a result of the 'lenity and equality of Charles's administration'. Meanwhile, '[t]heological controversy alone still subsisted, and kept alive some sparks of that flame, which had thrown the nation into convulsion'.[120] Presbyterianism and Episcopacy (or Prelacy), which was restored with the king, competed for superiority.

Religious struggle was the main 'party' competition that took place in English politics until a Court–Country polarity once again became apparent in the 1670s. That the Episcopalian and royalist party which now had the upper hand was a Church rather than Court party can be seen from the fact that 'when any real power or revenue was demanded from the crown, they were neither so forward nor so liberal in their concessions as the king would gladly have wished'.[121] The 'popular' or 'parliamentarian' 'party' had a long history of anti-Catholicism, which was often turned into anti-clericalism.[122] By contrast, 'a spirit of opposition, inclined the court and all the royalists to adopt a more favourable sentiment towards that sect'.[123] This came to the fore now as the king had during his exile 'imbibed strong prejudices in favour of the catholic religion', and perhaps was himself a closeted Catholic.[124] Charles II and his brother, the more 'zealously' Catholic James, Duke of York, formed a plan for a general toleration of sects, which would include Catholics.[125] This produced tension between the king and his parliament, which otherwise would have supported him.[126] 'Anti-popery' would be the main catalyst for the emergence of the Whig–Tory dichotomy that appeared at the Exclusion Crisis in 1679–81.

In the early 1670s, England attached itself to France in alliance against Holland. This alliance with a Catholic power against a Protestant country

---

[118] Ibid., 117, 132, 135.   [119] Ibid., 156.   [120] Ibid., 170.   [121] Ibid., 177.

[122] Ibid., V, 90, 175–6, 198, 201–2, 347, 373, 380.   [123] Ibid., VI, 185.

[124] Ibid. See also 175: 'The catholics, though they had little interest in the nation, were a considerable party at court.' Hume reported that Charles II received the sacraments from a Catholic priest on his deathbed (446).

[125] Ibid., 186. When perusing the memoirs of James II/VII at the Scotch College of Paris, Hume discovered that Charles II and his brother had aimed to change the religion of the country, which they believed was feasible seeing the propensity of the 'cavaliers' and the 'church party' for Catholicism. Hume also found that Charles II became a French pensioner from 1669–70 (286n). See also Hume to William Robertson, 1 December 1763, *New Letters*, 76.

[126] For the king's neglect to support 'loyalists', see Hume, *History*, VI, 189.

equalled a war 'against the religion and liberties of his own subjects, even more than against the Dutch themselves'.[127] The king had to resort to long and frequent prorogations of parliament. In the spirit of an absolute monarch, the king issued a declaration of indulgence, suspending penal laws against nonconformists, a measure 'laudable, when considered in itself; but if we reflect on the motive whence it proceeded ... it will furnish a strong proof of the arbitrary and dangerous counsels, pursued by the king and his ministry'.[128] It was around this time when government business was carried out by the notorious 'cabal', a group of ministers that sought to extend royal power. It was thus called after the first letter of the names of its five members,[129] and the word became a common term in eighteenth-century discourse as a synonym for 'faction'. In sum, Charles II alienated large chunks of his parliament, on which he was still dependent to raise money.

Anthony Ashley Cooper, the Earl of Shaftesbury, was Lord Chancellor and a leading member of the cabal, but when Charles II recalled the declaration of indulgence in the face of hostility from parliament, he sensed a weakness in the king and went into opposition himself. Now the Country–Court polarity re-entered the fray, and Shaftesbury emerged as a leader of the 'country party'.[130] At this point, the Country party became properly united with the Dissenting interest. The king continued to clash with parliament over the Dutch war for some time, but he shortly realised that he would not be granted supplies to carry on the war, and backed down as he had done over the declaration of indulgence.[131] The debate pointed to continuity in English 'party' division: 'The question, indeed, with regard to resistance, was a point, which entered into the controversies of the old parties, cavalier and roundhead; as it made an essential part of the present disputes between court and country.'[132] Hume continued to remark that few 'neuters' were to be found, but that those who could remain indifferent adopted sentiments different from either party, for the reasons we saw in Chapter 6.[133]

By the mid-1670s, '[t]he house of commons was ... regularly divided into two parties, the court and the country'.[134] Both sides boasted primarily men who intended the public good, but there was also a smaller number motivated by ambition, and, in the case of the Court party, offices or bribes. Many of the 'disinterested' who had the public good in mind

---

[127] Ibid., 252–3.   [128] Ibid., 254.
[129] Clifford, Ashley (later Shaftesbury), Buckingham, Arlington, and Lauderdale. Ibid., 239–40.
[130] Ibid., 276.   [131] Ibid., 281–2.   [132] Ibid., 293.   [133] Ibid., 293–4.   [134] Ibid., 307.

'fluctuated between the factions'.[135] There is a sense that Hume believed the regular English party framework to have 'arrived' at this point, in a similar structure to that we saw beginning to form in the early 1620s, and which he still thought played an important role in his own time.[136] Hume viewed this as the 'natural' party structure of England's mixed constitution. The civil war 'parties' – Roundhead and Cavalier – corresponded to this dichotomy to some extent, because it would be wrong to think that the Court and Country parties were free from religious dimensions. The civil war 'parties' were different, however, because they fought *pro aris et focis*. It can thus be said that Roundhead and Cavalier had stood in the way of the natural development of the English parties, which Hume on balance had seen as a positive event of the 1620s. Another fatal party division would now complement and to an extent eclipse Court and Country, namely that of Tory and Whig.

Exclusion, Whig and Tory, and Revolution

A great deal of discontent against the king stemmed from Charles II's perceived 'subservience' towards Louis XIV and France. Anti-French sentiments were related to fears of Catholicism and arbitrary power, which were both 'apprehended as the scope of all [the king's] projects'.[137] The general suspicion of and animosity against Catholics 'made the public swallow the grossest absurdities', including the Popish Plot, a fabricated conspiracy to assassinate Charles II contrived by Titus Oates.[138] Despite its absurdity, the plot dominated business in parliament. This can be said to have been a dress rehearsal for the Exclusion Crisis. The Commons introduced and passed a new test, which denominated Catholicism as idolatry. The openly Catholic Duke of York put in a motion to the upper house that an exception be made in his own case, and won by only two votes.[139] When Lord High Treasurer Danby was being impeached by parliament as part of the anti-French and anti-Catholic tide, the king proceeded in December 1678 to prorogue and shortly afterwards dissolve the so-called Cavalier Parliament.

Hume believed that the elections in March 1679 were 'perhaps the first in England, which . . . had been carried on by a violent contest between the parties'.[140] The Presbyterian *party* was particularly successful and 'the new representatives would, if possible, exceed the old in their refractory

---

[135] Ibid., 307–8.   [136] See Chapter 4.   [137] Hume, *History*, VI, 333.   [138] Ibid., 338.
[139] Ibid., 349.   [140] Ibid., 356.

opposition to the court, and furious persecution of the catholics'.[141] The king was now opposed by a numerous *party*, which comprised the populace, 'so credulous from prejudice, so blinded with religious antipathy', as well as leaders who sought to exploit these sentiments to further their own ambitions.[142] The king tried to stabilise the situation by what we may call a bipartisan approach through the selection of a new privy council of thirty members, half of whom were to be attached to the court and the other half unattached men with credit in both houses of parliament. Shaftesbury once again became a minister of the crown as Lord President of the Council.[143] It was evident that the popular leader only possessed the appearance of court favour, however, and Shaftesbury's main allegiance remained with the Country party. This party soon introduced a bill to exclude the Duke of York entirely from the succession to the crown, rejecting limitations suggested by Charles II.[144] It passed in the lower house by a majority of seventy-nine. At the same time, the same party continued to protest against the bribery and corruption of members of parliament.[145] The struggle against Catholicism and fears over arbitrary government went hand in hand with a Country programme of decreasing the executive influence over the legislature, according to Hume. The king prorogued parliament in the face of the opposition.

The king had managed 'to form a considerable party' at this time.[146] On his restoration, he had initially wanted to abolish distinctions of parties, but when he was faced with a 'general jealousy' he found it necessary 'to court the old cavalier party'.[147] The Exclusion Crisis made the succession to the throne a party question. According to Hume, the royalist party would always carefully guard the succession as a bulwark against encroachments of popular assemblies. Charles II received additional support from the Church of England by making the established clergy and their supporters believe 'that the old scheme for the abolition of prelacy as well as monarchy was revived'.[148] The memory of the civil war attached many impartial people to the crown.

Hume's description of how the 'petitioners' and 'abhorrers' acquired the lasting denominations of Whig and Tory was similar to the one in Rapin's *Histoire*, without the reference to *lait-aigre*, while differing from many more recently published accounts of the same events.[149] According to

---

[141] Ibid., 357.   [142] Ibid.   [143] Ibid., 363.   [144] Ibid., 365.   [145] Ibid., 365–6.
[146] Ibid., 375.   [147] Ibid., 376.   [148] Ibid.
[149] [Ralph], *The History of England* (2 vols., London, 1744–6), I, 473–5, 656; North, *Examen* (London, 1740), 320–4; Oldmixon, *The History of England* (London, 1730), 631. (Ralph and North are cited by Hume in other places of the second Stuart volume.)

Hume, the Court party reproached their antagonists for their affinity with 'the fanatical conventiclers in Scotland, who were known by the name of whigs', while '[t]he country party found a resemblance between the courtiers and the popish banditti in Ireland, to whom the appellation of tory was affixed'.[150] Hume added that 'these foolish terms of reproach ... even at present seem not nearer their end than when they were first invented'.[151] Against this background, and after the degree of abuse Hume received from both parties owing to his *History*, it is not surprising that he supported George III's attempt to abolish the distinctions of Whig and Tory.[152]

The two party positions crystallised as the Exclusion Crisis unfolded. The Whig party's case for exclusion rested on the fear that a Catholic successor would make mutual trust between king and people impossible. They argued that when theological principles 'become symbols of faction, and marks of party distinctions, they concur with one of the strongest passions in the human frame, and are capable of carrying men to the greatest extremities'.[153] Notably, Hume believed that it was the exclusionists who argued that '[i]n every government ... there is somewhere an authority absolute and supreme', which in England was the legislative body, comprising crown, Lords, and Commons.[154] All government matters, including the succession, should be subject to the same jurisdiction. On the other hand, in Hume's rendition, the Court (or Tory) party argued that '[a]n authority ... wholly absolute and uncontroulable is a mere chimera' and, in a Humean fashion, that '[a]ll government is founded on opinion and a sense of duty'.[155] If the popular assembly would 'shock' a fundamental opinion such as that of lineal succession, the obedience they themselves received would be undermined.[156] Hume stressed that denying the right to alter the succession did not equal rejecting any limitations to monarchy; in other words, not all Tories believed in arbitrary monarchy.[157]

This party division over exclusion came close to civil war, according to Hume.[158] As pro-exclusionist sentiments were as strong in the Commons as those against in the Lords, the division can also be likened to a constitutional wrangle between the upper and lower chambers. The king decided to assemble the parliament of March 1681 in Oxford instead of

---

[150] Hume, *History*, VI, 381.   [151] Ibid.   [152] *Letters*, I, 336, 368, 385.
[153] Hume, *History*, VI, 389.   [154] Ibid., 388.
[155] Ibid., 389; Hume, 'First Principles of Government', *Essays*, 32.
[156] Hume, *History*, VI, 389–90.   [157] Ibid., 390–1.   [158] Ibid., 399.

Westminster, as London was a hotbed for zealous Country party support. In the event, however, the new Commons consisted of nearly the same members as the old, and proceeded to pursue the same measures, including Exclusion and the impeachment of Danby. The king seized the first opportunity to dissolve parliament. Even if the Court party may have been inferior in numbers, without a parliament the Court held all the aces, and had 'every advantage over a body, dispersed and disunited'.[159] Hume's description of the royalist victory is nearly identical to Rapin's. In the process of defaming one another, both sides 'buried in their factious breasts all regard to truth, honour, and humanity', notably in their representations of the conspirator Edward Fitzharris.[160]

The dissolution of parliament was the end of the great and irregular party struggles of pre-revolutionary England. The king was now master and did not have to dread the Country party.[161] In this period, Hume's strongest praise was unsurprisingly reserved for men like Halifax, the great Trimmer, who 'affected a species of neutrality between the parties'.[162] By contrast, that Charles II acted as the head of a party ('a disagreeable situation for a prince, and always the source of much injustice and oppression'[163]) became clear when he departed from his previous maxim of toleration and allowed his Church friends to persecute their Dissenting 'enemies'.[164] Likewise, when ousting the Country party from its strong-hold in London, justice became subservient to the 'factious views' of the 'court and church party' as they began to dominate juries.[165] Most regular opposition ceased at this point, and was overtaken by extra-constitutional schemes such as the Rye-House Plot. The failure of this plot, for which Algernon Sidney was executed, was the final nail in the coffin for the Whig party, or the Country party as Hume more commonly referred to it, for the time being. This was reflected in its meagre success at the election of the House of Commons at the beginning of James II/VII's reign in 1685.[166]

We do not need to repeat all the familiar ways in which James managed to alienate a supportive parliament.[167] Hume is clear that if James only 'had embraced any national party [i.e. the Tories, which combined royalists and the Church], he had been ensured of success'.[168] Unfortunately for the king, the Catholics only made up one-hundredth of the nation's

---

[159] Ibid., 403.   [160] Ibid., 405–7.   [161] Ibid., 416.   [162] Ibid., 419.
[163] Hume's attitudes towards Halifax and monarchs being party leaders are identical to Bolingbroke's.
[164] Ibid., 419–20.   [165] Ibid., 421.   [166] Ibid., 453.   [167] For a summary, see ibid., 468.
[168] Ibid., 487.

population, according to Hume, and this was not a strong enough base. His attempt to court Protestant nonconformists, who were more numerous (one-twentieth, according to Hume), failed because they thought that history proved Catholicism to be incompatible with toleration.[169] The outcome is described in the same way as it had been by Rapin: a 'coalition of parties' formed against the king, consisting of Whigs and nonconformists on the one hand, and Tories and the Church of England on the other.[170] This coalition was not to last, however: the Convention Parliament was the scene of Whig–Tory division as the Revolution Settlement was hammered out.

Nevertheless, Hume was convinced that one species of 'party division' died with the Revolution Settlement. By settling fundamental questions in favour of liberty (Hume highlights the Bill of Rights),[171] and by deposing one king and establishing a 'new' family, 'it [the settlement] gave such an ascendant to popular principles, as has put the nature of the English constitution beyond all controversy'.[172] The 'fluctuation and contest' between prerogative and privilege, or king and parliament, which in the seventeenth century had been 'much too violent both for the repose and safety of the people', was now at an end.[173] What remained was a more limited tussle between the executive and legislative branches, or rather between parties within the legislature representing these branches, and this form of conflict became a regular feature of politics. Why did it not threaten civil war as in the seventeenth century? The court remained the executive branch, but since it had not yet acquired the power of 'influencing' parliaments on a sufficiently large scale in the seventeenth century, it instead had to resort to 'opposing' them.[174] Hume had in his essays defended this form of 'corruption', or influence, and it can now be seen that he believed this innovation to be one of the crucial differences that separated the eighteenth from the seventeenth century, and made the former more stable than the latter. Pre-revolutionary England was not just a time when the limits of the monarchy had been ill-defined, it was also a time when parliament had been 'uncontroullable'.[175] Bolingbroke was right that 'corruption' in the technical sense had increased since the

---

[169] Ibid.
[170] Ibid., VI, 502–3. As we have seen, this 'coalition' argument was developed by Rapin and became crucial for Macaulay and others following him. It has recently been put into question by Pincus in *1688* (New Haven, 2009), ch. 10.
[171] Hume, *History*, VI, 530.   [172] Ibid., 531.   [173] Ibid.   [174] Ibid., 532.   [175] Ibid.

Revolution, but this was what made government stable in the eighteenth century, according to Hume.[176]

Hume closed by remarking that the Revolution, which was carried out on Whig principles even if Tories had had at least an equal share in it, paved the way for the ascendency of the Whig party. By contrast, the Tory party became 'obliged to cultivate popularity' in opposition.[177] The Whig dominance may have been beneficial to the state, at least in some particulars, but it had 'proved destructive to the truth of history, and ... established many gross falsehoods'.[178] In particular, Whig writers had depicted the seventeenth century as a straightforward battle between liberty and tyranny, rather than the mutually dependent principles of liberty and authority.[179] In the process, they were 'forgetting that a regard to liberty, though a laudable passion, ought commonly to be subordinate to a reverence for established government'.[180] Seen in this context, Hume's dislike of Whiggism, at least vulgar Whiggism, which is more prominent than his aversion to Toryism, becomes comprehensible.[181] The later Hume's loathing of Whiggism, similar to an unhistorical form of English exceptionalism with which he, as a Scot, had little sympathy,[182] became more acute after the hostile reception of his Stuart volumes.[183] In later editions, Hume named Rapin, Locke, Sidney, and Hoadly in a footnote as examples of '[c]ompositions the most despicable, both for style and matter, [which have] been extolled, and propagated, and read; as if they had equalled the most celebrated remains of antiquity'.[184] Hume's standard excuse for delaying and in the end not writing a continuation of his *History* beyond the Glorious Revolution was party rage and in particular that Whigs in high places would not give him access to the necessary papers.[185] As set out in the introduction to this chapter, none of this should lead us to the conclusion that the *History* represented a move towards 'philosophic

---

[176] Other historians bemoaned the post-revolutionary developments of 'purchasing majorities' and 'managing parties', including [Ralph], *The History of England*, II, 1024.

[177] Hume, *History*, VI. 533. Compare with Hume's remark that the Tories had become quasi-republicans in Chapter 4.

[178] Ibid.   [179] Hume, 'Origin of Government', *Essays*, 40–1.   [180] Hume, *History*, VI, 533.

[181] *Letters*, I, 313, 317, 379, 415, 502, II, 150.

[182] Hume grew increasingly impatient with English nationalism, especially when it took an anti-Scottish turn in the 1760s. *Letters*, I, 378, 470, 491, 492, 497–8, 517; *Further Letters*, 64.

[183] *Further Letters*, 39, 44.   [184] Hume, *History*, VI, 533.

[185] *Letters*, I, 352, 359, 381–2, II, 98, 162. In the end, Hume is reported to have said that he was 'too old, too fat, too lazy and too rich' to continue his *History*; see Mossner, *The Life of David Hume* (Oxford, 1980 [1954]), 556.

Toryism'.[186] His intention was indeed to provide a more intellectually robust defence of the Revolution Settlement.[187]

To conclude this summary of Hume's *History*, the work dealt with party at two levels: it not only adumbrated the development of 'party' in the seventeenth century, but also wanted to show how partisanship and in particular Whiggism in history writing had corrupted our understanding of the past. By giving a fair hearing to both sides of the question, Hume hoped to correct the second defect and put the record straight. This intention had in some ways been identical to Rapin's, but Hume believed that the Frenchman's belief in the myth of the ancient constitution hindered him from properly understanding the issues at play in the seventeenth century. As Hume sought to correct the 'mistakes' of Rapin, many of his readers believed that he went too far in the other direction and he was specifically criticised for lacking the impartiality he aspired to, for example by William Rose.[188] Indeed, in the nineteenth century Hume was often accused of being dishonest and wilfully misleading his readers, notably by John Stuart Mill.[189] Hume's motivation was often singled out as being fame and fortune. Despite this, the endurance of the *History* is remarkable and Hume remained the writer whom nineteenth-century Whig historians felt that they needed to refute.[190] In the twentieth century the work was long out of print, but it eventually regained its reputation as a masterpiece, a process which has continued into the twenty-first century.[191]

Conclusion

One of the things Hume wanted to work out in his historical enterprise was how parliamentary opposition had arisen in England. The party terms that dominate the Stuart volumes are Court and Country, which essentially mean parties of government and opposition, or executive and

---

[186] This was the argument of Giarrizzo's *David Hume Politico e Storico* and repeated in Trevor-Roper's review of that work; see *History and the Enlightenment* (New Haven, 2010), 220–8.

[187] Duncan Forbes, 'Politics and History in David Hume', *HJ*, 6 (1963), 280–323.

[188] See Rose's review in *Early Responses*, VII, 160–72. On the continent, however, Hume was almost universally celebrated for his impartiality as a history writer, as documented in Bongie, *David Hume* (Indianapolis, 1998 [1965]), 12.

[189] Mill's review of Brodie's *History of the British Empire* (1822), *Westminster Review*, October 1824, in *Early Responses*, VIII, 292–8.

[190] Burrow, *A Liberal Descent* (Cambridge, 1981), 26.

[191] Although still primarily read by historians, Hume's *History* has in recent years received more attention from philosophers and political theorists; see Sabl, *Hume's Politics* (Princeton, 2012); Herdt, *Religion and Faction in Hume's Moral Philosophy* (Cambridge, 1997).

legislative, representing the centre of government and the localities, respectively. Like Rapin, Hume could perhaps be criticised for applying the eighteenth-century language of party to the first half of the seventeenth century, when, as he recognised, this terminology was absent. Hume was seeking to understand the *longue durée* of the rise of party, however, and for that history the beginning of the seventeenth century was arguably indispensable. Moreover, the ideological polarisation of the early Stuart period had continued into the eighteenth century, albeit in a less straightforward fashion, as we saw in Chapter 6. Simultaneously, the *History* served as a contrast. England's irregular constitution had continuously given rise to an oppositional Country party, and monarchs felt obliged to form a Court party as a counterweight. But as long as parliament was discontinuous, the history of party was disjointed. As a result of annual sessions of parliament, party competition had become more regular in the eighteenth century.

As we have seen, these parties were not purely constitutional but had religious dimensions. Indeed, Hume believed that they would never have materialised were it not for the Episcopalian–Puritan split within the Protestant church. One of his guiding principles was that religion, faction, and interest were mutually supportive.[192] The party struggle throughout the Stuart era centred on the questions of 'popery', the direction of the church, the balance of the constitution, and arbitrary monarchy. In other words, they touched on religion and politics, and to try and disentangle the one from the other is difficult and indeed unhelpful for the period. In this respect, we are led to disagree with the suggestion of Hume's most recent biographer that the Scotsman believed that 'party zeal replaced religious zeal as the engine of politics' after 1660.[193] As we have seen, the two had been continuously intertwined.

In all this, Hume was in broad agreement with Rapin. However, the Frenchman had also tried to show how the English parties could be split into religious and political categories, with each category containing extremists as well as moderates. According to Hume, separation between political and religious motivations made little sense for public figures in the seventeenth century. They were almost always confounded, often with disastrous consequences, as moderation was ignored when religious principles were at stake.[194] It has been powerfully argued that Hume's

---

[192] Hume, *History*, V, 347.

[193] Harris, *Hume*, 346. It is even doubtful whether this could be said even of the 1750s, to Hume's dismay.

[194] Hume, *History*, IV, 221. This is also something Hume often bemoaned in philosophical quarrels; see, e.g., Hume to Price, 18 March 1767, *New Letters*, 234. For Hume's dislike of party spirit among men of letters, see also *Letters*, I, 173, 360. This is a key theme in Harris, *Hume*.

controversial thought on religion was driven by the threat posed by religious fanaticism to society (not just in an abstract but in a specific sense) rather than epistemological concerns.[195] This threat had been extreme in the seventeenth century, but it was still relevant in the eighteenth century, particularly in his native Scotland. In the seventeenth century, the Country party had often aimed at limited government, but their 'extreme violence', fanaticism, and the spirit of persecution had 'disgrace[d] the cause of liberty'.[196] It should then not surprise us that Hume had earlier said that religious Whigs were much worse than religious Tories.[197]

Hume wanted to investigate why such parties tended to put the nation in danger. The fanaticism of religious principle was closely connected with this, but it also had to do with party mentality itself. As he had previously pointed out in his essays, honour as a check on behaviour was often removed when people acted in concert.[198] For Hume, the concept of party or faction, terms he continued to use interchangeably, was intertwined with civil war. This idea was not uncommon in the period. Emer de Vattel defined civil war as an event '[w]hen a *party* is formed in a state, who no longer obey the sovereign, and are possessed of sufficient strength to oppose him, – or when, in a republic, the nation is divided into two opposite *factions*, and both sides take up arms'.[199] In the words of a leading historian of Jacobitism, politics in the early eighteenth century still had a 'civil war edge', as was demonstrated by the frequent practice by new ministries of impeaching their predecessors.[200] This was not completely absent in mid-century Britain: Tory support for the short-lived Pitt–Devonshire coalition came with the expectation that Pitt would carry out 'strict inquiries into recent misfortunes' of the Newcastle ministry.[201] Even if Hume realised that the more controlled parliamentary conflict of his own day was different from the two sides that had fought in the civil war, he had good reasons to think that they were not entirely unrelated. While there is some truth in the statement that all of Hume's historical

[195] Herdt, *Religion and Faction*, 9. On this reading, Hume's wider philosophical project is strongly related to his political aspiration 'to render disagreement about religious matters innocuous by showing that no religious premises are required for reasoning about human nature, morality, politics, or history' (15).

[196] Hume, *History*, VI, 361.

[197] [Hume], *A True Account of the Behaviour and Conduct of Archibald Stewart* (London, 1748), 33–4.

[198] Hume, 'First Principles of Government', *Essays*, 33; Hume, 'Independency of Parliament', *Essays*, 43.

[199] Vattel, *The Law of Nations* (Indianapolis, 2008 [1758]), 427.

[200] Szechi, *1715* (New Haven, 2006), 34.   [201] Peters, *Pitt and Popularity* (Oxford, 1980), 64.

writings were guided by 'the question as to how [the] rare and fortunate state of affairs had come about in England',[202] we must recognise that Hume was far from starry-eyed about the British constitution. Indeed, he diagnosed potential weaknesses in the Hanoverian regime.[203]

Yet Hume agreed with Montesquieu that parties were a reflection of a mixed, or free, government. As he put it,

> In every mixed government, such as that of England, the bulk of the nation will always incline to preserve the entire frame of the constitution; but according to the various prejudices, interests, and dispositions of men, some will ever attach themselves with more passion to the regal, others to the popular part of the government.[204]

As Forbes argued, the point of Hume's *History* was to go beyond the rights and wrongs of the protagonists and antagonists.[205] Instead, Forbes believed that Hume attempted to show that the parties could be traced to the constitution, as he had done in 'Of the Parties of Great Britain'.[206] This is of course correct since having a parliament was a prerequisite for parties. However, it could equally be claimed, as by Nicholas Phillipson, that the Court and Country parties gave birth to the *mixed* constitution,[207] which was not conceived until the Petition of Right of 1628, and not functioning properly until after the Revolution. As no reader of Hume's *History* can fail to notice, unintended consequences and historical irony are its main themes.[208] That is why there is no all-out condemnation of 'party' as such in Hume's *History*, only of dishonest and dangerous behaviour associated with party. Indeed, there is even praise in volume five. The non-utopian observer of politics knew that parties would remain as long as Britain retained its parliament. All that a philosophically minded historian could do was to seek to understand them and mollify their worst extremes. As a historian, Hume disliked partisanship, especially the myths partisan historians created and sustained.[209] As political thinker, however, he had to accept them.

The seventeenth century presented a continuous conflict between authority and liberty, embodied by 'Court' and 'Country'. The question of 'party' was at the heart of Hume's enterprise. Indeed, it could be viewed as the 'organic connection' between politics and religion which Meinecke

---

[202] Meinecke, *Historism*, 163.
[203] Another prominent example is Hume's essay 'Of Public Credit' (1752).
[204] Hume, *History*, VI, 375–6.   [205] Forbes, *Hume's Philosophical Politics*, 299.   [206] Ibid., 284.
[207] Phillipson, *Hume*, 80.   [208] Sabl, *Hume's Politics*, 14.
[209] Hume held this in common with Rapin, Guthrie, and many others.

thought was missing in the *History*.[210] Ironically, it has been said that
Hume's historical work was a reflection of the decline in eighteenth-
century party strife, and contributed to a new 'establishment conservatism', which provoked the 'radicalism' of Catharine Macaulay's history.[211]
But as we have seen, Hume would not have recognised a decline in party
strife, either when he conceived of his historical project in the 1740s or
when he started writing it in the early 1750s.[212] Towards the end of the
1750s, however, after the publication of both Stuart volumes, he did see
encouraging signs of such an event when coalitions became the order of
the day. We now turn to the period of the Pitt–Newcastle coalition.

---

[210] Meinecke, *Historism*, 183.

[211] Okie, *Augustan Historical Writing*, 203. For Hume and Macaulay's disagreement, see *New Letters*,
80–2. See also Hill, *The Republican Virago* (Oxford, 1992).

[212] Hume referred to 'my historical Projects' in a letter to Kames in January 1747, *New Letters*, 23.

CHAPTER 8

Political Transformations during the Seven Years' War: Hume and Burke

> To abolish all distinctions of party may not be practicable, perhaps not desirable, in a free government.
>
> Hume, 'Of the Coalition of Parties' (1758)

Coalition Politics

Hume's essay 'Of the Coalition of Parties' (1758) has rightly been considered as an 'apologia' for the first volume of his *History*.[1] The essay opened with a restatement of the now familiar Humean view that it 'may not be practicable, perhaps not desirable', to abolish all distinctions of parties in a free, or mixed, government.[2] For Hume, '[t]he only dangerous parties are such as entertain opposite views with regard to the essentials of government', be it the succession to the crown as in the case of the Jacobites, or 'the more considerable privileges belonging to the several members of the constitution', as with the great parties of the seventeenth century, whose fate he had narrated in the *History*.[3] On such questions there could be no compromise or accommodation, and there was no room for such parties, since that type of party strife could easily turn into armed conflict. Recent tendencies to coalition government indicated that such fundamental conflicts had come to an end. To promote such an 'agreeable prospect', nothing could be better than to encourage moderation by 'persuad[ing] each that its antagonists may possibly be sometimes in the right, and to keep a balance in the praise and blame, which we bestow on either side'.[4] This had been Hume's intention in his essays on the original contract and passive obedience discussed in Chapter 6, and he now confirmed that he intended to promote the same political agenda in his history of the Stuarts. The rest of the essay was a summary of the argument

---

[1] Forbes, *Hume's Philosophical Politics* (Cambridge, 1975), 265.
[2] Hume, 'Coalition of Parties', *Essays*, 493.   [3] Ibid.   [4] Ibid., 494.

in his *History of Great Britain*, and some anticipations of his Tudor volumes (particularly appendix III), which he was working on at this time. 'The rule of government is the present established practice of the age', not some 'ancient constitution', of which people had little or no understanding, he concluded.[5]

George III's end to Tory proscription, which is dealt with in Chapter 9, was preceded by another shock to the Whig establishment: coalition with William Pitt the Elder. This is best described as a wide-ranging Whig coalition, however, and offices were not given to Tories, even if many Tories supported the coalition.[6] The unexpected death on 6 March 1754 of Henry Pelham, First Lord of the Treasury since 1744 – with the exception of the two-day 'ministry' of 1746 – ushered in a period of relative ministerial instability. As the leader of the ministry, Pelham had been the head of a system which Hardwicke saw as designed to 'preserve and cement the Whig party', a project Hardwicke was anxious to continue after his death.[7] This was the time when personal and family connections properly came to the fore in parliamentary politics. They had not been unimportant earlier, but for the first time they started to eclipse party politics. Namier's generalisations about eighteenth-century politics now become extra relevant, even if personal factionalism did not entirely supplant the entrenched Tory–Whig framework. These names continued to be used as self-identification as well as to describe others, even though their meanings had become increasingly ambiguous, as Namier recognised.[8]

Pelham was first succeeded by his brother, the Duke of Newcastle, who, unlike Pelham and Walpole, was a peer rather than a commoner. Newcastle's problems were intensified by the fact that two of the potential leaders in the Commons, Henry Fox and Pitt, were rivals. At the end of 1755, Pitt left the ministry and went into opposition in alliance with Leicester House (the Prince of Wales's connection). It has been argued that he would likely have remained in opposition if it had not been for two foreign policy developments: the threat of invasion and the loss of Minorca in June 1756.[9] Facing mounting pressure, from both within and out of parliament, Fox and eventually Newcastle resigned.[10] In the formation of a new administration with the Whig Devonshire, Pitt was hoping for Tory

---

[5] Ibid., 498.   [6] Hill, *The Early Parties and Politics in Britain* (Basingstoke, 1996), 103–4.
[7] Hardwicke to Pitt, 2 April 1754, *Correspondence of William Pitt* (4 vols., London, 1840), I, 91–2.
[8] Namier, *England in the Age of the American Revolution* (London, 1930), 207.
[9] Middleton, *Bells of Victory* (Cambridge, 1985), 4–5.
[10] Harris, *Politics and the Nation* (Oxford, 2002), 32–5.

assistance.[11] Pitt was not a Tory, but his father and uncle had been, until the latter left the Tory party with Gower in the 1740s. Viewing himself as an independent Whig, Pitt did not have qualms about cooperating with and being supported by Tories.[12] He had been part of the 'Country' and 'Patriot' tradition, the banner under which Whigs and Tories had cooperated periodically, albeit often uneasily, for decades. This tradition championed policies which united the disparate elements of the opposition, of which the Tories remained the largest single component. These policies included support for the militia and a blue-water strategy, and opposition to the standing army and foreign mercenaries,[13] which had been the key contrast between Whig and Tory visions of foreign policy since the Glorious Revolution.[14] A letter from the Duke of Cumberland to Henry Fox at the beginning of the Seven Years' War shows that the Hanoverians viewed 'Sea-warr' as a 'Tory Doctrine' even at this point.[15] What is more, Pitt's anti-Hanoverian rhetoric in opposition would have appealed to many Tories, although Pitt himself was eager to dissociate himself from Jacobitism. Many English Tories had themselves given up Jacobitism after the abandoned Elibank Plot in the early 1750s, when Charles Stuart managed to alienate diehard Jacobites, including William King.[16] However, even though Tories supported the government, we should note that they were not given administrative office, nor were they received at court.[17] Proscription did not end until the accession of George III.

Jacobitism and Toryism had a long association with 'City radicalism', which is why Fielding's literary Alderman declared himself 'a *Jacobite upon republican principles*'.[18] After the demise of Jacobitism as a serious force in *English* politics, this was one of the chief remnants of Toryism along with the country gentry.[19] For people such as Sir John Philipps, these worlds

---

[11] Peters, *Pitt and Popularity* (Oxford, 1981), 1–79; Middleton, *The Bells of Victory*, 6–7; Clark, *Dynamics of Change* (Cambridge, 1982), 295–300.

[12] Peters, *Pitt and Popularity*, 42; Colley, *In Defiance of Oligarchy*, 251, 266, 271. Pitt said in parliament in 1760 that 'I am neither a Whig not a Tory', but on other occasions he espoused independent Whiggism. See Black, *Pitt the Elder* (Cambridge, 1992), 203; Pares, *George III and the Politicians* (Oxford, 1970 [1953]), 55–6.

[13] In the event, Pitt's success in the war can be attributed to his realisation that the 'popular' maritime strategy had to be complemented with a continental one. See Kennedy, *The Rise and Fall of the Great Powers* (London, 1988), 146.

[14] Pincus, *1688* (New Haven, 2009), ch. 11; Black, 'Foreign Policy and the Tory World in the Eighteenth Century', in *The Tory World* (Farnham, 2015), 33–68.

[15] *Letters to Henry Fox* (London, 1915), 120.   [16] King, *Anecdotes*, 195–214.

[17] Brewer, 'Rockingham, Burke and Whig Political Argument', *HJ*, 18 (1975), 188–9.

[18] Fielding, *Dialogue between a Gentlemen from London and an Honest Alderman* (London, 1747), 9.

[19] Rogers, *Whigs and Cities* (Oxford, 1989), ch. 3; Peters, 'The *Monitor* on the Constitution, 1755–1765', *EHR*, 86 (1971), 706–27; Namier, *England in the Age of the American Revolution*,

overlapped.[20] In the 1750s, parliament still boasted around a hundred Tory members, but they were rudderless and ill-disciplined.[21] By studying the London newspapers in general and the *Monitor* in particular, Marie Peters has argued that the 'London-West Indians' William and Richard Beckford managed to transform Toryism, in its City as well as parliamentary forms, into support for Pitt. According to this reading, various strands of Toryism merged into a Patriot platform.[22] It needs to be acknowledged, however, that we do not yet have a comprehensive study of the relationship between metropolitan politics and Toryism for this period.[23] The Devonshire–Pitt coalition proved short-lived, partly because the parliamentary Tories were too fickle a base. As Henry Fox wrote to the diplomat Sir Charles Hanbury Williams in December 1756, 'Pitt is single, imperious, proud, enthusiastick; has engaged the Torys, who instead of strength are weakness'.[24] The main lesson of the Devonshire–Pitt administration appears to have been that Newcastle, as a manager and disposer of patronage, was necessary for any working government.[25] He was also needed to ensure Whig support; as T.B. Macaulay put it in a quotation which has stood the test of time, '[t]he great Whig families, which, during several generations, had been trained in the discipline of party warfare, and were accustomed to stand together in a firm phalanx, acknowledged [Newcastle] as their captain'.[26]

The Newcastle–Pitt coalition consisted broadly of two groupings: the Newcastle–Hardwicke Whig connection (the so-called Old Corps) on the

---

231. For the roots of the tradition of Tory populist opposition in London in the reigns of William and Anne, see De Krey, *A Fractured Society* (Oxford, 1985), chs. 1, 5, and 6. E.P. Thompson wrote about the conflation of Toryism and Painite 'radicalism' in the early nineteenth century; see *The Making of the English Working Class* (London, 2013 [1963]), 820–37. He became increasingly interested in the eighteenth-century roots of this form of Tory and Jacobite protest against the (Whig) establishment, as can be seen in *Whigs and Hunters* (London, 1975) and *Customs in Common* (London, 1991), ch. 2.

[20] Thomas, *Politics in Eighteenth-Century Wales* (Cardiff, 1998), ch. 8.

[21] Hill, *The Early Parties*, 106.

[22] Peters, *Pitt and Popularity*, 25. While Beckford cooperated with Tories such as Philipps against establishment Whigs, his most recent biographer has argued that he is better labelled as an 'independent Whig'; see Gauci, *William Beckford* (New Haven, 2013), 57–8. However, this might reflect the changing meaning of the political party labels in the 1760s to a greater extent than Gauci recognises.

[23] Connections can be identified, and there was policy overlap between the 'independent' City patriotism of the Beckfords, and eighteenth-century Toryism, e.g. support for the militia and blue-water strategy. Gauci, *William Beckford*, 68.

[24] BL Stowe MS 263, f. 13.

[25] Middleton, 'Newcastle and the Conduct of Patronage during the Seven Years' War', *ECS*, 12 (1989), 175–86.

[26] Macaulay, *Critical and Historical Essays* (3 vols., London, 1849), III, 531.

one hand, and the Pitt–Bute 'coalition' on the other, representing the Grenville family and Leicester House respectively. These political groups joined forces against a Court faction (in the neutral sense of the term), comprising the king and his close supporters, including Henry Fox and Bedford.[27] Newcastle–Hardwicke had the most supporters in parliament and were necessary to any workable solution, but Newcastle's reluctance to cooperate with Fox along with the unpopularity of Fox's patron, Cumberland, impeded George II's favoured solution.[28] One of the king's top priorities was to find a ministry that would protect the Hanoverian interest, which Hume had written about in 'The Protestant Succession' (1752).[29] It has been argued that one of Pitt's main political achievements was to shift focus from the Protestant Succession to the national interest, which was increasingly perceived as including an expanding empire.[30] The appointment and reappointment of Pitt also demonstrates that eighteenth-century monarchs did not have a completely free hand in forming governments.[31] The ministry had to maintain the confidence of parliament, in particular the House of Commons.[32] At the same time, in government Pitt proved willing and capable of supporting continental warfare and the Protestant interest in Europe, alongside his commitment to commercial and colonial interests beyond Europe.[33] The king's policy could never be run roughshod over.

As we have seen, Hume welcomed the development of coalition government. He lived in Edinburgh at the time but appears to have kept up to speed with events in London thanks to his several friends involved in Westminster politics. On the forming of the Pitt–Newcastle coalition, which succeeded the short-lived Pitt–Devonshire coalition, Hume wrote to his friend Gilbert Elliot of Minto, MP for Selkirkshire, to congratulate him on his reappointment as Lord of the Admiralty. In the letter, Hume expressed his '[w]ishes, that, both for your Sake and the Public's your Ministry, & that of your Friends, may be more durable than it was

---

[27] Middleton, *The Bells of Victory*, 15.   [28] Peters, *Pitt and Popularity*, 80–1.

[29] Middleton, *The Bells of Victory*, 18. For the Hanoverian aspect in British politics, see essays in Simms (ed.), *The Hanoverian Dimension in British History, 1714–1837* (Cambridge, 2007).

[30] Black, *Pitt the Elder*, ch. 2.   [31] Cf. Namier, *Crossroads to Power* (London, 1962), 77–93.

[32] This is why all 'prime ministers' with longevity in the eighteenth century sat in the lower house, including Walpole, Pelham, Lord North, and William Pitt the Younger. In Perceval's 1749–51 plans for a new administration after the future accession of Frederick, Pelham was top of the 'List of those who must if possible be kept out of the House of Commons', with the comment that he was 'to be obliged (if he can be made) to go up to the House of Lords'. *Egmont Papers*, 169. On the importance of the Commons, see Selinger, *Parliamentarism* (Cambridge, 2019).

[33] On this, see Gauci, *William Beckford.*

before'.[34] Hume described the ministry as consisting of a 'strange motley Composition', no doubt referring to the differences between Pitt and Newcastle, the patriot minister and the 'arch-corrupter'.[35] Although he supported the coalition, Hume appears to have been far from satisfied with its actual performance, writing of a 'sudden & total Failure of Capacity & true Spirit among the Great' at this very time.[36]

The Newcastle–Pitt coalition was an alliance that put the Old Corps of Whigs back into power together with Pitt. It was not a Whig–Tory alliance, even though many Tories supported the coalition because they disliked Fox and Cumberland even more than Newcastle.[37] Moreover, the string of victories in 1759 helped to reconcile people of different political persuasions. William King commented that '[a] continual success in the conduct of our public affairs, and a series of victories, may justly be alleged as one of the principal causes of uniting many of those (however they have been distinguished by party) who are real lovers of their country'.[38]

We have reasons to think that Hume in his essay may have been thinking about a 'coalition' of Whig and Tories rather than simply a coalition of various Whigs. Just like his *History* and his essays discussed in Chapter 6, 'Of the Coalition of Parties' was an attempt to defend the present establishment on moderate principles, ones which Tories could accept.[39] He was convinced that the 'spirit of civil liberty' had evolved from the religious fanaticism of the Puritans, who had been the enemies of what became the Tory party in the late seventeenth century. Liberty had now 'purge[d] itself from that pollution' of fanaticism, according to Hume.[40] It had instead come to embody a spirit of 'toleration' rather than 'persecution', with which Hume had on one occasion associated 'religious Whiggism' in the late 1740s.[41] The key essay is 'Superstition and Enthusiasm', in which Hume had contended that enthusiasm is more violent when it first arises, but becomes milder than superstition over time. Also, with the 'high claims of [royal] prerogative' reduced, and the

---

[34] Hume to Gilbert Elliot, 2 July 1757, *Letters*, I, 253.

[35] Ibid. Waldegrave put the matter more strongly: 'The Duke of Newcastle hated Pitt as much as Pitt despised the Duke of Newcastle'. *Waldegrave Memoirs*, 205–6.

[36] Hume to Strahan, 28 October 1757, *Further Letters*, 44. As the editor of the volume acknowledges, this may refer to Cumberland's resignation in October in the wake of the capture of Berlin, as well as divisions within the Pitt–Newcastle coalition.

[37] Peters, *Pitt and Popularity*, 87, 109.

[38] King, *Anecdotes*, 195. King attributed the decline of Jacobitism principally to other factors, however, which we return to in Chapter 9.

[39] Hume, 'Coalition of Parties', *Essays*, 500–1.   [40] Ibid., 501.

[41] [Hume], *A True Account* (London, 1748), 33–4.

constitution settled as described at the end of the second Stuart volume, 'a due respect to monarchy, to nobility, and to all ancient institutions' was still possible.[42] Hume clinched the argument by saying that 'the very principle, which made the strength of their party [i.e. the monarchical principle, perhaps even passive obedience, for the Tories], and from which it derived its chief authority, has now deserted them, and gone over to their antagonists'.[43] The constitution had been settled in favour of liberty, a liberty supported by the monarchy, and if the Tories threatened this settlement by seeking to restore the Stuarts, they would be the factious innovators.

The idea of a coalition between Whigs and Tories was not as outlandish as it might seem. The ministerialist Whigs' poaching of Gower, once the Tory leader, in 1745 was discussed in Chapter 6. Subsequently, Chesterfield continued to encourage Newcastle to 'please' reasonable Tory members: 'Though Gower has broke with the Torys, and the Torys with him, I still think they are worth managing to a certain degree. If they remain an unbroken party in the House of Commons, they will be resorted to by every dissatisfied Whigg there, and you will often be threaten'd with them.'[44]

We can thus identify a recurring theme across Hume's writings on party in the sense that he attempted to describe how the Tory party had gone from being the party of order to the party of opposition and innovation, while clinging on to principles incompatible with their new situation, and how the Whig party had gone in the opposite direction. He consistently attempted to give a fair hearing to both parties, and if he was often much harder on the Whigs it was because he wanted to convert Tories and Scottish Jacobites into supporters of the Revolution Settlement. The paradox was that this settlement could only be protected at the time on the Tory principle of passive obedience,[45] but in the past, in 1688–9, on the Whig principle of resistance. In other words, one had to defend resistance to ensure passive obedience to the present system of politics.

Once coalition had been shown to be practicable, Hume continued to recommend the measure, in opposition to the Old Corps' insistence on single-party government. For example, he would later applaud a speech by his fellow Scot Lord Bute, during the Rockingham ministry of 1765–6,

[42] Hume, 'Coalition of Parties', *Essays*, 501. [43] Ibid.
[44] Lodge (ed.), *Correspondence of Chesterfield and Newcastle* (London, 1930), 122.
[45] It was more common than is sometimes thought for Whigs to do exactly this; see Mischler, 'English Political Sermons 1714–42', *BJECS*, 24 (2001), 33–61.

which called for a ministry 'chosen from among all Parties, without Regard to former Attachments'.[46] Hume was not alone and it remained common well into the nineteenth century to speak of a coalition of all parties as desirable.[47] From a ministerialist perspective, preventing an alliance of opposition Whigs and Tories was imperative. As the Tories became less considerable, Chesterfield – who had himself cooperated with Tories in opposition – believed that it would be easier to reconcile them than the opposition Whigs.

Finally, while we have repeatedly seen that Hume consistently accepted party as a feature of the British government, he never offered an unqualified defence of its existence. Admittedly, it was not his ideal solution. In 'Of the Idea of a Perfect Commonwealth' (1752), Hume stated in yet another classic paradox that the main dangers of a senate were twofold: (1) its combination and (2) its division. His solution to the first conundrum was to make the suffrage more limited by ensuring that senators were elected 'by men of fortune and education' rather than the 'rabble', diminish their power, and institute a 'court of competitors' that would function as its 'rival'.[48] His solution to the second problem was to keep the senate small (only one hundred members), make them more dependent on the people (as distinguished from the rabble) by having annual elections, and give them the 'power of expelling any factious member'.[49] He repeated that '[t]he chief support of the BRITISH government is the opposition of interests; but that, though in the main serviceable, breeds endless factions'.[50] His 'perfect commonwealth' was designed to preserve the opposition of interests without having factions. Institutionalised rather than partisan, interparliamentary opposition was thus his preferred remedy in an idealised thought experiment. At the same time, Hume made it abundantly clear that such a utopian project could not be implemented in any state with an existing constitution. Accordingly, all that could be done was to mitigate the worst effects of party. Hume's philosophical politics would influence an Irishman who, before himself becoming a partisan proponent of party, started out as a commentator on politics

---

[46] Hume to Hertford, 20 March 1766, *Further Letters*, 66. Hume was deputy secretary of state for the Northern Department under Hertford's brother, Henry Seymour Conway. Conway stayed on as secretary of state in the Chatham administration, taking office in July 1766 with the aim to do exactly as Hume proscribed.

[47] This point is stressed in Pares, *George III and the Politicians*, 117.

[48] Hume, 'Idea of a Perfect Commonwealth' (1752), *Essays*, 523–4. Hume increased the property qualification of the franchise each time he edited the essay.

[49] Ibid., 524.   [50] Ibid., 525.

and a sceptical defender of party in a Humean mould. We now turn to the young Edmund Burke.

Burke's First Essay on Party

Edmund Burke's first essay on party was written in this same context, in 1757.[51] The essay was a defence of party, written before Burke had entered the world of politics and long before he became an MP in December 1765.[52] At this time he was a man of letters trying to make his way in London. He was acquainted with Hume, who admired Burke's writings and introduced Burke to Adam Smith.[53] Burke edited the *Annual Register* between 1758 and 1765, a publication which, as Butterfield has stressed, far from taking an extreme Whig stance on George III's accession, often wrote in favour of the new king, and aimed at what we can call 'Humean' impartiality regarding party.[54] In an unpublished essay on party, Burke described in familiar and conventional terms how 'the Whigs became friends to Royalty which they never had been before ... and the Tories became Enemies to [Hanover] because it was inconsistent with their Principles to have the new [royal family]'.[55] Jacobitism had 'kept Life in both Partys' ever since but was now entirely 'annihilated'.[56] Interestingly, the future Whig said that '[t]heir resisting Principle & their Practice of Submission has left the notion of Whiggistry [*sic*] as a party no better than a jest'.[57]

What Burke had to say about party in general in this early essay is of even more interest. 'Party' in Burke's understanding required a mixed constitution, since it needed to have the aggrandisement of one part of the constitution as its object. In unmixed constitutions there could only be 'factions', such as the Green and Blue factions in late Roman Empire, or those of York and Lancaster in the Wars of the Roses. Parties in mixed constitutions were 'absolutely necessary' because they keep matters even as each part of the constitution would check one another. Whereas factions were 'Cabals fomented by Ambition swelled up by popular madness &

---

[51] This essay was discovered and published by Richard Bourke in 'Party, Parliament and Conquest in Newly Ascribed Burke Manuscripts', *HJ*, 52 (2012), 619–52. The essay will be referred to as '[On Parties]'.

[52] Bourke's discovery of the essay forces us to reconsider the previously established interpretation that Burke developed his idea of party in the second half of the 1760s, for which see O'Gorman, *The Rise of Party in England* (London, 1975), 176; Cone, *Burke and the Nature of Politics* (2 vols., Lexington, 1957), I, 196.

[53] See Chapter 13.   [54] Butterfield, *George III and the Historians* (London, 1988 [1957]), 46–50.

[55] Burke, '[On Parties]', 644.   [56] Ibid.   [57] Ibid., 645.

nothing more', parties were constitutional and necessary to maintain the balance of the mixed constitution, according to Burke. As he put it, 'Party is always useful, factions always pernicious', adding that this fact had 'hardly been enough considered'.[58] Voltaire had written in the *Encyclopédie* the previous year that 'Le terme de parti par lui-même n'a rien d'odieux, celui de faction l'est toûjours', and his entry on 'faction' included many of the well-known historical examples that recurred in Burke's essay.[59] However, by pointing to the distinction between mixed and unmixed governments, Burke's discussion went well beyond Voltaire's brief entry. More specifically, Burke argued that those who believed that the loss of parties represented an improvement were entirely mistaken, because free, or mixed, governments were inseparable from parties.[60]

Since the parties of the seventeenth century were defunct, Britain had 'no Party properly so called' but 'mere factions: without any Design[,] without any principle[,] but only a junction of People intreaguing [*sic*] for their own Interest'.[61] The parties at the present, Burke argued, presumably with reference to the personal connections associated with Pitt, Fox, and Newcastle, were not much better than those of Marius and Sulla, or Caesar and Pompey. In the 'antient parties', with the exceptions of some Tories,[62] everyone knew what principle of government they espoused and what their goals were. That had now become entirely blurred, Burke complained.[63]

Although Burke had plenty in common with Hume, the emphasis of his essay is different, because while they both believed that the existence of parties was an inescapable part of a free government, Burke bemoaned the decline of principle whereas Hume believed that this development had brought about more stable politics. Instead of paving the way for stability, Burke argued that experience proved that if a nation was divided – and he stressed that Britain remained divided, despite the decline of party – without any real principle at stake, it 'came to a speedy & often terrible Destruction'.[64] The allusion was certainly to the conflict between Caesar and Pompey and their partisans, which he had already referred to twice in the short essay. He now mentioned the contention between nobility and plebs in free ancient states in Greece and Italy. In a Machiavellian

---

[58] Ibid. This early statement from Burke calls into question the tendency among historians to argue that Burke viewed party as a temporary solution rather than a permanent feature of politics. This is discussed at greater length in later chapters.

[59] *Encyclopédie* (28 vols., Paris, 1751–77), VI, 360.   [60] Burke, '[On Parties]', 646.

[61] Ibid., 645.   [62] Burke may here refer to the ambivalence of many Tories regarding Jacobitism.

[63] Burke, [On Parties], 646.   [64] Ibid.

argument, perhaps transmitted to him via Montesquieu whom he had studied carefully,[65] Burke argued that even if this conflict often endangered these states, it had helped to preserve the vigour of their constitutions.[66] This was a paraphrase of what Hume had said about the Court and Country parties in his first Stuart volume.

Conspicuously, the parties that were lacking according to Burke were proper Court and Country parties. Burke's *Annual Register* would later, with Hume, applaud George III's attempt to extinguish the Whig and Tory names.[67] It would have been nearly impossible for Burke to *wish* for a clearer Whig–Tory polarity, which would have implied a revival of Jacobitism. For Burke, Court and Country should be constitutional parties rather than parties of interest. He lamented that the Court party was currently no more than 'a Combination of the great Officers of the State become so by popular Influence & Authority', the officers under them and those expecting office, in other words, the ministry and its supporters.[68] The Country party, on the other hand, consisted of those who had been turned out and wanted to regain office, and a small, 'pitiful' Jacobite rump. Internal evidence suggests strongly that the essay was written during and possibly towards the end of the short-lived Pitt–Devonshire ministry,[69] as it argued that people currently 'are not grown great at Court by court favour but by popular influence ... They are those great Demagogue[s] ... To ascertain the Degree of Power any man has in great Britain, you must enquire, how many Boroughs he can influence, How is he versed in the Business of the house? Of what Powers of Oratory?'[70] To make sure that no one could miss that he referred to Pitt and Newcastle, he added 'Point me out the first Man in any of these particulars & I will shew you our first Minister [Pitt] or one that must be so shortly [Newcastle].'[71]

According to Burke, the current situation, in which a Court ministry depended on popularity, meant that Britain had grown 'into a perfect Democracy', without any counterweight.[72] George II had earlier

---

[65] Burke considered *Discorsi* and *Considérations* together in his second letter on a *Regicide Peace*; see *W&S*, IX, 282–3.

[66] Burke, [On Parties], 646.   [67] Butterfield, *George III and the Historians*, 48.

[68] Burke, [On Parties], 647.

[69] This ministry was formed in November 1756. Pitt resigned the following April, and Devonshire in June.

[70] Ibid., 646.

[71] Ibid. Like Hume, Burke was later to celebrate the coalition between Pitt and Newcastle. Bourke, *Empire and Revolution*, 203.

[72] Burke, [On Parties], 646–7. By sharp contrast, a Whig pamphlet five years later would criticise the new minister Bute for not possessing popularity; see *An Address to the Cocoa-Tree from a Whig* (London, 1762), 5.

complained in an interview with Hardwicke that 'Ministers are the king, in this country.'[73] Waldegrave wrote in his memoirs that George II during the Seven Years' War 'behaved to Pitt, as to a Prince who had conquer'd him'.[74] In Burke's mind, however, the minister was far from absolute and had become obliged to court and 'flatter those to whom he is to owe his Support', meaning the people, in opposition to the 'safety of the nation', the authority of the king, and even the king's own inclinations.[75] This was a scathing criticism of Pitt's reliance on popularity,[76] a new form of personal faction, as opposed to party connection. Although Burke appears here to be most concerned with the popular element of the constitution becoming too dominant by absorbing the Court, his real aim was to condemn the unaccountable power that would undermine representative and deliberative government.[77] Later in his career he would continuously attack the occasional and dangerous alliance between popularity with the Court, a combination that inevitably upset the balance of the constitution, for example after the rise of William Pitt the Younger.[78]

The vocabulary of Court–Country was still associated with Bolingbroke, even if Hume had made this terminology his own in his non-partisan analysis of politics. Burke was a careful reader, and a fierce critic, of Bolingbroke. His first publication, *A Vindication of Natural Society*, published in 1756 but written some years earlier, was a satire of Bolingbroke, in which the Irishman took aim at the Englishman's deism, politics, and bombastic writing style. Hume had earlier remarked of Bolingbroke that 'such an elevated stile has much better grace in a speaker than in a writer'.[79] The immediate occasion for Burke's satire, which captured his target's manner of writing so closely that some thought it was an actual production of Bolingbroke, was the posthumous publication of Bolingbroke's collected *Works* in 1754, which became a scandal on account of containing previously unpublished Deistic and anti-clerical writings. More relevant for our present purposes, Burke caricatured Bolingbroke as an anti-party writer, but to do that he needed to make *his* Bolingbroke revise his expressed admiration for mixed governments.[80]

---

[73] Coxe, *Memoirs of Pelham* (2 vols., London, 1829), I, 202.   [74] *Waldegrave Memoirs*, 212.

[75] Burke, [On Parties], 647.

[76] This is the main theme of Peters' study *Pitt and Popularity*. There is no doubt that Pitt was associated with 'popularity' in his lifetime. See, e.g., [Ralph], *The Case of Authors by Profession or Trade* (London, 1758), who said that 'Popularity, and Power are at present united' (69).

[77] Bourke, 'Party, Parliament and Conquest', 632.   [78] Bourke, *Empire and Revolution*, 442–4.

[79] Hume, 'Of Eloquence', *Essays*, 108.

[80] Edmund Burke, *A Vindication of Natural Society* (1756), *W&S*, I, 169, 171.

As we have seen, the *real* Bolingbroke regarded parties and a degree of turbulence as a price worth paying for having a mixed and free constitution. Burke paraphrased Bolingbroke's attacks on party in the *Patriot King*: 'the Spirit which actuates all Parties is the same; the Spirit of Ambition, of Self-Interest, of Oppression, and Treachery'.[81] As we saw in Chapter 3, this is a rather one-sided, but common, reading of Bolingbroke, which does not take his other writings into account.

Burke's refutation of Bolingbroke says much about the persistent fame of the latter as a political thinker, although his posthumously published views on religion would give him notoriety. The text is a *reductio ad absurdum*, and, naturally, it is a better guide to Burke's thought than Bolingbroke's. Even though the *Vindication* is a difficult text since Burke never overtly states his own opinions in it, it is fairly evident that he intended Bolingbroke's alleged condemnation of parties to be contrasted with his own view. It is also a clear indication that Burke saw himself as joining a longstanding conversation about party in British political discourse, one he would shape in the following decades. Crucially, Burke wrote his famous works on party, notably *Thoughts on the Cause of the Present Discontents* (1770), as an unapologetic partisan and member of the Rockingham Whig cadre in parliament. The *Present Discontents* was an explicit attack on the 'political school' of John 'Estimate' Brown, the eccentric Anglican who enjoyed literary fame in the early, unsuccessful stage of the Seven Years' War, and to whose work we now turn.

---

[81] Ibid., 170.

CHAPTER 9

'Not Men, But Measures': John Brown on Free Government without Faction

The narrow measure of governing by a party, which has, unfortunately attended the frequency of Parliaments, (a thing, in itself, most
desirable) seems to have been the occasion, that opposition has, too
frequently, changed its views, from the redress of grievances, (its
ancient, and only justifiable object) to a pursuit of private preferment, or private resentment.

George Bubb Dodington, Memorial for Frederick, the Prince of Wales
(1749)

The *Estimate*

An Estimate of the Manners and Principles of the Times (2 vols., 1757–8) by
John Brown (1715–66) has rarely been studied in depth by intellectual
historians, incongruent to its own initial popularity at publication. The
first volume went through numerous editions in its first year and was
followed by a second volume, intended as a clarification and elaboration of
the original argument.[1] According to an early biographical sketch of
Brown, the *Estimate* was 'almost universally read, and made an uncommon
impression upon the minds of great numbers of persons'.[2] The success was
so great that Brown's friend William Warburton, who was disparaging
about the performance, was worried that it had 'turned his head'.[3] It was
written in a declinist voice, following hard on the heels of Britain's defeat
by France at the Battle of Minorca in 1756. The *Estimate* should be read in
the context of a crisis in British politics, and can usefully be compared with

---

[1] Brown's modifications can be traced in an annotated copy of the first volume, held at TCD, Ireland,
MS 1448. I am grateful to the Board of TCD for letting me consult this material.
[2] Kippis, *Biographia Britannica* (5 vols., London, 1778–93), II [1780], 656. It was also met with
hostile comments; see, e.g., [Ralph], *The Case of Authors by Profession or Trade, Stated* (London,
1758), 13–4.
[3] *The Private Correspondence of David Garrick* (2 vols., London, 1831), I, 86.

Adam Ferguson's *Reflections Previous to the Establishment of a Militia* (1756), John Shebbeare's *Letters to the People of England* (1755–8), and E.W. Montagu's *Reflections on the Rise and Fall of the Antient Republicks* (1759).[4] It lost much of its urgency after the *annus mirabilis* of 1759. As Brown's title made clear, his primary target was the 'ruling Character of the present time', described as 'vain, *luxurious*, and *selfish* EFFEMINACY'.[5] He was convinced that Britain's initial bad fortunes in war against France were related to a general decline in manners and principles, exemplified by the spirit of party. This chapter will situate the *Estimate* in the context of debate about party in the eighteenth century in general and the beginning of the Seven Years' War in particular.

According to Harvey Mansfield, Brown was a 'disciple' of Bolingbroke who, in Mansfield's reading, had a single purpose: 'to be a party against parties'.[6] The evidence for Brown being a member of 'The Bolingbroke Party' is scanty, however, and rests chiefly on taking Burke's polemical arguments from thirteen years later at face value and reading them back in time. What is more, we cannot even be sure that Burke made this connection between Bolingbroke and Brown, let alone that one existed. Burke referred to the political writings of Brown in the *Thoughts on the Cause of the Present Discontents* (1770) as belonging to a political school seeking to recommend the court system to the public and forming a party known as the king's men.[7] On Mansfield's reading, this was the political school of Bolingbroke, and it was deeply anti-aristocratic, in contrast to Burke's idea of aristocratic party connection. Even if this is one potential reading of Bolingbroke's *Idea of a Patriot King*, and a connection others have made, we have to remember that Bolingbroke for Burke was first and foremost a dangerous religious thinker, and he may have, for good reasons, separated Bolingbroke's project from Brown's, while being critical of both. In contrast to Bolingbroke's freethinking, Brown was ordained and con-

---

[4] For contexts, see McDaniel, *Adam Ferguson in the Scottish Enlightenment* (Cambridge, MA, 2013), 163; Harris, *Politics and the Nation* (Oxford, 2002), ch. 2; Miller, *Defining the Common Good* (Cambridge, 1994), 102–17.

[5] Brown, *Estimate*, I, 67. Brown's argument has been called 'misogynistic' in Wilson, *The Sense of the People* (Cambridge, 1995), 187n129. 'Virtue' in its Latin form was derived from the qualities of the *vir*, meaning the man, and for many Latinist writers 'effeminacy' represented the opposite of virtue. As an illustration, it was not idiosyncratic of Thomas Gordon to refer to the 'The Manly Reign of Queen Elizabeth' in his manuscript draft of *The History of England*; see BL Add MS 20780 f. 385.

[6] Mansfield, *Statesmanship and Party Government* (Chicago, 1965), 86, 98. Mansfield's discussion of Brown is included in a chapter entitled 'The Bolingbroke Party'.

[7] See Chapter 11.

nected with major Anglican figures.[8] In the explicit connection he made
between religion and virtue, Brown leant on the authority of the 'excellent
and learned Prelate' Bishop Berkeley, who had said that 'a Believer [rather]
than an Infidel, have a better Chance for being Patriots'.[9]

It is also clear that Brown himself conceived of his project in opposition
to the political writings of Bolingbroke as well as those of Hume, whom he
bundled together and criticised for not paying enough attention to manners and principles.[10] Even though he noted that Bolingbroke was
'esteemed a capital Writer in Politics', he is likely to have seen
Bolingbroke and Hume as representing comparable and equally impious
interpretations of politics.[11] Brown's friend Warburton – famous as the
author of *The Alliance between Church and State* (1736) – had defended
revealed religion against the onslaughts from Bolingbroke and Hume in
1754 and 1757 respectively, in the latter case together with his disciple
Richard Hurd.[12] In the *Estimate*, Brown singled out Hume as particularly
pernicious as one of the 'two Champions of Luxury and Effeminacy',[13] but
he would later direct sharp criticism against Bolingbroke for going beyond
other religious freethinkers and attack 'not only *revealed* but *natural*
Religion', and against Hume for following in his footsteps.[14]

Leaving religion to the side, he believed that both Bolingbroke and
Hume had failed to look beyond political forms and institutions. In the
margins of the *Estimate*, he scribbled that 'modern Writers … seem to
think there is only one way by which a state can be destroy'd, by the Loss
of Liberty: indeed, their own Writings tend so strongly to bring out
Destruction from another Quarter [decline in principles and religion],
that in Charity one would believe they did not see their Tendency'.[15]
Integral to Brown's enterprise was the maxim that 'salutary Principles and

---

[8] Brown's Anglicanism is evident in his writings on education. He saw Anglicanism as a tolerant
religion but did not think that further toleration of Dissenters was required; see Crimmins,
'Legislating Virtue', *Man and Nature*, 9 (1990), 69–90.

[9] Brown, *Thoughts on Civil Liberty* (London, 1765), 10–11; [Berkeley], *Maxims concerning Patriotism
by a Lady* (Dublin, 1750), 3. Brown's early sermons, in the wake of the 'Forty-five' which he had
resisted, centred on 'the mutual connection between religious truth and civil freedom'. Kippis,
Biographia Britannica, 653–4.

[10] Brown, *Estimate*, II, 21.

[11] Indeed, this becomes evident when he lists Hume and Bolingbroke together with Shaftesbury,
Tindal, and Thomas Morgan as examples of '*Writers* of such Books as tend to overturn the
fundamental Principles of Religion' and led to 'Scenes of Licentiousness … [including] Pick-
pockets, Prostitutes, Thieves, highwaymen, and Murderers'. Ibid., 86, 88.

[12] Young, *Religion and Enlightenment in Eighteenth-Century England* (Oxford, 1998), ch. 5.

[13] Brown, *Estimate*, II, 174. The other was Mandeville, the criticism of whom he elaborated in *Civil
Liberty*, 16–17.

[14] Brown, *Civil Liberty*, 101–3.   [15] TCD MS 1448, 115.

Manners will of themselves secure the Duration of a State, with very ill-modelled Laws: Whereas the best Laws can never secure the Duration of a State, where Manners and Principles are corrupted'.[16] Only the second half of the 'penetrating' Machiavelli's maxim that good customs depended on good laws and good laws on good customs was true, and the first half 'a vulgar Error'.[17] In other words, moral and political conditions were closely related, an insight which he may have derived from William Temple, whom he frequently cited.[18] Brown's focus on manners was also indebted to Montesquieu, which he acknowledged.[19]

Mansfield's argument that Bolingbroke and Brown were united in their antagonism towards aristocracy is questionable, and does not take Bolingbroke's *Spirit of Patriotism* into account. Anti-aristocratic traits are more easily identified in Brown's writings, but still need qualification.[20] Brown was clear that a community derived its characteristics from its 'higher Ranks and leading Members', who could be a source of strength as well as weakness.[21] It remains true, however, that he thought that the upper echelons of society had grown effeminate and corrupt, and this was precisely what he wanted to correct with his intervention.[22] If the higher ranks improved, the lower ones would follow. We should note, moreover, that Brown believed that public appointments should be made on merit 'without regard to Wealth, Family, Parliamentary Interest, or Connexion', and this was a crucial part of his enterprise.[23] What is more, his tone became more anti-aristocratic after the partially hostile reception of the

[16] Brown, *Estimate*, II, 20.
[17] Ibid., 22; Machiavelli, *Discourses on Livy* (Chicago, 1998), 49. Brown excused the ruthless side of Machiavelli by saying that he 'only talked the Language of his Time and Nation'. *Estimate*, II, 46–7. In the marginal notes to the first volume of the *Estimate*, Brown made plenty more references to Machiavelli, and he wrote among other things that Machiavelli was at least the equal of Montesquieu, 'and seem to have been his Original'. While controversial, Brown was not the only Anglican clergyman to study Machiavelli closely. Carte had taken notes on various chapters in Machiavelli's *Discorsi*, especially in book one, where he had especially highlighted chapter twelve: 'of the importance of Religion to a State'. Carte MS 240, Bodleian, f. 197.
[18] This has been suggested in Crimmins, 'The Study of True Politics', *Studies on Voltaire and the Eighteenth Century*, 241 (1986), 65–86.
[19] Brown, *Civil Liberty*, 67.
[20] In his notes, Brown argued, against Hume, that power was only 'in appearance ... centering [*sic*] in the lower House, [but] in reality centring in the other [i.e. the Lords]' as 'The Great Nobility are swallowing up the House of Commons.' According to Brown, this was 'destroy[ing] all honest ambition in the young gentry'. TCD MS 1448, 121.
[21] Brown, *Estimate*, II, 17.
[22] For this reason, he argued that 'the united Voice of a People' was 'the surest Test of Truth in all essential Matters on which their own Welfare depends'. Ibid., 249.
[23] Ibid., 258.

Estimate.[24] But before concluding that Brown was in favour of more popular politics, we have to acknowledge that he would later castigate the 'corrupt' Athenians for instituting an unmixed democracy where 'the Dregs of the Community' ruled.[25] As we see later in this chapter, Brown separated 'the people' from 'the populace'. For now, it is enough to conclude that Brown viewed 'ranks', to use eighteenth-century parlance, as essential, even though he was critical of the current state of 'the great'.

There is no patriot king in Brown's *Estimate*, but instead an exhortation to a great minister,[26] unmistakably a reference to William Pitt who had recently risen to power.[27] In *Thoughts on Civil Liberty, on Licentiousness, and Faction* (1765), which I discuss later in this chapter, Brown put more emphasis on the 'Conduct of the Prince'. It was written after Pitt had fallen from power and before his return to office as the Earl of Chatham.[28] Remaining with the *Estimate*, like the patriot king, the great minister is encouraged to do away with parliamentary corruption and party distinctions.[29] Brown clarified that he addressed 'upright Men of all Parties', and fully embraced the Pittite 'not Men, but Measures' slogan.[30] There is some commonality between Bolingbroke and Pitt, and they had both been associated with the opposition to Walpole in the 1730s, although Bolingbroke had more or less retired when Pitt entered the fray as one of 'Cobham's cubs'. However, the suggestion that there is but 'a small difference' between Bolingbroke's 'patriot king' and Brown's 'great minister' is exaggerated.[31] Yet it is true that they both represent a sharp contrast with Burke's enterprise. Rather than sneering at Pitt's popularity, Brown hails the minister who is supported by 'the united Voice of an uncorrupt People' rather than party connection (and 'Humean' corruption).[32]

---

[24] He commented on the reception in the following way: ''Tis certain, that in Point of *Opinion* he hath a great *Majority* in his Favour; but he never expected to find that *Majority* among those Ranks, where the *ruling Errors* are supposed to *lie*.' Brown, *An Explanatory Defence of the Estimate of the Manners and Principles of the Times* (London, 1758), 45.

[25] Brown, *Civil Liberty*, 63–4.   [26] Brown, *Estimate*, I, 221; vol. II, part II, section XIX.

[27] The more optimistic conclusion of the *Explanatory Defence*, written after the second volume of the *Estimate*, can be attributed to the fact that this 'great minister' was now believed to have been 'found' (82).

[28] Also written after Pitt's failure to patronise Brown, as pointed out in Kippis, *Biographia Britannica*, 660.

[29] Brown, *Estimate*, II, 252.

[30] Brown, *Explanatory Defence*, 80. For Pitt and this slogan, see McGee, 'Not Men, but Measures', *The Quarterly Journal of Speech*, 64 (1978), 141–54. It should be recognised, however, that Pitt was often more prepared to compromise about measures than men, especially in 1756; see Black, *Pitt the Elder* (Cambridge, 1992), 124–6.

[31] Mansfield, *Statesmanship and Party Government*, 97. The same connection has also been made in Pocock, *The Machiavellian Moment* (Princeton, 2003 [1975]), 484–5.

[32] Brown, *Estimate*, II, 253.

The contemporary political literature had plenty of inspiration for Brown's emphasis on ministerial leadership, from Bolingbroke's discussion of states-manship in *Reflections on a Late State of the Nation* (1749) to Samuel Johnson's positive references to Colbert in the opening essay to the first issue of the Pittite *Literary Magazine* in May 1756.[33]

As Brown himself noted at the beginning of the second volume of the *Estimate*, some accused him of Toryism as well as republicanism after the first volume, and it is obvious that he viewed both labels as insults. His outlook was naturally more Anglican than Bolingbroke's,[34] and he also went well beyond Bolingbroke in his analysis of commerce, in dialogue with Montesquieu. In a word, he criticised Montesquieu's theory of *doux commerce* (for lack of a better term). Although we may be sceptical of Brown belonging to Bolingbroke's 'political school' or 'party', and indeed if anything as coherent as a Bolingbrokean party can be identified in this period, there is no doubt that Bolingbroke remained an influential writer in the late 1750s; nor is there any doubt that Brown used him to a certain degree. Brown was appalled by Bolingbroke's lack of religion, as well as his neglect of the importance of manners for politics, but this did not stop Brown from citing him for historical background. As he put it, Bolingbroke 'was a *great Historian*, tho' but a *poor Reasoner*'.[35] Bolingbroke's impact can be further teased out. For instance, on several occasions, Brown's key words are the same as Bolingbroke's. Notably, at the beginning of the first volume of the *Estimate*, Brown employs the Bolingbrokean terminology of 'the spirit of liberty',[36] a spirit which is incompatible with effeminacy and lack of principle.

Brown also echoed Bolingbroke when he spoke of a 'national Spirit of *Union*'. Such a union was naturally strong in absolute monarchies, where 'the *Prince* directs and draws every thing to one Point', and naturally weak in free countries, meaning those with mixed constitutions, 'unless sup-ported by the generous Principles of Religion, Honour, or public Spirit'.[37] A national union required that partial views and private interest would be sacrificed to general welfare.[38] For these reasons, Brown disputed the view

---

[33] Samuel Johnson, *Political Writings* (New Haven, 1977), 140–1.

[34] Brown's complaints about luxury combined with the decline of religiosity were comparable to those of Thomas Secker, Archbishop of Canterbury in 1758–68; see Ingram, *Religion, Reform and Modernity in the Eighteenth Century* (Woodbridge, 2007), 165.

[35] Brown, *Estimate*, II, 149. The Bolingbroke text he most frequently cited approvingly was *Remarks on the History of England*, particularly in his marginal notes; see TCD MS 1448, 105, 123.

[36] This phrase is from Brown's favourite work by Bolingbroke: the *Remarks*.

[37] Brown, *Estimate*, I, 102–3.   [38] Ibid., 103–4.

of 'the celebrated MONTESQUIEU', otherwise one of his favourite authors, 'that *Factions* are not only natural, but necessary, to *free* Governments', citing from the Frenchman's history of Rome, but as we know he could also have quoted from *The Spirit of Laws*.[39] The mistake Montesquieu had made was to offer this as a general rule 'without Restriction'. In its place, Brown suggested a distinction along the lines of Bolingbroke's distinction between party and faction, and in the second volume of the *Estimate* he actually cited letter two of Bolingbroke's *Remarks on the History of England* in this context.[40] When division in a free state stemmed from 'the Variety and *Freedom* of *Opinion* only; or from the contested Rights and Privileges of the different Ranks or Orders of a State, not from the detached and selfish Views of Individuals, a Republic is then in its *Strength*, and gathers Warmth and Fire from these Collisions'.[41] This was the case at an early stage of the history of the Roman republic. However, when 'Factions run high from selfish Ambition, Revenge, or Avarice, a Republic is then on the very Eve of its Destruction', referring to the later periods of contest between Marius and Sulla, Pompey and Caesar, and Antony and Augustus.[42]

Brown then moved from the Roman to the British context, and once again he touched on themes that had been central to Bolingbroke's political writings. Two consequences of the Glorious Revolution – annual sessions of parliament and annual supplies – made parliament an arena for place-hunters as the monarch needed to offer jobs to members in exchange for the granting of supplies. As a result 'the great Chain of political Self-Interest was at length formed; and extended from the *lowest Cobbler* in a *Burrough* to the *King's first Minister*'.[43] 'Faction' in Britain was 'established, not on *Ambition,* but on *Avarice*', although Brown would elsewhere stress the negative impact of the former as well.[44] Unlike Hume, Brown did not think that this was a stable foundation for a political system: the chain of self-interest was no better than a rope of sand, and instead of cohesion, it only created antipathy and repulsion between the parts of the constitution.

Brown was more eager than Bolingbroke to ascribe the system of corruption to the general decline in manners, as opposed to placing all blame on Walpole. Drawing on Machiavelli's maxim that an ill-disposed

---

[39] Ibid., 104–5. In the second volume, Brown acknowledged that his opinion regarding Montesquieu had been 'criticised, and shewn in some Sense to be *erroneous*, because too *general*', and that the Frenchman had borrowed this argument from Machiavelli's *Discourses*; see Brown, *Estimate*, II, 181.
[40] Ibid., 185–6.   [41] Ibid., I, 105.
[42] Ibid., 106. A similar distinction is found in Ferguson's *History of the Roman Republic* (1783).
[43] Brown, *Estimate*, I, 111.   [44] Ibid., 122.

citizen can do no great harm but in a corrupt city, he concluded that 'Bribery in the Minister supposes a corrupt People.'[45] Alluding to Walpole, Brown offered a partial defence of this 'noted Minister', arguing that he may have feared the virtue of the nation in opposing bad measures, but as often the lack of virtue in supporting good ones.[46] This more ambivalent attitude towards Walpole set Brown apart from Bolingbroke, and Brown was censured by the Tory-Jacobite William King on this basis.[47] In his marginal notes to the copy of the *Estimate*, Brown was bolder in his criticism of Walpole, scribbling that 'mr. Hume, in his Char-[acter] of S[i]r R. W[alpole] says, in his time that Liberty declined, and Learning went to Ruin. He should have said, Principles declined, and Religion went to Ruin'.[48] Edward Montagu's contemporary *Reflections* represented a more straightforward public condemnation of Walpole.[49]

Brown's main intention was not to rekindle a debate about Walpole's legacy, but to point out that the 'political System of Self-Interest is at length compleated; and a Foundation laid in our Principles of Manners for *endless Dissentions* in the State'.[50] The greatest danger of this state of affairs was not a bloody civil war, as had been the case in Athens and Rome, and indeed England in the seventeenth century. As the British had grown effeminate, the spirit of arms and honour was no longer strong enough to produce such an outcome.[51] The main threat was rather that Britain risked becoming susceptible to a foreign invasion. Division made consistency, vigour, and expedition in government impossible, in significant contrast with the 'united Enemy' of France.[52] The prospect that France would invade Britain was indeed a genuine fear at this time, before the year of victories in 1759.

Brown was naturally eager to emphasise that although the Williamite Revolution had paved the way for the rise of this form of dissension, he was not against the Revolution. 'Principle of [self-interested] *Faction* was a *natural* Defect, arising from a *noble Change* in the Constitution: Evils

---

[45] Ibid., 114.   [46] Ibid., 114–15.

[47] King, *Anecdotes*, 108. Brown ended up between a rock and a hard place, however, as his attempt at a balanced assessment upset one of his backers, the Court Whig Hardwicke. Kippis, *Biographia Britannica*, 660.

[48] TCD MS 1448, 115.

[49] Montagu, *Reflections on the Rise and Fall of the Ancient Republicks* (Indianapolis, 2015), 178.

[50] Brown, *Estimate*, I, 121. Indeed, in the second volume of the *Estimate*, Brown highlighted that his views of Walpole were '*different* from those of both his *Friends* and *Enemies*' (*Estimate*, II, 205). Brown saw his discussion of Walpole as being significantly different from Bolingbroke's partisan complaints.

[51] Ibid., I, 125.   [52] Ibid., 126.

infinitely greater were taken away', he argued.[53] To suggest anything else risked accusations of Jacobitism, which Brown was naturally eager to avoid as a staunch loyalist.[54] This could have serious consequences at the time; Shebbeare was sentenced to three years in prison and had to stand in the pillory at Charing Cross following the publication of his anti-Hanoverian *Sixth Letter to the People of England* in 1757.[55] While Brown intended to diagnose the flaws of post-revolutionary Britain, or rather explain how manners had been altered for the worse, it would be wrong to assume that his argument was an apology for the pre-revolutionary system of government, which he viewed as completely arbitrary. As he clarified in an explanatory publication, all he wanted to show was that 'our Constitution, excellent in its Nature, was liable to an Abuse [parliamentary corruption or influence], which arose from its Excellence'.[56]

In the second volume of the *Estimate*, Brown signalled that he was not restricted to Bolingbroke's distinction between faction and party and wanted to show that 'there is another Source of Faction, of which we have had most fatal Instances in our own Country, distinct from both that of public Spirit and selfish Interest'.[57] Brown referred to faction stemming from '*erroneous Conscience*', moving from the Bolingbrokean paradigm to a more Humean analysis of party systems. Brown did not refer to any kind of conscience, but particularly the idea that a certain person or race of men – that is, a certain royal family – had an '*unalienable Right* of governing', making explicit references to the conflict between Lancaster and York, as well as Jacobitism, in other words, what Hume would have categorised as a party (or faction) based on affection. This type of party had lost much of its force in more recent times, Brown argued, reflecting the real decline of particularly English Jacobitism since the early 1750s. For that reason, his main target remained the 'certain Party of Men ... who look no farther than themselves, and are watching to plunder the Public for their own private Emolument'.[58]

Brown concluded the second volume by delineating the ideal character of a political writer, the first characteristic of whom was impartiality.[59] Such a writer – who 'hath never yet existed; nor, probably, will ever

---

[53] Ibid., II, 194.
[54] Brown had 'distinguished himself by his zeal for government, and acted as a volunteer at the siege of Carlisle' during the 'Forty-five'. Kippis, *Biographia Britannica*, 653.
[55] Harris, *Politics and the Nation*, 89–90.   [56] Brown, *Explanatory Defence*, 8.
[57] Brown, *Estimate*, II, 187.   [58] Brown, *Explanatory Defence*, 58.
[59] Predictably, he was yet accused of 'blameable Partiality', which he laughed away in his appendix. Ibid., 34–5.

appear, in our own Country' – 'would chuse an untrodden Path of Politics, where no Party-man ever dared to enter'.[60] This section is a reminder that Hume was not alone in being obsessed with 'party' as an impediment to intellectual freedom and clear political thinking. The Tory–Whig framework may have started to disintegrate in the sphere of high politics, but 'party' remained at the heart of political debate in the late 1750s.

Brown's main contention was that the politics of parliamentary influence and party connection put the wrong sorts of people in power. This was fundamentally a challenge to Humean politics, and he was answered by Hume's fellow Scot Robert Wallace. Wallace's partial defence of the politics of party was essentially the same as Hume's but couched in more Whiggish and indeed nationalistic terms. No form of government was without inconvenience and a limited form of government had to tolerate 'parties and factions', which would still be infinitely better than absolute monarchy, Wallace concluded.[61] Brown agreed, but he became even more prepared to question the idea that 'faction' was inevitable under a mixed constitution after the accession of George III, a context to which we now turn, before returning to Brown's attempt to adumbrate the faction-less free state.

The Accession of George III

Notwithstanding Tory support for the governments in the late 1750s, the person who could really shake things up in eighteenth-century politics was the monarch. As long as George II was determined not to employ Tories, distrust between them and the political establishment subsisted. Only a few Tories had gained office since the onset of Whig ascendency, even if they were hopeful at the beginning of George I's reign and on the accession of George II in 1727.[62] One of the most radical actions of George III was to employ nominal Tories and people with such a background in his household.[63] The demise of Jacobitism as a potent political force had begun earlier; the abandoned Elibank Plot has already been referred to. Moreover, Pitt had managed to convert one of the last strongholds, the Scottish Highlands, by recruiting forces there during the Seven Years'

---

[60] Brown, *Estimate*, II, 260.
[61] Wallace, *Characteristics of the Present Political State of Great Britain* (London, 1758), 79–81.
[62] Colley, *In Defiance of Oligarchy* (Cambridge, 1982), ch. 2.
[63] I.e. Lord Litchfield, Lord Bruce, Lord Oxford, William Northey, George Pitt, and Norborne Berkeley. *Egmont Papers*, 226.

War.[64] The accession of George III, the first Hanoverian monarch who was Anglican and born in England, was symbolically important. William King described Gower's appointment as Lord Privy Seal in 1742 as a 'defection' and 'a great blow to the Tory party',[65] but he himself would make his peace with Hanoverian Britain after the accession of George III.[66] His enthusiasm for the Stuart cause had waned much earlier, however, and in his memoirs he attributed the decline of the Jacobite cause to the unattractive personality of Prince Charles Edward Stuart, with whom he had a series of meetings in the early 1750s.[67] There is little doubt, however, that the accession of George III had an impact on Tory opinion. Shebbeare's *History of the Excellence and Decline of the Constitution ... And the Restoration thereof in the Reign of Amaurath the Third, surnamed The Legislator* (2 vols., 1762), published five years after the author's imprisonment for Jacobite propaganda, has been described as a sign of 'Tory rapprochement with the Court'.[68]

It has been argued that George III ascended the throne as a man on a mission, determined to implement a 'drastic house-cleaning'.[69] In this he was assisted by his favourite John Stuart, 3rd Earl of Bute. Newcastle for one was certain that the king and Bute's treatment of him (as well as Devonshire and Hardwicke) from the accession was 'designed purely to drive Me out'.[70] As Newcastle made clear in a conversation with George Lyttelton, his departure was not only due to the fact he had been personally slighted but was also related to competing views about Britain's place in Europe after the Seven Years' War: 'my Difference of opinion with my Lord Bute, did not singly depend upon the Peace; For that I should be equally Zealous, after the Peace, for establishing some Plan of Connection with, & Support of, the Continent'.[71] In other words, Newcastle interpreted the situation as a traditional Tory–Whig split about Britain's involvement in continental Europe which stretched back to the 'rage of party' during the War of the Spanish Succession. When Lyttelton tried to lure Newcastle back to the king's service, the old statesman said that he had 'made one firm Resolution ... in everything, to consult the Interest, Inclination, & Wishes of the Body of The Whigs'.[72]

---

[64] *A Full and Free Inquiry into the Merits of the Peace; With some Strictures on the Spirit of Party* (London, 1765), 143–4; Fitzmaurice, *Life of Shelburne* (3 vols., London, 1875), I, 92. See also Brady, *Boswell's Political Career* (New Haven, 1965), 29. As Brady remarks, however, many retained their 'feeling for the Stuarts', Boswell among them.

[65] King, *Anecdotes*, 45.   [66] Greenwood, *William King* (Oxford, 1969), 300–1.

[67] King, *Anecdotes*, 195–214.   [68] Harris, *Politics and the Nation*, 94.

[69] McKelvey, *George III and Bute* (Durham, 1973), xi.

[70] Notes by Newcastle on a conversation with Lyttelton, BL Add MS 35422, f. 24.   [71] Ibid., f. 26.

[72] Ibid., f. 27.

The clash was one of men and measures. It is evident that the monarch was determined not to be enslaved to the Whig magnates as he believed his grandfather and great-grandfather had been. Waldegrave commented in his memoirs: 'The Spirit of Party or Faction which in former Reigns has caused so much disorder, and so much Malevolence, seems to be at its last gasp. Every Barrier is removed, the Road to Preferment lies open to every political adventurer.'[73] The idea to abolish party distinctions in the sense of Whig and Tory was not new but one that can be traced back to Bolingbroke's attempt to form a coherent Country party platform in the 1730s, if not earlier. Prince Frederick had made the same promise to opposition leaders in 1747.[74] Moreover, historians as far back as Robert Bisset have noted a correlation between Pitt and George III in this regard.[75] This principle had been a crucial component of George III's education when he was Prince of Wales. The pernicious influence of 'faction' is a key part of a prospectus for the prince's instruction from 1755–6, found among Bute's family papers.[76] This document, as described by James Lee McKelvey, bears all the hallmarks of Bolingbroke's political thought, with the replacement of a 'national party' by the Court Whig faction at its core.

Among the papers of George III, a document entitled 'Some Short Notes Concerning the Education of a Prince' can be found, probably written by his then tutor Bute.[77] This document also has many resemblances with Bolingbroke's writings, notably the suggestions that 'useful' history began at the end of the fifteenth century, with emphasis on the shift of 'Property and Power' from the great lords to the inferior ranks (the gentry and the yeomanry) in the reign of Henry VII.[78] This latter idea could of course be derived from multiple sources, from Harrington to Hume, but the short exposition that followed about the new system of balance of power in Europe, and competition between the House of Austria on the one hand, and the houses of Valois and Bourbon on the other, is reminiscent of Bolingbroke's *Letters on the Study and Use of History*, composed in 1735 but published for the first time in 1752, the

---

[73] He continued: 'This widening of the Bottom must undoubtedly be agreeable to the tories, whose attachment to their rightfull sovereign has seldom been equivocal, and who may find more solid satisfaction in the service of the Crown, than they have felt for some years past in the service of their Country.' *Waldegrave Memoirs*, 224.

[74] *Egmont Papers*, 90, 117, 119.

[75] Butterfield, *George III and the Historians* (London, 1988 [1957]), 220.

[76] McKelvey, *George III and Bute*, 85–7.   [77] RA GEO/ADD/32/1731.

[78] Bolingbroke, *Letters on the Study and Use of History*, in *Works*, II, 360–1.

year after the author's death. The document also contains subtle criticism of the post-1688–9 Whig continental vision of British foreign policy. Britain had a special role in maintaining the balance of power in Europe, and this had been neglected in the seventeenth century, especially from the Pyrenees Treaty of 1659 onwards.[79] Since the Revolution, however, the document states that Britain has fallen 'into another extreme, and have sacrificed ourselves beyond all proportion, not only to the common cause, but to the private Interest of an ally, [i.e.] the House of Austria', undoubtedly a reference to the Wars of the Spanish (1701–14) and Austrian Succession (1740–8).[80] Similarly, Bolingbroke had written that under William, England supported Austria against France and Spain with little concern for 'any national interest … either then, or afterwards'.[81]

George III's decision to employ Tories stemmed from his determination to pay no heed to party distinctions when awarding jobs and favours. Even if he may not have read the *Patriot King* himself,[82] it would not be an exaggeration to say that Bolingbrokean political principles had influenced his education. Horace Walpole, the minister's youngest son, infamously remarked that 'none but the friends and pupils of the late Lord Bolingbroke [were] entrusted with the education of a prince', referring to figures such as Andrew Stone and William Murray in the prince's household.[83] We should certainly not take Walpole at face value, especially not his accusations that the Hanoverian prince was educated in Jacobite principles. At the same time, however, we must recognise that Bolingbroke and his writings had been central to opposition politics, with which Leicester House had also long been associated. For one thing, he had given advice to George III's father when he had been leader of the opposition, perhaps as late as 1750, the year before they both died.[84]

---

[79] RA GEO/ADD/32/1731, f. 9. This is also singled out as a turning point in Bolingbroke, *Study and Use of History, Works*, II, 95.

[80] RA GEO/ADD/32/1731, f. 9.

[81] Bolingbroke, *Study and Use of History, Works*, II, 442. Bolingbroke's text was of course written in part to justify the Treaty of Utrecht (1713), in which he had played a key role as secretary of state and chief negotiator. It is one of the clearest statements of the Tory vision of foreign policy, with its critique of continental engagements.

[82] Butterfield, *George III and the Historians*, 231–7. In the newly released papers by the Royal Collection Trust, we find no evidence of George III having studied any of Bolingbroke's texts, at least not directly, as he had Montesquieu and Hume.

[83] Walpole, *Memoirs of George II* (3 vols., New Haven, 1985), I, 205. This was problematic for Walpole, who saw Bolingbroke as a straightforward Jacobite. However, while Murray had a Jacobite family background, and Scott was appointed on Bolingbroke's recommendation and other connections can be established, Brooke, the modern editor of the *Memoirs*, has disputed Walpole's charge that they were all 'disciples' of Bolingbroke (193n7).

[84] *Egmont Papers*, 174.

Moreover, the 'drastic house-cleaning' which George III and Bute managed to carry out to an extent on his accession was similar to the one which had been planned for his father by Perceval, and which Bolingbroke had recommended in the *Patriot King*.[85] It may be 'entirely imaginary' that George III was educated in Bolingbroke's 'arbitrary principles of government', as Walpole's editor John Brooke notes, but only because such principles had little to do with Bolingbroke's political thought.[86] Without evidence of direct influence, it is enough for us to acknowledge that George III shared some of Bolingbroke's key claims, the extinction of Whig and Tory being one of the most central. His supporters were also eager to associate him with Bolingbroke's ideal. In 1762, Bute's propaganda organ, the *Auditor*, published a piece entitled the 'Patriot Prince'.[87]

The accession sounded the death knell of the old Tory party, as it lost its identity as an oppositional Country party.[88] Former Jacobites went in all directions: Old Corps of Whigs (Peter Legh), the king's men (Westmorland), and even the supporters of John Wilkes (John Pugh Pryse).[89] Some country gentlemen with Tory backgrounds preferred to retain their independence even as they now broadly supported the king's government. Roger Newdigate, MP for Oxford University, wrote: 'I like the King and shall be with his ministers as long as I think an honest man ought, and believe it best not to lose the country gentleman in the courtier.' At the same time, Newdigate refused to join any Whig faction, stressing that 'men proscribed and abused for 50 years together [should] be presented with fools caps if they make ladders for tyrant Whigs to mount by'.[90] The leading words in Hume's correspondence on British politics in the 1760s, especially in 1766–9 when he was deputy secretary in the Northern Department and based in London, are 'confusion' and 'change'.[91] The party framework he had known and started to analyse in 1741 was disintegrating, and Hume welcomed this development. He

[85] Ibid., 106, 114–16. Hardwicke's son wrote in a memorial in 1771: 'Lord Bute had the sole power & influence, & he was determined to work out the old remnants of the Crown as soon as he could possibly bring it about'. BL Add MS 35428, f. 3.

[86] Walpole, *Memoirs of George II*, I, 193n7.

[87] Butterfield, *George III and the Historians*, 58. See also Burgh, *Remarks Historical and Political Collected from Books and Observations* (1762), BL King's MS 433, f. 21.

[88] Hume, *Letters*, I, 336, 368, 385.   [89] Szechi, *The Jacobites* (Manchester, 1994), 131.

[90] *Commons, 1754–90*, III, 197. As we saw in Chapter 3, Newdigate followed Bolingbroke in renouncing the Tory label in favour the Country party, but it is equally clear that he had numerous Tory ties, including William Bromley, his wife's brother John Conyers, the young William Blackstone, and his constituents at Oxford more generally. In 1754, he laboured to have the Tories James Dashwood and Viscount Wenman declared as MPs for Oxfordshire. *ODNB*.

[91] Hume, *Letters*, II, 144–5.

knew, however, that even if Whig and Tory were losing their former meanings, this did not mean that 'party' per se would vanish. Even if the old two-party framework had weakened and largely disappeared by 1760, party terminology was quickly revived.[92]

Importantly for Brown, George III's accession made it safe to criticise the legacy of the Old Corps of Whigs. Since the new Hanoverian king was himself a critic, such censure could no longer be dismissed as Jacobitism. Even anti-Hanoverian sentiments became more acceptable as they were shared by the king to some degree.[93] Having owed his church promotions in 1750s to the Whig establishment, in particular to Bishop Osbaldeston, Brown was now able to go further than in his previous publications in his attacks on the post-revolutionary, and particularly post-1714, Whig state.

Brown and the Faction-Free State

Brown returned to the subject of faction with his *Thoughts of Civil Liberty, on Licentiousness and Faction*, published in 1765, one year before he committed suicide. According to *Biographia Britannica* of 1780, the book was written at the beginning of 1765, and was 'little more than a party pamphlet; intended to censure ... the persons who at the time opposed the measures of the administration', in other words, the Rockingham Whigs, who replaced Grenville's ministry in the summer of 1765.[94] According to Warburton's judgement in February 1765, it was simply 'the old *Estimate* new turned'.[95] The work was not unambitious, however, as Brown now tried to do what many political writers had held to be impossible, including the principal ones discussed in this book, namely to demonstrate how a free state could exist without dissension. The basic idea behind *Thoughts on Civil Liberty* was that a free state could perish by two means: external or internal violence – in other words, foreign war or domestic faction.[96] Most of Brown's contemporaries agreed with this, but many, at least by 1765, would all the same contend that party division had to be permissible in a free state. In demonstrating the danger of internal violence, Brown followed Montagu's lead of analysing the central ancient republics, namely Sparta, Athens, and Rome.[97] Brown's main

---

[92] This is even noted in a recent Namierite study, which seeks to downplay the importance of party, written by Namier's final research student; see Thomas, *George III* (Manchester, 2002), 30–1.
[93] Blanning, *The Culture of Power and the Power of Culture* (Oxford, 2002), 322.
[94] Kippis, *Biographia Britannica*, 661.
[95] *Letters from Warburton to Charles York* (London, 1812), 59.   [96] Brown, *Civil Liberty*, 9.
[97] Montagu also looked at Thebes and Carthage.

source was also the same as Montagu's: Plutarch's *Lives*. As in the *Estimate*, Brown's concern remained to show how the politics of parliamentary influence and party were equally pernicious and mutually supportive.

Brown singled out Sparta, a republic where '*Manners* and *Principles*, all point[ed] to the *same* End, the *Strength* and *Duration* of the *State*'.[98] Crucially for our present purposes, he argued that the long duration of Sparta afforded evidence against Machiavelli's and Montesquieu's political maxim that divisions are necessary in a free state. On the contrary, Brown pointed out that 'intestine Divisions were unknown' for at least 500 years of Sparta's history, and once they appeared they caused the fall of that republic.[99] This was thus a 'mistaken Maxim (adopted by almost all political Writers)'.[100] It was founded on the supposition that freedom of opinion necessarily entailed division. Brown believed that Sparta demonstrated that 'Opinion may be *free*, yet still *united*', ensured by 'early and rigorous Education'.[101] He had made it clear at the outset of the text that he understood freedom of thought differently from freethinkers such as Mandeville and the authors of *Cato's Letters* (Trenchard and Gordon), the latter of whom he otherwise held in higher regard.[102] Civil liberty was derived from self-restraint and from giving up 'Every natural Desire, which might in any respect be inconsistent with the general Weal'.[103] Brown was convinced that licentiousness and faction had led to the ruin of both Athens and Rome. This time he made no mention of Montesquieu's and Machiavelli's positive treatment of division in the early history of Rome, which he had approvingly cited in the *Estimate*. Instead, he wholeheartedly embraced Montesquieu's other conclusion that overexpansion combined with the increased dominance of Epicureanism – for him, representing the decline of manners and principles – were instrumental in bringing about the downfall of Rome.[104]

Like Montagu, Brown included a section about 'How far these Facts can properly be apply'd to the political State of Great-Britain'. As Brown had already written in the *Estimate* but now made more explicit, 'Party rage' was one of the negative upshots of the by and large excellent

---

[98] Brown, *Civil Liberty*, 50.   [99] Ibid., 55, 58.   [100] Ibid., 55–6.   [101] Ibid., 56.

[102] Ibid., 16–19. Mandeville and *Cato's Letters* had made common cause against charity schools, designed to educate the poor, in the 1720s; Mandeville because education made the poor unfit for manual labour, and Trenchard and Gordon because they were hotbeds of Jacobitism and High Church sentiments. See Goldsmith, *Private Vices, Public Benefits* (Christchurch, 2001 [1985]), 97–8.

[103] Brown, *Civil Liberty*, 13.

[104] Ferguson would later adopt the same thesis in his history of Rome.

Revolution of 1688–9.[105] Brown took a particular swipe at 'the Dissentions that disgraced the Reigns of King WILLIAM and Queen Anne', known in modern historiography as the 'Rage of Party'.[106] That conflictual situation was 'essentially contradictory to the Principles of Freedom', but he repeatedly stressed that it was 'inevitable' because of the state of the manners and principles of those times.[107]

The accession of George I did not put an end to party rage. While 'the Advocates of Liberty [the Whigs] now assumed the Reins of Power ... The slavish Principle of absolute *Non-Resistance*, and an *independent Hierarchy*, were still prevalent in Part, especially among the *Clergy*.'[108] In other words, the Tory–Whig battle continued. The Whigs fought a press campaign against the remnants of seventeenth-century Toryism, but unfortunately religion was destroyed in the general onslaught on superstition. He singled out Trenchard and Gordon's anti-clerical *Cato's Letters* and *Independent Whig* along with the anti-Christian message he perceived in Shaftesbury and Mandeville as examples of this unhappy development.[109] Such publications 'tended ... to relax those Principles [religious institutions and prejudice] by which alone Freedom, either civil or religious, can be sustained'.[110] We can now understand how Brown believed that party rage had resulted in the sorry moral state of Britain in mid-century. The Whigs in power sought to 'sweep away *false Principles*, [but] imprudently struck at *all Principles*.'[111]

When Britain's degeneration led to a crisis in 1757, the year when Brown published the *Estimate*, 'NECESSITY gave a *temporary Union* to all Parties, and a *temporary Restoration* to the *State*.'[112] But as soon as the danger ceased, faction re-emerged, Brown lamented. It now arose on 'Foundations widely different from Those in the Reigns of WILLIAM and ANNE', when dissension was 'chiefly founded in *false Principles*'.[113] Toryism, Jacobitism, and 'bigoted' Dissent were all founded on 'mistaken Interpretations of Scripture', which were '*now* held in general Derision'.[114] Few among the aged clergy held 'despotic' principles and bishops had long been 'appointed by the Patrons of Liberty' and had become 'the *Friends* of

---

[105] Brown, *Civil Liberty*, 92, 88.   [106] Ibid., 93.   [107] Ibid., 92, 89, 94.   [108] Ibid., 94–5.
[109] Brown recognised that Shaftesbury's and Mandeville's systems were 'diametrically opposite' in the sense that the former held human nature to be excellent and the latter deprived, but they were both similar in the sense that they '*disgraced* CHRISTIANITY' (*Civil Liberty*, 100–1). For Brown's criticism of Shaftesbury in particular, see Crimmins, 'John Brown and the Theological Tradition of Utilitarian Ethics', *HPT*, 4 (1983), 523–50.
[110] Brown, *Civil Liberty*, 96.   [111] Ibid., 103.   [112] Ibid., 105.   [113] Ibid., 106.
[114] Ibid.

Freedom'.[115] By contrast, the dissension of the 1760s was founded 'on a *Want of Principle*', which was the dominant characteristic of the time, according to Brown.[116]

Competition for office led in particular the higher ranks of society into 'the Extremes of selfish Views, Ambition, Party-Rage, Licentiousness, and Faction'.[117] The uneducated populace in the cities, 'like the *Athenian Populace* of old', were 'liable to the *Seduction* of artful Men' and risked becoming 'the ready *Tools* of every unprincipled *Leader*'.[118] Distinguished from both these groups were those he called '*The* PEOPLE *of* GREAT BRITAIN', that is, 'Those who send Representatives for the Counties to Parliament', including the landed gentry, the Country clergy, the more prominent merchants and traders, and the freeholders and yeomen.[119] As was common in the eighteenth century, the people were distinguished from the populace, the political class from the dregs. This middle order would be alarmed by the '*factious Clamours* of the *Capital*' but only 'rowzed into *Action* ... on *singular* and *important* Emergencies'.[120] Brown's fear of the populace and the potential of demagogues from the upper ranks rising on their shoulders was shared by many of the Scottish literati, including Hume and Ferguson around this time, and this became particularly prominent after the outbreak of the 'Wilkes and Liberty' discontent.[121]

This new type of factionalism was even more pernicious than the one based on 'false principles', since it was less detectable. The reason for this was that people with false opinions naturally held them because they believed them to be true and were consequently not ashamed of them. By contrast, faction founded on lack of principle implied 'moral depravity' and would 'naturally attempt to *veil* itself'.[122] Brown emphasised that he was not against disagreement in politics. In all states, there were certain subjects and measures which were 'debatable', and on such 'even the Friends of Liberty may sometimes differ'.[123] As Berkeley, whom Brown

---

[115] Ibid., 106–7. Of the gradual diminution of Toryism among the clergy, see Gregory, *Restoration, Reformation and Reform, 1660–1828* (Oxford, 2000).
[116] Brown, *Civil Liberty*, 106.   [117] Ibid., 111.   [118] Ibid.   [119] Ibid., 87–8.
[120] Ibid., 114.
[121] Skjönsberg, 'Adam Ferguson on Partisanship, Party Conflict, and Popular Participation', *Modern Intellectual History*, 16 (2019), 1–28. Hume's late pessimistic phase is treated in Pocock, *Virtue, Commerce and History* (Cambridge, 1985), 125–42; Baumstark, 'The End of Empire and the Death of Religion', in *Philosophy and Religion in Enlightenment Britain* (Oxford, 2012).
[122] Brown, *Civil Liberty*, 115–16.   [123] Ibid., 116.

admired and cited, had written, 'honest Men may differ'.[124] The problem, however, was that 'The factious Man is apt to mistake himself for a Patriot.'[125] Brown's 'friend of liberty' would have no selfish ambitions and be 'rational, honest, equitable, in the Prosecution of his Wishes'. His (Brown uses the masculine possessive pronoun) primary concern would be to protect the 'just Balance of divided Power', that is to say, the integrity of the mixed and balanced constitution. When pursuing his goal, he will 'be attached to Measures, without respecting Men'.[126] Opposition had to be constitutional; a friend of liberty would 'not attempt to inflame an ignorant Populace against their legal Governors'.[127] Finally, he would respect other viewpoints and not seek to 'defame the private Characters of the Individuals who differ from him in Opinion'.[128]

On the other hand, a person motivated by the spirit of faction would be 'irrational, dishonest, iniquitous'.[129] Rather than upholding the mixed and balanced constitution, 'The Leaders of Faction (being naturally of the higher Ranks) would aim to establish an *aristocratic Power*, and *inslave* both *Prince* and *People* to their own Avarice and Ambition.'[130] Brown may here have alluded to the practice of 'storming the closet', whereby a powerful clique threatened a monarch with mass resignation to make him or her assent to their policies. This equalled 'usurp[ing] the *legal Prerogatives* of the *Crown*'.[131] Such people were 'attached to Men, to the Neglect of Measures', to the degree that they unconditionally backed each other in all public debates, even 'If the *Sovereign* had aimed to unite all *honest Men of all Parties*'.[132] As we have seen, this had been George III's explicit mission.

The attachment to the same party in and out of government regardless of changing circumstances would produce inconsistency and contradictory behaviour. Brown was careful to avoid 'particularities', but we can never-theless identify examples he is likely to have had in mind. It is clear from his language that he was not thinking, at least not primarily, of Bolingbroke's favourite example of how the Whig party had become more authoritarian in power. Rather he alluded to the Tories, who in opposition could be said to have condemned influence and dependence 'as a *despotic*

---

[124] [Berkeley], *Maxims concerning Patriotism*, 7. Berkeley's assumption that there are honest men in politics was a response to Hume's contention that we must suppose that everyone in politics is a knave. Berkeley wrote: 'He who saith there is no such Thing as an honest Man, you may be sure is himself a Knave' (5).
[125] Ibid., 7.   [126] Brown, *Civil Liberty*, 119.   [127] Ibid.   [128] Ibid., 120.   [129] Ibid., 117.
[130] Ibid., 121.   [131] Ibid.
[132] Ibid., 124. This language is reminiscent of Bolingbroke's *Patriot King*.

Measure in the *Servants* of the *Crown*, which They themselves *formerly* exercised when in *Power*, and still *continue* to exercise towards their *private Dependents*'.[133] In other words, the Tories' transformation into a Country party was as opportunistic as the Whigs' becoming a Court party.

The Whigs were not spared Brown's criticism, however. Brown evidently thought of events at the time of his writing, and perhaps also the Bolingbroke–Walpole conflict, when he said that it was the mark of faction to 'attempt to revive Animosities which Time had bury'd'.[134] There had been a time, he wrote, 'when All who presumed to *dissent* in any Degree from those in Power, were indiscriminately and unjustly branded with the Name of *Jacobite* or *Tory*'.[135] As we saw in Chapter 3, this had been a favourite Whig tactic when the Walpole press attempted to discredit Bolingbroke in particular, but also other members of the opposition. The same people (the Newcastle and Rockingham Whigs) now bestowed these appellations 'as freely round, on All those who *assent* to Those in Power'.[136] The words 'Jacobite' and 'Tory' had lost their meaning, according to Brown, and to use them to discredit political adversaries was clearly factious. Brown here referred to a new tendency to brand supporters of George III as Tories and even Jacobites,[137] as the new monarch sought to break the Whigs' power monopoly. The idea that there was a nascent Toryism in the early reign of George III was once taken for granted but refuted by historians in the twentieth century.[138] This should not blind us to the fact that many with Whig pedigrees continued to label their enemies Tories. In the 1760s, 'Tory' reverted to the way it had been understood at its inception, that is, a firm supporter of the royal prerogative. It was rare that people referred to themselves as Tories in this new setting, however, with some notable exceptions, including Johnson and Boswell. More than ever before, the term had now become an insult, which is reflected in Brown's writings.

Brown concluded his *Thoughts on Civil Liberty* with a series of proposals for 'checking the Growth of Licentiousness and Faction'. First and foremost, the monarch had to be steadfast and never yield to the demands of the leaders of factions. Second, the minister had to be equally firm in 'discouraging ... the Inroads of *Venality* and *Corruption*'.[139] Brown had

---

[133] Ibid., 126–7.   [134] Ibid., 132.   [135] Ibid.   [136] Ibid., 132–3.

[137] This was particularly true in the case of Bute, a Scot whose surname was Stuart. Pitt was among those who called the Bute-led ministry after May 1762 a 'Tory government'; see Black, *Pitt the Elder*, 236.

[138] Christie, *Myth and Reality in Late Eighteenth-Century British Politics* (London, 1970), 196–215.

[139] Brown, *Civil Liberty*, 142.

already written at length on this topic, as discussed in the previous section, but he now framed his views in opposition to Soame Jenyns's *Free Enquiry into the Nature and Origin of Evil* (1757).[140] Jenyns argued that a decrease in arbitrary power necessitated corruption in order to govern people successfully, since they were naturally and incurably wicked.[141] In other words, people had to be either 'beat or bribed into obedience'.[142] In lieu of this type of corruption, supported in even more cynical terms by Jenyns than it had been by Hume, Brown prescribed 'Virtue and Religion, upright Manners and Principles'.[143]

More surprisingly, Brown suggested 'some legal Limitation of Property' to reduce the inequality between the rich and the poor, which created a pernicious form of dependence.[144] As a good Harringtonian, he viewed as self-evident that power followed property, and that excessive property controlled by a few individuals meant excessive power and influence in the same hands. Harrington's maxim was a commonplace observation in the eighteenth century, embraced by Bolingbroke and in a more limited sense by Hume, yet few drew the same conclusion as Brown at a time when property rights were seen as sacred and redistribution as a recipe for social upheaval. Accordingly, Brown stressed that he spoke 'not of the Probability, but the Expediency of such a Measure'.[145]

No one wrote as evocatively about inequality in the period as Jean-Jacques Rousseau, and it may well have been the case that Brown was reacting to the writings of the Genevan citizen, even though he did not cite him directly.[146] Importantly for our present purposes, Rousseau's writings were among the most anti-party in the period with the idea of a total ban on 'partial associations' in the *Social Contract* (1762).[147] Brown also shared Rousseau's concern (and that of others, including Montesquieu) with the scale and size of states, as he drew attention to the fact that Rome had perished from overextension when highlighting that colonies could be a burden to the mother country. This was only if they became too much of a

---

[140] Jenyns was a parliamentarian and typical establishment Whig, who attained a seat with the aid of Hardwicke. His *Free Enquiry* was castigated by Samuel Johnson. Years later, Jenyns would compose one of the more practical schemes for abolishing party contest in the shape of annual administrations chosen by lot; see *A Scheme for the Coalition of Parties* (1772). The pamphlet was, however, a satire.

[141] *Free Enquiry into the Nature and Origin of Evil* (London, third edn., 1758), 139.

[142] Ibid., 133–4.   [143] Brown, *Civil Liberty*, 147.   [144] Ibid., 150.   [145] Ibid.

[146] We must remember, however, that even Rousseau saw private property as fundamental; see Rousseau, 'Discourse on Political Economy' (1755), in *The Social Contract and Other later Political Writings* (Cambridge, 2012), 4.

[147] Rousseau, *The Social Contract*, 60.

distraction, however, and generally speaking Brown supported the Chathamite and Beckfordite vision of a '[British] Empire of the Seas'.[148] The conjecture about Rousseau's impact on Brown also has to be weighted with another plausible speculation that Rousseau was one of '*two* authors now said to be living in these Kingdoms with impunity; who, in a better policed State, would ... [have] felt the full Weight of that public Punishment and Infamy, which is due to the Enemies of Mankind'.[149]

Be that as it may, Brown was at one with Rousseau in admiring the unity and strength of Sparta, and in stressing the importance of 'civil religion'. In short, Brown believed that 'National virtue never was maintained, but by national Religion'.[150] The necessary remedy as he saw it was improved education, which would centre on two mutually reinforcing principles: patriotism and Anglicanism. Brown concluded the text with an exhortation to all ranks and *parties* to unite, summarising some of the main points discussed in this section and emphasising the danger of the factious and tumultuous populace in the cities. Brown's thought was quintessentially Anglican in the sense that he associated party division with sectarianism and viewed schism as a threat to the unified church-state.[151] In his idolising of Sparta, the factionless state, Brown's Anglican vision was not entirely dissimilar to Rousseau's republicanism with its emphasis on civic education, civil religion, and patriotism.[152] The contrast with Hume, for whom Sparta's austere regime was simply against 'the common bent of mankind', could not have been starker.[153]

Conclusion

In the 1760s – decried by Brown for the lack of values combined with increased factionalism and job-hunting – an alternative vision of party emerged. This was Burke's party of principle, which is treated in

---

[148] Brown, *Civil Liberty*, 151.

[149] Ibid., 155 (footnote). Rousseau was fleeing persecution in France and Geneva at the time, taking refuge under the protection of Hume in England in 1765. The two fell out, leading to a famous public quarrel between the two philosophers. It is not implausible that Brown referred to Rousseau's *Émile* (1762), in that case 'The Professions of Faith of a Savoyard Vicar', when he wrote that one of the two authors had 'writ a Volume of execrable *Memoirs*, for the Corruption of Youth and Innocence'. The word *Memoirs* directs one's thoughts to the *Confessions*, which Rousseau had started writing around this time, but it is unlikely that Brown would have known about this at the beginning of 1765.

[150] Ibid., 154.   [151] On this theme, see Clark, *The Language of Liberty* (Cambridge, 1994), ch. 2.

[152] He directly influenced the French republican Mably; see Sonenscher, *Before the Deluge* (Princeton, 2007), 248.

[153] Hume, 'Of Commerce' (1752), *Essays*, 259–60.

Chapters 10–13. With political life having been essentially purged of Jacobitism, an unapologetic case for party was now possible. As was shown in Chapter 8, Burke had already laid the foundation for a defence of party in the 1750s, before entering politics. This defence was grounded in a critique of self-seeking and personal factions reliant on popularity, in other words, criticisms with which Brown would have agreed. Political *principles* had to be resuscitated in order for Whiggism, in its latest Rockinghamite guise, to have a reason for opposition other than replacing the government. Nearly all frontmen in politics now called themselves Whig, although many of them have later been mislabelled as Tories.[154] This was to a large degree the work of 'Wilkite' journalists, who have been credited with revitalising the Whig and Tory labels in the first half of the 1760s.[155] Crucially, issue forty-five of Wilkes's *North Briton* (1762–3) attacked George III's Scottish favourite Bute, as an old Tory and, by implication, a quasi-Jacobite. The spectre of Bute,[156] and later the threat of a system of secret influence, rallied the Rockingham Whigs, who turned their attention to what they viewed as a new form of Toryism, centred on increasing the personal power of the monarchy. This is the subject of Chapters 10 and 11.

This chapter has demonstrated that there was a rhetorically powerful, if unrealistic, alternative to this narrative: Brown's attack on self-interested factions. Burke may well have formulated his mature defence of party in the *Present Discontents* (1770) in opposition to Brown, although there had been similarities in their critiques of faction in the 1750s. In the 1760s, however, the two visions were irreconcilable. Burke viewed men and measures as interlinked and believed that a party had to seek office and negotiate with the monarch as a *corps*. This was diametrically opposite to the 'not men, but measures' slogan at the heart of Brown's writings and the Pittite patriot platform. As we saw in Chapter 3, however, it is doubtful whether the Pittite way of conceiving opposition should be traced back to Bolingbroke, at least in a straight line, since Bolingbroke, unlike Pitt, advocated general and concerted opposition, and stressed the connection

---

[154] This unfortunate practice has recently and deliberately been resuscitated in James Vaughn, *The Politics of Empire at the Accession of George III* (New Haven, 2019).

[155] Wilson, *The Sense of the People*, 212. This was more widespread than Wilkite journalism, however; see *A Letter From the Cocoa-Tree to the Country-Gentlemen* (London, 1762), 13; *An Address to the Cocoa-Tree from a Whig* (London, 1762), *passim*. For criticism of the revival of the Whig and Tory names, see [Jenyns], *Free Enquiry*, 148–52.

[156] Bute was not a MP between 1741 and 1761, and was widely regarded by the political class as a court creature; see Pares, *George III and the Politicians* (Oxford, 1970 [1953]), 100.

between men and measures. While Pitt's tendency to inflame the passion of the populace and insistence on only taking office on specific conditions would not have been to Brown's liking, his political writings are unquestionably closely linked to the figure of Pitt. The Chatham administration which replaced the Rockinghams in 1766 had as its goal 'to dissolve all factions & to see the best of all partys in Employment', an aspiration on which George III and Chatham saw eye to eye.[157] The experiment proved short-lived, however. Only a year after taking office, the Chatham administration, afflicted by its figurehead's illness, had to concede that the only road to political stability was to negotiate with the opposition as parties rather than as individuals.[158]

---

[157] Memorandum by the King, [July 1766?], in *The Correspondence of George III* (6 vols., London, 1927), I, 175. O'Gorman has demonstrated that the memorandum is misdated by the editor Fortescue as August 1765; see O'Gorman, *The Rise of Party* (London, 1975), 178, 548 (note 92).
[158] Duke of Grafton and Lord Northington to the King, 2 July 1767, in *The Correspondence of George III*, I, 495; O'Gorman, *The Rise of Party*, 206.

CHAPTER 10

Edmund Burke and the Rockingham Whigs

[Rockingham] far exceeded all other statesmen in the art of drawing together, without the seduction of self-interest, the concurrence and co-operation of various dispositions and abilities of men, whom he assimilated to his character, and associated in his labours; for it was his aim through life to convert party connexion, and personal friendship, (which others had rendered subservient only to temporary views, and the purposes of ambition) into a lasting depository for his principles; that their energy should not depend upon his life, nor fluctuate with the intrigues of a court, or with capricious fashions among the people; but that by securing a succession in support of his maxims, the British constitution might be preserved, according to its true genius, on antient foundations, and institutions of tried utility.

Burke on the Marquess of Rockingham

Introduction

This chapter's epigraph is an inscription by Edmund Burke on a statue of his political leader, the Marquess of Rockingham, at a mausoleum erected in Rockingham's memory, built between 1785 and 1789, in Wentworth Park, Rotherham. In the eighteenth century, Wentworth Woodhouse in south Yorkshire was the estate of the Rockinghams, one of the richest aristocratic families in the country. The Rockingham Mausoleum is naturally a monument created to honour not only Rockingham, but also his party, as Burke's inscription reflects. The mausoleum houses busts of key figures in the Rockingham party connection, including Burke, Charles James Fox, the Duke of Portland, Lord John Cavendish, Sir George Savile, Frederick Montagu, Admiral Viscount Keppel, and John Lee. Most of these figures held either senior or junior positions in the second Rockingham administration in 1782 and resigned upon the sudden death of Rockingham, three months into his second spell as head of the Treasury. They prided themselves on their Whiggism – understood as safeguarding the Revolution Settlement and the balance in Britain's mixed constitution – and attachment to one another; in other words, on public as well as private loyalty. This was a bundle of principles which Burke more than anyone else laboured to theorise and sanctify over several decades under the heading of 'party', as this chapter and Chapters 11 and 12 demonstrate.

As noted in the Introduction to this book, Burke is perhaps the best known writer on party, and he has been called the only classic defender of party among political philosophers.[1] He, rather than Bolingbroke, is often feted as the generator of the doctrine of parliamentary opposition in the sense of the 'promotion of a consistent program to be advocated in opposition and realized in office'.[2] As was shown in Chapter 3, Bolingbroke's *Letter on the Spirit of Patriotism* (1736) anticipated a principle of this kind. This is not to suggest that their respective theory of party and opposition were the same. To begin with, the political contexts in which they wrote were different. Burke's well-known defence of party was developed against the backdrop of three major historical events: the demise of Jacobitism as a serious political force,[3] the Seven Years' War, and the accession of George III.

These three events in combination introduced a degree of ministerial instability not seen in Britain since the reign of Queen Anne. Discussions of 'party' and 'opposition', although they had never disappeared, once again received a kind of prominence in political debate they had not been given since the heyday of Bolingbroke's pamphleteering and *Faction Detected*. At the same time, the relatively clear government versus opposition dichotomy of Bolingbroke's time had disappeared with the dissolution of the Tory party as a parliamentary bloc and intensified factionalism within the Whigs. When Burke wrote his mature defence of party in 1770, the political class was split into the 'king's men' on the one hand and several opposition groupings and Whig connections on the other. There were still individual Tories, but most of them were backbenchers with little interest in office. Burke's main intention was to unify the opposition under the leadership of his master Rockingham and under the label of 'the

---

[1] Rosenblum, *On the Side of the Angels* (Princeton, 2008), 5, 119–26; Muirhead, *The Promise of Party in a Polarized Age* (Cambridge, MA, 2014), 6.

[2] Waldron, *Political Political Theory* (Cambridge, MA, 2016), 102.

[3] In the wake of the death of the 'Old Pretender' in 1766, Burke stated that, despite Charles Edward Stuart, there was '[i]n effect, no pretender to the crown'. *W&S*, II, 208. He continued to use Jacobitism as a reference in his speeches, for example in the debate on Burke's first Bill for Economical Reform on 8 March 1780; see *W&S*, III, 556.

Whigs'. Although the Rockinghams, after brief periods in government in 1765–6 and in 1782, were the largest and most coherent opposition party, they were rarely the unthreatened central focus of the opposition. During much of the American Crisis, for instance, they shared the stage with the Chathamites.[4] Burke's ambition was for his party to take power as a corps and on the basis of shared principles rather than simply as the king's servants. This was finally achieved for a brief period in 1782.

Starting already in the eighteenth century, commentators have regretted Burke's involvement in partisan politics, especially since it was to entail many years in opposition. 'Had he devoted those powers and exertions to the illustration of the "noblest study of mankind," – of man, in his faculties, in his social and civil relations, which he applied to the *propagation of party creeds*', wrote Robert Bisset in his largely sympathetic biography from 1800, 'his utility to society must have been much greater than it was at *that* time'.[5] Bisset cited Oliver Goldsmith, who in his unfinished poem *Retaliation* from the year of the author's death (1774) had written: '[Burke] Who, born for the universe, narrow'd his mind | And to party gave up what was meant for mankind.'[6] In 1805, Burke's old friend Hannah More lamented that he had exerted himself violently and 'unworthily in party'.[7] However, More and Goldsmith, the latter being Burke's contemporary from Trinity College Dublin, knew that Burke was no simple party hack, and no minion of the Whig grandees, as Namier and his disciples believed.[8] What attracted Burke to the Rockingham Whigs was his conviction that Whiggism was beneficial for the country, and that party solidarity was necessary for principled politics to be put into action. In this chapter, we consider the formation of Burke's party connection and his first writings in the cause of this party. In Chapter 11, we look closely at Burke's most important statement on party, his *Thoughts on the Cause of the Present Discontents* (1770). In Chapter 12 we trace the fortunes of Burke's party and his writings on the topic after the *Present Discontents*, before briefly considering Burke in relation to other currents of eighteenth-century thought in Chapter 13.

---

[4] O'Gorman, 'The Parliamentary Opposition to the Government's American Policy', in *Britain and the American Revolution* (London, 1998), 97–123.

[5] Bisset, *The Life of Burke* (2 vols., London, second edn., 1800), I, 195. Burke as a 'party man' is a major theme in both volumes of Bisset's biography.

[6] Lee, 'Oliver Goldsmith', *Dublin Historical Record*, 26 (1972), 17.

[7] More, *Hints Towards Forming the Character of a Young Princess* (2 vols., London, 1809 [1805]), II, 204.

[8] Bourke, *Empire and Revolution* (Princeton, 2015), 223.

The Rockingham Whigs Are Formed

We saw in Chapter 8 that Burke's interest in the idea of party did not begin with his association with the Rockinghams in the 1760s, but can be dated back to an unpublished essay of 1757,[9] when Burke tried to make his way as a man of letters in London. At that time, his friends were Hume and Samuel Johnson rather than Rockingham and Charles James Fox. When he received an Irish pension of £300 from William Gerard Hamilton in 1763, Burke acknowledged that '[w]hatever advantages I have acquired ... have been owing to some small degree of literary reputation'.[10] As the editor and the principal writer of the *Annual Register* from 1758 until the mid-1760s, Burke became a close observer of politics.[11] In the early 1760s he wrote of government and opposition activity in relation to the peace negotiations ending the Seven Years' War. It is evident that parliamentary and party activity excited Burke. When parliament was in recess in December 1762, he wrote to his frequent correspondent Charles O'Hara in Dublin: 'the world here is dull enough; even faction is languid'.[12]

Burke's six-year association with Hamilton, which involved Burke with politics in both Dublin and London, ended unhappily at the beginning of 1765. Hamilton had become an Irish MP and chief secretary to the Lord Lieutenant of Ireland in 1761. Burke was infuriated that Hamilton appeared to want him to continue indeterminately in an inferior position and broke off the connection abruptly. He felt that the entire Hamilton episode had retarded his intellectual development and hurt his literary reputation.[13] Rather than returning to study, however, he became even more immersed in politics, perhaps in search of greater financial security. His close friend and writing collaborator William Burke introduced him to the circle of Charles Watson-Wentworth, 2nd Marquess of Rockingham, and when Rockingham took office as First Lord of the Treasury in July 1765, Burke became his private secretary. At the end of the year, Burke was elected as MP for Wendover, once again largely thanks to William Burke. He was to remain in the Commons, serving three different constituencies, for nearly three decades.

---

[9] Bourke, 'Party, Parliament and Conquest in Newly Ascribed Burke Manuscripts', *HJ*, 52 (2012), 619–52.

[10] Burke to Hamilton, March 1763, *Correspondence*, I, 165.

[11] Bourke, *Empire and Revolution*, 201.

[12] Burke to Charles O'Hara, 30 December 1762, *Correspondence*, I, 161.

[13] 'Burke's statement concerning Hamilton's Conduct', ibid., 184.

The Rockingham Whigs were linked to the Pelhamites, led by Pelham (until his death in 1754), his half-brother the Duke of Newcastle, and men such as Hardwicke, all three of whom had earlier been connected with Robert Walpole.[14] Scholars have identified both 'Court' or 'Country' roots and characteristics in the Rockinghams.[15] They viewed themselves as a party of government, the inheritors of the great Whig families who had been in government for most of the period since the Hanoverian Succession. After the accession of George III, however, the Whig grandees had to become accustomed to being in opposition and this is part of the reason why they resorted to Country tactics. They cannot thus be easily shoehorned into Namier's tripartite division of politicians into Court party, independents, and factions.[16] They viewed themselves as Whigs, and, as we shall see in this chapter and Chapters 11 and 12, constructed an identity as *the* Whig party. As one of their more recent historians has put it, '[i]f they and the society in which they lived believed they were Whigs, then surely they were'.[17]

The peace politics in the early 1760s was a crucial episode in the prehistory of the Rockingham party. The new monarch's favourite Lord Bute had piece by piece removed most of the remnants of the Newcastle–Pitt coalition. When Newcastle resigned from the Treasury in May 1762, Rockingham wrote to him: '[i]f that clamour arises which in my mind it certainly will, Your Grace will be called on & your assistance expected by all the Old Whigs'.[18] The events are described from a Whig perspective in a memorial drawn up by Hardwicke's son in 1771. After the dismissal of Devonshire in November 1762, 'the Duke of Newcastle strongly connected with the Duke of Cumberland, & in some measure with Mr Pitt, began a warm opposition to the peace, & all the neglect which ensued'. In consequence, most of '[Newcastle's] friends in and out of Parliament were turned out, & of course his Grace became more exasperated, & his

---

[14] O'Gorman, *The Rise of Party in England* (London, 1975), 46.

[15] Elofson, 'The Rockingham Whigs and the Country Tradition', *PH*, 8 (1989), 90–115; Browning, 'The Origin of Burke's Ideas Revisited', *ECS*, 18 (1984), 57–71. See also Pincus, *The Heart of the Declaration* (New Haven, 2016), 87, which links the Rockinghamites to the 'Patriot' tradition (which is of course strongly related to Country thanks to Bolingbroke). We must add, however, that Pincus's argument is problematic because of the differences between the Rockinghamites and Pitt/Chatham.

[16] Namier, 'Monarchy and the Party System', *in Crossroads to Power* (London, 1962). For criticism, see Thomas, 'Party Politics in Eighteenth-Century Britain', *BJECS*, 10 (1987), 201–10.

[17] Elofson, *The Rockingham Connection and the Second Founding of the Whig Party* (Montreal, 1996), 6–7.

[18] Rockingham to Newcastle, 26 May 1762, BL Add MS 32939, f. 16.

followers more violent in their Parliamentary conduct'.[19] Burke described the dismissals from the sidelines as 'the late violent measures'.[20] Further resignations – importantly, nearly all members of the Hardwicke/Yorke dynasty – followed in 1763. As we saw in Chapter 9, Newcastle was convinced that he served 'the Body of The Whigs' in opposition.[21] A correspondent wrote to him in May 1763 that 'the Genius of this Country is Whiggism ... the People will never be satisfied, but in the Re-establishment of the Old System'.[22] George III's attempt to abolish party distinctions, celebrated by the likes of Waldegrave, was resisted by the Old Corps of Whigs with Newcastle at the helm.

Rockingham was among those who resigned from a Court position in 1762 and joined Newcastle's opposition to the peace preliminaries as well as the Cider Bill. The latter was Bute's attempt to deal with the rising national debt by taxing cider production. This provoked riots in the cider-producing West Country in particular. A major aristocratic magnate in Yorkshire, Rockingham emerged as a leader thanks to the backing of Cumberland especially.[23] Another obvious reason was the fact that many of the Whig grandees were growing old, with Hardwicke, Devonshire, and Henry Legge all passing away in 1764. Newcastle was seventy-two years old in 1765 and played the role of an elder statesman, serving as Lord Privy Seal in Rockingham's first ministry. Not entirely happy with his new position, Newcastle complained during the negotiations in June 1765 that '[t]he Heads of the Party would use me very ungratefully, If they did not desire, That I should be consulted *In Every Step to be taken*, in the forming of a new Administration.'[24] The thrust of the disagreement was that, despite his personal difficulties with Pitt, Newcastle did not believe that an administration could be successful without the 'patriot minister'. Newcastle had relinquished leadership willingly, however, determined 'never to be a Minister, or a Bit of a Minister again', having served thirty years as secretary of state and eight years as head of the Treasury.[25] He lent his weight to the ministry and later the opposition, but his actual clout appears to have been slight, and he continued to complain to Rockingham that he was not consulted on affairs of state. In 1765, he seems to have viewed Cumberland rather than Rockingham as the ultimate 'head' of 'the Whole Whig party'.[26] But as the king's uncle,

---

[19] BL Add MS 35428, f. 5. [20] Burke to O'Hara, 30 December 1762, *Correspondence*, I, 162.
[21] BL Add MS 35422, f. 27. [22] Ne C 3417, University of Nottingham.
[23] Perhaps the most interesting recent research in relation to Rockingham concerns the political role of his wife, Mary (née Bright); see Chalus, *Elite Women in English Political Life* (Oxford, 2005), 71–7.
[24] Newcastle to Rockingham, 19 June 1765, BL Add MS 32967, f. 69. [25] Ibid.
[26] Ibid., f. 70.

Cumberland could hardly lead a party in parliament, and was himself to die at the age of forty-four in October 1765. Be that as it may, until his death the administration was sometimes referred to as 'The duke of Cumberland's administration'.[27]

Born in the same year as Burke (1730),[28] Rockingham was relatively inexperienced in contrast with major figures such as Pitt and Grenville, though several years older than the alternative leaders Grafton and Portland.[29] Although related to the Earl of Strafford, the seventeenth-century royalist, Rockingham's own Whig credentials were impeccable. At the young age of fifteen he had fought in the 'Forty-five' against the Jacobites as a colonel in his father's voluntary regiment.[30] Somewhat ironically considering their later posture, the Rockinghams assumed power in 1765 thanks to Court intrigue, more precisely because George III had fallen out with George Grenville.[31] Even though the ministry turned out to be one of the shortest in the century, it became vital for the Whig tradition and indeed Whig mythology, including Burke's political identity and writings. We saw in Chapter 9 that Newcastle wanted more continental involvement on Britain's part. The Rockingham administration worked to forge a closer Anglo-Prussian alliance against France and Austria, continuing wartime commitments into peacetime. The administration fell when Pitt and his followers withdrew their support, vindicating Newcastle's conviction that the 'great commoner' could undo any government of which he did not form a part.[32] According to Burke, Pitt wanted to construct a 'Patriot' administration 'against any sort of personal connections',[33] which is what he duly did as Lord Chatham.[34] Burke later disparagingly described this ministry as

> [S]o checkered and so speckled; he put together a piece of joinery, so crossly indented and whimsically dovetailed; a cabinet so variously inlaid; such a piece of diversified Mosaic; such a tesselated pavement without cement; here a bit of black stone, and there a bit of white; patriots and courtiers, kings friends and republicans; whigs and tories; treacherous friends and

---

[27] Langford, *The First Rockingham Administration* (Oxford, 1973), ch. 3.
[28] For the revised birth date of Burke, see Lock, *Edmund Burke* (2 vols., Oxford, 1998–2006), I, 16–17.
[29] Langford, 'Introduction', in Burke, *W&S*, II, 16–17.
[30] Hoffman, *The Marquis* (New York, 1973), 3–4.
[31] Langford, *The First Rockingham Administration*, 6–8.
[32] *W&S*, II, 54; BL Add MS 32967, ff. 69–70.
[33] Burke to O'Hara, 23, 24 (?) [April 1766], *Correspondence*, I, 252.
[34] Brooke, *The Chatham Administration, 1766–68* (London, 1956).

open enemies ... indeed a very curious show; but utterly unsafe to touch, and unsure to stand on.[35]

The Rockingham leaders were proscribed, and those of 'our Party that has staid in has taken great Offence at it', Burke told O'Hara.[36] Henry Seymour Conway, Hume's chief in the Northern Department, was one of those who stayed on in the Chatham ministry and held talks with Burke about potential job offers. Burke responded that 'I had begun with this party ... the point of honour lay with that division which was out of power'. He added that he could only accept a job offer provided that he 'must be understood to belong not to the administration, but to those who were not'. If Rockingham and his followers went into formal opposition, he would have to resign and join it, he added.[37] Unsurprisingly, no formal job offer materialised. After his split with the Foxite Whigs in 1791, Burke would look back and stress that he at this time had been 'free to choose another connexion' but that 'he cheerfully took his fate with the party'.[38]

After the dissolution of the administration of 1765–6, Hardwicke's son described how 'Lord Rockingham's party ... [and] Newcastle's few remaining followers formed a sort of concerted opposition.'[39] Their numbers have been estimated at as many as eighty-five members of the Commons. It should be noted, however, that many included in such a guesstimate were independent country gentlemen, some of them Tories and former Tories, who sometimes united with the Rockinghams to criticise the government. Moreover, the Rockinghams were only one of the groupings in opposition, and one of Burke's major tasks in his political speeches and writings was to make the case that his party had the best claim to be the centre of opposition and was the most natural government in waiting. It was key for the Rockinghams to take office on the right terms and not as court creatures. They had opportunities to enter government, especially in 1767, if they had been more willing to compromise, especially on imperial policy.[40] At this point, Rockingham had emerged as the undisputed leader. Newcastle wrote in a letter to Lord Mansfield in 1767: 'My Lord Rockingham is entirely Master of my Political Conscience, & Conduct ... I shall always be ready, to give Him my

[35] Burke, *Speech on American Taxation* (1774), *W&S*, II, 450.
[36] Burke to O'Hara, 29 July and 19 August 1766, *Correspondence*, I, 262, 265.
[37] Burke to O'Hara, 11 November 1766, ibid., 279.
[38] Burke, *An Appeal from the New to the Old Whigs* (1791), *W&S*, IV, 408.
[39] BL Add MS 35428, f. 12.
[40] Ibid., f. 13; O'Gorman, *The Rise of Party*, 210; Du Rivage, *Revolution against Empire* (New Haven, 2017), 155–6.

Opinion, if He desires it; But [I] am determined to abide by whatever He shall finally resolve upon.'[41] After he had retired from politics at the start of 1768, Newcastle let it be known '[t]hat all His Friends should concur with My Lord Rockingham, in such Measures, as He shall take, for the Support of the Whig Cause, (which has always been the Duke of Newcastle's great Object,) & for the Interest of The Nation'.[42] Rockingham's party was to remain in opposition until 1782. Burke predicted lengthy opposition already in December 1766, and he liked that his party did not appear desperate for office.[43] By contrast, the Bedford party (also known as the Bloomsbury gang) entered government in 1768. In the next section we turn to Burke's first pamphlets written in defence of the Rockinghams in the early years of opposition.

Burke's *Observations*

Burke said that '[a]ccidents first threw me into this party',[44] but he certainly treated his new vocation seriously. The eighteenth century was a time when many, notoriously those of 'country' ilk, treated politics as a burdensome duty and a part-time occupation at best. Burke, however, was from the start a 'full-time politician', attending every parliamentary session between 1766 and 1774 and in near-constant attendance at Westminster.[45] Moreover, between sessions the Whig magnates of the Rockingham connection depended on Burke for news from the metropole. Burke was not the party's leader in the Commons, even less so before the death of William Dowdeswell in 1775.[46] He was, however, a frequent debater and a key spokesperson for the Rockinghamites. In the eighteenth century not all members of parliament spoke in parliament. Edward Gibbon, for example, MP in 1774–80 and 1781–4, never gave a single speech. However, even though Burke quickly established himself as an orator in Commons, he was by no means always successful. As his

---

[41] Newcastle to Mansfield, 20 December 1767, BL Add MS 32987, f. 364.

[42] BL Add MS 32988, f. 23.   [43] Burke to O'Hara, 23 December 1766, *Correspondence*, I, 285.

[44] Burke to Dr William Markham, 9 November 1771, ibid., II, 263.

[45] Langford, 'Introduction', in *W&S*, II, 3. By contrast, Rockingham was 'notoriously unbusinesslike, even by the leisured standard of the time'. He was also a nervous and infrequent speaker in parliament. See Langford, *The First Rockingham Administration*, 19.

[46] O'Gorman, *The Rise of Party*, ch. 11. Perhaps influenced by 'Namierites' such as John Brooke and Richard Pares, O'Gorman exaggerated Burke's unimportance. Contemporaries such as Horace Walpole suggest that Burke had more clout even in the later 1760s. See *Memoirs of George III*, III, 390–1. As one of the editors of Burke's letters pointed out, the frequent correspondence between Burke and Rockingham is characterised by mutual respect as well as observance of differences in rank; see Burke, *Correspondence*, III, xv–xvi.

acquaintance Hume reported to Adam Ferguson regarding a parliamentary debate in 1767: 'Burke did very ill, which I am sorry for.'[47]

Burke quickly became a vital publicist for the Rockingham Whigs. Within days of the Rockingham-led ministry leaving office, he wrote *A Short Account of a Late Short Administration*. This brief pamphlet outlined the Rockingham ministry's commercial achievements, chief among them the repeal of the Stamp Act and the cider tax, which the Grenville administration had pushed through. Burke argued that in only just over a year the Rockinghams had managed 'to accomplish many Plans of public Utility ... having left their King and their Country in a much better Condition than they found them'.[48] One of Burke's key arguments was that the Rockingham ministry had been far removed from the court sycophancy and corruption embodied by the figure of Bute, with whom the ministry 'had no personal Connection; no Correspondence of Councils'.[49] Horace Walpole, who was to become critical of the Rockingham party and Burke's writings, referred to the *Short Account* as a 'small, well written tract'.[50] Others were more critical. The Chathamite Charles Lloyd ridiculed Burke's pamphlet in *A True Account of the Late Short Administration* (1766), countering that the ministry had abandoned the interests of Britain in favour of those of the Colonies, and had generally caved in to the commercial lobby. In brief, 'the landed Gentlemen were partially sacrificed to the Interests of Traders and Colonists'.[51] Bolingbroke had championed trade and commerce along with land, but Lloyd's argument suggests that the 'Patriots' – if such a coherent platform can indeed be identified over time – did not wish to see the trading interest take precedence over landed wealth, as Steve Pincus has suggested.[52] Burke certainly exaggerated the ministry's achievements, but, as Richard Bourke has argued, many political historians, in reaction against nineteenth-century Whig historians, have tended to go too far in the other extreme.[53]

In 1769, Burke published the longer *Observations on a Late State of the Nation*, intended to distinguish the Rockingham connection from the Grenvilles. Its immediate occasion was a riposte to the Grenvillite William Knox's *The Present State of the Nation* (1768).[54] Knox's pamphlet

---

[47] Hume to Ferguson, March 1767, *Letters*, II, 127.
[48] Burke, *Short Account of a Late Short Administration* (1766), *W&S*, II, 57.
[49] Ibid., 56. On Bute and the Rockinghams, see Brewer, 'The Misfortunes of Lord Bute', *HJ*, 16 (1973), 3–43.
[50] Walpole, *Memoirs of George III*, II, 357–8.
[51] [Lloyd], *A True Account of the Late Short Administration* (London, 1766), 22.
[52] Pincus, *The Heart of the Declaration*.   [53] Bourke, *Empire and Revolution*, 234.
[54] Grenville had commented on drafts of the pamphlet; see HMC, *Report of Manuscripts in Various Collections* (7 vols., Dublin, 1901–14), VI, 95–6.

is in itself an interesting text, expressing a degree of nostalgia for the old Whig–Tory dichotomy: 'the abolition of party-names seem to have destroyed all public principles among the people, and the frequent changes of ministers having exposed all sets of men to the public odium, and broke all bands of people'.[55] When Whig and Tory, Court and Country, and High Church and Low Church dichotomies had divided the country, according to Knox, 'both acted from principle'. Since the decline of principled division and its substitution for the scramble for office, the 'great men' had lost their standing in the country, the monarchy had become more extensive, and parliament had lost its reverence among the people. The voice of the multitude was now at odds with the legislature. Rather than elaborating on the need for principled Whiggism to return to the fore, Knox simply recommended the reappointment of his patron Grenville, who had led the ministry from 1763 to 1765. In recommending Grenville on the basis of his experience and financial expertise, Knox wanted to counter the cynical view that 'all ministers are alike, and that the measures proposed by all will have the same tendency'.[56] In the final pages of the pamphlet, Knox stressed the importance of men *and* measures in order to root out corruption.[57] In this recommendation, Knox's text differed from John Brown's earlier pessimism treated in Chapter 9. However, in analysing the decline of political principle, and in his dire depiction of the state of the country, Knox shared much common ground with Brown. Like Brown, he complained of '[a] people luxurious and licentious'.[58]

Since Grenville had been dismissed in favour of Rockingham – even though Rockingham was subsequently replaced by Chatham – Knox's pamphlet invited comparisons between the two ministries. This was unfortunate since Rockinghamites and Grenvillites were discussing cooperation in 1768.[59] Burke's response, helped by Dowdeswell's financial expertise, sought to refute Knox and defend the record of the Rockingham ministry. Burke's *Observations* has rarely been much noticed in scholarship, however, partly because it has been overshadowed by the *Present Discontents*, published a year later. In the *Observations*, Burke took issue with Knox's bleak and exaggerated portrayal of the state of Britain, which suggests that the initial provocation on this score came from Knox

---

[55] [Knox], *The Present State of the Nation* (London, third edn., 1768), 64–5.   [56] Ibid., 64.
[57] Ibid., 102–3.   [58] Ibid., 65.
[59] Burke, *Observations on a Late State of the Nation*, *W&S*, II, 104. Horace Walpole believed that the *Observations* did more honour to Burke as a writer than as a politician since it alienated the Grenvilles; see *Memoirs of George III*, III, 334.

rather than Brown. Comparing Britain in the late 1760s with civil war-ridden France under Henry IV as Knox had done was disingenuous, according to Burke: 'there is some likeness between a summer evening's breeze and an hurricane; they are both wind: but who can compare our disturbances, our situation, or our finances, to those of France in the time of Henry?'[60] Britain's circumstances may have been bad but they were ultimately those 'of a strong and mighty nation'.[61] Richard Whatmore has rightly pointed out that there were plenty of dire predictions about Britain's future, even after its successes in the Seven Years' War.[62] We must remember, however, that doomsday prophecies were neither universal nor unopposed, as Burke's response to Knox shows. At the same time, Burke would only a year later sound more pessimistic himself about Britain's standing abroad.[63]

Burke's main criticism was directed against Knox's vague and meaningless appeal to 'men of virtue and ability'. Instead, Burke recommended party. In the *Observations*, he put forward the argument, which he had already made in an unpublished essay in 1757 (see Chapter 8), that party was inseparable from free governments. In fact, he opened the pamphlet with these very words.[64] By this time the notion that party division was a natural part of politics had become widespread, even though anti-party rhetoric had certainly not disappeared. 'In all governments which are in any degree popular, faction must make as necessarily and unavoidably a part, as trumps do in the game of whisk [i.e. whist]', wrote one pamphleteer in 1765.[65] Burke said that the inevitability of party was a truth which had 'been established by the uniform experience of all ages'.[66] The question, as Burke presented it, was instead what part people should play in divisions. He concluded that '[p]rivate men may be wholly neutral' but that 'they who are legally invested with public trust, or stand on the high ground of rank and dignity', in other words, members of the Commons, the Lords and potentially local officeholders, 'can hardly in any case remain indifferent, without the certainty of sinking into insignificance'.[67] Sinking into insignificance did not only have ramifications for the individual politician, but also meant 'in effect deserting that post which … the laws and institutions of their country have fixed them'.[68] Burke thus contended that partisanship was compulsory for public figures. He did not only

[60] Burke, *Observations*, *W&S*, II, 207–8.   [61] Ibid., 213.
[62] Especially in his 2019 Carlyle Lectures delivered at the University of Oxford.
[63] Burke, *Present Discontents*, *W&S*, II, 285.   [64] Burke, *Observations*, *W&S*, II, 110.
[65] *An Essay on the Constitution of England* (London, 1765), 57.
[66] Burke, *Observations*, *W&S*, II, 110.   [67] Ibid.   [68] Ibid.

qualify his embrace of partisanship by excluding 'private men', but also by stressing the importance of decent conduct of party members. For politics to be effective, a balance needed to be struck between zeal and detachment. 'In a word, we ought to act in party with all the moderation which does not absolutely enervate that vigour, and quench that fervency of spirit, without which the best wishes for the public good must evaporate in empty speculation', he wrote.[69]

The most interesting part of the *Observations* for our present purposes comes towards the end of the pamphlet. Here Burke condemned proscriptions of other parties, while defending the Rockinghams' 'unwilling[ness] to mix in schemes of administration, which have no bond of union, or principle of confidence'. This implied 'the necessity of having the great strong holds of government in well-united hands, in order to secure the predominance of right and uniform principles'.[70] Coalition was certainly possible, indeed the Rockingham ministry of 1765 had been a coalition of sorts,[71] but it could not be a coalition 'which, under the specious name of independency, carries in its bosom the unreconciled principles of the original discord of parties'.[72] Instead, the administration needed to be 'established upon the basis of *some set of men*, who are trusted by the publick, and who can trust one another'.[73]

These views concurred with the long-held policy of the Rockingham party. As indicated above, Rockingham had an opportunity to gain office in 1767, but not as the leader of the administration. Burke wrote to Rockingham in 1767: '[Y]our Lordships Opinion of the duty of a Leader of party [is] to take more care of his friends than of himself . . . the world greatly mistook you, if they imagind, that you would come in otherwise than in Corps'.[74] Taking office as an isolated individual would only serve 'to disunite the party', according to Burke.[75] Everyone in the party capable of judging would see this, he assured his leader. Whether his advice was decisive or not, Rockingham's decision not to take office shows that he went along with Burke's reasoning.

In the *Observations*, Burke described the Grenville administration as embodying 'a spirit of disorderly despotism' in domestic affairs. Grenville had been appointed on the recommendation of Bute, and to an extent continued with the same measures as the king's favourite. In the prosecution of John Wilkes for seditious libel, the ministry had issued general

[69] Ibid., 110–11.   [70] Ibid., 210.   [71] Langford, *The First Rockingham Administration*, ch. 1.
[72] Burke, *Observations, W&S*, II, 210.   [73] Ibid. (My emphasis.)
[74] Burke to Rockingham, 1 August 1767, *Correspondence*, I, 317.   [75] Ibid.

warrants for the seizure of papers, and attacked the liberty of the press and the privilege of parliament. Its actions were, in a word, 'wholly repugnant to our laws, and the genius of the English constitution', Burke insisted.[76] In economic affairs, the Grenville ministry had added a plethora of regulations and taxes, chief among them the Stamp Act and the cider tax. Burke once again outlined the achievements of the Rockingham administration, elaborating on his earlier and briefer *Short Account.* Repealing the Stamp Act had restored both peace and trade, and if the Rockinghams had had the chance to continue in office, they would have strengthened the British government of America.[77] Burke also reiterated his defence of the party's unashamed canvassing of opinion among merchants[78] – a practice which had been subject to attacks such as Lloyd's response to Burke cited earlier. 'Never were points in trade settled upon a larger scale of information', he concluded.[79] This practice of consulting merchants is noteworthy considering the social make-up of the Rockinghams as great landowners, and important for their identity as a national party.

Terminology conspicuously absent from Burke's writings at this time was that of Whiggism. Indeed, the word does not appear in the *Observations.* However, it is hinted at, when he gestures at an area of commonality between himself and Knox: 'I admit there is a cankerworm in the rose ... This is nothing else than a spirit of disconnexion, of distrust, and of treachery, amongst public men.'[80] However, there were still many examples 'of an unshaken adherence to principle, and attachment to connexion, against every allurement of interest'.[81] He here referred to the Rockingham connection, many of whom were 'of the first families, and weightiest properties, in the kingdom', but first and foremost characterised by 'their zealous but sober attachment to the constitution of their country'.[82] Burke appealed to floating 'Whigs' (the Bedfords) who had shifted their allegiance from Rockingham to Chatham in 1766.[83] What Burke shared with Knox, as well as Brown, was an uneasiness with the ministerial instability since the late 1750s and in particular since the beginning of George III's reign. In this new situation, public figures had become accustomed to relinquishing one set of men for another and had grown indifferent to human feeling and moral obligation alike. For all their

---

[76] Burke, *Observations*, *W&S*, II, 185.   [77] Ibid., 198.
[78] This is a key theme in Marshall, *Burke and the British Empire in the West Indies* (Oxford, 2019).
[79] Burke, *Observations*, *W&S*, II, 201.   [80] Ibid., 208.   [81] Ibid., 209.   [82] Ibid.
[83] Ibid., 211n.

other differences, one of Burke's major fears was identical with Knox's and Brown's: the disappearance of political principle. But his other concern, the effacement of sentiment, distinguished him from both of them and enabled him to recommend party connection as the solution.[84] As he put it: 'Private life . . . is the nursery of the commonwealth', and, unlike Knox and Brown, he believed that it had in general remained 'pure'.[85] After the death of Rockingham in 1782, Burke would write in the Marquess's memory that '[t]he virtues of his private life, and those which he exerted in the service of the state, were not, in him, separate principles . . . He was devoted to the cause of freedom, not because he was haughty and intractable, but because he was beneficent and humane.'[86]

Burke's appeal to party unity was more concrete than what Knox had offered. According to Burke, Knox's *'men of ability and virtue'* meant nothing at all since '[a]ll parties pretend to these qualities', including the present government they both wanted to replace.[87] In Knox's response to the *Observations*, he attacked Burke with the standard anti-party rhetoric, calling him a 'party writer' three times and a 'party man' twice.[88] Already in the *Observations* in 1769, then, Burke had put forward the argument that party was not only natural and inevitable, but potentially a boon and an instrument for good. However, Burke's argument was less tangible than it could have been, especially since he refrained from making use of the 'Whig' label. Who exactly were his 'large body of men, steadily sacrificing ambition to principle', and what exactly were their key principles? True, he referred to the Rockinghams' record in office rather than relying on empty moralism in a Brownian manner, but Knox had also emphasised Grenville's prior achievements. Burke's 'zealous but sober attachment to the constitution of their country' was arguably as generic as Knox's 'men of ability and virtue', since all parties would pretend to possess such qualities as well. According to Walpole, the tract showed that Burke's party 'was composed of impracticable men', whose raison d'être was their attachment to Rockingham.[89] Burke had to raise his game, and so he did. In the *Thoughts on the Cause of the Present Discontents*, to which we turn in Chapter 11, his arguments would be more strongly formulated.

---

[84] Ibid., 212.   [85] Ibid., 214.

[86] Burke's inscription at the Rockingham Mausoleum, Wentworth.

[87] Burke, *Observations*, W&S, II, 210.

[88] [Knox], *An Appendix to the Present State of the Nation. Containing a Reply to the Observations on that Pamphlet* (London, 1769), 7, 51, 52, 56, 59.

[89] Walpole, *Memoirs of George III*, III, 334. What made this worse was that Walpole viewed Rockingham as 'a weak, childish, and ignorant man, by no means fit for the head of Administration'.

Burke's Thoughts on the Cause of the Present Discontents

[D]uty demands and requires, that what is right should not only be made known, but made prevalent; that what is evil should not only be detected, but defeated.

Burke, *Thoughts on the Cause of the Present Discontents* (1770)

Introduction

What Burke intended to spell out in the *Present Discontents* was simply 'the political Creed of our Party'.[1] In October 1769, Burke described in correspondence his aim in the pamphlet as 'shewing the ground upon which the Party stands; and how different its constitution, as well as the persons who comprise it are from the Bedfords, and Grenvilles, and other knots, who are combined for no publick purpose'.[2] The pamphlet was discussed with Rockingham and other leading members of the party.[3] The difficult task of the *Present Discontents* was to strike a double blow: against the government as well as other opposition groups.[4] For this reason, Burke was eager that the text be supported and conceived as a 'Common Cause'.[5] However, he indicated that the final version was 'every word good and bad his own'.[6] The pamphlet was written for two audiences: for the Rockingham party itself and for potential converts who could convince the monarch of the strength of the party. Rockingham's expectations on the pamphlet were remarkably high. He wrote to Burke:

---

[1] Burke to Richard Shackleton, 6 May 1770, *Correspondence*, II, 136.
[2] Burke to Rockingham, 29 October 1769, ibid., 101.
[3] For discussion of its composition, see Bryant, 'Burke's *Present Discontents*', *Quarterly Journal of Speech*, 42 (1956), 115–26.
[4] Burke to Rockingham, 6 November 1769, *Correspondence*, II, 109.   [5] Ibid.
[6] This is what Burke scribbled on a letter from Thomas Leland, 11 June 1770. He further wrote 'no such thing!' under Leland's suggestion that Burke had 'accepted the thoughts of other people'. See WWM, Burke Papers. 160 P/1/305.

I am exceeding anxious, that the Pamphlet which you shewed me in such forwardness ... should make its appearance as early as possible. In all respects – now is the time – I wish it read by all the members of Parliament. I think it would take universally, and tend to form and to unite a party upon real and well founded principles – which would in the end prevail and re'establish order and Government to this country.[7]

The title of the famous pamphlet refers to the Middlesex election dispute, wherein John Wilkes was continuously expelled from parliament by the government and re-elected by the voters.[8] While suspicious of Wilkes and his followers, the Rockinghams supported Wilkes's right to take his seat in parliament and more precisely the right of the electorate to choose him as their representative. For Burke, it was important that his party defended 'the Cause not the Person'.[9] He referred in private to parliament's selection of Henry Luttrell as the MP for Middlesex as 'this New, usurped, and most dangerous power of the house of Commons, in electing their own Members'.[10] In this context, other members of the Rockingham connection advocated opposition on grounds similar to Bolingbroke's many years earlier. William Dowdeswell, who had a Tory background,[11] wrote in a 1769 pamphlet: 'The first principles of the constitution should be often looked to ... A guard should ... be constantly kept, each deviation from them met in the first instance, and (by every opposition that our constitution will justify) resisted and controlled.'[12] In language reminiscent of Bolingbroke, Dowdeswell called for '*constant* jealousy, and apprehension of abuse'.[13] Sir William Meredith MP, who had drawn up division lists for Newcastle and been Lord of the Admiralty in Rockingham's administration, also addressed the Middlesex dispute in a pamphlet. 'These are the Times ... that call for the Attention, Vigilance, and Authority of grave, moderate, and important Men', he wrote.[14] Neither pamphlet, however, used the language of either party or connection. It fell on Burke to build on his argument in the *Observations*

---

[7] Rockingham to Burke, 15 October 1769, *Correspondence*, II, 92.

[8] Thomas, 'The House of Commons and the Middlesex Elections of 1768–69', *PH*, 12 (1993), 233–48.

[9] Burke to O'Hara, 13 June 1768, *Correspondence*, I, 353.

[10] Burke to O'Hara, 31 May 1769, ibid., II, 26–7.

[11] Langford, *The First Rockingham Administration* (Oxford, 1973), 30.

[12] [Dowdeswell], *The Sentiments of an English Freeholder on the Late Decision of the Middlesex Election* (London, 1769), 6.

[13] Ibid., 52.

[14] [Meredith], *The Question Stated, whether the Freeholders of Middlesex lost their right, by voting for Mr. Wilkes at the Last Election* (London, second edn., 1769), 69.

from the previous year to take his party argument forward. He now argued that party was necessary to address the problem of the Court system, in other words, what he dubbed the 'double cabinet'.[15]

The 'Double Cabinet'

Some members of the Rockingham party disagreed with Burke's approach in the *Present Discontents*. The Duke of Portland wanted a more head-on attack on Bute: 'for surely at the time you are declaring war and irreconcilable enmity to the whole party of *Kingsmen*, it must appear very strange to show any tenderness to their chief.'[16] This was the tactic adopted by other opposition organs. 'Junius', for example, wrote in 1771: 'Did you [George III] imagine that the whole body of the Dissenters, that the whole Whig interest of London, would attend at the levee, and submit to the directions, of a notorious Jacobite [Bute]?'[17] Burke's own suspicion of Bute went back further than his connection with the Rockinghams, as a letter from 1763 demonstrates.[18] Moreover, in August 1767 he told Rockingham that he had been informed that Bute 'personally confers with the Ministry', four years after his formal resignation.[19] Modern research has dismissed this as a myth, but it was perceived to be real by Burke and his political friends. Burke for one did not think he was writing 'fiction' in the *Present Discontents*.[20]

The greatest part of the *Present Discontents* is made up of an analysis of the corrupt court system and exposure of the so-called 'double cabinet'. This entailed an examination of the system of government and the shock to the Whig establishment introduced at the accession of George III. While the existence of a 'double cabinet' has been called a fallacy which misled many generations of scholars,[21] it should not surprise us that

---

[15] Burke, *Present Discontents*, *W&S*, II, 274.

[16] Portland to Rockingham, 3 December 1769, in *Memoirs of Rockingham and his Contemporaries* (2 vols., London, 1852), II, 146.

[17] *The Letters of Junius* (London, 1786), 272 [28 May 1771]. To his dismay, Burke was suspected by some to be the author of *Junius*; see Burke to Charles Townshend, 17 October 1771, *Correspondence*, II, 249.

[18] Burke to John Ridge, 23 April [1763], *Correspondence*, I, 169.

[19] Burke to Rockingham, 1 August 1767, ibid., 316.

[20] This 'Namierite' accusation is repeated in Pocock, 'Political Thought in the English-Speaking Atlantic, 1760–1790', in *The Varieties of British Political Thought* (Cambridge, 1993), 255.

[21] John Brewer, 'Party and the Double Cabinet: Two Facets of Burke's *Thoughts*', *HJ*, 14 (1971), 479–501; Christie, *Myth and Reality in Late Eighteenth-Century British Politics* (London, 1970), ch. 1.

George III's accession produced such a reaction.[22] Wilkes's issue forty-five of the *North Briton* had accused Bute of being a Jacobite because of his nationality (Scottish), surname (Stuart), and family background.[23] The Rockinghams believed that Bute and George III had resuscitated Toryism by patronising Tories and increasing the powers of the crown.[24] Bute had at first been appointed as leader of the government on the basis of his personal relationship with the Court rather than his standing among the wider political class. After his resignation, it was claimed that he continued to pull the strings behind the scenes, since he still had the king's ear. This is what was meant by the 'double cabinet', which was viewed as nefarious because of its unaccountability and potential to increase the power of the crown at the expense of the other parts of the mixed constitution. Protection of the constitution was integral to Burke's political thought and his Whiggism. He understood the British constitution as delicately and precariously balanced: 'Our constitution stands on a nice equipoise, with steep precipices, and deep waters upon all sides of it.'[25]

Burke's pamphlet certainly alluded to Bute,[26] but rather than calling out Bute frequently, he focused on what he described as 'a cabal of the closet and back-stairs', which had been 'substituted in the place of a national administration'.[27] He pre-empted criticism that he did not spend more time on attacking Bute by arguing that '[w]here there is a regular scheme of operation carried on, it is the system, and not any individual person who acts in it, that is truly dangerous'.[28] Not making more effort to criticise Bute was a mistake according to Horace Walpole, who called the double cabinet a 'vague idea'.[29] Burke had also been wrong to not go further back, according to Walpole, whose politics rather surprisingly in some ways were closer to the 'radicalism' of Catharine Macaulay than the Whig aristocracy. 'The canker had begun in the Administration of the Pelhams and Lord Hardwicke, who, at the head of a proud aristocracy of Whig Lords, had thought of nothing but establishing their own power', Walpole argued.[30] While he thus implicitly exonerated his father by not mentioning him, he did not let Robert Walpole's key supporters and heirs off the hook. In

[22] For Burke's preoccupation with the court system, see Bourke, *Empire and Revolution* (Princeton, 2015), 348–50, 360.
[23] According to the Alexander Carlyle, Bute thought he was descended from the Stuart royal family; see Carlyle, *Anecdotes and Characters of the Times* (London, 1973), 182. Bute's son and heir, Lord Mountstuart, told Boswell that he would never have taken the oaths under George I and George II; see Sack, *From Jacobite to Conservative* (Cambridge, 1994), 120.
[24] Brewer, 'The Misfortunes of Lord Bute', *HJ*, 16 (1973), 39.
[25] Burke, *Present Discontents*, *W&S*, II, 311.   [26] Ibid., 260.   [27] Ibid., 261.   [28] Ibid., 275.
[29] Walpole, *Memoirs of George III*, IV, 135.   [30] Ibid., 136.

brief, for Horace Walpole the Pelhams had been an 'aristocratic faction'.[31] By contrast, Burke, whose party connection had included Newcastle (until his death) and the Hardwicke family, was not interested in tracing corruption back to the glorious days of Whiggism.[32] For him the root cause of the problem was the system established when the Whig families had been turned out of government. In order for the new system to make Parliament subservient, '[a]ll connexions and dependencies among subjects were to be entirely dissolved'.[33] Whereas 'hitherto business had gone through the hands of leaders of Whigs or Tories', the new king appointed one of his 'footmen', meaning Bute, as his minister. 'Every thing would be drawn from its holdings in the country to the personal favour of the Prince', Burke concluded.[34] In this new environment, there was no check on the power of the Court, which effectively became 'arbitrary'.[35]

Although Burke's attack on the 'double cabinet' as a conspiracy against the constitution was naturally exaggerated, it represented a genuine difference of opinion about what the accession of George III had meant, and how Britain's uncodified constitution was to operate in practice. The system of Court 'favouritism' and 'influence' meant that 'neither office, nor authority, nor property, nor ability, eloquence, council, skill, or union, are of the least importance'.[36] All that mattered was subservience to the Court. The 'double cabinet' – the separation between the administration and an 'interior cabinet' – had created a confused and feeble government which had sullied Britain's reputation abroad, created discontent at home, and had not even benefited the monarch himself.[37] What was worse, the system seriously risked disturbing the balance of the constitution, which Burke believed had been protected by the Whigs since the Revolution.

Reviving Whiggism

Besides an analysis and critique of the court system, Burke's main intention in the *Present Discontents* was to elaborate on his defence of party connection set out in the *Observations* a year earlier, and more precisely to specify the principles of the Rockingham cadre. As part of the latter enterprise, he effected a revival of Whiggism. This was not something he did entirely on his own. The Rockinghams viewed themselves as the inheritors of the 'Old Corps' with Newcastle – who had followed the Rockinghams into opposition in 1766 – as crucial linkage. Both

---

[31] Ibid., 137.   [32] He referred favourably to Pelham in the *Present Discontents*, *W&S*, II, 306.
[33] Ibid., 261.   [34] Ibid.   [35] Ibid.   [36] Ibid., 271.   [37] Ibid., 274–91.

Dowdeswell and Meredith cited Locke's *Second Treatise of Government* (often known as *Essay on Government* in the eighteenth century) in their Middlesex pamphlets.[38] However, neither used the 'Whig' label in their pamphlets, and nor had Burke in the *Observations*. In the *Present Discontents*, however, 'Whig' occurs nine times. He specifically referred to the short-lived Rockingham administration of 1765–6 as an attempt 'to restore the principles and policy of the Whigs'. This Whiggism was understood as an antidote to the Court faction ('the king's men') and a perceived new form of Toryism. As Edward Gibbon, who was from a Jacobite family, commented in his memoirs:

> The accession of a British king reconciled them [the Tories and the Jacobites] to the government and even to the court; but they have been since accused of transferring their passive loyalty from the Stuarts to the family of Brunswick; and I have heard Mr Burke exclaim in the house of Commons: 'They have changed the Idol, but they have preserved the Idolatry!'[39]

The Rockinghams' priority of principle over power attracted Burke. As he wrote to O'Hara:

> [they are] by a good deal the strongest, of any, separated from Government, and their connection the closest. They certainly stand fairest in point of Character; but that fairness which they have kept, and are determined still to keep, goes against their practicability ... I look therefore upon our Cause, viewed on the side of power, to be, for some years at least, quite desperate.[40]

Rockingham himself wrote to Dowdeswell in 1769: 'we and *we only* of all the parts now in Opposition are so on system and principle'.[41] As we saw in Chapter 10, Newcastle believed that they carried on the torch of the 'Whig cause'. At the early stage of the composition of the *Present Discontents*, Burke considered framing it as an epistle addressed to John White, one of Newcastle's loyal supporters.[42] Burke's letters to

---

[38] For Burke as a 'Lockean', see Dreyer, *Burke's Politics* (Waterloo, 1979). Cf. Browning, 'The Origin of Burke's Ideas Revisited', *ECS*, 18 (1984), 57–71, who focuses on the influence of Court Whigs such as Hardwicke. The impact of Locke in eighteenth-century America has been debated by historians from Pocock to Kramnick and beyond. His importance for mid to late eighteenth-century Whigs is undisputed; see, e.g., Mitchell, *The Whig World* (London, 2005), 26–7.

[39] Gibbon, *Memoirs of My Life* (London, 1966), 111. According to Gibbon, the revived militia during the Seven Years' War cured families such as his own from the 'prejudices' of Jacobitism.

[40] Burke to O'Hara, 15 January [1767], *Correspondence*, I, 290.

[41] Cited in Foord, *His Majesty's Opposition* (London, 1964), 315.

[42] Burke to Rockingham, 30 July 1769, *Correspondence*, II, 52.

Rockingham in the late 1760s show that he was privately thinking of members of parliament in Whig and Tory terms.[43] Although they cooperated with the other major Whig connection in the late 1760s, the Grenvilles, Burke was convinced of 'the extreme difference between the Spirit of that political School, and the party with which we act'.[44] At the same time, unity was of the essence; Rockingham wrote to Burke in October 1769: 'I think as you do ... that the appearance of a thorough union in all the Parties now in opposition – would increase the weight of opposition'.[45] For the purpose of unity against the Court system, Burke omitted '[t]he whole attack on Pitts Conduct' in the final draft.[46] In a letter to Chatham, Rockingham described the intention of Burke's pamphlet as 'pointing out how necessary it is – that Honest men should now unite – in order to save this Country from the Power of a System – which has been established in great part on the Foundation of dividing and subdividing all Parties & all Connexions in this Country'.[47]

Reviving Whiggism necessitated demonstrating that the Rockinghams were the heirs of an existing Whig tradition. This was a response to the attack on the Whig establishment which Burke and his party friends (not entirely unreasonably) viewed George III's accession as representing. One of the few pamphlets Burke mentioned in the *Present Discontents* was John Douglas's *Seasonable Hints* published at the beginning of the reign.[48] In this pamphlet, Douglas had argued that

> however favorable to national freedom the true genuine principles of *whiggism* be, some individuals of that denomination, (who, in times happily at an end, got possession of the royal family) were the great promoters, if not the first introducers of such a plan of wicked policy, as had a natural tendency to sap the firm foundation of British liberty, and to destroy the independence of the constitution.[49]

He believed that Whig leaders had set themselves up as a 'fourth estate' which controlled the other three and monopolised power. According to Douglas, that the Whigs had been outraged that a few Tories had been appointed demonstrated amply that 'party is the madness of the many, for

---

[43] See, e.g., Burke to Rockingham, 9 September 1769, ibid., 76.
[44] Burke to James Barry, 8 October, 1769, ibid., 85–6.
[45] Rockingham to Burke, 15 October 1769, ibid., 91.
[46] Burke to Rockingham, 6 November 1769, ibid., 109.
[47] Rockingham to Chatham, [1770], WWM, Rockingham Papers 1/1328.
[48] Burke, *Present Discontents*, *W&S*, II, 265.
[49] [Douglas], *Seasonable Hints from an Honest Man on the Present Important Crisis of a New Regime and a New Parliament* (Dublin, 1761), 19–20.

the gain of the few', citing Swift's *Thoughts on Various Subjects*.[50] George III's reign enabled the 'abolishing [of] all the distinctions of party, by accepting with paternal affection the assistance of every honest man, to support the throne'.[51] For Burke and his fellow Whigs, this smacked of old-fashioned Toryism.

What had paved the way for this nascent Toryism was the position of George III. 'His Majesty came to the throne of these kingdoms with more advantages than any of his predecessors since the Revolution', Burke argued, 'even the zealots of hereditary right, in him, saw something to flatter their favourite prejudices; and to justify a transfer of their attachments, without a change in their principles'.[52] In a stroke this had obliterated Jacobitism as a powerful force, according to Burke. His friend Samuel Johnson is a good example of a likely Jacobite who made this transition.[53] In short, Burke believed that by 1760 '[t]he person and cause of the Pretender were become contemptible; his title disowned throughout Europe, his party disbanded in England'.[54] Nor was there any 'reversionary hope' since George III ascended the throne at the age of twenty-two.[55] The end of Jacobitism was a prerequisite for Burke's mature defence of party. As he put it, 'the great parties which formerly divided and agitated the kingdom are known to be in a manner entirely dissolved'.[56] The legacy of Jacobitism, however, made the Whigs slow to become accustomed to their new situation. 'To the great Whig families it was extremely disagreeable, and seemed almost unnatural, to oppose the Administration of a Prince of the House of Brunswick', Burke wrote.[57]

The Whigs had to become acclimatised to the new state of play, however. Since the Whig families had independent strength and did not rely solely on the monarch, it was in the interest of the 'Court faction ... to get rid of the great Whig connexions'.[58] The Whigs could boast '[l]ong possession of Government, vast property, obligations of favours given and received, connexion of office, ties of blood, of alliance, of friendship ... the name of Whig, dear to the majority of the people, the zeal begun and steadily continued to the Royal Family'.[59] To stamp out this threat to royal

---

[50] Ibid., 26. This quote has often been attributed to Swift's friend Pope.   [51] Ibid., 23.
[52] Burke, *Present Discontents*, *W&S*, II, 262.
[53] On this, see Clark, *Samuel Johnson* (Cambridge, 1993).
[54] Burke, *Present Discontents*, *W&S*, II, 262.   [55] Ibid., 263.
[56] Ibid., 253. Mansfield is mistaken that the Revolution Settlement 'destroyed the basis of the great parties', since Jacobitism survived; see *Statesmanship and Party Government* (Chicago, 1965), 6.
[57] Burke, *Present Discontents*, *W&S*, II, 263.   [58] Ibid., 264.   [59] Ibid.

supremacy, 'the whole party was put under a proscription'.[60] All dependencies apart from those of royal favour had to be destroyed.

Part of what Douglas and other pamphleteers had done was to paint the reign of George II in bleak colours as a time when corruption had triumphed. As we saw in Chapter 9, this had also been the tactic of John Brown. In the *Present Discontents*, Burke singled out Brown along with his entire 'political school' which had been outraged about 'the growth of an aristocratic power'.[61] Instead, he argued that George II's thirty-three years on the throne had been a time when the monarch 'maintained the dignity of his Crown with the liberty of his people, not only unimpaired, but improved'.[62] His legacy of defeating the Jacobite rebellion of 'Forty-five', increasing Britain's commerce and reputation abroad, and carrying the country's glory and prosperity to the new heights set a gold standard, according to Burke.[63]

Burke referred to even earlier periods in the history of the Whig party in the *Present Discontents*. 'In one of the most fortunate periods of our history this country was governed by a *connexion*; I mean, the great connexion of Whigs in the reign of Queen Anne.'[64] These Whigs 'believed that no men could act with effect, who did not act in concert; that no men could act in concert, who did not act with confidence; and that no men could act with confidence, who were not bound together by common opinions, common affections, and common interests'.[65] Burke specifically referred to Somers, Sunderland, Marlborough, and Godolphin. Somers had been a member of the Whig Junto, with whom Sunderland was associated. Marlborough and Godolphin were at least initially nominal Tories, but they later became Courtiers who cooperated closely with the Whig Junto. Marlborough and his wife Sarah became a Whig power couple after the former's military victories against the French and the latter's strict partisanship. In Burke's history of Whiggism, all four were members of the 'ambitious Junto', resolved 'to stand and fall together'.[66]

In summary, Burke and his party friends feared that the revived Tory attitudes towards the monarchy combined with antipathy towards Whiggism risked making the Court powerful enough to dominate the constitution. What was needed was party connection. Since party implied dependence between party members it would make them independent from the Court. This is how Whigs could be employed by the monarch and carry out his or her business of government on mutually beneficial

[60] Ibid.   [61] Ibid., 267.   [62] Ibid., 266.   [63] Ibid., 266–7.   [64] Ibid., 316.
[65] Ibid., 317.   [66] Ibid.

terms, and ultimately serve the national interest rather than the interest of the Court. Not only did they have to oppose royalists such as Douglas, but also the Chathamite 'not men, but measures' platform, which Burke singled out in the concluding pages of the *Present Discontents* as 'cant ... by which many people get loose from every honourable engagement'.[67] As we saw in Chapter 9, this doctrine had been given prominent expression in Brown's Pittite *Estimate* (1757) and his anti-Rockingham *Thoughts on Civil Liberty* (1765).

A Note on the Composition of the *Present Discontents*

As the question of the composition of the *Present Discontents* has been treated at length elsewhere, I will simply make one additional and rather speculative point. John Brewer argues that Burke's party argument was conventional by pointing out that none of the Rockingham leaders who discussed the composition of the *Present Discontents* remarked on Burke's notion of party.[68] But as Lucy Sutherland as editor of the second volume of Burke's correspondence had previously pointed out, this argument may not have been present in the early and non-surviving draft read by Rockingham's circle at the end of 1769.[69] George Savile warned Rockingham in December 1769 that 'whoever answers it would say that its all about who shall be in and who shall be out'.[70] In other words, the draft of the pamphlet looked hardly different from Grenvillite pamphlets such as Knox's *The Present State of the Nation*, according to Savile. It is plausible, I would suggest, that Burke elaborated on his argument about party in response to such worries. It is supported by the fact that Burke wrote to Rockingham on the same day as Savile said he had 'in a rough way got near to a conclusion' of the pamphlet.[71] This suggests strongly that Savile had seen an earlier draft without the concluding pages with Burke's party argument.

The Party Argument

According to Burke, the British political system allowed two safeguards against royal supremacy: 'power arising from popularity, and power arising

---

[67] Ibid., 318.   [68] Brewer, 'Party and the Double Cabinet', 487.
[69] Burke, *Correspondence*, II, 118.   [70] Savile to Rockingham, 18 December 1769, ibid., 120.
[71] Burke to Rockingham, 18 December 1769, ibid., 122.

from connexion'.[72] The former was associated with Chatham and the latter with Rockingham. Out of the two, Burke unsurprisingly contended that connection was much preferable, since it was more deeply 'rooted in the country', whereas popularity was 'personal, and therefore transient'. Burke claimed that George III and the Court faction had struck at the first power by discharging Pitt and the second power by dismissing Newcastle and then proscribing the entire Whig party. In short, the Court system – as illustrated in Douglas's *Seasonable Hints* – wanted to do away with party entirely.[73] The Court cabal had successfully propagated the doctrine that 'all political connexions are in their nature factious, and as such ought to be dissipated and destroyed; and that the rule for forming Administrations is mere personal ability, rated by the judgements of this Cabal upon it'.[74] Burke alluded to a speech in parliament by Bute in 1766, which Hume had celebrated, demonstrating the intellectual and political distance between them at this time.[75] Burke's most significant intervention in the *Present Discontents* was to argue that party connection was necessary for effective politics and that it could restore the balance in the constitution.

Party connection was necessary for the fulfilment of public duty, Burke claimed. Without concert and bonds of friendship and trust, political action would lack 'uniformity, perseverance, [and] efficacy'.[76] In a party, 'the most inconsiderable man, by adding to the weight of the whole, has his value, and his use'. No parties meant that 'the greatest talents are wholly unserviceable to the publick'. A single, isolated individual would carry little weight in politics, and had no chance standing up to the Court cabal. 'When bad men combine, the good must associate', Burke wrote, 'else they will fall, one by one, an unpitied sacrifice in a contemptible struggle'.[77] Good intentions on their own were of little use in public life, unless they could have a tangible effect: 'duty demands and requires, that what is right should not only be made known, but made prevalent; that what is evil should not only be detected, but defeated'.[78] Politics was not about having a clean conscience but making a difference. Burke complained that too many in politics aspired to 'angelic purity' rather than simply being 'good men'.[79]

The Court cabal propagated the doctrine that party connections and faction were equivalent terms.[80] As we saw earlier in this book, Rapin and

---

[72] Burke, *Present Discontents*, *W&S*, II, 264.   [73] Ibid., 265.   [74] Ibid., 314.
[75] Hume to Hertford, 20 March 1766, *Further Letters*, 66.
[76] Burke, *Present Discontents*, *W&S*, II, 314.   [77] Ibid., 315.   [78] Ibid.   [79] Ibid., 320.
[80] Ibid., 314.

Hume had also treated 'party' and 'faction' interchangeably, whereas Bolingbroke was more eager to distinguish between the two, even though he did not do so as consistently as Burke. All professions had their vices and virtues and politics was no different, according to Burke. Party connections in politics were 'essentially necessary for the full performance of our public duty, [but] accidentally liable to degenerate into faction'.[81] Similarly to Bolingbroke in *The Spirit of Patriotism*, Burke equated opposition with duty: 'he trespasses against his duty who sleeps upon his watch, as well as he that goes over to the enemy'.[82] Like Bolingbroke, he cited Solon's outlawing of neutrality.[83] The major difference between Bolingbroke and Burke, however, was that the latter had a stronger commitment to the notion that party solidarity was needed even in government. This view had been prefigured theoretically in the *Observations*, and to a degree in practice in the Rockingham ministry. The fact that not all Whigs resigned with Rockingham and Newcastle and instead went over to Chatham – true to the 'No Men, but Measures' Patriot slogan – had deepened the country's problem, according to Burke.

Burke further argued that party was needed because it connected government with the people. He believed that it would be unnatural for the lower house to be completely detached from the sentiments of the people. 'By ... want of sympathy they would cease to be an House of Commons', Burke wrote, highlighting that the lower house was meant to be a control *for* the people, not *on* the people.[84] The Court system risked undermining this principle by making the Commons obsequious. If everyone depended on Court favour, no independence could be expected, and 'indiscriminate support to all Ministers' would become the rule.[85] Moreover, the example of Wilkes's expulsion demonstrated that the 'King's friends' really intended to separate the Commons from the will of the people.[86] Defenders of the expulsion of Wilkes such as Johnson argued that Parliament had the right to regulate its members, a right it had exercised in the past.[87] By contrast, Burke contended that '[t]he true contest is between the Electors of the kingdom and the Crown'.[88] A government founded on 'public opinion' could achieve 'stability', but one built on 'private humour' had 'quicksand' as its foundation.[89]

---

[81] Ibid., 315. [82] Ibid., 320. [83] Ibid., 316. [84] Ibid., 292. [85] Ibid., 293.
[86] Ibid., 295–8.
[87] Johnson, *The False Alarm* (1770), in *Political Writings* (Indianapolis, 2000 [1977]).
[88] Burke, *Present Discontents*, *W&S*, II, 302. [89] Ibid., 312.

What was needed was an administration 'composed of those who recommend themselves to their Sovereign through the opinion of their country'.[90] Such people would provide a stronger executive power, 'because they will add to the weight of the country to [its] force'.[91] Public principle separated party connections from cabals. The latter were simply knots of men who come together only 'in order to sell their conjunct iniquity at the higher rate'.[92] For this reason, it was vital for Burke that the Rockinghams were 'attached in office to every principle they had maintained in opposition'.[93] Rockingham's record in office was thus of paramount importance. In his inscription at the Rockingham Mausoleum, Burke wrote that '[Rockingham] employed all his moments of power in realizing every thing which he had proposed in a popular situation'.

Loyalty is a key element of Burke's party thought. Generalising from his experience of the Rockingham administration in 1765–6, he argued that '[a]s there always are many rotten members belonging to the best connections, it is not hard to persuade several to continue in office without their leaders'.[94] Conway – Hume's chief in the Northern Department – had stayed in the Chatham administration which succeeded Rockingham. As we saw in Chapter 10, Burke had himself been canvassed for a job and, as we shall see in Chapter 12, he prided himself for the rest of his political career on his loyalty after Rockingham's departure from office. Public principle had to be supported by private honour, in the way that Romans such as Cicero had theorised and practised.[95] Public and private virtues were supposed to be mutually supportive, Burke argued, citing from Cicero's *De Amicitia* (*On Friendship*). Indeed, a common term in the correspondence of Burke's party was 'our friends' as a euphemistic synonym for party.[96] As has already been alluded to, Burke believed that the Whig Junto under Anne had exemplified party loyalty.

Burke's famous definition of party comes towards the end of the pamphlet: 'Party is a body of men united, for promoting by their joint endeavours the national interest, upon some particular principle in which they are all agreed.'[97] He concluded by arguing explicitly that it is the duty of parties to contend for political power.[98] The doctrine of party government, meaning that the principal offices had to be in the hands of people

---

[90] Ibid., 322.   [91] Ibid.   [92] Ibid., 280.   [93] Ibid., 275.   [94] Ibid., 270.
[95] Ibid., 316.
[96] See, e.g., Rockingham to Newcastle, 16 April 1768, and Newcastle to Rockingham, 26 April 1768, BL Add MS 32989, ff. 342, 384.
[97] Burke, *Present Discontents*, *W&S*, II, 317.   [98] Ibid., 318.

of the same ilk, had already been foregrounded in his *Observations* the previous year. 'Without a proscription of others, they are bound to give to their own party the preference in all things; and by no means, for private considerations, to accept any offers of power in which the whole body is not included'.[99] A party could not allow itself to be 'controuled' and 'over-balanced' in government.

Burke's party argument has sometimes been interpreted as a temporary measure rather than a permanent institution. It is true that Burke rarely expressed a wish to preserve the parties of his political opponents. For instance, when discussing unity among the Whig elements of the opposition with a Chathamite at the end of 1769, Burke stated that 'no union could be formed of any Effect or Credit, which was not compacted upon this great principle, "that the Kings men should be utterly destroyed as a Corps"'.[100] We should note, however, that Burke viewed the 'Court party' as unconstitutional and nefarious. Although he occasionally referred to the 'Court party', the more common words Burke used for pernicious political connections in his published works were 'cabal' and 'faction'. To argue that his Whig party amounted to a 'party to end all parties' would be missing the point. He firmly believed that the Whig party had to be made permanent to sustain the balance of the constitution. His point above against the Chathamites was itself an argument about the importance of party unity, a question upon which Chatham had proved himself untrustworthy during the 1760s.

Burke recommended party connection in the same breath as he dismissed parliamentary reform measures, including more frequent elections and the eviction of Court employees from parliament.[101] It should be noted, however, that he stressed that 'people ought to be excited to a more strict and detailed attention to the conduct of their Representatives' and that '[s]tandards, for judging more systematically upon their conduct, ought to be settled in the meetings of counties and corporations'.[102] He did not have instructions to representatives in mind – which he would famously reject in his *Speech to the Electors of Bristol* (1774) a few years later – but rather the publication of voting records so that the electorate could identify MPs who supported the administration indiscriminately. As we shall see below, this did not satisfy the more extreme elements of the broad-church opposition. But before we turn to consider the criticisms from the group Burke referred to as the 'Bill of Rights people', and the

---

[99] Ibid.   [100] Burke to Rockingham, 24 November 1769, *Correspondence*, II, 113.
[101] Burke, *Present Discontents*, *W&S*, II, 308–11.   [102] Ibid., 312.

reception of Burke's pamphlet more broadly, we will consider Burke's party argument as a point about the importance of intermediate powers.

Intermediate Powers

In 1760s Britain, Montesquieu was widely conceived as the greatest political genius of the age. Adam Ferguson hailed 'President Montesquieu' in his *Essay on the History of Civil Society* (1767), reviewed favourably by Burke in the *Annual Register* and well read in political circles in London.[103] Grenville cited *L'esprit des lois* in parliament in the context of Wilkes.[104] As we saw in Chapter 7, Bath had already done so. Even the young George III had studied Montesquieu before his accession.[105] Both as a man of letters and a politician, Burke would have studied Montesquieu carefully.[106] The brother of his father-in-law is believed to have translated *The Spirit of Laws* in 1750.[107]

One of the most influential arguments in Montesquieu's book was his argument about intermediate powers (*pouvoirs intermédiaires*) as a bulwark against despotism – royal, aristocratic, or democratic.[108] Burke would later famously deploy this argument in his *Reflections on the Revolution in France* (1790). But before that, it had been important in the *Present Discontents*, in which he wrote that '[i]t is in the nature of despotism to abhor power held by any means but its own momentary pleasure; and to annihilate all intermediate situations'.[109] Under the first two Georges, Burke argued, the Whigs had been an intermediate power between the people and the Court. He also used the Montesquieuean language of 'spirit' when he treated the Commons 'not with regard to its *legal form and power*, but to its *spirit*, and to the purpose it is meant to answer in the constitution'.[110]

By celebrating the legacy of the Whig supremacy, bemoaned by a host of writers including Brown and Douglas, Burke has sometimes been accused of behaving obsequiously towards aristocracy. In a classic

---

[103] Ferguson, *Essay on the History of Civil Society* (Cambridge, 1995 [1767]), 66.

[104] Courtney, *Montesquieu and Burke* (Westport, 1975 [1963]), 79.

[105] GEO/ADD/32/1044–7, RA.

[106] Bourke, *Empire and Revolution*, esp. introduction. As Selinger has argued, however, Burke departed from Montesquieu on fundamental constitutional questions. In advocating strict separation between the executive and legislative powers, Montesquieu had been inspired by Bolingbroke, whereas Burke's position is closer to Hume's; see Selinger, *Parliamentarism* (Cambridge, 2019), 68–9.

[107] McBride, 'Burke and Ireland', in *The Cambridge Companion to Burke* (Cambridge, 2012), 189.

[108] Montesquieu, *The Spirit of the Laws*, (Cambridge, 2015 [1748]), 17–19, 78.

[109] Burke, *Present Discontents*, *W&S*, II, 259–60.   [110] Ibid., 291.

treatment, Alfred Cobban called Burke's conception of government 'oligarchic'.[111] The core of Burke's party was made up of major Whig aristocratic families such as Cavendish and Devonshire. The First Rockingham ministry had been taunted at the time for being 'unusually aristocratic',[112] although such accusations should be moderated with Lloyd's charge that the Rockingham ministry had sacrificed the landed interest for the benefit of the merchant community in the cities. In the *Present Discontents*, Burke pre-empted criticisms on this score by stating that he was 'no friend to aristocracy, in the sense at least in which that word is usually understood', that is to say, as 'austere and insolent domination'.[113] What the Whig aristocrats possessed was property, rank, and quality which gave them a degree of independence, enabling them to stand up to the Court. The Whig cause (preservation of the Revolution Settlement) had united them in defence of the common good rather than any specific branch of the constitution. Outside of the Whig party, there were many peers who were Court creatures, as Burke pointed out.[114] In this sense, Burke's conception of party was indeed aristocratic, but it was not aristocracy for its own benefit but for the sake of the whole.

The Whig party which Burke wanted to revive was certainly not exclusively a party of the House of Lords. This would have been absurd since he himself sat in the lower chamber, as did many of Rockingham's followers. Many of the members of the Commons were gentry, but there was also space for relatively 'new men' such as himself.[115] For Burke, the Whig party enabled the aristocracy to make common cause with the people's representatives. The usual way of analysing the British constitution was of course as consisting of king, lords, and commons. In May 1768, Burke had in a parliamentary debate described the British constitution as consisting of king, parliament, and people, with parliamentary members (both Lords and Commoners) as a 'middle class' that would mediate between popular turmoil and royal domination.[116] This middle class played the role of an intermediate power capable of keeping despotism at bay in the way that Montesquieu had theorised. This was only possible, however, if it was sufficiently independent from the Court and

---

[111] Cobban, *Burke and the Revolt against the Eighteenth Century* (London, 1960 [1929]), 69. More recently, see Lock, *Edmund Burke* (2 vols., Oxford, 1998–2006), I, 282.
[112] Langford, *First Rockingham Administration*, 15.   [113] Burke, *Present Discontents*, *W&S*, II, 268.
[114] Ibid.
[115] With reference to Cicero, Burke often referred to himself as a *Novus homo*; see William Burke to William Dennis, [3, 6] April [1770], *Correspondence*, II, 128.
[116] Bourke, *Empire and Revolution*, 255.

the people alike. Party loyalty would enable such independence. It is unlikely that Burke viewed popular participation in partisan politics as desirable, however. He had already argued in the *Observations* (1769) that partisanship was a duty for this 'middle class' and not for everyone. We return to the place of aristocracy in Burke's thought on party and constitutionalism in Chapter 12. As we see in the following section, however, Burke had been accused of promoting 'aristocratic faction' already in 1770.

Reception and Impact

Burke was nervous about the reception of the pamphlet, writing to Rockingham during the drafting process that 'I am very far from confident, that the doctrines avowed in this piece (though as clear to me as first principles) will be considered as well founded, or that they will be at all popular. If so, we lose upon every side.'[117] The *Present Discontents* was eventually published on 23 April 1770 and is estimated to have sold at least 3,000 copies in six weeks. Within a few months it had been printed in a second edition in three impressions.[118] Although it was published anonymously, Burke was immediately identified as the author, as had been the case with the *Observations*.[119] Burke commented to friends that it was 'well-received', even 'beyond [his] expectations'.[120] But the pamphlet certainly had many detractors as well. Even though Burke had removed 'the attack on Pitts Conduct', Chatham was unhappy with Burke's appeal to party. 'The *Whole* alone can save the *Whole*', he wrote to Rockingham in November 1770. The pamphlet had done 'much harm to the Cause [of opposition], in the wide and extensive Publick', Chatham feared.[121] Reviewing the letter in July 1792, Burke scribbled that '[t]he pamphlet is itself, by anticipation, an answer to that grand artificer of fraud. *He* could not like it.'[122]

Horace Walpole bemoaned that the *Present Discontents* 'tired the informed, and was unintelligible to the ignorant'. More seriously, '[i]n point of judgment it was totally defective'.[123] Walpole suggested that the fact that the Court did not respond to the pamphlet was strong evidence of its 'demerit'.[124] Walpole was mistaken, however, and there were plenty of

---

[117] Burke to Rockingham, 6 November 1769, *Correspondence*, II, 109.
[118] Brewer, 'Party and the Double Cabinet', 495.   [119] Lock, *Burke*, I, 293.
[120] Burke to Shackleton, 6 May 1770, and Burke to O'Hara, 21 May 1770, *Correspondence*, II, 136, 139.
[121] Chatham to Rockingham, 15 November 1770, WWM, Rockingham Papers 1/1327.
[122] Ibid.   [123] Walpole, *Memoirs of George III*, IV, 129.   [124] Ibid., 130–1.

hostile ministerial responses in the press, which have been canvassed by Brewer. Most of the 'Court' criticisms concentrated on the 'fiction' of 'secret influence'.[125]

As Burke pointed out in a letter to Richard Shackleton, however, the bitterest attacks did not come from the Court but from a section of the broad Whig opposition: 'the republican faction' or 'the Bill of rights people'.[126] Prominent in this context was Catharine Macaulay, whose short attack made a significant impression on Walpole. Macaulay argued that the *Present Discontents* 'fine turned and polished periods carry with them a poison sufficient to destroy all the little virtue and understanding of sound policy which is left in the nation'.[127] What Burke promoted was nothing less than 'Aristocratic faction and party, founded on and supported by the corrupt principle of self-interest'.[128] Similarly to Brown, Macaulay believed that

> the flaws in the Revolution system left full opportunity for private interest to exclude public good, and for a faction [the Whigs], who by their struggles against former tyrannies [James II/VII], had gained the confidence of the people, to create, against the liberties and the virtue of their trusting countrymen, the undermining and irresistible hydra, court influence, in the room of the terrifying, yet less formidable monster, prerogative.[129]

While the form of the constitution was preserved, its 'spirit' was annihilated, according to Macaulay. Her complaints included all the familiar ones from Bolingbroke's Country platform: the national debt, the standing army, placemen and pensioners in parliament, the Septennial Act (1716), and heavy taxes. In the wake of the Revolution, the Whigs became a 'state faction'.[130] The new system favoured this state faction as long as the monarch was 'weak', but it gave '[h]is stronger and more confirmed successors [George III]' the opportunity 'to make use of the superior advantages of their situation, to throw off the fetters of former obligations'.[131] Macaulay believed that the Commons needed to be purified to reclaim its proper function as a check on executive power. For her, Burke ignored the wider problems and instead argued that the reinstatement of the 'friends of liberty' to government was the panacea.

---

[125] Brewer, 'Party and the Double Cabinet', 496–7.
[126] Burke to O'Hara, 5 June 1770, and Burke to Shackleton, 15 August 1770, *Correspondence*, II, 140, 150.
[127] Macaulay, *Observations on a Pamphlet, Entitled, Thoughts on the Cause of the Present Discontents* (London, fourth edn., 1770), 6–7.
[128] Ibid., 7.   [129] Ibid., 12–13.   [130] Ibid., 17.   [131] Ibid., 18.

Walpole believed that Macaulay's short riposte exposed the Rockinghams' 'folly' of adhering to men and not to measures.[132] This attack on Burke resurfaced during his election campaign for Bristol in 1774, when one critic in the local press wrote:

> Are you acquainted with Mr. Burke? Do you know that he is the agent and instrument of the Rockingham party? Do you know that he has written a book recommending the principles of that party? That they amount to this ... that they will kindly take the Government of this kingdom on themselves. That they will invest themselves with the peoples rights, who shall be free in their power, but no otherwise, for that they shall have virtue and ability enough for you all. That you shall have no other security, no other resource but in them, and in particular, that the ancient Constitution by short Parliaments shall never be restored.[133]

Some modern scholars have followed Catharine Macaulay and other critics in arguing that Burke simply inverted the 'measures, not men' slogan.[134] This has an air of plausibility, especially since Burke cited Brown as one of his targets. However, if read in conjunction with Burke's *Observations*, in which he criticised Knox for making such a simple inversion, we see that Burke's theory of party was more sophisticated. In a sense, however, Macaulay's criticisms are apposite. Burke's first and largely sympathetic biographer commented on the *Present Discontents* that Burke 'contends less for change of measures than change of men. Indeed he proposes no material change of measures.'[135] If parliament had become as corrupted as Burke portrayed in the *Present Discontents*, how could he remain so hostile to reform?[136] Although disparaging about the 'Bill of Rights people', calling them 'a rotten subdivision of a Faction amongst ourselves', Burke was not dismissive of Macaulay's attack: 'the Amazon is the greatest champion among them ... You see I have been afraid to answer her.'[137]

Despite Chatham's dissatisfaction with the *Present Discontents*, the opposition 'coalition' held together for the rest of 1770 and managed to put up a relatively common front. For example, Burke applauded Chatham for speaking out against triennial parliaments. The death of Grenville in November 1770, however, gave the Court ample opportunity to weaken the opposition, with Alexander Wedderburn leaving the

---

[132] Walpole, *Memoirs of George III*, IV, 131.
[133] Cited in Weare, *Burke's Connection with Bristol* (Bristol, 1894), 45. [134] Lock, *Burke*, I, 278.
[135] Bisset, *The Life of Burke* (2 vols., London, second edn., 1800), I, 191. [136] Ibid., 193.
[137] Burke to Shackleton, 15 August 1770, *Correspondence*, II, 150.

Grenvillite splinter group to become solicitor general in January 1771. By December 1770, Burke had become disillusioned. The *Present Discontents* had not had the impact he envisaged because the party had failed to step up the propaganda campaign. 'We lost much of the advantage of the Last Pamphlet', he wrote to Rockingham, 'because the Idea was not kept up by a continued succession of papers, seconding and enforcing the same principle.'[138] The Court and the Rockinghams were irreconcilable. What is more, Burke mistrusted Chatham and his companion William Petty, the Earl of Shelburne, who had become more influential in London politics, for 'endeavouring to discredit [Rockingham] with the people'.[139] Finally, 'the sober, large-acred part of the Nation', the Rockinghams' mainstay in many ways, were 'either entirely indifferent about us, or of no considerable weight in the publick Scale'. Burke had no doubt that the solution was increased activity: 'To lye by occasionally may be prudent for an individual; it never can do for a party; which will immediately purifye and dissipate, if not kept healthy and compact by continual agitation and enterprise.'[140] If the party did not step up its game, their opposition risked serving the nation without helping the party. As long as the Rockinghams remained excluded from office, the nation was stuck with the 'mischievous [Court] System', he concluded.[141]

Did Burke's writings on party have any impact beyond his own party? Frederick Barlow's *Dictionary* from 1772 stated that party could be 'used in a good or a bad sense according to the object of the association'.[142] This definition – reminiscent of the opening lines of Burke's *Observations* – represented a change of tone, although a modest one, from Johnson's neutral definition from 1755. But by no means had Burke won a universal victory. A Bristol pamphlet in 1784, a constituency Burke had represented for six years in the 1770s, warned of 'the degrading effects of party in religion and politicks ... better would it be that their very names were obliterated from the ideas and languages of men'.[143] Within his own party,

---

[138] Burke to Rockingham, 29 December 1770, ibid., 175.
[139] Ibid. For instance, Burke and the Rockinghams tried hard to cultivate the West Indian interests in London, but Beckford and his 'successor' Richard Oliver, who represented these interests in the 1760s and 1770s, were close allies of Chatham and Shelburne, and tended to support more reformist politics; see Marshall, *Burke and the British Empire in the West Indies* (Oxford, 2019), 126. See also Gauci, *William Beckford* (New Haven, 2013).
[140] Burke to Rockingham, 29 December 1770, *Correspondence*, II, 175.   [141] Ibid., 176.
[142] Barlow, *The Complete English Dictionary* (2 vols., London, 1772).
[143] Dawes, *Observations on the Mode of Electing Representatives in Parliament for the City of Bristol* (London, 1784), 41.

however, Burke's argument exerted a lasting influence, as will be demonstrated in Chapter 12.[144]

Burke did not so much invent something *ex nihilo* as to formulate clearly what many in the Rockingham group already felt. His views were rooted in the Court Whig tradition, which had – as Bolingbroke had rightly complained in the 1730s – worked hard to keep party names and party loyalty alive. As Reed Browning has pointed out, Hardwicke had distinguished 'honorable connexion' from 'faction' before Burke.[145] Since this was a private remark, however, and as Hardwicke died the year before Burke joined the Rockinghams, Browning may have gone too far in suggesting direct influence. Even more importantly, among the 'Old Corps', Hardwicke, unlike Newcastle, was repulsed by opposition activities, and undertook them unwillingly.[146] In any event, establishment Whigs such as Hardwicke and Newcastle bequeathed to the Rockingham connection a sense of Whig unity and party solidarity. Among the Rockinghams, no one understood this importance more acutely, and none did more to propagate it, than Burke. Like much successful writing, Burke simply reminded readers – especially those in his own group – of what they already knew.

Conclusion

Many discussions of Burke on party boil down to the question of whether he had a theory of modern party politics.[147] His definition of party is indeed similar to many relatively modern ones, including Karl Loewenstein's of party as a 'combination of persons holding similar ideological beliefs and possessing, for their realization, a permanent organization'.[148] What Lowenstein meant by organisation would of course have been unfamiliar to Burke. The (slow and uneven) rise of mass politics in the nineteenth century, although prefigured to a great extent by popular politics in the eighteenth century, separates Burke from modern parties. This is the reason why analysts of party at the turn of the century – Weber and Ostrogorsky among them – had little time for the aristocratic party connections of Burke's day. At the same time, as Nancy Rosenblum has

---

[144] See also Richard Champion's *Comparative Reflections on the Past and Present Political, Commercial, and Civil State of Great Britain* (London, 1787), chs. 3–4.
[145] Browning, 'The Origin of Burke's Ideas Revisited', citing BL Add MS 35422, ff. 243–4.
[146] BL Add MS 35428, ff. 5–6.   [147] See, e.g., Conniff, *The Useful Cobbler* (Albany, 1994), 164–7.
[148] Loewenstein, *Political Power and the Governmental Process* (Chicago, 1957), 75.

stressed, the argument in favour of partisan division has independent merit.[149]

Scholars have disagreed about whether Burke promoted party as a permanent feature of politics, or whether he simply promoted his own party not dissimilarly to Bolingbroke. In general, intellectual historians from Harvey Mansfield to Richard Bourke fall into the former category, whereas political historians such as Paul Langford, Frank O'Gorman, Archibald Foord, and Warren Elofson have tended to make the latter case.[150] In a word, the question is whether the *Present Discontents* is political theory or an occasional pamphlet. F.P. Lock has written that to speak of Burke's 'theory of party' is to fall into Skinner's 'mythology of doctrine'.[151] According to Richard Bourke, such an approach to Burke makes a mockery of his political thought.[152] Bourke's biography has a good claim to be the first book which relates Burke's political thought to his political practice.[153] The chapters on Burke in this book are intended as a contribution in a similar spirit, although perhaps with even greater emphasis on political practice. Burke himself wrote that '[i]t is business of the speculative philosopher to mark the proper ends of Government, [and] ... of the politician, who is the philosopher in action, to find out proper means towards those ends, and to employ them with effect'.[154] Burke tried to do both, in the *Present Discontents* and throughout most of his political life.

Another question is whether Burke justified 'party government' or simply an 'opposition party'.[155] While he doubtlessly argued for the latter, the former is somewhat more complicated. He did not envisage single-party government in the sense of an administration which would exclude all courtiers or the king's party, who voted with the administration of the day. When the Rockinghams were in government in 1765–6, Egmont (formerly Perceval) and Lord Northington were carried over from the previous administration. However, Burke did implicitly celebrate the

---

[149] See this book's Introduction.
[150] Mansfield, *Statesmanship and Party Government*; Bourke, *Empire and Revolution*; Langford, 'Introduction' to *W&S*, II; O'Gorman, *Edmund Burke* (London, 1973), 32 (but cf. 144); Foord, *His Majesty's Opposition*, 318; Elofson, 'The Rockingham Whigs and the Country Tradition', *PH*, 8 (1989), 101, 112. The latter view is also expressed in Macpherson, *Burke* (Oxford, 1980), 23.
[151] Lock, *Burke*, I, 295–6.
[152] Bourke, 'Edmund Burke and the Politics of Conquest', *Modern Intellectual History*, 4 (2007), 406.
[153] Bourke, *Empire and Revolution*, 224–5. Marshall has recently stressed the importance of not neglecting Burke as a practical politician in *Burke and the British Empire in the West Indies*. This interpretation is compatible with Bourke's, since the latter portrays Burke as a realist with multiple commitments rather than a single-minded moral crusader.
[154] Burke, *Present Discontents*, *W&S*, II, 317–18.
[155] Mansfield, *Statesmanship and Party Government*; Brewer, 'Party and the Double Cabinet', 488.

legacy of the proscription of the Tories after 1714, and explicitly argued for 'the necessity of having the great strong holds of government in well-united hands, in order to secure the predominance of right and uniform principles'.[156] The *Present Discontents* may have been a defence of opposition, but the Rockinghams had by no means given up hope of re-entering government as a body of men. In the pamphlet, he argued that every party connection ought 'to pursue every just method to put the men who hold their opinions into such a condition as may enable them to carry their common plans into execution, with all the authority of the State'.[157]

What Burke had in common with Bolingbroke rather than Hume – at least in 'Politics a Science'[158] – was confidence in the idea that politics is at least in part about making sure that the right people end up in government. In other regards, Mansfield has stressed the intellectual distance between Bolingbroke and Burke, which, even though I disagree in some details, is broadly correct.[159] We should remember, however, that the views of contemporaries were often more complicated. When a new edition of Bolingbroke's political works was published in 1775, the bookseller Thomas Davies dedicated it to Burke as an exemplar of patriotism. 'Blest with the copious and commanding eloquence, and all the various abilities of a Bolingbroke, your conduct has been, and, I doubt not, ever will be, more steady and uniform than his', Davies wrote of Burke.[160]

Bolingbroke believed that men of virtue, meaning those who adhered to the 'Country party' and the Patriot King, would devote themselves to the common good. Plato had previously been as confident about philosopher-kings, and Marx would later prophesise that the proletariat would put an end to exploitation after it had overthrown the bourgeoisie.[161] It is tempting to think that Burke held similar unrealistically high hopes about the Whigs. We have to recognise, however, that by recommending party connection rather than men of virtue, Burke's intention in the *Present Discontents* was precisely to argue against such utopian schemes as Plato's *Republic* and Harrington's *Oceana*, both of which he alluded to,[162] and implicitly Bolingbroke's *Patriot King*. In any event, Burke's partisanship

---

[156] Burke, *Observations on a Late State of the Nation*, *W&S*, II, 210.
[157] Burke, *Present Discontents*, *W&S*, II, 318.   [158] See Chapter 4, note 171.
[159] Mansfield, *Statesmanship and Party Government*.
[160] Bolingbroke, *Letters on the Spirit of Patriotism: On the Idea of a Patriot King: and On the State of Parties at the Accession of George III* (London, 1775), viii.
[161] Runciman, *Great Books, Bad Arguments* (Princeton, 2010).
[162] Indeed, he cited Plato's *Republic* as an example of the ambitions of Douglas and Court writers; see Burke, *Present Discontents*, *W&S*, II, 265. For Harrington, see ibid., 269.

makes Hume come across as a more detached and soberer analyst of politics. As a non-partisan, Hume was able to strike this chord in a way that Burke, as the chief publicist of a party connection, could not. We must remember that Burke was drawn to this position. He chose the Rockingham Whigs because he was convinced that Whig principles were beneficial for Britain. We should thus be careful about exaggerating his intellectual proximity to Bolingbroke. Since the latter had to distance himself from the High Toryism of Queen Anne's last ministry, he tended to appeal to airy principles of Country opposition politics. By contrast, Burke referred to concrete achievements of the Whigs, especially the Rockingham ministry of 1765–6, which he had served, and the Whig Junto earlier in the century.

The aim of Burke's early party writings, especially the *Present Discontents*, was even more ambitious than to simply recommend party connection, difficult as that could be. In the face of factionalism among Whigs and a new kind of Court party which excluded the great Whig families, Burke set himself the task of bringing about a renewal of Whiggism. In doing this, he did not so much look forward to later opposition parties as backwards, especially to the Whig Junto of Anne's reign, and also to Walpole and the Pelhams. Having an ideological enemy was necessary for a new party of principle to be viewed as relevant. At a time when pedigree and tradition were all-important, this party had to present itself as being involved in the perpetual struggle between liberty and authority in the British constitution. In the *Appeal from the New to the Old Whigs* more than two decades later, Burke would return to the legacy of earlier generations of Whigs. At that time, however, Burke had broken off from many of his former party friends, mainly as a result of the French Revolution. In Chapter 12, we trace Burke's thought on party after the *Present Discontents*, and beyond his split with the Whigs. In the latter context, it is argued in Chapter 13 that the differences between Hume and Burke on party were diminished.

Burke and His Party in the Age of Revolution

My party principles ... must lead me to detest the French Revolution.

Burke to William Weddell, 31 January 1792

Burke and the Rockingham Whigs, 1771–1782

This chapter does not treat every significant event in Burke's career for the remaining twenty-seven years of his life after the *Present Discontents*, as this has already been done by others.[1] Instead, it focuses on the fortunes of Burke's party engagements and his views on party after his classic statement on the subject. America, India, and especially the French Revolution will be referred to, but only insofar as they are related to 'party'. A full treatment of Burke's reaction to these late eighteenth-century events is beyond the scope of this chapter and book.

The Rockinghams stuck together as a party for sixteen years in opposition until they finally re-entered government in 1782. The American Crisis gave coherence to both government and opposition, and because they had repealed the Stamp Act, the Rockingham Whigs could present themselves as the real friends of America.[2] Members of the local Whig association the Union Club helped Burke become MP for Bristol in 1774, but his Westminster party attachment was by no means universally seen as a blessing in the city. One broadside in 1774 warned: 'Will Mr. Burke be answerable to you? ... He is answerable another way to the Rockingham party, with whom he is too closely connected to regard your demands.'[3]

---

[1] Bourke, *Empire and Revolution* (Princeton, 2015) and the second volume of Lock, *Burke* (2 vols., Oxford, 1999–2006).

[2] However, it is important to note that they originally favoured conciliation rather than American independence, and that the repeal of the Stamp Act had been accompanied by the Declaratory Act, which confirmed parliamentary sovereignty over the colonies.

[3] Cited in Weare, *Burke's Connection with Bristol* (Bristol, 1894), 48.

Another Bristolian pamphleteer, echoing Catharine Macaulay, accused the Rockingham party of 'want[ing] to establish Aristocratic Government, to keep the King in leading strings, and dragoon the people'.[4] Burke defended his party attachment in *A Letter to the Sheriffs of Bristol* (1777). 'The only method which has ever been found effectual to preserve any man against the corruption of nature and example, is an habit of life and communication of councils with the most virtuous and public spirited men of the age you live in', Burke argued. 'Such a society cannot be kept without advantage, or deserted without shame.'[5] His description of the Rockinghams – 'those incomparable persons, living and dead, with whom for eleven years I have constantly thought and acted' – was characteristically rhetorical and exaggerated.[6] 'I shall never blush for my political company', Burke wrote, going on to list many of the members of the Rockingham cadre.[7] He reiterated in the pamphlet his conviction that party connection was necessary because of each person's 'inability to act alone'. Those who complained that party was simply an instrument for the gratification of personal ambition knew 'nothing of the world', Burke continued, suggesting that parties in opposition had to sacrifice personal ambition for loyalty and principle. Loyalty and principle went together for the Rockinghams, which entailed 'grafting public principles on private honour'.[8] As we see later in this chapter, Burke would return to the question of aristocratic party in the 1790s.

Charles James Fox was a rising star within the Rockinghams in the late 1770s.[9] With his first and middle names suggesting a Tory and Jacobite family background, Fox's transition to Whiggery has been described as 'a slow and halting process'.[10] His father Henry Fox, later 1st Baron of Holland, had not been a committed Jacobite but a royal manager under the Hanoverian family, and the young Fox made his first strides in politics in that tradition until the death of his father and his resignation from his junior office in 1774. Fox's nephew said that Burke's *Present Discontents* played a key role in converting Fox to the Rockinghams.[11] Burke himself attempted to convert Fox to the party, writing to him in October 1776 that

---

[4] Ibid., 60.   [5] Burke, *Letter to the Sheriffs of Bristol* (1777), *W&S*, III, 324–5.

[6] In his defence, Burke's praise of his fellow partisans could be as heightened in private: 'it is my happiness to act with those that are far the best that probably ever were engaged in the publick service of this Country, at any time'. Burke to Richard Shackleton, 25 May 1779, *Correspondence*, IV, 80.

[7] Burke, *Letter to the Sheriffs of Bristol* (1777), *W&S*, III, 325.   [8] Ibid.

[9] Mitchell, *Charles James Fox* (London, 1992), ch. 2. Fox's nephew said that Burke's *Present Discontents* played a key role in converting Fox to the Rockinghams; see *Fox Memorials*, I, 69.

[10] Mitchell, *Fox and the Disintegration of the Whig Party* (Oxford, 1971), 7.

[11] *Fox Memorials*, I, 69.

'[I] wish you a firm ground in the Country; and I do not know so firm and sound a bottom to build on as our party.'[12]

Unlike Burke and Rockingham, Fox was tempted by what looked like an opportunity to allow elements of the party into government in 1778. The offer was rejected because the Rockinghams did not receive assurances about changes in policy, notably on America. Fox wrote to Burke at the start of 1779 that 'I think as I always did, that without Lord Rockingham and his friends being in power, this country never can be upon the *best possible* footing.'[13] He further tried to convince Burke that 'I hate the power of the Crown', but '[t]o lessen that power by continued Opposition seems to be an attempt of the wildest kind after all we have seen'.[14] A month in government would be enough for the party to cut a stronger figure in opposition afterwards, Fox argued. He also believed that the Rockinghams had to be more pragmatic in their dealings with the monarch: 'Are they [Rockingham and his friends] to say that because we can not have the *best possible* system, we will have the *worst possible*[?]'[15] Burke persuaded Fox in person that continued opposition was the best policy for the time being. In the summer of 1780, Lord North wanted to let Rockingham into government in a coalition, but it fell through because Rockingham's party and George III were irreconcilable on the questions of America and economical reform.[16] The Rockingham Whigs continued to put principle before office.

Hostility to the American War provided a foundation for a coherent opposition to the policies of North's administration. Historians have argued and presented evidence suggesting that America renewed earlier Whig–Tory divisions, with High Church Anglicans and former Jacobites favouring coercive measures, and merchants and manufacturers conciliation.[17] Burke for one certainly continued to analyse what he saw as a revived form of Toryism since the 1760s in tandem with American politics. As he wrote to Fox in 1777:

> There are most manifest marks of the resurrection of the Tory party ... The Tories do universally think their power and consequence involved in the Success of this American business. The Clergy are astonishingly warm in it – and what the Tories are when embodied, united with their natural head

[12] Burke to Fox, 8 October 1777, *Correspondence*, III, 385.
[13] Fox to Burke, 24 January 1779, ibid., IV, 39.   [14] Ibid., 39–40.   [15] Ibid., 40.
[16] Christie, *Myth and Reality in Late Eighteenth-Century British Politics* (London, 1970), ch. 3.
[17] Gould, *The Persistence of Empire* (Chapel Hill, 2000), 153. For the revival of Oxford High Toryism after the accession of George III, see O'Flaherty, *Utilitarianism in the Age of Enlightenment* (Cambridge, 2019), 182–3.

the Crown, and animated by their Clergy, no man knows better than yourself. As to the Whigs I think them far from extinct. They are what they always were (except by the able use of opportunities) by far the weakest party in this Country. They have not yet learnd the application of their principles to the present state of things; and as to the dissenters, the main effective part of the Whig strength; they are, to use a favourite expression of our American Campaign Style – not all in force.[18]

This analysis of the fundamental party division, that is, church and crown on the one hand and Protestant Dissenters on the other, would have fitted into the reign of Anne.[19] Burke also emphasised what other commentators had remarked on earlier in the century, namely, that the Whigs were the natural minority party, since they were the party of Dissent rather than that of church and king. This had always been the case, but luckily for the country the party had managed to make 'able use of opportunities'. The problem, as Burke argued, was that while Toryism had been made acceptable after the end of Jacobitism it was now the Whigs who had failed to adapt to the new circumstances. This was despite Burke's best efforts in the *Present Discontents*, which, as Burke complained to Rockingham, had not been followed by a sustained propaganda campaign.

Reform, both political and religious, emerged as a common cause in which the broad Whig coalition and Protestant Dissenters could potentially once again unite. There was to be a bumpy road ahead, however. Burke had rejected the traditional Country measures in the *Present Discontents*, notably shorter parliaments. In the late 1770s, however, the Rockinghams became seriously involved in reformist politics. As an opposition party, they had already cooperated with movements 'out of doors' such as the petitioning movement, whereby people around the country were encouraged to petition the monarch to dismiss the Grafton ministry after its handling of Wilkes.[20] At the same time, they were not tempted by

---

[18] Burke to Fox, 1777, *Correspondence*, III, 382–3.

[19] Burke was committed to religious toleration, not only for Protestant Dissenters but also for Catholics, Jews, and pagans; see Burke, *W&S*, III, 376. At the same time, he supported the integrity of the Church of England and sided with Roger Newdigate, MP for the High Church seat of Oxford University, in defeating the Feathers Tavern Petition which demanded an end to mandatory subscription to the Thirty-Nine Articles in 1772. While Burke differed with many of his party friends on the question – notably Rockingham – it was not uncommon to view the issues of toleration and tests as distinct and insist on both. For Paley's similar position, see O'Flaherty, *Utilitarianism in the Age of Enlightenment*, ch. 9.

[20] However, Burke's biographer wrote that '[i]n his heart, Burke agreed with Johnson. Expediency, more than conviction, drew him into the petitioning movement.' See Lock, *Burke*, I, 273. On the episode, see Rudé, *Wilkes and Liberty* (Oxford, 1962), esp. chs. 7–8. See also Wilson, *The Sense of the People* (Cambridge, 1995), ch. 4.

the far-reaching reforms proposed by 'proto-radicals', unlike other opposition leaders such as Shelburne. The Rockinghams' proposals have been described as the most 'conservative' among the opposition groupings to North, as they did not want to undermine the constitutional framework established by their Whig precursors.[21] Other associates of the Rockinghams became increasingly entwined with more far-reaching reform, in particular the Duke of Richmond.[22] The party was thus pulling in different directions well before the French Revolution, as it was seeking to adjust to its identity as a longstanding opposition party.

The death of Chatham in 1778 paved the way for cooperation between Rockingham and Shelburne, and a commitment to American independence on the part of the opposition.[23] The question of reform remained a source of disagreement, however, and Burke was an obstacle because he and Shelburne mutually mistrusted each other. Shelburne complained that 'there is no dealing with Mr Burke, he is so violently attach'd to his own opinion that there is no arguing with him, and has got so much ascendency over Lord Rockingham that I protest I see no method of doing anything'.[24] Shelburne's follower Isaac Barré also criticised Burke's influence over Rockingham. '[W]hen [Burke's] wanderings come to be adopted seriously and obstinately by men of far higher description than himself, they then become alarming indeed', he told Richmond.[25] The duration of parliament was a particular bugbear for Burke, who had offered a qualified defence of the Septennial Act (1716) in the *Present Discontents*.[26] This Act had been one of the important milestone pieces of legislation which had secured the Whig supremacy and the Hanoverian settlement.[27]

Burke was not dogmatically against reform measures, however, commenting in 1770 that '[i]ndeed the idea of short parliaments, is I confess plausible enough; so is the idea of an Election by Ballot, but I believe neither will stand their Ground when entered into minutely and with reference to actual existing circumstances'.[28] In the late 1770s, Burke began to develop a programme of 'economical reform', the purpose of which was to reduce the influence of the executive, or the crown, over the

---

[21] Elofson, 'The Rockingham Whigs and the Country Tradition', *PH*, 8 (1989), 110.

[22] See, e.g., O'Gorman, *The Rise of Party in England* (London, 1975), 420–1.

[23] O'Gorman, 'The Parliamentary Opposition to the Government's American Policy', in *Britain and the American Revolution* (London, 1998), 116–19.

[24] Cited in Burke, *Correspondence*, IV, xiii.   [25] Cited in ibid., xiv.

[26] Burke, *Present Discontents*, in *W&S*, II, 293.

[27] Skjönsberg, 'Ancient Constitutionalism, Fundamental Law, and Eighteenth-Century Toryism in the Septennial Act (1716) Debates', *HPT*, 40 (2019), 270–301.

[28] Burke to Shackleton, [*ante* 15 August 1770], *Correspondence*, II, 150.

legislative process. This coincided with the 'county movement' starting with the meeting of Christopher Wyvill in Yorkshire. Cooperation between Wyvill and the Rockinghams looked possible for a while, but ultimately Wyvill advocated parliamentary reform rather than economical reform. This included shorter parliaments (annual or at least triennial) and an addition of one hundred County members to the Commons. For Burke, this was an attempt to overturn the established constitution the Whigs were meant to protect. By contrast, Shelburne was more attracted to Wyvill, contributing to a breach between him and Rockingham in 1780–1.

Rockingham and Shelburne reconciled after the fall of Lord North in 1782 and the formation of the second Rockingham administration. Although Rockingham was head of the Treasury and had a larger following, Shelburne had more influence with George III. The king remained suspicious of the Rockingham Whigs, and had tried everything he could to avoid inviting Rockingham.[29] In the new ministry, Burke as paymaster general managed to push through a bill on economical reform – the Civil List Act 1782 – abolishing a swathe of sinecures and redundant Court positions, the third Secretaryship of State, and the Board of Trade. Burke's Act also regulated the monarch's household budget and transferred its management to the Treasury. The Rockingham reform programme may have been 'very mild' by late eighteenth-century standards.[30] We should note, however, that unlike many other reform aspirations the Rockinghams and Burke actually managed to carry out their measures. It marked the beginning of reform in Britain and turned the Whigs into a party of reform. Between 1714 and 1760, parliamentary reform had largely been Tory politics.[31]

Rockingham's sudden death on 1 July 1782, just three months after he had taken office, split the ministry as Burke and many of Rockingham's followers resigned, refusing to serve under Shelburne, whom they called 'Malagrida', after the Portuguese Jesuit Gabriel Malagrida involved in a plot to assassinate King Jose I at Lisbon in 1758.[32] Under the new leadership of Portland in the Lords and Fox in the Commons, Burke's party, together with Lord North and his followers, brought down Shelburne's ministry the following year over the generous peace

[29] Cannon, *The Fox–North Coalition* (Cambridge, 1969), ch. 1.
[30] Elofson, *The Rockingham Connection*, 7.
[31] Sack, *From Jacobite to Conservative* (Cambridge, 1994), ch. 6.
[32] Whatmore, 'Shelburne and Perpetual Peace', in *An Enlightenment Statesman in Whig Britain* (Woodbridge, 2011), 249–50.

preliminaries Shelburne had negotiated with the Americans. Burke was back in office with his party in the Fox–North coalition, once again as paymaster of the forces (a position below Cabinet level). Portland – the new torchbearer of aristocratic Whiggism[33] – was head of the Treasury, Fox foreign secretary, and North home secretary. Without Rockingham, Burke's position within the party was weakened, and he eventually broke with his party friends under the critical circumstances of the French Revolution.

Burke and the Foxite and Portland Whigs, 1782–1791

The Fox–North coalition did not survive for much longer than the second Rockingham administration. It was eventually brought down by the monarch over regulation of the East India Company, with the king declaring that everyone voting for Fox's India Bill was his enemy. The Bill would have placed the East India Company under the control of a commission appointed by parliament rather than the crown. With the first members of the commission named in the Bill all being supporters of the Fox–North Coalition, it naturally gave rise to the accusation that it was a party measure. In a famous speech, Burke defended the Bill by pointing out that future nominations would be made by the crown. In the same speech, he also defended the politics of party. He told the Commons:

> The kingdom is divided into parties, and it ever has been so divided, and it ever will be so divided; and if no system for relieving the subjects of this kingdom from oppression, and snatching its affairs from ruin, can be adopted, until it is demonstrated that no party can derive an advantage from it, no good can ever be done in this country.[34]

George III – still no friend of the formerly Rockingham and now Portland Whigs – replaced the coalition with William Pitt the Younger at the end of 1783, who bolstered his position at the general elections of 1784. This election had been called early, after only half of the potential lifetime, to give Pitt a majority. The court system had won the day, and Burke was mightily disappointed since it looked as if the king's interpretation of the constitution had prevailed, and party had failed.[35] 'We have been

---

[33] His Dutch great grandfather, William Bentinck, had been one of William of Orange's closest men, and was ennobled as the Earl of Portland after the Glorious Revolution. George I made his son – who had been tutored by Rapin as we saw in Chapter 2 – a duke in 1716. In the 1760s, he had been Newcastle's protégé. See Wilkinson, *The Duke of Portland* (London, 2003), ch. 1.

[34] Burke, *Speech on Fox's East India Bill* (1783), *W&S*, V, 447.   [35] Lock, *Burke*, I, 281.

labouring for near twenty years to make [the Commons] independent', he wrote to William Baker, 'for me to look forward to the event of another twenty years toil – it is quite ridiculous.'[36] It has been argued that the events of 1782–4 split the political landscape into the proponents of party, on the one hand, and those of management and patronage, on the other.[37]

What emerged after 1784 was a clearer dichotomy between an opposition party and a broad-bottom Treasury party, and at least the semblance of a two-party framework.[38] The opposition Whigs under Portland and Fox became bigger than they had been under Rockingham, with approximately 145 MPs out of 183 members of the opposition belonging to this connection after the election of 1790. This was largely thanks to better party organisation and electoral management of Portland and his assistant William Adam.[39] However, many commentators, including Horace Walpole and Edward Gibbon, believed that the party names lost meaning after the American war.[40] There are indications that both sides viewed themselves as Whig and accused the other side of being Tory. Pitt never described himself as a Tory, but as an 'independent Whig'.[41] In 1784, he was supported by the Whig Union Club in Bristol, which had championed Burke's candidacy in 1774.[42] Having started his career as a reformer, he disliked party connections as much as his father, and became a royal servant who eventually gathered a personal following of 'Pittites'. In the nineteenth century, Tories such as Benjamin Disraeli claimed Pitt, despite Pitt's own efforts to associate himself with independent Whiggism.[43] When Pitt became 'prime minister', however, 'Tory' had long since become reduced to an insult in national, parliamentary politics, even if it survived in a more positive sense in local politics and occasionally in public discourse.[44] From Burke's perspective, there was little doubt that the opposition were the true Whigs and that Pitt represented Toryism. The

---

[36] Burke to William Baker, 22 June 1784, *Correspondence*, V, 154.

[37] Mitchell, *Fox and the Disintegration of the Whig Party*, 190.

[38] Hilton, *A Mad, Bad, and Dangerous People?* (Oxford, 2006), 47.

[39] Ginter, 'The Financing of the Whig Party Organization, 1783–1793', *American Historical Review*, 71 (1966), 421–40; Ginter (ed.), *Whig Organisation in the General Election of 1790* (Berkeley, 1967).

[40] Sack, *From Jacobite to Conservative*, 81.

[41] Ehrman, *The Younger Pitt* (3 vols., London, 1969–96), I, 58 and II, 389. See also Christie, *Myth and Reality*, ch. 7.

[42] Poole and Rogers, *Bristol from Below* (Woodbridge, 2017), 276.

[43] Disraeli, *Vindication of the English Constitution* (London, 1835), 173, 192, 195.

[44] O'Gorman, *Voters, Patrons, and Parties* (Oxford, 1989), ch. 6.

founding of the Whig Club at Westminster to aid Fox's election was part of an effort to confirm this interpretation and monopolise the term.[45]

At least at the start of the new campaign, Burke showed himself more than willing to continue in a spirited opposition to the crown and its new minister. On 14 June 1784, he criticised the monarch's meddling in the business of Fox's India Bill in a lengthy speech which he later described as a 'defence of the Whigs'.[46] In the context of the coalition's significant defeats at the general election earlier in the spring, Burke restated his doctrine set out in his *Speech to the Electors of Bristol* (1774) when arguing that representatives had to be responsive but not submissive to the 'sense of the people'.[47] Burke's speech in 1784 had only been supported by his disciple William Windham. The death of Rockingham was a heavy blow for Burke and it greatly impacted his position within the party. The man who had written and spoken so fervently and eloquently of party loyalty and unity would eventually become responsible for creating a fundamental schism within the Whigs. Johnson had said of Burke to Boswell: 'I remember being present when [Burke] shewed himself to be so corrupted, or at least something so different from what I think right, as to maintain, that a member of parliament should go along with his party right or wrong ... It is maintaining that you may lie to the publick.'[48] Johnson misunderstood Burke, who had written in the *Present Discontents* that if one disagreed with one's party more than one time out of ten, one had chosen the wrong connection. 'Men thinking freely, will, in particular instances, think differently', he had argued. What was crucial was agreement on *'leading general principles in Government'*.[49] Burke had chosen freely to associate with his party, knowing the principles upon which it was founded. In such groupings, 'crises of conscience ought not normally to arise', but if they did, 'honourable men would break off the relationship'.[50] This is what eventually happened in the early years of the French Revolution.

Before the outbreak of revolution in France, Burke had taken an independent position on the Regency Crisis in 1788–9 during George III's mental illness, arguing that the Prince Regent should attain full

---

[45] Hilton, *A Mad, Bad, and Dangerous People*, 50–1.
[46] Burke, *Appeal*, *W&S*, IV, 404. Windham described Burke's speech on 14 June 1784 as 'a defence both of the late Parliament and of the party, against the calumnies of the court and nation'. See Burke, *W&S*, IV, 181.
[47] Burke, *W&S*, IV, 183.   [48] Boswell, *The Life of Johnson* (2 vols., London, 1791), I, 398.
[49] Burke, *Present Discontents*, *W&S*, II, 319.
[50] Canavan, *The Political Reason of Burke* (Durham, 1960), 155.

monarchical authority.[51] Many Whigs waited for the king to die because as long as he was alive there was little hope that he would let them back into power.[52] As Adam Ferguson commented on the matter, 'the more they are offensive to the present Reign the more they will direct their hopes to a succeeding one'.[53] By the time of the Regency crisis, the opposition Whigs had forged an alliance with the Prince of Wales using classic 'reversionary interest' tactics. While Pitt and the administration wanted to impose restrictions on the Prince Regent, Burke argued that the British constitution vested executive power in the crown, and that the hereditary right to the throne in the House of Hanover had been established by the Act of Settlement. Pitt had no right to impose any restrictions since no legislation could be executed without royal assent. Burke feared that parliament was usurping powers which belonged to the executive, and that Pitt would effectively make himself king during the Regency.[54] In the process, Burke went to great rhetorical lengths in portraying Pitt as a power-hungry innovator and a threat to the constitutional equilibrium. Burke's advice to his party was that the Prince should have taken the lead by announcing his intentions to parliament, which would have made his friends (the Whigs) the 'proposers' and Pitt and the administration the 'opposers'.[55] But Fox and others in the party believed this tactic to be too extreme, which allowed Pitt's ministry to keep the initiative. In any event, George III recovered in February 1789, and the regency question became less relevant until 1810 when the king became irremediably insane.

In addition to the Regency Crisis, Burke's involvement in the impeachment of Warren Hastings, former governor-general of India, created distance between him and the Foxites. As he famously wrote to Mary Palmer, his friend Joshua Reynolds's niece and heiress:

> [I]n India affairs, I have not acted at all with any party ... I have no party in this Business, my dear Miss Palmer, but among a set of people, who have none of your Lilies and Roses in their faces; but who are images of the great Pattern as well as you and I. I know what I am doing; whether the white people like it or not.[56]

---

[51] Derry, *The Regency Crisis and the Whigs* (Cambridge, 1963), ch. 4.
[52] O'Gorman, *The Whig Party and the French Revolution* (New York, 1967), 5; Cannon, *The Fox–North Coalition*, 229.
[53] Ferguson to John Macpherson, 26 April 1788, BL MS Eur F291/97, f. 3.
[54] Derry, *The Regency Crisis*, 161–2.
[55] Burke to Windham, c.24 January 1789, *Correspondence*, V, 437–8.
[56] Burke to Mary Palmer, 19 January 1786, ibid., 255.

Fox did not like Burke's obsession with Hastings, whose trial went on for much longer than initially expected. What made matters worse was that Pitt refused to make it a party question by offering limited support to the prosecution, and Fox lost interest. When Fox was planning for a new ministry during the Regency Crisis, he left out Burke's name as the proposed head of the Board of Commissioners for the Affairs of India.[57] Burke was once more going to be offered the office of paymaster general, below cabinet level.

There are few signs that Burke had lost his conviction of the importance of party, however. As late as August 1789, he wrote that 'Party is absolutely necessary at this time. I thought it always so in this Country ever since I had anything to do in publick Business'.[58] As we saw above, Burke had viewed the Dissenting constituency as the mainstay of the Whig party. In 1784, however, many Dissenters had supported Pitt and helped him win an overwhelming majority at the general election.[59] In a letter from 1792, Burke argued that the Dissenters 'had long shewn themselves wholly adverse to, and unalliable with the Party. They had shown it ... signally in 1784.'[60] It is clear, however, that Burke for a while had sought to win them back. As late as September 1789, he wrote to Fox advising him to publish a volume of essays by Joseph Priestley, dedicated to the Prince of Wales, for electioneering purposes: 'Dr P. is a very considerable Leader among a Set of Men powerful enough in many things, but most of all in Elections ... It would be material to you to gain entirely some of these dissenters.'[61] This seems to suggest that Burke's complete alienation from the Dissenters happened later than Pocock surmised (1780).[62] In the wake of the French Revolution, however, Burke sharply diverged from the Dissenters. Writing to Richard Bright, a prominent Dissenter from Bristol, in February 1790, Burke said that he had become 'less desirous, than formerly I had been, of becoming active in the Service of the Dissenters'.[63] The reason, as he described it, was that he had 'observed' and 'felt' that the Dissenters were turning themselves into 'a party which seems to have contention and power much more than Piety for its Objects'.[64] What made things even worse, this party was 'proceeding

---

[57] Ibid., xvii.   [58] Burke to Charlemont, 9 August 1789, *Correspondence*, VI, 9–10.
[59] Clark, 'Introduction' to Burke, *Reflections on the Revolution on France* (Stanford, 2001), 56.
[60] Burke to Weddell, 31 January 1792, *Correspondence*, VII, 55–6.
[61] Burke to Fox, 9 September 1789, ibid., VI, 15.
[62] Pocock, 'Political Thought in the English-Speaking Atlantic, 1760–1790', in *The Varieties of British Political Thought* (Cambridge, 1993), 289.
[63] Burke to Bright, 18 February 1790, *Correspondence*, VI, 83.   [64] Ibid., 84.

systematically, to the destruction of this Constitution in some of its essential parts', in 'imitation' of events in France.[65] In March 1790, Burke astonished Fox and many of his friends by actively opposing a new motion to repeal the Test and Corporation Acts.[66]

The *Reflections on the Revolution in France*, published in November 1790, is Burke's most famous condemnation of the French Revolution. More specifically, it was a response to the Dissenting section of the broad Whig landscape and more precisely to Richard Price's *Discourse on the Love of Our Country* (1789).[67] In this address, which Burke called a sermon, the Dissenting minister compared the French Revolution with 1688–9, and seemed to be calling for general revolutions across Europe: 'I see the ardor for liberty catching and spreading ... the dominion of kings changed for the dominion of laws, and the dominion of priests giving way to the dominion of reason and conscience.'[68] Burke had earlier bundled Price together with his nemesis Shelburne in a letter to Philip Francis in February 1790.[69] But Burke was also increasingly concerned with his own colleagues' sympathetic attitudes towards the French efforts. Fox periodically praised the Revolution publicly, and in private said that the storming of the Bastille was the 'greatest' and 'best' event in world history.[70] Francis wrote to Burke about the *Reflections*: 'you dread and detest commotion of every Kind. And so should I ... But, tell me, has not God himself commanded or permitted the Storm to purify the elements?'[71] Burke's first major quarrel was with Richard Sheridan, his Irish compatriot whose relationship with Burke had cooled since the Regency crisis. A letter from Burke's son Richard to Fitzwilliam, Rockingham's nephew, is worth quoting at length:

> [Sheridan] thinks it advisable, to throw himself into a new line of politics, different from that which has been pursued by the party, that is, the principle of recommending themselves to the public favor, by administering ably and conscientiously the *actual existing government*, when in place – and when out of place, by the resistance of all bad measures, and above all things adhering to and maintaining both the form and substance of our present constitution. This I take to have been the principle of Lord R[ockingham]'s

---

[65] Ibid., 83.   [66] O'Gorman, *The Whig Party and the French Revolution*, 49.

[67] He wrote that '[i]n reality, my Object was not France, in the first instance, but this Country.' See Burke to Charles-Alexandre de Calonne, 25 October 1790, *Correspondence*, VI, 141.

[68] Price, *Discourse on the Love of Our Country* (London, second edn., 1789), 50.

[69] Burke to Francis, 20 February 1790, *Correspondence*, VI, 91. For Shelburne's association with Price, see Whatmore, *Terrorists, Anarchists, Democrats and Republicans* (Princeton, 2019), ch. 8.

[70] Fox to Fitzpatrick, 30 July 1789, *Fox Memorials*, II, 361.

[71] Francis to Burke, 3–4 November 1790, *Correspondence*, VI, 154.

party, of the same party under the present head [Fox]. The new line –
I call – an endeavour to recommend ourselves not by conduct only, but by
seeking favor with various descriptions of men [the Dissenters and
reformers] by flattering them with hopes of real or pretended improvements
of the constitution; And by disgusting them by the representation of the
vices or supposed vices of that constitution, to excite such a popular spirit,
as shall give the power to correct them[.][72]

One can question whether this tactic was a 'new line' at all; some of
Burke's earlier letters to Fox suggest otherwise. What was particularly
problematic for Richard Burke, and, presumably his father,[73] however,
was that Sheridan had allegedly said that the French Revolution should be
celebrated by all 'without *any distinction of parties – on general principles*'.[74]
Richard Burke reminded Fitzwilliam that '*General principles without distinction of parties*, never I believe was the principle of the present
opposition.' As we saw in Chapter 11, if that had been Burke's argument
in the *Present Discontents*, it would have made it virtually indistinguishable
from Bolingbroke's 'Country party'. '[W]hat is the meaning of *general
principles without distinction of parties*, but – the formation of *a new party*
upon *new principles*', Burke's son asked rhetorically.[75]

Fox and Burke fell out dramatically during the debates on the Quebec
Bill in May 1791, an occasion which moved Fox to tears.[76] The French
question arose when Parliament debated the establishment of a constitution for a French province under British dominion. In the debate, Fox
'condemned [the *Reflections*] both in public and private, and every doctrine
contained in it'.[77] Defending himself, Burke contended that 'there was not
one step of his conduct, nor one syllable of his book, contrary to the
principles of those men with whom our glorious revolution originated, and
to whose principles as a Whig, he declared an inviolable attachment'.[78] Six
months earlier, when the *Reflections* had been first published, Burke
assured Sir Gilbert Elliot that he had received from Portland,
Fitzwilliam, Devonshire, Cavendish, and Montagu 'and a long et cetera
of the old Stamina of the Whiggs a most full approbation of the principles
in that work and a kind indulgence to the execution'.[79] Lord John

---

[72] Richard Burke Jr. to Fitzwilliam, 29 July 1790, ibid., 127.
[73] Burke's son said: 'I know I speak his [Burke's] sentiments'. Ibid., 130.   [74] Ibid., 128.
[75] Ibid.
[76] *Parl. Hist.*, XXIX, 388. Less than a year earlier, they had celebrated Fox's victory at the Westminster
polls together; see Burke to Charlemont, 2 July 1790, *Correspondence*, VI, 124.
[77] *Parl. Hist.*, XXIX, 389; Burke to Fitzwilliam, 5 June 1791, *Correspondence*, VI, 273–4.
[78] *Parl. Hist.*, XXIX, 396.   [79] Burke to Elliot, 29 November 1790, *Correspondence*, VI, 178.

Cavendish had indeed ensured Burke on 14 November 1790 that 'all men of sense must I think feel obliged to you for shewing in so forcible a manner, that confusion is not the road to reformation', adding that 'there are a few points (& but a few) in which you go rather too far for me; & a few expressions which I wish had been softened'.[80] Portland later referred to the *Reflections* as 'the true Whig Creed'.[81] To Burke's disappointment, when he clashed with Fox 'not one of the party spoke one conciliatory word'.[82] Burke had dismissed Fox's suggestion that there need not be any loss of friendship as pretence.[83] The Whig press reported that Fox had got the better of Burke in their exchanges in the Commons.[84] Burke continued to vindicate his position after the rupture in *An Appeal from the New to the Old Whigs*, published just within a few months of the Quebec debates. This pamphlet would reiterate what Richard Burke had told Fitzwilliam the previous year: Burke had not abandoned the party's principles, it was the Foxite Whigs who had morphed into a *new party*.

An Appeal from the New to the Old Whigs

The *Appeal* can be viewed as Burke's political testament. In this pamphlet he addressed his erstwhile party friends whom he privately described as 'incurable, for they will not allow that there is any sort of disease in it [the party], except the difference between Fox and me'.[85] Written in the third person, Burke said of himself that he was 'known indeed to have been warmly, strenuously, and affectionately, against all allurements of ambition ... attached to the Whig party'.[86] To former party friends, he stated his intention as 'mak[ing] it manifest to the world, that those [Whigs] who condemn me, condemn their predecessors in principle whom they so highly and justly honour and esteem'.[87] He celebrated the memory of Rockingham in the *Appeal*,[88] but his main focus was on the 'Old Whigs' of the reigns of William and Anne. 'I shew myself [in the *Appeal*] no worse

---

[80] Ibid., 161.
[81] Portland to Laurence French, 30 August 1791, Pw F 6241, University of Nottingham.
[82] Burke to Fitzwilliam, 5 June 1791, *Correspondence*, VI, 275.
[83] O'Gorman, *The Whig Party and the French Revolution*, 67.
[84] Leslie, *Fox and the Disintegration of the Whig Party*, 165.
[85] Edmund and Jane Burke to Richard Burke, 10 August 1791, *Correspondence*, VI, 335.
[86] Burke, *An Appeal from the New to the Old Whigs* (1791), *W&S*, IV, 373.
[87] Burke to Charlemont, 8 August 1791, *Correspondence*, VI, 331.
[88] Burke, *Appeal*, *W&S*, IV, 406.

a Whigg than the Somer's, Godolphins, and Jekylls', he wrote to Lord Charlemont.[89] Having joined the party in his mid-thirties, he had been perfectly aware of the differences between Whig and Tory principles, and he knew that his conformed to the former. He had also understood that joining the Whigs at that time would not be 'a road to power', especially not for someone of his status.

Burke's predicament now was that this party – via 'the mouth of him [Fox] who must be regarded as its authentic organ' – had not only disapproved of him but indeed disavowed him.[90] This was unreasonable, he contended, since he had only expressed private and not party opinions in the *Reflections*. Moreover, he argued that the French Revolution could not determine the character of any British party which had been formed before that event, 'unless they choose to imitate any of its acts, or to consolidate any principles of that revolution with their own opinions'.[91] Because the new-modelled French constitution had become an object of comparison and imitation for 'factions, at home and abroad', scrutinising it was certainly a proper enterprise, Burke argued. The risk was indeed that people would be tempted to sacrifice 'the good, of which they had been in assured possession, in favour or wild and irrational expectations'.[92] In other words, Burke believed that he was sticking to the tenets of Whiggism by defending the British constitution.

Fox could of course claim, as he had done, that he was the true Whig since he celebrated the fall of absolute monarchy. Lafayette and other French revolutionaries viewed Fox and other Whigs as their natural allies.[93] Burke anticipated this argument with 'Montesquieuan' political science: France had not just seen the dissolution of absolute monarchy but also 'the utter ruin of whole orders and classes of men', in other words, the removal of intermediate powers.[94] He also evoked Hume's notorious description of France as a civilised monarchy where property was secure,[95] which had been anathema for many orthodox Whigs.

The main charge against Burke was one of inconsistency. He countered such accusations in the *Appeal* by saying that 'if he could venture to value himself upon any thing, it is on the virtue of consistency that he would value himself the most'.[96] Burke contended that the three parts of Britain's

---

[89] Burke to Charlemont, 8 August 1791, *Correspondence*, VI, 331. Godolphin was not a nominal Whig but became associated with the Whigs during the War of the Spanish Succession.
[90] Burke, *Appeal*, *W&S*, IV, 372.   [91] Ibid., 374.   [92] Ibid., 380.
[93] See, e.g., Lafayette to Fox, 6 Nivôse 1800, BL Add MS 51468, f. 47.
[94] Burke, *Appeal*, *W&S*, IV, 381. Montesquieu is mentioned at the end of the *Appeal* (473).
[95] Hume, 'Of Civil Liberty', *Essays*.   [96] Burke, *Appeal*, *W&S*, IV, 391.

mixed constitution had to be defended in distinct ways, and the friends of the whole would not hesitate to support the part in most need of defence. There was thus no contradiction in a constitutional Whig defending monarchy, Burke argued, referring to his record on 'economical reform' aimed at reducing the influence of the crown when it had been 'too great'.[97] Moreover, by citing from his famous speech to the electors of Bristol seventeen years earlier, Burke demonstrated that he had never been a partisan of any one part of the constitution exclusively but rather a partisan of all of them.[98] In any event, many continued to criticise Burke on account of perceived apostasy. John Millar, Smith's student, condemned Burke in *An Historical View of the English Government*, which was dedicated to Fox, referring to 'the distinction between the *old* and the *new* whigs, by which a famous political character endeavoured lately to cover the desertion of his former tenets'.[99]

More specifically, Fox had accused Burke of inconsistency in supporting the Americans against Britain and not the French struggle against absolute monarchy. '[I]t was evident the American states had revolted, because they did not think themselves sufficiently free', Fox had told the Commons during the Quebec debate.[100] Burke disagreed, clarifying in the chamber that '[h]e was favourable to the Americans, because he supposed they were fighting, not to acquire absolute speculative liberty, but to keep what they had under the English constitution'.[101] As an 'Old Whig', Burke's key reference point was frequently the Glorious Revolution. In the *Appeal*, Burke stressed that '[h]e considered the Americans as standing at that time, and in that controversy, in the same relation to England, as England did to king James the Second, in 1688'.[102] The Americans had been on the 'defensive footing'. The same analysis had allowed him to separate the French Revolution from 1688–9 in the *Reflections*. Burke wanted to stress in the *Appeal* that it was his party which had shifted ground and abandoned its principles, whereas he was still defending the legacy of the Glorious Revolution and Whiggism. He still supported a 'rational plan of free government', meaning a 'tempered' and 'balanced' monarchy.[103]

Burke acknowledged that it was with regards to the Revolution of 1688–9 that those 'who speak in the name of party have thought proper to censure him the most'.[104] He admitted that 'he must be defended on

---

[97] Ibid., 399.   [98] Ibid., 394; Burke, *Speech to the Electors of Bristol* (1774), *W&S*, III, 59.
[99] Millar, *Historical View of the English Government* (Indianapolis, 2006), 806n.
[100] *Parl. Hist.*, XXIX, 425.   [101] Ibid., 395.   [102] Burke, *Appeal, W&S*, IV, 396.
[103] Ibid., 401–4.   [104] Ibid., 407.

party grounds too', in other words, he must show that his interpretation of that 'leading event' was 'in perfect harmony with that of the ancient Whigs'. The party he had joined 'did not affect to be better Whigs, than those who lived in the days in which principle was put to the test'.[105] He once again emphasised his version of a linear story from the *Present Discontents* of how the Whiggism of the Revolution was transmitted, via the Whigs under Anne and the two Georges, to Rockingham's connection. As the clearest statement of Whig tenets, Burke returned to the period in which he believed that British party ideologies had matured: the reign of Anne. More exactly, he returned to the 'great constitutional event' of the impeachment of Henry Sacheverell in 1710. Sacheverell was an Anglican High Church clergyman who had preached a notorious sermon on 5 November 1709 entitled *The Perils of False Brethren, in Church, and State* at St Paul's Cathedral to commemorate Gunpowder Plot Day. The printed version of the sermon became a bestseller, and infuriated the Whigs because it attacked religious toleration and, according to Whigs, the Revolution Settlement as a whole. Sacheverell was impeached, but received a very light sentence, and the episode is believed to have swung much of the country behind the Tories and paved the way for their landslide election victory in 1710.[106]

The purpose of the trial, Burke claimed, was that of 'stating the true grounds and principles of the Revolution'.[107] By comparing his *Reflections* with the published speeches from the trial, from which he cited at length, Burke's expressed intention was naturally to show that he had not diverted from the 'Old Whigs'. In the *Reflections*, Burke had argued that the subversion of the 'ancient constitution' – 'inviolably fixed in King, Lords and Commons' – had justified the Revolution. It had been carried out 'from necessity'.[108] Rather than modelling a new government, it sought 'to derive all … as *an inheritance from our forefathers*'.[109] Citing extracts from the managers of the trial, including Nicholas Lechmere, James Stanhope, Robert Walpole, and Joseph Jekyll, Burke wanted to show that the Whigs of the trial believed that the Revolution had not fundamentally changed

---

[105] Ibid., 409.
[106] Holmes, *The Trial of Doctor Sacheverell* (London, 1973); Knights (ed.), *Special Issue: Faction Displayed: Reconsidering the Impeachment of Dr Henry Sacheverell, PH*, 31 (2012), iv–vi, 1–132; Cowan (ed.), *Special Issue: Texts and Studies Series 6: The State Trial of Doctor Henry Sacheverell, PH*, 31 (2012), vii–xiii, 1–307.
[107] Burke, *Appeal, W&S*, IV, 409.　　[108] Ibid., 411. See also Burke, *Reflections, W&S*, VIII, 77–8.
[109] Burke, *Reflections, W&S*, VIII, 81.

the nature of the monarchy. The Act of Settlement (1701) did not create an elective monarchy but the safeguarding of the hereditary principle in a Protestant line.[110] Jekyll, for instance, had put the Revolution and the Restoration (1660) 'exactly upon the same footing'.[111] Burke took the opportunity to celebrate Walpole's legacy as a 'sound Whig' and 'safe minister', who governed by 'party attachments' rather than corruption as Bolingbroke and others of the (mostly) Tory-Jacobite opposition had claimed.[112] Walpole's financial acumen had laid the foundation for Britain's later military glory, Burke argued. For 'old Whigs', Britain's military strength relative to Catholic and absolutist France had always been a top priority, and, as we shall see, for Burke this remained a priority for the rest of his life.

Having explained and defended the principles of the 'old Whigs' – those he viewed as the 'constitutional ancestors' of his party[113] – Burke proceeded to attack the books of the 'new Whigs', citing from Thomas Paine's *Rights of Man: Part the First* and Mary Wollstonecraft's *Vindication of the Rights of Men*, written against Burke's *Reflections*.[114] His purpose was that '[t]he Whig reader may make his choice between the two doctrines'.[115] In private, Burke wrote to his son that he believed that the great majority of his party were of his opinion and that he wanted to 'get the better of their inactivity, and to stimulate them to a publick declaration of, what every one of their acquaintance privately knows, to be as much their Sentiments as they are yours and mine'.[116] Burke's main attention was fixed on Paine, who had stated that the Septennial Act (1716) showed that Britain had no constitution.[117] When responding to Paine, Burke associated him with quasi-Jacobitism: the modern Whigs 'represent the king as tainted with principles of despotism, from the circumstance of his having dominions in Germany'.[118] As J.C.D. Clark has recently argued, Paine's anti-monarchical writings relied to a large extent on an earlier anti-Hanoverian discourse with Jacobite elements.[119] Paine did certainly not identify with either Whiggism or the appeal to party. In the preface in the second part of *Rights of Man*, Paine ridiculed the Whig tradition in which

---

[110] Burke, *Appeal, W&S*, IV, 421.   [111] Ibid., 425.   [112] Ibid., 416. See also ch. 3.
[113] Ibid., 476.
[114] Ibid., 432–9. Others who responded to Burke included his old republican nemesis Catharine Macaulay, Priestley, James Mackintosh, and William Godwin.
[115] Ibid., 432.   [116] Burke to Richard Burke, 5 August 1791, *Correspondence*, VI, 316–17.
[117] Paine, *Rights of Man: Being an Answer to Mr. Burke's Attack on the French Revolution* (London, 1791), 59.
[118] Burke, *Appeal, W&S*, IV, 438.   [119] Clark, *Thomas Paine* (Oxford, 2018), ch. 2.

Burke took so much pride, and condemned all parties as self-seeking in the same breath:

> But who are those to whom Mr. Burke has made his appeal? A set of childish thinkers and half-way politicians born in the last century; men who went no farther with any principle than as it suited their purpose as a party; the nation was always left out of the question; and this has been the character of every party from that day to this.[120]

While portraying himself as an undisputable Whig in the *Appeal*, Burke did not shy away from drawing attention to his previous disagreements with his party under Rockingham's leadership, including on questions of parliamentary reform and the Thirty-Nine Articles of the Church of England.[121] In these cases, he had gone against the opinion and even the solicitations of some of his 'best friends'.[122] His point was that ultimately principle must be put before party. Party could uphold principles in politics, but it could also become an engine for destructive ones. As he had made clear from his early writings on the subject, including in the *Present Discontents*, party could operate for good as well as for ill. Against the backdrop of the French Revolution, Burke came, as he had put it in a letter to Fitzwilliam between his split with Fox and the appearance of the *Appeal*, 'totally and fundamentally to differ with that party in constitutional and publick points of such moment, that all those, on which I have hitherto ever differd from other men and other Parties, are, in comparison, mere toys and Triffles'.[123]

Burke became increasingly alarmed about the body of the Dissenters in particular. In a letter to Henry Dundas, he described the Dissenters as a 'more united' party than the Jacobites and the Republicans had ever been. Like Rapin, he said that the Republicans had only been prominent during the Wars of the Three Kingdoms and 'never formed themselves into any thing like a party ... Until [the French Revolution] they were individuals who hung upon the whigg party, and by that party were lookd upon as absurd and visionary men of no sort of consequence.'[124] Although Burke viewed the Whigs as the natural protector of the Dissenting interest, they were not supposed to represent solely this section of the population, especially not when the Dissenters had become seduced by principles he

---

[120] Paine, *Rights of Man; Part the Second.* (London, 1792), preface.
[121] See note 19 in this chapter.   [122] Burke, *Appeal*, *W&S*, IV, 393.
[123] Burke to Fitzwilliam, 5 June 1791, *Correspondence*, VI, 275.
[124] Burke to Dundas, 30 September 1791, ibid., 420.

deemed destructive for the whole. The question then naturally arises: what and who did Burke think that the true Whigs were supposed to represent?

Aristocratic Party?

Burke and Paine not only disagreed about monarchy but also about aristocracy.[125] As we saw in Chapter 11, the Rockinghams were a party of the major Whig aristocratic families, the Cavendish's and the Devonshire's, even if there was space for an Irish self-made *novus homo* such as Burke. Burke referred to the landed aristocracy in a letter to Richmond as 'the great Oaks that shade a Country and perpetuate your benefits from Generation to Generation'.[126] Burke was, however, no sycophant, writing early in his career to Portland that '[w]hatever advantages I have had, have been from friends on my own Level; As to those that are called great, I never paid them any Court; perhaps since I must say it, they have had as much benefit from my Connection, as I have had'.[127] Towards the end of his life, Burke presented himself as a self-made man in a pamphlet responding to the aristocratic Bedford and Lauderdale, who had criticised Burke's pension:

> I was not, like the Grace of Bedford, swaddled, and rocked, and dandled into a Legislator ... I was made for a minion or a tool ... At every step of my progress in my life (for in every step was I traversed and opposed), and at every turnpike I met, I was obliged to shew my passport ... I had no arts, but manly arts. On them I have stood, and, please God, in spite of the Duke of Bedford and the Earl of Lauderdale, to the last gasp I will stand.[128]

In the *Appeal*, Burke had argued that '[a] true natural aristocracy ... is an essential integrant part of any large people rightly constituted'.[129] An aristocracy was naturally 'elevated', but it also needed '[t]o look early to public opinion', which is what the Rockinghams had done, both in government and opposition, as was seen in Chapter 11.[130] Aristocracy had been attacked alongside monarchy and the church in the French Revolution, and his former Whig friends had failed to side with him in

---

[125] Burke, *Appeal*, *W&S*, IV, 433. On this point, Fox and Paine disagreed as well; see Mitchell, *Fox and the Disintegration of the Whig Party*, 175–6.
[126] Burke to Richmond, 15 November 1772, *Correspondence*, II, 377.
[127] Burke to Portland, 22 April 1770, ibid., 131.
[128] Burke, *Letter to a Noble Lord* (1796), *W&S*, IX, 160.   [129] Burke, *Appeal*, *W&S*, IV, 448.
[130] See also Brewer, *Party Ideology and Popular Politics at the Accession of George III* (Cambridge, 1976), 237–8; Sutherland, 'The City of London in Eighteenth-Century Politics', in *Essays Presented to Namier* (London, 1956), 49–74.

condemning this attack. The party in which he had acted had always had the 'reproach' as well as the 'estimation' of being an 'Aristocratick party', he wrote to Fitzwilliam. 'Such I always understood it to be, in the true Sense of the word; that is to say, a party grave and moral, equally removed from popular giddiness and profligacy on the one hand, and from servile Court compliances on the other.'[131] As was argued in Chapter 11, aristocracy properly understood equalled independence for Burke. In a letter to William Weddell, the other MP for Malton, Burke argued that the purpose of the Whigs was to support 'aristocratick principles' and 'aristocratick interests' for the sake of 'the real Benefit of the Body of the people, to which all names of party, all Ranks and orders in the State, and even Government itself ought to be entirely subordinate'.[132]

Burke told Fitzwilliam that many of the party leaders had given him written assurances that the *Reflections* would be both honourable and useful to the party,[133] until Fox had encouraged a complete change of tone. What had happened since was that the leaders had started 'to propagate the principles of French Levelling and confusion'.[134] After the example of Burke, no one dared to speak out against the events in France. The party was no longer safe for principled disagreement. Burke assured Fitzwilliam that he would not stay in parliament 'one hour after' the Hastings trial had been concluded.[135] However, Burke's references to Portland towards the end of the letter shows that he suspected that enthusiasm for the French Revolution among the Whig aristocracy was waning.

The French Revolution showed Burke's readiness to differ and depart with the Whig aristocracy when he believed that they were condoning doctrines which would ensure their own destruction and that of the mixed and balanced constitution. Burke was not only committed to the aristocratic part of the constitution. As we have seen, he viewed himself as defending all its branches, including the democratic part, which he represented himself in the Commons, and the monarchical element. As he had argued in the *Appeal*, this was his longstanding commitment and the core of his Whiggism.

In May 1768, Burke had in a parliamentary debate described the British constitution as consisting of king, parliament, and people, with

---

[131] Burke to Fitzwilliam, 21 November 1791, *Correspondence*, VI, 450. He repeated this verbatim in a later letter to Weddell, 31 January 1792, ibid., VII, 52–3.
[132] Burke to Weddell, 31 January 1792, ibid., VII, 543.   [133] See note 80 in this chapter.
[134] Burke, *Appeal*, W&S, IV, 451.   [135] Ibid., 452.

parliamentary members of both the Lords and Commons described by
Burke as a 'middle class' that would mediate between popular turmoil and
royal domination. Central to his argument, starting with the *Observations*
(1769), was that partisanship was a duty for this middle class. In the
Appeal, Burke argued that parties themselves contained 'a middle sort of
men; a sort of equestrian order', undoubtedly with reference to people of
more humble pedigrees such as himself.[136] This 'equestrian order', standing 'between the principal leaders in parliament, and the lowest followers
out of doors ... are the fittest for preventing things from running to
excess'. The problem, however, was that even they tended to go along with
their leaders. And what made things worse, the leaders were themselves
'blindly led' by the whims of the multitude.[137] Like Bolingbroke had done
in the *Patriot King*, Burke referred to his own experience of the inner
workings of parties in his analysis.

The aristocratic part of the constitution was important insofar as it held
a middle position between people and monarch. Burke was often censured
for being rhetorical and exaggerated, whether he was denouncing British
abuse in India or the excesses of the French Revolution. This was part of
his brief as an orator whose job for most of his thirty years in parliament
was to criticise the government of the day. At the same time, the avoidance
of extremes is an organising theme in many of Burke's writings, especially
in the *Appeal*. 'The whole scheme of our mixed constitution is to prevent
any one of its principles from being carried as far, as taken by itself, and
theoretically, it would go', he wrote.[138] This applied as much to aristocracy
as the other two branches. The British constitution was one of 'perpetual
treaty and compromise'.[139] Once again using Montesquieuean language,
Burke said that only '[p]rofound thinkers will know its reason and
spirit'.[140] By castigating the British constitution, the 'new teachers', or
the 'New Whigs', sought 'to deprive men of the benefit of the collected
wisdom of mankind'.[141]

Burke's key argument for the boon of an aristocratic party was its ability
to be relatively independent from both the populace and the monarch.
Ultimately, Burke also wanted individuals in the parties to think freely and
not be blindly led by either their leaders or their followers. Burke seems at
least at this stage of his career to have agreed with the earlier (and later)
calumnies of parties that they involved a form of herd mentality. Despite
this, the *Appeal* itself and his subsequent activities demonstrate that he had

---

[136] Ibid., 449.   [137] Ibid., 448.   [138] Ibid., 470.   [139] Ibid., 471.   [140] Ibid., 472.
[141] Ibid., 473.

not given up entirely on his party, as we see in the final section of this chapter.

Burke and the Portland Whigs after 1791

Burke was disappointed with the reception of the *Appeal*. 'Not one word from one of our party', he wrote to his son. 'They agree with me to a title – but they dare not speak out for fear of hurting Fox.'[142] In fact, the pamphlet had insulted some of Burke's potential allies. Crucially, Portland was mightily upset, and worried that it could 'injure & annihilate the remains of the Old Whig Party'.[143] For a while it looked as if Burke was the only discontented Whig in the Portland–Fox connection, which he had now left. Even his disciple Windham hesitated at first. The truth, however, was that Burke was right in thinking that Portland and many others did not share Fox's views on the French Revolution. But they were too attached to the idea of party unity to break publicly. In other words, they were too attached to the doctrine of the *Present Discontents*. Burke even suggested in a letter that he believed that Fox was himself more ambivalent than he appeared, but that it would be difficult for him '[t]o abandon all the young and energetick part of the Party, and the whole body of the Dissenters, upon whom he has lately built his principal hopes'.[144]

The French Revolution had yet to enter the era of violence which Burke had predicted – accurately as it turned out – in the *Reflections*. In September 1791, Louis XVI accepted the new French constitution. In the opening months of 1792 political societies dedicated to reform proliferated in Britain, many drawing on 'plebeian' support. The forming of the Association of the Friends of the People by younger Whig parliamentarians caused particular alarm among the Whig aristocrats.[145] Fitzwilliam would later write to Portland: 'I never will *act in party* with men who call in 40,000 weavers to dictate political measures to the Govt'.[146] Fox was caught between a rock and a hard place. In this new environment, Pitt invited Portland into discussions about measures to pacify the country. The Portland Whigs supported Pitt's Proclamation against seditious writings in May 1792. Astonishingly, this produced no 'rupture' and only

---

[142] Burke to Richard Burke Jr., 18 August 1791, *Correspondence*, VI, 360.
[143] Portland to French Laurence, 30 August 1791, Pw F 6241, University of Nottingham.
[144] Burke to William Burke, 3 September 1792, *Correspondence*, VII, 193.
[145] O'Gorman, *The Whig Party and the French Revolution*, 82–3.
[146] Fitzwilliam to Portland, 22 September 1793, WWM, F.31a.

'vexation' between Fox and Portland.[147] During the summer, the Portlands negotiated to join the government in a coalition with Pitt. Burke, from the sidelines, supported the attempts to form a coalition and even entertained the notion that Fox and Pitt could serve in the same cabinet for a while.[148] Fox, on his part, viewed Pitt's resignation from the Treasury as a *sine qua non*, although this was never formally proposed. It all ended in failure in any case. Portland was disappointed, writing to Burke that Henry Dundas's associates 'do not wish for power for the only purpose which makes that wish justifiable, They have no principle, They know not what *party* is, but for the desire of annihilating it'.[149] Burke would presumably once have agreed, but at this point his greatest fear was rather that Portland was 'more and more in Foxes power'.[150]

Fox had in fact tried to maintain a relatively moderate position on the French Revolution, seeking to persuade his colleagues that the domestic events of 1782–4 rather than French affairs ought to underpin the fundamental division in British politics. But events in France were to take a more extreme turn with the September Massacres of 1792. On 19 November, France made explicit its intention to export the Revolution. Loyal Associations were now formed in opposition to the reformist ones. However, unlike many of the Whig aristocracy, Fox remained convinced that the French did not pose a threat. In a speech at the Whig Club in December 1792, Fox declared himself openly 'to be an advocate for "*The Rights of the People*"'.[151] It was reported that Portland cheered the speech,[152] but the truth was that he had not heard it and wanted to disassociate himself from it.[153] A few months later, after the execution of Louis XVI, Burke, his son, and forty-one others signed an open letter withdrawing their names from the Whig Club because of their unhappiness with Fox's leadership.[154] The letter was meant to put pressure on the notoriously indecisive Portland to dissociate publicly from Fox. Against all odds, the connection between Fox and Portland remained for another twelve months. A self-styled 'Third Party' – led by Windham – had broken away, however, and the Old Whig party began to crumble.[155]

---

[147] Burke to William Burke, 3 September 1792, *Correspondence*, VII, 192.
[148] Burke to Loughborough, 13 June 1792, ibid., 151.
[149] Portland to Burke, 12 September 1792, ibid., 206.
[150] Burke to William Burke, 3 September 1792, ibid., 194.
[151] *The Speech of the Right Honourable C.J. Fox Containing the Declaration of his Principles, Respecting the Present Crisis of Public Affairs* (London, n.d. [1792]), 7.
[152] Ibid., 10.   [153] Wilkinson, *The Duke of Portland*, 93.
[154] Burke, *Correspondence*, VII, 353–5.
[155] O'Gorman, *The Whig Party and the French Revolution*, 121.

After Fox openly supported the Friends of the People in May 1793, and pushed for peace with France in June, the Portland Whigs moved closer to the 'Third Party'.[156] In the autumn, Burke wrote *Observations on the Conduct of the Minority*, addressed to Portland and Fitzwilliam. The pamphlet opened with a letter to the former, in which Burke wrote that '[n]o man can be connected with a party which professes publickly to admire, or may be justly suspected of secretly abetting the French Revolution'.[157] Whigs had been deluded into thinking of the revolution 'as an ordinary party squabble about place and patronage'. A general war against Jacobinism at home and abroad was the only way of 'saving Europe', according to Burke.[158] Portland responded that his and Burke's principles were 'exactly the same', but that he was 'not Christian enough to turn the other cheek to the man [Pitt] who has given me a blow nor can I lick the hand which has endeavoured to destroy me'.[159]

In January 1794, Portland finally took the step of committing himself to 'a full, firm, unequivocal support, both of the war and of its conductors'.[160] In essence, this meant that the Portland Whigs separated from the Foxites and joined Windham's 'Third Party'. Burke held out lingering hopes, in vain as it turned out, that Fox could be saved when 'he sees that the Body of his party is melting away very fast'.[161] According to Fox, the Portland Whigs supporting the administration equalled 'the separation, or rather the dissolution, of the Whig party'.[162] Portland himself was worried about breaking up the unity of the Whigs. His understanding of what the Whig party stood for was close to Burke's. In 1779, Burke had reported to Richard Shackleton that 'a very wise and a very good man, the Duke of Portland, said to me in a conversation on this Subject [of party], that he never knew any man disclaim party, who was not *of* a party, that he was ashamed of'.[163] He wrote to Windham in January 1794 that they must consider 'what our Duty to the publick requires us to do as Whigs, that is, as members of a Party, or as unconnected Individuals'.[164] The question was whether they should support the government from the outside or the inside, in other words, whether or not they should form an active coalition with Pitt. Burke had long tried to convince members of the opposition to

---

[156] Ibid., 135–6, 144–5.   [157] Burke, *Observations on the Conduct of the Minority*, *W&S*, VIII, 405.
[158] Ibid., 404.   [159] Portland to Burke, 10 October 1793, *Correspondence*, VII, 448.
[160] Windham to Burke, 19 January 1794, ibid., 526.
[161] Burke to Richard Burke, 10 January 1794, ibid., 515–16.
[162] Fox to Lord Holland, 9 March 1794, in *Fox Memorials*, III, 65.
[163] Burke to Shackleton, 25 May 1779, *Correspondence*, IV, 80.
[164] Portland to Windham, 11 January 1794, BL Add MS 37845, f. 17.

join the government in the war effort against France. Portland was hesitant about joining the administration, since he believed that it would hurt the party to which he was devoted.[165] As he wrote to Windham:

> '[T]he existence of a Whig Party is essential to the well being of this Country, as well as to the preservation of its Constitution, & allow me, my dear Windham, when the name of Whig has been so prostituted & counterfeited, as We have seen it, to deposit with you in a very few words my definition of The Whig Party, which I have always understood to be, an Union [sic] of any number of persons of independent minds & fortunes formed & connected together by their belief in the principles upon which the Revolution of 1688 was founded & perfected; & by the attachment to the present form of our Government to all its Establishments & Orders Religious and Civil.[166]

Part of Portland's reluctance to join the administration stemmed from his understanding of party and the importance of an independent aristocracy. His differences with George III on this score went back to the beginning of the reign, and this had remained more important for Portland than for Burke. '[T]he characteristick feature of the present Reign has been to ... debase & vilify the natural aristocracy of the Country, &, under the proper pretence of abolishing all party distinctions, to annihilate, if possible, The Whig Party.'[167] At the same time, supporting the war without joining the government would 'vindicate the cause of Whiggism', which he, like Burke, feared had been hijacked by Fox and his followers.[168]

In the event, however, leading members of the Portlands joined Pitt's administration in the early summer of 1794. Portland had changed his mind and was now convinced that 'the true Spirit of Aristocracy and the true Principles of Whiggism may be revived and re-established' if his party joined the coalition.[169] Fitzwilliam conceded that even though the formation of Pitt's government had originally been 'destructive of true Whiggism', a coalition could become 'the cause of the renewal of power in an Aristocratic Whig party'.[170] Portland's and Fitzwilliam's understanding of the importance of aristocratic party was similar to Burke's. They did

---

[165] Ibid., ff. 20–1.   [166] Ibid., f. 18.

[167] Ibid. Whigs frequently lamented that the sharp rise in ennoblements in the late eighteenth century was part of a conscious attempt on the part of George III and Pitt to weaken the independent aristocracy; see Mitchell, *The Whig World* (London, 2005), 22–4.

[168] Portland to Windham, 11 January 1794, BL Add MS 37845, f. 23.

[169] Portland to Fitzwilliam, 14 June 1794. WWM, F.31b.

[170] Fitzwilliam to Portland, 15 June 1794. WWM, F.31b.

not advocate for the ascendency of a distinct interest but of an independent section of society, held together by party loyalty, and with sufficient wealth and virtue to stand up to the monarch and the people alike to preserve the balance in the constitution and the prosperity of all. Despite Portland's and Fitzwilliam's resolution that the coalition would not sound the death knell of the party, the press reported this development as a coalition between Whigs and Tories which extinguished these older labels and introduced the new ones of royalists and republicans.[171]

In the coalition, Portland became home secretary, Windham secretary at war, Spencer Lord Privy Seal, and Fitzwilliam Lord President of the Council, with a promise to take over the Irish policy as soon as expedient. The 2nd Earl of Mansfield (before 1793, the Viscount Stormont) took a seat in the cabinet without portfolio. The Whigs now made up around half of the positions in the efficient cabinet which had been in development during George III's reign.[172] Portland had to use all his skills of persuasion to make sure that his key political allies accepted office. Burke, having stood down from parliament in June, played no official role in the new coalition, but he supported it and offered advice on Irish politics in particular, which came under the Portland Whigs' remit. On the news of naval victories in June 1794, Portland wrote to Burke that the British were finally 'advancing to restore Order Religion and Law to that unhappy Country and tranquillity and security to the rest of the civilized World'.[173] 'Order, religion and law' were also key words in Burke's correspondence and pamphlets at this time, but he stressed that they were not new concerns. For Burke, as for Hume, order had a close relationship with liberty, which is discussed in Chapter 13. In *A Letter to a Noble Lord* (1796), Burke argued that the Rockinghams had loved liberty as much as the aristocrats such as Bedford and Lauderdale who were favourable towards the French Revolution. 'The Liberty they [the Rockinghams] pursued was a Liberty inseparable from order, from virtue, from morals, and from religion'. What this meant in practice was '[t]o preserve the Constitution entire ... not in one single part, but in all it's parts [sic]'.[174]

Burke supported the Portlands' joining the government. He had earlier said in private that the pamphlets he had written since his split with Fox had 'one single principle to guide me – namely that the extinction of

---

[171] Mitchell, *Fox and the Disintegration of the Whig Party*, 237.

[172] On this, see Christie, *Myth and Reality*, ch. 2.

[173] Portland to Burke, 11 June 1794, *Correspondence*, VII, 549.

[174] Burke, *Letter to a Noble Lord*, *W&S*, IX, 153.

Jacobinism in France was the sole worthy object of Arms and politicks of this time'.[175] The mid-1790s was the time when Immanuel Kant and others wrote famous essays on perpetual peace, following the Abbé de St Pierre earlier in the century. Burke did not write about perpetual peace but rather about war against the French. In the War of the Spanish Succession, peace with France had been a Tory policy, whereas the Whigs had prioritised protecting the Protestant interest and the balance of power in Europe.[176] As we saw in Chapter 9, such considerations still impacted Newcastle's disagreement with Bute at the conclusion of the Seven Years' War. At least it was an argument to which Newcastle resorted, and it was crucial in turning Portland away from Fox. In November 1792, Portland wrote to Fitzwilliam: '[Fox] is in a manner insensible to the effects of the increasing power of France & to that lust of Dominion which is to me as evident in their present Republican Government as in the Zenith of their Monarchical Glory.'[177]

Burke returned to this orthodox Whiggism in his *Letters on a Regicide Peace* (1795–7), written at the end of his life. Burke had been committed to the idea that Britain must defeat France on the battlefield since his *Letter to a Member of the National Assembly* in May 1791. The key was to make sure that the Protestant powers – chiefly Britain, Prussia, and the Dutch – and Catholic Austria, would counterweigh the power and influence of France, the greatest power in Europe. Burke's *Reflections* is often seen as a defence of the French *ancien régime*. In the last years of his life we can see that Burke was as worried about French preponderance in Europe as the early Whigs had been. The spectre of the universal monarchy of Louis XIV had been replaced by the threat of the universal doctrine of Jacobinism. By contrast, Fox viewed war against France as part of a scheme to extend the power of the executive in Britain.[178] Both sides could be interpreted as holding on to Whig orthodoxy, and both sides could accuse each other of apostasy.[179]

Portland's biographer has argued that the Duke in office made the transition into a nineteenth-century Tory in the coalition government and later as prime minister in 1807–9.[180] Rockingham's widow was confounded when Portland and Fitzwilliam joined the government in

---

[175] Burke to Loughborough, 13 January 1794, *Correspondence*, VII, 517–18.
[176] See also Chapter 5.   [177] Portland to Fitzwilliam, 30 November 1792, WWM, F.31a.
[178] Mitchell, *Fox and the Disintegration of the Whig Party*, 217–18.
[179] The Whig response to the French Revolution is more one-sidedly summarised in Mitchell, *The Whig World*, 86–7.
[180] Wilkinson, *The Duke of Portland*, 138.

1794. For her, it 'seems such a completion of Lord Bute's system at the first of this reign, *to blend Whig and Tory, to break all connection* and to disperse *all parties*'.[181] This is what the Rockinghams and their inheritors the Portlands had resisted since the early days of her husband's leadership.[182] As we have seen, Portland had only a few years earlier expressed the same worries to Burke. What made matters worse was that Lady Rockingham viewed the Pitt administration as Tory. This is also how the Portland Whigs had become accustomed to think of Pitt. He had been their ideological counterpart and was viewed as a Court creature, as evidenced in 1783–4. For Burke and now also Portland, however, the struggle against the French Revolutionaries at home and abroad to save the British constitution and the balance of power in Europe took precedence over old party battles. Burke and Portland thus helped bury the party names which they, and especially the former, had helped revive in the 1760s and 1770s. As Portland's followers either died, retired, moved to the Lords, or abandoned their leader, the Portland connection was reduced to a tiny faction, and by the time he led the government in 1807–9, he relied on Pittites and the 'king's men'. It should be remembered, however, that the Foxite rump was not much more impressive, with Fox mustering only forty-four votes, mainly representing rotten boroughs, in favour of his motion for peace on 10 May 1796. The size of his following in the years after the Whig schism has been estimated at around fifty-five MPs.[183]

Had the Whigs become Tories or the Tories Whigs? This was the question people asked at the time. Fox's nephew, Lord Holland, for instance, suggested that 'the Duke of Por: ... may call & think himself a Whig & yet be a Tory'.[184] But only a Foxite would maintain that the Portlands had abandoned the Whigs. From Burke's and (eventually) Portland's perspective it was Fox who was the deserter of the Whig cause. It can indeed be argued that the split between Portland and Fox, foreshadowed first by Burke's 'disownment' and later by Windham's breakaway party, ended the eighteenth-century Whig party, and the last vestiges of the eighteenth-century party framework.[185] The principle of party, promoted by Burke, had kept it alive for longer than most observers in the early 1760s would have predicted. The party names were so

---

[181] Cited in ibid., 139.
[182] Mitchell's *Fox and the Disintegration of the Whig Party* puts plenty of emphasis on the formative events of 1782–4, but Lady Rockingham's remarks remind us that many leading Whigs were thinking about party battles in an even larger framework.
[183] Ibid., 247.   [184] Holland to Caroline Fox, 9 November 1792, BL Add MS 51731, f. 99.
[185] Mitchell, *Fox and the Disintegration of the Whig Party*, 166, 183, 205–6.

entrenched that a new party framework would later emerge in the nine-teenth century with the same names. Most recent research has rightly stressed Burke's lifelong commitment to Whiggism.[186] Towards the end of his life, however, there are some minor signs of Burke entering 'Toryland', as James Sack puts it in a noteworthy study of the creation of British conservatism.[187] Writing to an unnamed correspondence in an undated letter, probably composed in the wake of the *Appeal*, Burke said that if his principles 'are Tory principles, I should always wish to be thought a Tory'.[188] But this was a restatement of Burke's commitment to consis-tency in principle, which he believed to be more important than the changing meaning of party names. As he stressed in the same letter: '[w]hether [my principles] are allowed to be Whigg principles, or not, is a very small part of my concern. I think of them exactly such as the sober, honourable, and intelligent in that party [the Whigs], have always pro-fessed.'[189] In his *Fourth Letter on a Regicide Peace* (1795), Burke referred to '*us* poor Tory geese'.[190] This humorous remark alluded to a famous story with roots in Livy, whereby the crackling of geese woke Manlius to defend Rome against the Gauls. It is likely to be a tongue-in-cheek comment with a nod to Alexander Pope's *Dunciad*, in which Pope turned 'The silver goose before the shining gate | There flew, and, by her crackle, sav'd the state', from Dryden's Virgil, into 'rob the *Roman* geese of all their glories, | And save the state by crackling to the Tories'.[191] Burke was an eighteenth-century Whig who believed that the French Revolution and its consequences took precedence over older party divisions. Moreover, his support for Catholic emancipation and his Irishness in general made him an unlikely hero figure among Tories before 1830.[192]

Fox was also an eighteenth-century Whig, who, in contrast with Burke, interpreted the British response to French events as a continuation of older party disputes.[193] The Whig cause understood as restraining the executive had not lost its relevance, according to Fox. 'I remain of opinion . . . that

---

[186] Bourke, *Empire and Revolution*; Clark, 'Introduction', 23–48; Bromwich, *The Intellectual Life of Burke* (Cambridge, MA, 2014), 19.

[187] Sack, *From Jacobite to Conservative*, 66n13.

[188] Burke to [Dr Richard Brocklesby?], n.d. [1791–2?], *Correspondence*, IX, 446.   [189] Ibid.

[190] Burke, *Fourth Letter on a Regicide Peace*, *W&S*, IX, 105. (My emphasis.)

[191] Virgil, *Aeneid*, trans. Dryden (New York, NY 1909), 294; Pope, *The Dunciad* (London, 1728), 14.

[192] Sack, 'The Memory of Pitt and the Memory of Burke', *HJ*, 30 (1987), 623–40.

[193] Note that Fox has and can be interpreted as carrying on the 'reform' agenda of earlier Tory-Jacobite oppositions. His friend the Earl of Carlisle wrote of him: 'He was ever in his heart more inclined to Tory, than what in these times are called Whig principles.' Cited in Hilton, *A Mad, Bad, and Dangerous People*, 50. Many Tories and former Jacobites, including Samuel Johnson, supported Fox against Pitt; see Sack, *From Jacobite to Conservative*, 82.

party is by far the best instrument, if not the only one, for supporting the cause of liberty in this country', he wrote to Lord Holland a few months into the life of the Portland–Pitt coalition.[194] Party persisted as the supreme instrument for standing up to the monarchy, he argued in a Burkean fashion, almost *plus royaliste que le roi*, even though he cited Hume's phrase of the 'euthanasia of absolute monarch' in the letter. Fox was now worried that this instrument risked being destroyed, and he held that his duty was 'to use the utmost endeavours to preserve together what little remains of this system [of party], or to revive it if it is supposed to be quite extinct'.[195] Fox conceded that the party may become divided again in the future since he believed that people are fundamentally driven by interest and ambition. When politicians act in party, however, they would be less frequently tempted with office and allurements. 'In short, it appears to me that a party spirit is the only substitute that has been found, or can be found, for public virtue and comprehensive understanding; neither of which can be reasonably expected to be found in a very great number of people', Fox concluded.[196] In the same letter, he also cited from Rockingham's epithet, written by Burke: 'his virtues were his means'.[197]

We should note, however, that Burke – somewhat surprisingly considering the role he had played – shared Fox's fears that the coalition had wrecked party. Burke was far from content with Portland's performance in the coalition. As originally promised, Fitzwilliam became Lord Lieutenant of Ireland six months into the coalition, in December 1794. However, supporting full Catholic emancipation to the horror of the administration in Britain, he was recalled after only a few months in the position. Burke, who also supported emancipation, was distraught over the sacrifice of Fitzwilliam and the cause of the Catholics, describing Portland as 'the very man who destroyed the Catholicks, and his own friend [Fitzwilliam], and himself, for ever'.[198] In a letter to Fitzwilliam in September 1796, Burke argued that the coalition had indeed destroyed party. 'I was in serious hopes that party which was at last rallied under its proper standard ... might, either in Ministry, or out of Ministry ... become some sort of Asylum for principles moral and political', he wrote to Rockingham's nephew and heir. Instead, politics had evolved into a straight choice between Pitt and Fox. 'This extinguishes party, as party ... Every thing is forced into the shape of a mere faction, and a

---

[194] Fox to Lord Holland, 5 October 1794, *Fox Memorials*, III, 88.   [195] Ibid., 89.
[196] Ibid., 90.   [197] Ibid., 91. The inscription actually says: 'his virtues were his arts'.
[198] Burke to Bishop Hussey, 27 November 1795, *Correspondence*, VIII, 352.

contest for nothing short, in substance and effect, than the sovereign authority, for one or the other of the chieftains', Burke lamented.[199] He added that he believed Britain would be 'undone' under either leader, but 'much more certainly, much more rapidly, and in a way beyond cure' under Fox.[200] It has been argued that Burke rejected party,[201] and in a way he did, but it was only because he believed that the Whigs in coalition had not lived up to his expectations of principle and loyalty.

The fundamental disagreement and schism within the Whigs at the end of the eighteenth century close this chapter in the history of party. Many of the 'old Whigs' – including Windham but crucially not Portland, who turned into a royal servant – returned to the Foxite opposition a few years after Burke's death, but this alliance was fragile.[202] Since Burke (unlike Fox) at least occasionally appeared to argue that the old parties had become irrelevant, it was naturally Fox rather than Burke who became synonymous with Whiggery, although this point could be exaggerated. While nineteenth-century Whigs regretted the split between Fox and Burke, they continued to regard Burke as providing the intellectual foundations for the still important ideal of aristocratic independence under the banner of the Whig party, and cite the *Present Discontents* as setting out the theory of party solidarity.[203] In Chapter 13, the final chapter of this book, Burke's political thought is considered in the context of some of the earlier thinkers discussed in this book, along with others, with particular emphasis on what is known as the Scottish Enlightenment.

---

[199] Burke to Fitzwilliam, 2 September 1796, ibid., IX, 78.   [200] Ibid., 79.
[201] O'Gorman, *The Whig Party and the French Revolution*, 234.
[202] Smith, *Whig Principles and Party Politics* (Manchester, 1975), ch. 9.
[203] See, e.g., Russell, *Essay on the History of the English Government and Constitution* (London, 1823), 178–9. See also Jones, *Burke and the Invention of Modern Conservatism* (Oxford, 2017), 28–34.

CHAPTER 13

Burke and the Scottish Enlightenment

The spirit of party prevails less in Scotland than in England.
Adam Smith, The Wealth of Nations (1776)

Burke and the Scots

Following the work of Isaiah Berlin and others, Burke is often read as a counter-Enlightenment thinker.[1] One of his late twentieth-century editors, for example, writes that Burke 'all[ied] himself with the ancients, with classical modes of education and feeling, against the Enlightenment'.[2] But Burke was not the only 'enlightenment' luminary to be confounded by the French Revolution. Edward Gibbon was equally appalled, and it eventually disappointed the likes of Paine and Sieyès as well.[3] Throughout his life, Burke moved in literary circles, and he had particularly interesting connections with what has become known as the Scottish Enlightenment. The Scottish thinkers particularly relevant for Burke were the usual suspects, especially Hume, Adam Smith, Adam Ferguson, and William Robertson. Burke liked travelling to Scotland, and in 1784 he was named Lord Rector of the University of Glasgow, although by this stage Smith had long been succeeded by Thomas Reid in the professorship of moral philosophy.[4]

---

[1] Berlin, 'The Counter-Enlightenment' (1973), in *Against the Current* (London, 1979), 1–32. Bourke's *Empire and Revolution* (Princeton, 2015) has pushed back significantly against this interpretation. See also Himmelfarb, *The Roads to Modernity* (London, 2008 [2004]), 71–92.

[2] Burke, *Further Reflections on the Revolution in France*, ed. Daniel E. Ritchie (Indianapolis, 1992), 28.

[3] For discussion, see Whatmore, 'Rights after the Revolutions', in *Philosophy, Rights and Natural Law* (Edinburgh, 2019), 338–65.

[4] Burke dined with Smith in Edinburgh after his ceremonial admission at Glasgow in 1785; see *The Diary of Windham* (London, 1866), 64.

Although Burke was more eager to stress the negative aspects of party after his split with Fox, he never juxtaposed 'party' and the 'common good' in the way Josiah Tucker had done.[5] In the *Third Letter on a Regicide Peace* (1797), written towards the end of his life, Burke gave his most non-partisan statement in favour of parties. He now argued that the old Whig and Tory parties had sustained the British mixed and balanced constitution 'by their collision and mutual resistance'.[6] Richard Bourke has cited this passage to signal intellectual distance between Burke (and Montesquieu) on the one hand, and Hume on the other.[7] However, Burke's words are reminiscent of a key quotation from Hume's *History of England*,[8] even if Hume speaks of the Court and Country parties, as giving 'life and vigour' to politics (rather than Whig and Tory). In Chapter 7, I suggested that this phrasing in Hume's *History* may have been inspired by a similar wording in Montesquieu's *Spirit of Laws*. Which one of them influenced Burke's argument is more difficult to determine – perhaps both or neither. The key point is that it brings these three thinkers together on the question of party. Towards the end of his life, freed from party allegiance, Burke once again adopted the kind of independent analysis of politics, which no doubt had characterised his entire career to an extent, but which was particularly marked in the 1750s and 1790s when he was out of parliament.

Robert Bisset, Burke's first biographer, wrote at length about Burke's low opinion of Hume. He speculated that Burke had early planned to refute Hume's sceptical philosophy (along with Berkeley's).[9] This is not entirely implausible, but we have reasons to believe that Burke's engagement with Hume's writings was respectful even if it was occasionally critical. The *Annual Register*, with which Burke was continuously associated, wrote highly of Hume after his death, calling his *History* 'one of the most excellent productions of human genius, and . . . certainly the greatest

---

[5] Tucker, *Treatise Concerning Civil Government* (London, 1781), 254.
[6] Burke, *W&S*, IX, 326. This statement anticipates Butterfield's classic argument *against* Whig history: '[The Whig historian] is apt to imagine the British constitution as coming down to us by virtue of the work of long generations of whigs and in spite of the obstructions of a long line of tyrants and tories. In reality it is the result of the continual interplay and perpetual collision of the two.' See *The Whig Interpretation of History* (New York, 1965 [1931]), 41. It is also noteworthy that Burke in the same context refers to the Glorious Revolution as a 'union' between Whigs and Tories rather than a Whig affair.
[7] Bourke, *Empire and Revolution*, 22–3. In other respects, Bourke has made a strong case for Hume's actual influence on Burke; see, e.g., ibid., 193.
[8] Hume, *History*, V, 556.
[9] Bisset, *The Life of Burke* (2 vols., London, second edn., 1800), I, 33, 77.

historical work of modern times'.[10] The entry made no references to Hume's irreligion, and sided with the Scotsman over Rousseau in their famous quarrel. In the *Reflections*, Burke reported a conversation he had had with Hume about Rousseau,[11] and in a later publication he said that he 'had good opportunities of knowing [Rousseau's] proceedings almost from day to day' when he was in England in 1766, presumably from Hume, who had taken Rousseau under his wing before they dramatically fell out.[12] It is fairly evident that Burke's acquaintance with Hume did not develop into a close friendship as was the case with Smith, although it was actually Hume who introduced the two to each other. Later in life, Burke seems to have suggested that he had indeed been the person Hume had had in mind when he wrote of an 'Irish Catholic, who denies the massacre in 1641'.[13] At one point, however, Hume told Smith that he was 'very well-acquainted' with Burke and described him to friends as 'a very ingenious Irish gentleman'.[14]

Burke shared with Hume several basic philosophical and political commitments. When Burke wrote that 'reason is but a part and by no means the greatest part' of human nature, he came close to Hume's infamous statement that '[r]eason is, and ought only to be the slave of the passions'.[15] Moreover, he agreed with Hume that government is ultimately founded on opinion, as well as on the importance of balancing liberty and authority.[16] Hume's most explicit statement on the interrelationship of liberty and authority was his posthumous 'Of the Origin of Government' (1777), published after Burke had linked them in his *Speech at Arrival at Bristol* (13 October 1774), which he auto-cited in the *Appeal*.[17] As we saw in Chapter 12, the linkage between order and liberty became important in the critical circumstances of the 1790s, for Burke and the likes of Portland. As Burke put it in the *Appeal*: 'none, except those who are profoundly studied, can comprehend the elaborate contrivance of a fabric fitted to unite private and public liberty with public force, with order, with peace, with justice, and, above all, with the institutions formed for bestowing

---

[10] *The Annual Register for the year 1776* (London, 1777), 31.

[11] Burke, *Reflections*, *W&S*, VIII, 219.

[12] Burke, *Letter to a Member of the National Assembly* (1791), ibid., 314.

[13] Bisset, *The Life of Burke*, II, 426; Hume, *History*, IV, 395.

[14] Hume to Smith, 28 July 1759 and Hume to Hugh Blair, 19 September 1763, *Letters*, I, 312, 400.

[15] Burke, *Observations*, *Works*, II, 196; Hume, *Treatise*, 415. See also Burke, *Philosophical Enquiry*, *Works*, I, 221.

[16] For Burke's agreement with Hume on the importance of 'opinion' in government, see *Letter to the Sheriffs of Bristol* (1777), *W&S*, III, 314–15.

[17] Hume, 'Of the Origin of Government', *Essays*, 40–1; Burke, *W&S*, III, 59, IV, 394.

permanence and stability through ages'.[18] In a letter he explained his intention of the *Reflections* as 'to distinguish the Ideas of a sober and virtuous Liberty, (such as I thought our party had ever cultivated) from that profligate, immoral, impious, and rebellious Licence, which, through the medium of every sort of disorder and calamity, conducts to some kind or other of Tyrannick domination'.[19]

This was a fairly standard establishment Whig doctrine, and had indeed been prefigured by Court Whig writers before Hume.[20] Hume would, however, have been a natural interlocutor for Burke. The influence of Hume on Burke was stressed by Friedrich Meinecke and G.H. Sabine in the middle of the twentieth century but this was criticised by Pocock since they could not show that Burke had read Hume at a critical time.[21] Considering their acquaintance in the 1750s, it is likely that he had, however. There are not only echoes of Hume in Burke's writings but also citations, for example in Burke's *Letter to the Sheriffs of Bristol* (1777), where he quotes from Hume's essay 'Of Civil Liberty'.[22] There are also many instances where Burke cites Hume in respectful disagreement in a way which suggests careful engagement, as in *Thoughts on French Affairs* (1791).[23] In the *Reflections*, Burke repeated many familiar Humean arguments, including the critique of enthusiasm,[24] and the relationship between democracy and Caesarism.[25] Moreover, Burke's moderate defence of resistance to government shares similarities with Hume's. For both, resistance could only be justified on the basis of necessity, and they both stressed that '[t]he superlative line of demarcation, where obedience ought to end, and resistance must begin, is faint, obscure, and not easily definable'.[26]

The similarities between Hume and Burke should not be exaggerated. For most of his life, Burke was a partisan and a rather conventional Whig. Moreover, Burke, who remained friends with Samuel Johnson despite

---

[18] Burke, *Appeal*, *W&S*, IV, 473.

[19] Burke to William Weddell, 31 January 1792, *Correspondence*, VII, 55.

[20] Browning, 'The Origin of Burke's Ideas Revisited', *ECS*, 18 (1984), 66n.

[21] Pocock, *Politics, Language and Time* (Cambridge, 1989 [1971]), 203–4.

[22] Burke, *W&S*, III, 299.   [23] Burke, *W&S*, VIII, 369.

[24] Pocock, 'Political Thought in the English-speaking Atlantic', *The Varieties of British Political Thoughts* (Cambridge, 1994), 304.

[25] Bourke, 'Popular Sovereignty and Political Representation', *Popular Sovereignty in Historical Perspective* (Cambridge, 2017), 229–30.

[26] Burke, *Reflections*, *W&S*, VIII, 81; Hume, 'Of Passive Obedience', *Essays*, 490; Hume, *History*, V, 544–6.

their political differences, appears to have shared Johnson's suspicion of Hume's irreligion. Burke's personal faith was sincere, and he further thought religion to be vital for society.[27] However, he was against the readiness of High Churchmen *and* Radical Dissenters such as Richard Price to mix politics and religion, writing in the *Reflections* that '[p]olitics and the pulpit are terms that have little agreement. No sound ought to be heard in the church but the healing voice of Christian charity.'[28]

Superficially, Burke's belief in the 'ancient constitution' might appear to have had more in common with Bolingbroke than Hume. When we examine the details, however, we see that this is not the case. In a draft of a parliamentary speech, Burke rejected the Bolingbrokean 'ancient constitution' argument in favour of reform. The county movement, including the Younger Pitt as well as writers such as Major Cartwright and James Burgh, justified reform on the basis that the constitution had fallen away from its original principles.[29] This had been a fundamental principle of Bolingbroke's Country party opposition, which continued to inspire writers around this time.[30] For Burke, the constitution could not be restored to its original principles because '[a] prescriptive government, such as ours, never was the work of any legislator, never was made upon any foregone theory'.[31] We can only know the principles of the constitution from its structure and since it is 'immemorial', we know little about its original foundation. As Pocock pointed out, this is reminiscent of seventeenth-century common lawyers such as Matthew Hale.[32] It has little to do with the ancient constitutionalism of Bolingbroke, largely derived from Rapin and used for accusing Walpole's Whigs of corruption. Burke's response to the Bolingbrokean argument was different from Hume's, who, like Hervey before him and Josiah Tucker afterwards,[33] held that the past was barbarous and irrelevant. But Burke's was nevertheless a different and less bold take on the ancient constitution than Bolingbroke's.[34]

Burke's understanding of society and politics was similar not only to Hume's but to that of many eighteenth-century Scottish thinkers. Although the Scottish literati had many differences, they shared

---

[27] Harris, 'Burke and Religion', *The Cambridge Companion to Burke*, 92–103.
[28] Burke, *Reflections*, *W&S*, VIII, 62.   [29] Pocock, *Politics, Language and Time*, 229.
[30] His continued salience is reflected in [de Lolme?], *Essays on Constitutional Liberty* (London, 1780).
[31] Burke, *Speech on Parliamentary Reform*, 16 June 1784 [previously dated as 7 May 1782], *W&S*, IV, 220.
[32] Pocock, *Politics, Language and Time*, 228–9.   [33] Ibid., 248.
[34] As Pocock has rightly stressed, Burke's English common-law thinking is a significant area where Burke and 'the great Scottish theorists' talked past each other; see *Virtue, Commerce, and History*, 297–8.

commitments to empiricism and wrote philosophical works about the history of human nature and civilisations.[35] Burke's major contribution to aesthetics and philosophy, his *Philosophical Enquiry into the Origin of Our Ideas of the Sublime and Beautiful* (1757), infused with ideas of sentiment and feeling, fits neatly with the works produced by the Scottish literati in the second half of the eighteenth century. Like Smith in *Theory of Moral Sentiments* (1759), Burke gave sympathy a major role, calling it one of the three main links in 'the great chain of society'.[36] Hume referred to Burke's book as 'a very pretty Treatise' in a letter to Smith.[37] He also gave a copy of Smith's *Theory of Moral Sentiments* to Burke in the year of its publication. 'I am not only pleased with the ingenuity of your Theory', Burke wrote to Smith, 'I am convinced of its solidity and Truth'.[38] His review of the book in the *Annual Register* was similarly enthusiastic, calling it 'one of the most beautiful fabrics of moral theory, that has perhaps ever appeared'.[39] According to Smith's student Dugald Stewart, Smith had been equally admiring of Burke's *Philosophical Enquiry*.[40]

The *Annual Register*'s positive review of the *Wealth of Nations* is believed to have been written by Burke. The close intellectual affinity between Burke and Smith is worth emphasising, especially since there is a tradition in the intellectual history of political economy which emphasises their differences.[41] Burke and Smith appear not to have met in person until 1775, but they eventually formed a longstanding friendship, with Burke addressing Smith as 'My dear friend'.[42] Smith is believed to have said that Burke 'was the only man, who, without communication, thought on these topics [political economy] exactly as he did'.[43] It is further likely that Burke had Smith and the *Wealth of Nations* in mind (especially its later editions with additional material on India) when he

---

[35] The best works which treat the eighteenth-century Scots as one unit are those of Berry, including *The Idea of Commercial Society in the Scottish Enlightenment* (Edinburgh, 2015) and *The Social Theory of the Scottish Enlightenment* (Edinburgh, 1997). These works downplay the differences between the various Scottish thinkers, however.

[36] Burke, *Philosophical Enquiry*, W&S, I, 220.   [37] Hume to Smith, 12 April 1759, *New Letters*, 51.

[38] Burke to Smith, 10 September 1759, *Correspondence*, I, 129.

[39] *The Annual Register ... for the year 1759* (London, sixth edn., 1777), 485.

[40] Bourke, *Empire and Revolution*, 139–40.

[41] Stedman Jones, *An End to Poverty?* (London, 2004); Rothschild, *Economic Sentiments* (Cambridge, MA, 2001); Winch, *Riches and Poverty* (Cambridge, 1996); Winch, *Adam Smith's Politics* (Cambridge, 1978), 187.

[42] Burke to Smith, 7 December 1786, *Correspondence*, V, 296–7.

[43] Bisset, *The Life of Burke*, II, 429.

said in *A Letter to a Noble Lord* (1796) that '[g]reat and learned men thought my studies [in political economy] were not wholly thrown away, and deigned to communicate with me now and then on some particulars of their immortal works'.[44] Burke's posthumous *Thoughts and Details on Scarcity* (1800) is a classic statement of enlightenment free market economic theory, but the importance of free trade for Burke goes at least as far back as his *Speech on Conciliation with America* (1775).[45] Smith may have indirectly referred to the French Revolution in the last edition of his *Theory of Moral Sentiments* when he criticised the 'man of system'.[46] A comparable analysis was part of Burke's hostile views of the revolutionaries.[47]

Burke also wrote a positive review of Ferguson's *Essay on the History of Civil Society* (1767) in the *Annual Register*. In the *Appeal*, Burke repeated one of the key phrases and arguments from Ferguson's *Essay*: '[a]rt is man's nature'.[48] Ferguson has sometimes been interpreted as a republican nostalgic, but he was committed to modernity on balance.[49] One illustration of this is his discussion of the 'system of chivalry' – the 'marvellous respect and veneration to the fair sex' – which meant that the moderns had 'greatly excelled any of the celebrated nations of antiquity'.[50] Robertson produced a more extensive but overall similar analysis in his celebrated introductory essay to *The History of Charles V* (1769), as did John Millar in *The Origin of the Distinction of Ranks* (1771).[51] When writing about chivalry in his *Reflections*, Burke drew on a panoply of Scottish Enlightenment arguments, including these Scottish histories of chivalry.[52]

Robertson asked his printer William Strahan to send a copy of the *History of America* (1777) to Burke, describing him as 'one of the best judges in the Kingdom of the subject on which it is written'. Burke was enthusiastic about the performance, and demonstrated his awareness of

---

[44] Burke, *W&S*, IX, 160.   [45] Burke, *W&S*, III, 137–8.

[46] Smith, *The Theory of Moral Sentiments* (Indianapolis, 1982), 233–4. An alternative interpretation is that this refers to the Physiocrats. For the best reading, combining the two perspectives, see Hont, *Jealousy of Trade*, ch. 5.

[47] See, e.g., Burke, *Appeal W&S*, IV, 460.

[48] Ibid., 449; Ferguson, *Essay on the History of Civil Society* (Cambridge, 1995 [1767]), 12.

[49] Smith, *Adam Ferguson and the Idea of Civil Society* (Edinburgh, 2019).

[50] Ferguson, *Essay*, 191–3.

[51] Robertson, *The History of the Reign of the Emperor Charles V* (4 vols., London, 1802 [1769]), I, 82–6; Millar, *The Origin of the Distinction of Ranks* (Indianapolis, 2006 [1771]), 142.

[52] Pocock, 'Political Thought in the English-Speaking Atlantic', 304–5; Winch, *Riches and Poverty*, 175–85.

Robertson's other historical works when thanking Robertson for the book: 'Every thing has been done which was so naturally to be expected from the author of the History of Scotland and the Age of Charles the fifth.'[53] Burke's letter to Robertson reveals his continued interest in enlightenment writings about stages of civilisation:

> We need no longer go to History to trace [human nature] in all its stages and periods ... now the Great Map of Mankind is unrolled at once; and there is no state or Gradation of barbarism, and no mode of refinement, which we have not at the same instant under our View ... You have employd Philosophy to judge on Manners; and from manners you have drawn resources for Philosophy.[54]

In return, Burke sent Robertson his *Letter to the Sheriffs of Bristol*, almost apologising for sending 'a triffling temporary production, made for the occasion of a day, and to perish with it, in return for your immortal Work'.[55]

When postulating that Burke was particularly influenced by Scottish thought, we should bear in mind that the Scottish Enlightenment did not have a unified political programme in party-political terms. Many of them were active in the 'moderate party' in the Scottish Kirk. Indeed, Robertson was for many years its leader.[56] Many were 'Whig' in the general sense of defending the Glorious Revolution, the Union of 1707, and the Protestant Succession. Others (James Steuart) were Jacobites. Some were associated with the Rockingham and later Foxite Whigs (John Millar), others with Lord North's administration (Ferguson). They reacted in different ways to the American War and, the ones who survived, to the French Revolution. Hume and Smith appear to have stayed largely clear of party politics. Shelburne attempted to patronise both Hume and Smith with little luck. Thanks to his association with the Hertford/Conway family, Hume worked in the Northern Department in the Chatham administration despite despising its leader. Many of his political friends in his youth had been opposition Whigs and Jacobites, and many in his later life belonged to the 'king's men'. There was not one unified political thought in eighteenth-century Scotland just as there has not been one in any other century. The Scottish Enlightenment was to a large extent characterised by political disagreement.

There was no set attitude to political parties among the Scottish literati. No one was more intrigued by the politics of party than Hume and his contribution to the debate about party has been investigated at length

---

[53] Burke to Robertson, 9 June 1777, *Correspondence*, III, 350.   [54] Ibid., 351.   [55] Ibid., 352.
[56] See, especially, Sher, *Church and University in the Scottish Enlightenment* (Edinburgh, 2015 [1985]).

earlier in this book. I have treated Ferguson's writings on party elsewhere, and concluded that he was more negative about party, especially the form of opposition party embodied by the Rockingham Whigs and defended by Burke, than the previous literature has suggested.[57] As noted by Duncan Forbes, most of what Smith had to say about the origin and principles of the Tory and Whig parties in the *Lectures on Jurisprudence* was taken from Hume's *Essays*.[58] This is not the only discussion of factionalism in Smith's works, however. In the next section, we take a closer look at Smith's engagement with the subject.

Smith on Faction

Smith's attitude towards the Glorious Revolution was more Whiggish than Hume's, and although the two are often bundled together, Smith is better described as a more straightforward Whig.[59] At least, this is the case if we consider the student notes of his lectures on jurisprudence. There is a streak in Smith, however, which is deeply critical of 'party spirit' as such, a hostility he shared with his teacher Francis Hutcheson, and indeed with his friend Hume.[60] In short, party spirit impaired the moral sense, the hinge of Hutcheson's moral philosophy, and perverted 'our Natural Notions of Good and Evil'.[61] Like Hutcheson's, Smith's moral philosophy had a political dimension. Similarly to Hutcheson, Smith believed party spirit to be destructive of his moral system as set out in *The Theory of Moral Sentiments*. 'Of all the corrupters of moral sentiments … faction and fanaticism have always been by far the greatest', Smith wrote.[62] The reason was that '[a] true party-man hates and despises candour; and, in reality, there is no vice which could so effectually disqualify him for the trade of a party-man as that single virtue'.[63] 'The … impartial spectator', Smith continued, 'is, upon no occasion, at a greater distance than amidst the violence and rage of contending parties.'[64] Like Rapin, Smith highlighted

---

[57] Skjönsberg, 'Adam Ferguson on Partisanship, Party Conflict, and Popular Participation', *Modern Intellectual History*, 16 (2019), 1–28; Skjönsberg, 'Adam Ferguson on the Perils of Popular Factions and Demagogues in a Roman Mirror', *HEI*, 45 (2019), 842–65.

[58] Forbes, 'Sceptical Whiggism, Commerce and Liberty', in *Essays on Adam Smith* (Oxford, 1975), 181.

[59] Winch, *Riches and Poverty*; Winch, *Adam Smith's Politics*; Phillipson, *Adam Smith* (London, 2010).

[60] Although they had intellectual disagreements, Smith referred to his former teacher as 'the never to be forgotten Dr Hutcheson' near the end of his life, see *The Correspondence of Adam Smith* (Indianapolis, 1987), 309. For Smith and Hutcheson, see Phillipson, *Adam Smith*, 24–55.

[61] See Introduction.   [62] Smith, *The Theory of Moral Sentiments*, 156.   [63] Ibid., 155.

[64] Ibid., 155–6.

that party spirit inevitably came to dominate political life and engulfed nearly everyone, since those who remained detached would have little sway over public affairs. He was convinced that only 'a very few' would be able to 'preserve their judgment untainted by the general contagion' and '[t]hey seldom amount to more than, here and there, a solitary individual, without any influence of either party, and who, though he may be one of the wisest, is necessarily, upon that very account, of the most insignificant men in the society'.[65] Consequently, '[t]he animosity of hostile factions, whether civil or ecclesiastical, is often still more furious than that of hostile nations; and their conduct towards one another is often still more atrocious'.[66]

Smith warned that the partial and biased nature of party spirit extended to the realm of religion. Nicholas Phillipson has argued that Smith should be regarded as a mainstream enlightenment critic of organised religion. As in the case of Hume, this was bound up with his worries about factionalism.[67] Rightly understood, religion could enforce the natural sense of duty, according to Smith, as the idea that 'we are always acting under the eye, and exposed to the punishment of God, the great avenger of injustice, is a motive capable of restraining the most headstrong passions'.[68] Such religious beliefs, however, are beneficial only as long as 'the natural principles of religion are not corrupted by the factious and party zeal of some worthless cabal'.[69] However, party politics and religion were closely linked. 'Even to the great Judge of the universe, they [party men] impute all their own prejudices, and often view that Divine Being as animated by all their vindictive and implacable passions', Smith wrote in a Humean vein.[70]

Even when party sprit was not inflamed by religion, it could still have a negative effect on public policy. When Britain was governed by the Newcastle–Pitt coalition, Smith told Shelburne that he was glad that there was no faction in parliament at the time, echoing Hume's essay 'Of the Coalition of Parties' (1758).[71] 'For tho' a little faction now and then gives spirit to the nation the continuance of it obstructs all public business and

---

[65] Ibid., 155.   [66] Ibid.
[67] Whether Smith's views on religion should be equated with the scepticism of his friend Hume is a debated subject. For two contrasting views, see Phillipson, *Adam Smith*, and Hill, 'The Hidden Theology of Adam Smith', *European Journal of the History of Economic Thought*, 8 (2001), 1–29.
[68] Smith, *The Theory of Moral Sentiments*, 170.   [69] Ibid.   [70] Ibid., 156.
[71] One day earlier, Robertson attributed the success of his *History of Scotland* (1759) to the absence of faction: 'I have luckily made my appearance at a time when there is no faction in Parliament'; cited in Smitten, *The Life of William Robertson* (Edinburgh, 2017), 117.

puts it out of the power of [the] best Minister to do much good', he wrote to Shelburne.[72] In the same way as special interest groups such as merchants could conspire against the public, political parties could act against the public interest for self-interested purposes. On such grounds, Smith was critical of what he perceived as the factious spirit that had animated Bolingbroke's opposition to Walpole in the 1730s. 'Even Sir Robert Walpoles administration would, I imagine have been better had it not been for the violence of the opposition that was made to him, which in its beginnings had no great foundation', Smith continued in the same letter to Shelburne.[73] He would return to this context in the *Wealth of Nations*, in which Smith suggested an excise scheme similar to Walpole's proposal to extend taxation to wine and tobacco in 1733. As we saw in Chapter 3, this scheme was defeated by the Bolingbroke–Pulteney opposition platform that combined Tories and opposition Whigs. 'Faction, combined with the interest of smuggling merchants, raised so violent, though so unjust, a clamour against that bill, that the minister thought proper to drop it; and from a dread of exciting a clamour of the same kind, none of his successors have dared to resume the project', Smith reflected.[74]

In the conclusion of the *Wealth of Nations*, when Smith discussed the possibility of a parliamentary union between the thirteen colonies of America and Britain, he argued that one of the benefits of such a union was that the colonies would escape the 'spirit of party', a spirit 'which commonly prevails less in the remote provinces than in the centre of the empire'.[75] London would be the centre stage of factional disputes and party rage. 'The distance of those provinces from the capital, from the principal seat of the great scramble of faction and ambition', Smith continued, 'makes them enter less into the views of any of the contending parties, and renders them more indifferent and impartial spectators of them all.'[76] The prime example before Smith's eyes was his native Scotland, which as a result of the Acts of Union of 1707 had abolished the notoriously factious Scottish parliament. 'The spirit of party prevails less in Scotland than in England', Smith concluded, leaving no reader in doubt that this was a great advantage in his mind.[77] Smith believed that the colonies would enjoy 'a degree of concord and unanimity at present unknown in any part of the British empire' if they entered the union he proposed.[78] As John Robertson has pointed out, this was an exemplary

---

[72] Smith to Shelburne, 21 February 1759, *Smith Correspondence*, 28. [73] Ibid.
[74] Smith, *Wealth of Nations* (2 vols., Indianapolis, 1981 [1776]), I, 886. [75] Ibid., II, 945.
[76] Ibid. [77] Ibid. [78] Ibid.

rather than a practical proposal, as he kept this section in the third edition of the *Wealth of Nations*, published in 1784 after the colonies had become independent.[79]

Smith's final strike at party and faction came in his significant addition to the sixth edition of *The Theory of Moral Sentiments*, published shortly before his death in 1790. Like many of his countrymen of similar temperament, Smith was alarmed over developments in France since 1789. Smith appears to have believed that a 'spirit of system' had been let loose in France, a spirit that could lead to the 'madness of fanaticism'.[80] He did not refer to France specifically but discussed a hypothetical party attempting large-scale constitutional change. When the leaders of such a 'discontented party' propose to reform the constitution root and branch, 'the imaginary beauty of this ideal system' would intoxicate the great body of the party, he argued.[81] The party leaders may start out only seeking to aggrandise their power, but some of them would become 'dupes of their own sophistry' in the process, while others might remain free from fanaticism but yet 'obliged, though contrary to their principles and their conscience, to act as if they were under the common delusion'.[82] The spirit of such an aggressive reform agenda is counterproductive, Smith argued, as '[t]he violence of the party, refusing all palliatives, all temperaments, all reasonable accommodations, by requiring too much frequently obtains nothing'.[83]

Appealing to the patriotism of his fellow Britons, Smith said that love of country involved two principles: respect and reverence for the existing constitution and a concern for the welfare of the entire society of one's fellow citizens or subjects. In times of public discontent, faction, and disorder, however, these two different principles may appear to be pulling in different directions. In such cases, 'it often requires . . . the highest effort of political wisdom to determine when a real patriot ought to support and endeavour to re-establish the authority of the old system, and when he ought to give way to the more daring, but often dangerous spirit of innovation'.[84] Smith conceded that '[s]ome general, even systematical, idea of the perfection of policy and law, may no doubt be necessary for directing the views of the statesman'. However, the man of system 'is apt to be wise in his own conceit; and is often so enamoured with the supposed beauty of his own ideal plan of government, that he cannot suffer the smallest deviation from any part of it'.[85] For such a man of

---

[79] Robertson, *The Scottish Enlightenment and the Militia Issue* (Edinburgh, 1985), 220.
[80] Smith, *The Theory of Moral Sentiments*, 232.   [81] Ibid.   [82] Ibid., 233.   [83] Ibid.
[84] Ibid., 231–2.   [85] Ibid., 233–4.

system 'to insist upon establishing ... all at once, and in spite of all opposition, every thing which that idea may seem to require, must often be the highest degree of arrogance', Smith argued. In short, '[i]t is to erect his own judgment into the supreme standard of right or wrong'.[86]

A wise reformer, according to Smith, would not attempt to subdue people by force if 'he cannot conquer the rooted prejudices of the people by reason and persuasion ... like Solon, when he cannot establish the best system of laws, he will endeavour to establish the best that people can bear'.[87] Curiously, Smith is often described as an implacable enemy of aristocracy, although he defended rank and distinction here and elsewhere in *The Theory of Moral Sentiments*.[88] In this context, Smith sounds almost like his friend Burke when arguing that '[t]he man whose public spirit is prompted altogether by humanity and benevolence, will respect the established powers and privileges even of individuals, and still more those of the great orders and societies, into which the state is divided'.[89] Few of Smith's contemporaries would have failed to recognise that he must have had events in France since 1789 in mind when making these arguments against the fanatic potential of party spirit, and in particular the democratic fervour in opposition to established orders.

It is important to point out, however, that Smith was not a categorical enemy of either reform or party. In a qualifying remark, he wrote that '[f]oreign war and civil faction are the two situations which afford the most splendid opportunities for the display of public spirit'.[90] Success in the former would 'almost always' attain a 'more pure and more splendid' glory than the latter, however, as the war hero would be celebrated by the entire nation, while 'the leaders of the contending parties, though they may be admired by one half of their fellow-citizens, are commonly execrated by the other'.[91] The paragraph that follows is striking:

> The leader of the successful party, however, if he has authority enough to prevail upon his own friends to act with proper temper and moderation (which he frequently has not), may sometimes render to his country a service much more essential and important than the greatest victories and the most extensive conquests. He may re-establish and improve the constitution, and from the very doubtful and ambiguous character of the leader of

---

[86] Ibid., 234.   [87] Ibid., 233.
[88] For Smith on rank, see ibid., 50–61, 226, 230–1. Notably, he held that 'The distinction of ranks, the peace and order of society, are, in a great measure, founded upon the respect which we naturally conceive for the former.' Smith's student John Miller wrote *Observations Concerning the Distinction of Ranks in Society* (1771).
[89] Smith, *The Theory of Moral Sentiments*, 233.   [90] Ibid., 232.   [91] Ibid.

a party, he may assume the greatest and noblest of all characters, that of the reformer and legislator of a great state; and, by the wisdom of his institutions, secure the internal tranquillity and happiness of his fellow-citizens for many succeeding generations.[92]

The paragraph shows that for all his dislike of parties, Smith was not prepared to offer unreserved criticism. It is possible that Smith in this instance thought of his friend Burke, who had not yet broken off his connection with his party at this stage. When Rockingham died in 1782, Smith, in London at the time, wrote a letter of condolence to Burke, in which he expressed his 'hope and trust that you will exert your usual firmness and that your friends and you will immediately plight unalterable faith to one another, and with unanimous consent chuse a leader whose virtues may command the same confidence with that which you all had in the worthy man whom it has pleased God to take from you'.[93] This letter shows that Smith had both understanding of and insight into party politics. The editors of Smith's correspondence and his biographer have indicated that Smith had Shelburne in mind as the new leader,[94] but he must have known Burke and other Rockinghamites better than that.

Smith never advocated anything as radical and unrealistic as the abolition of parties. Presumably he agreed with Hume that it would not have been practical, however unpalatable and pernicious extreme factionalism may have been. On balance, however, he was more eager to stress the perils of party spirit and faction as opposed to their potential utility. The focus in the chapter in which the paragraph cited above occurs is firmly on the dangers of party and faction, in addition to violent reform. The emphasis in part VI of the *Theory of Moral Sentiments* more generally is on the virtues of the prudent man, whom Smith defines as someone 'averse to enter into party disputes, hates faction, and is not very forward to listen to the voice even of noble and great ambition'.[95] While Smith believed that the prudent citizen should not decline to serve '[w]hen distinctly called upon', he should 'not cabal in order to force himself into it'.[96]

Smith was a thinker with deep worries about the potential negative effects of party spirit. Political parties posed a double threat, according to

---

[92] Ibid.
[93] Smith to Burke, 1 July 1782, *Smith Correspondence*, 258. This letter also illustrates the relative closeness between Smith and Burke, with the former writing: 'When I first heard of the misfortune [of Rockingham's death] my first movement was to run to your house; but I restrained myself for fear of disturbing your sorrow.'
[94] *Smith Correspondence*, 258 (note 3); Ross, *The Life of Smith* (Oxford, 1995), 351.
[95] Smith, *The Theory of Moral Sentiments*, 216.   [96] Ibid.

Smith. First, they risked undermining the fabric of society by corrupting moral sentiments. Party membership produced strong partialities and biases that undercut the workings of the impartial spectator and thus impeded the ability to sympathise with others. This was especially a problem when politics and religion were mixed, which is why Smith, like Hume, usually discussed parties, factions, and religious sects in the same context. Second, party spirit will always be an obstruction to the pursuit of truth. That is why Smith referred to party pamphlets as 'the wretched offspring of falshood and venality'. This was a dislike shared by Hume. One of Hume's main aversions was the partiality prevalent in history writing, which Smith had also stressed in his *Lectures on Rhetoric and Belles Lettres*.[97] Smith also dreaded that party spirit could become an obstruction to good policy, similarly to that posed by monopolies and special interest groups conspiring against the public.

For all their similarities, Smith's policy for managing the politics of religious sects differed from Hume's. They were both worried about the dangerous potential of religious sectarianism, but whereas Hume believed that a state church was the best policy for supervising the nation's zealots, Smith proposed the multiplication and free competition of sects, not so that the best opinion would win out, as in J.S. Mill's free market of ideas, but in order for them to cancel each other out and check one another.[98] James Madison combined Hume's argument in 'Of a Perfect Commonwealth' about the beneficial effects of size and scale on factions with Smith's arguments about the free competition of sects to produce his own sceptical solution to factionalism in the *Tenth Federalist*.[99]

Unintended Consequences

Burke did not derive an attitude towards party, nor did he receive a set of political opinions from the Scottish Enlightenment, because there was no *one* attitude nor such a set to be found.[100] What he shared with the Scots (and Montesquieu) was a historical and systematic way of thinking about institutions and society. He further shared the Scots' interest in the non-rational and emotional dimension of human experiences. In relation to

---

[97] Smith, *Lectures on Rhetoric and Belles Lettres* (Indianapolis, 1985), 116.
[98] Hume, *History*, III, 134–6; Smith, *Wealth of Nations*, 791–5.
[99] Spencer, *David Hume and Eighteenth-Century America* (Rochester, 2005), ch. 6.
[100] His writings on party were, however, influential for the next generation of Scottish writers in the *Edinburgh Review*; see Fontana, *Rethinking the Politics of Commercial Society* (Cambridge, 1985), 45; Mitchell, *The Whig World* (London, 2005), 135.

party, Burke believed that bonds and trusts rested fundamentally on feelings and sentiments.[101] A vital idea integral to Burke's statement about the benefit of the dialectic between opposing parties from the *Letters on a Regicide Peace*, cited at the beginning of this chapter, is the notion of unintended consequences. The idea of spontaneous order was crucial for the eighteenth-century Scottish intelligentsia.[102] In a key formulation of the idea, Ferguson wrote that 'nations stumble upon establishments, which are indeed the result of human action, but not the execution of any human design'.[103] Smith, when writing of the rise of manufacturing and commerce, said that '[a] revolution of the greatest importance to the publick happiness, was ... brought out by two different orders of people [great landowners and merchants], who had not the least intention to serve the publick'.[104] Chapter 7 of this book demonstrated that for Hume, 'British history appeared as a contingent succession of unintended consequences driven by the dynamics of party strife.'[105] As stressed by Richard Bourke – from whom this formulation is borrowed – this entailed a sceptical theory of politics and human nature. When freed from party allegiance, Burke showed himself to have more in common with this philosophical outlook than may usually be assumed.

The belief in the importance of unintended consequences is usually viewed as incompatible with mythical lawgivers and social contract theory, concepts which the eighteenth-century Scots had generally little time for, especially after Hume. As Ferguson put it, 'we ascribe to a previous design, what came to be known only by experience, what no human wisdom could foresee'.[106] Although Burke as a good Whig used the rhetoric of social contract, as we have seen he also stressed that '[a] prescriptive government, such as ours, never was the work of any legislator, never was made upon any foregone theory'.[107] When he restated contract theory in the *Reflections*, he reformulated it so as to give little weight to, and deter from, constitutional design and innovation, in a way that would have satisfied many of the Scottish literati: 'Society is indeed a contract ... As the ends of such a partnership cannot be obtained in many generations, it becomes a

---

[101] See, e.g., Burke, *Present Discontents*, *W&S*, II, 301, and Burke to Fitzwilliam, 2 September 1796, *Correspondence*, IX, 77.

[102] Smith, 'The Scottish Enlightenment, Unintended Consequences and the Science of Man', *Journal of Scottish Philosophy*, 7 (2009), 9–28. See also Hamowy, *The Scottish Enlightenment and the Theory of Spontaneous Order* (Carbondale, 1987) and Berry, *The Social Theory of the Scottish Enlightenment*.

[103] Ferguson, *Essay*, 119.   [104] Smith, *Wealth of Nations*, I, 422.

[105] Bourke, 'Pocock and the Presuppositions of the New British History', *HJ*, 53 (2010), 763.

[106] Ferguson, *Essay on the History of Civil Society*, 120.   [107] Burke, *W&S*, IV, 220.

partnership not only between those who are living, but between those who are living, those who are dead, and those who are to be born.'[108] Burke and the Scots, then, were at one in downplaying rational deliberation and putting a premium on unintended consequences.

The notion of unintended consequences – sometimes secularised but often simply a synonym for providence – impacted the way Hegel and Marx thought about history in the nineteenth century.[109] It had earlier brought together Burke with Hume, Smith, Ferguson, and Robertson. It paved the way for a sceptical acceptance of party by Hume and later Burke in the *Letters on a Regicide Peace*. On this understanding, parties did not have to be purer than pure to serve the public good. By following their own principles and interests they naturally checked and counterweighed the opposite party. 'Ambition must be made to counteract ambition', as James Madison put it in a Humean phrase.[110]

---

[108] Burke, *Reflections*, *W&S*, VIII, 146–7.
[109] Waszek, *The Scottish Enlightenment and Hegel's Account of 'Civil Society'* (Dordrecht, 1988).
[110] *The Federalist Papers with the Letters of 'Brutus'* (Cambridge, 2003), 252.

Conclusion

> [I]n forming our hopes we must not forget that we live in Face
> Romuli not in Republica Platonis; We are a land of Party & when
> we cease to have Parties we shall scarce be alive.
>
> Adam Ferguson to John Macpherson, 10 May 1789, BL MS EUR F. 291/97,
> f. 39

Party was widely regarded in the eighteenth century as an enduring and crucial part of British politics. As one foreign commentator wrote towards the end of the century: 'Various causes, since the latter part of the reign of king James I have occasioned state-parties to subsist in England without interruption.' The names of these parties were changeable. This particular writer mentioned Whigs and Tories – the two most persistent ones – along with High-flyers, Jacobites, Patriots, Courtiers, and Ins and Outs. What had been continuous, however, was one party representing monarchy and one the people, or one party of government and one of opposition, referred to by this writer as Ins and Outs, but by most eighteenth-century British commentators as Court and Country.[1] In many cases this was an unenthusiastic admission, as this chapter's epigraph illustrates. However, as we saw in Chapter 9, the way John Brown framed his argument about unity demonstrates the limitations of the common characterisation of the eighteenth-century debate on party as one of nearly universal condemnation before Burke realised the necessity of political parties. Partial acceptance of party had indeed become established political wisdom by the time of Burke's writing, even though most writers qualified their case, and Burke did more than anyone else to make party allegiance honourable. A typical mid-century case would be the anonymous pamphleteer who, writing at the time of Brown's *Estimate*, said that 'Parties, which in Time

---

[1] Wendeborn, *A View of England* (2 vols., London, 1791), I, 49–51. The author cites Rapin and Hume, including their dissertations, essays, and histories (ibid., 33, 36–8, 81–2, 88–90, 97, 204, 272, 281, 336, 360–1, 386).

of publick Tranquility are useful, and perhaps essential to our Constitution, are as destructive when we are threatened by a foreign Enemy.'[2] As we saw, Brown himself believed that it was a 'mistaken Maxim (adopted by almost all political Writers)' that internal division had to be tolerated in a free state. He referred directly to Machiavelli and Montesquieu in this context, but many of the major thinkers in this study – Rapin, Bolingbroke, and Hume – could also have been mentioned. In opposition to this idea, and by pointing to the example of Sparta in ancient Greece, Brown tried to show that a state could both be free, in his particular understanding of liberty, and unified at the same time. In any case, however, 'party' had to be examined and discussed; rarely was it taken for granted.

This book has underlined the importance of the idea of party for political debate throughout the eighteenth century. Against the backdrop of Britain as a rising power, Rapin argued that the country's party conflict could determine European affairs, as evidenced by the War of the Spanish Succession and its conclusion. He believed that Europeans had to learn about British party politics to prepare themselves for the future. Bolingbroke argued for concerted opposition under the banner of the 'Country party', against what he viewed as an oligarchic one-party government of Court Whigs, founded upon an anti-Tory alliance with the Hanoverian monarchs. Hume placed party at the heart of his investigations into both contemporary politics and British history. Particularly fearful of parties based on speculative principles, Hume was concerned that political convictions, in contrast with interest, tended to make human beings fanatic. Party spirit thus represented a continuation of the religious sectarian politics of the previous two centuries. At the same time, Hume believed that the constitutional parties of Court and Country, or government and opposition, were natural concomitants of Britain's mixed constitution and had the potential to give 'life and vigour' to politics. By contrast, Brown (and others) believed that the longevity of the Whig Supremacy had divested politics of principle. Burke revived the notions of Whiggism and party solidarity in the new political climate after the accession of George III and the end of the Whig ascendency. At the end of the period, politicians on both sides of the Whig divide justified their behaviour with reference to party. Fox, Burke, Portland, and Fitzwilliam all wanted to be consistent with the Whig party's principles and history. Pitt the Younger and his supporters, on the other hand, had little time for

---

[2] *Party Spirit in Time of Public Danger Considered* (London, 1756), 11.

party – much like his father and his own followers. Anti-party rhetoric remained prominent among those who called for reconciliation between Fox and Pitt after the example of North and Fox in 1783.[3] Even though the party question was never settled, party consistently dominated political discourse.[4]

This book has shown that the question of 'party', which once dominated political history, deserves to be returned from the background and foregrounded in the history of eighteenth-century British political thought. Much emphasis in this work has been placed on Hume's extensive writings on party, and this needs to be justified. Hume believed that determining the nature of these British parties was 'perhaps, one of the most difficult problems, that can be met with, and is a proof that history may contain questions, as uncertain as any to be found in the most abstract sciences'. A key reason for this was that politics in this period was mixed with religion, which tended to make it more capricious. If human beings had *only* been motivated by Epicurean self-interest, and were not prone to seduction by speculative principles and enthusiasm, human affairs would have been more predictable.[5] Alas, most were not and such a scenario played no part in Hume's political thought.

For Hume, experience was the main guide to thinking about politics, which is why history was fundamental for his enquiries. It has been shown that Hume modified his emphasis in some important instances, but we should not let a 'mythology of coherence' mislead us into searching for absolute consistency, at least not over time.[6] Acquisition of new data and changing circumstances produce refined conclusions – a realisation which demonstrates the strength and not the weakness of Hume as a politico-historical thinker. His writings on party are unified by the intention to demonstrate the danger of speculative principles, political as well as religious. These had the potential to undermine moderation and bring about political instability and even implosion. This framework fits neatly with Pocock's characterisation of 'Enlightenment' as an intellectual enterprise centred on the necessity of preventing a repetition of the wars of religion.[7] Moreover, the way of thinking about party as such in terms of pros and

---

[3] Macpherson, *Two Letters to a Noble Earl* (London, 1797).

[4] As recent research has indicated, anti-party rhetoric remained prominent well into the nineteenth century; see Conti, *Parliament the Mirror of the Nation* (Cambridge, 2019), 343–58.

[5] See Pocock, 'Enthusiasm: The Anti-self of Enlightenment', *Huntington Library Quarterly*, 60 (1997), 7–28. Cf. Robertson, *The Case for the Enlightenment* (Cambridge, 2005), 316–24.

[6] Skinner, *Visions of Politics* (3 vols., Cambridge, 2002), I, 67–8.

[7] Pocock, *Barbarism and Religion* (6 vols., Cambridge, 1999–2015), I, 1–10.

cons, as well as in its specific guises, can be seen as a typical enlightenment way of approaching the subject – part of the Baylean *règne de la critique*.[8] This was an approach that Hume perfected, and to a surprising degree had in common with Rapin, Bayle's fellow Huguenot. While it is well established that Hume differed from Rapin in extending his criticism to the myth of the ancient constitution, and their differences should not be minimised, this book has pointed to the early Hume's reliance on Rapin's writings on party, which has been underestimated in the existing literature.

Hume believed that he was living in 'the historical age' and 'the historical nation'.[9] This study has reflected the prominence of histories of England as a crucial idiom of political discourse in the early to mid-Hanoverian period. These politically minded historians were searching for the origins of party in British politics. The era of Rapin, Bolingbroke, Carte, and Hume, who published the final volume of his *History of England* at the end of 1761, was followed by the golden age of conjectural history as practised by Rousseau and philosophical universalist history as embodied by the works of Montesquieu and Adam Smith. The great historical works of the second half of the century were written on feudalism and Rome, with the exceptions of the Edinburgh historian Robert Henry and the all-too-frequently underestimated Catharine Macaulay.[10] The works of Mandeville, Montesquieu, Rousseau, Smith, and Ferguson were intended to address such questions in political philosophy as the nature of human sociability, the basis of political authority, the importance and place of international trade and commerce, and the differences between the ancients and the moderns, especially regarding liberty and luxury.[11] All these questions also interested Hume, who arguably did more than anyone, including Montesquieu, to shape these debates, particularly

---

[8] Koselleck, *Kritik und Krise* (Sinzheim, 2013 [1959]), 89–90. As we have seen, however, Hume and Bayle disagreed on the question of religious motivation. Rapin's position on self-interest was closer to Bayle's, although he, like Hume, distinguished between the main motivation for party leaders and the rank and file.

[9] Hume to William Strahan, August 1770, *Letters*, II, 230.

[10] The French revolutionaries certainly took her seriously, as did many contemporaries in Britain; see Bongie, *David Hume* (Indianapolis, 1998 [1965]), 132–40. Burke was of course contracted to write an *Abridgement of English History*, which he never finished, although a 90,000-word fragment was published posthumously.

[11] These and related questions have been prominent in research on the history of political thought in the last decade; see, e.g., Hont, *Politics in Commercial Society* (Cambridge, MA, 2015); Douglass, *Rousseau and Hobbes* (Oxford, 2015); Brooke, *Philosophic Pride* (Oxford, 2012); Nakhimovsky, *The Closed Commercial State* (Princeton, 2011); Sagar, *The Opinion of Mankind* (Princeton, 2018); Stuart-Buttle, *From Moral Theology to Moral Philosophy* (Oxford, 2019).

in what has become known as the Scottish Enlightenment.[12] However, Hume can also be seen as belonging to an earlier tradition of historical and political enquiry, which dealt with one of the most basic questions in politics, namely that of internecine division. The most important genres for such enquiries were narrative history and politico-historical arguments in pamphlets and essays.

Although Hume came to dislike his predecessor Rapin's rhetoric, and to disagree with him on the Stuart kings and in particular the transition from Elizabeth I to James I/VI, the French Huguenot was in many respects the architect of how the seventeenth-century party framework was understood in the eighteenth century. For this reason, Rapin was crucial for Bolingbroke (who adopted ancient constitutionalism wholesale) as well as for Hume. Others had written about party in the seventeenth century and its relevance for the eighteenth century before Rapin, but none had matched the lucidity of his *Dissertation sur les Whigs et les Torys*. Rapin's achievement was to show that Whig and Tory represented a continuation of the Reformation in Britain, stemming from division within Protestantism in England and Scotland. This is not an entirely implausible conclusion, since modern historians are becoming increasingly engaged with the afterlife of the Reformation and its impact well into the eighteenth century.[13] It was certainly not out of antiquarian concern that Bishop Burnet wrote a history of the Reformation in three volumes between 1679 and 1715, or indeed that William Cobbett did the same in instalments from 1824 to 1826. On the back of this, the influential thesis that political economy in the eighteenth century, significant though it was, supplanted constitutional, religious, and dynastic discourses as the dominant language of politics cannot be sustained.[14] We cannot thus accept, at least not in its entirety, Steve Pincus's argument that '[p]arty political dispute in the late 17th and early 18th centuries was as much about political economy as it was about religion and the constitution'.[15]

---

[12] Hont, *Jealousy of Trade* (Cambridge, MA, 2005); Berry, *The Idea of Commercial Society in the Scottish Enlightenment* (Cambridge, 2013).

[13] Ingram, *Reformation without End* (Manchester, 2018); Bulman and Ingram (eds), *God in the Enlightenment* (New York, 2016), introduction; Sirota, *The Christian Monitors* (New Haven, 2014); Ahnert, *The Moral Culture of the Scottish Enlightenment* (New Haven, 2014), 81; Tyacke (ed.), *England's Long Reformation, 1500–1800* (London, 1998).

[14] Cf. Hirschman, *The Passions and the Interests* (Princeton, 2013 [1977]), 37. It should be noted, however, that the volume of legislation concerning economic life expanded exponentially in the eighteenth century, in particular after 1760; see Hoppit, *Britain's Political Economies* (Cambridge, 2017), chs. 2–3.

[15] Pincus, 'Addison's Empire', *PH*, 31 (2012), 101.

This does not appear to have been the way most contemporaries understood party conflict. From within the prism of party, no contexts are more central than the 'long Reformation' and Britain's constitutional history for understanding eighteenth-century British politics.

As much as both Rapin – himself a victim of the continental counter-Reformation – and Hume emphasised the significance of religion for party strife, so did Bolingbroke seek to downplay it. What Bolingbroke promoted instead of Whig and Tory were constitutional parties: those of 'Court' and 'Country', representing the executive and legislature, but also the parties of government and opposition. This was a key dimension of British politics and not a figment of his imagination, although it was frequently overridden by Whig and Tory because of religious and dynastic politics. The Country party had a recognisable ideology consisting of a body of arguments used to legitimise opposition, most of which centred on attacking corruption and the growth of executive power. It is far from clear whether the same can be said of the 'Court party', however, since government policy was the result of negotiations between the leaders of the ruling party and the monarch. Bolingbroke was drawing on his own parliamentary career, the beginning of which he spent in close alliance with Robert Harley, the one-time paradigmatic Country politician. In fact, the Tory party in general increasingly came to adopt Country party rhetoric and the language of ancient constitutionalism after the Hanoverian succession. Bolingbroke was part of a longstanding political tradition, which was predominantly Tory, as much as he was a borrower of Whig and 'neo-Harringtonian' arguments.[16] Be that as it may, his impact, as has been shown, was monumental. As we have seen, this anti-executive language of opposition was bequeathed to Burke and the Rockingham Whigs. In opposition, the alliance between former Tories and those of Tory families such as Dowdeswell and Charles James Fox with undisputable Whigs such as Rockingham and Portland was surprisingly seamless, partly because of self-interest and political manoeuvring but also because of the strength of the Country tradition.

The need Bolingbroke felt to argue against the relevance of Whig and Tory becomes fully understandable when his works are considered in their particular contexts, as a partisan attack on Walpole, and an attempt to unify Tories and discontented Whigs against the Court Whigs. Although Bolingbroke never managed to break the Whig ascendency, he made a

---

[16] This is discussed in Skjönsberg, 'Ancient Constitutionalism, Fundamental Law and Eighteenth-Century Toryism in the Septennial Act (1716) Debates', *HPT*, 40 (2019), 270–301.

distinctive mark on political debate and in the sphere of political ideas as he offered the most sustained defence of a concerted opposition party before Burke. Even such a staunch Anglican Tory-Jacobite as Carte, who had been critical of Bolingbroke and the *Craftsman* for capitulating to Whiggism, eventually followed his lead. In 1742, when Carte made the case for a continued alliance between opposition Tories and Whigs, he stressed that the Tories were 'as determined to support dissenters in the enjoyment of the Toleration indulged to consciences truly scrupulous, as we are the Church in her establishment'.[17] This policy was incidentally one that had been favoured not only by Rapin and Burke, but also by the religious sceptic Hume, who was more worried about violent competition among sects than the potentially oppressive nature of a state church.[18] As a philosophical exercise, Hume speculated about 'a society of atheists', like Bayle and Mandeville had done.[19] For all his heterodoxy and many attacks on religion, however, Hume's political position in favour of a strong state church combined with toleration was mainstream, and motivated by his overriding 'Hobbesian' obsession with the need to avoid civil and religious strife. Although this argument may have been controversial in his native Scotland with its anti-Erastian Kirk,[20] it was part of his realisation that he could not write as if his contemporaries were unbelievers when religion dominated and pervaded eighteenth-century life.[21] The fact that his most relentless attack on Christianity – the *Dialogues Concerning Natural Religion* – was held back for twenty-five years before it was posthumously published to the dismay of most of his friends supports this interpretation. In any event, in his *History* Hume prescribed an establishment Whig solution to the Reformation problem of the direction of the reformed English church, and its relationship to the state.[22]

Even though the Carte quotation above may suggest that even Tories, following Bolingbroke, began to accept toleration, sectarian strife none-theless continued to plague the British state.[23] The debate over the Jewish Naturalisation Act 1753, repealed the following year, has been dubbed 'a

---

[17] Carte MS 230, Bodleian, ff. 201–2.   [18] Hume, *History*, I, 311, III, 134–6, IV, 352.
[19] Robertson, *The Case for the Enlightenment*, 308–16.
[20] Kidd, *Union and Unionism* (Cambridge, 2008), 216.
[21] Robertson, *The Case for the Enlightenment*, 374.
[22] On this, see also Ingram, *Religion, Reform and Modernity* (Woodbridge, 2007), ch. 6.
[23] Langford, *Public Life and the Propertied Englishman, 1689–1798* (Oxford, 1991), 71–98. Some Jacobites continued to argue against toleration, as did Sir James Steuart in opposition to Hume. Steuart, 'Notes upon Hume's Elizabeth', NLS MS 9376, ff. 78–9.

doctrinal issue in the old Whig and Tory tradition'.[24] The same can be said of the 1754 election in Oxfordshire, reflected in Hogarth's *Election* paintings, in which Whig and Tory politicians and antisemitic Tory crowds feature prominently (see Figures 1.1–1.4). William Warburton went as far as to describe church politics as 'warfare upon earth' in 1763.[25] Domestic religious strife certainly saw a reduction in bloodshed compared with the previous century, but events such as the Subscription Controversy and Catholic relief and emancipation continued to cause division in the second half of the century and the beginning of the next. Burke was a champion of religious toleration, and his career in Bristol was promoted by some of the city's prominent Quakers and Presbyterians. Many Anglicans in Bristol viewed him as overly friendly to Protestant Dissenters and Catholics, and the established clergy walked in procession to the polls to vote against him in 1774.[26] By the time of the French Revolution, however, he had come to regard the British Dissenters as politically extreme and posing a risk to the survival of the constitution. In the international sphere, religious tension never really went away. Even if most eighteenth-century wars were dynastic and imperial, the fundamental division in Europe remained Protestantism versus Catholicism. After the Anglo-French alliance between 1716 and 1731, Britain's central rival was once again what it had always been in the eyes of many: Catholic France. Rhetoric about universal monarchy and balance of power and trade complemented, rather than eclipsed, religious discourse.[27]

The intention behind this book has been to understand the politics and political thought of eighteenth-century Britain through the prism of party. The transformation of politics after the advent of modern democratic politics, along with the impact of socialism in the late nineteenth and early twentieth centuries, means that it is unhelpful to view Whig and Tory of the eighteenth century as forerunners to later progressive and conservative ideologies, parties, or movements – although even Namier appears to have believed this was possible.[28] Since the nineteenth century, and especially since the aftermath of the Second World War, the demands

---

[24] Perry, *Public Opinion, Propaganda and Politics in Eighteenth-Century England* (Cambridge, MA, 1962), 178.

[25] Warburton, *Letters from a Late Eminent Prelate to One of His Friends* (London, second ed. 1809), 346.

[26] Weare, *Burke's Connection with Bristol* (Bristol, 1894), 48–9, 77.

[27] Claydon, *Europe and the Making of England, 1660–1760* (Cambridge, 2007), 192–219; Smith, *Georgian Monarchy* (Cambridge, 2006), 21–32. For a Catholic perspective, see Burkhardt, *Abschied vom Religionskrieg* (Tübingen, 1985).

[28] Namier, *England in the Age of the American Revolution* (London, 1930), 207, 212.

of states and their bureaucracies have increased beyond the imagination Whigs and Tories alike. However, modern politics inherited the institutions of the eighteenth century, and one of the most important ones was the political party, the characteristics of which had already been defined by the political thinkers and writers treated in this book. There are thus reasons beyond historical understanding why we may be interested in the eighteenth-century debate about party. Although most take parties for granted, the debate about party politics has never completely disappeared. The idea of democracy without parties is still periodically raised. The chief objection against party politics has often been that it offers a superficial conflict to voters, and that it fails to address real issues with clarity. This is by no means a new objection,[29] but in the 1990s and early 2000s it was frequently remarked that all major parties were gravitating towards the centre. More recently, especially against the backdrop of 'populism', parties and partisanship are blamed for increased polarisation. For these reasons, we are likely to ask ourselves continuously how much partisan conflict our political systems can handle. It may then be enlightening to revisit the eighteenth century. This was not only a time of continuous party change but also one when some wondered whether parties were a distraction and even pernicious, and if free politics without parties was possible. As I have demonstrated, most acute observers quickly concluded that it was not. The key instead was to pacify parties and make them serviceable by keeping conflicting forces balanced through mutual checking. This is how the equilibrium of Britain's mixed and balanced constitution had been maintained, as Rapin and the older Burke emphasised. The younger Burke, and Bolingbroke before him, had further argued that parties could concentrate opposition to government and empower isolated individuals. Hume, echoing Montesquieu, contended that constitutional party strife was a sign of liberty, which could give life and vigour to politics. This could generate discordant harmony and be as close an approximation of the common good as the imperfections and diversity of human society permit. But for this to materialise, we must also ensure that the debate remains civil.[30] With Hume, we must persuade partisans 'not to contend, as if they were fighting *pro aris & focis*'. This is

---

[29] A similar point was made fifty years ago in Hofstadter, *The Idea of a Party System* (Berkeley, 1969), 271.

[30] For a discussion of civility in the seventeenth century and modern political theory, see Bejan, *Mere Civility* (Cambridge, MA, 2017). On the importance of civility in the context of group life and factionalism, with treatments of thinkers from Hobbes to Hayek (including Hume and Burke), see Boyd, *Uncivil Society* (Lanham, 2004).

especially important in party politics since, as Hume stressed, when people act in party, honour as a restraint on behaviour is all too often ignored.[31] Our ultimate allegiance must be to what he called 'the *party* of humankind'.[32]

---

[31] Hume, *Essays*, 31, 43.
[32] Hume, *Enquiry Concerning the Principles of Morals* (Oxford, 1975 [1751]), 275. (Emphasis in the original.)

Bibliography

MANUSCRIPTS

Aberdeen University Library

MacBean Collection: Jacobite material.

Bodleian, Oxford

Ballard MS 38: William Bromley letters.
Carte MS 175: Papers in relation to the financing of Carte's *History*.
Carte MS 227: Carte Letters.
Carte MS 230: Various papers and pamphlets.
Carte MS 231: Notes on people and events.
Carte MS 237: Pamphlets and papers.
Carte MS 240: Various papers and letters.
Carte MS 263: Notes on the king's evil.
Carte MS 266: Notes on various conversations.
English History MS C 374: Various pamphlets, published and unpublished.
Rawlinson MS 909: Jacobite tracts.

The British Library, London

Add MS 20780: Thomas Gordon's *History of England*.
Add MS 21500: Carte's correspondence with Corbett Kynaston MP.
Add MS 22628: Pulteney letters.
Add MS 32939: Newcastle papers.
Add MS 32987: Newcastle papers.
Add MS 32988: Newcastle papers.
Add MS 32989: Newcastle papers.
Add MS 32967: Newcastle papers.
Add MS 33954: Privy Council order.
Add MS 34495: *Mackintosh Collections*.
Add MS 35422: Hardwicke papers.
Add MS 35428: Hardwicke papers.
Add MS 37845: Portland-Windham correspondence.

Add MS 51468: Holland papers.
Add MS 51731: Holland papers.
Add MS 61136: 'History of Whigs and Tories in Scotland'.
Egerton MS 1706: Letters related to Rapin.
EUR F. 291/97: Adam Ferguson Correspondence.
King's MS 433: James Burgh, *Remarks Historical and Political Collected from Books and Observations. Humbly Presented to the King's Most Excellent Majesty* (1762).
Lansdowne MS 885: Rapin letters.
Stowe MS 155: Political correspondence.
Stowe MS 230: Rapin letter to Robethon.
Stowe MS 242: Political correspondence, including unpublished Bolingbroke letters.
Stowe Ms 263: Political correspondence.

East Sussex Record Office, The Keep, Brighton

DAN/394: Unpublished Bolingbroke letter.

Edinburgh University Library

La.II.96/6: Robert Wallace MS.
La.II.97/5: Robert Wallace MS.

National Library of Scotland, Edinburgh

MS 293: Jacobite material.
MS 296: Jacobite material.
MS 9376: Sir James Steuart, 'Notes upon Hume's Elizabeth'.

Royal Archives, Windsor Castle

GEO/ADD/32/1731: George III essay.
GEO/ADD/32/1044–7: George III papers.

Senate House Library, London

MS 533: [Bolingbroke, *On the Character of a Great Patriot, c.*1731].

Sheffield City Archives

Wentworth Woodhouse Muniments, F.31a: Fitzwilliam papers.
Wentworth Woodhouse Muniments, F.31b: Fitzwilliam papers.
Wentworth Woodhouse Muniments. Bk 160 P/1/305: Burke papers.
Wentworth Woodhouse Muniments. R1/1327: Rockingham papers.
Wentworth Woodhouse Muniments. R1/1328: Rockingham papers.

Trinity College Dublin, Ireland

MS 1448: John Brown's annotated *Estimate of the Manners and Principles of the Times* (vol. I, 1757).

University of Nottingham

Ne C 3417: Newcastle correspondence.
Pw F 6241: Portland correspondence.

PUBLISHED PRIMARY SOURCES

Debates and Documents

Andrew, Donna T. (ed.). *London Debating Societies, 1776–1799* (London, 1994).
Archaeologia, or Miscellaneous Tracts relating to Antiquity (110 vols., London, 1770–1992).
True Copies of the Papers wrote by Arthur Lord Balmerino, Thomas Syddall, David Morgan, George Fletcher, John Berwick, Thomas Deacon, Thomas Chadwick, James Dawson, and Andrew Blyde; and delivered by them to the Sheriffs at the Places of their Execution (N.p., 1746).
Cobbett, William (ed.). *The Parliamentary History of England from the earliest period to the year 1803* (36 vols., London, 1802–20).
HMC, *Report of Manuscripts in Various Collections* (7 vols., Dublin, 1901–14).
  Calendar of the Stuart Papers belonging to his Majesty the king, preserved at Windsor Castle (7 vols., London, 1907–23).
Holmes, G. and Speck, W.A. (eds). *The Divided Society: Party Conflict in England, 1694–1716* (London, 1967).
Taylor, Stephen and Jones, Clyve (eds). *Tory and Whig: The Parliamentary Papers of Edward Harley, 3rd Earl of Oxford, and William Hay, MP for Seaford, 1716–53* (Woodbridge, 1998).
Williams, E.N. (ed.). *The Eighteenth-Century Constitution* (Cambridge, 1960).

Diaries, Memoirs, and Correspondence

Letters to and from Henrietta, Countess of Suffolk, and her second husband, the Hon. George Berkeley (2 vols., London, 1824).
Letters and Correspondence, Public and Private, of the Right Honourable Henry St. John, Lord Viscount Bolingbroke (4 vols., London, 1798).
The Correspondence of Henry St. John and Sir William Trumbull, 1698–1710, ed. Adrian Lashmore-Davies, *Eighteenth-Century Life*, 32 (2008), 23–179.
The Unpublished Letters of Henry St John, First Viscount Bolingbroke, ed. Adrian Lashmore-Davies (5 vols., London, 2013).
Boswell's Edinburgh Journals 1767–1786, ed. Hugh Milner (Edinburgh, 2013).
The Correspondence of Edmund Burke, ed. Thomas W. Copeland et al. (10 vols., Chicago, 1958–1978).

Campbell, John. *The Lives of the Lord Chancellors and Keepers of the Great Seal of England* (10 vols., London, 1846).

Carlyle, Alexander. *Anecdotes and Characters of the Times* (London, 1973 [1860]).

Cazenove, Raoul de. *Rapin-Thoyras, sa famille, sa vie et ses œuvres: études historiques suive de généalogies* (Paris, 1866).

Characters by Lord Chesterfield contrasted with Characters of the Same Great Personages by other Respectable Writers (London, 1778).

Lodge, Richard (ed.). *Private Correspondence of Chesterfield and Newcastle, 1744–46* (London, 1930).

Chesterfield, Lord. *Letters*, ed. David Roberts (Oxford, 1998).

Coxe, William. *Memoirs of the Life and Administration of Sir Robert Walpole, Earl of Orford, with Original Correspondence and Authentic papers, Never Published Before* (3 vols., London, 1798).

   Memoirs of the Administration of the Right Honourable Henry Pelham, Collected from the Family Papers, and Other Authentic Documents (2 vols., London, 1829).

Correspondence of William Pitt, Earl of Chatham (4 vols., London, 1840).

The Diary of the Late George Bubb Dodington (London, third edn., 1785).

Fitzmaurice, Lord Edmond. *Life of William, Earl of Shelburne, afterwards first Marquess of Lansdowne* (3 vols., London, 1875).

Letters to Henry Fox, Lord Holland, ed. Lord Ilchester (London, 1915).

Memorials and Correspondence of Charles James Fox, ed. Lord John Russell (4 vols., London, 1853–7).

The Correspondence of King George III, ed. Sir John Fortescue (6 vols., London, 1927).

The Private Correspondence of David Garrick (2 vols., London, 1831).

Ginter (ed.), Donald E. *Whig Organisation in the General Election of 1790: Selections from the Blair Adam Papers* (Berkeley, 1967).

Harris, George. *The Life of Lord Chancellor Hardwicke; with sections from his Correspondence, Diaries, Speeches, and Judgments* (3 vols., London, 1847).

Remarks and Collections of Thomas Hearne, ed. C.E. Doble et al. (11 vols., Oxford, 1885–1921).

Hervey, Lord. *Some Materials towards Memoirs of the Reign of King George II*, ed. Romney Sedgwick (3 vols., London, 1931).

Lord Hervey and His Friends, 1726–38: Based on Letters from Holland House, Melbury, and Ickworth, ed. Giles Stephen Holland Fox-Strangways, Earl of Ilchester (London, 1950).

Letters of Eminent Persons addressed to David Hume (Edinburgh, 1849).

The Letters of David Hume, ed. J.Y.T. Greig (1932) (2 vols., Oxford, 2011).

New Letters of David Hume, ed. Raymond Klibansky and E.C. Mossner (1954) (Oxford, 2011).

E.C. Mossner, 'New Hume Letters to Lord Elibank, 1748–76', *Texas Studies in Literature and Language*, 4 (1962), 431–60.

Further Letters of David Hume, ed. Felix Waldmann (Edinburgh, 2014).

The Letters of Sir William Jones, ed. Garland Cannon (2 vols., Oxford, 1970).

Memoirs and Correspondence of George, Lord Lyttelton, from 1734 to 1773, ed. Robert Phillimore (2 vols., London, 1845).

A Selection from the Papers of the Earls of Marchmont, in the Possession of the Right Honourable Sir George Henry Rose: illustrative of events from 1685 to 1750 (3 vols., London, 1831).

The Letters and Works of Lady Mary Montagu, ed. Lord Wharncliffe with corrections by W. Moy Thomas (2 vols., London, revised edn., 1898).

Memorials of John Murray of Broughton, Some-time Secretary to Prince Charles Edward, 1740–1747, ed. Robert Fitzroy Bell (Edinburgh, 1898).

Newman, Aubrey N. (ed.), 'Leicester House Politics, 1750–60, from the Papers of John, 2nd Earl of Egmont', *Camden Fourth Series*, 7 (1969), 85–228.

The Correspondence of Alexander Pope, ed. George Sherburn (5 vols., Oxford, 1956).

Memoirs of the Marquis of Rockingham and his Contemporaries: with original letters and documents now first published, ed. George Thomas, Earl of Albemarle (2 vols., London, 1852).

Saussure, César de. *A Foreign View of England in the Reigns of George I and George II*, ed. Madame Van Muyden (London, 1902).

The Correspondence of Adam Smith, ed. E.C. Campbell and I.S. Ross (Indianapolis, 1987).

The Memoirs and Speeches of James, 2nd Earl Waldegrave, 1742–63, ed. J.C.D. Clark (Cambridge, 1988).

Walpole, Horace. *Memoirs of the Reign of King George III* (4 vols., London, 1845). *Memoirs of King George II*, ed. John Brooke (3 vols., New Haven, 1985).

Warburton, William. *Letters from a Late Eminent Prelate to one of his Friends* (London, second edn., 1809).

Letters from the Reverend Dr Warburton to the Hon. Charles York (London, 1812).

The Diary of the Right Hon. William Windham, 1784–1810 (London, 1866).

Newspapers and Journals

Common Sense, or the Englishman's Journal.
The Country Journal, or the Craftsman.
The Daily Gazetteer.
Fog's Weekly Journal.
The Free Briton.
The Gentleman's Magazine.
The London Journal.
Mist's Weekly Journal.
Mitre and Crown.
The National Journal, or Country Gazette.
The Spectator.

Pamphlets and Books

The Works of Joseph Addison (3 vols., New York, 1845).

Anon, *A Letter from a Person of Quality to his Friend in the Country* (London, 1675).

The Character of an Honest Man; whether stiled Whig or Tory, and his Opposite, the Knave (1683), in *A Collection of Tracts on all Subjects: But chiefly such as relate to the History and Constitution of these Kingdoms* (London, 1748).

The Whigs Appeal to the Tories in a Letter to Sir T[homas] H[anmer] (London, 1711).

A Letter to a Country Gentleman, shewing the inconvenience, which attend the last part of the Act for Triennial Parliaments (London, 1716).

Whig and Tory Principles of Government fairly stated in a Dialogue between an Oxford Scholar and a Whig Parson (N.p., 1716).

The Duty of Benevolence and Brotherly Love, and the ill Effects of a Party Spirit. Considered in a Sermon Preached at the Assizes held at Newcastle upon Tyne, on Tuesday the 8th of August, 1727 (N.p., 1727).

The Grand Accuser the Greatest of All Criminals (London, 1734).

The Present Necessity of Distinguishing Publick Spirit from Party (London, 1736).

An Historical View of the Principles, Characters, Persons, &c of the Political Writers in Great Britain (London, 1740).

The Desertion Discussed: Or, the Last and Present Opposition placed in their True Light (London, 1743).

The Detector Detected (London, 1743).

Opposition not Faction: Or the Rectitude of the Present Parliamentary Opposition (London, 1743).

A Defence of the People (London, 1744).

The Opposition Rescued from the Insolent Attacks of Faction Detected (London, 1744).

An Expostulatory Epistle to the Welsh Knight, on the Late Revolution in Politics (London, 1745).

The Present State of Scotland Consider'd: And its Declining and Sinking Condition Charged upon the Conduct of the Landed Gentlemen (Edinburgh, 1745).

The Surprising History of a Late Long Administration (London, 1746).

Admonitions from the Dead, in Epistles to the Living . . . to Promote the Cause of Religion and Moral Virtue (London, 1754).

Party Spirit in Time of Public Danger Considered (London, 1756).

An Address to the Cocoa-Tree from a Whig (London, 1762).

A Letter from the Cocoa-Tree to the Country-Gentlemen (London, 1762).

The True Whig Displayed. Comprehending Cursory REMARKS on the Address to the Cocoa-Tree. By a TORY (London, 1762).

An Essay on the Constitution of England (London, 1765).

A Full and Free Enquiry into the Merits of the Peace; With Some Strictures on the Spirit of Party (London, 1765).

Fallacy Detected in a letter to the Rev. Mr. John Wesley (London, 1775).

The Letters of Junius. Complete in One Volume (London, 1786).

[Arnall, William]. *Remarks on the Craftsman's Vindication of his Two Hon[oura]ble Patrons Remarks on the Craftsman's Vindication of His Two Honourable Patrons, in his paper of May 22, 1731* (London, 1731).

[Arnall, William]. *Opposition No Proof of Patriotism: With Some Observations and Advice Concerning Party-writings* (London, 1735).

Astell, Mary. *Political Writings*, ed. Patricia Springborg (Cambridge, 1996).

Barlow, Frederick. *The Complete English Dictionary* (2 vols., London, 1772).

Bayle, Pierre. *Miscellaneous Reflections, Occasion'd by the Comet, which appear'd in December 1680* (London, 1708).

    A Philosophical Commentary on These Words of the Gospel, Luke 14.23, 'Compel Them to Come In, That My House May Be Full' (Indianapolis, 2005 [1686–8]).

    Political Writings, ed. Sally L. Jenkinson (Cambridge, 2012).

Bentham, Jeremy. *A Fragment on Government*, ed. Ross Harrison (Cambridge, 1988 [1776]).

[Berkeley, George]. *Maxims Concerning Patriotism, by a Lady* (Dublin, 1750).

Blair, Hugh. *Lectures on Rhetoric and Belles Lettres* (Carbondale, 2005 [1783]).

Blanc, Abbé Le, *Lettres d'un François* (3 vols., The Hague, 1745).

The Works of the Late Right Honourable Henry St. John, Lord Viscount Bolingbroke, ed. David Mallet (5 vols., London, 1754).

Bolingbroke, *Letters on the Spirit of Patriotism: On the Idea of a Patriot King: and On the State of Parties at the Accession of George III* (London, 1775).

    Contributions to the Craftsman, ed. Simon Varey (Oxford, 1982).

    Political Writings, ed. David Armitage (Cambridge, 1997).

Bossuet, Jacques-Bénigne. *Discours sur l'histoire universelle* (Paris, 1966 [1681]).

Boswell, James. *The Life of Samuel Johnson* (2 vols., London, 1791).

Boyer, Abel. *The History of King William the Third* (3 vols., London, 1702–3).

    The History of the Reign of Queen Anne Digested into Annals (11 vols., London, 1703–13).

    The Political State of Great Britain, being an Impartial Account of the most material occurrences, Ecclesiastical, Civil, and Military, in a monthly letter to a friend in Holland (38 vols., 1711–29).

Brady, Robert. *An Introduction to the Old English History, Comprehended in Three Several Tracts* (London, 1684).

Brown, John. *An Estimate of the Manners and Principles of the Times* (2 vols., London, 1757–8).

    An Explanatory Defence of the Estimate of the Manners and Principles of the Times: Being an Appendix to that Work (London, 1758).

    Thoughts on Civil Liberty, on Licentiousness, and Faction (London, 1765).

Burke, Edmund. *The Annual Register ... for the year 1759* (London, sixth edn., 1777).

    The Annual Register for the year 1776 (London, 1777).

    The Annual Register, or a View of the History and Politics and Literature for the Year 1758 (London, eighth edn., 1791).

    The Writings and Speeches of Edmund Burke, ed. Paul Langford et al. (9 vols., Oxford, 1970–2015).

    Further Reflections on the Revolution in France, ed. Daniel E. Ritchie (Indianapolis, 1992).

    Reflections on the Revolution on France, ed. J.C.D. Clark (Stanford, 2001 [1790]).

Burnet, Gilbert. *The History of the Reformation of the Church of England* (3 vols., 1679–1715).

Bishop Burnet's History of His Own Time (2 vols., Dublin, 1724–34).

[Carte, Thomas?]. *A Defence of English History, against the Misrepresentations of M. de Rapin Thoyras, in his History of England, now publishing weekly* (London, 1734).

[Carte, Thomas]. *A Full Answer to the Letter from a Bystander* (London, 1742).

[Carte, Thomas?]. *The Case Fairly Stated: In a Letter from a Member of Parliament, in the Country Interest, to one of his Constituents* (London, 1745).

Carte, Thomas. *A General History of England* (4 vols., London, 1747–55).

Chambers, Ephraim. *Cyclopaedia: Or an Universal Dictionary of Arts and Sciences* (2 vols., London, 1738).

Champion, Richard. *Comparative Reflections on the Past and Present Political, Commercial, and Civil State of Great Britain* (London, 1787).

Cize, Emmanuel de. *Histoire du Whiggisme et du Torisme* (Leipzig, 1717).

Cleghorn, William. *The Spirit and Principles of the Whigs and Jacobites Compared* (London, 1746).

Coke, Roger. *A Detection of the Court and State of England during the Four last Reigns, and the Inter-regnum* (2 vols., London, 1694).

[Davenant, Charles]. *The True Picture of a Modern Whig* (London, 1701).

[Davenant, Charles]. *The Old and Modern Whig Truly Represented. Being a Second Part of His Picture. And a Real Vindication of his Excellency the Earl of Rochester and of Several Other True Patriots of our Establish'd Church, English Liberty, and Ancient Monarchy* (London, 1702).

Dawes, M. *Observations on the Mode of Electing Representatives in Parliament for the City of Bristol* (London, 1784).

Disraeli, Benjamin. *Vindication of the English Constitution in a Letter to a Noble and Learned Lord* (London, 1835).

Sybil; or the Two Nations (London, 1845).

[Douglas, John]. *Seasonable Hints from an Honest Man on the Present Important Crisis of a New Regime and a New Parliament* (Dublin, 1761).

[Dowdeswell, William]. *The Sentiments of an English Freeholder on the Late Decision of the Middlesex Election* (London, 1769).

Dubourdieu, Jean Armand. *Apologie de nos Confesseurs qui etoient aux galères, au mois de Janvier 1714* (London, 1717).

Echard, Laurence. *The History of England* (3 vols., London, 1707–18).

An Appendix to the Three Volumes of Mr. Archdeacon Echard's History of England (London, 1720).

The History of the Revolution and the Establishment of England, in the year 1688 (Dublin, 1725).

Eden, William. *Four Letters to the Earl of Carlisle* (London, 1779).

Encyclopédie ou dictionnaire raisonné des sciences, des arts et des métiers, par une société de gens de lettres, ed. Diderot and D'Alembert (28 vols., Paris, 1751–77).

Ferguson, Adam. *An Essay on the History of Civil Society*, ed. Fania Oz-Salzberger (Cambridge, 1995 [1767]).

The History of the Progress and Termination of the Roman Republic (5 vols., Edinburgh, 1825 [1783]).

Fielding, Henry. *A Dialogue between a Gentlemen from London and an Honest Alderman of the Country Party* (London, 1747).

The Jacobite's Journal and Related Writings, ed. W.B. Coley (Oxford, 1974).

Filmer, Robert. *Patriarcha and Other Writings*, ed. Johann Sommerville (Cambridge, 1991).

[Forbes, Duncan]. *Some Considerations on the Present State of Scotland* (Edinburgh, 1744).

Forman, Charles. *Protesilaus: Or, the Character of an Evil Minister. Being a Paraphrase of the Tenth Book of Telemachus* (London, 1730).

The Speech of the Right Honourable C.J. Fox Containing the Declaration of his Principles, Respecting the Present Crisis of Public Affairs (London, n.d. [1792]).

Gibbon, Edward. *Memoirs of My Life* (London, 1990).

Gordon, Thomas. *The Works of Tacitus. Containing the Annals. To which are Prefixed Political Discourses upon that Author* (4 vols., London, 1728–31).

Political Discourses on Tacitus and Sallust: Tyranny, Empire, War, and Corruption, ed. David M. Hart (Indianapolis, 2013 [1728–44]).

English Jacobite Ballads, Songs & Satires, etc. From the mss. at Towneley hall, Lancashire, ed. Alexander Grossart (printed for private circulation, 1877).

Guthrie, William. *A General History of England* (4 vols., 1744–51).

Halifax, George Savile, 1st Marquess of. *Complete Works*, ed. J.P. Kenyon (London, 1969).

Hamilton, Alexander, Madison, James, and Jay, John. *The Federalist Papers with the Letters of 'Brutus'*, ed. Terence Ball (Cambridge, 2003).

Harrington, James. *The Commonwealth of Oceana*, ed. J.G.A. Pocock (Cambridge, 2001 [1656]).

[Hervey, Lord]. *Ancient and Modern Liberty: Stated and Compar'd* (London, 1734).

[Hervey, Lord]. *The Conduct of the Opposition and the Tendency of Modern Patriotism* ... (London, 1734).

Hoadly, Benjamin. *The Original and Institution of Civil Government, Discuss'd*, ed. William Gibson (New York, 2007 [1710]).

Hobbes, Thomas. *On the Citizen*, ed. Richard Tuck (Cambridge, 1997 [1642]).

Leviathan, ed. Richard Tuck (Cambridge, 1991 [1651]).

Holberg, Ludvig. *An Introduction to Universal History ... with Notes Historical, Chronological, and Critical by Gregory Sharpe* (London, 1755).

Hume, David. *A Treatise of Human Nature*, ed. L.A. Selby-Bigge and P.H. Nidditch (Oxford, 1978 [1739–40]).

Essays, Moral and Political (Edinburgh, 1741).

Enquiries Concerning Human Understanding and Concerning the Principles of Morals, ed. L.A. Selby-Bigge and P.H. Nidditch (Oxford, 1975).

A True Account of the Behaviour and Conduct of Archibald Stewart (London, 1748).

The History of England from the Invasion of Julius Caesar to the Revolution in 1688 (6 vols., Indianapolis, 1983 [1754–61]).

Essays, Moral, Political and Literary, ed. Eugene F. Miller (Indianapolis, 1987).

Early Responses to Hume, ed. James Fieser (10 vols., Bristol, 2005).

Hutcheson, Francis. *An Inquiry into the Original of our Ideas of Beauty and Virtue* (Indianapolis, 2004 [1725]).

[Jenyns, Soame]. *Free Enquiry into the Nature and Origin of Evil* (London, third edn., 1758).

A *Scheme for the Coalition of Parties, Humbly Submitted to the Publick* (London, 1772).

Johnson, Samuel. *Dictionary of the English Language in which Words are Deduced from their Originals and Illustrated in their Different Significations by Examples from the Best writers* (2 vols., London, 1755).

To the Hebrides: Samuel Johnson's Journey to the Western Iceland of Scotland and James Boswell's Journal of a Tour of the Hebrides, ed. Ronald Black (Edinburgh, 2007 [1775 and 1785]).

Political Writings, ed. Donald J. Greene (Indianapolis, 2000 [1977]).

[Kames, Lord]. *Essays upon Several Subjects concerning British Antiquities. . . With an appendix upon Hereditary and Indefeasible Right. Composed anno MDCCXLV* (Edinburgh, third edn., 1747).

King, William. *Political and Literary Anecdotes of His Own Times* (London, 1818).

Kippis, Andrew. *Biographia Britannica* (5 vols., London, 1778–93).

[Knox, William]. *The Present State of the Nation: Particularly with respect to its Trade, Finances, etc. etc. addressed to The King and both Houses of Parliament* (London, third edn., 1768).

An Appendix to the Present State of the Nation. Containing a Reply to the Observations on that Pamphlet (London, 1769).

Larrey, Isaac de. *Histoire d'Angleterre, d'Ecosse et d'Irlande; avec un abrégé des événements les plus remarquables arrivés dans les autres états* (4 vols., Rotterdam, 1697–1713).

Leslie, Charles. *A View of the Times, their Principles and Practices, in the First Volume of the Rehearsals* (3 vols., London, 1750).

The English Levellers, ed. Andrew Sharp (Cambridge, 1998).

Livy, *History of Rome: Volume I* (Cambridge, MA, 1989).

Lolme, Jean-Louis de. *A Parallel between the English Constitution and the Former Government of Sweden; containing some observation on the late revolution in that kingdom; and an examination of the causes that secure us against both aristocracy, and absolute monarchy* (London, 1772).

[Lolme, Jean-Louis de?]. *Essays on Constitutional Liberty: Wherein the Necessity of Frequent Elections of Parliament is shewn to be Superseded by the Unity of Executive Power* (London, 1780).

[Lloyd, Charles]. *A True Account of the Late Short Administration* (London, 1766).

Machiavelli, Niccolò. *Discourses on Livy* (Chicago, 1998).

Mallet, David. *Memoirs of the Life and Ministerial Conduct, with some Free Remarks on the Political Writings of the Late Lord Viscount Bolingbroke* (London, 1752).

Macaulay, Catharine. *Observations on a Pamphlet, Entitled, Thoughts on the Cause of the Present Discontents* (London, fourth edn., 1770).

[Macpherson, John]. *Two Letters to a Noble Earl, from a Member of Parliament* (London, 1797).

[Meredith, William]. *The Question Stated, whether the Freeholders of Middlesex lost their right, by voting for Mr. Wilkes at the Last Election* (London, second edn., 1769).

Millar, John. *The Origin of the Distinction of Ranks* (Indianapolis, 2006 [1771]).

An Historical View of the English Government, ed. Mark Salber Phillips and Dale R. Smith (Indianapolis, 2006 [1787]).

Montagu, E.W. *Reflections on the Rise and Fall of the Ancient Republicks: Adapted to the Present State of Great Britain*, ed. David Womersley (Indianapolis, 2015 [1759]).

Montesquieu, *Considerations on the Causes of the Greatness of the Romans and their Decline* (Indianapolis, 1999 [1734]).

The Spirit of the Laws, ed. Anne M. Cohler et al. (Cambridge, 2015 [1748]).

More, Hannah. *Hints Towards Forming the Character of a Young Princess* (2 vols., London, 1809 [1805]).

North, Roger. *Examen: Or, An Enquiry into the Credit and Veracity of a Pretended Complete History; shewing the Perverse and Wicked Design of it. . .All tending to Vindicate the Honour of the late King Charles II, and his Happy Reign . . .* (London, 1740 [1713]).

Oldmixon, John. *The History of England, during the Reigns of the Royal House of Stuart* (London, 1730).

The History of England during the Reigns of William and Mary, Anne and George I (1735).

Memories of the Press, Historical and Political, for Thirty Years Past, from 1710 to 1740 (London, 1742).

Orléans, Pierre-Joseph de. *Histoire des révolutions d'Angleterre depuis le commencement de la monarchie* (3 vols., Paris, 1693–4).

Paine, Thomas. *Common Sense* (Boston, 1856 [1776]).

Rights of Man: Being an Answer to Mr. Burke's Attack on the French Revolution (London, 1791).

Rights of Man; Part the Second. Combining Principles and Practice (London, 1792).

Paterson, William. *An Enquiry into the State of the Union of Great Britain* (London, 1717).

[Perceval, John (2nd Earl of Egmont)]. *Faction Detected* (London, 1743).

Pope, Alexander. *The Dunciad: An Heroic Poem. In Three Books* (London, 1728).

[Pownall, Thomas]. *A Treatise on Government: Being a Review and Doctrine of an Original Contract* (London, 1750).

Price, Richard. *Discourse on the Love of Our Country* (London, second edn., 1789).

Priestley, Joseph. *Lectures on History and General Policy* (Birmingham, 1788).

Pulteney, William. *A Review of the Excise Scheme* (London, 1733).

[Ralph James]. *The History of England during the Reigns of K. William, Q. Anne and K. George I, with an Introductory Review of the Reigns of the Royal Brothers, Charles and James . . .* (2 vols., London, 1744–6).

The Case of Authors by Profession or Trade, Stated (London, 1758).

Rapin, *Dissertation sur l'origine du gouvernement d'Angleterre, et sur la naissance, les progres, les vues, les forces, les interets, et les caracteres des deux partis des Whigs et des Torys* (The Hague, 1717).

An Historical Dissertation upon Whig and Tory, translated by Mr. Ozell (London, 1717).

Histoire d'Angleterre (10 vols., The Hague, 1724–7).

The History of England, translated by Nicholas Tindal (15 vols., London, 1726–31).

Thomas Reid on Society and Politics: Papers and Lectures, ed. Knud Haakonssen and Paul Wood (Edinburgh, 2015).

Rees, Abraham. *The Cyclopaedia: Or, Universal Dictionary of Arts, Sciences, and Literature* (39 vols., London, 1819).

Robertson, William. *The History of the Reign of the Emperor Charles V* (4 vols., London, 1802 [1769]).

Rousseau, Jean-Jacques. *The Social Contract and Other Later Political Writings*, ed. Victor Gourevitch (Cambridge, 2012).

Ruddiman, Thomas. *A Dissertation concerning the Competition for the Crown of Scotland...wherein is proved, that by the Laws of God and of Nature...at that time, and ever since, the Right of Robert Bruce was preferable to that of John Baliol, in answer to the author of a late pamphlet, intitled, The Right of the House of Stewart to the Crown of Scotland considered; to the Reverend Mr. Logan's Two Treatises on Government, and to three anonymous Papers in the Scots and British Magazines* (Edinburgh, 1748).

Russell, John. *An Essay on the History of the English Government and Constitution* (London, 1823).

Sacheverell, Henry. *The Perils of False Brethren, both in Church, and State: Set forth in a Sermon preached before the Right Honourable the Lord Mayor, Alderman, and Citizens of London, at the Cathedral-Church of St. Paul, on the Fifth of November, 1709* (London, 1710).

Salmon, Thomas. *The History of Great Britain and Ireland ... The Second Edition, with a Preface wherein the Partiality of Mons. Rapin and other Republican Historians, is demonstrated* (London, 1725).

Secker, Thomas. *A Sermon preach'd before the University of Oxford, at St Mary's, on Act Sunday in the afternoon, July 8. 1733* (1733).

Sidney, Algernon. *Discourses concerning Government* (Indianapolis, 1996 [c.1698]).

Sieyès, Emmanuel Joseph. *Political Writings*, ed. Michael Sonenscher (Indianapolis, 2003).

Shaftesbury, 3rd Earl of. *Characteristicks of Men, Manners, Opinions, Times* (3 vols., Indianapolis, 2001 [1711]).

Shippen, William. *Moderation Displayed* (London, 1704).

Smith, Adam. *The Theory of Moral Sentiments* (Indianapolis, 1982 [1759]).

An Inquiry into the Nature and Causes of the Wealth of Nations (2 vols., Indianapolis, 1981 [1776]).

Lectures on Jurisprudence (Indianapolis, 1978).

Lectures on Rhetoric and Belles Lettres (Indianapolis, 1985).

Smollett, Tobias. *Continuation of the Complete History of England. Volume the First* (London, 1760).

[Squire, Samuel]. *An Historical Essay upon the Ballance of Civil Power in England, from its first Conquest by the Anglo-Saxons, to the Time of the Revolution; in which is introduced a new Dissertation upon Parties* (London, 1748).

[Steele, Richard]. *A Letter to Sir Miles Wharton, Concerning Occasional Peers* (Fleet Street, 5 March 1713).

Swift, Jonathan. *A Discourse of the Contests and Dissensions . . . in Athens and Rome* (London, 1701).

Project for the Advancement of Religion and the Reformation of Manners (London, 1709).

The Conduct of the Allies (London, 1711).

The Public Spirit of the Whigs (London, 1714).

Gulliver's Travels (London, 2003 [1726]).

The Works of Sir William Temple (2 vols., London, 1720).

Toland, John. *The Art of Governing by Partys, particularly in Religion, in Politics, in Parliament, on the Bench, and in the Ministry* (London, 1701).

The State-Anatomy of Great Britain (London, 1717).

Trenchard, John and Gordon, Thomas. *The Independent Whig* (4 vols., London, 1741–7 [1720–47]).

Cato's Letters, ed. Ronald Hamowy (2 vols., Indianapolis, 1995 [1720–3]).

Tucker, Josiah. *Treatise Concerning Civil Government* (London, 1781).

Tyrrell, James. *Bibliotheca Politica: or An Enquiry into the Ancient Constitution of the English Government; both in respect to the Just Extent of Regal Power, and the Rights and Liberties of the Subject* (London, 1718 [1694]).

Vattel, Emer de. *The Law of Nations* (Indianapolis, 2008 [1758]).

Virgil. *Aeneid*, trans. John Dryden (New York, 1909).

Voltaire. *Philosophical Letters, Or, Letters Regarding the English Nation (1733–4)* (Indianapolis, 2007).

Wallace, Robert. *The Doctrine of Passive Obedience and Non-resistance Considered* (Edinburgh, 1754).

Characteristics of the Present Political State of Great Britain (London, 1758).

Wendeborn, Friedrich August. *A View of England towards the Close of the Eighteenth Century. Translated from the Original German by the Author Himself* (2 vols., London, 1791).

PUBLISHED SECONDARY SOURCES

Abbott, Wilbur C. 'The Origin of English Political Parties', *American Historical Review*, 24 (1919), 578–602.

Ahn, Doohwan. 'From Idomeneus to Protesilaus', in *Fénelon in the Enlightenment: Traditions, Adaptations, and Variations*, ed. Christoph

Schmitt-Maaβ, Stefenie Stockhorst, and Doohwan Ahn (Amsterdam, 2014), 99–128.

Ahnert, Thomas. *The Moral Culture of the Scottish Enlightenment, 1690–1805* (New Haven, 2014).

Allan, David. *Scotland in the Eighteenth Century: Union and Enlightenment* (Abingdon, 2002).

The Making of British Culture: English Readers and the Scottish Enlightenment, 1740–1830 (London, 2008).

Armitage, David. 'A Patriot for Whom? The Afterlives of Bolingbroke's Patriot King', *JBS*, 36 (1997), 397–418.

The Ideological Origins of the British Empire (Cambridge, 2000).

Civil Wars: A History in Ideas (Padstow, 2017).

Ashcraft, Richard and Goldsmith, M.M. 'Locke, Revolution Principles, and the Formation of Whig Ideology', *HJ*, 26 (1983), 773–800.

Ball, Terence. 'Party', in *Political Innovation and Conceptual Change*, ed. Terence Ball, James Farr, and Russell L. Hanson (Cambridge, 1989), 155–76.

Barber, Giles. 'Bolingbroke, Pope, and the Patriot King', *The Library*, 19 (1964), 67–89.

Baumstark, Moritz. 'The End of Empire and the Death of Religion: A Reconsideration of Hume's Later Political Thought', in *Philosophy and Religion in Enlightenment Britain: New Case Studies*, ed. Ruth Savage (Oxford, 2012).

Bejan, Teresa. *Mere Civility: Disagreement and the Limits of Toleration* (Cambridge, MA, 2017).

Bennett, G.V. *The Tory Crisis in Church and State, 1688–1730: The Career of Francis Atterbury, Bishop of Rochester* (Oxford, 1975).

'English Jacobitism, 1710–15: Myth and Reality', *Transactions of the Royal Historical Society*, 32 (1982), 137–51.

Bentley, Michael. *Politics without Democracy: Great Britain, 1815–1914* (Oxford, 1984).

Berlin, Isaiah. *Against the Current: Essays in the History of Ideas* (London, 1979).

Berry, Christopher. *The Social Theory of the Scottish Enlightenment* (Edinburgh, 1997).

The Idea of Commercial Society in the Scottish Enlightenment (Cambridge, 2013).

Beyme, Klaus von. 'Partei, Faktion', in *Geschichtliche Grundbegriffe: Historisches Lexikon zur politisch-sozialen Sprache in Deutschland* (7 vols., Stuttgart, 1972–92), IV (1978), 689–90.

Bisset, Robert. *The Life of Edmund Burke* (2 vols., London, second edn., 1800).

Black, Jeremy. *The English Press in the Eighteenth Century* (London, 1987).

'An Underrated Journalist: Nathaniel Mist and the Opposition Press during the Whig Ascendency', *ECS*, 10 (1987), 27–41.

Pitt the Elder (Cambridge, 1992).

'Foreign Policy and the Tory World in the Eighteenth Century', in *The Tory World: Deep History and The Tory Theme in British Foreign Policy, 1679–2014*, ed. Black (Farnham, 2015), 33–68.

Blanning, Tim. *The Culture of Power and the Power of Culture* (Oxford, 2002).

Bongie, Laurence. *David Hume: Prophet of the Counter-Revolution* (Indianapolis, 1998 [1965]).

Bourke, Richard. 'Edmund Burke and the Politics of Conquest', *Modern Intellectual History*, 4 (2007), 403–32.

'Theory and Practice: The Revolution in Political Judgement', in *Political Judgement: Essays for John Dunn*, ed. Richard Bourke and Raymond Geuss (Cambridge, 2009), 73–109.

'Pocock and the Presuppositions of the New British History', *HJ*, 53 (2010), 747–70.

'Party, Parliament and Conquest in Newly Ascribed Burke Manuscripts', *HJ*, 52 (2012), 619–52.

Empire and Revolution: The Political Life of Edmund Burke (Princeton, 2015).

'Popular Sovereignty and Political Representation: Edmund Burke in the Context of Eighteenth-Century Thought', *Popular Sovereignty in Historical Perspective*, ed. Richard Bourke and Quentin Skinner (Cambridge, 2017), 212–35.

'What is Conservatism? History, Ideology and Party', *European Journal of Political Theory*, 17 (2018), 449–75.

Boyd, Richard. *Uncivil Society: The Perils of Pluralism and the Making of Modern Liberalism* (Lanham, 2004).

Bradley, James E. *Religion, Revolution and English Radicalism: Non-Conformity in Eighteenth-Century Politics and Society* (Cambridge, 1990).

Brady, Frank. *Boswell's Political Career* (New Haven, 1965).

Brewer, John. 'Party and the Double Cabinet: Two Facets of Burke's Thoughts', *HJ*, 14 (1971), 479–501.

'The Misfortunes of Lord Bute: A Case-Study in Eighteenth-Century Political Argument and Public Opinion', *HJ*, 16 (1973), 3–43.

'Rockingham, Burke and Whig Political Argument', *HJ*, 18 (1975), 188–201.

Party Ideology and Popular Politics at the Accession of George III (Cambridge, 1976).

The Sinews of Power: War, Money, and the English State, 1688–1783 (London, 1989).

Brewer, John and Hellmuth. Eckhart (eds). *Rethinking Leviathan: The Eighteenth-Century State in Britain and Germany* (Oxford, 1999).

Brolin, Per-Erik. *Hattar och mössor i borgarståndet, 1760–66* (Uppsala, 1953).

'Svenskt och engelskt sjuttonhundratal: en jämförelse', *Historielärarnas föreningsårsskrift* (1971), 77–97.

Bromwich, David. *The Intellectual Life of Edmund Burke: From the Sublime and Beautiful to American Independence* (Cambridge, 2014).

Brooke, Christopher. *Philosophic Pride: Stoicism and Political Thought from Lipsius to Rousseau* (Oxford, 2012).

Brooke, John. *The Chatham Administration, 1766–68* (London, 1956).

Browning, Reed. *Political and Constitutional Ideas of the Court Whigs* (Baton Rouge, 1982).

'The Origin of Burke's Ideas Revisited', *ECS*, 18 (1984), 57–71.

Bryant, D.C. 'Burke's *Present Discontents:* The Rhetorical Genesis of a Party Testament', *Quarterly Journal of Speech*, 42 (1956), 115–26.

Buckle, Stephen and Castiglione, Dario. 'Hume's Critique of the Contract Theory', *HPT*, 12 (1991), 457–80.

Bulman William J. and Ingram, Robert (eds). *God in the Enlightenment* (New York, 2016).

Burkhardt, Johannes. *Abschied vom Religionskrieg: Der Siebenjährige Krieg und die päpstliche Diplomatie* (Tübingen, 1985).

Burrow, J.W. *A Liberal Descent: Victorian Historians and the English Past* (Cambridge, 1981).

'Introduction', in *Macaulay, History of England* (London, 2000).

Burtt, Shelley. *Virtue Transformed: Political Argument in England, 1688–1740* (Cambridge, 1992).

Butterfield, Herbert. *The Whig Interpretation of History* (New York, 1965 [1931]).

The Statecraft of Machiavelli (London, 1960 [1940]).

George III and the Historians (London, 1988 [1957]).

Canavan, Francis P. *The Political Reason of Edmund Burke* (Durham, 1960).

Cannon, John. *The Fox–North Coalition: Crisis of the Constitution, 1782–4* (Cambridge, 1969).

Cannon, John (ed.). *The Whig Ascendancy: Colloquies on Hanoverian England* (London, 1981).

Carlsson, Ingemar. *Frihetstidens handskrivna politiska litteratur: En bibliografi* (Göteborg, International, 1967).

Parti – partiväsen – partipolitiker, 1731–43: Kring uppkomsten om våra första politiska partier (Stockholm, 1981).

Chalus, Elaine. 'Elite Women, Social Politics, and the Political World of Late Eighteenth-Century England', *HJ*, 43 (2000), 669–97.

Elite Women in English Political Life, c. 1754–1790 (Oxford, 2005).

Champion, Justin. *Republican Learning: John Toland and the Crisis of Christian Culture, 1696–1722* (Manchester, 2003).

Christie, Ian. *Myth and Reality in Late-Eighteenth-Century British Politics* (London, 1970).

Ciardha, Eamonn O. *Ireland and the Jacobite Cause, 1685–1766: A Fatal Attachment* (Dublin, 2000).

Clark, J.C.D. 'A General Theory of Party, Opposition and Government, 1688–1832', *HJ*, 23 (1980), 295–325.

Dynamics of Change: The Crisis of the 1750s and English Party Systems (Cambridge, 1982).

'The Politics of the Excluded: Tories, Jacobites and Whig Patriots 1715–1760', *PH*, 2 (1983) 209–22.

Samuel Johnson: Literature, Religion and English Cultural Politics from the Restoration to Romanticism (Cambridge, 1993).

The Language of Liberty: Political Discourse and Social Dynamics in the Anglo-American World (Cambridge, 1994).

English society, 1660–1832: Religion, Ideology, and Politics during the Ancien Regime (Cambridge, 2000 [1985]).

'Church, Parties, and Politics', in *The Oxford History of Anglicanism, Volume II: Establishment and Empire, 1662–1829*, ed. Jeremy Gregory (Oxford, 2017), 289–313.

Thomas Paine: Britain, America, and France in the Age of Enlightenment and Revolution (Oxford, 2018).

Claydon, Tony. *William III* (London, 2002).

Europe and the Making of England, 1660–1760 (Cambridge, 2007).

Cobban, Alfred. *Edmund Burke and the Revolt against the Eighteenth Century* (London, 1960 [1929]).

Colley, Linda. 'The Loyal Brotherhood and the Cocoa Tree: The London Organization of the Tory Party, 1727–60', *HJ*, 20 (1977), 77–95.

In Defiance of Oligarchy: The Tory Party, 1714–60 (Cambridge, 1982).

Britons: Forging the Nation 1707–1837 (Avon, 1992).

Cone, Carl B. *Burke and the Nature of Politics: The Age of the American Revolution* (Lexington, 1957).

Conniff, James. 'Hume on Political Parties: The Case for Hume as a Whig', *ECS*, 12 (1978–9), 150–73.

The Useful Cobbler: Edmund Burke and the Politics of Progress (Albany, 1994).

Conti, Gregory. *Parliament the Mirror of the Nation: Representation, Deliberation and Democracy in Victorian Britain* (Cambridge, 2019).

Cooke, George Wingrove. *The History of Party; from the Rise of the Whig and Tory Factions, in the Reign of Charles II., to the Passing of the Reform Bill* (3 vols., London, 1836–7).

Cottret, Bernard and Martinet, Marie-Madeleine. *Partis et factions dans l'Angleterre du premier XVIIIe siècle* (Paris, 1987).

Courtney, C.P. *Montesquieu and Burke* (Westport, 1975 [1963]).

Cowan, Brian (ed.), *Special Issue: Texts and Studies Series 6: The State Trial of Doctor Henry Sacheverell*, *PH*, 31 (2012), vii–xiii, 1–307.

Crimmins, James. 'John Brown and the Theological Tradition of Utilitarian Ethics', *HPT*, 4 (1983).

'"The Study of True Politics": John Brown on Manners and Liberty', *Studies on Voltaire and the Eighteenth Century*, 241 (1986), 65–86.

'Legislating Virtue: John Brown's Scheme for National Education', *Man and Nature*, 9 (1990), 69–90.

Cruickshanks, Eveline. *Political Untouchables: The Tories and the '45* (London, 1979).

'Lord Cornbury, Bolingbroke and a Plan to Restore the Stuarts 1731–1735', *Royal Stuart Papers*, 27 (1986), 1–12.

'Religion and Royal Succession – The Rage of Party', in *Britain in the First Age of Party, 1680–1750*, ed. Clyve Jones (London, 1987), 19–43.

'Tory and Whig "Patriots"', in *Samuel Johnson in Historical Contexts*, ed. J.C.D. Clark and Howard Erskine-Hill (London, 2002), 146–68.

'Jacobites, Tories and "James III"', *PH*, 21 (2002), 247–54.

Cruickshanks, Eveline and Erskine-Hill, Howard. *The Atterbury Plot* (Basingstoke, 2004).

Cruickshanks, Eveline, Handley, Stuart, and Hayton, David (eds), *The History of Parliament: The House of Commons, 1690–1715* (5 vols., Cambridge, 2002).

Daly, James. 'The Idea of Absolute Monarchy in Seventeenth-Century England', *HJ*, 21 (1978), 227–50.

De Krey, Gary S. *A Fractured Society: The Politics of London in the First Age of Party, 1688–1715* (Oxford, 1985).

Derry, John W. *The Regency Crisis and the Whigs, 1788–9* (Cambridge, 1963).

Dickinson, H.T. 'Henry St. John: A Re-appraisal of the Young Bolingbroke', *JBS*, 7 (1968), 33–55.

Bolingbroke (London, 1970).

Liberty and Property: Political Ideology in Eighteenth-Century Britain (London, 1977).

Dickson, P.G.M. *The Financial Revolution in England: A Study in the Development of Public Credit, 1688–1756* (London, 1967).

Douglass, Robin. *Rousseau and Hobbes: Nature, Free Will, and the Passions* (Oxford, 2015).

Downie, J.A. *Robert Harley and the Press: Propaganda and Public Opinion in the Age of Swift and Defoe* (Cambridge, 1979).

Dreyer, Frederick A. *Burke's Politics: A Study in Whig Orthodoxy* (Waterloo, 1979).

Duke Henning, Basil (ed.), *The House of Commons, 1660–90* (3 vols., London, 1983).

Duncan, Douglas. *Thomas Ruddiman: A Study in Scottish Scholarship of the Early Eighteenth Century* (Edinburgh, 1965).

Dunn, John. 'The Identity of the History of Ideas', *Philosophy*, 43 (1968), 85–104.

Dwan, David and Insole, Christopher J. (eds). *The Cambridge Companion to Edmund Burke* (Cambridge, 2012).

Eagles, Robin. 'Loyal Opposition? Prince Frederick and Parliament', *PH*, 33 (2014), 223–42.

'Frederick, Prince of Wales, the "Court" of Leicester House and the "Patriot" Opposition to Walpole, c. 1733–42', *The Court Historian*, 21 (2016), 140–56.

Ehrman, John. *The Younger Pitt* (3 vols., London, 1969–96).

Elofson, Warren. 'The Rockingham Whigs and the Country Tradition', *PH*, 8 (1989), 90–115.

The Rockingham Connection and the Second Founding of the Whig Party (Montreal, 1996).

Emerson, Roger. *Academic Patronage in the Scottish Enlightenment: Glasgow, Edinburgh and St Andrews Universities* (Edinburgh, 2008).

An Enlightened Duke: The Life of Archibald Campbell (1682–1761), Earl of Ilay, 3rd Duke of Argyll (Kilkerran, 2013).

Erskine-Hill, Howard. 'Literature and the Jacobite Cause: Was There a Rhetoric of Jacobitism?', in *Ideology and Conspiracy: Aspects of Jacobitism, 1689–1759*, ed. Eveline Cruickshanks (Edinburgh, 1982), 49–69.

Erskine May, Thomas. *The Constitutional History of England since the Accession of George III* (2 vols., New York, 1874 [1861]).

Feiling, Keith. *A History of the Tory Party, 1640–1714* (Oxford, 1924).

Ferente, Serena. 'Guelphs! Factions, Liberty and Sovereignty: Inquiries about the *Quattrocento*', *HPT*, 28 (2007), 571–98.

Fieldhouse, H.N. 'Bolingbroke and the Idea of Non-party Government', *History*, 23 (1938).

Fontana, Biancamaria. *Rethinking the Politics of Commercial Society: The Edinburgh Review 1802–1832* (Cambridge, 1985).

Germaine de Staël: A Political Portrait (Princeton, 2016).

Foord, Archibald. *His Majesty's Opposition, 1714–1830* (Oxford, 1964).

Forbes, Duncan. 'Politics and History in David Hume', *HJ*, 6 (1963), 280–323.

'Introduction', in Hume, *The History of Great Britain: The Reigns of James I and Chares I (1754)* (Middlesex, 1970).

Hume's Philosophical Politics (Cambridge, 1975).

'Sceptical Whiggism, Commerce and Liberty', in *Essays on Adam Smith*, ed. Andrew Skinner and Thomas Wilson (Oxford, 1975), 179–201.

'The European, or Cosmopolitan, Dimension in Hume's Science of Politics', *BJECS*, 1 (1978), 57–60.

Franchina, Miriam. 'Entering the Republic of Letters: The Backstage of Paul Rapin Thoyras' *Histoire d'Angleterre*', *Erudition and the Republic of Letters*, 3 (2018), 315–47.

Franklin, Michael J. *'Orientalist Jones': Sir William Jones, Poet, Lawyer, and Linguist, 1746–1794* (Oxford, 2011).

Fritz, Paul. 'The Anti-Jacobite Intelligence System of the English Ministers, 1715–45', *HJ*, 16 (1973), 265–89.

Fry, Michael. *The Dundas Despotism* (Edinburgh, 1992).

Gascoigne, John. *Cambridge in the Age of the Enlightenment: Science, Religion and Politics from the Restoration to the French Revolution* (Cambridge, 2002 [1989]).

Gash, Norman. 'The Organisation of the Conservative Party, 1832–46. Part II: The Electoral Organisation', *PH*, 2 (1983), 131–52.

Gauci, Perry. *William Beckford: First Prime Minister of the London Empire* (New Haven, 2013).

Gerrard, Christine. *The Patriot Opposition to Walpole: Politics, Poetry, and National Myth, 1725–1742* (Oxford, 1994).

Giarrizzo, Giuseppe. *David Hume politico e storico* (Turin, 1962).

Ginter, Donald E. 'The Financing of the Whig Party Organization, 1783–1793', *American Historical Review*, 71 (1966), 421–40.

Girard d'Albissin, Nelly. *Un précurseur de Montesquieu: Rapin-Thoyras, premier historien français des institutions anglaises* (Paris, 1969).

Glickman, Gabriel. 'The Career of Sir John Hynde Cotton (1686–1752)', *HJ*, 46 (2003), 817–41.

The English Catholic Community, 1688–1745: Politics, Culture and Ideology (Woodbridge, 2009).

'Parliament, the Tories and Frederick, Prince of Wales', *PH*, 30 (2011), 120–41.

'Political Conflict and the Memory of the Revolution in England, 1689-c. 1750', in *The Final Crisis of the Stuart Monarchy: The Revolutions of 1688–91 in their British, Atlantic and European Contexts*, ed. Tim Harris and Stephen Taylor (Woodbridge, 2013), 243–71.

Goldgar, Bernard A. *Walpole and the Wits: The Relation of Politics to Literature, 1722–42* (Lincoln, 1976).

Goldie, Mark. 'Edmund Bohun and *Jus Gentium* in the Revolution Debate, 1689–93', *HJ*, 20 (1977), 569–86.

'The Revolution of 1689 and the Structure of Political Argument', *Bulletin of Research in the Humanities*, 83 (1980), 473–564.

'The Roots of True Whiggism, 1688–1694', *HPT*, 1 (1980), 195–236.

'Danby, the Bishops and the Whigs', in *The Politics of Religion in Restoration England*, ed. Mark Goldie, Tim Harris, and Paul Seaward (Oxford, 1990), 75–105.

'Priestcraft and the Birth of Whiggism', in *Political Discourses in Early Modern Britain*, ed. Nicholas Phillipson and Quentin Skinner (Cambridge, 1993), 209–31.

'Introduction', in *The Reception of Locke's Politics* (6 vols., London, 1999).

'The Damning of King Monmouth: Pulpit Toryism in the Reign of James II', in *The Final Crisis of the Stuart Monarchy: The Revolutions of 1688–91 in Their British, Atlantic and European Contexts*, ed. Tim Harris and Stephen Taylor (Woodbridge, 2013).

Goldsmith, M.M. 'Faction Detected: Ideological Consequences of Robert Walpole's Decline and Fall', *History*, 64 (1979), 1–19.

Private Vices, Public Benefits: Bernard Mandeville's Social and Political Thought (Christchurch, 2001 [1985]).

Gould, Eliga H. *The Persistence of Empire: British Political Culture in the Age of the American Revolution* (Chapel Hill, 2000).

Graham, Aaron. *Corruption, Party, and Government in Britain, 1702–13* (Oxford, 2015).

Green, David. *Queen Anne* (London, 1970).

Greenwood, David. *William King: Tory and Jacobite* (London, 1969).

Gregg, Edward. *Queen Anne* (New Haven, 2001 [1970]).

Gregory, Jeremy. *Restoration, Reformation and Reform, 1660–1828: Archbishops of Canterbury and their Diocese* (Oxford, 2000).

Grene, Marjorie. 'Hume: Sceptic and Tory?', *Journal of the History of Ideas*, 4 (1943), 333–48.

Gunn, J.A.W. (ed.). *Factions No More: Attitudes to Party in Government and Opposition in Eighteenth-Century England: Extracts from Contemporary Sources* (London, 1971).

Gunn, J.A.W. *Beyond Liberty and Property: The Process of Self-Recognition in Eighteenth-Century Political Thought* (Kingston, 1983).

Haase, Erich. *Einführung in die Literatur des Refuge: Der Beitrag der französischen Protestanten zur Entwicklung analytischer Denkformen am Ende des. 17. Jahrhunderts* (Berlin, 1959).

Habermas, Jürgen. *The Structural Transformation of the Public Sphere: An Inquiry into a category of Bourgeois Society* (Cambridge, 1989 [1962]).

Hallam, Henry. *The Constitutional History of England from the Accession of Henry VII to the Death of George II* (2 vols., Cambridge, 2011 [1827]).

Halliday, Paul D. *Dismembering the Body Politic: Partisan Politics in England's Towns, 1650–1730* (Cambridge, 1998).

Hamburger, Philip. 'The Development of the Law of Seditious Libel and the Control of the Press', *Stanford Law Review*, 37 (1985), 661–765.

Hammarlund, Bo. *Politik utan partier: Studier i Sveriges politiska liv, 1726–1727* (Stockholm, 1985).

Hammersley, Rachel. *The English Republican Tradition and Eighteenth-Century France: Between the Ancients and the Moderns* (Manchester, 2016 [2010]).

Hamowy, Ronald. *The Scottish Enlightenment and the Theory of Spontaneous Order* (Carbondale, 1987).

Hanman, Andrew. '"So Few Facts": Jacobites, Tories and the Pretender', *PH*, 19 (2000), 237–57.

Harris, James. *David Hume: An Intellectual Biography* (Cambridge, 2015).

Harris, Michael. *London Newspapers in the Age of Walpole* (Toronto, 1987).

Harris, Robert (Bob). *A Patriot Press: National Politics and the London Press in the 1740s* (Oxford, 1993).
  Politics and the Nation: Britain in the Mid-Eighteenth Century (Oxford, 2002).

Harris, Tim. 'Party Turns? Or, Whigs and Tories Get Off Scott Free', *Albion*, 25 (1993), 581–91.
  Politics under the Later Stuarts: Party Conflict in a Divided Society, 1660–1715 (London, 1993).

Hart, Jeffrey. *Viscount Bolingbroke: Tory Humanist* (Toronto, 1965).

Hawkins, Angus. *British Party Politic, 1852–86* (Basingstoke, 1998).

Hayton, David. 'The "Country" Interest and the Party System', in *Party and Management in Parliament, 1660–1784*, ed. Clyve Jones (Bath, 1984), 37–85.
  'Moral Reform and Country Politics in the Late Seventeenth-Century House of Commons', *Past and Present*, 128 (1990), 48–91.
  (ed.) *The Irish Parliament in the Eighteenth Century: The Long Apprenticeship* (Edinburgh, 2001).
  Ruling Ireland, 1685–1742: Politics, Politicians and Parties (Woodbridge, 2004).

Hayton, David, Kelly, James, and Bergin, John (eds). *The Eighteenth-Century Composite State: Representative Institutions in Ireland and Europe, 1689–1800* (New York, 2010).
  Conservative Revolutionary: The Lives of Lewis Namier (Manchester, 2019).

Herdt, Jennifer. *Religion and Faction in Hume's Moral Philosophy* (Cambridge, 1997).

Hicks, Philip. *Neoclassical History and English Culture: From Clarendon to Hume* (Basingstoke, 1996).

Hill, Brian. *Robert Harley: Speaker, Secretary of State and Premier Minister* (New Haven, 1988).

The Early Parties and Politics in Britain, 1660–1832 (Basingstoke, 1996).

'Parliament, Parties, and Elections 1688–1760', in *A Companion to Eighteenth-Century Britain*, ed. H.T. Dickinson (Oxford, 2002), 55–68.

Hill, Bridget. *The Republican Virago: Life and Times of Catharine Macaulay, Historian* (Oxford, 1992).

Hill, Lisa. 'The Hidden Theology of Adam Smith', *European Journal of the History of Economic Thought*, 8 (2001), 1–29.

Hilton, Boyd. *A Mad, Bad, and Dangerous People? England, 1783–1846* (Oxford, 2006).

Himmelfarb, Gertrude. *The Roads to Modernity: The British, French and American Revolutions* (London, 2008 [2004]).

Hirschman, Albert O. *The Passions and the Interests: Political Arguments for Capitalism before its Triumph* (Princeton, 2013 [1977]).

Hochstrasser, Tim. 'The Claims of Conscience: Natural Law Theory, Obligation, and Resistance in the Huguenot Diaspora', in *New Essays on the Political Thought of the Huguenots of the Refuge*, ed. John Christian Laursen (Leiden, 1995).

Hoffman, Ross J.S. *The Marquis: Study of Lord Rockingham, 1730–82* (New York, 1973).

Hofstadter, Richard. *The Idea of a Party System: The Rise of Legitimate Opposition in the United States, 1780–1840* (Berkeley, 1970).

Holmes, Geoffrey. *The Trial of Doctor Sacheverell* (London, 1973).

Religion and Party in Late Stuart England (London, 1975).

Politics, Religion, and Society in England, 1679–1742 (London, 1986).

British Politics in the Age of Anne (London, 1987 [1967]).

Making a Great Power: Late Stuart and Early Georgian Britain, 1660–1722 (London, 1993).

Hone, Joseph. *Literature and Party Politics at the Accession of Queen Anne* (Oxford, 2017).

Hone, Joseph and Skjönsberg, Max. 'On the Character of a "Great Patriot": A New Essay by Bolingbroke?', *JBS*, 57 (2018), 445–66.

Hont, Istvan. 'Commercial Society and Political Theory in the Eighteenth Century: The Problem of Authority in David Hume and Adam Smith', in *Main Trends in Cultural History: Ten Essays*, ed. Willem Melching and Wyger Velema (Amsterdam, 1994), 54–94.

Jealousy of Trade: International Competition and the Nation-State in Historical Perspective (Cambridge, MA, 2005).

Politics in Commercial Society: Jean-Jacques Rousseau and Adam Smith (Cambridge, MA, 2015).

Hoppit, Julian. *A Land of Liberty? England 1689–1727* (Oxford, 2000).

Britain's Political Economies: Parliament and Economic Life, 1660–1800 (Cambridge, 2017).

Hundert, E.J. *The Enlightenment Fable: Bernard Mandeville and the Discovery of Society* (Cambridge, 1994).

Ihalainen, Pasi. *The Discourse on Political Pluralism in Early Eighteenth-Century England* (Helsinki, 1999).

Agents of the People: Democracy and Popular Sovereignty in British and Swedish Parliamentary and Public Debates, 1734–1800 (Leiden, 2010).

Ingram, Robert. *Religion, Reform and Modernity in the Eighteenth Century: Thomas Secker and the Church of England* (Woodbridge, 2007).

Reformation without End: Religion, Politics and the Past in Post-revolutionary England (Manchester, 2018).

Innes, Joanna. *Inferior Politics: Social Problems and Social Policies in Eighteenth-Century Britain* (Oxford, 2009).

'Polite and Commercial's Twin: Public Life and the Propertied Englishman, 1689–1798', in *Revisiting the Polite and Commercial People*, ed. Elaine Chalus and Perry Gauci (Oxford, 2019), 241–58.

Jones, Clyve. 'The Parliamentary Organisation of the Whig Junto in the Reign of Queen Anne: The Evidence of Lord Ossulston's Diary', *PH*, 10 (1991), 164–82.

Jones, Clyve (ed.). *Special Issue: British Politics in the Age of Holmes*, PH, 28 (2009), vii, 1–208.

'The Extra-Parliamentary Organisation of the Whig Junto in the Reign of William III', *PH*, 32 (2013), 522–30.

Jones, Emily. *Edmund Burke and the Invention of Modern Conservatism: An Intellectual History* (Oxford, 2017).

Jones, George Hilton. 'The Jacobites, Charles Molloy, and *Common Sense*', *The Review of English Studies*, 4 (1953), 144–7.

Jones, J.R. *The First Whigs: The Politics of the Exclusion Crisis, 1678–1683* (Oxford, 1970 [1961]).

Jupp, Peter. *The Governing of Britain, 1688–1848: The Executive, Parliament and the People* (New York, 2006).

Kalyvas, Andreas and Katznelson, Ira. *Liberal Beginnings: Making a Republic for the Moderns* (Cambridge, 2008).

Kelley, Donald R. *The Beginning of Ideology: Consciousness and Society in the French Reformation* (Cambridge, 1981).

Kendrick, T.F.J. 'Sir Robert Walpole, the Old Whigs and the Bishops, 1733–1736: A Study in Eighteenth-Century Parliamentary Politics', *HJ*, 11 (1968), 421–45.

Kennedy, Paul. *The Rise and Fall of the Great Powers: Economic Change and Military Conflict from 1500 to 2000* (London, 1988).

Kenyon, J.P. *Revolution Principles: The Politics of Party, 1689–1720* (Cambridge, 1977).

The History Men: The Historical Profession in England since the Restoration (London, 1993 [1983]).

Kidd, Colin. *Subverting Scotland's Past: Scottish Whig Historians and the Creation of an Anglo-British Identity, 1689–c.1830* (Cambridge, 1993).

Union and Unionism: Political Thought in Scotland, 1500–2000 (Cambridge, 2008).

Kjellin, Gunnar. 'Gustaf III, den patriotiske konungen', in *Gottfried Carlsson* (Lund, Sweden, 1952), 323–38.

Kluxen, Kurt. *Das Problem der Politischen Opposition: Entwicklung und Wesen der Englischen Zweiparteienpolitik im 18. Jahrhundert* (Munich, 1956).

Knights, Mark (ed.). *Special Issue: Faction Displayed: Reconsidering the Impeachment of Dr Henry* Sacheverell, *PH*, 31 (2012), iv–vi, 1–132.

Koselleck, Reinhart. *Kritik und Krise: Eine Studie zur Pathogenese der bürgerlichen Welt* (Sinzheim, 2013 [1957]).

Futures Past: On the Semantics of Historical Time (New York, 2005 [1979]).

Kramnick, Isaac. *Bolingbroke and His Circle: The Politics of Nostalgia in the Age of Walpole* (Ithaca, 1992 [1968]).

Landau, Norma. *The Justices of the Peace, 1679–1760* (Berkeley, 1984).

Langford, Paul. *The First Rockingham Administration, 1765–1766* (Oxford, 1973).

The Excise Crisis: Society and Politics in the Age of Walpole (Oxford, 1975).

A Polite and Commercial People: England 1727–1783 (Oxford, 1989).

Public Life and the Propertied Englishman, 1689–1798 (Oxford, 1991).

Lee, Gerard A. 'Oliver Goldsmith', *Dublin Historical Record*, 26 (1972), 2–17.

Lenman, Bruce. *The Jacobite Risings in Britain, 1689–1746* (London, 1980).

'The Scottish Episcopal Clergy and the Ideology of Jacobitism', in *Ideology and Conspiracy: Aspects of Jacobitism, 1689–1759*, ed. Eveline Cruickshanks (Edinburgh, 1982), 36–48.

Lock, F.P. *Edmund Burke* (2 vols., Oxford, 1998–2006).

Lockwood, Thomas. 'The Life and Death of *Common Sense*', *Prose Studies*, 16 (1993), 78–93.

Loewenstein, Karl. *Political Power and the Governmental Process* (Chicago, 1957).

Macaulay, T.B. *Critical and Historical Essays, Contributed to the Edinburgh Review* (3 vols., London, 1849).

The History of England from the Accession of James II (5 vols., Chicago, 1890 [1848]).

Macinnes, Allan. 'Jacobitism in Scotland: Episodic or National Movement?', *Scottish Historical Review*, 86 (2007), 225–52.

Macpherson, C.B. *Burke* (Oxford, 1980).

Mansfield, Harvey. *Statesmanship and Party Government: A Study of Burke and Bolingbroke* (Chicago, 1965).

Marshall, John. *John Locke, Toleration and Early Enlightenment Culture* (Cambridge, 2006).

Marshall, P.J. *Edmund Burke and the British Empire in the West Indies: Wealth, Power and Slavery* (Oxford, 2019).

McDaniel, Iain. *Adam Ferguson in the Scottish Enlightenment: The Roman Past and Europe's Future* (Cambridge, MA, 2013).

McKelvey, James Lee. *George III and Lord Bute: The Leicester House Years* (Durham, 1973).

McLynn, Frank. 'The Ideology of Jacobitism on the Eve of the Rising of 1745', *HEI*, 6 (1985), 1–18.

Bonnie Prince Charlie: Charles Edward Stuart (London, 2003).

Meinecke, Friedrich. *Historism: The Rise of a New Historical Outlook*, translated by J.E. Anderson (London, 1972 [1936]).

Melton, James van Horn. *The Rise of the Public in Enlightenment Europe* (Cambridge, 2001).

Metcalf, Michael. 'The First "Modern" Party System? Political Parties, Sweden's Age of Liberty and the Historians', *Scandinavian Journal of History*, 2 (1977), 265–87.

'Hattar och Mössor 1766–72: Den sena frihetstidens partisystem i komparativ belysning', in *Riksdag, Kaffehus och Predikstol: Frihetstidens politiska kultur, 1766–72*, ed. Christine Marie Skuncke and Henrika Tandefelt (Stockholm, 2003), 39–54.

Middleton, Richard. *Bells of Victory: The Pitt-Newcastle Ministry and Conduct of the Seven Years' War 1757–1762* (Cambridge, 1985).

'The Duke of Newcastle and the Conduct of Patronage during the Seven Years' War, 1757–63', *ECS*, 12 (1989), 175–86.

Miller, Peter N. *Defining the Common Good: Empire, Religion and Philosophy in Eighteenth-century Britain* (Cambridge, 1994).

Mischler, Gerd. 'English Political Sermons 1714–42: A Case Study in the Theory of the "Divine Right of Governors" and the Ideology of Order', *BJECS*, 24 (2001), 33–61.

Mitchell, Leslie. *Charles James Fox and the Disintegration of the Whig Party, 1782–94* (Oxford, 1971).

Charles James Fox (London, 1992).

The Whig World, 1760–1837 (London, 2005).

Monod, Paul. 'Jacobitism and Country Principles in the Reign of William III', *HJ*, 30 (1987), 289–310.

Jacobitism and the English People, 1688–1788 (Cambridge, 1989).

Mossner, E.C. 'Was Hume a Tory Historian? Facts and Reconsiderations', *Journal of the History of Ideas*, 2 (1941), 225–36.

The Life of David Hume (Oxford, 1980 [1954]).

Muirhead, Russell. *The Promise of Party in a Polarized Age* (Cambridge, MA, 2014).

Murdoch, Alexander. *'The People Above': Politics and Administration in Mid-Eighteenth-Century Scotland* (Edinburgh, 1980).

Nakhimovsky, Isaac. *The Closed Commercial State: Perpetual Peace and Commercial Society from Rousseau to Fichte* (Princeton, 2011).

Namier, Lewis. *The Structure of Politics and the Accession of George III* (2 vols., London, 1929).

England in the Age of the American Revolution (London, 1930).

Conflicts: Studies in Contemporary History (London, 1942).

Personalities and Powers (London, 1955).

Crossroads to Power: Essays on England in the Eighteenth Century (London, 1962).

Nelson, Eric. *The Royalist Revolution: Monarchy and the American Founding* (Cambridge, MA, 2014).

Nilzén, Göran. *Studier i 1730-talets partiväsen* (Stockholm, 1971).

Nordmann, Claude. 'Choiseul and the Last Jacobite Attempt of 1759', in *Ideology and Conspiracy: Aspects of Jacobitism, 1689–1759*, ed. Eveline Cruickshanks (Edinburgh, 1982), 201–17.

O'Brien, Conor Cruise. *The Great Melody: A Thematic Biography and Commented Anthology of Edmund Burke* (London, 1992).

O'Brien, Karen. *Narratives of Enlightenment: Cosmopolitan History from Voltaire to Gibbon* (Oxford, 1997).

O'Flaherty, Niall. *Utilitarianism in the Age of Enlightenment: The Moral and Political Thought of William Paley* (Cambridge, 2019).

O'Gorman, Frank. *The Whig Party and the French Revolution* (New York, 1967).

Edmund Burke: His Political Philosophy (London, 1973).

The Rise of Party in England: The Rockingham Whigs, 1760–82 (London, 1975).

Voters, Patrons, and Parties: The Unreformed Electoral System of Hanoverian England, 1734–1832 (Oxford, 1989).

The Long Eighteenth Century: British Political and Social History 1688–1832 (London, 1997).

'The Parliamentary Opposition to the Government's American Policy 1760–1782', in *Britain and the American Revolution*, ed. H.T. Dickinson (London, 1998), 97–123.

Okie, Laird. *Augustan Historical Writing: Histories of England in the English Enlightenment* (Lanham, 1991).

Ostrogorsky, Moisey. *La Démocratie et l'organisation des partis politiques* (2 vols., Paris, 1903).

Owen, John. *The Rise of the Pelhams* (London, 1957).

Pares, Richard. *George III and the Politicians* (Oxford, 1970 [1953]).

Paulson, Ronald. *Hogarth. Volume 3: Art and Politics, 1750–64* (Cambridge, 1993).

Peltonen, Markku. *Rhetoric, Politics, and Popularity in Pre-revolutionary England* (Cambridge, 2013).

Perry, Thomas. *Public Opinion, Propaganda and Politics in Eighteenth-Century England: A Study of the Jew Bill of 1753* (Cambridge, MA, 1962).

Peters, Marie. 'The *Monitor* on the Constitution, 1755–1765: New Light on the Ideological Origins of English Radicalism', *EHR*, 86 (1971), 706–27.

Pitt and Popularity: The Patriot Minister and London Opinion during the Seven Years' War (Oxford, 1980).

Petrie, Charles. 'The Elibank Plot, 1752–3', *Transactions of the Royal Historical Society*, 14 (1931), 175–96.

Phillipson, Nicholas. *David Hume: The Philosopher as Historian* (London, 2011 [1989]).

'Propriety, Property and Prudence: David Hume and the Defence of the Revolution', in *Political Discourse in Early Modern Britain*, ed. Nicholas Phillipson and Quentin Skinner (Cambridge, 1993), 302–20.

Adam Smith: An Enlightened Life (London, 2010).

Pincus, Steve. *1688: The First Modern Revolution* (New Haven, 2009).

'Addison's Empire: Whig Conceptions of Empire in the Early 18th Century', *PH*, 31 (2012), 99–117.

The Heart of the Declaration: The Founders' Case for an Activist Government (New Haven, 2016).

Plassart, Anna. *The Scottish Enlightenment and the French Revolution* (Cambridge, 2015).

Plumb, J.H. 'The Organization of the Cabinet in the Reign of Queen Anne', *Transactions of the Royal Society*, 7 (1957), 137–57.

The Growth of Political Stability in England, 1675–1725 (London, 1967).

Pocock, J.G.A. *The Ancient Constitution and the Feudal Law: A Study of English Historical Thought in the Seventeenth Century, a Reissue with a Retrospect* (New York, 1987 [1957]).

The Machiavellian Moment: Florentine Political Thought and the Atlantic Republican Tradition (Princeton, 2003 [1975]).

Virtue, Commerce, and History: Essays on Political Thought and History, Chiefly in the Eighteenth Century (Cambridge, 1985).

Politics, Language and Time: Essays on Political Thought and History (Cambridge, 1989 [1971]).

The Varieties of British Political Thought, 1500–1800 (Cambridge, 1993).

'England's Cato: The Virtues and Fortunes of Algernon Sidney', *HJ*, 37 (1994), 915–35.

'Enthusiasm: The Anti-self of Enlightenment', *Huntington Library Quarterly*, 60 (1997), 7–28.

Barbarism and Religion (6 vols., Cambridge, 1999–2015).

Discovery of Islands: Essays in British History (Cambridge, 2005).

Poole, Steve and Rogers, Nicholas. *Bristol from Below: Law, Authority and Protest in a Georgian City* (Woodbridge, 2017).

Rivage, Justin du. *Revolution against Empire: Taxes, Politics and the Origins of American Independence* (New Haven, 2017).

Robbins, Caroline. '"Discordant Parties": A Study of the Acceptance of Party by Englishmen', *Political Science Quarterly*, 73 (1958), 505–29.

The Eighteenth-Century Commonwealthman (Indianapolis, 2004 [1959]).

Roberts, Michael. *Swedish and English Parliamentarism in the Eighteenth Century* (Belfast, 1973).

Robertson, John. *The Scottish Enlightenment and the Militia Issue* (Edinburgh, 1985).

'Universal Monarchy and the Liberties of Europe: David Hume', in *Political Discourse in Early Modern Britain*, ed. Nicholas Phillipson and Quentin Skinner (Cambridge, 1993), 349–74.

The Case for the Enlightenment: Scotland and Naples 1680–1760 (Cambridge, 2005).

Robson, R.J. *The Oxfordshire Election of 1754: A Study in the Interplay of City, County and University Politics* (Oxford, 1949).

Rogers, Nicholas. 'The City Elections Act (1725) Reconsidered', *EHR*, 100 (1985), 604–17.

Whigs and Cities: Popular Politics in the Age of Walpole and Pitt (Oxford, 1989).

Rosenblum, Nancy. *On the Side of the Angels: An Appreciation of Parties and Partisanship* (Princeton, 2008).

Ross, I.S. *Lord Kames and the Scotland of His Day* (New York, 1972).

The Life of Adam Smith (Oxford, 1995).

Rothschild, Emma. *Economic Sentiments: Adam Smith, Condorcet, and the Enlightenment* (Cambridge, MA, 2001).

Rudé, George. *Wilkes and Liberty: A Social Study of 1763 to 1774* (Oxford, 1962).

Runciman, W.G. *Great Books, Bad Arguments: Republic, Leviathan, and the Communist Manifesto* (Princeton, 2010).

Sabbadini, Lorenzo. 'Popular Sovereignty and Representation in the English Civil War', in *Popular Sovereignty in Historical Perspective*, ed. Richard Bourke and Quentin Skinner (Cambridge, 2016).

Sabl, Andrew. *Hume's Politics: Coordination and Crisis in the History of England* (Princeton, 2012).

Sack, James. *The Grenvillites 1801–29* (Urbana, 1979).

'The Memory of Pitt and the Memory of Burke: English Conservatism Confronts its Past, 1806–1829', *HJ*, 30 (1987), 623–40.

From Jacobite to Conservative: Reaction and Orthodoxy in Britain, c. 1760–1832 (Cambridge, 1994).

Sagar, Paul. *The Opinion of Mankind: Sociability and the Theory of the State from Hobbes to Smith* (Princeton, 2018).

Scarrow, Susan E. 'The Nineteenth-Century Origins of Modern Political Parties: The Unwanted Emergence of Party-Based Politics', in *Handbook of Party Politics*, ed. Richard S. Katz and William Crotty (London, 2006), 16–24.

Schmitt, Carl. *Politische Theologie II. Die Legende von der Erledigung jeder politischen Theologie* (Berlin, 1970).

Scott, Jonathan. *Algernon Sidney and the Restoration Crisis, 1677–1683* (Cambridge, 1991).

Sedgwick, Romney (ed.). *History of Parliament: The House of Commons, 1715–54* (2 vols., London, 1970).

Selinger, William. *Parliamentarism: From Burke to Weber* (Cambridge, 2019).

Shackleton, Robert. *Montesquieu: A Critical Biography* (Oxford, 1961).

Sharp, Richard. '"Our Church": Nonjurors, High Churchmen, and the Church of England', *Royal Stuart Papers*, 57 (2000), 1–21.

Sher, Richard. *Church and University in the Scottish Enlightenment: The Moderate Literati of Edinburgh* (Edinburgh, 2015 [1985]).

The Enlightenment and the Book: Scottish Authors and Their Publishers in Eighteenth-Century Britain, Ireland and America (Chicago, 2006).

Simms, Brendan (ed.). *The Hanoverian Dimension in British History, 1714–1837* (Cambridge, 2007).

Sirota, Brent S. *The Christian Monitors: The Church of England and the Age of Benevolence* (New Haven, 2014).

Skinner, Quentin. 'The Principles and Practice of Opposition: The Case of Bolingbroke versus Walpole', in *Historical Perspectives: Studies in English Thought and Society in Honour of J.H. Plumb*, ed. Neil McKendrick (London, 1974), 93–128.

Visions of Politics (3 vols., Cambridge, 2002).

Skjönsberg, Max. 'Adam Ferguson on Partisanship, Party Conflict, and Popular Participation', *Modern Intellectual History*, 16 (2019), 1–28.

'Adam Ferguson on the Perils of Popular Factions and Demagogues in a Roman Mirror', *HEI*, 45 (2019), 842–65.

'Ancient Constitutionalism, Fundamental Law, and Eighteenth-Century Toryism in the Septennial Act (1716) Debates', *HPT*, 40 (2019), 270–301.

Smith, Craig. 'The Scottish Enlightenment, Unintended Consequences and the Science of Man', *Journal of Scottish Philosophy*, 7 (2009), 9–28.

Adam Ferguson and the Idea of Civil Society (Edinburgh, 2019).

Smith, E.A. *Whig Principles and Party Politics: Earl Fitzwilliam and the Whig Party, 1748–1833* (Manchester, 1975).

Smith, Hannah. *Georgian Monarchy: Politics and Culture, 1714–60* (Cambridge, 2006).

Smith, Paul. *Disraeli: A Brief Life* (Cambridge, 1996).

Smith, R.J. *The Gothic Bequest: Medieval Institutions in British Thought, 1688–1863* (Cambridge, 1987).

Smitten, Jeffrey R. *The Life of William Robertson: Minister, Historian, and Principal* (Edinburgh, 2017).

Sonenscher, Michael. *Before the Deluge: Public Debt, Inequality, and the Intellectual Origins of the French Revolution* (Princeton, 2007).

Soulard, Delphine. 'The Reception of Locke's Politics: Locke in the République des Lettres', in *Politics, Religion and Ideas in Seventeenth- and Eighteenth-Century Britain: Essays in Honour of Mark Goldie*, ed. Justin Champion, John Coffey, Tim Harris, and John Marshall (Woodbridge, 2019), 201–18.

Speck, W.A. *Stability and Strife: England, 1714–60* (London, 1977).

'The Whig Schism under George I', *The Huntington Library Quarterly*, 40 (1977), 171–9.

Spencer, Mark. 'Hume and Madison on Faction', *The William and Mary Quarterly*, 59 (2002), 869–96.

David Hume and Eighteenth-Century America (Rochester, 2005).

Stedman Jones, Gareth. *An End to Poverty? A Historical Debate* (London, 2004).

Stephan, Deborah, 'Laurence Echard – Whig Historian', *HJ*, 32 (1989), 843–66.

Straka, Gerald. 'The Final Phase of Divine Right Theory in England, 1688–1702', *EHR*, 77 (1962), 638–58.

Stuart-Buttle, Tim. *From Moral Theology to Moral Philosophy: Cicero and Visions of Humanity from Locke to Hume* (Oxford, 2019).

Stuart Shaw, John. *The Political History of Eighteenth-Century Scotland* (New York, 1999).

Sullivan, M.G. 'Rapin, Hume and the Identity of the Historian in Eighteenth-Century England', *HEI*, 26 (2002), 145–62.

Sullivan, Vickie B. 'Walter Moyle's Machiavellianism, Declared and Otherwise, in *An Essay upon the Constitution of the Roman Government*', *HEI*, 37 (2011), 120–7.

Sutherland, Lucy. 'The City of London in Eighteenth-Century Politics', in *Essays Presented to Sir Lewis Namier*, ed. Richard Pares and A.J.P. Taylor (London, 1956), 49–74.

Szechi, Daniel. *Jacobitism and Tory Politics, 1710–14* (Edinburgh, 1984).

The Jacobites: Britain and Europe, 1688–1788 (Manchester, 1994).

1715: The Great Jacobite Rebellion (New Haven, 2006).

Targett, Simon. 'Government and Ideology during the Age of Whig Supremacy: The Political Argument of Sir Robert Walpole's Newspaper Propagandists', *HJ*, 37 (1994), 289–317.

Taylor, Lily Ross. *Party Politics in the Age of Caesar* (Los Angeles, 1968 [1949]).

Taylor, Stephen. 'Sir Robert Walpole, the Church of England, and the Quakers Tithe Bill of 1736', *HJ*, 28 (1985), 51–77.

'"Dr Codex" and the Whig "Pope": Edmund Gibson, Bishop of London, 1716–1748', in *Lords of Parliament, 1714–1914*, ed. R.W. Davis (Stanford, 1995), 9–28.

Thomas, P.D.G. 'Sir Roger Newdigate Essays on Party, c.1760', *EHR*, 102 (1987), 394–400.

'Party Politics in Eighteenth-Century Britain: Some Myths and a Touch of Reality', *BJECS*, 10 (1987), 201–10.

'The House of Commons and the Middlesex Elections of 1768–69', *PH*, 12 (1993), 233–48.

Politics in Eighteenth-Century Wales (Cardiff, 1998).

George III: King and Politicians (Manchester, 2002).

Thompson, E.P. *The Making of the English Working Class* (London, 2013 [1963]).

Whigs and Hunters: The Origin of the Black Act (London, 1975).

Customs in Common (London, 1991).

Thompson, Andrew C. *Britain, Hanover and the Protestant Interest, 1688–1756* (Woodbridge, 2006).

Tocqueville, Alexis de. *Democracy in America*, trans. and ed. Harvey Mansfield and Delba Winthrop (Chicago, 2000 [1835–40]).

The Ancien Régime and the French Revolution (Cambridge, 2011 [1856]).

Tolonen, Mikko. *Mandeville and Hume: Anatomists of Civil Society* (Oxford, 2013).

Townend, G.M. 'Religious Radicalism and Conservatism in the Whig Party under George I: The Repeal of the Occasional Conformity and Schism Acts', *PH*, 7 (1988), 24–44.

Towsey, Mark. *Reading History in Britain and America* (Cambridge, 2019).

Trevelyan, G.M. *The Two-Party System in English Political History* (Oxford, 1926).

Trevor-Roper, Hugh. 'Our First Whig Historian: Paul de Rapin-Thoyras', in *From Counter-Reformation to Glorious Revolution* (London, 1992), 249–65. *History and the Enlightenment*, ed. John Robertson (New Haven, 2010).

Tyacke, Nicholas (ed.). *England's Long Reformation, 1500–1800* (London, 1998).

Urbinati, Nadia. *Representative Democracy: Principles and Genealogy* (Chicago, 2006).

Vaughn, James. *The Politics of Empire at the Accession of George III* (New Haven, 2019).

Vile, M.J.C. *Constitutionalism and the Separation of Powers* (Indianapolis, 1998 [1967]).

Waldron, Jeremy. *Political Political Theory: Essays on Institutions* (Cambridge, MA, 2016).

Waszek, Norbert. *The Scottish Enlightenment and Hegel's Account of 'Civil Society'* (Dordrecht, 1988).

Weare, G.E. *Edmund Burke's Connection with Bristol, from 1774 till 1780* (Bristol, 1894).

Weber, Max. *Political Writings* (Cambridge, 1994).

Whatmore, Richard. 'Shelburne and Perpetual Peace: Small States, Commerce, and International Relations within the Bowood Circle', in *An Enlightenment Statesman in Whig Britain: Lord Shelburne in Context, 1737–1805*, ed. Nigel Aston and Clarissa Campbell Orr (Woodbridge, 2011).
Against War and Empire: Geneva, Britain, and France in the Eighteenth Century (New Haven, 2012).
'Rights after the Revolutions', in *Philosophy, Rights and Natural Law*, ed. Ian Hunter and Richard Whatmore (Edinburgh, 2019), 338–65.
Terrorists, Anarchists, Democrats and Republicans: The Genevans and the Irish in Time of Revolution (Princeton, 2019).

Whelan, Frederick. 'Hume and Contractarianism', *Polity*, 27 (1994), 201–24.

White, Jonathan and Ypi, Lea. *The Meaning of Partisanship* (Oxford, 2016).

Wilkinson, David. *The Duke of Portland: Politics and Party in the Age of George III* (London, 2003).

Willman, Robert. 'The Origins of "Whig" and "Tory" in English Political Language', *HJ*, 17 (1974), 247–64.

Wilson, Kathleen. *The Sense of the People: Politics, Culture, and Imperialism in England, 1715–1785* (Cambridge, 1995).

Winch, Donald. *Adam Smith's Politics: An Essay in Historiographic Revision* (Cambridge, 1978).
Riches and Poverty: An Intellectual History of Political Economy in Britain, 1750–1834 (Cambridge, 1996).

Winton, Patrik. *Frihetstidens politiska praktik. Nätverk och offentlighet* (Uppsala, 2006).

Wootton, David. 'Hume, the Historian', in *The Cambridge Companion to Hume*, ed. David Fate Norton (Cambridge, 2006).

Wulf, Steven J. 'The Skeptical Life in Hume's Political Thought', *Polity*, 33 (2000), 77–99.

Yardeni, Myriam. 'The Birth of Political Consciousness among the Huguenot Refugees and their Descendants in England (c. 1685–1750)', in *From Strangers to Citizens: The Integration of Immigrant Communities in Britain, Ireland and Colonial America, 1550–1750*, ed. Randolph Vigne and Charles Littleton (Portland, 2001), 404–11.

Young, Brian. *Religion and Enlightenment in Eighteenth-Century England: Theological Debate from Locke to Burke* (Oxford, 1998).

DISSERTATIONS

Goldie, Mark. *Tory Political Thought, 1689–1714* (PhD thesis, Cambridge, 1977).

Thomson, David. *The Conception of Party in England, in the Period 1740 to 1783* (PhD thesis, Cambridge, 1938).

Index

absolutism, 21–2, 25, 48–9, 51–2, 55–6, 60–4, 70–1, 86–7, 89, 122–3, 129, 135–6, 154, 180, 186, 189, 219, 223, 230, 291–2, 294

Acts of Parliament
Act of Settlement (1701), 52, 95, 162–3, 165–6, 168, 286, 294
Act of Uniformity (1662), 50
Acts of Union (1707), 3, 34–5, 316, 319
City Elections Act (1725), 141
Civil List and Secret Service Money Act (1782), 282
Corporation Act (1661), 288
Declaratory Act (1720), 36
Jewish Naturalisation Act (1753), 332–3
Licensing of the Press Act (1662), 7
Occasional Conformity Act (1711), 56, 75, 132
Riot Act (1714), 81, 172
Schism Act (1714), 75, 93, 132
Septennial Act (1716), 44, 81, 96, 143, 177, 270, 281, 294
Stamp Act (1765), 251, 277
Test Act (1673), 56, 288

Adam, William, 284
Addison, Joseph, 12, 28, 113–14, 138
America, 6, 240, 251, 277–81, 284, 292, 315–16, 319
ancient constitution, 34, 41, 49, 53, 66, 71, 87, 177–80, 196, 202, 271, 293, 313, 330–1
Anglicans, 16, 28, 37, 44, 48, 54–5, 65–6, 68, 71, 79, 125, 129, 131, 134, 168, 185, 216, 219, 224, 235, 279, 293, 332–3
Anne, Queen, 5, 7, 36–7, 43, 49, 52, 57, 68–9, 80, 84, 92, 112–13, 125, 148, 162, 164, 166, 230, 239, 247, 276, 280, 290, 293
Argyll, Archibald Campbell, Duke of (Earl of Ilay), 35
Arnall, William, 93
Athens, 94, 221, 228–9
Atterbury, Francis, 47, 79, 127, 177
Austria, 58, 145, 225–6, 244, 304

Bacon, Nathaniel, 88
Barlow, Frederick, 16, 272
Barré, Isaac, 281
Barrymore, Lord, 149–50
Bath, Earl of. See Pulteney, William
Bayle, Pierre, 56, 138, 175, 182, 329, 332
Beaufort, Charles Somerset, Duke of, 32, 148
Beckford, Richard, 204
Beckford, William, 204, 235
Bedford, Francis Russell, 5th Duke of, 296
Bedford, John Russell, 4th Duke of, 246, 251, 253
Berkeley, George, 216, 231–2, 310
Bisset, Robert, 225, 240, 310
Bodin, Jean, 154
Bolingbroke, Henry St John, Viscount, 8, 16, 38, 41–3, 57, 62, 112–14, 116, 119, 121, 123–6, 128, 130, 133–4, 139, 141–3, 145–7, 149, 153, 166, 179, 183–4, 195, 212–13, 215–22, 225–7, 233, 237, 239, 247, 254, 264, 270, 273, 275, 289, 294, 313, 319, 327, 329, 331–2
  A Dissertation upon Parties (1733-34), 73, 84, 89–94, 120
  A Letter on the Spirit of Patriotism (1736), 97–100, 239
  A Letter to Sir William Windham (1717), 43, 79, 96
  Letters on the Study and Use of History (1735), 82, 226
  Remarks on the History of England (1730-31), 83–9
  The Idea of a Patriot King (1738), 102–6, 298
Bossuet, Jacques-Bénigne, 21
Boswell, James, 29, 177, 233
Bourke, Richard, 174, 247, 274, 310, 324
Boyer, Abel, 47
Brady, Robert, 41, 177
Brewer, John, 38, 95, 262, 270
Bristol, 15, 271–2, 278, 284, 287, 333
Bromley, William, 32

CPSIA information can be obtained
at www.ICGtesting.com
Printed in the USA
LVHW080432210422
716714LV00003B/61

9 781108 841634